SURVIVED
The Journey

Memuna Barnes

Survived; The Journey

© Memuna Barnes 2013

Reprinted 2014, 2015.

ISBN: 978-0-473-24624-2

Published by Memuna Barnes and Ocean Reeve Publishing

Ocean
REEVE
PUBLISHING

DEDICATION

CHAPTER ONE

The Beginning

This book is dedicated to my family for their steadfast prayers and faith during these scary and uncertain times. To my parents thank you for having me and for being there. To my sisters, thank you for sticking together.

Mainly, thank you to the most important women in my life; my mother and Mrs. Memuna A. Barnes (Menah). You two ladies are humanly responsible for my strength.

Thank you to my father for fasting and praying and keeping faith that we would return.

Thank you to the rest of my Grandmothers, Mrs. Adama Barnes, Mrs Irene Kande and Mrs. MaNgaya Barnes.

Most of all I thank you my Heavenly Father; it was by your amazing grace I survived the journey.

PART ONE

CHAPTER ONE

The Beginning

I was born in Monrovia - Liberia in 1980, to Cynthia Diarra and Samuel Barnes. As I grew up both of my parents were in the work force and our mother employed a lady called Ma Cecilia. We lived in the duplexes in Barnersville Estate in Monrovia, a humble middle class neighbourhood, with plumbing and electricity-although sometimes we had power cuts which would last days.

Samia and I attended different schools in town. I went to J. L. Gibson Memorial Elementary school while my sister went to Hilton Van E. Elementary - now renamed Early Learning. I was an interesting child. Michael Jackson was my favourite singer. I had the Thriller video and one of his albums on cassette tape. I would tell people that Michael Jackson was my boyfriend. I would try to copy his dance moves.

We always got new toys at Christmas. One time I got a bicycle. I remember having lots of toys. Our mother always gave us whatever we wanted. We weren't rich but we never wanted for anything. She went to all of our school programs and she took us with her almost everywhere she went. I loved clothes and shoes. My mother bought us a lot of clothes. Every morning before we left for school, Mama would ask us to choose what we wanted to have for dinner that night. Our father did not mind. I did not like eating. I would play with my food and go to bed on peanut buttered toast and Cool Aid if my father was not home early enough to force me to eat. He was the only one who could make me eat. Mama did not like to force me to do anything. I loved my school and that was why our mother put me into that school when I came back from Sierra Leone.

When I was four years old, I went to live in my father's home town of Sembehun Nancy Tucker (locally called Sembehun Nes Tucker). I lived with my paternal grandmothers. My grandfather had four wives and three were still alive. Sembehun was a small town with no plumbing or electricity. People were able to buy generators to supply them with electricity.

Everyone in the town used kerosene lamps. We had drums (barrels) and huge clay pots to store the water. The clay pots were usually used for drinkable water as they kept water cool. At the Barnes home we had three drums which we filled with water for daily use. As I was a young child, I never went to the wells. At first I did not like Sierra Leone. Mama made sure I had my favourite things with me. She packed a huge suitcase filled with clothes and another filled with toys, shoes.

I was a sickly child -I had problems with my eyes and suffered from 'pink eye' every year. I missed Mama and Papa. I stayed with Grandmas Memuna and Ngaya for about a year before Mama came back for me. When I returned to Barnersville Estate in Monrovia, I was a completely different person. I stopped eating cheese, apples and some other things I liked before I went to Sierra Leone. Mama tried to get me back into my routine and I think she succeeded.

I had to try to catch up with my friends in the Estate. It seemed like life on the Estate had move on without me while I was way. I caught up with my best friend Enzo. I also made friends at school. Leah was the daughter of the principal of the school we went to. I also became friends with a girl called Ngaima and a boy called Luke. We were the centre of attention as all of the girls in our class. Some of the other girls wanted to be like us. Sometimes, we came to school wearing the same style of shoes and hair baubles. I remember the time Leah talked her father into letting her turn her school dress into a skirt and a top. As soon as I saw her wearing it I went home and asked Mama to talk to Mr. Gibbins and ask if I could do the same. A week later, Ngaima and I went to school in the same outfits. Mama used to teach me things like writing and reading when she was home. She taught me how to read the Bible and every night before we went to bed she would kneel by the bed between my sister and I and pray and then recite Psalm 23. I used to have recurring nightmares when I was young and she told me to say Psalm 23 whenever I felt scared, confused or sad.

When I was about eight years old, my parents separated and my mother moved out taking us to her grandmother's house in Capitol Hill in Monrovia. My father came to see us and pleaded that she come back home. My maternal grandmother Irene lived in Lofa and anytime my mother went to see her during the holidays she would take us with her.

However, one day in 1989 our mother went to Lofa and did not take us with her because we had to go to school. She kissed us goodbye in the car park and said she was coming back in a few days. *(She told us her mother was ill, but we found out years later, it was my mother who was ill and needed native treatment she did not want to worry us)*. She asked us to be good to her younger sister Auntie Yvette. Ma Cecilia was not looking after us anymore as we were now far away.

The following day, after school, as soon as we got home, we heard shooting and after a few shots, the soldiers and the people they were shooting at ceased firing. That evening our father drove from his office on

Front Street about fifteen minutes' drive away from Capitol Hill and came to pick us up and took us back to the Estate.

A few days later the rebels arrived in Barnersville Estate. It was so scary; they were people like us yet looking at them I thought these rebels must be what the devil looks like. The rebels ordered us all to get out of our homes and stand in single files so they could look for military men among us and kill them. They had their guns pointed at us, some had their guns in the air and they smelt bad and looked rough, mean and sweaty. They beat a few men and shot into the air. I was so scared I almost wet my pants. Paralysed with fear all I thought of was 'Mama where are you? I want you.' They looked very frightening and they were not all Liberians. We stood there with our hands up for hours while they beat some of the men and women.

That evening after the rebels finally allowed us we went home, had dinner and went to bed. No-one could really sleep but it was safer being in the dark. I could not sleep; the rebels were still brutalising people around the Estate and there were cries and screams coming from every corner in the darkness of the Estate – a suburb which once had street lights at night with all the houses lit at night was now a dark hell.

I heard them beating a man and asking him for his car keys and his money. He told them he did not have any money but they continued beating him. During all this I peered through the curtains. They cut the power lines so there was no power but the moonlight was bright enough to see. They could not see that in a house nearby there was a little girl spying on them. They took the man to the basketball court near the old dump site and shot him a few times. Shocked and in awe I fell back on the bed clutching the pillow tightly to my face so I would not scream.

The violence got worse in the Estate and we had to leave. Only a couple of weeks later, there were dead bodies on the streets and the rebels were still killing and people were dying from hunger and illnesses. We walked about three to four miles to Jacksonville and stayed with my father's friend's family. On our way to Jacksonville, we went through lots of rebel checkpoints and there was always one dead body or more at every checkpoint.

Monrovia bore the stench of decomposed bodies and there seemed to be more flies than people. In some areas there were vultures pecking at dead bodies. As we walked it seemed as if the whole of Liberia smelt that way. My heart broke seeing our father carry his luggage on his head; to see the happy people of Liberia so broken and sad and others so full of hate that they could end a life in the blink of an eye.

Before the rebels had entered Barnersville Estate, I saw my father sitting in the bathroom, burning his documents one after another and flushed the ashes. It was a sad, heart breaking sight. He did not want them to come and find his pay slip. They would ask him for the money and if he failed to provide it, they would kill him. We finally arrived at Jacksonville and at the last checkpoint they accused my father of being an ECOMOG; they said the he was a Ghanaian. They took him aside and we stayed a long time, but they let him go. A few weeks later he had to hide away in the forest because they were looking for him – like all other ECOMOG contributing citizens - to kill him.

ECOMOG, the Economic Community Monitoring Group, was the military arm of ECOWAS – the Economic Community of West African States – first established as a Peace Enforcement force and headquartered in Nigeria. This force was considered a threat to the advances of Charles Taylor's National Patriotic Forces of Liberia – the NPFL. It vowed to kill five citizens from any of the sixteen West African states for any Liberian killed by ECOMOG.

My sister and I used to visit our father in the forest and come back to town. We stayed there until 1990 when, President Samuel K. Doe was caught and killed. After a few months, we moved back to the Estate. Some of the rebels gave us a lift in someone's Land Rover and there were about six rebels in a taxi behind us protecting our Land Rover. We didn't stay in the Estate for more than a couple of weeks, we went to a displaced camp across the street from Free Port and lived in a container for a week or two and then moved to a hotel – Island Hotel, about five metres away. It was 1990, that was the year Lucky Dude's album 'Remember Me' was released in Liberia.

One morning I almost got killed. I had just got out of the bathroom and on to the balcony trying to hang my undies to dry when a rocket flew passed me, went into Free Port and killed a lot of people. The impact shook the building we were in. Our father grabbed us, taking us downstairs until the scare of the bomb had settled and then we went back upstairs. We stayed at Island Hotel for a while until it was time for Auntie Stina (Dad's younger sister) to take us to Sierra Leone on board a Sierra Leone gunboat. I was nine years old at this stage.

We woke early the following morning to get ready to board the Sierra Leone army gunship for our journey to Sierra Leone. I felt resentful, scared and sad that I was leaving Liberia without my mother. However, there was no-one for me to confide in, but Samia and I, looking at each other and knew exactly what the other was thinking. We did not want to go but we did not have a choice. As I looked at my sister, I knew I had to grow up and be a big sister. When we were alone, I talked to her. I told her not to worry; we would see our mother one day. She said she did not want to go to Sierra Leone and began to sob. I covered her mouth so her crying would not be heard, as I forced myself not to also cry out loud.

Auntie Stina did not like our mother and she sometimes directed her feelings for our mother toward us. Our father was also preoccupied with something else and I felt like we were alone with no adult to talk to. I felt scared and alone the moment the war started in Monrovia. At first, I would tell myself my mother would be back and then I would not have to be so scared anymore but when I found out we were going to Sierra Leone, I felt completely empty. I had to learn how to be there for my little sister as she was really spoilt and did not know how to take care of herself.

We got dressed in a hurry to be at Free Port in time for if we were not, we would be left behind. Samia and I wore dresses and sandals and we had some sweaters to keep us warm at sea. I felt numb when we got to the wharf. I refused to say a word as I was screaming inside; wishing and screaming inside of me that the war would end. I wanted to go and search for my mother. I wanted to stay until I found our mother. I wanted to tell someone that I did not want to go to Sierra Leone; I did not want to leave Monrovia without my mother. I needed to talk to someone but I knew our father would not listen to me. I clung to my sister and in terror watched the chaos in the city, as about a thousand or more people fought to get on the ship.

People wanted to leave Liberia so much they were willing to hurt or kill each other to get a seat or even a standing space on the ship. As I watched, I wished that another family would take our seats and we would stay. A woman got pushed so hard that her baby almost fell into the sea. The child fell and rolled onto the stairs of the ship and the woman screamed for her child. A man was pushed into the sea off the ship. On the other side, another man was getting beaten up.

As we watched all this in horror, around midday we finally boarded the ship. I looked at my father thinking I cannot believe you are sending us away. He promised to look for our mother and he waved at us promising to see us soon. His promises gave me some hope and I felt alright enough to get on the ship. I was sure that we would go back to Liberia as soon as my mother was found.

Before this day, I always thought travelling on a ship would be a great adventure and I had wished for it. Before the war, when I went to Free Port to shop or just passing through on our way home with our mother I'd always wanted to go to the wharf to look at the ships. She always promised to take us and on the days she did, I did not want to leave. But this day, as the ship got ready to leave for Sierra Leone, Samia and I leaned on the banister and waved to our father. I stopped waving when the captain blew the horn one last time and started to depart the harbour. The day my mother took us to see the ship replayed in my head; I could see her face.

I could not breathe; the reality of leaving Monrovia without my mother hit me hard. As the ship departed Free Port I felt something in me break, like a huge piece of flesh inside me was being cut out. The song 'Sweet Liberia' played in my head as I watched the port and my father get smaller.

"Goodbye Monrovia, Liberia and Mama," I muttered.

At that moment, I did what I call 'adult cry'. I was hurting so much inside but I could not cry out, I just stood and watched as tears rolled down my cheeks. Samia cried out when she saw me crying; she hugged me as she cried. One of our father's cousins Auntie Mia held and comforted her. At that moment, I did not know where Auntie Stina was.

We sat on the front balcony of the ship which was great. I liked the view, but at times the smell of the sea made me sick. I was seasick the whole journey vomiting everything I ate and struggling to let something out even when I had nothing left in my stomach. Auntie Mia was friendly with a few of the men who worked on the ship as they were all Sierra Leoneans. They suggested we sit on the balcony in the open as I needed fresh air. Before we left Free Port, they had caught a huge fish about six feet long and everyone on the ship was to have a piece to eat once it was cooked.

I threw up at the first sight of the food that one of Auntie Mia's friends brought us. He was very kind to my sister and me. I hung my head over the side and vomited into the sea and he whispered consoling words in my ear. He rushed into the ship and brought me a glass of cold water and some tablets. He told Auntie Stina and Auntie Mia what the pills were for; I heard him but I did not understand as they spoke in Krio and, at the time, I only spoke English with a Liberian accent.

I was frightened to death as all I thought about were sharks but when I saw the sea gulls on the sea I forgot about the sharks and looked at them instead. Auntie Mia talked to my sister and me trying to encourage us. She told us that everything would be alright and we would see our mother again. Sometimes on the ship I felt numb and completely blanked out not knowing where I was. I only willingly spoke to Samia.

In the warm night I slept a little and threw up a lot. Three days later it was said that the captain had lost his way at sea with our ship. Rumour had it that his girlfriend distracted him and he was taking us somewhere else. It was frightening and a little chaotic. We found out before the other people as our aunties were talking about it and we heard them after one of the men told Auntie Mia. The others on the ship noticed the captain's mistake but only after we had been at sea for five days and six nights. Before we left Liberia, we were told that the journey would be four days long.

A week later, a few miles away from the Sierra Leone harbour, we saw lights and everyone on the ship rejoiced. Samia and I were quiet and in that moment, I just wished my mother were there for me to hug her. All I could hear was, 'finally we are here,' and 'oh God, thank you.' People were happy. They rejoiced while I vomited for the last time.

"This is Freetown, girls, we are getting off here and your seasickness will stop," Auntie Stina told us.

I looked at her, the lights that the ship was going towards and back at her, forcing myself to smile. Inside, I was the saddest child at the time, I thought. Although I was in Sierra Leone, a different country which was safe at the time, I felt like I was still in the war. I could not imagine being happy knowing that my mother could be killed at anytime.

About half an hour later, somewhere around 9.30pm or so, we arrived in the night at Government Wharf in Freetown. There were many Sierra

Leoneans waiting for the ship's arrival. Some were waiting for their loved ones who had been displaced by the Liberian war and some were waiting to take advantage of the helpless refugees. It was noisy; everyone but my sister and I had something to say. We got off the ship and stood there, watching the chaos, while Auntie Stina tried to find our luggage. Thinking 'I love Liberia more than anywhere in the world.'

"I miss Monrovia," Samia said forcing back her tears.

I could see the tears in her eyes and I started to cry too. I forced myself to stop crying. We waited hours for one of our aunties whom Samia and I had never seen before or our cousin Tenneh.

As we waited in the cold evening air, I watched how heartless some people could be. Some of the people waiting at the wharf were thieves. They stole from some of the people who arrived with us. Other people had plates of food which they gave to the Liberian refugees with no-one to help them in exchange for suitcases full of their belongings. Some of them complained that they did not want Liberians in their country and they were shameless enough to say it in English so we could all understand. I was angry and I wished I could go back. Auntie Stina argued with one of the women who tried to exchange a plate of rice for a full suitcase. I did not understand everything she said to the woman but I knew she was telling her off.

Auntie Stina and Auntie Mia stopped a Liberian woman from selling her suitcase; they invited her to eat with us at a little eatery on the wharf. I did not eat much of my food; too tired and too devastated. I wanted my mother. After the meal, I do not know where the Liberian lady went and I think Auntie Stina and Auntie Mia gave her some Leones (Sierra Leone currency). We sat for a while but neither Tenneh nor the other person we were waiting for showed up. Auntie Stina did not know the address, so she, Samia and I had to wait. Fortunately one of their friends, who worked on the ship we arrived in, offered us a room on their ship; it was a different ship. We stayed at the wharf for about five days and I really liked the ship but I was too sad to be normal and excited so I remained quiet. This ship was a bit smaller than the other one we travelled in. It was white and clean and everything in it seemed new.

There was another big yellow ship some feet away from ours and it only had men on it. They were Asians. At the time, I only knew about Chinese, Japanese and Indians so I thought these men on the big yellow ship were Chinese. I was definitely sure they were not Indians, as they did not look Indian. One day Auntie Stina went out in the morning after breakfast, I think in search of Tenneh. She only left us on the ship alone about three times and for a few hours in total. While she was out, I would take my sister to the balcony of the ship so we could look at the men as they were fascinating to me. They were all the same height and they looked alike to me. In the mornings they all wore the same riding tights, all black and seem really busy on their ship; they also made lots of noise. The noise went on for hours but I did not hear them speak English. One day I asked my auntie why all those Chinese men were in Sierra Leone. She told me that they were Malaysians, not Chinese and that they were probably there on business.

Finally, one morning while we were in town, we saw Tenneh but I did not recognise her. She and Auntie Stina jumped into each other's arms screaming with joy. She greeted Samia and me and said that she had been looking for us, that someone told her we were in the country. Tenneh looked good with her makeup and her hair done, manicured nails and she wore high heels and a nice outfit with a nice leather handbag. As I looked at her, my heart broke and I cried inside myself as I remembered our mother all dressed up in the morning for work. I was really sad.

Tenneh was a bubbly person and very loud when she talked. She and Auntie Stina talked and talked but my sister and I did not know what they were talking about. At some point, they started talking about Liberia and our father. I knew this because I heard Tenneh say, 'oh, God …oh Liberia.' Then she called our father's name. I did not know what they said as they spoke in Krio and Mende.

Samia and I remained quiet while we got a taxi from town to the wharf, got our luggage and finally went to Tenneh's house. Anytime my sister and I were alone we used to sit and cry for our mother as we did not want to cry in front of anyone. We did not know what would happen if we cried in front of our Auntie. We cried every day.

Tenneh was a very busy woman, we only got to see her in the morning on her way out and at night when she got back from work. She went to work very early. Her house was well furnished; she had flowers outside in the yard, some outdoor furniture and a hammock on the veranda. We stayed with her for about a week and then we moved to Baba-Dorry, Lumley into Auntie Nyahanga's house.

This house was huge and so was the yard. There were no flowers in the yard as almost the whole yard was paved and beautiful, with only a few yards of land left for gardening where she grew sweet potatoes and other vegetables. The house was a large brick two story building and the fence around the whole compound was seven feet high with a big steel gate. There was also an apartment in the backyard which was rented out to someone else. I liked the place and I liked Auntie Nyahanga and her younger brother Sorie. It was my first time to meet them but they were nice.

There was also Mahmoud who was staying with her. Both Mahmoud and Sorie were in their twenties and they did all the domestic work in the week. Sorie and Mahmoud did everything they could to distract us and keep us smiling once they found out we cried any time we were left alone. I was later told that another one of my father's younger sisters, Auntie Yenie, lived in that home but the time we arrived she was in the hostel on campus at university till the holidays.

Every morning Auntie Nyahanga reminded me of our mother. She was always well dressed and she always smelled good. She would shower, do her makeup, dress up and wear her perfume and leave the house smelling so nice and feminine, every morning before she went to work. She also had her hair neatly done.

"Memuna, look, she has lots of shoes like Mama!" Samia cried one morning.

I burst into tears as I agreed with my sister. Anytime we talked or thought of our mother, we cried. Even when someone asked us about our mother, we would cry in despair as we did not know where she was. It was really hard for us to say we did not know where our mother was. Samia and I were always left with Mahmoud and Sorie, while all the grown women went out to work and other things. Auntie Stina was still trying to settle in her own way.

It was nice in Freetown but hot at night. The view from our house from upstairs was nice at night. One could see the sea, the boats and other houses and lights down the hill. Since my sister and I had not started school yet, we got to go to the market about three times a week with Mahmoud and Sorie; we would go in the morning after breakfast. They would teach us Krio all day before the others got home. Our aunties did not want us speaking too much Krio out of fear we would forget English because we had to study in English like we did in Liberia. In Liberia, my sister and I only got to go to the market on the weekends and two weeks before Christmas for our Christmas shopping with our mother. I had liked going to the market but I was not always allowed.

There was a kitchen in the house but we only used the outdoor kitchen to cook. The one in the house we used when it rained or at night if we had to. There was a tenant called Kumba living in the backyard apartment with her husband. I did not know her husband's name. He was always away for work. Kumba was fond of me; she liked to hear me speak Krio and she would laugh. Isata used the outdoor kitchen all the time and that was how we got to spend time together. Some days when my aunties stayed out late, the boys would allow Kumba to take Samia and me out to sit with her friends who were vendors. She would buy us peanuts, biscuits and candy all evening. Sorie and Mahmoud used that time to catch up with their girls and other boys' stuff. If Kumba was busy we would sit in the living room and read books while the two boys used the balcony or down stairs to entertain their guests. All we had to do if we needed them was call out.

I made lots of friends in the neighbourhood; it was a middle class neighbourhood. One of my close friends in Lumley was Loretta. She was only home on holidays as she lived on campus as a boarder. Her mother and sisters were kind and I think Sorie liked her older sister. Their house was as huge as ours and their fence was just as high on one side. It was lower in the front. Their house was opposite ours and they could stand upstairs in their backyard and see us in the front balcony. I used to visit Loretta without my aunties consent, especially Auntie Stina's. She only wanted us to stay home and read. When Auntie Nyahanga found out one day that I went to visit Loretta, she was glad that I was making friends and she told Samia and me not to get carried away and forget our books. Auntie Stina did not find out. I got to know lots of people in the neighbourhood and my aunties could now send me down the road to the shops.

A week later, Auntie Yenie came to the house on a long holiday; she wanted to spend time with us. She was happy to see us and she was in tears. She asked me about my childhood boyfriend Enzo. My father's sisters would ask lots of questions but none were about my mother. I assumed that it was because they knew exactly what I was going to say but I did not really know why they never asked. Auntie Yenie came home with one of her friends. The lady was quite fond of me. She did not stay; she went to her house and came to visit. One day while she was over visiting, I proudly told her that I knew lots of words in Krio.

"I'm proud of you, that you are so enthusiastic to learn Krio but don't forget English," she said.

I nodded and told her I would not forget. That day when she visited, she brought two storybooks containing a collection of fairy tales.

A few weeks later our father came from Liberia. He came to Lumley in the morning and found me in the outdoor kitchen trying to help Sorie make the fire in the coal pot.

"Get away from that fire," he said, when he walked into the yard and saw me blowing the fire in the coal pot with my mouth.

I looked up and ran into his arms as I called out to Samia who was upstairs. I hugged him and asked him about my mother. He said he had not seen her but we should not worry and keep praying until we find her. He stayed a few hours talking with his sisters and us but left as he was leaving for Liberia again that night. He stayed behind to look for Mama. He assured us things will get better and he would come back to Sierra Leone soon.

A few weeks after he left for Liberia, Samia went to live in Sembehun with our grandmothers. We were not happy they were separating us but we had no choice. I completely shut down when my sister went away. If it was possible, I was sadder than before. I cried for my sister and Mama every day. Auntie Nyahanga told me I did not have to worry about Samia; she was going to be spoiled by the old ladies and she would be happy. Before Samia left, sometimes the house used to be so hot we had to sleep in the living room on blankets on the carpet. If the two of us were left without Sorie and Mahmoud we were scared to be in the house alone. All four of us would sleep on the balcony on mats and blankets in the evening breeze. The boys would make space for Samia and me in front of the front door upstairs on the balcony and they would lay their mat on the far end. The beds in the house were empty. We had fans in the room but the power was never stable, so I preferred to sleep in the living room or on the balcony.

When Samia went to Sembehun, I was left alone with the boys and Isata. Sometimes my aunties would take me with them to weddings and baby showers but I hated the weddings because of the noise. Kumba took me for a walk any time she could, when my aunties were out and that put a smile on my face. Loretta and I visited each other more often. A few weeks went by and one morning I was asked to go down the road to buy two big loaves of bread and a box of cube sugar. Everyone in the house was busy as it was Saturday. They were cleaning, doing the laundry and preparing to cook, so I was the only one who had nothing to do. But this day something invaded our new normalcy. As I walked down the lane to the shops I heard people screaming and the sound of a vehicle engine roaring. I saw some men dressed in army uniform brutally beating a couple of Liberian young men who had come as refugees and found a place to live in Lumley. They were trying to settle, they seemed relaxed and some of the people in the neighbourhood knew and liked them. There was a man who was introduced to me by Kumba. He was called Kabineh. He was involved in the beating. They beat those young men until they were bloody and helpless. It was chaotic in Lumley. I saw Kabineh beat the helpless young men with a baton and asking them for their partners. Some of the people who knew them cried and screamed for the beating to stop.

"They are just refugees, not rebels," one woman cried.

As I stood on the lane looking at Kabineh, feeling sorry and scared with tears in my eyes, he turned and looked at me. Our eyes locked. I could not believe what I saw. Kabineh was a military man in the Sierra Leone army but all this time had posed as a civilian watching people. In that instant I hated him, Freetown and Sierra Leone. I stood there numb and stiff with fear and anger. I watched Kabineh and his cruel army colleagues tie those men and throw them in the army truck; the engine had been running the whole time. Kabineh was enjoying himself beating those young men. He had a huge smile on his face. He walked up to me and I could see splashes of blood on his T-shirt.

"Liberian girl!" he yelled in my face when he reached me.

I screamed and ran as fast as I could back up to our house and I heard someone yell at him to leave me alone. I was very scared, I could not stop screaming. I got home and wrapped my arms tightly around Auntie Yenie's waist. She was the first person I bumped into.

"What's the matter, Memuna?" She asked. "Where are the things you went to buy?"

I could not talk, so I unfolded my right fist and showed her the money I had clutched in it. I was so scared my hands were clenched in fists. I showed my aunt the money, I pointed frantically to the street where the noise was coming from. Sorie and Mahmoud were on the other side of the house doing the laundry and making noise.

Auntie Stina was upstairs standing on the front balcony, she could see down the lane and she saw the chaos.

"What is going on down there? Where is Memuna?" she asked, as her voice grew anxious. Auntie Yenie told her I was in the yard. She pulled me from the stairs downstairs to show me to her sister.

"But she is scared and I think she saw what is going on down there," said Auntie Yenie.

Auntie Stina asked me if I got hit by anyone and I shook my head, looking up at her.

"Why are you scared then? Did you buy the things?" she asked.

"They beat those Liberian men, there was blood everywhere," I cried. "I think they killed them or they are going to kill them."

Auntie Yenie coaxed me. "Hush…. now I'm sure they did not kill them," she said.

"They took them…. in the army truck," I cried.

She wiped my tears and took me upstairs. Apart from the time I was seasick, that day was the second time Auntie Stina was patient with me. She hugged me and coaxed me. She assured me the two men were alright but I could not believe them after what I saw.

Later that day we learned all young Liberian males in Freetown were in trouble. They were accused of being rebels as the war had started on the Sierra Leone/Liberia border and the rebels were entering Sierra Leone through Pujehun. Foday Sankoh had formed the Revolutionary United Front - RUF. Innocent refugees who had fled for a peaceful life were paying for it. I lived in fear for weeks and I stopped going down the road with Kumba. She knew why and she was regretful about what her friend, Kabineh, had done.

Soon, I was taken to Bo Town, to live with Tenneh's father Bishop J. Samuels and the rest of the family. At first, I did not like being there as none of the people in the house were familiar. But the lady of the house, Mammy Sallay, was so kind and gentle to me that slowly I grew to like the place. She would always have me with her in the kitchen when she was cooking. She would talk and give me courage to believe that by God's grace I would see my mother again. She wanted to enroll me in school, but I arrived in Bo in the middle of the last term of the school year. So she promised to do it the following year, after she got the chance to speak to my father.

There were other young people in the house. Aminatu, Mammy Sallay's daughter and I were close but I would often feel very sad and lonely when I saw Mammy Sallay and Aminatu together. I wanted my mother so badly that, most of the times, I would run to the mango trees in the backyard, sit on the ground, cry bitterly and then pray. When I was six years old, our mother taught me to recite the 23rd Psalm whenever I was in trouble. So any time I felt sad or scared I would recite it. I missed Samia too but at least I knew where she was.

Pa Samuels spent his time at the church leading prayers and undertaking other spiritual works of God for people. At other times he would remain in his room doing just that or reading the Bible. He was a very observant old man. Just when you think he knows nothing he lets you realise you are wrong. He was aware of everything that went on in the home and he knew who did what although he was hardly there. He surprised me by letting me know he knew I was unhappy. When he was less busy and at home, he would talk to me. He had his own pet name for me – Tinny. He would tell me everything would be alright, no matter how long.

I grew to like the house, but there was something I did not like. There were lots of domestic animals - poultry, ducks, sheep, pigs and guinea pigs. There were also two dogs: one big old one belonging to the old man and one puppy that always had bare sores on its ears. The guinea pigs were kept in a cage in the vacant outdoor kitchen, while Mammy Sallay used the other for cooking. The sheep would sometimes come into the house and poop around and the pigs were always where they were meant to be, in a puddle of mud. We all loved the old dog; he was so old that he could not bark anymore, though he tried. I did not like the puppy that had sores on its ears and I would kick it or move away anytime it came near me. The others would growl at it when it got near them. One day Mammy Sallay felt sorry for the dog when she saw me kick him, she told me not to do it again and she said that animals were from God. Two days later she assigned the Guinea pigs to me and told me how to look after them. I stopped kicking that dog but I always moved away when he came closer because of the flies that followed the sores on his ears. Mammy Sallay made several attempts to treat the sores but the dog would not let her.

I fell sick a couple of times; once I had a fever and the other time I woke up one morning with about six medium bumps on my face. In a day or two, they developed into big, sore, ripe boils and my whole head hurt. I could hardly open my mouth to eat but Mammy Sallay took her time to treat and feed me. I had sleepless nights; I would stay up crying for my mother because I was in a lot of pain. My face and head hurt.

Weeks after the scars on my face from the boils healed, one afternoon while we were in the kitchen cooking, a petite old lady came to the house. The moment I saw her I told myself I was not getting out of that hot kitchen. As scary as she was, she seemed pleased to see me. She greeted me and said my name but I remained silent and stared at her. Mammy Sallay took her to the veranda to where Pa Samuels was sitting and they talked; they all seemed happy to see each other. I hid myself in the kitchen because I was afraid of old people, especially ones that had grey hair and wrinkles. This old lady had all of those. She was dressed in a West African outfit with a scarf tied around her head. I was afraid of old people because I thought every old person was a witch. I made this conclusion because all the stories I had read and was told featuring old women were witches - stories like

Hansel and Gretel. At this time, the only elderly person I was used to was my mother's mother who was not old at all.

While I hid in the kitchen, Mammy Sallay came to get me out. She told me my grandmother wanted to talk to me. When I pleaded with her not to make me go out to talk to the old lady, she assured me it was alright, she was my grandmother called Mama Adama. I screamed, telling her I remember Mama Adama and the last time I saw her she was not that old. I refused and cried, while Mama Adama and Mammy Sallay watched me in disbelief. Pa Samuels came and talked me into coming out of the kitchen. Finally I came out covered in sweat. Mama Adama tried to touch me but I moved away. In an effort to convince me that she was really who they said she was, she started to talk about our family and she even mentioned my mother. They spent hours talking to me. I was supposed to go with Mama Adama to her house as we were travelling to Sembehun in the morning.

I did not want to leave Mammy Sallay as she loved me very much and I loved her too. It hurt me to realise that from the day the war started, my best friend, my family and I all went our separate ways, people were being snatched out of my life. I cried bitterly, but I went with Mama Adama. I did not know what was going on and I did not ask. At that moment I just wanted Mama to come and ease my pain. Mama Adama took me to her house and, only when we got there, I believed that she was really my grandmother Mama Adama Barnes. I remembered the house, from when I went to live in Sierra Leone when I was 4. My cousin Maada was there; he picked me up the moment he saw me. He was very happy that I recognised him. Maada was my father's younger brother's son. He put a smile on my face and we played all night. I gave him two of my note pads that I brought from Freetown and some of the money that Pa Samuels gave me. Everyone in the yard was gushing over how grown up I was and how much I looked like both of my parents. By then I was good at Krio. Maada and I played all night and fell asleep early in the morning. I had two hours of sleep and it was time to get ready for the trip to Sembehun which was roughly a thirteen hour drive from Bo Town.

Everyone in Sembehun was happy to see us; Mama Adama was greeted with so much respect. We arrived in the afternoon; the driver of the Toyota stopped on the main road, not so far from our house and carried on with his journey. Memories flashed as soon as I got out of the vehicle. There were screams and people running to us, others stood and watched. As they saw me, they screamed 'oh…. you are so grown.' That was all I could hear. I was hugged from one person to the other and several times I was picked up. They carried our luggage and between the hugs and totes we got to our house. Samia and I hugged for a long moment. She seemed very happy and she had put on so much weight.

I remembered all my cousins and all the others whom I spent time with when I lived in Sierra Leone when I was four years old.

All of our aunties except Auntie Soko – my dad's youngest sister were there. There were drummers entertaining the guests, there was a huge tent in the front yard and there were huge pots on the fires in the kitchen. I greeted my paternal grandmothers. My paternal grandfather married four wives but one died, I had three left. They were all at the house on that day. It was a scary sight for me. Mama Adama told them about our little problem when she went to get me.

Our houses were filled. My siblings, aunties, uncles, grandmothers, cousins, other relatives and other people from around Sembehun were all there. It was Auntie Yenie's engagement ceremony. She brought her friends, her in-laws, Auntie Nyahanga, her parents and a few of her siblings. That day I had to meet so many family members and I managed to smile at the old ones, but I did not shake hands. I remembered my Grandmother Ngaya very well although she was grey now too. When I was first taken to Sierra Leone I lived with her and Grandma Memuna for almost two years, so I was not afraid of those two. As for Mama Adama I only spent a few days with her, so that was why I could not recognise her and I did not think she would be so grey so fast. She was a very strong old lady because at this time she was over eighty years old and she could still do chores on her own.

Grandma Memuna was very busy; she felt like she had to cook for everyone. It was her kitchen in her marital home and it was her daughter's engagement. Grandma Ngaya and Mama Adama were busy making sure things were well organised and that every guest had a room, took a bath and were comfortable. Mee Mariama, my other grandma- she was my grandfather's dead brother's wife but my grandfather cared for her after his brother died. She was the very loud one. She was up the hill at her house doing what she was meant to do and she came down to the other house to help do other things. They all got help from my aunties, uncles and us the grandchildren. At first, I did not know what to do but I was given something to do. Auntie Yenie got emotional quite easily. She had a lot on her plate and everyone wanted to talk to her. They called her from one corner to the other. Some old ladies gave her marital advice. The Barnes home was like a little village; people kept coming including some who were drummers coming from nearby villages. Our grandmothers made sure that we ate and they told us the younger children were to go across the compound to Auntie Satta's house and stay there. The older ones from fifteen up stayed to help serve the guests and do other things. Gbondo was not feeling well so she did not do much; she joined us with the younger children. I was very happy to spend time with two of my siblings and cousins but I was so tired all the drums and singing could not keep me awake.

There were more arrivals in the morning. Our father had arrived over night with my oldest brother Sam, one of my uncles with his wife and some other people. Later that morning, two more of my siblings, Nafiatu and

Mahein, arrived. It was a busier day even than the one before. My grandmothers were happy to see almost all of their children, especially my father and his brother with whom he arrived, because they had not seen them in years. We all had to dress up. It was easier to get the boys to dress up because they had already had haircuts. Between other things, Auntie Yenie did Samia and my hair. It was easier to do Nyalay's hair because her hair was cut too. Auntie Yenie straightened our hair with a hot iron comb and put in baubles. She asked Nafiatu to help us pick out our outfits. I was 10 years old by now as it was already a few months into 1991. I wore a beautiful blue dress I was able to bring from Liberia and a pair of slippers. Gbondo, Nafiatu and our older teenage cousins did their own hair and got dressed on their own.

This was the evening of the ceremony which I was unaware of until my grandmother, my father, his brothers, and some other relatives gathered in the living room with Auntie Yenie's in-laws. My aunties, my female cousins, my sisters and I were told to go into two rooms in the house and close the door. A man knocked on the door of the rooms we were in asking for something he wanted from our family. Each time he knocked the wrong person came out and each time this happened he gave the wrong woman some money and she would go outside. It went on almost an hour, until finally the right woman, being the only one left in the rooms, came out. He held her hand and led her to the living room where both families were waiting. The two families spent almost an hour talking then the ring was finally placed on her finger.

This was not a formal marriage but a traditional engagement. Auntie Yenie's partner was in England but they knew each other before he travelled. So his brother, deputising for him, put the ring on her finger. Everyone wanted to see the diamond on her ring; the old people blessed the ring. Those who had cameras took pictures. Our family asked her new family by marriage to take good care of her before they gave her away. The drums and singing got louder in the tent. There was lots of alcohol and some people were already drunk. I hate being stepped on and I got stepped on by a lot of people. I got upset and started to cry. When Auntie Yenie found me crying she reached for my hand and took me to the living room. She went outside again to look for Samia, Nyalay and my other younger cousins so she could put us in bed.

Some of the guests from Freetown who had jobs to return to started to leave in the morning. In a few days all the guests were gone. Some of the drummers went back to the villages and some stayed. They played a few more days. Everyone went and left the bride-to-be and her family to work through other things. My father did not stay long; he fell sick so he left for Freetown. Auntie Yenie left soon after my father. She had to arrange herself to go to England. The engagement took place during midterm break (September), so when school reopened I was enrolled at United Methodist Church Primary school (U.M.C) with Samia and my other cousins. It was the school that my father and almost all of his siblings had gone to. I liked the school. One of our uncles was one of the teachers and I had other relatives who were teachers there as well. That did not mean that any of my cousins or I were special. I had lots of cousins in Sembehun, they were also my friends and I made some other friends.

It was a little hard for me in the beginning but I had my grandmothers and they made me feel at home. Auntie Satta was there and she kept her eyes on us all along with her children. She put us in our place when we tried to give the old ladies a hard time. Gbondo was taken to Freetown so that she could continue high school. Nafiatu went back to Moyamba eighteen miles away from Sembehun, where she was a boarder living on campus at one of the high school for girls. Sony went to Freetown with Uncle Charles my father's youngest brother. Nyakeh left long before they did with our father. So there were six grandchildren left with our grandmothers and we were not all teenagers. I was ten years old, Samia was seven years old, the others were ages six, twelve and thirteen years old.

Every day I went to school I would become upset and Memuna would fight for me. The other children at school teased me because I did not know how to speak Mende. One time I cried and reported a group of girls to one of our teachers, Mrs. Bangalie. She told them that they were laughing at themselves because we were not taught in Mende. We were taught in English and she gave them a second chance after she made them apologise. Sometimes they would attack me in the schoolyard and tease me. At first I would just look at them and laugh as I did not want them to get the best of me. One day, it got too much though and it did not take much effort to upset me. A girl teased me calling me a white woman in Mende. Before she could complete her words I gave her a hard slap across her face. She was shocked and began to cry. I looked in her eyes, nodded and I walked away. I did not know how to fight so I had been beaten lots of times when I got into fights but I was not scared. I slowly learned the art of fighting by my mistakes and soon I was left alone because I beat lots of people on Samia's and my behalf.

A month after the engagement Auntie Soko came home; no-one knew where she had been. She arrived at night and when she saw Samia and me she burst into tears. She was happy that we made it through the war. Someone told her that we were in Sembehun and they told her that my father was there too. She asked for her brother and they told her that he had gone back to Liberia. The old ladies were angry with her for not coming home in years especially when she did not come to her sister's engagement even though she was in the country. It was also a family gathering.

"How do you think your father would have felt?" Grandma Memuna asked.

She apologised and the old ladies continued reprimanding her, but all she said was she was sorry and that it would not happen again. Luckily she arrived on the weekend so we stayed up late talking. I did not have much to say, neither did Samia. She asked us about our mother and I told her we did not know where she was. I told her our father asked us not to worry, that we would see her again. I told her about my mother's younger brother, and how we saw him before we boarded the ship for Sierra Leone. He told us our mother was stuck in Lofa and that she was doing ok but she was worried about us. She put her arms around us and told us that things would be fine.

My grandfather, Joseph C. Barnes, had passed away but his family kept his memory alive with the firm hands of his wives. He made all the locks on the doors in the house; he built the house, most of the trunks that his children used when they were boarders in high school were made by him. He made some of the furniture in the house and he made his own spoon and engraved his initials on the handle and his bedroom was still kept clean and respected as if he were still alive. All of these things were well taken care of. My father's and his siblings' trunks were kept in their father's room and in the ceiling. They contained their books, letters and academic results. We kept our clothes in some. Auntie Soko and her friend slept in her father's room. They stayed about three weeks and she went back – to Rutile where she said she was living, promising to go to Freetown to catch up with her brothers and sisters and hoping to see Auntie Yenie before she left.

A few months later, it was Christmas 1991. All the family members came back to spend Christmas at the family house. My father was in Liberia so he did not come but everyone else came. We all had some new outfits for Christmas. There was lots of food and drinks. This was the best Christmas for me since 1989 - the last Christmas I spent with my mother. I did not unwrap any presents but I had new things and I had my paternal grandmothers, my siblings, my aunties and uncles and my cousins. I cried for my mother when I heard the carols being sung and Gbondo wiped my tears. I love all of my siblings and I believe they feel the same about me. Gbondo and I love each other, though she would act like she does not like me. We snapped at each other when we were young, but she did not let anyone take advantage of me.

"Don't bother my little sisters," she would say.

When we were not teasing or snapping at each other, she would tell me about the things I did when I was very young and taken to Sierra Leone. She did not like to do my hair, she said I whined too much and I did not sit still. Sembehun was crowded as everyone who had family in Sembehun came along with friends to spend Christmas and New Year with their family. It was awesome and there were parties everywhere. They brought their city life to Sembehun. They made sure they went to the night club every Friday and Saturday and there were movies at U.M.C school hall every Wednesday if Christmas did not fall on those days.

My father's younger brother, Uncle Kalu, would not allow my older sisters and my cousins to go to the clubs but the older boys were allowed to roam around town all night. So Gbondo and the other older girls would pretend as if they were going to bed, they would say their goodnights and go to the other house. Sometimes if our main house was full, they would go and sleep at Gbondo's' friend, Hafsatu house but they would give me their clothes and shoes to push through the window; they already had their makeup at the other house.

There was a delicious aroma of food coming from every kitchen in the town. On Christmas day we woke up at around 5am to start cooking and get ready to go to church for Christmas service. There was always so much food at our house especially on special days. Apart from our own food, our relatives around town and the neighbours brought dishes to our house. My cousins, my sisters and I would focus on the food that Grandma Memuna cooked and also the dish from Auntie Satta because we were used to their cooking. That was what we ate everyday so it was a must to us. There were only two reasons I would not eat Grandma Memuna's food – if I was hiding out at another relative's house because I had done something wrong and did not want to go home because I was dodging punishment for something I had done or because I was ill otherwise it was like I did not eat at all.

I lived with my grandmothers for two years in Sembehun. I was a good student and I enjoyed living with them. I gave them a lot of work to do as I was a very energetic child and I fell ill occasionally. I did not get to climb trees, go fishing or go to farms in Liberia but I could do all of these things in Sembehun and it was exciting. My family did not have a farm; our food came from Freetown along with money for everything from Auntie Yenie, Auntie Soko and sometimes my father (as he was still settling in at Freetown). It was monthly and we were well cared for.

We had everything we wanted although we did not have electricity and it was by choice. Sembehun is a town with three primary schools and a high school, there were no supermarkets (but there were convenience stores and a market). The people lived happily even without electricity. Those who wanted it bought generators. In our house, we sometimes had power but only on special occasions. Auntie Yenie's engagement was one of those special occasions and on some Christmas holidays. Grandma Ngaya did not want a light bulb in her bedroom, she used her lantern as she always done despite there being power through the rest of the house.

The people of Sembehun did not think it was important to have electricity. Only a few families had a generator and they did not use it every day. Pa Madou, who owned one of the biggest shops in Sembehun, had a generator for his business. He sold everything from tea bags, sugar and milk to shoes, underwear, clothes and fabric. He didn't sell meat of any kind or fish. We always had kerosene in the house for our lanterns and some people used kerosene fridges. We had used electricity in Monrovia before the war started and the lines were cut.

My Grandma Memuna's brother, Pa Kanu whom we all called Kaynya (Mende for 'uncle'), had a farm every year (after harvest he usually used a different piece of land – not sure how he obtained the land but everyone did that) and we went to his farm when we felt like it. I only went a few times; I was so excited to be there. The second time we visited his farm we got caught in a heavy rain and I was so upset I vowed never to go to a farm again. I liked it though, I was only upset about the rain and that was why I made a vow.

My cousin Komeh and I used to go to the bridge with our friends to go fishing for mudskippers and crabs. We would not tell Auntie Satta or the old ladies where we were going because they would not have let us. One day I almost drowned and I was not going to tell either of my grandmothers with whom I lived, but somebody saw me and told Grandma Memuna before I got home. She told me she wanted that to be the last time I went to the bridge and I apologised. Every day I came home with a sore body either because I rode bicycle with the boys, got into serious fist fights with some other girls or I tried to jump from a tree and landed hard on my feet. Other times I would sprain my leg or toes by playing soccer bare foot. I was always very busy.

From Monday to Friday, when we woke in the morning, we would brush our teeth and freshen up, have breakfast and go to school. From 8am to 2.30pm, we would be at school. After school we went straight home, got out of our uniforms and had some food. Grandma Memuna always had a proper meal ready for all of us by that time every day. She would also set some aside for dinner. After we ate, we would clean the kitchen and the lantern shades and then we would check the drums to see if we had enough water and if they were clean. If we needed to clean the drums and fetch more water, we would do it as fast as we could and then run off to our various social activities. By 5pm we knew to be home, bathe, light the lanterns, give our grandmothers water to bathe, have dinner, read a book, do homework and then go to bed. If we did not have enough wood in the kitchen when we got home from school we would go with Grandma Memuna to a farm nearby and fetch some. She would ask the owner of the farm first. She did not just use any kind of dried tree as wood; she had some she was completely against using.

On Saturdays we would sit outside and tell tales into the night. We would spend the day cleaning and doing laundry washing our uniforms and ironing them for Monday. Every Sunday morning we went to church. After church we would go home, eat, and then corn row our hair for the school week. About once a month there would be a movie showing at U.M.C. school hall in the evening and we would go and watch and then come back home.

I loved it in Sembehun. I grew to like old people and found them interesting. It was awesome living with my grandmothers; I loved them. After I passed class five, Auntie Soko took me crying and kicking to live with her in Kongoma about thirty miles away. I did not like it one bit. I was happy when I was at school with my friends Jennie, Osman and Bashir. I always looked forward to the holidays because that meant I would go and be with my grandmothers, Samia and my cousins.

CHAPTER TWO

Taken

I came from school on a Tuesday in May 1995. I helped my Auntie Soko whom I lived with, to fill the water drum we had in our kitchen for our everyday use. After that I went to my room to write in my diary with my friend Jennie. We were talking about our boyfriends from class six.

Suddenly we heard Jennie's mother, whom everyone called Sissy and some other people talking unusually loud.

"Memuna, I think there's a quarrel going on out there?" Jennie said. "Let's go out so we won't miss the excitement."

I saw Ella, Jennie's younger sister and asked her what the fuss was about.

"They just listened to the five o'clock BBC news and everyone just went mad after they heard it," Ella said.

"What was the news about," I asked.

"I think it was about the rebels. They said they will enter Moyamba in a few weeks," she replied.

Shocked, Jennie asked, "How close is Moyamba to us here in Kongoma, Memuna?"

"About eleven or twelve miles," I replied.

"Oh good," she said, "by the time those bastards get here I'll be gone to Freetown."

Auntie Jenneh had come down from her house.

"Soko if the rebels come to this town we should not be afraid to hit them with sticks," she said.

She had a stick in her hand and she demonstrated as she spoke. I looked and thought she did not know what she was talking about. As a matter of fact I was the only one, a fourteen year old child, who knew exactly what the word 'war' meant. Although I was still trying to understand why it happened, I was the only one who had any idea of what was coming our way.

I was frustrated and terrified knowing I was going to have to flee my home yet another time because of rebels. Then I started thinking of my mother picturing everything that went on with us in Monrovia during the war. For a minute I was totally lost in my thoughts and I could not hear what Jennie was saying. It was early 1995. As I stood there listening to them and drifting away from their conversation I relived the pain in my heart of leaving Monrovia for Freetown, the pain I felt thinking I might not see my mother again and all the horrific things I saw in Monrovia – horror a child should not have to see.

That night Auntie Soko called me to her room and asked me whether I preferred to go to Freetown with her or go to Sembehun to my grandmothers.

"Let me think about it," I said.

"Okay, goodnight then," she said.

I gave her question a long hard thought all night and made up my mind I was going to my grandmothers to be with my younger sister Samia and my cousins, especially Komeh. The following morning I told Auntie Soko that I'd rather go to Sembehun.

"Okay I'll discuss it with Amadu(her fiancé)," she said.

Two weeks later she got me ready to take me to Sembehun. All of my cousins and Samia were happy to see me. Auntie Soko and I saw Grandma Memuna on her way to Kongo-Lorlu.

"Ngor (a word used in reference to one's older brother or sister - what Grandma Memuna's children and grandchildren called her), where are you going?" Auntie Soko asked her mother.

"I'm going to Kongo-Lorlu, Jebbeh just died," said Grandma Memuna.

"What did you say? When did she die?" asked Auntie Soko. "What happened to her, could I come with you?"

"No, go home you must be tired," Grandma Memuna said. "She died two hours ago of malaria. Go home I'll be back in the evening."

I was sorry that my grandmother had lost her close friend. She came home in the evening and told Grandma Ngaya and the others about the funeral. Ma Jebbeh was a Muslim so she had to be buried the same day. I was scared of the whole dead body conversation so Samia, my cousins and I sat outside in the moonlight and talked about different things. Auntie Soko went back to Kongoma the following day to get ready for her trip to Freetown.

I spent a week in Sembehun and Grandma Ngaya got desperate to send me to Freetown. She said I was wasting time in the village; I should have been in school because I was already in secondary school.

"Karimu, child, can you please tell Kenawova that I would like to see him before he leaves tomorrow?" Grandma Ngaya said. Karimu was my father's relative who was in his early thirties, he lived with my grandmothers.

Karimu told Grandma Ngaya he would try to get Kenawova before dawn.

"Please Papa, because this child should be in Freetown going to school," Grandma Ngaya said.

I wanted more than anything to go back to school, but I only had two places to stay - either with our grandmothers in Sembehun or with Auntie Soko because Samia and I did not know where our mother was. We did not know whether she was alive or not and our father was back and forth between Liberia and Sierra Leone, although the war in Liberia had long ago taken over the country.

The next morning Kenawova came to the house around 7.30am. I was still asleep but when I heard his voice I woke up. I wanted to see him but when I greeted him his response was "What are you doing here?"

"Spending holidays," I said.

"It's not school holidays yet, Soko shouldn't have let you make your own decision," Kenawova said.

"This is what I was saying, how could she let this child make decisions about where she wants to go and where she doesn't want to go," Grandma Ngaya said.

"Hey, get ready tomorrow I'm taking you to Freetown," Kenawova said, pointing at me.

"It's God who told her to let me decide where I want to go because she can't keep her hands off me," I said. "I'm sure even her own mother did not beat her as much as she beats me. Even my mother did not beat me but that is all that Soko does, so I'm not going if my father isn't in Freetown."

I cried and stormed into the girls' room and threw myself on the bed with my fingers in my hair. Everyone was upset with me for being in Sembehun instead of going to Freetown to go to school. Kenawova said bye to Grandma Ngaya on his way to the backyard to say hello to Grandma Memuna.

"Ngeiwo ee wu jia paanda (Mende for 'May God walk you safely')," Grandma Ngaya said.

"Memuna," called Grandma Memuna from the back veranda. "I think you'll like to wake up now."

I got out of bed wiping my tears with the back of my hand as I walked through the house to the back veranda.

"Ngor buwaa (Mende for 'hello')," I said, leaning on the back door.

"Bie yea yie?" (Mende for 'how did you sleep.' In other words 'how was your night') she said.

Samia and Nyalay were eating rice from the day before in a medium pot.

"Memuna you really enjoyed your sleep, huh?" Nyalay teased.

"You like sleeping too much," Samia said.

I knew that they liked bothering me anytime I was in Sembehun so I said nothing.

28

"Are you being a snob?" Samia asked. "Or you did not hear what we said."

"I don't want to talk I just woke up," I replied.

Ngor took the lid off the plate she had in front of her on the table and asked me if I wanted some pancakes.

"Yes," I said.

Unlike Samia and my cousins I did not like eating rice in the morning especially when I had it the day before. I ate the pancakes before brushing my teeth, usually Ngor would tell me off for eating before brushing my teeth but she did not say anything this time. Instead Samia and Nyalay decided to do it for her.

"Won't you two leave her alone?" said Wale Jr., Uncle Sylvester's son (one of my father's younger brothers).

So I took my plate of pancakes and went next door to Auntie Satta's house, as they had really started getting on my nerves. I could not think with all of them talking. Komeh was in her room, I went there to her and we both ate the pancakes. We stayed in the room for hours. When we got out I washed up and we went up the hill to see Grandma Mariama. I had not been to greet her since I arrived from Kongoma so that was what I went to do. The first thing she said as soon as I said hello was,

"You're here in this town again with your walking about, aren't you?"

"No, I just came up here to greet you," I said.

She asked me some questions and she told me everyone is worried about the rebel news, so we should not go too far with our walking about. I assured her we would not.

"Mee (Mende for 'granny' or 'mama') Mariama, I'll tell the rebels not to come here," Komeh said. Komeh never took anything seriously.

"Clear out," Mee Mariama said.

We laughed and ran off to Abibatu house which was just three houses away from Mee Mariama's house. She was happy to see us, especially me.

"Hey, you look taller to me. You'll soon be a woman, how old are you now?" she said.

"Fourteen, I'll be fifteen soon," I said.

We talked a while and left. Two weeks later I dreamt the rebels captured me, I managed to escape and hide in an unfinished house. From there I climbed up our kitchen ceiling till the rebels went away. Two days later we heard heavy gun fire from Rutile. Rutile was a beautiful town; it was where the mineral rutile was mined. The town was named after the mineral. The firing was so heavy the army troops that were sent to guard Sembehun panicked and left the following morning leaving some of their belongings behind. One soldier left his pregnant girlfriend behind.

Kenawova could not come for me. The rebels took over the Moyamba road and the other road. The night after the army left some people came from the nearby villages. They said the rebels were in Moyamba and they were capturing young people. The next morning Sembehun was full of people from the surrounding villages. Within the next week, the villagers went to the other villages behind Sembehun. Late one night, some more displaced people arrived in Sembehun, waking up everyone in our area. They said they were from Moyamba. They said they had been in the forest for the past week. We stayed up to listen to what they were saying. They had so much to say and I was sleepy so I went back to our room and found Komeh already in bed.

"What are we going to do? Those bastard monkeys who call themselves rebels," she asked.

I could not say anything, I was confused. Bewildered I could not really put anything together.

I took the cloth I had wrapped around me. I wore a T-shirt and one of my shorts and my sneakers. Katumu walked into the room and saw me dressed; she could not help herself laughing.

"Memuna.... What are you doing?" she said. "They are not here yet."

Komeh looked at Katumu and me and the three of us burst out in laughter.

"Hey, you know what?" I said. "I know what those displaced people are talking about. I have seen rebels in Liberia before and I don't want it to happen again. I wish those rebels could just go blind and then there wouldn't be any war."

We laughed about it and went back to bed but all this time I was so confused and sad I could not believe it was happening to me again. I felt the horror from the war in Liberia was following me. I laid awake in bed for hours wishing, hoping and praying they would not come to Sembehun. The next morning most of the displaced people and residents of Sembehun moved their families and friends to the nearby villages to stay with relatives. Sembehun was now very quiet as only my family and some other families stayed behind.

3rd June 1995, a Saturday morning; I woke up, with a craving for pepper soup and sweet potatoes. I had to wait for Grandma Memuna to come back from the market to give me some fish and other ingredients so I could cook my stew. When she got back I asked her to give me the things I needed for my stew.

"I don't have any fish to give to you because you won't cook it properly. Too much of a hurry to eat it which is not good for your health," she said.

"Ok, just give me two pieces, I'll cook it very well before eating it," I said.

"No, you don't know how to cook and eating half cooked fish gives people worms. So please, you're not having it," she said.

I left her and went to Auntie Satta's house, I asked her to give me some fish. She knew I could cook very well for my age, so she gave me some fish. I spent two hours cooking my stew. Once the food was ready I went to our room to talk to mine and Komeh's friend, Katumu. She had hurt her foot by stepping on a rusty nail the day before. Her second treatment had been at the clinic that morning; she had just got back and was resting.

She was lying in bed staring up at the ceiling. I got in and asked her how she was feeling.

"I thought you did not care," she said.

That made me upset with her again, she had ignored me for another friend the day she got hurt.

"See, you're not ready to talk to me yet. There's some potatoes and stew in the two little pots in the kitchen, you can have some if you want," I said on my way out.

I went up to the schoolyard for a bicycle ride with my cousins and friends. It was our own form of racing. Suddenly there were people running and crying. Mikailu asked what was going on,

"The rebels are coming, they are in our town."

I did not believe them. There was no shooting and it was not the first time a group of people had run around town crying and screaming that the rebels were in town. I gave Mikailu his bicycle then Wale Jr., Daddy and I walked back home. I was really sick and tired of the false alarms but some part of me believed they were in town. Our grandmothers and some of the town's people were confused. Auntie Satta and our grandmothers urged us to run as fast as we could, especially Komeh, Katumu and me. Komeh and Katumu had huge breasts and mine had just started growing it felt like a little nut on my chest. Katumu was in her early twenties, I was fourteen and Komeh was six months older than I was. So she was already fifteen and she grew faster.

But that day, Komeh was not at home. She had gone to the market to sell some vegetables in the morning and was still in the market. She did not believe the rebels were in the town either. We were all at home at this moment and her mother and our grandmothers thought she had ran home too, so all this time they were talking to us she was not there. They called out to her but she was nowhere around. We found out that, this time it was true the rebels were actually in Sembehun. I was confused and speechless. Shaking and tongue-tied, I was so frightened I could hardly breathe. Flashbacks of what happened to us in Barnersville Estate in Monrovia, spilled through my brain leaving me numb. Tears streamed down my cheeks. Nyalay, Samia and Katumu packed up some things. Nyalay packed some clothes in my school bag.

"All of you can run to Manni and leave us here, they won't do anything to us," Grandma Memuna said.

"It's true, run they are coming…. Run!" Grandma Ngaya said.

For a few minutes we could not leave them and run off but they kept yelling at us, crying for us to run. I had not seen my grandmother cry until that day.

We ran to the other side of town, but the rebels were everywhere. Horrified, we saw them running toward us, yelling,

"Where are you all going? Stay where you are."

We kept running searching for a place to hide. We ran to the UMC school yard where we had spent half of the day racing on bicycles but there was a group of rebels lying in the elephant grass. They had surrounded the town before we knew anything about it. All in dark-coloured outfits, some wore army trousers and army T-shirts, some wore just dark T-shirts while others wore dark jeans and Army T-shirt or dark-coloured T-shirts. Most of them wore sneakers and some wore boots. No matter what the rebels wore, they were all well-armed. As we ran up the street, they kept yelling:

"Where are you all running to? Stay where you are."

We ran anyway. We ran into a group of them lying in the elephant grass between R.C and U.M.C School. A lot of them were running behind us in the street, some of them stopped running and pointed their guns at us. Each time I looked behind me I yelled to Samia and Nyalay to keep running. One of the rebels got out of the grass with his gun pointing at Katumu.

"Drop your bag or I'll shoot you," he ordered.

We stopped. They had surrounded us. Twenty AKs were pointed at Katumu, Samia, Nyalay, and me. Benjie, Wale Jr. and Joe ran faster; they were already in the forest on their way to Manni. I was terrified. I could not feel. I was standing but I felt as if I was floating in the air. Katumu, shaking like a leaf in the wind, threw her bag to the ground. Komeh had bumped into another group of them in the street as she tried to run home from the market. Those rebels brought her to the group we ran into in the schoolyard. I was standing next to Katumu, my eyes wide with fear, my sister Samia and my cousin Nyalay stood next to me holding each other tight. Then Grandma Memuna came running up behind us with a loaf of baguette in her hand.

Just when we thought there were no more of them in the school yard, one of the rebels suddenly came out of the elephant grass and said to us,

"Where are you all going? Do you run away when you see the Sierra Leone army?"

We watched silently.

"Answer me, arseholes!" he yelled.

I felt angrier because we were all females, my grandmother was there and he called us arseholes.

"No," we said.

"We are the RUF rebels, Foday Sankoh's children," he said. "And where are you going Mama?"

"Nowhere," said Grandma Memuna.

"My name is Foday, can we have some food?" he asked.

The rebel, who had just insulted us, was called Foday.

"What kind of food would you like?" asked Grandma Memuna.

Foday said he wanted some bread, because he saw my grandmother with the baguette in her hand.

"I don't think this would be enough for you, don't you want some rice instead?" replied Grandma Memuna, as she looked from the bread in her hand and then at Foday.

We were all frozen under gunpoint except Foday and my grandmother. Grandma Memuna was terrified but was a very strong old lady. She hid her fear well and used her motherly instinct to talk to Foday like a mother talking to her upset teenage son. For a moment it was like this terrible ordeal was not happening.

"Yes, do you have some rice but I guess your house isn't around here, is it?" Foday asked.

"Yes, my house is just around the corner, I'm here to take my grandchildren home," said Grandma Memuna.

"Where are they?" he asked, as if he could not see us.

She pointed at us when he asked. We were standing still but Foday was being cold hearted pretending as if there was nothing going on.

"Where are they going and why are they running, is it because of us?" he said. "Now, I don't want to see any of you here. Go back home. Run!"

We ran home praying we would not get shot in the back. The rebels did not shoot but they were behind us. They came to our house. Foday and two of his friends went to our dining room; one went to Grandma Memuna's room, one to Grandma Ngaya's room and four to my Uncle Karimu's room. They took his travel bag and his money that he had in the room. They did not go into the most important room in the house- my grandfather's room - where we kept all of our important things including money and our school results.

"Come fellows, come and eat," Foday said to the others.

They went to the dining room and ate all the cooked food in sight. Then they went next door to Auntie Satta's house. They looked around and told us to go inside the house and do not think of hiding or running out. I was so scared but at the same time ready to give up my life. I thought they were going to burn the house with us in it. Then the rebel who took Katumu's bag said,

"If we come back and don't find you here, you'll all be in big trouble because we will kill everyone we see and burn all the houses in this town."

We went into Auntie Satta's bedroom without saying a word. Nyalay wanted to hide in the ceiling, but I pulled her down. We could all run, as we were young, but not our grandmothers and Ngor Sabatu Sandy's mother came from the Sandy family house. She was their grandmother who was very old and deaf. All the young people ran off in time and left her but she got up and came to our house. So I stopped Nyalay from hiding in the ceiling so the rebels would not kill any of the old people. We sat on Auntie Satta's bed hunched, frightened while the four old ladies (Grandma

Memuna, Grandma Ngaya, Ngor Sabatu's mother and Granny - Auntie Satta's mother-in-law) and Auntie Satta sat in the living room crying.

CHAPTER THREE

Hell visits A Small Town

It seemed to me like we were the only ones left in the whole of Sembehun. It felt so sad and lonely as if even God himself had left us to die saying, 'There, survive this on your own, I'm tired!'

After an hour or so the rebels came back and took us girls, Auntie Satta and Grandma Menah to a big shop owned by Pa Madou. They broke into his shop and looted his things he had worked hard for. One of the rebels gave me a pair of plastic slippers (flip-flops) from Pa Madou's shop and I told him that I did not want them. He yelled at me, ordering me to take off my sneakers and put the slippers on. It took me a second or less to kick off my sneakers and put on the slippers.

I was frightened out of my mind because I knew the rebels from Liberia would not tell me to take the slippers a second time. I would have probably been killed the moment I refused them. So I was surprised and shocked at my own cheekiness in refusing the slippers because I knew very well that it was not a good idea to argue with a cold blooded rebel and a very ugly one too. As I shoved my feet into the slippers I prayed that God would forgive me for using Pa Madou's things that he had worked hard for. Although I felt like God had left us to dry in the sun and wind, I still asked for His mercy. After yelling at me, the rebel went to Mafo, a girl who was pregnant by one of the soldiers who fled Sembehun.

"Why are you pregnant, whose baby is it?" he yelled.

Mafo was a very smart and fast thinker. "A student," she said. "The father is a student but he isn't here."

While I stood there murmuring Psalm 23, another one of the rebels came and said to me:

"Hello, what's your name?"

"Memuna," I said.

"What did you say?" he asked. "Tell me again."

35

"Memuna," I said, thinking, 'you idiot it's just a word and you don't understand it.'

"Ok, my name is Ndaiima (Ndaiima is Mende for anonymous)," he said. He went back to the other two who had sent him to ask me, came back and said to me, "You see those two men over there? They want to ask you some questions, so come with me."

One of the men was very dark and handsome like a Mandingo man and the other good looking too, but he was light skinned.

"Hello Memuna, are you Mandingo?" asked the darker one.

"No," I said.

"But you look Mandingo, tell me the truth," he said, "Where were you born?"

"Liberia," I said.

He asked me to tell him what part of Liberia I was born in and I told him I was born in Monrovia.

"I was born in Bo Njaila and I'm Mandingo. My name is Lansana but they call me Eagle and this is Magic," he said, pointing to the light-skinned one next to him. "I'm leading this troop, would you like to go with me?"

I was in shock all this time but I was trying to put on a brave face but as soon as he asked me that question I burst into tears and begged for him not to take me.

"No please don't take me," I pleaded as I shook my head. He was so cold he did not care.

"Are those girls your sisters?" he asked, pointing at Komeh, Katumu, Samia and Nyalay.

I nodded. I did not think that such normal looking people could do something so evil, as the rebels I saw in Liberia seemed quite abnormal. I stood in front of them wondering what they were doing being rebels.

Lansana stood up and asked:

"Fellows are you ready to move it?"

The rest of the rebels said that they were ready to continue their journey. He asked Auntie Satta whether the next town, Shenge, was far. Auntie Satta thought that by lying she was going to save us, so she told Lansana that Shenge was forty-five miles away. She thought that Lansana would have changed his mind on taking us with him thinking it was too far to carry hostages, but he did not. Lansana ordered Ndaiima and two other rebels to tell us that we were going with them. We looked at Auntie Satta and Grandma Memuna and we all broke down. My grandmother and auntie went down on their knees begging Lansana to leave us but it was in vain.

"Please don't take my grandchildren, they are only children," Grandma Memuna said. "Please for God's sake."

"Please don't take my children, please…. Please," Auntie Satta cried.

Lansana looked at them and walked away smiling. The boys told us to move, start walking. As we walked away very frightened and in tears, our grandmother and auntie were on the ground crying and blessing us.

"May God go with you all," cried Grandma Memuna.

We crossed the bridge and went passed the graveyard. I stood on the road for a moment to look at my grandfather's grave one last time.

"If you hear a heavy sound of a plane, you go back to your family," Lansana said.

I started praying in my heart for the jet-fighter to come, as we already knew that the plane he was talking about was the jet-fighter. We had seen it a few times flying toward Rutile when the rebels newly attacked that place. When Lansana said that, I knew they were afraid of the jet-fighter.

Thirty minutes later we arrived in Kongo-Lorlu. Kongo-Lorlu was a little village on the highway just about a mile and a half away from Sembehun. It had about a hundred or fewer houses. We had family in Kongo-Lorlu as well. Everyone in the village had a farm in the forest and a garden in their backyard. Everyone had fled the village leaving Mama Yebu and Pa Kottu who were blind. Mama Yebu used to visit my grandmothers but I was afraid of her as she had elephantiasis. She was always nice to me though and her voice was very gentle. Any time Mama Yebu visited us in Sembehun she always took vegetables, poultry (a hen or a cock) or some oil (palm kernel or palm oil) for us. I was confused when we arrived in Kongo-Lorlu. While Nyalay, Komeh, Katumu and Samia were crying I had no more tears to cry. I stood there staring for a moment as I did not understand what was going on. After a while Ndaiima and two other rebels brought a lot of hens, which the villagers had reared for so many years. The rebels took control of everything in minutes. Some of them were sitting at my cousin Wale Jr.'s maternal grandmother's house climbing her orange trees and ruining her garden. The rebels killed three hens and brought them to Katumu and Komeh asking them if they knew how to cook.

"I don't know how to cook," said Komeh,

The other rebel who came with Ndaiima looked at her and said. "What, you are a girl and you say you don't know how to cook?"

She nodded.

"Well your sister will teach you," Ndaiima said, referring to Katumu. As they walked away we looked at each other and started crying again. "We have to do it," I said. Katumu nodded as she cried.

The rebels that brought the hens came back a few minutes later with a bucket of water each.

"Here, we brought some water for the cooking," Ndaiima said.

We looked at them but said nothing. I helped Katumu and Komeh clean the hens. While we were cooking the stew they brought some rice. One of the two rebels who was with Ndaiima, came to us in the kitchen and gave the rice to Katumu trying to develop a conversation.

"My name is Soja, what are your names?" He said, pointing at me,

"I know your name, your name is Memuna."

I was disgusted by how they all knew my name. Komeh introduced the others and herself to him. Soja was very small, carrying an AK– 47. He had on a pair of baggy jeans and a NIKE T-shirt. Without the gun he looked like a sweet little boy. They stood for a while but we said nothing more, so they left.

One of the teenage rebels came up to us.

"My name is Jusu and I was captured not too long ago and I did exactly what you are doing," he said. "But I'm used to everything and accepted it when I went to the training base. So I want you to stop crying."

He took Nyalay aside to talk to her; we could still see them from the kitchen. They talked and he called me.

"Nyalay is feeling sick and she wants to go back home," he said. Nyalay was crying but I could not say anything, so I started crying too. He held me by my shoulders and said. "You've cried too much, I think you should stop crying. If I were the one who captured you I would have let you go home by now. So don't worry. I'm here and nothing will happen to you. Lansana is a nice person."

Komeh, Samia and Katumu saw him holding my shoulder so they came to find out what was going on.

"If he is a nice person as you say, he would have left us when my mother and grandmother were crying and begging him on their knees." Komeh said, sounding very bitter. "We don't owe him a thing for him to capture us."

"It's ok. That happened to almost all of us here. You have to take care of each other," Jusu said.

He gave Nyalay some Panadol tablets and told us that he will be around if we needed him.

There was a huge three-legged pot in the corner of the kitchen.

"We can use that pot to cook the rice," I said.

Komeh and I took the pot, washed it, set it on the fire and poured some water in it. Katumu was so confused that when she cooked the rice some was cooked and some was not.

"Is the food ready yet?"

This time the rebels who had brought the food for us to cook came with two others but they left as soon as we gave them their food. They could not leave us alone fast enough.

"Did you leave some food for yourselves?" Soja asked as they turned to leave. Katumu shook her head and Ndaiima asked her why and if we were not hungry.

"We are not hungry," Komeh answered.

"They want to say that RUF rebels are greedy," Soja said and they laughed.

"We won't eat if you don't, so you will have some," Ndaiima said.

I was angry that they were making fun of us. Katumu dished some rice from the big bowl we had put the rebels' food in, back into the pot for us before they left us alone.

"I don't want any," I said.

"Neither do I," said Katumu and Komeh.

I asked Nyalay and Samia whether they were hungry and they said they were. We gave them some stew and the rice from the bottom of the pot as that bit was properly cooked.

It was getting dark so we left the kitchen and went to where Lansana was standing, leaning on a little tree. Nyalay, Samia and Katumu sat on the ground while Komeh and I remained standing. Komeh and I stared at each other wanting to say something but we were afraid of saying what we wanted to say. The rebel who gave me the slippers came up to me and gave me a lappa (wrap around cloth for women), "Here, wear it," he said.

I was afraid of him.

"I don't know how to tie it," I said.

"Throw it away then," he snapped.

Lansana heard him snapping at me. "Hey, Two-five, what's wrong?" he asked.

Two-five was his name. "Nothing Sir," He answered and turned to leave. Lansana went around for a walk and left us.

"I want to go home," said Nyalay.

"Me too," Samia agreed.

I still did not have anything to say. I looked at them and cried. "By God's grace they will let us go so let's just pray". Komeh said.

"By God's grace" Katumu agreed.

I nodded and cried. Magic, Ndaiima and another rebel came who resembled Magic. "Hello my name is Hawk. What are your names? Memuna, I already know your name," he said.

I felt so angry and something in me knew that they were going to take me away because all of Lansana's boys knew my name - which indicated significant interest in me. Komeh introduced them again.

"Has anyone been bothering you?" He asked looking at me.

I shook my head.

"Stop crying" he said in a low tone.

"We want to go home to our family," I said.

"Okay but don't cry. Come we will show you where you will spend the night."

We followed them. They took us to Mama Yebu's house. There were so many rebels in her house playing reggae music, smoking marijuana and talking over their lungs while she was sitting in her room on her bed.

"I want you to wait for us here," said Hawk.

As soon as they left two other rebels came to us. One was slim and of medium height and the other was tall and well built.

"Hello my name is Spider and he is Julius," said the short one. We remained silent. Then they took Katumu into the house with them and we didn't see her all night.

Magic, Ndaiima and Hawk came back with two mattresses and four bed sheets. We made our bed and sat on it.

"Where is Katumu?" Magic asked.

"They took her," I said.

"They, who?" Hawk asked.

"They said they are Julius and Spider," Komeh replied.

"Those bastards!" Ndaiima shouted. "We should get someone to watch these girls or else those men won't leave them alone," said hawk. "We should look for their sister" said Hawk.

They left and Magic stayed with us. He kept staring at me and I was so angry but I could not speak.

"Have you been crying Memuna?" he asked.

"We want to go home and stop looking at me!" I said.

He laughed and said "Okay I won't look at you anymore but you should stop crying" he said.

Hawk came back with Soja and Ndaiima and told them to watch us all night.

"See you all tomorrow. Memuna please don't cry all night," said Magic.

"Watch them and don't leave them by themselves. We will try and find Katumu" said Hawk.

Komeh and I sat all night wondering what they were doing to Katumu.

"I hope they don't rape her," said Komeh.

"The other one with his stinky breath kept telling me his name was Spider as if I asked him," I said.

"Don't you want to sleep?" Soja asked.

We looked at him in disgust and said nothing. Samia and Nyalay slept. Hawk came back

"We could not find them but we will look for her," he said.

He left soon after. Even though I was scared of her, I went to Mama Yebu's room. She was sitting on her bed alone.

"Mama Yebu," I said as I walked in.

"Who is it?" she asked in Mende.

"It's me Memuna," I said.

"Come in. What are you doing here child?" she whispered.

"I'm not here alone. I'm here with Samia, Nyalay, Komeh and Katumu. They caught us this afternoon," I said.

I went in and she asked me whether they killed anyone in Sembehun. I told her they hadn't.

"Did they rape you?" she asked pulling me closer.

I told her about how they took Katumu away and she started crying and praying. I also told her about Karimu, Briama, Samba, Ngor Siaka and the other men they captured from Sembehun. We both cried and she prayed for us to be safe. She asked for God to bless us and told us to take care of each other. I went back to my sisters and told them what she said.

Katumu arrived early the next morning. It was around 5am when we had woken up, ready for the journey. Katumu came to us crying. Komeh hugged her and asked what had happened to her. I could tell from the look on her face that something had happened to her. "I will tell you girls when we get home and this morning they told me they would let us go."

Although we wanted to go home she did not have to suffer for our freedom. We all cried again. Soja brought us some water.

"Wash your faces. We're going," he said.

"We want to go home," said Komeh.

On the front porch we saw Lansana. Komeh and I begged him to let us go. He refused.

"No you are going with us. You will make a lot of friends. There are lots of friends on our base."

We started crying and begging him to let us go but he would not listen to us. Julius called Katumu and offered her a bicycle and told her to go home.

"What about my sisters?" she asked.

Lansana said "your leg is hurting that's why I am letting you go home. If it's too dark for you to go you can stay till whenever you want but we are going with your sisters." We cried and said bye to Katumu. 'Tell our family to pray for us'.

Watching us leave, she got on the bicycle and went home. We walked to the next village. The path was very rocky but we kept walking till we arrived at a very lonely town. The town was abandoned except for two young girls looking after their grandmother in her sickbed. The rebels captured them but the girls begged so much to be let go that Lansana let them go while on our way to Mosakki, about four to five miles away from there. When we got to Mosakki everyone was silent. They captured another little girl called Kayma, who was about 8 years old at most. She was sitting next to her grandmother all cuddled up when one of the rebels captured her. He ordered her to take off the clothes she was wearing in exchange for the ones he had looted. He took her from her grandmother. Nyalay cried for a while and then she joined us in trying to console each other.

An hour later, one of the town's men could not control his anger and frustration. He took a machete and jumped one of the rebels called Alimamy. "Come on men, the guns are empty. They don't have bullets in them. Let's fight!" he said screaming in Mende, calling on the other men in the town. No-one helped because they were afraid. Alimamy fought and took the machete off the man using it to kill him by slitting his neck from the side. There was blood everywhere. This was the second killing I had witnessed since the one I saw in Monrovia in 1990. We shook in fear and shock. Samia, Nyalay and Kayma all covered their faces.

A few hours later we went down to the river which divided the town to try and cross to the other side of Mosakki. While we sat there the villagers on the other side of the river and the rebels on our side, were arguing about canoes. The villagers hid their canoes so the rebels would not use them to enter the town. As we sat there Lansana's bodyguards were talking about their girlfriends they left behind and Magic was talking about his girlfriend Bintu and how he did not want her anymore. They gave us tooth brushes and tooth paste and some water to brush our teeth. I was shocked to see Magic gladly using the tooth brush I had used, when there were so many new tooth brushes. I spaced out so many times while we sat by the river on the beach towels they had looted. The devastation was unbelievable and we had seen so many horrific things within the last few days.

On our way to the river, Julius had caught an old man and was torturing him. He ordered the old man to kneel in the gravel while he tried to climb and stand on the old man's shoulders but he was old between 70 to 75 years old, so he fell to the ground each time Julius tried to stand on his shoulders. Julius decided that was not enough so he used the lighter he had to light the old man's beard on fire. He set the old man's beard on fire three times laughing as each time the man struggled to cut out the fire. I was very angry. Angry at God and humanity. Why should anyone be able to do such things to another human being? I kept asking myself.

A few hours later the rebels found some canoes and we crossed to the other side of the town. It was chaos, within minutes that half of Mosakki was on fire and the cold day became hot on that side of the village. As the houses burned and people screamed I stared in shock and horror with tears streaming down my cheeks. The young men and women had left the town when they saw us in the canoes. Lansana kept a close eye on us. We crossed with him in the canoe. Lansana had arranged for some of the rebels to stay behind and watch their backs while they went ahead to set up an ambush. They arranged for the rest of us to go to a nearby farm in the forest next to Mosakki.

As we walked in the muddy paths to the farm, one of the rebels called Sahr started talking to me. He said that I would be fine that Lansana was a nice person.

"If he was such a nice person why did he take us?' I asked not caring about his reaction.

He continued trying to console me but I kept quiet. My Uncle Karimu and the other male captives carried the rest of the looted goods. When we finally got to the farm which was approximately three miles away from the village, the rebels gathered the male captives in the farm hut and, as the men sat on the floor against the walls, tied their hands behind their backs and tied their legs too. We were all devastated and Karimu was really angry as most of the rebel boys were his age or younger but they had the power of the gun. Hawk had a shelter outside the hut and a radio. He called us to sit with him, because Lansana had left him behind to look after us and make sure no-one harmed us.

Later that day, we had biscuits with cheese and milk. The day was as sad, horrifying and dangerous as the previous; so was the night. The only difference was that the rebels untied the male captives. Minutes later the rebels brought a goat to the farm and they asked Komeh to cook. She did not want to cook but Two-five insisted that she cooked the goat. They made a fire with wood outside the hut. There were two huge three legged pots on the farm. The rebels also fetched water for Komeh to use for the cooking. It was getting late I think it was around 7pm and the rebels wanted quiet, they did not know who was in the area. So Two-five told Komeh to make sure there was no noise whilst she cooked. Unfortunately, when she tried to cover the pot the lid made a sharp sound as it hit the pot. Two-five was so angry he slapped Komeh hard across her face. I look at our uncle (who saw what had happened) and he moved slightly from his space on the floor of the hut. I was angry and I started to cry as I ran out to Hawk. Hysterical, I could not speak or catch my breath.

Although Hawk was younger, he was Two-Five's superior, a sergeant and one of Eagle's bodyguards. As soon as the others realised he was coming to the hut they struggled to hide the marijuana they were smoking although Hawk was doing the same thing when I ran to him. "Two-five what is going on here?" Hawk said. "Komeh, why are you girls crying?"

"He just slapped me because I made some noise while I was cooking," she sobbed out her reply.

"Two-five what the fuck is wrong with you?" Hawk demanded. "Lansana will kill you. He left me here to look after these girls. They are not here to work for any of you and yet you want to start beating them. Your arse is in trouble!"

He told us to leave the hut as he sniffed around. "So you've been smoking marijuana and you know we are not allowed to do that any longer?" Hawk said. "All of that will be reported. Man you just can't do that."

Two-five tried to beg but it was in vain. Hawk was really angry and they almost got into a fist fight over the slap. But Two-five continued the cooking and we went outside with Hawk till late, until we were cold and went into the hut to be by the fire. We stayed on the farm for two days and there were lots of tension between Hawk and Two-five.

Two days later, in the afternoon, Lansana and the rest of the rebels came back from the ambush. So we walked from the farm back to the village again. It was sunny and hot; Lansana wore a white vest designed with holes to allow for air. The rebels saluted Lansana and his response was "rest". After that they exchanged greetings and shook hands like normal people. They seemed arrogant. Miles, At-the-end, Acid-moe, Laser and Soja saluted Hawk and then they hugged afterwards.

Lansana carried a white towel with red stripes that he used to wipe his sweat. He walked to us and asked Hawk whether we were alright.

"Well maybe," Hawk said.

"What do you mean?" Lansana asked.

Hawk explained what had happened to Komeh on the farm. Lansana was furious; he looked at Komeh's face for fingerprint.

"Sorry Komeh, I will deal with the dog," Lansana said.

Lansana was so angry he could not keep his eyes open. He kept batting them. The other rebels carried on harassing the old people in the village. Lansana later sent Soja to get Two-five.

"Sir," Soja said, standing erect.

Two-five did the same as Soja when he came and then he stood normally.

"You know what? Don't you ever touch any of those girls again? They are not here to be beaten and they are not your children," Lansana said. "Who knows, maybe their parents did not hit them. You saw how they were when we first saw them. They did not look like they have been suffering. So please respect yourself and keep your fucking hands off them. You can go."

"Thank you Sir I'm sorry Sir, it won't happen again," he said.

I was shocked but happy at the way Lansana had reprimanded Two-five. Two-five saluted Lansana.

I found Two-five scary and Miles, Lansana's bodyguard, I thought rude, even very rude. Everyone else seemed normal. Sahr looked like a boxer. He was short with bowed legs and big muscles. Lansana was a lieutenant. He treated his bodyguards like they were his friends, involving them in decision making and behaving in a jocular mood. He was a handsome Mandingo man who, like Hawk was always smiling. Even so, as I sat on a mat on the front veranda of one of the houses which they had not burned, in silence, praying and hoping that Lansana would miraculously decide to let us go, I noticed that all of his bodyguards had two things in common - they were handsome and silly. I was confused; they were rebels and executing evil actions. Miles was very arrogant and he always tried to look tough by walking with his chest up, but still, the appearance they were putting up did not make sense as everyone but me was scared of them. I simply did not care anymore. I felt like there was no situation worse than being a rebel's captive. Hawk, Miles, Magic, Acid-moe, Bayo and At-the-end came to cheer us up. They started asking questions. Anger rose inside me, I just wanted to scream at them. They said we could ask questions if we wanted to.

"How old are you Memuna?" Hawk asked.

"I'm 14 years old, Komeh is 15 years old, Samia is 11 years old and Nyalay is 8 years old," I said.

To stop myself from screaming (I did not know what the consequences would be if I did), I decided to talk. I knew he was going to ask the same question three more times so I decided to answer for them.

It was obvious both Hawk and Acid-moe seemed to be attracted to Komeh but she did not want to see their faces any more than any one of us did.

"Oh so Komeh is older than you?" Acid-moe asked.

"Yes, by just a few months as I will be 15 very soon. We are both just children," I replied, tersely. At-the-end took a bullet out of something on the gun that I later learned was called a magazine. He pointed the bullet at my shoulder and yelled.

"Pow, you just got shot."

I jumped with shock when he yelled but they all laughed. Shuddering, I shook my head thinking "don't touch me!"

"I'm just joking," he said.

During this time Lansana was sitting outside with Karimu and the other male captives, with Soja guarding him. The other rebels were torching buildings in the town bringing heat on our side of the town. There were two old and fragile ladies sitting in their verandas crying, as they were too old to escape but they did not get burnt. The house opposite theirs was. I stood straight against the wall as I watched in astonishment and anguish. Magic and his friends changed the topic. This time they talked about how useless one of Magic's girlfriends was and talked about the other who made up a song that rhymed with his name. They carried on their conversation indifferent to the indiscriminate arson perpetrated by their subordinates. As I stared at the burnt out village with smoke still rising from some houses, I heard everything they said. At-the-end talked about how much he missed his girlfriend and how he could not wait to see her.

"Hey, Laser why do you pick on Yema, do you miss her?" Magic asked, rubbing Laser's head.

"Yes, I miss her. I don't pick on her, she drives me crazy," Laser said. "She wants me to be with her all the time. I have things to do myself."

"To God (instead of saying 'I swear to God', in Sierra Leone people say 'to God' when speaking in Krio) Laser, Yema is beautiful. I'd die for her dark complexion," Acid-moe said.

I looked at him and I did not know what he was talking about, as he was dark as well. "Acid-moe man that is enough, she's your boy's woman," Magic teased and they laughed and shook hands.

"To God," Hawk added.

Lansana called Magic and said something to him. Magic called Hawk, At-the-end, Acid-moe and Miles. They whispered something. Then Lansana pointed out some of the male captives and decided to let them go. He gave them some tobacco leaves, cigarettes and some other things from Pa Madou's shop. Komeh and I went to Lansana and pleaded with him to let us go but he refused. Karimu, Briama, Samba and three other men were not released. Lansana decided they were young and strong enough to become rebels. Komeh and I went back to the veranda in tears, devastated, all over again.

CHAPTER FOUR

Captivity

It was time to continue the journey. A couple of young men abducted from Mosakki decide to confront the rebels for their abduction. One of them was among the men who refused to give the rebels their canoes. Karimu and our grandmothers knew him and his family. I had seen them talking so many times in Sembehun, but I always forgot his name. The two men tried to attack the rebels with sticks. I thought that was foolhardy and a stupid mistake they should have never made. It was obvious they did not discuss their plans with any of the other villagers. The rebels had guns and these men had sticks. Some of the rebels had the village men under gunpoint while the others fetch stones to throw at them. The men ran into the coffee farm with the rebels chasing after them. One of the running men was hit so hard with a huge stick at the back of his neck; he could not run any more. Falling to the ground they hit him with sticks.

A few of the rebels chased the one that Karimu knew and brought him back. They beat him and told him to get up and run. He was weak, he struggled but got up hoping he could run and save his life. As soon as he got to where the other man was lying, Laser threw a huge rock that knocked him down. He was on the ground badly beaten and fighting for his life. His breathing was laboured and his body bleeding. Magic hit him with a long thick stick and left him for the others.

Sick at the sight of the blood and frightened to death, angry tears were streaming down my cheeks. I held tight onto a wooden pillar on the veranda, my fingers clenching tighter every time they hit the men. Samia and Nyalay clung to each other. It was a nasty sight watching those men get killed.

The torched village was still smoking when we departed for Gbangbatoke. The long walk took up the whole morning and half of the afternoon I had never walked that long a distance before. We walked through some abandoned villages and towns with beautiful houses. The doors were open and there were belongings everywhere. The people of the town had packed and fled in a great hurry.

The male captives were made to carry the looted property for the rebels. It was a long walk. Komeh, Samia, Nyalay and I were tired and emotionally drained but we continued walking. My memory replayed the murder and arson in Mosakki over and over again. There was a coffee and cacao farm, or just a coffee farm at the entrance of every small town or village. Each time we saw a few coffee trees we knew we were approaching a town or a village which, at times, meant we could rest. Once we arrived in one of the villages, one of the male captives requested that he wanted to pee. Hawk helped him put his load down by the path and Lansana told Hawk to keep an eye on the man. He walked among the coffee trees pretending to look for a private spot to stand.

"Stand there and pee," Hawk said.

The man did as he was told; he pretended to unzip his pants and as Hawk turned his face, he ran off. Hawk called to the others for help as he chased the man. I was happy that this man had taken this step and I hoped they would not catch him. But they did. They brought him to the village, laid him on the ground and beat him with the pestle which the villagers used in their kitchens for pounding. The old man did not die but he was covered in his own blood. I was physically sick and my sisters and I were petrified. They gave him the load to carry again and we continued walking.

We arrived in Gbangbatoke after hours of walking. We rested a little and Lansana told us to cook something to eat. He told Soja and Laser to help us. We went with them and got some potato greens for us to cook. We saw an old man and an old lady standing on the veranda of their house and we went to them.

"Mama, do you have two big pots we can borrow?" Laser asked, politely.

"How big?" she asked.

"Big enough to cook for twelve or more people," he replied.

We were only cooking for us, the captives, Lansan and his bodyguards and a few others. The old lady went into her house and dragged out two big three legged-pots, exactly the size we needed. The boys took the pot to a kitchen near the house where Lansana, the other captives and some of the rebels were. The rebels were all over town and some were in ambush.

The old people were obviously scared of us. We told them that we were not rebels but we were captives. We explained everything to them and the old lady started to cry. "Mama," I asked her, "do you know some young men called Ishmael, Alusine and Alfred? They owned a boat," I said.

"Yes," she said.

She turned around to point their house out to me. As she did she saw a little boy in the arms of one of the rebels. She was shocked and she stood with her eyes stretched and her mouth agape.

"Oh, my God, I know that little boy his name is Ishmael Jr.," she cried.

"Even that child," Komeh whispered as she covered her mouth with her hand, she did that sometimes when she cried.

"I heard about Ishmael Jr. but this is my first time to see him. I told them, looking at the rebel carrying the little boy.

The old people cried. "God will destroy them," the old man cried and shook his head.

Soja called out to me from the kitchen that everything was ready for us to start cooking. We got to the kitchen as fast as we could and they went to fetched us some water from the well for cooking. The thought of seeing Ishmael captive made me shake in fear and worry.

"Wait for me here; I'm going to see who's got Ishmael's child and I will talk to him," I said bursting into tears.

"What are you going to say? Maybe he's as evil as Two-five. Don't go," Komeh said. She was scared.

"I don't know what I'm going to say but I'll know when I get there. He won't do anything to me because Lansana is there," I assured her as best as I could.

I left my sisters in the kitchen pleading for me not to go.

"Come back, please don't go."

I had this voice in my head urging me to go, telling me that nothing would go wrong. So I went, running past Lansana (who had developed flu) sitting on the veranda.

"Hey, where are you going Memuna?" Magic asked.

I ignored him and carried on to the lounge as I jumped over bags and boxes. I paused and took a deep breath to calm down a little. Looking around I saw Ishmael sitting on the rebel's knee like he was his own son. I went over to him.

"Hello Ishmael," I said.

He looked at me "Hello."

I was in tears as I looked at the child.

"What's your name?" the rebel asked.

I looked at him thinking at least one of them does not know my name.

"My name is Memuna," I said.

"Oh so you are Memuna? I've heard Lansana talking about you but I did not know it was you. So how do you know Ishmael?" he asked. "Anyway my name is Viking, they call me Viking King."

"Ishmael's father is a friend of my older sister's," I said.

"Lansana and I live in the same town so you can visit Ishmael anytime you want," he said. I hugged Ishmael and left.

As I turned to walk away, I saw Magic looking at me. Wiping my tears with the back of my hand I walked passed him. Komeh was in the kitchen with Nyalay and Samia cutting the greens. As soon as they saw me they started asking.

"What happened? What did you say to him?"

I sat down on the log next to Komeh to help with the greens while I told them what Viking and I talked about.

"That bastard! Son of a bitch! Does he have to take that boy away?" Komeh asked.

In anger, she threw the knife in the bowl with anger, took the rice to wash it and put it in the pot.

"If I had some poison now I could just put it in this food and watch them die as they eat like a bunch of sick chickens."

Jusu came to the kitchen. "Oh my sisters, it's been so long since we talked in….what was the name of the town?" he pointed his finger to his temple trying to remember.

"Kongo-Lorlu," I said. Nyalay and Samia were happy to see him. We talked and it lessened the tension a little. He told us he was going to the stream to bathe and left.

Bayo came to the kitchen as Jusu left.

"How are you young women doing? I saw you crying Memuna, what's wrong? You need to stop crying. I know how hard it is but you just have to accept it and stop crying," he said, calmly with a smile.

"Hey Komeh, is that stew delicious?"

As I looked at him in angry silence I thought, was he kidding me asking me 'what is wrong'? Everything, including himself, was wrong.

"Maybe as I don't know how to cook, our family never sent us to the kitchen to do the cooking and I never did like cooking," Komeh said, raising her voice.

Bayo did not mind the harshness I guess he knew that they deserved it. He knew what we were going through.

"Who knows how to cook among you then?" he asked.

"Here," Nyalay said, pointing at me.

"Oh Memuna, but she is tense at the moment," he said.

Nyalay knew what was going on; she dealt with the situation her way as she was only 8 years old. Bayo took Nyalay for a walk, he had his rocket-propelled grenade (RPG) rifle on his shoulder and they stood somewhere where we could see them.

I asked Komeh to dish some food for Ishmael and Jusu.

"Of course, maybe because of Ishmael if I had the poison I won't put it in the whole pot of food. Can you go and call Laser for me please?" Komeh said.

When I got back from calling Laser I found those two in the kitchen talking to Komeh. Anger boiled up inside me again but, I completely ignored their presence.

"Hey Komeh, Laser is coming, he's looking for something," I said.

"Hello Memuna," Julius said.

I looked at him in disgust and looked away. I hated him for what he had done and the old man he had tortured.

Laser came to the kitchen and Julius and Spider were still there.

"Spider and Julius, Eagle doesn't want you near these girls. So you better leave or I will go and tell him," Laser said.

"Fuck off, man Laser," Spider said.

"What, do you think we are going to eat them?" Julius said, but they turned away and left.

"Don't talk to those men anymore," Laser said. "They are nasty, nasty."

He went to the old people to borrow some trays. Komeh dished some food for Ishmael and I took it to him. I had two spoonfuls of the food and the stew did not taste good. It was what I expected because that was what always happened when Komeh was forced to do something let alone the situation we were in.

After we ate, we cleaned the pots and took them back to the old lady. Lansana came to the kitchen smiling.

"Why are you crying?" he asked.

"We want to go home," Komeh cried. "Please let us go."

"No," he said. He turned to leave and then he came back.

"Did you eat any of the food and did you dish some out for your uncle and the other men? Do you want to go and bathe?"

"Yes I dished some food for them and we ate too," Komeh said. "We want to wash our bodies."

"Come with me then, come and take the things you need," he said.

Lansana gave us some new undies, shorts and four T-shirts and a bar of bathing soap. All of these things were from Pa Madou's shop. As I got angrier I could feel my face getting hot. I did not want to use the things but I had to. The clothes I had on had been on me from the day we were captured four days ago. My skin had started itching. Lansana gave Komeh a bra and he handed me one too.

"Memuna do you need a bra too?" he asked. I took it from him and dropped it on the floor as I fixed a cold hard look on him.

"I don't need a bra," I said and walked away.

He sent Magic and Miles to follow us so that we would not run away.

We went to a beautiful waterfall. The water came from rocks in the hills and it was clean. Samia took off her clothes but left her undies on, Nyalay got naked. She said she wanted to wash her undies. Komeh and I took off our clothes leaving our undies on like Samia did. I walked into the water. It was cool and refreshing. Komeh stood by the water holding the large T-shirt with a picture of Malcolm X on it I was wearing when we were captured. It belonged to her boyfriend Oscar who had left it in our room the day before I was wearing it with a pair of green shorts on the day that we were captured. He was not in Sembehun on the day of the attack having gone to a nearby village to test his new XL motor bike. She cried as she looked at the T-shirt clutched in her hands. I went to her, took the T-shirt from her and hugged her. I told her to stop crying and that everything that starts must have an end. I told her that it would all end one day and she and

Oscar will be together again. She wiped her tears and followed me into the water.

Magic and Miles could not get their eyes off us. They stood by the water talking, staring at us and laughing. I was irritated even here, their staring reminded us we were prisoners. We sat in the water and took off our underwear to wash them.

"I'm going to keep this underwear till I get back home," I said.

Samia, Komeh and Nyalay agreed that they were going to do the same.

"Keep the T-shirt too, ok?" Komeh suggested.

"Of course, these are all we have from our family for now. I don't even want to undo my braids Nadine (Oscar sister) did," I said.

As Nyalay walked out of the water she asked if we wanted her to bring us our towels in the water for us. Those boys were peering at us and talking about our bodies. Normally I had no problem being naked but they made me uncomfortable.

"Yes thank you very much, Nyalay," Komeh said.

Komeh, Samia and I walked out of the water with the towels around us. Nyalay dried her skin and put on the huge shirt that Lansana gave her. It seemed like she was wearing a dress and fortunately the undies were a fit. The things that Lansana gave to Samia, Komeh and I fitted well but I felt guilty and scared to wear them but had no choice.

Lansana and his rebels had managed to turn the house into a ghetto while we were at the waterfall. We could hear the loud reggae music from the end of the town. There was too much noise and there was marijuana and cigarette smoke coming from every corner. Due to the rebel attack, Gbangbatoke was like a ghost town. The people of the town had fled and there was only the old couple, the captives and about eighty rebels, so every noise echoed. Gbangbatoke was a big town with beautiful houses, known as a very busy town full of business people and farmers.

In the evening, the rebels went from house to house in Gbangbatoke looking for mattresses for us all to sleep on. Lansana's bodyguards brought four mattresses; they gave Komeh, Samia, Nyalay and me the king sized one. They spread some sheets they had looted from Pa Madou's shop on the mattresses and they gave us two to cover ourselves with. Pa Madou owned one of the biggest shops in Sembehun. He sold almost everything including food, clothes and radios. His shop was the only shop they looted. The radios the rebels were using to make noise in Gbangbatoke were all from Pa Madou's shop including the batteries.

We spent the night on the veranda on our mattresses with Lansana and his bodyguards, Bayo and Acid-moe so we were safe. We were too tired to resist sleeping. Komeh and I slept a little despite the noise. Samia and Nyalay slept through the night. Komeh woke up and saw that I was not asleep.

"I wonder what's happening to Karimu, Briama, Samba and the other men. I wonder where they are," Komeh whispered.

"Me too, I know that they are in the house inhaling the marijuana and cigarette smoke," I whispered back, looking angrily at Lansana's back.

Lansana was on the other mattresses near ours. We put Samia and Nyalay in the middle while Komeh and I slept on the edges of our mattress so that was how I ended up lying close to Lansana. "They will survive, God will be with them and us all," Komeh said, hopefully.

It was my first time to see my cousin Komeh taking something seriously. The stoic look on her face showed that she was sad but ready for any challenges.

We whispered to each other all night how much we wished to escape, how much we hated the rebels and how we wished the jet-fighter could come, kill all of them but leave all the captives alive. Lansana must have heard us whispering, he turned around.

"I thought you were sleeping, in fact someone can hardly sleep in this noise," he said. He looked at Samia and Nyalay as if they were his children and it made me angrier. "Those men can't stop smoking," Laser said. "I guess they are making use of their chance to smoke marijuana freely."

Laser and the rest of Lansana's bodyguards had just finished smoking with Lansana, Bayo and Acid-moe but he did not want the others to smoke. I looked at him thinking, 'you just did the same thing. Who do you think you are?'

CHAPTER FIVE

In Rebel Territory

At the crack of dawn they turned their music off and started to pack. It was time to continue walking. The smoke cloud in the house had disappeared. I was tired and drained. Lansana stood on the veranda and called out to the rebels as they had all come around to the house for their meeting.

"Listen gentlemen, we have from now till 6pm to get to our destination," he said. "That is if we don't get attacked on our way."

I was frightened and deep down I was screaming inside calling out to the Sierra Leone Army to please come and help us. At least we were still (relatively) close to Sembehun. I looked at Lansana with wide eyes, imagining them engaging with the army and us girls escaping with Ishmael and the male captives but it was all just day dreaming.

Viking hugged and played with Ishmael Jr. like a father would play with his son and I got angry again, feeling jealousy and grief on behalf of Ishmael. He called Ishmael Jr. "Little Man". I guess he knew that the little stolen boy needed to be entertained. He carried Ishmael everywhere and the child liked it. As I watched them I prayed that the army would attack the rebels. Viking passed behind me holding Ishmael's hand. As they walked past Ishmael touched my hand and brought me back out of my imagination. As I turned to see who had touched me, Ishmael waved with a big smile on his face. I waved back and greeted him. I realised he was very innocent and it saddened me.

While we waited for what fate had in store for us, the rebels held formation. Lansana sat on a high stool in front of them all with a red beret on his head. First Viking stood in front of them leading them to do their parade and addressed them. Then he fell back into his line and Lansana stood up. They saluted him and greeted him. Lansana told them how we were going to travel and that the troop was going to be led by the same advance team that they came with. They said what we were taught was The Lord's Prayer in English and Arabic (Afatia).

"What do they think they are doing? So they think they can just stand there with their cigarette and Marijuana breath and say the Lord's Prayer and be forgiven after they killed those people in Mosakki and they are ready to kill some more," I whispered to Komeh.

"Don't mind those sons of bitches," Komeh said.

"Gentlemen, let's move!" Lansana said.

They untied the male captives; Lansana was in the advance team as he was leading the troop. He led the way with Bayo, who was operating one of the RPGs, Miles, Laser, Small Soja, At-the-end, Magic and Acid-moe and some other rebels. Like before, Hawk stayed behind with us, the male captives and the rest of the rebels. Viking stayed behind this time because of Ishmael.

There was a young woman left in the village next to Gbangbatoke and she was captured by one of the rebels upon our arrival. Lansana got upset when he found out that the rebel had captured the woman. He yelled at him and ordered him to let her go. He and his friends thought that Lansana was being unfair because he had us and Viking had Ishmael and one of the other rebels had Kayma from Mosakki. They grumbled for a while but Lansana did not hear them. He had passed his order and that was it.

We got to a wide but not too deep river and there were no canoes. There was no other way to cross the river but to swim or walk in the water. Lansana carried Nyalay on his back; the river almost reached his chest. Lansana was six-feet and a few inches tall. At-the-end crossed with Samia on his back and his gun slung on his chest. Acid-moe held Komeh with his arm around her and they crossed, Hawk carried me on his back across the river. It was then I knew that Lansana and his boys would do anything to take us with them; no amount of crying or any pleading we could do would save us from being taken away. Karimu and the rest of the male captives walked in the water with the loot on their heads. All the rebels took off their jeans and walked in the water with their underwear on. Nyalay and Samia did not have to take off their clothes because they did not get wet. Komeh and I took off our shorts. Magic had already crossed; and was sitting on the root of a big tree on the other side of the river. He took off his wet boxer-shorts to wring them. He stood up and yelled out to Hawk when he saw him crossing with me.

"Hey sergeant, take care of that girl," he said. They all laughed.

"Sir!" Hawk said.

I was disgusted thinking that they laughed about stupid things. I thought that 'they did not have any problems as they were causing the problems.' I thanked Hawk for crossing with me, which I later regretted because I saw no reason for being polite to any one of them. I walked up the hill and put on my shorts. I looked up to watch Karimu and the others crossing but I saw a rebel naked down to his brief in front of me and our eyes met.

"Don't look at me little girl, turn your face to the other side," he said.

I ignored him and looked passed him.

"Don't yell at her," Magic said. "You can go behind the tree and do what you are doing."

As Magic started defending me I turned and walked past him on my way up to the village.

Upon our arrival, there were only pigs, sheep, goats, a dog and some poultry left in the village. We spent what seemed like fifteen minutes resting in the muddy little village and we set off again. After hours of walking we arrived in another small town with new houses. It seemed as though the town was just being built. We could still smell the paint on some of the houses and the roofs shone in the sunlight. Everything in the town was new. A tree branch struck Lansana in his face and one of his eyes upon our arrival. His eye swelled and became red so he decided we would rest and wait for the sun to go down a little as his eye hurt in the sunlight. Magic, Hawk and Laser asked Komeh to help them cook some rice so we could eat with some sardines. The house we were in was clean and new but all the furniture was outside in the backyard.

We sat on a couch looking at each other in hunger. I did not mind being hungry. Nyalay was rubbing her hair and sucking her tongue. I remembered our grandmothers telling her to give her tongue a break, but when I saw her doing that I smiled.

"What's funny?" Komeh asked.

I pointed at Nyalay and we smiled. Komeh asked Nyalay if she was hungry. She nodded.

Hawk came out with some rice to cook and some biscuits and cheese. He gave the rice to Komeh for her to cook.

"Komeh please, for God's sake don't spoil this rice," Hawk said. "If you want me to stay here and talk to you while you cook, I will. So is that what you want?"

Komeh snatched the rice bowl of from him and remained silent. He did not mind that she had snatched the rice from him.

"Memuna do you think I should stay here with you?" he asked.

"I think we want to go home where we don't have to cook," I replied tersely. "I don't care about that rice."

Hawk found me funny. He ran to the others and told them what I said. I thought they were all very stupid and wicked. They came to the backyard and asked me what was going on. I ignored them completely.

"Ok, let's sit with them since she doesn't want to talk," Magic suggested.

They sat for a while waiting to hear what I would say but I did not say a word, so they started their own conversation. My eyes ran really fast as I scanned the town to see if my sister, my cousins and I could escape but on Lansana's order, we continued the journey as soon as they ate the rice and we dished out some for Samia and Nyalay. The sun was still hot.

"It's Wednesday now, I don't think these girls will have the strength to walk tomorrow," Lansana said.

We walked faster than before. Samia, Komeh, Nyalay and I were so tired I had corns developing on my last toes. We had never walked such long distances. It seemed as though we had walked about sixty miles that day. We walked through three abandoned villages and when we arrived in a village on the main road we had a rest. Magic and most of the rebels who were in the advance team sat by the road; some sat in the middle of the road with their guns ready.

'What is this about' I thought. I was curious and scared but I could not resist asking. "Hawk, why are they sitting in the road like that looking so serious?" I asked.

"They are the advance team, they are on guard," he replied.

"Oh," I said, nodding.

"That is good, asking questions," he said.

Samia, Komeh and Nyalay were very quiet. They sat on a bench on the veranda of a mud house just looking ahead of them. It was time to start walking again. I was hungry but we hardly had time to have a drink of water. This time we walked with the advance team. Jusu and I had a long conversation.

"I can tell from your face that you are tired. Don't worry we are almost there," Jusu said.

"I'm not only tired; I'm scared and worried and I won't be happy even when we get to wherever it is that we are going," I said. "What do you expect? I have never walked so far in my life. Why should we be here with rebels? We are children and we should be home with our family and going to school."

"I know. I felt the same way when I was captured. I used to cry all the time and all they did was laugh at me," Jusu told me. "I had two more years left for me to finish high school, my parents aren't rich but they have enough to provide for me and my siblings. My father was thinking of sending me to a good college if I had the chance to finish high school. Now, look at me with a gun."

He told me not to worry, that my sisters and I would be fine as the rebels did not bother girls like they used to. He told me that it was an advantage that we were going to live with Lansana because he was a Commanding Officer.

"They are so wicked. They just want everyone to be like them. Look at us, we are going to be with them until the end of the war or maybe we will die," I cried. "Maybe I won't be disturbed by anyone else but Lansana himself, so if that happens who do I report to?"

"Lansana is a nice man. Don't worry he won't bother you. Take me as your brother, I'll always be there for you when you need me," he said.

Crying as I walked, I told him that I had a brother called Jusu too. I also told him I was scared I was going to be forced to have sex with someone and that I would get pregnant by someone whom I hated. I was crying, as we walked. Viking passed us with little Ishmael and I became hysterical.

"Look at that little boy Jusu, do you think he should be taken away from his family?" I said. "They are going to be hurt for the rest of their lives thinking about him. I know that boy's father."

As we arrived in yet another town, we saw a burnt van, a burnt car on the side of the gravel road and the street was quiet still and lonely. I could only hear our footsteps, our quiet conversation and the birds singing in trees on the sides of the road. Lots of bullets and bullet shells scattered everywhere on the ground.

"The battle was heavy here," Jusu said.

"Memuna," Komeh called from behind us. I turned to her as she pointed at the two burnt vehicles and the bullets and shells in the road. I nodded and waved to her, Nyalay and Samia. They were walking with Hawk, Acid-moe and the other rebels. Nyalay and Samia ran to join me. As we walked across a bridge we looked down into the water and saw lots of decomposing corpses of babies, older children and adults. The stench was putrid. I turned to Jusu we just looked at each other. I wondered if he was involved in that killing or if he knew any of those people. I felt sadder and numb. The sight and smell frightened Nyalay and Samia. We walked even faster to get away from the odour.

"We are very close now. See, it's 5pm," Jusu said, looking at his watch.

As we got closer to another town we saw a bloated body. It was an army man; he was still wearing his army shorts. He died lying on his stomach on the side of the street with his head in the bush. One of his legs already had maggots. The body smelt really bad. The sight made me sick and I had to cross over to the other side of the street so I would not look at it though I could still smell the odour. The horror was too much for Samia and Nyalay.

Finally we got to the rebels' territory. A rebel was standing very alert at the roundabout. There were three corpses of army men around the roundabout, one at each junction. The one at the road we arrived on was swollen and very black. Seeing it, I screamed inside, too scared and shocked to let it out. The body on the street we turned onto that entered the next town was sun dried. The third one was swollen. Everyone else except us captives acted as if it was normal to have decomposing bodies lying around.

"This is Yangatokee, but we call it Africa's Ground because the ground commander is called Africa," Jusu informed us.

Jusu greeted the guard at the roundabout and we continued walking. I felt I was walking into hell; my legs shook and my face was hot in fear.

"Why ground commander, is Yangatokee the town we are going to live in?" I asked.

"No Lansana lives in Kabbaty, his woman, his sister and his son live in Mattru Jung. That's where I live too," Jusu said.

He told me that Mattru Jung was his hometown and is where he was captured. He told me it was a crowded town, always busy and there were plenty of girls.

"Ground commanders are like chiefs but they are rebels too," Jusu said.

"Oh," was all I could say.

I had so many questions to ask, but I knew that Jusu was tired and I was scared and distracted so I stopped talking. He met some of his friends who thought that he had captured me. Most rebels treated captives (especially female captives) like they were game from a hunting trip. They were happy to see a few girls and were betting on who will get to be first with us. They greeted Jusu, told him that I was beautiful and asked him who I was. He told them to stay away and leave me alone. As Lansana and his bodyguards walked down the streets all I could repeatedly hear was 'good evening Sirs'. They saluted our captors from every corner. Hawk and the other rebels hugged and shook hands with their friends in Yangatokee. My sisters and I became angry again at the sight of our uncle and the other male captives carrying heavy loads and looking so drained and tired. My heart broke.

Lansana walked so fast we had to walk faster to catch-up with him. Upon our arrival in Yangatokee, Jusu bid us good-bye. He said he was going to his friend's house to bathe and have a rest.

"I will see you girls on my way to Mattru Jung and I mean what I said, Memuna," he said. "I'm here for you."

I started crying when he turned his back, although he was a rebel, he was the one stranger I could relate to and was comfortable with at this point. He hugged me and left. I became annoyed at how giggly the girls in Yangatokee were. They were all over the boys and they called Hawk from all corners. He left Samia, Komeh, Nyalay and me with Laser sitting outside a veranda of a beautiful house and went to talk to a group of girls on another veranda.

Yangatokee was full. There were lots of girls. Lansana's bodyguards were very popular as the girls were all over them and were happy to see them. As I watched in disgust, four girls came and took Laser from us. They had all gone and left us sitting outside alone. I was frightened and angry as someone could have taken us. We later learned that Lansana, Hawk, Laser, Acid-moe, Magic, Bayo, Soja and At-the-end had gone to Two-five's house. We did not see Karimu, Briama, Samba and the other captives. We sat there wondering where they were and what the rebels were doing to them or what would become of them. Julius and Spider came and found us sitting outside by ourselves. They took Komeh with them.

"Come with us Memuna," Spider said.

I screamed "No, I don't want to go with you. Komeh don't go, Hawk told us to wait here. Leave her alone."

Komeh was afraid; she was ready to do anything they told her to do. I watched them deeply sad as they went around the house to the next house.

"He just can't get my name out of his dirty mouth," I grumbled, as I turned around.

I told Samia and Nyalay not to go anywhere. I was about to tell them that if anyone other than Lansana and his boys comes to take them, they should scream. I was about to follow and see where they were taking Komeh. Nyalay saw At-the-end coming.

"Hey, At-the-end is coming," Nyalay interrupted pointing at him. I was strangely grateful.

"Good," I said.

"Where is Komeh? We are going to eat and wait for the driver to come and take us," he said

I could not talk fast enough, pointing frantically in the direction they went as I spoke. "Julius and Spider had taken her away!"

"Where did you see them go? Eagle will kill those dogs," At-the-end exclaimed.

"Let's go, show me where they went."

At-the-end was upset and anxious. He took the radio Hawk had left with Komeh, held Nyalay's hand, Samia held Nyalay's other hand and I walked by them. I pointed at the house I saw them go to.

Rushing into the house he called, "Komeh....Komeh, where are you? Answer me."

One of the girls who lived in the house came up to us.

"At-the-end, are you looking for the girl who was with Julius and Spider?" she asked.

"Yes, where is she, where are they?" He asked.

We were all thinking the worst; we thought they were raping her.

"She is bathing and they are on the veranda. Why are you so tense?" she said.

I ran to where she pointed. Komeh was in the zinc bathroom bathing from a bucket.

"Komeh, get out, let's go," I yelled at her. "Have you lost your mind? Why could you not refuse? Those boys are so desperate for women especially young girls."

"Just pour the whole bucket on your body and come out!" At-the-end said angrily. Spider came to the backyard to talk to At-the-end.

"What's happening here? At-the-end, we are sorry," he said.

"Go to hell Spider, say that to Lansana," At-the-end yelled at him.

Komeh finally came out crying and we left. I felt sorry that I yelled at her, I knew she was frightened and that was why she did not resist when Spider and Julius took her.

Komeh and I walked behind At-the-end, Samia and Nyalay.

"Did they do anything to you?" I asked.

"No, they only gave me a bucket of water, soap and towel to bathe," she said.

"Why you so scared you could not say no? You know what they did in Kongo-Nani. They would have done the same to you if At-the-end hadn't come in time," I said.

"I was too scared to say no. Thank God At-the-end came," she said.

We got to Two-five's house.

Lansana asked At-the-end what took him so long to get us to the house. He told Lansana what had happened and he was furious.

"God those sons of bitches are playing with me. Komeh did they do anything to you?" Lansana asked.

Komeh slowly shook her head.

"The next time they call you just ignore them or tell them to leave you alone," Lansana told her.

I was so tired. I stood and leaned on the wall inside Two-five's room. The room was huge with light yellow painted walls, a king sized bed, a chess of drawers a cupboard, a huge dressing mirror and some chairs. Bayo, Magic, Hawk and Lansana sat on the bed. The bodyguards sat on the linoleum floor with Two-five. They were tired too but they did not seem as tired as we were. Lansana looked at me and smiled, he reached out his hand.

"Come and sit here," he said, pointing to the space near him with his other hand.

I turned to Samia, Nyalay and Komeh and invited them to sit as well. As we sat, Lansana held my right hand, looking at my fingers and saw that I had been biting my nails.

"Why is this, are you hungry?" he asked, sounding sarcastic.

I snatched my hand from him and looked at him badly.

"I'm not hungry," I said, "and if I was I wouldn't eat my nails."

A girl walked into the room smiling with a big tray of rice with cassava leaves stew. I thought she was a beautiful young girl, older than I was though. Lansana introduced us.

"Mariatu, this is Memuna and meet her sisters Samia, Komeh and Nyalay. Girls, this is Mariatu, she is Two-five's girlfriend."

I looked at her for a while when Lansana said that she was Two-five's girlfriend imagining how mean he must be to her because of what he did to me and Komeh. Mariatu was welcoming.

"You are so beautiful and look at your hairdo. Who did it for you?" she said.

"My cousin did it," I said.

She tried to cheer us up. "Can we be friends? I'll come to Kabbaty to visit you," she said. "You are all beautiful,"

I nodded and looked at her like she was not there.

"They are tired," Lansana said.

Hawk told her that I was angry with her man and she asked why, sounding curious. Hawk told her what Two-five did to Komeh.

"Oh, Komeh I'm sorry. Two-five why?" she asked, looking at him.

One-five did not say anything.

Hawk gave us spoons to eat with. I took a couple of spoonfuls of the food then laid the spoon on the table.

"Why are you not eating?" Magic asked.

"What's wrong?" Lansana asked.

Everyone in the room had their eyes on me. I hated the attention and I hated that they kept asking me what was wrong when they knew what was wrong. They were wrong and it was wrong that they took us from our home.

"Nothing," I said, shaking my head thinking "if you don't know what is wrong when it is so obvious then I don't think I can make it any clearer."

"She doesn't like cassava leaves," Komeh informed them.

Hawk gave me four pieces of meat on a plate. I ate the meat and drank some water and fell on the bed to relax. I felt like my head was going to explode from all the thoughts running through my mind. Then I heard this voice calling out to Lansana. "Eagle, man where is Eagle?'

"Tricks is here," Magic said, laughing.

A tall masculine man walked into the room. He smelt of marijuana and he seemed high.

"Hey, Tricks how is it?" Lansana said. They shook hands. Tricks greeted all the men in the room. He was a noisy Liberian man.

"I heard you brought some beautiful girls, can I have one?" Tricks said.

My heart thumped as he said those words. The four of us just sat there looking at Lansana. He introduced us to Tricks and told him that we were tired and we did not want to talk.

"Ok, then let's get ready to go," Tricks said.

He followed Mariatu out of the room asking her whether she had anything for him. He wanted some food to eat too.

Lansana told us Tricks was the driver and he was going to take us to the town where he lived.

"You girls can then bathe and rest," Lansana said. "My sister is there so don't worry, she will look after you."

No sooner had he said that we heard Tricks honking from outside. He was already in the car waiting for us.

"Eagle let's go, man," he called out.

We said good-bye to Two-five and thanked Mariatu and went out. We got into a pickup. I sat in the front seat with Lansana, Nyalay and Tricks, Nyalay sat by the gear and I sat between her and Lansana. Samia and Komeh sat in the back seat with Hawk. The rest of the boys sat in the truck. Nyalay had one of her legs almost on the gear.

"Hey little girl, push your little leg to the other side," Tricks said, laughing rudely.

I thought he was disgusting. Lansana told him to be nice and stop yelling, because we did not like it.

"She will be afraid of you if you yell at her," Lansana said.

"Yeah, ok. Sorry small girl," Tricks said.

He increased the speed and we arrived at a town in, I think, twenty minutes or less. Almost everyone was in bed.

"Little girl come, I'll take you inside. What's your name again?" Tricks asked, reaching for Nyalay.

She went to him silently. Lansana let me out. At-the-end told Tricks Nyalay's name. Hawk let Samia and Komeh off. Lansana told us that the town we were in was called Kabbaty and that it was where he lived.

Tricks squatted in front of Nyalay when he took her into the house. He told her not to be afraid of him, that he would not harm her. He held out his hand to shake on what he said to her

"Let's be friends, ok," he said.

Nyalay nodded and shook his hand. We were very sleepy and exhausted. Nyalay was sucking her tongue and rubbing her eyes while Tricks talked to her. Tricks took Nyalay to Lansana's room and I walked behind them as I refused to leave her with him for a second.

"Where is the other radio?" Hawk asked.

He asked everyone, no-one knew what had happened to the radio.

"Maybe Two-five stole it," Laser suggested.

"If he did I will take something from him," Hawk said.

They were very upset about the missing radio. As I looked at them I thought, 'how Pa Madou would be feeling because he was the actual owner of everything the rebels brought back to their base, including the radios.' I leaned over to Komeh and whispered, "Stealing from the thief makes God laugh." She smiled and nodded.

Lansana introduced us to his sister Yewa who was pregnant. She was a petite woman and I liked her smile. She looked good pregnant. Her skin glowed and she had the same complexion as Magic and Hawk. I thought she was pretty. A few minutes later she brought us some food.

"Memuna, it's time for you to eat. You did not eat the food Mariatu cooked for us," Lansana said "eat and freshen up then you can get some sleep."

I was so tired and angry with them I did not want to even hear their voices but it was all I heard. I could not hear myself think. I was screaming inside for them to shut up. I covered my face with my hands. Hawk pulled me off the wall in Lansana's bedroom by my hand and sat me on his lap. The room was full of loot. Hawk fed me, as I was too tired and it was also too late in the night for me to eat. I managed to eat a few spoonfuls of the rice and leaned on Hawk and fell asleep. Lansana tried to wake me up.

"Memuna wake up you can't sleep on empty stomach," he said.

"I can't eat by this time, it's too late," I told him.

They did not understand what I was talking about.

"It's true, that's how she is," Komeh said.

Yewa suggested I went with her behind the house so she could give me some water to bathe.

In West Africa younger people are not allowed to say an adults name as if they are equals, they will appear cheeky. Some of us though, have adults we just call by their names without a title. So we either say Auntie or Uncle if they are related to us or very close to the family. For just another adult we say Ma or Pa if they are old, or Sissy (big sister). Among Mende people Ngor is another word we use before saying an adult's name. It means big sister or big brother. Komeh, Samia, Nyalay and I started to call Yewa Ngor Yewa.

I got off Hawk's lap and went with her. She took a lantern and we went to the backyard. It was dark and somehow windy. There was already a bucket of warm water waiting for me. I wondered how she did that but I did not ask as I got undressed and squatted by the bucket. I tried to rub the soap on my skin but it was too cold. The air was chilly outside and I started to shiver. Fortunately Ngor Yewa was standing there waiting for me with the lantern. For a while she did not hear me put water on my skin and she turned around to see what was going on. She found me asleep on the bucket and shivering.

"Memuna stand up," she said.

She set the lantern on the steps on the veranda and walked to me. I held her hand and stood up. She was very gentle; she rubbed the soap onto my skin and used a little bowl that was in her soap dish to pour the water from the bucket on my skin. She told me to rub my skin and my other parts she could not touch as she poured the water. It was fast and I felt fresh and clean.

"You are so tired from the walking; the warm water and a long sleep will bring you back," she said.

Ngor Yewa wrapped a towel around me and gave me some clean undies. She told me to go in and call Samia or Nyalay as she got their bathing water ready for them also. She said that she would do Komeh's water last. Everyone had gone except Samia, Nyalay and Komeh which was a relief for me.

I asked Komeh if she knew where Lansana had gone because I only had a towel around me and wanted something to wear.

Komeh said "He is on the front veranda smoking."

I went outside to him standing on the veranda with a bath towel around his neck, smoking and enjoying the breeze. He seemed to be enjoying a quiet moment. I stood at the door for a while staring at his back. I thought Lansana was a very attractive and handsome man. As I was looking at him I wondered why he captured us, why he put our family and us through such anguish. Again I was angry at how unfair it was.

"I want something to wear," I said.

"I was waiting to see if you will say something," he said. He knew I had been standing behind him.

"You are ready for bed now," he said. throwing the rest of his cigarette away and led me to the bedroom. Kabbaty was quite dark.

He pointed at a bag on the floor and told me to check in it for what I wanted. I stared at the bag for a moment, feeling guilty because it was from Pa Madou's shop. Samia, Komeh and Nyalay were outside with Ngor Yewa bathing.

"Where are your sisters?" Lansana asked.

"They are with Ngor Yewa behind the house," I said.

He walked out leaving me to get dressed. I opened the bag and took a pair of shorts and a big T-shirt. I got dressed and sat on the bed hunched in fear. There were no such things as pyjamas. The girls came back into the room and I showed them the bag so they could get into some clean clothes.

"Oh…Pa Madou's things, we are wearing them for free," Komeh said, as she shook her head feeling sorry for Pa Madou.

We all sat in Lansana's king-sized bed and Komeh and I tried to calm Samia and Nyalay. We fell asleep. Lansana was with us in the same bed. I did not have enough sleep. I could not dare to relax I was too scared. I was like a watchdog that night. I thought I was going to get raped by Lansana, as I was his main attraction. He had got dressed after he bathed and got into the bed and slept. He did not do anything to any of us.

CHAPTER SIX

Meeting Other Captives

Early the next morning around 6am, Lansana tuned on the BBC news. He sat up in the bed listening. I was not asleep; he looked over at me and saw my eyes opened. He smiled.

"Morning," he said.

"Morning," I whispered.

Komeh was lying next to me and I did not want to wake her. He asked me how I was and I told him that I was fine.

"What day is it?" I asked.

"It's Thursday. You are not going outside now. It's too early, you need to sleep and get your energy back," he said.

"I did not say I was going out, you woke me up with your news," I said.

He apologised and promised to turn the radio off after the news, with a smile. I closed my eyes and slept till 10am.

We had cassava and gravy for brunch. After we sat and talked to Ngor Yewa about our family for a while, by midday we fell asleep again. Lansana was not home but he came back a few minutes later. I opened my eyes and saw that he seemed busy. He got out some tobacco leaves from a big bag and rushed out quietly.

"That was Pa Madou's tobacco," I muttered.

I lay in bed staring at the ceiling. I heard the door open slightly but I did not look.

"Are you girls ready to eat yet?" Ngor Yewa asked.

"No," I said.

"I'm outside, tell me when you are ready," she said.

I nodded. She went out and closed the door quietly. Lansana got back in the afternoon. He asked "Did you girls have enough sleep and something to eat?" I told him I was not hungry and I did not know about Samia, Komeh and Nyalay, they were asleep. He asked if I had been crying because my eyes were red. I did not want to talk to Lansana. The more I heard his

66

voice, the more I hated him. I looked at him for a moment in silence then I told him that my eyes were red because I was still sleepy.

"You should sleep, did you know when I came in?" he asked, trying to start a conversation.

"Yes, I want to go home," I said.

"It's not true, you were dead asleep" he said.

"What makes you think I am lying?" I asked. "Do you want me to tell you what I was doing when you came in?"

"Yes," he said, "if you really saw me."

"Okay" I said. "You took some tobacco leaves and went out again."

"Don't you sleep at all?" he asked. "I see why your eyes are red." I lay in the bed and covered my head with the pillow.

"Where is my red shirt" muttered Lansana to himself searching through the big travelling bag. He went out to ask Ngor Yewa because she did his laundry. He came back into the room and went out again.

"Bastard!" Komeh sighed.

"Who?" I asked.

"Lansana" she said. "I heard everything the two of you said."

"We will eat together when your sisters wake up" Lansana said as he came in.

"Oh Komeh, you are awake. Did you dream?" he asked.

"I don't dream!" She answered angrily.

"Why don't you dream?" he asked smiling.

"I don't know!" she answered harshly.

Nyalay and Samia woke up from the noise of the conversation. Lansana spoke to them but Samia did not say anything. He went to the door and opened it slightly.

"Yewa can you please bring some food.? Lansana requested.

She brought rice with meat and fish stew. After eating we went outside and sat on the mat in the hut with his bodyguards. They were playing loud reggae music. A very fair complexioned woman introduced herself to us.

"My name is Maria. I heard that you were from Sembehun. How was it there?"

"Sembehun was good," Komeh said. We introduced ourselves to her.

"Which family are you from?" She asked us

"The Barnes' Family, and you?" Komeh asked.

Maria told us the name of the family she belonged to in Sembehun. She asked if Komeh knew her sister Angela. I told her that I knew her sister and their younger brother. Maria had been captured with her younger sister Sue who had a little son. Sue introduced herself to us and she and I became friends. She was beautiful.

There were a few people from Sembehun in Kabbaty who had been captured in Rutile and Moyamba. Sue and her sister Maria introduced me to them. We went to the creek with Hawa the landlord's daughter and Sue. Hawa asked if we knew how to swim and we told her we did not.

"The water is not deep so you have nothing to worry about."

I was sad. I wanted to go home. I took off my clothes and stood looking at the water wondering what I could have done not to be captured. Sue distracted me by pulling me into the water.

"Don't look so sad," she said. "Komeh, Samia and Nyalay take off your clothes and jump in."

The water was clean and cool; we almost spent the rest of the evening at the creek. A woman met us there, she greeted us and introduced herself to us, saying her name was Sabatu Sowah. She asked Sue if we were the girls Lansana had brought from Sembehun.

"Yes, I told them that I was going to take them to your house," Sue said.

We told her our names and she too asked which family we were from and we told her. She told us that she was from another family in Sembehun. She asked whether we knew her grandfather. I said no as I did not quite remember but Komeh reminded me that I knew him. I knew her grandfather when I was a child and I was taken to Sierra Leone to know my paternal grandmothers. He was our neighbour. Sabatu Sowah was very excited. I was cold and I did not want to talk to anyone but I forced myself not to direct my anger at fellow captives. She told us that we were always welcome to her house. Sabatu Sowah asked how old we were and Komeh told her. I gave random answers to questions most of the time. This was so because I wanted to end whatever conversation it was a person was trying to engage me in.

It was getting late and Sue suggested we went back to the house. Lansana, his bodyguards and his friends were in his room smoking cigarettes and marijuana.

"Man, Eagle, it's true," one of his friends said, as soon as we walked into the room. "I'm Lieutenant Strong; you can call me Strong."

He offered his hand for me to shake and I did. The room was cloudy with smoke.

"Gentlemen, this is Memuna, Komeh, Samia and Nyalay," Lansana introduced us. "Meet Lt. Universe, Lt. Sky…well you already know Strong's name."

I was disgusted by their attention. All I wanted was to go home and be a normal child. Instead I was some kind of trophy that Lansana showed off to everyone and they all peered at my sister, my cousins and me. We left them in the room and went outside to Ngor Yewa for our dinner. After dinner we sat on the veranda and talked with Sue and Hawa then we went to Lansana's room to sleep. He was in the room with Hawk, Laser and Magic. They talked to us but I ignored them. Lansana asked me if I was making friends in Kabbaty. I told him that I did not want any friends and that I wanted to go home. He held my shoulder and shook me slightly in an effort to cheer me up.

"I want to sleep," I said. I shook his hands off my shoulders.

He talked with his bodyguards for a while; they went to their rooms and left us with him.

"Have any of you been to Mattru Jung?" he asked.

We told him we had never been to Mattru Jung.

"Do you want to go and see?" he asked. We looked at each other and said we wanted to.

"Ok, I will make time for that. I'm very busy at the moment," he said.

Lansana woke up at the crack of dawn and came back in the afternoon. He found the four of us, Hawa and Laser in her mother's shop, which was now a room. Laser was sleepy and tired. Sue asked him what was wrong with him, as he seemed unwell. He said that he felt sick and weak.

"You remember those people you and those other rebels killed? They are haunting you, you can't kill Sembehun people," Komeh said.

"They will haunt you," I added.

He told us not to try and scare him because he was not scared but he was. I said that we were not lying.

"You will see," Komeh said.

Hawa laughed at him, Laser was trying to seem brave but the fear was too obvious in his eyes. He reached into his back pocket and took out a little blue Bible. He started to read it. I tried to take it from him.

"You should be afraid of God, he won't forgive you," I told him. "No - one is allowed to take another person's life. So you shouldn't touch the Bible.'

Lansana walked into the shop and saw Laser and I wrestling over the Bible and he got angry. He ordered Nyalay and Komeh to get ready that he was taking them to Mattru Jung.

"Why, what about Samia and me?" I asked.

"You will be fine. I need to keep an eye on you," he said. "You can visit each other; Yewa is here so don't worry."

"Ngor Yewa is not a part of our family," Komeh reminded him. "We feel better when we are together; we have always been with our family."

Komeh was angry and so was I. Samia and Nyalay were crying.

"What are you two crying for? Nothing bad is going to happen to any one of you so stop crying," Lansana said.

Tricks came and drove them to Mattru Jung. We cried bitterly for each other, we did not believe we were going to see each other again.

As they drove off I ran into the house crying and Samia followed me.

"Don't cry…they will be fine. Naffie is a nice person she is Lansana's woman," Ngor Yewa stammered. She stammered when she said every word. We continued crying.

"Lansana has a little son, his name is Boys and Naffie is pregnant again. Our little sister lives with Naffie in Mattru Jung; her name is Hafsatou and she is friendly too," Ngor Yewa continued. "Komeh and Nyalay will be fine, they will come here to visit and you can go there too, I will make sure that happens."

"I don't believe anything, it's not true," I said.

"No, it's true. Anytime you want to go to them ask Lansana or me." She tried to assure us.

"Ok, I want to go to them now," I said.

She laughed. "Not just yet," Ngor Yewa said. "But believe me, you will all be fine," she hugged Samia and me and wiped our tears. We went to the shop with Hawa and talked.

Laser came in and saw me lying on the mattresses giggling as I had been tickled by Hawa and Samia.

"The three of you make too much noise, the sun is hot; it's time to relax," he said. Hawa told him that we did not want to relax. He ignored us and laid on the bed. He started reading his Bible again. He read the Lord's Prayer and laid the Bible on his chest. I looked at him in disbelief.

"Laser, what did you just do?" I asked.

"Nothing, I only read Our Father," he said.

"You are not serious; you have the brave mind to touch the Bible after everything I have told you?"

He said "I did not kill anyone. Besides, is your father a pastor?"

"I saw you. Why are you praying?" I asked.

Laser said "It was for God's protection and forgiveness."

"You want God to forgive and protect you?" I asked looking at him seriously.

"Yes, why?" he said.

So I asked if I could ask him a question. I held his hand and asked him to sit up.

"Laser, if I pinch you would you forgive me?" I asked, as I pinched him.

He said he would forgive me and tell me not to do it again. I pulled his ear and asked him if he would forgive me.

"Hey ouch, stop it. That's enough what is this about?" he asked getting very annoyed.

"It's about forgiveness. How can you expect God to forgive you when you keep killing and capturing people over and over again? You won't let me pull your ear or pinch your hand for the second time," I said.

Hawa stared and started laughing.

"You act too old for your age, where do you get your ideas?" he asked. "You think like an old woman for a person so little,"

I told him my size had nothing to do with my thoughts.

"You are bigger than I am but you think like a goat," I said.

I asked him to let me look at his Bible but he refused. I told him that I wished the people he killed would haunt him.

Lansana returned and found Laser and me wrestling over the Bible again and again he got angry. He ordered me to go with him to his room. I was close to tears but I forced them back. We got into his room and he slammed the door behind us. I was so frightened I squeezed myself against the wall. I thought he was going to hit me.

"Sit down," he said.

I was too scared to refuse; I sat on the chair and looked at him.

"What are you doing with Laser?" he asked.

I told him we were only wrestling over a Bible.

"Who does the bible belong to?" he asked.

"It's Laser's, but I wanted to read it," I said.

He told me that he never wanted to see me playing with boys anymore.

"When I'm not here you stay with Yewa," he said. "You like little boys don't you?"

I felt sick and angry. I was always allowed to play with whomever I wanted to play with and most of my friends were boys when I was home.

"I don't want boys around something I want," he sighed.

At that moment I started to cry, I could not hold it anymore. I felt like I was being made a woman before I was ready to become one. Anger welled up inside me.

"I was allowed to play with anyone when I was home and my grandmothers did not mind" I cried.

"I don't care, I don't want to talk anymore," Lansana said.

He ordered me to stand in the corner and turn my face to the wall. He turned on the radio and lay in bed.

"I don't want you, I don't want anyone," I cried. "Please don't want me I'm only fourteen and you are too big for me."

"Come, come on," Lansana beckoned me. "Sit down."

"I don't want to sit," I said, shaking in fear.

"Why don't you want me or anyone?" he asked

I fixed my eyes to the floor while he looked at me.

"But I want you," he said.

"No, don't want me please," I looked at him in his eyes as I pleaded.

"I will take care of you until you are ready to be my woman," Lansana said.

I looked at him in silence imagining myself being raped by him. I thought of my family and how horrible my grandmothers said sex was when one did it at a young age, grandma Ngaya said it perforated one's ovaries, in turn making pregnancy impossible. I looked at Lansana feeling nothing for him but hate and disgust. He asked me why I was looking at him the way I was, but I said nothing. I just kept staring at him. He got up and changed his jeans.

"You are not going outside today," he said.

He walked out locking me in his room. I sat on the floor and cried again.

Samia came into the room after a while. Ngor Yewa let her in. She said that she had been looking for me.

"Since when?" I asked.

Samia, noticed that I had been crying, she asked me what was wrong; she thought I was still crying for Nyalay and Komeh. I did not want to add to her worries so I told her that nothing was wrong but she insisted and I told her what Lansana did.

"Is he stupid? He is shameless and wicked", she said. "God will curse him."

She looked at me for a moment and asked me what I told Lansana so I told her.

He came back a few minutes later and asked whether we had eaten but we ignored him.

"Since neither of you want to talk to me, you can ask Yewa for anything you want," he said. "I'm going to Mattru Jung. Again, do you have anything you want to say to your sisters?"

Samia told him to greet them for us. He said bye and rushed out.

Ngor Yewa asked if we wanted some food and we told her we did. We followed her to the kitchen where she gave us a medium-sized bowl of rice and some fish stew. I looked at her as she ran around giving us food. Her stomach was big and I was feeling sorry for her. She caught me looking at her and she asked why but I said nothing.

"I know what you are looking at, I have four more months to go," she said.

I nodded and continued eating. I would have made a conversation but I knew nothing about pregnancy at the time.

I was sad for the rest of the evening, I was thinking of what Lansana had said to me. Samia and I went to the creek with Hawa and Sue. I was not the usual me but they did not ask. We played a lot in the water and went back to the house. I wished I could have spent the night at the creek. We sat on the veranda and talked for a while with the mosquitoes flying around and biting us. As I felt sleepy, I thought of Lansana and I felt afraid to go to sleep in his room. I was scared he would rape me. Samia and I went to sleep in his room; there was nowhere else to sleep. Everyone shared his or her room with someone. Samia tried not to sleep but she slept. I stayed awake all through the night, watching over my sister and myself. Luckily Lansana did not return that evening. By the time I closed my eyes to sleep I heard the cockcrow and the people at the mosque were calling for the 6am prayer. Then I knew that I had been up till the next day and I was sad that I had to worry about being raped and I started crying. I cried till I fell asleep and I woke up at sunrise.

Ngor Yewa was not at home when I woke up. She had gone to a nearby village. Samia and I were hungry, so I decided to cook. I put some wood in the fireplace and made the fire, poured some water and palm oil into the pot and put it on the fire. When the pot boiled I washed the rice and put it in the pot with salt, which was too much but I did not realise. Samia and I sat in the kitchen struggling to eat the salty rice. We saw a young couple walk in. The woman was beautiful, fair skinned, big eyes and hair the same length as mine just pass shoulder length at the time and was a thick afro. And she wore a nice smile. She greeted us in Mende and we replied.

"Where is everyone," she asked. I stopped eating and stood up with my right hand behind me. We told her that some were asleep and others were gone out. She was surprised that we were alone.

"My name is Magainda, what are yours?" she asked.

I told her our names and relation. She smiled the whole time and I liked her. The young man she came with was not really tall. He was dark and masculine and he had a low haircut I thought he looked neat, though he was a rebel. I liked Magainda the moment I saw her. She took us to the mud house opposite the house Lansana lived in. She opened her room; we went inside and sat on the bed. She took a deep breath and said she was very tired. The young man came into the room and introduced himself; he said his name was Amara. He told us Hawk and Magic were his brothers and that he lived in Mattru Jung but he came to escort Magainda so that she could be with us.

"I saw your sisters," he said. "You are all pretty."

He smiled and went back outside. He looked like he was bored and lonely without his brothers and the others.

Magainda asked us which family we were from and we told her. She asked us whether we knew Joseph Aruna Bangura or whether we had heard about him. He was a famous politician in Sierra Leone. I told her that I met him once and that he had children with one of my cousins. I told her that my cousin's last name was not Barnes.

"He is my uncle," she said. "I know all his children."

She asked me who my cousin was and I told her. She said that she missed the children.

"I remember one night when uncle came with them and one of your cousins Aminatu and another girl called Memuna," Magainda said.

I remembered the night she was talking about as I was there. It was the night I got to meet Joseph Aruna Bangura.

"Magainda, I'm Memuna," I said. "I went to the house with the children and Aminatu."

I recited the children's names and she believed me. She gave Samia and me a big hug and said that she was happy to see us. She asked why I did not tell her earlier.

"I did not know it was you and I had totally forgotten about that night," I said.

"We are family!" Magainda said. "We will look after each other."

Amara went back to the room and saw us excited. He asked what was going on and Magainda explained to him as fast as she could. He was happy for us.

"That is good then, maybe they will feel more confident around you," Amara said.

Indeed I did, I felt easy with Magainda around. Amara said goodbye as he was going back to his assignment in Mattru Jung. He got on his bicycle and rode off. Magainda emptied a plastic bag of vegetables she had brought. One of the many things I love about Sierra Leone is that it is easy to be related to someone. You can be related to someone only by marriage but that someone will treat you like a blood relative if the relationship is good.

"I saw you two eating some food out there which I know you did not want to eat," Magainda said.

"It's Memuna, she put too much salt in the rice," Samia complained.

Magainda laughed and asked me whether I knew how to cook. I told her that I was learning and that I enjoyed cooking. She asked us to go with her to the kitchen and help her cook then after we ate we could do our hair. Her presence in the house made us feel so much better. She told us she met Nyalay and Komeh in Mattru Jung and said that Nyalay had lots of fans in Mattru Jung, as she was very active. Nyalay was just an 8-year-old child and she handled the situation the way she knew best as so did all of us. Magainda said she was worried about Komeh as she was still worried and angry but also assured me that eventually Komeh would be fine.

"Sunshine and Bintu are there and, they will make friends with her," Magainda said.

I thought the name Sunshine was weird and for a moment I thought I heard Magainda wrong so I asked her,

"Magainda who is Sunshine ?"

She told me that Sunshine was Lansana's sister. "Her name is Hafsatou but they call her Sunshine," Magainda said.

It was time for all the other women to go to the kitchen and cook. There were six women in the house including Magainda. Sue went to the kitchen to help Maria, while Hawa helped her mother in the kitchen as well. Sahr's girlfriend Mabinti, cooked alone. They all conversed with each other. Hawa's mother, called Mama by everyone in the house, was the oldest woman in the house. She was happy that Magainda had come because that day was the first time she saw me smile. She thanked Magainda for coming. Soon Ngor Yewa arrived back from the village and she also thanked Magainda for coming to Kabbaty so she could help her look after us.

Samia told her about the rice I cooked. She asked where the rice was and we told her that I threw it away and everyone laughed at me.

"You better be careful, Memuna and don't get me in trouble," Ngor Yewa said. "If you burn yourself, Lansana will be looking for someone to blame."

I got worried that she knew about her brother's feelings for me and had not talked to him to stop feeling that way as I was a child. After cooking we went back to the room.

"Now it's time to undo the hair," Magainda said. "Who wants to go first?"

She helped Samia undo her hair while I did mine alone. Magainda liked Samia's hair. We went to the creek with Magainda to wash our hair with bathing soap. When we got back we were too tired to braid our hair so Magainda promised to do it first thing in the morning.

As we sat in Lansana's room chatting I was in hell; I thought of Lansana the whole time. Mabinti Sahr - that was what we called her because there was another with the same name - came and joined us in Lansana's room. Around 9pm Ngor Yewa went to bed and soon after we went to our room too. Samia slept and left Magainda and I talking. We talked about our families and for a while I was in denial. I felt like I was on holiday and that I could go home anytime I wanted to. I went outside to use the toilet and instantly I was back to reality I was a captive living with rebels.

CHAPTER SEVEN

A Strange Way Of Life

Lt. Universe was in charge of the artillery and he had some crazy bodyguards. They guarded the 50-calibre gun mounted in a pickup truck under a mango tree in front of Magainda's house. The pickup truck was spray painted in military camouflage to avoid ready detection by the roaming jet-fighter. The artillery calibre was black with a long chain full of up to a thousand huge bullets mounted on it. The guards changed shift on a daily basis.

We had our little kerosene lantern and the artillery calibre guards could hear us talking and laughing, they already knew Magainda. I wanted to tell Magainda that Lansana had locked me in his room all day and spoke of having me as his wife after the war and that now I was his girlfriend but I still did not fully trust her. Lansana returned at around midnight; there was a lot of noise. One of Lt. Universe's bodyguards called out to us and said that Lansana was back. We already knew. My heart had begun to pound. Anxiety took over my reality. As I did not want Magainda to ask what was wrong, I controlled it. I was not ready to tell her. We heard them give him a salute – which they referred to as "courtesy". We heard them talking to Lansana's bodyguards. When the rebels gave courtesy, they would stand still like the army and say 'it's for you Sir', or 'I'm to myself (something the rebels said to show respect and praise to their superiors) Sir', or 'good afternoon Sir' if it was afternoon, etc. When the female rebels gave courtesy, they either knelt down on one knee with their arms straight down by their sides or they did it like the men and said those words. In RUF the female rebels were also referred to as Sir since according to them there is no woman in the army. Magainda suggested we went out to Lansana's room to say hello. I did not want to go but I forced myself to. I got into some clothes as I was only wearing a huge t-shirt and we went outside.

"Hey Bullet, my sister is asleep in that room please don't let anyone go in," Magainda said to one of the calibre guards.

It was daytime for Lansana, his friends and his bodyguards. They smoked and made lots of noise. Tricks was in Lansana's room too. They were all stoned high and their eyes were red. Tricks was on his way out as we walked into the room. He said goodnight and got into his pickup and drove off. They kept quiet and stared at us for a moment when they saw us. Then they said hello. Lt. Strong and Lt. Sky shook our hands. I was scared but I shook their hands. Lansana and his friends were pretty boys, only Lt. Universe looked like a real soldier but they were all strong fighters. We sat for a while and Lansana could not stop looking at me. His friends asked me one stupid question after another. They asked my age, I told them and then they asked me whether I missed home. I thought it was cold and stupid of them.

"Lansana man, she is pretty," Lt. Strong said. "She looks a little like you."

Lansana carried on staring at me as he nodded. Magainda saw that I was uncomfortable, she said goodnight and we went back to our room to go to bed.

Magic, Hawk and Soja followed us to Magainda's room. At-the-end was in Mattru Jung spending time with his girlfriend. Acid-moe lived on the other side of Kabbaty with his commanding officer, called Titanium, who was said to be Lansana's cousin. He had two women and they both lived in the same house as Naffie. They were both called Rugiatu, which was a total coincidence. They both had a child by him. The younger Rugiatu had a son and named him after Blazing Spares. The older one had a daughter and named her Umu. We stood on the veranda to talk, because Samia was asleep. Hawk asked me whether I had missed him and I told him I did not miss any of them. He saw that I was smiling.

"You missed me I know," he said. "I'm back now I just went to see some girls."

"How about Karimu, Samba, Briama and the other men you people captured with us?" I asked.

"They are gone to the training base, to train and fight for their country," he said.

"They don't want to be rebels," I said.

"Well I really don't know anyone wanting to become a rebel, but this is just how it is around here for men," he replied.

He told me not to worry that my uncle would be alright. He went into the room and got some clean clothes for him and Magic. Soja had left us standing earlier and went to their room to bed. Hawk and Magic said goodnight and went away. "They have a secret house that I don't know about," Magainda said.

She complained that they took other girls to the house so she would not see them and she was determined to know where it was. Amara was the oldest amongst the boys.

"They all use that room, from Laser to Amara," she said.

One of the calibre guards laughed and told us that he heard everything. Magainda told him that she did not care all she cared about was to find that house. We went to bed and woke up late the next morning. Samia woke up before us. She went to the kitchen and helped Ngor Yewa in the kitchen to make breakfast. Magic and hawk came to our room with Acid-moe and three other young rebels. One had a towel wrapped around his head; and he wore baggy jeans with a singlet. He looked like Magic. The others wore shorts. They woke us to introduce me to them, as they already knew Magainda.

"These are our brothers, Ghost, PJ. and Rebel Daddy and boys this is Memuna," Magic said.

They all seemed normal and as I looked at them, I felt sorry for their parents. They were good looking boys. They shook hands with me. The one with the towel was called Rebel Daddy.

"You can call me Daddy that's what everyone calls me. I've heard a lot about you Memuna," He said.

Acid-moe funny and love to joke a lot he made it so easy for me to get used to him and so did Ghost. They made so much noise in the room. Magainda asked them to please excuse us so that we could put on some clothes as we only had our undies on under the blanket. It was a very hot night.

"Magainda, looks beautiful every day. Twelve-round (Amara's nickname) is lucky," Acid-moe said.

They went to the veranda and continued making noise.

Magainda pulled her bag from underneath the bed. "I've got lots of clothes here and they are all mine; I was captured in Mattru Jung so I just took my things to my mother's in Ndogbohun - a village just across the river. Since the rebels decided to live in Mattru Jung, they did not take us anywhere else. I have two suitcases full of clothes in Ndogbohun in my mother's house. We can share them," she said.

"Where is Ndogbohun?" I asked.

"Ndogbohun is my village; it's close to Mattru Jung and the Teli-yeh (Mende for black water. Teli-yeh is the name of the river that separates Mattru Jung from Ndogbohun). Would you like to go to Ndogbohun?"

"Yes," I nodded. I thought to myself "I'd do anything to be among normal people."

I sat for a while wondering why they call the river Teli-yeh. "Magainda, why is the river called Teli-yeh?"

"The water seems black but when you dip it, it's just like ordinary water. So they named it Teli-yeh because of its colour," she explained.

"Oh, ok," I said.

"Have you sat in a canoe before?" She asked.

"Yes, but I'm afraid of canoes. Why? Are we going to sit in a canoe to go to Ndogbohun?"

"We will cross the Teli-yeh in a canoe it will only take five minutes. There are men who row the canoes."

"Hmm ok," I said, but I was still afraid.

The boys came back into the room after we had dressed.

"Magic, Memuna wants to go to Ndogbohun," Magainda said.

"When would she want to? I'll talk to Lansana about it or Magainda you can tell him," Magic suggested.

I sat on the bed thinking who on earth is he, why is Magainda asking his permission to take me to where I wanted to go, why not Lansana. Magic and the others said good-bye and left the three of us.

We talked about our trip to Ndogbohun all night; Samia fell asleep and left us talking. I started thinking of Lansana telling me that he wanted he and I to be a couple and I cannot play with boys, this was worrying me and I could not hold it in any longer so I tried to make a conversation

"Magainda, why did you have to ask Magic's permission to take me to Ndogbohun?" I asked.

"He is Lansana's senior bodyguard," She answered.

"Oh, I see. So suppose he agrees and Lansana doesn't?" I said.

"Well they agree a lot; even if Lansana doesn't want you to go Magic will talk him into it," Magainda said.

I nodded in surprise and said nothing for a while.

Lying on the bed staring at the ceiling, Magainda turned to face me.

"I think we should sleep now," she whispered.

I nodded.

She closed her eyes while I still stared at the ceiling. I thought of my mother whom we thought we had lost in the war in Liberia and then I started sobbing. I did not want Samia to see me crying so I tried to stop.

"God what's next, after losing our mother in the war in Liberia and now being captured by a bunch of rebels? What's next?" I whispered.

This time I cried even harder, I did not want Magainda or Samia to hear me cry because I needed to be strong so I covered my head with the pillow. I cried till I fell asleep.

The next morning Magic and Magainda's whispers and laughter awakened me at sunrise. Magic chuckled when I opened my eyes "Magainda she's up," he said.

She looked at me and I smiled back at them.

"How many dreams did you have?" Magic asked.

I looked at him. "Five," I said. "Where is Samia, Magainda?"

"She is washing up and you can go after her if you want, or you can wait to go to the creek with me," Magainda said.

"I'll go to the creek with you then," I said.

Magainda nodded.

On our way I asked Magainda whether we could go to Mattru Jung when we got to Ndogbohun.

"Sure, we will," she said.

Magainda and I dilly-dallied in the water for half an hour. Samia did not want to get in so she sat in the shade underneath a tree by the creek waiting for us.

Later in the afternoon Magainda, Samia and I met Lansana in the hut with David on guard and Magainda told Lansana about our trip to Ndogbohun.

"Magic told me," Lansana said. "So, How long are you going for? Are you taking Samia and Memuna with you?"

"No, I don't want to go I'm tired," Samia interrupted.

"Okay, I'll go with Memuna," Magainda said.

"Tell Magic when you are ready to go he'll sign your passes for you," Lansana said. Magainda thanked him and we went to our room.

By then the weather was getting a bit chilly and the sun had begun to set. Everyone, especially women and children were sitting on their verandas. That night after dinner Magainda told Magic about our conversation with Lansana. Samia and I were sitting in the bed playing a game of cards. It was a bit cloudy outside and we were expecting rain. I suggested the card game to cheer Samia up a little. She was very sad and she started isolating herself while I was trying to hide my feelings and accept what life had pushed at my face instead of being sad. I could not think of anything more we could do but accept it. I suggested the game to find a way to tell her that it was not the end of our lives.

"So, Memuna you sure you want to go to Ndogbohun?" Magic asked.

"Yes I'm sure," I replied, sounding a little angry. "Why?"

"Nothing," he answered.

"Memuna likes walking about. She gets bored staying steady," Sami informed him.

"Okay," Magic said.

"When are we going Magainda?" I asked.

"In two weeks I want you to rest," She said.

I nodded.

I had all my attention to the game as Samia had started cheating. We talked a while and then Magic left. Magainda and I talked about Ndogbohun almost all night and fell asleep.

It was just the same routine the next morning as usual but it was a little cold and wet as it rained a bit the night before. Later in the afternoon Magic, Samia, Magainda and I played Ludo in the hut. We played twice and Magainda won both games, after that she and Samia got bored and went to our room. I still wanted to play so Magic played with me. He let me win the first game, then we played again and he won.

"You are a cheat. You cheated your way through that game," I said.

"Ok, let's play another game," he said, "an easier game this time."

Lansana had come out of the house to the hut for some air. I cheated the game and Magic took the dice.

"Stop cheating, tell me you won't cheat again," he said.

I told him I would not cheat anymore and we continued the game. Magic had three seeds left to win while I had five. He started laughing at me, so I began the cheating again. This time it was not working for me so I took the dice and ran off to Magainda and Samia in the room.

"What is going on?" they asked.

But I could not talk as I was giggling and trying to catch my breath. I hid behind the door but when he walked into the room, I ran outside giggling. He ran after me and caught me. He held my hands and we were both laughing.

"Hey, we are going to finish the game," He said.

"No, you want to win. So I'm not playing," I said.

"But you cheated a lot, so keep cheating and maybe you will win," he said.

I cheated but it still was not any good, so I disarranged the game and ran off again with both dice. He ran after me and caught me again. "We are going to start a new game, someone must win," he said.

"Okay, okay. Can we play later? I'm tired now," I said.

He agreed. "You and Magainda cheat a lot," he said.

Lansana got very angry watching Magic and me play like that. He went to his room and sent David to call me. David stayed on the veranda, as I walked into the room

"You forgot what I told you about those boys, haven't you?" he said.

I stood there looking at him without saying a word. I was so confused and angry at the same time and I wondered 'why me? With all the women in that town who were ready for a man why me?' It was unfair. I felt like his property and that he could do anything to me and I would have no-one to protect me, just the thought was horrifying.

"You are sleeping here again tonight," he snapped.

Luckily this time he let me go out. I did not let him see me all evening, I told Magainda about his reaction to Magic and I playing. I told her that when Lansana asked for me, to tell him I was asleep. I slept in our room. Magic, the other bodyguards and his friends came over and Magainda told him what I told her to say. Magic got angry and told Hawk, Laser, At-the-end, Acid-Moe and their friends that he did not want to stay. They knew he was angry so they left. Magainda and I talked almost all night, this time I told her what Lansana told me the time he saw me playing with Laser. Lansana and all his bodyguards were very good-looking especially Magic and Hawk, one could hardly tell when those two were angry. Hawk would try to frown and swear when he was angry, Magic would get really serious, smoke and stay quiet.

"Magainda, I've never had a boyfriend before so what will I be doing with Lansana as big and tall as he is. I'm only 14 Years old I don't want a boyfriend. When I was in Sembehun, my aunties and my grandmothers did not mind me playing with boys so I'm used to it. That doesn't mean they are going to put their hands in my pants," I said.

"I will make sure that won't happen," said Magainda.

In the morning all the boys came to the house, as usual. I only realised it was a Saturday because everyone was doing his or her laundry. It was a hot sunny day, the breeze was cool and there were food smells everywhere. Some women were cooking while others were cleaning. It did not seem like a war zone except for the boys and their guns that we saw around. Magainda packed our clothes as well as some of Lansana's and some of the boys'. The atmosphere in the house was not really good; the boys were still angry with Lansana but they did not tell him. Ngor Yewa asked Magic what was wrong with him. He said he felt sick. We left them and went to the creek to do the laundry. When we arrived, Magainda arranged the clothes. She put all the jeans and two of her denim skirts aside and the tops one side and the bedding on the other.

"Do you know how to do laundry, Memuna?" Magainda asked.

Samia stared and laughed because she knew how bad my laundry was.

"No," I said.

"Okay, I'll wash them and you will rinse them, is that okay?" Magainda said.

"Yes," I said.

"Let's wash the jeans first," she suggested.

We took off our clothes and got into the water. I was left with a T-shirt and my undies on. Magainda wore shorts and a T-shirt. Magainda gave me the jeans that Magic and Hawk wore and the T-shirts Laser, Lansana and Miles wore when they went to Sembehun.

As I spread the jeans in the water to rinse them, I was angry as the day of my capture replayed in my head. I was angry so often that it scared me and I always had a headache. There were two girls beside me; one light - skinned and chubby the other one dark like me but chubby too. The light-skinned one saw the jeans; she looked at them and pinched the dark one to look at the jeans.

"Aren't those Magic's pants?" She asked.

"Yes, it looks like the one he had on when they came back from the mission," the dark one said.

The light-skinned one wanted to be sure of what was going on. She stood in front of me in the water.

"Afternoon, do you know Magic, Hawk and At-the-end?" she asked politely.

I did not know what to say and I could not be bothered. So I looked at Magainda wanting her to say something because they understand each other.

"Yes. We live together I'm his brother's girlfriend," Magainda said.

"Who, Hawk?" the light-skinned girl asked.

"No, Amara," Magainda said.

"Okay…." They both said nodding, giving us the impression they have heard about Magainda.

"My name is MaHawa and that's my cousin Marion." The light-skinned one said, introducing her and the dark one.

"Oh, I'm Magainda and these are my cousins Memuna and Samia," Magainda said.

"Oh, I like your hair it's quite long," Marion said.

"Thank you," I said.

They were doing their laundry along with Magic's, Hawk's, At-the-end's and Laser's too. We talked and became friends.

"We live in Captain Barrie's house. I'm his daughter. We can visit each other sometime, Marion suggested.

We finished and left them at the creek.

On our way back to the house, Magainda and I started laughing.

"Magic is going to face court martial board today," she said. "One of them is his girlfriend. They must know where the secret house, I'm sure."

"They are jealous," Samia said.

The boys spent the whole day at the house, as it was the main house. They sat in Lansana's room arranging the things they looted from Pa Madou's shop. They put some aside for us to use. We went into the room and Magic saw us first. He tapped me on my shoulder and thanked me for helping with the laundry. Lansana was with them in his room, he looked at me.

"You look tired, your eyes are red," he noted.

"I'm not really tired. My eyes are red because I spent most of the time in the water trying to swim," I said.

Magic tried to give Magainda a hug, but she smiled and pushed him out of her way.

"Don't hug me, you boys are in trouble with us, especially me," she said. "Some of the secret is out; we will talk about it tonight if you are not going with Bra." (Bra is what the boys called Lansana, slang - meaning big bro or boss.)

"I'm not feeling very well so I'm not going anywhere. Bra is going with Laser and Miles," Magic said without any care in the world as to what was going on.

Laser mistakenly stepped on a box of NATCO biscuits while packing and talking. "Laser, man, be careful these are government properties," At-the-end said.

"Magainda what is this trouble we are in or am I not a part of it?" Laser asked.

"Yes, you are. Go and come back and face court martial board, you rabbit ear" Magainda said with a smile.

They all laughed. They made us feel at ease. We were very lucky in a bad situation, to fall in the right hands. Not like we needed it but if that was how it was going to be, then we were lucky, because some girls got beaten every day for nothing.

"Well I think it is tougher on my boy Laser. Maybe it is entirely his fault. Oh Yes Magainda it's his fault. I told him not to do it but he wouldn't listen," Hawk joked.

"You don't even know what it is, so why are you trying to blame it all on him? Maybe it's entirely your fault. The only person who I think is not involved in this is David," she said.

David was one of those quiet mysterious people; he only talked when he had to. Magainda was the only girl who hung out with them since they came to Mattru Jung before we were captured, apart from all the other girls outside, so they liked her very much.

That evening, after dinner, Lansana went out. He was busy delivering the things they looted from Pa Madou's shop around. He took a lot to Mattru Jung and some to Africa's Ground that was originally called Yangatokee. They all came to our room laughing and talking about something.

"Okay, Queen Magainda, tell us what this problem is. But just know, it's not my fault," Magic said, jokingly.

"This room is too small for us; let's go to Lansana's room," Magainda said.

When we got to Lansana's room, Magic turned the radio on loud he was playing Bob Marley's track 'Could You Be Loved'

"Turn it down a bit," Magainda said.

Magainda explained what had happen at the creek while Samia and I just sat listening. Every time I was quiet my brain ran a thousand miles per hour and sadness got stronger inside me. They started laughing, they all tried to be innocent but Magainda insisted.

"Magic man, tell Magainda what happened, how they got our jeans," At-the-end said.

"I don't know I don't even know those girls," Magic said.

"You are the only Magic here, in Kabbaty. The other two are gone to Freetown Highway. So don't say you don't know," Magainda objected. "You better tell me."

"True, I don't know them. You know there are so many girls…from Africa's Ground to Sumbuya. So many girls are dying for the Colonel (that's what his friends, brothers and Lansana called him, but Magic was not a colonel). So maybe they saw me and made up a story," Magic said.

"Okay, I'll tell you Magainda. The colonel is lying. See the MaHawa girl, she is his on-and-off bitch but he doesn't want anyone to know," Hawk said.

"Who is the Marion one?" she asked.

"Well um…let's leave that," he said.

"You want the girl, man say it," At-the-end interrupted.

84

While talking in Lansana's room, Ngor Yewa yelled my name from the veranda. She said there was someone there for me. I went out and it was MaHawa, I could not help laughing when I saw her. 'Speak of the devil,' I thought. We greeted each other and she said she was passing by so she thought she could drop in and say hello to us. I took her into the room, but as we walked in Magic gave MaHawa a hard look and walked out. MaHawa sat with us for a while and left. When I walked her out, we found Magic standing outside in the front yard smoking marijuana. He never smoked cigarettes. As I walked passed him with MaHawa, he reached and held my hand and looked at MaHawa in the eyes. She stared back at him and said goodnight to him and me and she left us standing there.

"I'll see you tomorrow, MaHawa," I said.

I turned to him, looked at his hand holding mine and looked him in the eyes; I did not know what was going on.

"Don't be friends with her," he said.

"Why? She is nice, she is your girlfriend," I said.

He took a puff and dropped the remaining of his smoke.

"That was long ago. Though she still wants me," he said.

"Well, go back to her. I think she's nice," I said.

"No, I don't want her anymore. I want someone else," he said.

"Who, is she here in Kabbaty?" I asked.

"Maybe," he said thoughtfully.

The others laughed louder as we walked into the room to join them.

"Man, you are a coward," Hawk said.

"Why did you walk out?" Magainda asked. "Memuna where is she?"

"She's gone home. He wouldn't let me walk her half way," I said.

"She came here to see you man," At-the-end said to Magic.

"No, she said she was walking by so she thought she could drop by," I said.

"Walking by going where and from where? She won't say she went to the bridge at this time of the night or maybe she went to visit the skull at the guard post. Or she is coming from Mattru Jung tonight on foot." Hawk interrupted, making everyone in the room laugh.

He said this because the house we lived in and Lt. Universe's house were the two last houses on the other side of Kabbaty. We stopped talking about Magic and MaHawa and listened to some loud reggae music. Magic, Hawk and At-the-end were smoking cigarette and marijuana. Lansana went with Soja, Miles, David and Laser. "Hawk, what's government property? I heard At-the-end saying those things were government properties," I asked.

"Government property is something that belongs to the government," he started to explain.

"I know what government property is. I was wondering why he said they are government properties. They don't belong to the government, they belong to Pa Madou," I interrupted.

"Okay now they belong to RUF. When we go on a mission and bring back something, we give some to the RUF government for our wounded soldiers," he said.

Samia left us talking and went to bed.

CHAPTER EIGHT

Teli-yeh (Mende for Black-water) River

Within a week I made lots of friends. A lot of people liked me. MaHawa and I visited each other. At times Magainda, Samia and I went to visit Marion and MaHawa. When it was time to go to Ndogbohun; Lansana went to Africa's Ground again with more "government properties". While he was away Magic took us to the Kabbaty ground commander, a clerk who was a rebel and in charge of what the town commander (a civilian in charge of other civilians who did not live with rebels - mainly old people) could not handle. They gave us the passes and Magic took them, signed them and put them in his pocket.

"Magic, those passes should be in my hands not in your pockets. Give them to me now," Magainda said.

"Magainda, why do we need them?" I asked.

"To show as identification and as a pass allowing us to go where we are going," she answered, holding her hand out to Magic waiting for our passes. He leaned over to her and whispered something in her ear and she looked at him with her mouth open in surprise with a little mischievous smile and she opened her eyes wide. I stared at them wondering what was going on and Samia stood without saying a word. He gave Magainda the passes a few minutes later.

"Samia you sure you don't want to come?" I asked.

"Yes Samia are you sure?" Magainda added.

"She will be alright, I'll see to that," Magic said.

"No, I will be with Ngor Yewa. I don't want to walk any more long distances," Samia said.

"She will be fine I swear. Magainda say hello to everyone for me," Magic said.

"Memuna bring something back for me okay and make sure you come back tomorrow," was all Samia said.

"Okay," I said.

"Samia you are right, they should make sure they are here tomorrow," Magic said.

"Hey, say bye to Hawk and At-the-end," Magainda said to Magic.

"Okay, be back tomorrow," he said.

"Why, do we have to breast-feed you?" she asked.

We laughed and we both hugged Sania, said bye to Ngor Yewa, Ngor Maria and Sue and left.

We walked through farms and forests; I was very scared. All I could think of was snakes. Magainda kept asking me whether I was alright. When we got to the river just the sight of it scared me and I held Magainda's hand tight.

"Don't be scared. We will be fine. It's only five minutes to cross and my cousin is coming to cross us," she said.

"Samukai, how are you?" she greeted the man who came for us in a canoe.

"Samukai, this is Memuna. Memuna, this is Samukai," she politely introduced us.

"Hello Memuna, how are you?" Samukai asked.

"Good and you?" I asked.

I sat in the canoe and held tight and took a deep breath when we finally got to Ndogbohun. "Ah, Samukai, before I go up there, is everyone okay and alive?" Magainda asked.

Samukai laughed, "Yes, Magainda everyone is fine."

Ndogbohun was a little village on the hill surrounded by forest and the Teli-yeh River with about eight to ten houses and it was pretty muddy at that time of the year because it was June - raining season. Magainda took me around the village introducing me to everyone and they were so happy to see me. I was not surprised at how happy they were to welcome me. Mende people are very good at that; they like strangers. Magainda has an auntie called Yea Nnasu (Yea is Mende for mama). She was so happy she gave me a cuddle when we arrived.

Yea Nnasu's son was a nice, happy boy. He told me his name but I never remembered as it was not a common name.

Magainda's mother took us to her nice round hut.

"God, I've been waiting to enter this kind of hut for so long," I said to myself.

Inside the hut was cool and it felt good to be in it. I felt a sense of peace being with Yea Gbassay (Magainda's mother), I felt protected. I felt like my grandmothers were just around the corner and I could just see them whenever I wanted.

"Sit on the bed my child and make yourself comfortable. This is your next home, Magainda is your sister," Yea Gbassay said.

I sat on the bed then I saw Magainda sitting on the floor

"Oh it's so nice and cool on the floor," she said. "Yea, I want to look in my suitcase for some clothes for me and Memuna."

I sat on the floor too and it felt good and soothing. Magainda took some clothes out for us to take to Kabbaty.

"I have some food ready for the strangers!" In came smiling Yea Nnasu.

"You girls seem very tired, look at you on the floor," she said rubbing my head.

We spent the night at Magainda's house, which she had not finished building yet. All she had left to do was the painting and the living room windows properly fixed. She told me all about the house and how she left the house in the care of Samukai's mother. That night we had food from every home in Ndogbohun so we ate a bit from each dish. The house was so hot and there were too many mosquitoes so we could not sleep. We sprayed some mosquito spray, locked the door and went to Yea Gbassay 's hut for a while. There were still a few mosquitoes when we came back to sleep, so Magainda lit a mosquito coil.

"Listen, Magainda, some of them did not die. Those are the rebel ones," I said.

She laughed "Why are they rebels?" she asked.

"They are stubborn. Upon all the spray they still did not die. Now we have to sleep with a coil lit and wake up tomorrow with our noses blocked," I said.

"It's still very hot in here," Magainda said.

We both took off our clothes and went under the blanket. Magainda took a magazine from the pile of old ones she had in her room on a little table. "I bought these from Bo," She said.

"Can I look at one please?" I asked.

She gave me one. As I went through the magazine, I did not know anyone in it. I was actually looking for styles. "Hey Magainda look, I like this one." I pointed at a woman wearing a West African outfit.

"Yes. I had that style but it's at our house in Bo Town. I have another one I know you will like," she said this not taking her eyes off the page she was reading.

There was a knock from outside our room. Magainda and I looked at each other. Magainda raised her eyebrow and pouting her lips.

"Huh, now we'll have some more mosquitoes in this room. They will come in as this person comes in and more will come in as the person walks out," Magainda said.

"It's time to sleep but Mende people will never know time," I teased in Mende, sounding sleepy and funny.

We always teased other tribes and our own. We both laughed.

"Come in!" Magainda said in Mende.

It was Amina. She was very pretty; her skin just glowed in the candlelight. She was one of those sociable people but very shy too. She could only speak Mende. When she saw us in bed she felt embarrassed for visiting us so late. She apologised and turned to leave but we asked her to stay because we were leaving for Mattru Jung the next morning.

"Do you still remember my name, Muna?" she asked in Mende.

"Yes…. Why would I forget?" I said smiling.

"What's my name then?" she asked.

"Amina!" I said.

She laughed. "I thought you forgot," she said.

"No, I have not. I forget very few names," I said.

Amina and Magainda talked while I read some old magazines. They talked about Magic a lot. I did not pay much attention.

"Memuna, do you like Ndogbohun?" Amina asked.

"Yes. I actually asked Magainda to bring me here," I said.

"Oh really," she giggled. "Well, I think I'll let you sleep now. Goodnight Magainda, Memuna, may God make us sleep well."

"Okay Amina, may God make us sleep well. See you tomorrow," I said in Mende.

"Amina is such a nice girl. It would have been even better if she had a bit of education," Magainda said.

I was very sleepy by now so I just nodded and went beneath the covers.

Before sunrise we went to the river to bathe and get ready for the walk to Mattru Jung but it was just across the river. Magainda laughed at the mosquito bites I had on my cheek and arms. "Will you come to Ndogbohun again?" she asked.

"Yes, I will. Everyone likes me and I like the place. Next time let's spend two nights," I said. "Magainda, you are teasing me but you got some bites on your back too. You know you are light skinned, the bites look like tomatoes," I said.

All of us girls were naked to our undies at the river. When we got there, Magainda and some other girls threw themselves into the river screaming but I was too cold; I wanted a bucket of hot water to bathe. I hated the bathroom in Magainda's house. It was outside at the backyard and muddy. So the best option I had was the river.

"Get in and the cold will go away as soon as you are in," Magainda encouraged me.

"But look at my body, the bumps from the cold," I said running my hands over my upper body.

"Well, you are standing in the cold breeze with only your undies on so what do you expect," Magainda said.

I carried on rubbing my body to get the chill out of my skin and paid no attention to her.

"Hey," she said splashing some water on me. I screamed and turned to run up the hill. As I turned I saw Amina right behind me, she giggled and patted me on the shoulder.

"I was looking for you, did you sleep well?" she asked in Mende.

I told her I had a goodnight's sleep but it was too cold for me to bathe.

"How is the morning, Amina?" Magainda asked.

"Thank God." She answered.

"Hey Memuna, come and bath or you will be like that all day except you want to stay here in Ndogbohun," Magainda said.

"I want to come back but I don't want to stay here," I said.

"Well you know how you feel when you don't bathe in the morning," Magainda said.

During all this conversation, I wrapped my arms around myself. Magainda finally convinced me to get into the river.

"Put some soap on the face towel, rub it on your skin, jump into the river and you will be just fine," Magainda said, as she threw a face towel at me.

I did it and it worked, but I did not stay long in the water. Magainda wrung her towel.

"Okay, spending two nights here is up to Magic," she said.

I told her to please ask Magic to let us spend two nights on our next visit. As we walked up the hill, we talked about how excited Komeh and Nyalay would be when they saw me in Mattru Jung, as we took pauses to say hello to everyone who went past us. In West Africa, we always greet people and when a younger person sees an adult they initiate the greetings. So you are either responding to someone's greeting or initiating one.

We had fish stew and cassava for breakfast. There was nothing like bread or cereal but there was enough coffee, as they had the village surrounded by large coffee, cacao and cola nut farms. Magainda's mother brought us some vegetables from her garden, Samukai's mother brought us some vegetables and smoke-dried fish, Yea Nnasu brought some smoke-dried meat, fresh pepper and vegetables and Samukai gave us two big catfish he caught that morning from the river.

"It's time to cross the Teli-yeh again Yea Nnasu and this time you will row the canoe," he said.

"Okay, Samukai I'm not coming to Ndogbohun again," I said.

They all laughed.

"Don't mind him, he will row the canoe," Yea Nnasu said putting her arm around me. Amina gave us some new rice kanya (Sierra Leonean snack, made of toasted and pounded young rice).

"Um Magainda, give Issa this please," Amina said.

Magainda was busy packing the things the women gave us.

"Give it to Memuna," she said.

I took the kanya from Amina and smiled, I was not sure who Issa was but I did not ask Amina. As she turned her back on me to talk to Magainda and the others, I sniffed the kanya to see what kind it was, whether it was the one made of toasted new young rice or the peanut and rice one. It was the one made from young toasted rice which we called ngaifae in Mende. I liked the smell of it. When I turned to join the conversation I caught

Magainda looking at me. She knew what I was doing; she smiled and shook her head, as sniffing food is considered a bad and unaccepted behaviour. I smiled back and joined the conversation.

We went down to the river with our things in two little bamboo baskets. Magainda carried our clothes in a bag on her back. Yea Gbassay and the other women prayed for us and told us to be careful. As Samukai got in the canoe to row us, Magainda told him to row us to the main wharf which was going to take about ten to fifteen minutes.

"No Magainda, Doodoo-bird (as the jet-fighter was called) might come and bomb us. Let's just cross here and then walk the rest of the journey so that when it comes we will be walking in the bush. That way it won't see us," I said.

I was so afraid that I started shaking in the canoe. We crossed safely then Magainda started laughing at me.

"I did not want to laugh at you in the canoe because I know you would get very angry at me and you won't speak to me," she said.

Samukai laughed and said bye to us. He promised to visit us in Kabbaty.

"Magainda, stop annoying Memuna," he chuckled.

"Samukai please go straight home before Doodoo-bird sees you," I said.

We arrived in a big field with a lot of elephant grass that was higher than us.

"Where is this Magainda? I did not see this on our way yesterday," I said.

"Well maybe it's because you were only thinking of the river yesterday and that's why you can't remember what you saw yesterday," she said.

"Hey, who told you that, you remember that crazy farm? I can tell you everything we came across yesterday if you want," I said.

"Oh, I don't want you to strain your brain because we both know you can't remember…you lost your mind because of the Teli-yeh. I saw the way you were sitting in the canoe," she said laughing.

I pinched her on her back and ran past her. As I ran I stepped in the mud and fell on the side of the path.

"See, I said you've lost your mind but you don't believe me." She laughed even harder.

"Why are you laughing? You don't see me laughing. It says in Mende "ba ngele lor colar mui lar."(When a person falls, see them laugh before you laugh)," I said.

"But I know you won't laugh because you are too busy thinking about the river. I got news for you," she said giggling.

"No, I don't want to hear any news. All I want to know is where this place is," I interrupted.

"Well that's the news but since you don't want to hear it, I won't tell you," she sighed.

"Tell me, I want to hear it," I said.

"Okay, you said you wanted to go to Mattru Jung. Did you not?" she asked.

"Yes," I answered.

"Well, this is the way to Mattru Jung. We did not pass through here yesterday. We'll get to Mattru Jung in twenty minutes…. if you stop falling," she giggled again.

"But it was not my fault I fell and I don't find it funny," I protested but I could not help giggling.

I found the structure of Matru Jung beautiful. Some of the houses had been burnt as the jet had bombed some too. Magainda took me to a big house.

"When they captured us, this is where they brought us. They captured me from up town," she said.

She introduced me to all the girls in the house. As they touched my hair, cheeks and shoulders all they said was, 'Oh, she is so beautiful. Look at her hair!'

Magainda took me outside to a young man sitting on the veranda with an AK on his lap looking so lonely; he looked like he needed to bathe. She asked him how he was doing and introduced me to him.

"Magainda, will you give me your cousin?" he asked.

"No," she said.

As they laughed, I looked at him in disgust thinking you need to bathe and have a haircut.

"Okay people, see you the next time we come," Magainda said.

They waved "Bye Memuna."

"Bye to everyone," I said.

"You see the man who said I should give you to him?" Magainda asked.

"Yes, why is he like that? I think he needs to bathe and have a haircut and besides I don't even want anyone; why are they so desperate for girls?" I asked.

Magainda laughed as she shook her head. "You are a woman and a half trapped in a girl's body. One tough woman! You know he used to be clean and he likes to joke a lot. But he was under punishment for launching his girlfriend with an RPG," Magainda said.

I was shocked to hear that. "What? No, Magainda you are joking," I said.

"I swear," she said, pointing to the sky. "She was my friend and we all lived in that house when they captured us. He was jealous, but I don't think he really wanted to launch her. Did you see the broken part of the veranda? That's where it happened; it cut one of her legs off and left the other one dangling. They took her to the hospital but she started getting rotten after a few days and she died after a week."

I had my hand slapped over my opened mouth in disbelief as I listened to Magainda. I could not say a word.

"Don't tell me you are scared now, Memuna," Magainda said.

"No, I'm not scared I just can't believe a human being could be so cruel and what did the bastard eat today, asking you to give me to him. So he would launch me with three RPGs? Because I won't even talk to him and I will play with other boys," I said.

As we walked up the hill Magainda pointed at a beautiful large compound painted in something that looked green or aqua.

"This is the chief's compound."

Half of the compound was broken down.

"So what happened here?" I asked.

"The battle was heavy," she said as she pointed at the bullet shells on the ground.

Goosebumps ran all over me as I looked around. It was eerily quiet and desolate in that part of town; there were broken houses, burnt houses with grass growing in and around them and burnt vehicles. Looking at the houses I could only imagine what it was like before the war with the children running around. Now everything was taken away from them just like that. Tears streamed down my cheek as Magainda took me to the other side of town.

"We came here just to sit around at lunch time and in the evenings during normal days," she said.

We referred to the days before the war as normal days. Now all I saw was grass but as we walked further I could smell the stench of a dead decomposing body.

"There must be a dead body around here, can you smell it?" Magainda asked.

"Yes, let's not go further down," I said.

So we walked on the other side. It was bushy everywhere.

As we walked up town, Magainda pointed at a big building surrounded by grass and filled with scattered books.

"That was my school. It was a secondary school and a very good one too. It was called Centennial," she said.

As I looked at the building tears were swelling in my eyes, I only just managed to keep them from streaming down my cheeks. Magainda was well known in Mattru Jung, where she grew up and some of her friends were held captive as well. She was also a happy and friendly person who made friends easily.

"Hello, Magainda!" was all I could hear from every corner and street.

She took me to another half-blasted house where there were a lot of young boys and a few girls armed with an AK or a bomb.

"So, how is Mattru Jung? I mean, did I miss anything?" she asked as she hugged some of them and shook hands with others introducing me as we went through the group.

"This is my cousin Memuna, everyone," she introduced me.

"Ooh, Magainda what's happening in your family? Are all the women in your family beautiful?" asked one of the boys, making everyone laugh.

"I went up town and saw the others; the little one is beautiful. She has a hard side to her and she looks like a Soja and I saw the older one too, Komeh. Is that her name?" he asked.

I nodded.

"As for her, if you don't want to sin don't look at her and she is so crazy," he added, gesticulating as he tried to talk about how big Komeh's breasts were.

"Hey! So?" Magainda interrupted, "You go all the way to town to eye my sisters. I'll tell the boys about you."

We all laughed.

"Hey, it is good to know that we are all trying to survive the struggle. I'll see you people later…by God's grace," Magainda said.

"Hey, we will come see you one day in Kabbaty Magainda," said one of the boys with a NIKE headband around his head. He had his AK hanging on his shoulder.

"Okay," Magainda replied.

The sun was hot and the breeze was cool. As we walked up the hill Magainda put her arms around my neck.

"Having lots of friends is the only way to survive in RUF. Especially when they are boys, they can help you through tough times. Just be nice to them," she said. "We will soon reach Naffie's house. We are going to make so many friends. Before you girls came, I was stuck with those crazy boys but I'm glad to have you. It's better because we are always together."

I nodded and smiled. "But I wish we were somewhere else, not here waiting to die at any time or wondering how you will die. I'm…I'm not saying that I'm not happy to see you Magainda, it's always good to see a relative," I said.

"God is in heaven watching. He knows why this had to happen. Let's just look up to him. Okay?" she said.

All I did was nod. As I heard those words I didn't think our situation could get any worse or there could be any more sadness worse than what we were going through. I could not say anything, as I did not trust my voice to not break into a cry.

We finally got to Naffie's house. All the adults went about their business leaving Guy (Lansana's son who was around three to four years old), Nyalay and another girl, Kona, in the house by themselves. The moment I saw 'Guy', I knew then and there who he was. He wore a pair of cute little jeans, a T-shirt and trainers.

"That's Guy," Magainda whispered pointing at the cute, innocent little figure.

"I know…it's obvious," I said nodding and smiling.

He ran to Magainda as soon as he spotted us. She picked him up, hugging him tight. She sniffed his neck making him giggle.

"Guy, man, you smell good. Say hello to Memuna. She's Nyalay, Komeh, Samia and my sister," Magainda said.

He gave me a shy look, dangled his hand at me pretending to wave and snuggled to Magainda.

"Hello Guy how are you?" I said.

"He talks a lot, asks lots of questions too," Magainda whispered, "Where is everyone? Why are you alone?" she asked him as she put him down.

"Naffie is gone to the hospital, Komeh and Sunshine are gone somewhere, Nyalay and Kona are inside there," he said.

"Guy, did you see Amara and Magic today?" Magainda asked.

"Yes, they are in Bayo's room," he answered.

"Let's go Guy," I said reaching for his hand.

Nyalay came running shouting my name "I saw you through the window. Oh I miss you so much. Komeh and I were crying for you and Samia," she said, giving me a tight hug, not wanting to let go.

"Yes we were crying for you too. Where is Komeh? Are you alright, Nyalay? Have you been sick?" I asked and I started crying again.

She eventually let go of me.

"Where is Samia?" she asked.

"She did not come."

Trying to tell her that Samia said she was tired, Magic interrupted me. He was wearing a pair of shorts and a T-shirt; it was a hot day. He came from behind me and hugged me.

"Hello, who said you girls could come here?" he asked looking at Magainda searching for an answer then he smiled.

"Memuna wanted to come see Mattru Jung," she answered.

"Okay," he said.

All of a sudden everyone came.

Komeh slapped me slightly at the back of my head. "What are you doing here? Oh, I miss you so much," she said also giving me a tight hug.

"Tell her you've been crying for them. Don't be shy, I already told her," Nyalay interrupted making everyone laugh.

"Hey, there is Naffie. Her stomach is so big," Guy said, pointing at his pregnant mother coming towards us.

Sunshine introduced herself to me and hugged me. Naffie greeted and hugged Magainda and myself. She panted from walking.

"I walked very fast from the hospital. Oh the sun is so hot," she said.

She commented on my looks too, saying my sisters and I are beautiful girls. She ushered us into the house and introduced us to Titanium's women, the two Rugiatus. The house was very noisy, everyone shouting and laughing boisterously. When we had time to be together, my sisters and I laughed, joked and made as much noise as possible because we spent a lot of time crying and worrying. Komeh had so much to tell me, she was pulling me into a room trying to explain something when Magic came.

"Memuna please come, Komeh come too. Someone wants to meet your sister," he said. He introduced me to one of his brothers. He was very handsome and dark he looked so much like Lansana - the eyes, long face, straight nose.

"This is Maximilian. Man, this is Memuna, Komeh's sister," Magic said, in Krio. He smiled shyly and gently shook my hand.

"So, how are you?" he asked.

He had one of his arms in a bandage.

"I'm good and you?" I asked.

"I'm trying," he said looking at his bandaged arm.

I smiled at him then Komeh and I went back to the room and left Maximilian and Magic on the veranda.

As we entered the room, we saw Magainda and Amara kissing and rolling in the bed with the music so loud almost bursting the roof.

"Knock, knock," Komeh said.

They stopped and we all giggled. Trying to find somewhere to talk in private, we went to the veranda as, fortunately, Magic and Maximilian had left. They had gone to Naffie's room.

"Good, now we can talk in private," Komeh said.

I nodded giving her my undivided attention.

"Hey, how can you leave Nyalay alone before you start and go about your business like that? You know very well that when we were in Sembehun, we were never left alone let alone in this war zone. Anything could happen and Nyalay is only eight, she won't know what to do. Someone else might capture her and we will be separated forever. We should look after each other, Komeh. I know that you and I are still only kids but we are older than they are so let's look after them. Okay?" I said.

She nodded trying not to cry. I held her hand to give her strength.

"Okay, you know what I want you to know?" she asked giving me a hard cold look with her tearful eyes.

I shook my head.

"I think I'm going to kill myself," she said.

"What?" I interrupted looking around us to see if anyone else heard what she had just said.

"What's going on?" I whispered.

"I just want to die right now where I'm standing. I can't stand it anymore," she cried.

I started crying too, though I tried not to.

"Please don't think of that, we need you to survive this. When they took us from our family home in Sembehun, it was Komeh, Memuna, Samia and Nyalay so please let's stay that way until God takes us home," I pleaded with her "What.... what's wrong?"

"Everything! They want me to be that dog Maximilian's girlfriend and I'm supposed to sleep with him and I still love Oscar. I don't want anyone else, especially not a rebel. Memuna, I'm scared," she said, looking very sad.

"What should I do?"

"Let me think about something. But at the same time can you please think of something better than killing yourself and please try to put on a happy face for Nyalay's sake. I'm going through the same thing in Kabbaty with Lansana, but I'm doing my best to be strong for Samia's sake. So please, let's be strong for each other. Like our grandmothers would say "nothing lasts forever"; so Komeh please hold on to that," I said, nodding and searching her eyes for her to say she would think about it.

Finally she nodded then we went inside and joined the others.

As soon as we got into Naffie's room I was pulled from one person to another.

"Why are you called Sunshine?" I asked Hafsatou.

"I don't know. They've been calling me Sunshine for quite a long time now," she said, as she smiled.

Komeh pulled me by my skirt to the room that was supposed to be for her and Maximilian.

"So is this room for both of you? I thought it was just for you," I whispered.

She nodded. It was the room we had found Magainda and Amara kissing in. As we fell on the bed she turned the music up. The house was like a West African marketplace - noisy. She started tickling me as we both giggled and shouted. Nyalay came in and jumped on us, we tickled her too.

"I miss you so much," I said looking at them both, from one to the other.

Sunshine came in the room with a short, dark, chubby girl and Kula. They stood looking in amazement at the way the three of us were on each other. They joined us on the bed trying to start a conversation.

"This is Bintu, Memuna. You've met Kona, haven't you?" asked Sunshine.

I nodded and shook hands with Bintu. Bintu kept staring at me then I knew she was Magic's girlfriend - the one they were talking about by the river in Mosakki. I got sick of her looking at me.

"Komeh let's go and join Magainda," I suggested. Leaning over, whispering so only she would hear, I told her, "I'm still thinking of what you should do about that thing."

CHAPTER NINE

Hiding Place

The boys were in Bayo's room smoking and Magainda was in the kitchen with the other girls talking. Magainda introduced me to all the girls in the kitchen.

"Memuna this is Ruby, Lt. Husain's woman," she said.

"Well all of you know my name; I'm very happy to meet you all," I said.

As we walked to the room where the boys were, we could hear the girls in the kitchen murmuring gossips.

"I think that's the Memuna girl they have been talking about," one of them commented.

"Oh Komeh's sister! The rumour is true, she's beautiful," the other one said.

We went to the room filled with loud reggae music and clouds of Marijuana and cigarette smoke.

"Did you hear those girls?" I asked.

"Yes, get used to their penchant for gossip and ignore them," Magainda said.

Nyalay and Kula left us and went out to play.

"Don't go far away from the house, Nyalay," I said over my shoulder.

"Okay, I'm just out here," she replied.

"Magainda, the passes I signed were for Ndogbohun not here," Magic said, as we walked into the room.

Magainda rolled her eyes and shook her head and brushed passed him in the doorway.

"Why? You don't want us to see what you are doing?" she said as she entered the room. "I told you, Memuna said she wanted to come and guess what, she was scared in the canoe."

He grinned and reached for my hand as she told him about how frightened I was on the river.

Hawk sat with his three-magazine-fitted AK next to him, Miles had a grenade, Bayo had his RPG next to him as usual and Acid-Moe had a bomb that looked like a hammer. The others had no weapons. Storm, Bayo's girlfriend, entered the room. She was happy to see us, especially Magainda. She knew who I was as soon as she saw me.

"Hello Memuna, I've finally met you."

The music was so loud, she was yelling at me so hard the vein on her neck showed. "How are you?"

She told me her name and we shook hands, she whispered something to Magainda and Magainda held my hand and took me out.

"I want you to meet someone; she is Lansana's friend, Lt John's woman. She is such a hard case," Magainda said.

We went to the kitchen again. "Rabiatu, how are you? How's the baby. This is Memuna," Magainda said.

Rabiatu had a very cute baby. She was a Fullah girl and very light-skinned, as was her son. He had bulging gorgeous eyes. Rabiatu was a very beautiful girl with long hair.

"Hello Memuna, I've heard so much about you. How are you coping?" she asked kindly.

"Fine…I'm fine," I said looking at her baby. "He is so handsome; he looks like a little angel."

"Okay, Rabiatu we will join those men. See you before we leave," Magainda said.

"Oh, you leaving tonight?" she asked.

"Yes," Magainda replied.

Hawk cheered loudly and hugged me; he sat me on his lap. Storm sat next to her boyfriend and Magainda sat on Amara's lap.

"Did you like Ndogbohun?" Hawk asked me.

I nodded and told him I'd love to visit the village again.

"Wow, so, Magainda what happened in Ndogbohun that makes Memuna wanting to visit again?" he asked.

"Oh, oh. Magainda what happened." They all asked. At-the-end, Maximilian and Amara looked at Magic and looked at me.

"Man, Magic you got taste," Acid-Moe said.

"Yeah!" said Hawk.

But I did not take notice of anything they were saying. Magic took me from Hawk and made me sit next to him.

"I dream of her every day, since the day I saw her" he said.

The rest of them looked at us and went "hmmm," laughing.

"Oh Magic," Magainda said.

We got tired of sitting in their noise and smoke so we left them and went to Naffie's house. We had a bit of chat; I was too busy with the children. Both of Titanium's women had a child each. The younger Rugiatu was dark and slim and very pretty and friendly. Rumour had it she was found in bed with her army boyfriend the day she was captured but he was lucky to escape. The other Rugiatu taller, a bit bigger and not as pretty, was good looking. The two women had something in common; they were both very happy and noisy people.

While playing with the children and Guy, Nyalay came running to me.

"Memuna come let me show you something," she pleaded.

"What is it Nyalay?" I asked.

"My hiding place. This is where I hide when I miss you and Samia and when I want to go home. I go there to hide when Doodoo-bird comes, that is if I get the chance to run there without it spotting me."

My heart ached as she told me about her hiding place, but I tried not to cry. She took me to a burnt down house behind the house she and Komeh lived in. The house was full of grass; it was as if no-one had lived there.

"This is where I hide," she said pointing at a corner in the house.

Deeply hurt and still trying not to cry, I took a deep breath.

"Ok Nyalay that is very clever to have your own hiding place and a private place, but it's not good to try to come outside when Doodoo-bird comes. It's good to stay where Komeh is and don't come here when you feel sad; go and talk to Komeh. Anything could happen and we won't be able to find you if you are in your secret place," I said. "So don't come to this place anymore okay?"

She nodded and we went back to the house. I could see that she was a little disappointed but I talked to her to forget about her secret place and she agreed.

We went back to the boys to tell them that it was time we left for Kabbaty. Amara hugged and kissed Magainda passionately and we all hugged each other.

"So, when are you coming to Kabbaty?" Magainda asked.

She asked Amara, Bayo and Maximilian when they were going to visit us in Kabbaty, as they were assigned in Mattru Jung but they had time to visit us. These boys were strong fighters. Other RUF rebels respected them and their bosses very much. They were very popular in RUF as well. Some people heard their names but did not know them.

"Hey Magainda, don't worry we are coming in two days; it's just that we have something to take care of. Can I talk to you in private, please?" Magic said.

The boys were so close and they liked joking, it was hard to stay angry with them. "Hey Magic we all know what you want to tell Magainda. So why don't you say it here," Hawk said, pulling a face behind his cousin.

"Yeah man," They all went. Miles laughed out so loudly.

"Sorry sojas, but I said it was private," he said.

As he said that they laughed even louder. I stood there wondering what was going on.

Magic whispered something to Magainda and she laughed out loud.

"I knew it all along," she said.

Outside the boys laughed when they heard her. They went with us to Naffie's house. We said bye to the two Rugiatus and Naffie.

"Ask Lansana if he has time to look after Guy for a while, I'm tired. As you can see, my stomach is very big now Magainda," she said. "Memuna you can come whenever you want okay, this is our house. We should look after each other. Magainda you two should look after yourselves and tell Samia I want to see her." Naffie hugged us and we left.

"Tell Bra I want to come," Guy said.

Magainda knelt in front of him, "Okay, Guy."

We both hugged him one after the other. Naffie saw us out and went back to her room. The boys, Guy, Nyalay, Komeh, Kona, Sunshine and Bintu walked us down to the other side of the Teli-yeh down town Mattru Jung. From here we could catch the ferry and get in the pickup so Tricks could take us to Kabbaty. The boys stopped half way; Magic gave me a hug and said he was coming in two days. Then he joined his brother to go back to town leaving Guy with the girls. Bintu gave me a very nasty look as Magic hugged me. Tricks's pickup was parked in the little village across the river.

"This time Memuna, it's not a canoe, it's a ferry. Then Tricks will take us home," Magainda pointed out.

We hugged each other as the ferry came for us.

"I'll ask Lansana to let you come and visit us, okay?" I said to Nyalay cupping her face in my hand as I kissed her on the lips.

She wanted to cry but I told her not to as she will soon come to us. Komeh held her hand and wiped her face.

"Tell Samia we'll see her soon," Komeh said.

"Tell her I miss her," Nyalay added.

I nodded trying not to cry as we got on the ferry. I was scared and sad, I kept wondering if we were going to see each other again. I also felt anger. We waved till the ferry got to the other side; we could still see each other. Then they turned away and walked up the hill out of sight.

Tricks was there, waiting, bad-mouthing a couple of girls.

"Rude bastard, I'll go and ask him to take us to Kabbaty," Komeh said.

He said he would take us and that we should go and sit in the pickup.

"Magainda, is this place a part of Mattru Jung?" I asked.

"Well, not really. It has its own name."

She told me the name of the little village but I have since forgotten it.

Tricks was a crazy man, always high.

"Wait, do you girls follow your men wherever they go?" he asked.

I smiled and chuckled. Magainda smiled, looked at me, but shook her head as I stretched my eyes wide.

"When are we leaving this place Tricks ?" Magainda asked.

"We will leave soon. I'm only waiting for those guys," he said pointing at some men in the ferry. We got in the pickup and Tricks drove with reckless abandon, as the road was full of potholes from the rain and bombs. We sat in the front seats with him.

"Hey, girl, who is your man?" he asked me.

"My name is Memuna. I've told you so many times and I don't have a man," I said.

I was a ball of anger – if there is ever anything as such. Sometimes I didn't care what the rebel's reaction would be to me, I was so angry and not afraid to answer back.

"Hey, just tell me the truth. I want to know. Magainda then, please tell me if she can't," he said.

"She already told you the truth Tricks , nothing else to tell," Magainda said.

"Okay, Tricks will know the truth one day," he said, referring to himself in the third and went on Marionng the Bob Marley song on the cassette that was playing.

"Thank God I'm not pregnant. Then by now I'll either deliver the baby in this pickup or lose it," Magainda commented, the ride was so bumpy.

He entered Kabbaty in high speed raising dust and making a sudden stop in front of our house.

"Tricks !" everyone cheered loudly. I was happy to be alive. We were as tired as if we had walked from Mattru Jung to Kabbaty. We thanked him and took our luggage. "Memuna," he called, "tell me when you ready to tell me? Is Lansana there, say hello to him and tell him I'll see him later," he said in Liberian colloquial.

He got into his pickup and drove off again leaving dust behind looking like a tornado.

As we got into the house we were pulled from one person to the other. All were glad to see us. We told them the trip was good; we went to Mattru Jung. We gave Ngor Yewa the vegetables, meat and fish we brought back.

"How was your trip? You two look tired," Lansana said.

"Good."

We followed him to his room to get away from the questions. Samia came with us.

"The trip was good and we went to Mattru Jung. Naffie wants you to take Guy for a while. She says she is very tired," Magainda explained.

"How is she? How are Nyalay, Komeh and everyone?" He asked.

"They are fine and Naffie's big now," Magainda said.

"Nyalay and Komeh want to come here for a while. Can you arrange that?" I interrupted. There was a long pause.

"Oh, yes they can come next week. Before you start crying on me again," He said.

Samia was so happy to hear it she got off her chair, tilted her head and jumped around the room giggling.

"What day next week?" I asked.

Smiling, he looked at me. He knew I was doing this to give him a hard time and I was demanding instead of asking, that he let my sisters come to Kabbaty. At least for a visit; after all that's the least he could do.

"Well, I'm going to Mattru Jung with Tricks ; then on Monday they'll come back with me," he said.

That evening the atmosphere - Samia had some smile on her face. We cleaned up while Ngor Yewa cooked dinner. After dinner we sat with Lansana in his warm room for what seemed like an hour then we went to bed. As we walked towards our room from Lansana's house, Magainda tapped me on the shoulder. "I have a message for you," she whispered.

I nodded. "Yes Magainda, but can you please tell me tomorrow? I'm too tired right now," I said.

I was so tired that no sooner did I fall on the bed, I slept.

When we woke it was lunchtime and a sunny and hot day. Things seemed slow that day. We went to the creek and freshened up.

The water was cool and I could feel the tiredness coming out of me.

"Did you enjoy the trip?" Magainda asked.

"Yes" I said nodding, "but the mosquitoes were annoying. That won't stop me from going there again though."

"I can't wait for our sisters to come; especially tongue-sucking Nyalay," Samia said.

It was hot so we did not want to get out of the water. We stayed there for what seemed like two hours. When we finally got out, all I wanted was to eat and go back to sleep. I had forgotten all about the message Magainda said she had for me.

The house was filled with loud noise. Lansana and his friends were in his room smoking and laughing loudly over the loud reggae music. We went and sat in the hut with Ngor Yewa and the other women. Some of us played the game of Ludo while the rest sat on mats talking. Magainda sat in the only hammock, eating lots of oranges as we discussed our trip. Magainda told Ngor Yewa how big Naffie had gotten.

"Is she bigger than me?" she asked, making everyone laugh

"What, Ngor Yewa, are you looking for someone who is bigger than you are? Well I am," I said.

They all laughed at me. Magainda said the baby Ngor Yewa was carrying was probably my size, as I was very thin. I have always been thin. We all laughed and talked about different things as though we were home.

We went for a little walk to Mahawa and Marion, spent some time with them and returned quite late. Samia was sleepy, she left Magainda and myself in the hut and went to bed. Magainda got to the hammock before me so I climbed and sat on the banister while she swung in the hammock. We could hear the monkeys and birds in the trees far away. The night was cool and calm.

"What a beautiful night! I miss Sembehun Nes Tucker, times like these we would sit in the moonlight and tell stories. I wished we were there now and everything was normal."

"What did you do on a night like this?" Magainda asked.

"Well we did some interesting and troublesome things really. You know those old women. They prefer leaving their fruits on the trees for them to look at, or till they have a special reason to pick them including having guests or…something like that," I said.

"Yes…" Magainda replied giggling and nodding.

"Well, we would climb the trees or go to their gardens and cut their sugar canes. Eat, make a lot of noise and litter the whole place. We did not care about studying because we would be on holidays by then. Our grandmothers and Auntie Satta, knew the things we got up to so in the morning they'd make us sweep the whole yard. The old women knew what we got up to so they would come to Ngaya to complain and threaten to put a curse on us. She would tell them to go ahead as we were all related (our grandfather had done almost every family in Sembehun a favour or two).

She'd say, "Yes, put all the curses in the world on them. We will all suffer because we all are their grandmothers. They should bother us all."

We both laughed, my laughter ended up with crying as memories reminded me where I was now. Magainda did not notice. We fell silent enjoying the cool breeze.

"Oh, your message Memuna. Well first of all before I give you the message I'll tell you something about this place. You, Samia, Komeh, Nyalay and I, we all fell into good hands. Some girls your age are pregnant and at the same time get beaten for every mistake they make. Some got raped the moment the rebels laid hands on them. But God blessed us. He is with us. Okay, this is your message. Magic asked me to tell you that he really loves you. He could imagine your reaction that's why he asked me to tell you since I'm your sister," Magainda explained.

I jumped off the banister interrupting.

"What! He wants me? Oh my God, why me?"

I stood there looking straight ahead, tears streaming down my cheeks. I took a deep breath and wiped my tears with the back of my hands.

"I know…I know Memuna, but soon you will have to have a man to stand up for you and I think, as we are all together, we should stay together and pray for God to take us through. I've been with these boys for a long time and I think I know them very well. They are all nice boys. I know no-one expects a rebel to be nice but these are. They are only mean when they are on the warfront. I don't want you to be with someone else outside of our group. It won't be good for any one of us as we won't be able to keep an eye on each other if that happened and I know you don't want Lansana," Magainda said.

"I don't want anyone Magainda," I interrupted frantically.

"Yes I know, but take time to think about it. He is a nice person though. The two of you have been nice to each other these past weeks. Hold me responsible for anything that goes wrong if you agree," Magainda encouraged me and gave me a hug. "Let's stay in the family."

"Okay. Magainda let's go to bed now," was all I said.

I thought of it all night. It seemed like the only option available to me so I decided to say yes and give him a chance.

Magainda and I woke up and smiled at each other. Samia was lying between us still sleeping though the sun had already risen. She opened her eyes and said good morning to Magainda.

"I'm here too, can't you see me?" I said jokingly.

"No," Magainda said.

Samia moved closer to Magainda and put her arm around her. I got up, turned the radio on, went back and sat in the bed.

"Oh. What a nice day! Let's go and clean up and help Ngor Yewa in the kitchen," Magainda said.

It was time for Lansana to go to Africa's Ground and Mattru Jung with Soja and Laser again.

"Magainda, Yewa or any one of you, tell Magic to take care of my room. He should sleep in here and no outsider is allowed in here. Take care of each other and I'll see you later. Memuna don't start crying like a baby while I'm not here," he commanded.

I just looked at him, thinking that was what I do when I'm frustrated with my new life. He had a late lunch and left.

"Magic and all of them should be here tomorrow," Magainda said.

That evening Ngor Yewa, Magainda, Samia and I sat in Lansana's room, ate six packets of NATCO biscuits and drank a tin of Peak milk each. Later we listened to loud music. We went to our rooms when we were full. We took off our clothes and wore something thin. Magainda wore a pair of shorts and a T-shirt, Samia wore a big T-shirt and I wore one of Magainda's little T-shirt and shorts we had brought from Ndogbohun. Lying there talking and listening to music I whispered to Magainda that I would give Magic a chance. She promised it would be alright and she was going to be with me step by step.

We sat in bed playing cards. The opened window let in the refreshing air.

"Wait, I hear Magic," Samia said.

Magainda told her to look out the window and check if it was he. My face got hot and my stomach churned as I sat praying Samia was wrong. Then we heard him and the calibre guards greeting each other outside. He came into the room and smiled at me.

"How are you young ladies doing?' he asked.

As he sat on the bed playing with his thick silver ring on his finger. Leaning over, he touched my hand and asked if I liked Ndogbohun.

Nodding I looked at him. Magainda gave him the message Lansana had left for him and asked him for Hawk, Miles, At-the-end and Acid-Moe.

"Miles is staying to wait for Bra, the others are coming tomorrow," he said.

"How are Komeh and Nyalay?" I asked.

Normally I would say his name but this time I did not. He looked at me, said they were fine and can't wait to come.

"They wanted to come with me but I told them to wait for Bra," he said.

"They are coming soon. Magic, what did you bring for me," Samia said.

"Sorry Samia, I came in a hurry, but next time. Magainda do we have some water there, I'm hot. I want to freshen up," he said.

He took off his T-shirt showing off his muscles, as he bit his nails

"Stop biting your nails you, Memuna does the same," Magainda said teasing him.

He went with her to the other house. I could not play anymore I felt like vanishing. Samia still wanted to play so I forced myself to play a game with her. Magainda came back ten minutes later with a smile. She knew I was worried.

"You look tired, Memuna."

I did not say anything. She sat on the bed with us. Hawa inched our door open and popped her head in.

"Hey Magainda, Magic is calling the three of you," she said.

"Okay, tell him we will be there," Magainda replied.

"Wait for me, Hawa," Samia said, as she hurried to get out of the bed.

"I know you don't want to go," Magainda said, tilting her head looking at me.

I shook my head looking at her pleadingly. "Magainda, can I stay please?" I asked.

"I already told him and he seems happy. He wants to talk to you. You are a big girl, just be normal and talk to him. Okay?" she said giving me that cute big sister smile.

Magic was lying on the bed listening to Burning Spear. He smiled when we walked in. Everyone but me seemed to be in high spirits that night. Magainda sat on the bed by him, Ngor Yewa, Samia and I sat on the chairs. The four of them chatted away while I got lost in my wishes.

"Can we talk, Memuna, please?" he asked.

I nodded, nervous, but trying to keep my cool. Holding my hand, he led me out to the hut. I lay in the hammock and he sat in a chair someone had left there. He drew it closer and sat by me. He attempted to hold my hand but I quickly laid both hands on my head.

"How are you?" he asked.

"I'm fine," I said.

"Did you get your message from Magainda?" he asked.

I nodded.

There was a long silence. "So what do you think?" he asked.

"Did not Magainda tell you what I told her?" I said, not wanting to say it myself.

"I will take care of you and I won't push you to do anything you don't want to do. So what did you tell Magainda to tell me? I want you to tell me," he said.

"Well I'm not saying it. Whatever she told you, was what I said," I said.

He grinned and slightly pulled one of my braids. "I know you are shy. Okay then I understand. I came back running here just to see you," he said.

I did not say anything, as I could not think. I could not believe it was happening.

"Let's join the others," he said, "you look tired."

He held my hand as I got out of the hammock and led me back to the room.

Samia, Magainda and I stayed with Magic for what seemed like forever. When we finally went to our room I was a bit upset but did not say anything. I went straight to bed. The next morning I did not want to go outside, as I did not want to meet eye-to-eye with Magic in the day. Magainda got up, went to the other house and came back.

"What, are you sick or you don't want to go out?" Samia asked.

"I'm only tired but I'll come out later," I said.

As she went out Magic walked into the room. I was lying covered except for my feet. "Good morning girls," he said.

"Good morning, Magic," Magainda replied. But I did not say anything.

Magic held one of my feet "Your feet are so little and beautiful," he said "Magainda look."

"Yes, those are a woman's feet," she said.

I was so shy I pulled one foot away from him and curled up under the cover.

"So, Magainda what's there to eat this morning? I'm really hungry," he said.

"Go and ask Ngor Yewa," she replied.

He climbed into the bed and sat between us.

"Your sisters are coming today so you two better start getting food ready for them. That crazy Komeh doesn't like being hungry," he said.

"Our family never kept us hungry. Magic, I've told you this so many times. So if RUF wants to keep us you should have enough food for us," Magainda said.

"Okay, spoilt children," he chided us, "Get up, the sun is up. You two are so spoilt, small Samia is up and you are still in bed," he said.

We went to the creek, washed up quickly, came back and met Ngor Yewa in the kitchen trying to make something to eat that morning.

"I...I heard the girls are coming today with Guy. Samia is really happy," she stammered.

I was so nervous I did not feel like eating. I sat with Samia, Magainda and Magic in Lansana's room. While they ate, I sat in the bed. Magic leaned over and whispered.

"Why are you not eating?" he asked.

I told him I did not feel like it and I would eat something later. By midday I got feverish. I was burning and my head was throbbing. Everyone was worried. Magainda took me to the zinc bathroom outside and poured some cold water on me. Later, she rubbed some Chinese balm on me and tucked me into bed.

"Maybe it's the mosquitoes in Ndogbohun or it could be the long walk from Sembehun," Magainda said, trying to figure out what was happening to me. She was confused because I was crying. They wanted to take me to the nurses but I refused.

"Why don't you want to go to the nurse? It will be better if you go and see them and they will give you some medication." Magic tried to encourage me.

"No, I don't trust them. I just need some Panadol and some sleep," I said.

They sat by me until I fell asleep. Hours later I woke soaking wet in sweat with Magic sitting next me.

"Hello," he said when I opened my eyes. He felt my forehead.

"Do you feel better now?"

I nodded. "Where is everyone" I asked.

They were at the other house, he told me and we could go there if I wanted but he thought I should rest a bit more.

"Please don't get sick," he said. He held my hand while we sat in total silence.

"I'm a bit hungry," I said to him.

He took me to the other house. I sat on Lansana's bed eating NATCO and laughing cow cheese and drinking milk.

"Do you want some tea or some rice pap?" Magainda asked.

"No, I'll vomit if I drink tea and that I don't want to do."

Sitting in Lansana's room talking; we heard the jet flying over the town. Everyone outside frantically ran to clear their laundry. Others quickly poured water in the kitchen fireplaces because the jet would bomb us if it detected smoke. It came back and flew around the town three times. We were all terrified. Magainda wanted to run out to the forest. Magic told her it was too late to run out, that if the jet spied her we would all die. Magainda, Samia and me sat in the bed clinging to each other.

"Are you strong enough, Memuna? This could be it," Magainda said nervously.

I nodded praying for it to go away without bombing us. Eventually it went away without bombing. Magainda said thanks to God and we carried on as if nothing had happened. The fear stayed within me.

Magic decided to play music for the whole house. He opened Lansana's room door and turned the music up to the maximum volume. Mahawa (Magic's girlfriend) came to visit us as she wanted to talk to Magic. He was so confused; he did not know what to do. I did not even care. I liked him cheating at first because that way I will have my space, but he did not know.

"Mahawa is here; don't you want to talk to her?" I asked.

"Don't be sarcastic. I don't have anything to say to her. She is here to visit you and your sister," He said, sounding irritated.

I took her out to the veranda to talk to her. Inside, the music was too loud and the room too hot for me causing my heart to palpitate. She told me I looked sick and I told her I had fever.

"Oh, I am sorry. How do you feel now? Did you go to the nurse?" she asked.

I told her I felt much better and I did not need to go to the nurse because I just needed some sleep. Magic came and kissed me on my cheek interrupting our conversation. Magainda was too busy helping Ngor Yewa in the kitchen so she could not be with Mahawa. Mahawa felt badly when she saw what Magic did. She tried to hide her feelings but it was obvious. She left and as I took her halfway she said it was okay I shouldn't go too far, as I was not feeling too well.

By five o'clock in the evening Acid-Moe came. He met Magic and me standing outside trying to get some fresh air. My headache started again. Acid-Moe greeted us both; he shook my hand and asked me if I was well. He could see the weakness in my eyes.

"Hey, Memuna don't die, please try and get well," he said jocularly.

I smiled and nodded. He took Magic aside and asked him something. Then they both shook hands and laughed even louder. I could tell Acid-Moe was asking him whether he succeeded in asking me out.

"Memuna I have a message for you. Magic has a girlfriend in Mattru Jung and she is coming tonight with your sisters. Her name is Bintu; she said she will shoot you if she sees you around him," Acid-Moe said.

"Okay," I nodded.

Magic laughed and held my hands in both of his. "Don't mind him. It's not true," he reassured me.

"Even if it was I don't care. It takes two to fight and she would have to deal with Komeh's crazy side first," I said.

"Acid man go and don't come back," Magic said.

"Man I'm joking. Bintu did not say that but she is coming though. Memuna knows I'm joking," Acid-Moe laughed.

We talked for a while then he left promising to come back.

Tricks arrived hours later with Nyalay, Komeh, Guy, Sunshine, Bintu and Lansana. I ran to them and, hugging each other, we went inside. Ngor Yewa told Lansana I was not feeling well. He felt my forehead, neck and cheeks and asked if I went to the nurses. I told him I did not but I took Panadol and rested. He told me not to get sick and I should stop crying, as if that could be the reason why I got sick. He seemed to be in a hurry. He changed his top and told us to expect him in two days.

"Magic, make sure Memuna is alright," he said as he waved and got in the pickup with Tricks. Nyalay and Samia were so happy they jumped around the room like monkeys. Komeh took me aside.

"So, what did you come up with?" she asked.

"There is something I want to tell you. It is the answer to what you want to know," I said.

"What is it?" she interrupted.

I told her what was going on with Magic and I and the reason why I agreed.

"So you want me to do the same?" she asked seemingly disappointed. "Be careful," she advised.

"I'm so scared and nervous. Maybe that's why I got sick yesterday. You know the pressure of knowing that I have a boyfriend for real and he is a rebel. But like Magainda said, eventually it's going to happen whether I liked it or not. So since he is a few years older and we are all in the same group," I shrugged my shoulders.

"It's important for us to stay together. What do you think?"

She stood for a while as if thinking of something to say.

"Well I think it's ok. So do you think I should do the same? Well Maximilian hasn't done anything bad to me. Even the first time we slept together, I was so angry I told him not to touch me and he stayed away. I was surprised considering he's a rebel," she said.

Interjecting, I told her, "In every situation there is always the bad and the good."

"The next day I did not see him for two days," she said.

"Well give him a chance, but there should be a limit. Don't be too nice and I'm sure you can handle the whole boyfriend thing because you've already had one before. I've only had those kiddie boyfriends that I shared letters with and rode bicycles with," realising the strange comparison between this simple thing in life which now had come to mean something so different.

"Yes but you know how to write boyfriend letters better than me. Anyway we will do anything in our power to stay together," Komeh agreed.

"Yes and by God's grace we will survive."

We smiled and went inside.

"Hey, do you know about Magic and Bintu?" Komeh asked.

"Yes, but I don't know how to be jealous over a man. Besides I never had one so they can carry on" I told her.

Ngor Yewa and Magainda were already through with cooking the rice and meat stew. All of them ate but me. Bintu could not keep her eyes off me; she must have heard the news. We all went to the creek to wash after eating, came back and listened to music while we played with Nyalay and

Samia. Sunshine pulled me into a corner and begged me to go out with her brother. "Lansana is good-looking and he is a good person too and please be my friend, I like you," she said.

I looked at her wondering what was wrong with her.

"I don't want anyone. Yes I can be your friend," I said and went back to my sisters. Komeh, Magainda and I sat in the room to talk. Magic came and sat on my lap and made everyone laugh.

"Get off! I'm too tired," I scolded.

He wanted to sit next to me but the chair was too small so we sat on the bed.

"You see. I don't want Bintu anymore," he said.

I nodded thinking "I don't care," I was wondering if I was ever going home again.

CHAPTER TEN

Love In Dangerous Places

Bintu and Sunshine spent the night at Lt Titanium's. While Komeh, Magainda, Guy, and I went to our room to sleep, Guy and Komeh slept on a double mattress on the floor Nyalay and Samia slept with Ngor Yewa. Around nine o'clock in the morning Magic was in our room claiming he was lonely. We followed him to Lansana's room. Magainda sat in the chair with Komeh. I lay in the bed with him and little Guy went to his auntie. Magic sat in the bed next to me while Komeh and I fought for the cover. When Bintu saw us sitting in the bed she got angry and walked out.

"Okay, poppies, let's go to the creek. Memuna call Nyalay, Samia and Guy," Magainda ordered.

Bintu went with us to the creek but she did her best to stay away from me. When we got back to the house she had forgotten to bring spare undies so she asked everyone else but none of them had any.

"I have some new ones. You want one?" I asked.

She nodded and thanked me

I gave her two pairs of new undies that Lansana had given us from Pa Madou's shop.

The rest of the boys came that morning and it was so noisy. At-the-end picked me up and yelled my name and Hawk hugged me. Everyone made noise besides David who was always smiling and very quiet. He was always by Lansana's side. They hugged all of us and went to the room. They accorded each other military courtesies and all I could hear was Hawk and At-the-end say to Magic was "all the others have to go."

They seemed to be in high spirits because they were happy about me and Magic being together. They laughed out loudly. Magic, At-the-end and Hawk had a very cute boyish way of laughing which was liked by all of us. We made a lot of noise. We adjusted and went with the flow. I was scared of losing them. I guess myself, my sister and my cousins were. I was not very worried about myself. I was instead more worried about them and our

113

family who were on the other side. I was scared but I kept it inside of me. I never let it rise to the surface. We got used to the marijuana smoke and the loud reggae music.

The next morning was the same. PJ and Daddy came over and we all made lot of noise as usual. They liked Guy because he was a brilliant little boy. He also went with the flow just as we did. It could have something to do with the fact that that was the only way of life he knew. He was used to all of them as he was born in their midst. Magainda cooked a big pot of venison stew; some men had shot an antelope for Lansana. She made it so spicy that though all the boys were complaining, they wouldn't stop eating the stew. I ate some of mine keeping the rest for when my appetite was restored. Magic came to me with a piece of meat on a plate and offered me a bite.

As I opened my mouth he averted the meat and ran off so I ran after him for it.

"You two are always chasing each other like dogs," Magainda said jokingly.

"They are enjoying. Life is short," At-the-end said. "And I've not seen my man like this."

We all laughed and he gave me a bite of the meat. We made noise till it was bedtime.

Next morning, in the early hours Lansana came with a very beautiful young woman with long hair. He introduced her to me as his girlfriend, telling me her name was Josephine. She touched my hair and said we both have lots of hair. I nodded thinking that I wouldn't have long hair for much longer, as I was thinking of shaving my head. Ngor Yewa did not like the idea of Lansana cheating on Naffie but there was nothing she could do. It seemed like RUF had more women and children than they did men. The next afternoon Komeh, Nyalay, Bintu and Sunshine went back to Mattru Jung leaving Guy with us. Lansana saw us crying and promised he would let them come and visit us whenever they wanted.

We visited Mahawa and Marion that evening. There were a couple of girls who did not want to see us. They were the bodyguards of Lansana's friend, Lt. Isha . We all called her Old Ma'am Isha. Her bodyguards were pompous and thought that everyone feared them but they did not scare us. Marion's mother welcomed us. We met her in the kitchen with some other women cooking and gossiping. We did not stay long, as we did not want to eat their food. The visit did me some good though as it helped me take my mind off my sisters a bit; I was missing them.

"So where have you two been?" Magic said.

Magainda told him where we were. "Lansana was looking for you. Memuna are you alright?" he said.

Feeling tired, I nodded and climbed into bed.

"There is a battle around the Rutile area and they want us to go there but I don't think Bra will take the mission," Magic said.

"You just came from Sembehun. You people should take a break," Magainda advised him.

"Yeah it's not that serious. They will send some other sojas there," Magic replied.

Among themselves they referred to themselves as soldiers. That day Magic had his three-magazine AK47. Samia was with Lansana, Guy and his girlfriend Josephine. Magic and Magainda decided to teach me some things about RUF. They taught me how to parade and their anthem. Magainda demonstrated the parade; Magic commanded while I sat and watched. They told me to try it; I did it twice before I got it right. They sang the anthem and told me to repeat after them. It went like this:

RUF Anthem
RUF is fighting to save Sierra Leone
RUF is fighting to save our people
RUF is fighting to save our country
RUF is fighting to save Sierra Leone
Chorus
Go and tell the President, Sierra Leone is my home
Go and tell my parents they may see me no more
When fighting in the battlefield I'm fighting forever
Every Sierra Leonean is fighting for his land
Verse2
Where are our diamonds, Mr. President?
Where is our gold, APC? - (When the RUF started, it was the APC –
All People Congress government that was in power).
RUF is hungry to know where they are
RUF is fighting to save Sierra Leone
Chorus
Go and tell the President, Sierra Leone is my home
Go and tell my parents they may see me no more
When fighting in the battlefield I'm fighting forever
Every Sierra Leonean is fighting for his land
Our people are suffering without means of survival
All our minerals have gone to foreign lands
RUF is hungry to know where they are
RUF is fighting to save Sierra Leone
Chorus
Go and tell the President, Sierra Leone is my home
Go and tell my parents, they may see me no more
When fighting in the battlefield I'm fighting forever
Every Sierra Leonean is fighting for his right
Sierra Leone is ready to utilise her own
All our minerals will be accounted for

The people will enjoy in their land
RUF is the saviour we need right now.
Chorus
Go and tell your President Sierra Leone is my home
Go and tell my parents, they may see me no more
When fighting in the battlefield I'm fighting forever
Every Sierra Leonean is fighting for his land.

After the anthem, Magic said I was a fast learner and I was easy to teach. So he thought he could teach me how to identify myself in case I came across a bully. "There are some people who like harassing new faces around here. So in case you meet one such person and none of us is around, they will say, "you soja?" Don't say "yes" then they will know that you are lying. Say "Sir". They will ask, "What makes you soja?" Say "arms, discipline and courtesy". While saying all this, you should stand still with both hands straight by your sides in attention. That way they will let you go. But if they find out that you are a civilian, tell them that you are my girlfriend or just mention any one of us. That way they will stay away. We still have some guys who don't care about the laws they still harass the other soja's girls but they do their best to stay away from us," he said.

Hawk walked in. "So you are training Mrs?" he asked, teasing us.

They told him that I could do the parade and I could sing the anthem.

"Stand, let me try you, Memuna," he said.

I did not want to do it; I told him I was tired.

"Okay, I know you are shy, because Magic is here. Let's pretend he is not here."

He pulled me to stand. I got serious and stood up.

"Attention!" he commanded.

I raised my right foot and stamped it putting it together in a V-shape with my left foot and stood straight with my arms squeezed to my sides.

"Right.... Turn!" he said.

My arms squeezed to my side and turned right with my left foot following my right foot then I took a step, stepping my left foot next to my right in a v-shape.

"Left.... Turn!" he said.

I did likewise only this time I turned left and my right foot followed the left. "About...turn!" he said.

I kept my hands clung to my side and turned right around, but by my left. Facing them again and stamped my right foot by the left foot in a v-shape. He clapped "You pass!" We sat down and talked again about the battle going on in Rutile.

"Hawk, how are my uncle and the other men doing? Where are they? When are we going to see them again?" I asked.

"They are still on the training base. They will be there for three more weeks or a month. After that they could ask their CO for permission to come and see you."

It was Magic who answered me.

Hawk told me not to worry about my uncle, that he was a man and he would be just fine.

Josephine, Lansana's girlfriend stayed for two days. Magainda, Ngor Yewa and I got sick of her. All she did was stay indoors and eat. The evening after she left, Lansana gave me a book, 'Chike and the River.'

"Your sister Komeh said you'd like this book. She said you like reading."

I took the book from him and grinned.

"We used to read this in our literature class. It's a good book," I told him.

"Well you can have it. Maybe it will help stop the daily crying," he said.

I spent half of the day reading the book. It was hard to focus with all the surrounding noise. Magainda wanted to read the book too so after dinner we lay in bed and read it. When we got to the part where Chike got on the bus with a sign on it that says SMOG (Save Me Oh God) we said it out loud. Samia listened to music and fell asleep.

The next morning I was in such a bad mood. I guess the book made me even more homesick. I was so bitter I wouldn't talk to any of the guys including Lansana.

In the afternoon he started complaining again about the boys and me. I did not say anything as I just stood there with my hands behind me staring at him coldly. He was jealous of Magic. Once again, he let me go. I went to the backyard, sat all alone and sobbed. When he went to the hut for some fresh air, I got an idea. There was a hole underneath his bed; it was like a grave. The first time I saw it I asked what it was and he told me it was a grave. I was so frightened I wondered how he could sleep over a grave but then I kept telling myself that he was a rebel and all they did were scary things. One day I told Hawa about the grave. She laughed at me as if I was crazy.

"Are you that scared?" she said, staring at me as if I was an alien. "That hole," she said and went on giggling.

"Stop laughing at me or I won't tell you anything again," I said.

"Okay…. Okay, I won't laugh… we dug that hole," she said.

"What?" I interrupted.

"Yes. We dug the hole, when we heard about the rebels. We were going to hide our valuable belongings in that hole, but we were too late. They attacked us as soon as we got through digging the hole. Don't mind him. It's not a grave," she explained and went on laughing at me.

"You will pay for laughing at me like this, Hawa," I said.

So I thought of the conversation I had with Hawa about the hole and thought I would do something.

That afternoon everyone was on the veranda or in the hut. I was alone. So I went to the room. Lansana had stacked about five big cartons of 555 cigarettes in the hole for themselves. I went underneath the bed, came out and wore a pair of shorts. I took a tin of milk and a packet of NATCO biscuits and returned underneath the bed. I lay in the hole on top of the cigarette boxes and sobbed. Hours later Lansana started looking for me. It got serious as he thought I had run into the forest finding my way back to Sembehun. He told his bodyguards to look for me. Magic, Samia and Magainda were devastated. Samia, Ngor Yewa and Magainda came to Lansana's room; they tried to console Samia, as she was hysterical. I did not move a muscle and I let them look for me for hours. no-one thought I would be in the hole as they all thought I was afraid of the "grave". I felt sorry for Samia though so I came out. Samia jumped and hugged me tightly.

"She's here. She's still here," she said shaking.

"Where have you been?" Lansana demanded, shaking me.

I pulled myself away from him, staring at him coldly.

"I… was there," I said pointing underneath the bed. He looked at me and shook his head.

"You got us looking everywhere for you. I thought you ran into the forest," he said.

Ngor Yewa hugged me saying sorry.

"I…I want to go home….!" I cried.

They saw that Lansana wanted us to be alone so they went out. He held my hand and said he was sorry, that we will all go home one day.

"Why did you bring us here in the first place?" I cried.

Embarrassed, he bowed his head and shook it; he looked up at me and begged me to stop crying. There was a long silence.

"Are you hungry?" he asked.

I shook my head.

"Please talk if you are hungry. So do you like the book?" he said.

I nodded.

He ran out of words, so we sat staring at each other. I went out to Magainda and the others. We went to our room. Magic gave me a very pathetic look and sat next to me.

"I'm sorry. I know how you feel," he told me.

"Why are we here? We want to go home," I cried.

"If you cry I'll be confused, please don't cry. Stop crying. The day will come," he said.

"We need to go to school. Our time is running out, we are wasting time Magic. We miss our family so much," I cried.

He sat behind me and put his arms around me. Magainda held my hand and Samia cried and asked me to please stop crying.

I nodded and tried to stop.

That night Samia slept with Ngor Yewa. It rained heavily, so Magic slept with us. That night we had our first passionate kiss.

"How come you know how to kiss so well? You are supposed to be a virgin and virgins don't know how to kiss," he said.

I just looked at him and said goodnight. I turned to the wall, covered my head and fell asleep. It rained ceaselessly all night until the next afternoon. Two hours after the rain had ceased, the jet came. This time was better because it just passed straight through. That evening Lansana had taken Guy back to Mattru Jung. He came back later that night.

"Your sisters are coming in two weeks. They will bring Guy again to give Naffie time off," he said.

We spent some time with him and then went to our room. Samia continued sleeping with Ngor Yewa. I asked her whether it was alright with her and she said yes. It was for the best because Ngor Yewa needed someone to be by her as she was pregnant.

Magic went on about the kiss all evening. I told him not to push it. I had no reason to lie about my virginity. He apologised and we talked about something else with Magainda and Hawk. Magic slept in our room again but this time I refused to kiss him. He knew I was upset so he apologised but I did not say anything, neither did Magainda. The next morning when he apologised again, I told him it was okay. Magainda and I went to the creek.

"Hey Magainda why do men like having sex? I know a bit about it because I was taught at school. But I just don't feel it's okay to do it at this age. I think I'm still too young Magainda. My Auntie Satta says one never runs out of time to do it but you run out of time for education," I said.

"I don't know why they like it so much, either. I wish I knew. Tell him you are not ready. He will listen. I have so much energy today, let's do something," Magainda said. We spent hours at the creek. From the creek we visited Sabatu Sowah, Mahawa and Marion and came back to listen to loud music. The jet came and disrupted our lively day, but fortunately it did not bomb.

Yea Gbassay, Yea Nnasu and one of Magainda's other aunties were due to visit us. Two days after their visit, Laser's Aunties were due to visit. Three days thereafter, we were expecting Komeh, Nyalay, Sunshine and Guy again. Yea Nnasu and the others came with lots of vegetables, dried meat and fish. They saw the disorderly life we led but they understood. Once again Amina sent a special delivery for Magic. I was there when Yea Nnasu gave it to him but he wouldn't look at me. I did not let that spoil my day. Yea Gbasay and Ye Nnasu decided to give Ngor Yewa and Magainda a break in the kitchen. They said they wanted to cook but Ngor Yewa and Magainda refused to leave it all to them; so they did it together. I was there talking and laughing with them.

Later in the evening, while talking with our guests, Yea Nnasu asked Magainda why Issa and his brother haven't been to Ndogbohun for so long.

Magainda said she did not know and thought they were too busy. It was then that I knew who this Issa was but I did not say a word. On our way to our room I asked Magainda to tell me who Issa was. She did not say anything until we got to the room.

"We have two Issa among us - At-the-end and Magic. Magic's name is Issa, which Yea Nnasu and others prefer to call him by,' she explained. I was angry with Magainda because she encouraged me to get involved with Magic despite her awareness that he had so many girlfriends.

"So, why does Amina always send him things?" I asked, pretending not to know.

"She was his girlfriend but they are not together anymore," Magainda answered.

"Well, it doesn't seem like it," I said.

"Well that's what he told me," Magainda said.

"He told you but obviously he did not tell her. Let him try, I don't care. He can be with whoever he wants to be with," I said.

We stopped talking about Magic and talked about our day instead. He did not come around that night.

The next morning, Kabbaty was filled with new faces. Reinforcements had come for the Rutile battle. Hawk and At-the-end brought some other rebels to introduce to us. They were handsome young men wasting.

"Morning Magainda and morning Memuna. This is Sergeant Sly and this is corporal Fuck-it but you can call him Tiger and this is Dirty-boy. They are our brothers," Hawk said.

They were good-looking but they tried to look tough. The day was a busy one. Magainda got angry because she was tired of the cooking, cleaning, smoking and the noise. We cooked twice. Magic tried to make it up to me but I did not pay much attention. That evening the jet came twice due to the ongoing war in Rutile. The reinforcements got ready and went to war that evening. Lansana and his boys did not go. We spent time with our guests once more. We were all too worried though, as the battle could extend to where we were or maybe extend to our families on the other side. Magic came to our room and sent Soja to call me. When I walked into the room, he sat on the bed staring at me. He looked so guilty. He held my hand and sat me next to him. He apologised about Amina.

"This is not the time to remain upset at someone," he said, "you might not get the chance to resolve it. So I'm sorry please forgive me. Amina and I had something once but not anymore I swear. I'm sorry you have to know all of this. I need you to forgive me please."

I nodded and told him that his apology was accepted. He gave me a hug and did not let me go.

Yea Gbassay and the others left before our other guests arrived. Laser tried to be a good boy when he saw his aunties. He was so nervous he told us not to call him Laser but by his real name Alpha. We spent time with them in the day and gave them their space at night as we did not know them very well. We packed our things and gave them our room. That evening the reinforcement team retreated. It was a cool night with the breeze blowing gently and the air was filled with marijuana and cigarette smoke from every doorway as loud voices of both men and women and loud reggae music sounded throughout the heart of the little village -Kabbaty. Sunshine, Komeh, Nyalay and Guy came with Maximilian.

The house was once again a typically very noisy West African market. During this time Sergeant Sly and Tiger loosened up a bit and we all talked. We discovered that Tiger knew Komeh and Nyalay so we all laughed and joked together. There was a girl called Maggie who was so confused she did not know who she liked. She had a boyfriend who liked her so much but he was wounded. She left him hospitalised in Mattru Jung and came to Kabbaty.

At-the-end, Hawk, Magic, Miles and Laser gave up their secret room for their brothers. Maximilian slept at Lt. Titanium's house. Magainda, Sunshine, Hawa, Maggie and I slept in the shop store with Hawk, At-the-end, Laser, Amara, Magic, Salifu (Lansana's cousin) and Soja. We had two double mattresses and a bed. Amara, Hawk and Magic slept on the bed. Magainda, Laser, Small-Soja and I slept on one of the mattresses while Hawa, Sunshine, Maggie and Salifu slept on the other. Hours later Magainda pinched me and whispered, telling me to listen. While everyone was supposed to be asleep, she noticed something was going on. I raised my head to see who it was. It was Maggie and Hawk at it. Her moaning awakened everyone. We all watched but did not say anything. I stayed awake from then till morning wondering what a worrisome life we were living in. So different from what my parents had hoped for us.

In the morning we went to the creek as usual. Magainda, Hawa, Sunshine and I put on funny smiles but did not say anything. Hawa was embarrassed; she went back to Mattru Jung that afternoon. After she left, Laser's aunties followed. He was so happy because he regained the chance to be the rebel he was. After lunch I fell sick again so I went to our room to sleep. Instead of sleeping, I got depressed. I missed my mother. I cried for what seemed like two hours. Magic saw me crying. He looked at me and lay beside me.

"One of those days again?" he said as he wiped my tears, "I've been looking for you."

"Leave me alone. I feel sick," I said.

"You need to stop crying. I can't leave you to cry," he said.

I looked at him but turned around facing the wall.

"Just say you don't want to be guilty for bringing us here," I said "Why am I here Magic? And don't tell me it's because I'm beautiful. Why?"

"I'm sorry. We will talk about this later, when you stop crying," he said.

I continued to lay crying for a while but then stopped.

There was a long silence. I broke the silence by asking where Nyalay, Samia and Komeh are.

"They are fine don't worry. I left them with Magainda in Bra's room. Are you okay now?"

I nodded.

We lay looking at the ceiling for a moment.

"You know, we were all captured. It was very nasty for some of us and it was even worse for others but my brothers and I just decided to go with the flow."

Now he got my attention. I sat in the bed leaning against the wall.

"Where and when were you captured?" I asked.

"Do you really want to know?" he asked.

I nodded.

"Okay. I went home to Pendembu from Freetown. My father had called me to come home because I was too wild, well at least that's what he said I was. After some days I was in the hut in the afternoon with my father arranging my trip back to Freetown, when some rough looking men came up to us. They had zagay (voodoo) hanging all over them. Soon we heard people running and crying followed by the sound of gunfire. My mother and sister had gone out. Hawk, Mustapha and others were somewhere in town. So, these men asked my father in English but with Liberian accent to tell them where the paramount chief was or who he was. My father said he did not know but they did not believe him. Because of the way my father looked and dressed they thought he was the paramount chief. They threw us both on the floor," he explained with tears streaming down his cheeks.

"Don't tell me anymore. You are crying," I cried.

It was sad. Then and there I felt myself liking Magic more. I stroked his short hair begging him to stop crying. He held me tight and stopped crying.

But he continued.

"When they threw us to the floor they killed my father and took me away. By then, the town was on fire with rebels everywhere. Guy and girls were captured, some girls were raped, some killed because they resisted. Adults got killed. Some other men like my father, got killed because they were wealthy. My father was a devout Muslim and he was wealthy too. They captured Amara, Hawk, Sandy, Mustapha, Daddy and some other guys, later up town. From that morning when I saw my mother and my sister going out, I haven't seen them up till now. I don't even know where they are but I know by God's grace they are alive. It's because of my sister Hawk likes you so much," he explained.

"So you and Hawk are really related?"

"Yes and we have been together since the day they captured us," he said.

"Who are Sandy and Mustapha?" I asked.

"Sandy is my older brother and Mustapha is my younger brother. He is the darkest. If you see him you will think I'm lying about him being my brother, but he is. You will see them one day. They are both on Blama Highway; Sunshine knows them,' he affirmed as if I did not believe him.

"Do I look like your sister?" I asked him gently.

"Not really, but Hawk says he sees her when he sees you. I don't know how, but that's what he says," he explained shrugging his shoulders.

"So... what sort of job did your father do? Did you ever see those rebels that killed your father?" I asked.

"Oh, as for those dogs, we killed them. After killing my father, we were their rangers. They trained us and when we got a bit older we paid them back. My father was a diamond dealer. We had lots of money," he said.

"I can tell you and your brothers are from a wealthy family. You are very spoilt," I said.

He laughed. "Oh, no, I'm not spoilt. Maybe Hawk and Amara are but not me. Magainda accuses me of being spoilt all the time," he said faking indignation.

"Well, you see. I'm not the only one who thinks so. You are a brat, a very spoilt one too," I said, laughing at him.

Tickling me he chided. "You are spoilt too! You pick the food you eat, you always want things your way and you always bite your nails. You and your sisters are just as spoilt. I knew from the moment I saw you that you are spoilt," he said.

We played and kissed and he begged me once again not to sit lonely and cry.

"I will never let anyone take advantage of you as long as I'm around. .... Even if I'm not there my brothers will be there for you. Please let me know if you have a problem. I have never trusted a girl as much as I have trusted you."

I started feeling better after I took some Panadol. I wore Magic's jeans and a big T-shirt and snuggled under the cover, as I was cold. Every time I got sick I was scared that I could die and I always cried for my parents or grandparents.

"So I've got you to stop crying, now can I get you to go to the nurses?" Magic asked.

"No. Please don't make me go there. I don't trust the job they do, the medicine might have expired and the needles not sterilised," I protested.

"I'm not sure about the medicine but that can be solved. We will check the expiry date and as for the needles I will make sure they use a new one," he said.

"Can I think about it?" I said "I mean I don't think I'm that sick."

"You've caught fever three times in two weeks and you are telling me you don't think you are that sick. How sick do you want to get?" He asked.

I looked at him thinking he really does care. He has been keeping an eye on me. "Okay, I'll go but I need to rest a bit more," I said.

He went outside to talk to someone, I wanted to rest but I did not want to be alone so I got out of bed and went to the other house. As I entered the living room to go to Lansana's room, I felt like throwing up. I ran to the backyard and did it; Magainda helped rub my back for me to get it out.

I was so weak everyone was scared, as I could not talk. I felt like I was in a different place and I felt dizzy.

"Let's take her to the nurse; she doesn't need to say yes," Ngor Yewa stammered.

"Memuna, you are going to the nurse okay. Antonia is there she will make sure you are well treated," Lansana said.

I nodded and started crying. I thought it was the end for my life. Burning up I could not talk or see properly. Antonia was one of Foday Sankoh's girlfriends but she lived in Kabbaty. She visited him irregularly because it required four to five days' walking and one needed tight security. She and Nurse Florence were very fond of me. They had about ten patients waiting but when I got to the clinic – which was someone's home before the war, about a block away from the house we occupied, Gbasay took me in to Florence. She treated me and asked me whether I was allergic to Chloroquine. I told her I was not and she asked me to lick some sugar after I took the tablets. She gave me an injection for malaria because that was what she diagnosed. Much later about an hour and half, I went home to rest. By late afternoon I was feeling better and really hungry. Antonia came from the clinic to check on me. Rumours started spreading around that I was pregnant with Magic's child because I got sick so often. Magainda told him and he laughed.

"I will love that but not now and not here. I don't want my child to go through this war," he told her.

CHAPTER ELEVEN

Stay Alert

Two weeks later, Komeh, Nyalay and Sunshine came to spend time with us again. Heartbroken and stressed, Komeh saw a bottle of valium tablets in Lansana's bedside drawer and decided to take fifteen of them. Though she was drugged she did not want to lie down. Maximilian was very angry with her for taking the drugs. Despite her condition Komeh demanded to cook her own food so she went to the kitchen and while trying to stir the pot she almost fell into the fire. Quickly I pushed her away. Magainda and I took her to the room with the help of Hawk. Maximilian sat in the hut very angry, looking straight ahead as if he was in a trance. Hawk left us to talk to her.

"Why are you making a fool of yourself Komeh?" Magainda asked.

"Why did you take those pills? Do you want to start doing drugs now? Don't you ever want to go home anymore? Why are you doing this to us?" I demanded.

She looked at us both and said she was sorry but before we could say another word, she fell asleep. We tucked her in, locked her in and went to the other house.

Magainda told me to give the key to Maximilian so I went to the hut and gave him the key to the room.

"I'm very sorry Maximilian for all of this," I told him. "She won't do it again. Here is the key; you might want to check on her. Also just in case Doodoo-bird comes," He nodded and walked towards the room.

The house was noisy. Magainda was so upset at Komeh that she started beating herself.

"I wish I were there to stop her. Anything could happen right now. At times like these one needs to always stay sober. What are we going to do?" she asked me.

"I will chastise her very seriously when she recovers. Let's just pray to God for Doodoo-bird not to come and bomb us. She is just a crazy person right now," I said.

Magic came up behind me and slightly bit my ear.

"Your sister will be okay. She might sleep for a day or two though but she will be fine," he said.

Magainda just stood there helplessly looking at Magic. Nyalay and Samia were worried and they asked us over and again if she was going to die. Lansana told them that Komeh would be alright.

We had dinner and checked on Komeh. Later in the evening we all went in the room. Though we made so much noise, she did not wake up. She was sound asleep. Maximilian sat by her while he ate.

"No sooner than she recovers we are going to Mattru and she won't be coming here for a long time," he said.

Magainda and I looked at each other as he said that. Samia and Nyalay sat on the bed by her. We stayed together till late then Nyalay and Samia went to bed. Komeh woke up two days later one afternoon and we all had lunch. Then it was time for them to go back to Mattru Jung.

A week after they left - I had lost track of the date, Magainda and I made our second trip to Ndogbohun. Lansana asked us to bring Guy on our way back. We got ready to leave Ndogbohun for Mattru to pick Guy up. Samukai crossed us in the canoe once again, I was still really very scared as I did not trust this canoe. As soon as we got off the canoe into the elephant grass, we saw a crazy man walking up and down the path talking to himself.

"How are you this morning?" Magainda asked.

"I'm fine," he said, nodding

"Did someone bother you?" she asked.

This crazy man was allowed to live because he was genuinely mentally impaired. The rebels found him like that when they attacked Mattru Jung. He was the only crazy person in Mattru Jung while we were there. The rebels did not trust any new crazy person, as they could be on reconnaissance. That was one of the surveillance tricks the RUF used to get to know about a town before attacking it. Some would pose as businessmen, some as crazy men or women and some as visitors who do not know where to go.

This man kept walking up and down the path, punching in the air and talking to himself in Mende.

"He will fight for us...he will fight for us,"

That's all I could understand him saying amongst so many other things as he spoke really fast.

"Who will fight for us?" Magainda asked.

He stood for a while head down staring at the mud he was standing in. Then he pointed up to the sky. Magainda nodded and told him to calm down, that things will be back to normal one day. He nodded but did not raise his head.

Suddenly we heard this loud noise. We looked at each other.

"That could be Tricks …." Magainda said.

"We need to walk faster Magainda if that is him so he won't leave us behind. I don't want to walk anymore," I said.

Magainda touched the crazy man on the shoulder trying to talk to him, as she had known him for years. The sounds of bombing came from the direction of Mattru Jung. Then the jet came flying very low over us. Having bombed Mattru Jung, it came around Ndogbohun, made a U-turn, went back and did some more bombing. Scared to death I was shaking like a leaf in the wind. I held tight to Magainda, so tightly that I was pinching her but did not realise it. The crazy man kept walking the path only this time he said, "I did not do anything, don't kill me."

She grabbed him by the arm and we all lay in the tall elephant grass. "He won't kill you if you lie in the grass and don't make a move," Magainda said.

Still shaking all I could say was "God…Mama…my God please save us."

Magainda was so calm; we lay in the grass for what seemed like twenty minutes. The jet made three sorties to Mattru Jung dropping some bombs, which did not explode and then went away. Luckily Magainda and I met Hawk as we walked vary fast on our way to Mattru Jung. Naffie did not want us to take her son but she agreed anyway

"Magainda, you all should stay off the main road please, anyway you know that and please don't spoil Guy too much. I don't let him have his way so you do the same. I'm pregnant but I don't know what the future holds so at the moment he is my only child and he is a boy," Naffie spoke her fear. "Be careful all of you." She hugged her son and we left.

Hawk held Guy, while Magainda and I carried the vegetables that were given to us by her mother and aunt in Ndogbohun.

We still had to cross to the other side of the river. We had to walk in the bush just as everyone else was in the bush. We had to plead with one of the RUF boys to cross us.

"The jet just killed two young boys and a dog. The worse of it was both boys were innocent civilians. So I don't think it's a good time to get on the river now," one of the guards said.

"Look, we need to be in Kabbaty as soon as possible. So let's cross quickly and forget about it," Hawk said.

We crossed.

"I owe you man," Hawk said, to the man who crossed us. Warning him to wait for hours before crossing back to Mattru Jung, Hawk told him, "Find a place to sleep if you have to. I got the feeling that that bastard is coming back!"

We could not walk on the road, so we walked in the forest. An hour later the jet came back still sounding desperate.

"Keep walking," Hawk said. "The forest is thick enough to cover us."

The jet went to Mattru Jung once more.

We walked through the bushes and swamps. Guy sat on Hawk's shoulders, Magainda and I walked beside them. The last swamp we had to walk through near Kabbaty was so deep the mud almost reached my chest. Feeling disgusting as my skin itched from the mud and grass, I swore never to go to Ndogbohun again. We finally reached Kabbaty at night around 7pm; everyone was on the veranda waiting for us.

"Oh thank God you are here," Ngor Yewa stammered, "Are you alright?"

Their questions went on for five minutes but it seemed like forever as Magainda and I stood there covered in, now drying, stinking mud. Getting irritated we managed to nod and to pass them.

"Welcome to RUF, Memuna," Lansana said.

"I'm sorry that happened. You still have fear in your eyes," Magic said.

"I need to clean up. My skin is itchy," was all I said.

Magic rubbed my head, consoling me as we went along to mine and Magainda's room to get a towel so I could bathe.

"Don't be too scared, that's how it is around here. This is my first time seeing you so scared. Clean up and have a rest," he said trying to soothe me.

Still in a state of shock I was too upset and scared to say anything. Anger burned inside me. Why did I have to experience that terror? I had no hand in their meaningless war. This was not my war and I shouldn't have to know that terror.

But thank you, God. What if we had died? 'Oh God please don't let them capture any of my grandmothers or any other family member. I do not wish this on my enemy.' That is, if I ever have one. 'Please save us' was all I thought of.

Magic kept trying to cheer me up, but it was to no avail. I could see him talking, feel his hands on me but I was in a trance. I had never been so terrified and tormented in my life. I started to cry with Samia holding my hand. I looked at her, forced a smile and nodded.

Magainda did not utter a word. She was tired, terrified and angry. She took some clothes out of the bag for both of us then sighed.

"Memuna, let's go and try to clean up."

I looked at her and suppressed my tears.

'What a life! God why?' I thought. I nodded to myself. Ngor Yewa got Guy ready for bed. The little boy was just as terrified as we were. Guy normally asks a lot of questions but that evening he said very little. Hawk cleaned up and had dinner as if nothing had happened. They looked worried but not so much about themselves but about us.

Magic kept on trying to calm Magainda and me. Samia was too scared to go to Ngor Yewa's room to sleep.

"The room is just there," I said pointing in the direction of the room, assuring her that no matter what I will make sure we run together.

"Don't be afraid. Lansana is there with you and nothing will happen," Magainda assured her.

"Okay. Goodnight then, but I'm still scared. Ngor Yewa needs someone to be with her too. See you tomorrow by God's grace," Samia said bravely.

I walked with her across the yard to the house and made sure she was in. I said goodnight to her and went to bed.

"If anything happens, we will be together so go and sleep. Don't worry," I said, mirroring her bravery.

Magic, Hawk, Miles, At-the-end and Acid-Moe were in our room. Acid-Moe never took anything seriously. He tried to make fun of what had happened and he succeeded. He made us all laugh.

"We will bring that one down one day just like their helicopter," At-the-end said.

I looked at them in surprise.

"Yes, we brought one down and we will again," Magic whispered. He sat behind me in the bed and put his arms around me.

The next morning Magainda and I did not want to go outside. We stayed in the room till around 10am. The jet-fighter came again later in the afternoon and flew to Mattru Jung twice, after that it flew around Kabbaty then left. It was a sunny day.

Lansana's friends came and again they kept talking about my hair and how dark my skin was.

'You people are sick; we are all black and all you do is sit and admire my skin?' I thought. I rolled my eyes and left the room. Lansana was getting ready for a meeting in Africa's Ground. Lt. Strong, Lt. Sky and Lt Universe were in the room. They were all talking about me. Magic was busy too; he had to go with Lansana. I found him in our room with his brothers.

"Don't be scared, we are going to Africa's Ground and we will be back in a day or two. Hawk and Laser are staying with you girls and Amara is coming in case of anything," he said.

Hawk pulled me to him. "We will be fine," he said as if he cared.

Magic kissed me and went to Lansana's room.

"Let's follow him," Hawk said.

Tricks drove the pickup for them. As he got into the pickup, Lansana winked his eye at me.

"Look after yourself, I will be back. Hawk man, sleep in my room and make sure they are alright. Guy, man I will be back soon. Yewa, Magainda, Samia," he said waving as he got into the pickup.

"I wonder what's happening," Ngor Yewa thought out loud.

"Nothing to worry about, it is just a little thing," Hawk said.

"Just a little thing and this bastard of a jet keeps on threatening the life out of us?" Magainda said sharply.

"Okay… okay, let's not worry, we will be fine. Amara is coming soon. Guy man, come here."

Hawk took Guy in his arms.

"Is Doodoo-bird going to bomb Mattru Jung? Tell Lansana to bring Naffie, Komeh, Sunshine, my sister Nyalay and everyone in our house from Mattru Jung here," Guy pleaded.

He told everyone that Nyalay and Samia were his sisters because his mother told him to say so. Sometimes he would call me his sister too, at other times I'm either his auntie or his father's girlfriend. As for Komeh, Ngor Yewa, Sunshine and Magainda, he would always say they were his aunties. He was about five years old, but he handled most situations very well.

Amara gave Magainda a big hug and then he greeted us all.

"A-A-Amara what's happening?" Ngor Yewa stammered.

Amara told her not to get stressed, as she was heavily pregnant. He assured us that everything would be alright.

That evening everyone cooked quickly and put their fire out because of the fear of the jet. Fear filled me to the point where the atmosphere seemed dark and cold to me. We had dinner and Magainda did my hair in colourful rubber bands. She did the same for Samia. We sat in the hut with Sue, Hawa, Mabinti and Ngor Maria talking and playing Ludo. They went on about how long and nice our hair was. I did not mind women talking about my looks because they only said it, but they did not want anything out of it.

I felt my scalp itch, so I scratched slightly and went on playing the game but it did not stop itching. I went to Lansana's room to get some water to drink and, rubbing my finger through the parts on my head, caught a lice.

"Magainda!" I screamed. "Come…come quickly."

Everyone went to the room. "What's wrong? Are you alright? What's wrong?"

"I'm fine I only want Magainda, Samia can come too. Don't worry I'm fine," I assured them.

"What's wrong?" she asked.

I laid the lice on a piece of paper for her to see.

"Ewww…lice! Where did you get that? Don't tell me…" she said.

"Yes," I nodded.

"See, that's why Magic told you to stop playing with Hawa. You got it from her; you can play with her but not too close. Now your nice hair…" Magainda said

"So what am I going to do?" I asked.

I felt so disgusted I started scratching all over my body. "Magainda what am I going to do? Let's shave it…" I said.

"What?" she asked.

"Let's shave my hair," I repeated, determined.

"You lost your mind? When you shave your hair you need product to take care of the new hair that will grow and we don't have any here, besides I don't want to get in trouble with your man and his family," she said.

"Magainda, Magic is not my father nor my husband and the hair is mine so let's shave it," I said.

"Tell Lansana and Magic before we shave it. Let's forget about shaving, we can find something to kill them. After that we can cut your hair if you want. But shaving? No way," she said.

"Magainda, I feel so awful. From where and when are we going to get this medicine? Let's hurry before they eat me up,"

"Alright, they won't eat you up. We will find the medicine soon,"

"Well let's undo the hair," I suggested.

"No, you don't want them asking you too many questions, so let's leave it as it is. Scratch if you want," Magainda suggested.

We went back to the hut. All of the women looked at us wanting us to tell them what happened but we did not.

The next day was the same, though the jet did not come. The afternoon was a scorcher and all in our household went to bed. Hawa and I sat in the hut and played Ludo. I was a bit upset with her but I did not tell her.

"I want to relax my hair, it's getting too thick I can't even comb it out, it's so painful," she complained.

"Where are you going to get the relaxer from?" I asked.

"I will make the native one."

"But it's too harsh. I've seen some girls lose their hair because of that thing. Do you know how to make it? Do you know how to use it? It is going to wipe your hair off, Hawa," I said.

"I know how to make it; wait and you will see. You never used it before, have you?" she said.

"No, I've only stretched my hair with the hot comb; one of my older sisters did it for me. I was so scared; I kept wiggling till she scorched my ear. My aunt relaxed my hair before but she did not let it go straight," I explained.

"Ok, I'll show you how to make it and you might like to try some," she said.

"No, Hawa…" I said.

Then I thought. Since it's that harsh, it might kill the lice. "Yes, make it. I'll try some…Magainda is asleep and by the time she wakes up I would have done it," I said.

Hawa went to her mother's room and brought some caustic soda and a bar of bathing soap. She brought a big bowl half full of water, a smaller bowl and a wooden ladle. She put the bathing soap in the bowl of water and started creating foam.

"What's the foam for?" I asked.

"Wait, you will see. I need you to whip the foam that I'm going to put in the other bowl till it looks like cream," she said.

She made lots of foam and I started blowing bubbles.

"Here, whipping time. Do it with all your strength, I'll help you when I'm through," she said, to me handing over the bowl and ladle.

We whipped the foam till it was creamy and I was surprised.

"Oh, I see! So this is how they make this thing. I see why it's so cheap. What are we doing with the soda?" I asked.

"We will put the soda into the creamy foam and mix it until it turns into relaxer," she said.

"How is that going to happen?" I asked.

"Watch, you'll see," she said. "Please pour the soda here for me. Be careful not to touch it with your bare hands."

She whipped faster as I poured the soda. I poured about one fourth of the packet.

"Ok, it's enough," she said. Ten minutes later it turned into relaxer - it looked like very thick cream.

"Look!" she said "This looks harsh; we will put some palm oil in to calm it."

"Let's go to the creek and do it," I said.

I was so eager I could not wait. Good-bye lice, I thought. I took the rubber bands off my hair as fast as I could.

Hawa took four plastic bags, "We will need these for our hands," she said.

We took our towels and ran to the creek. Hawa did hers and washed it ten minutes later. I did mine and as I washed my hair I saw a hand full of my hair floating in the water. Some of my fringe was wiped off. It looked as if I shaved it. When I touched the side, it was the same.

"Oh God.... Magainda is going to kill me," I screamed. I wanted my hair shaven but this was horrible. Hawa stood with her hand to her mouth. Luckily it was only the two of us at the creek that afternoon or else the news would have reached the town before me.

"It's my entire fault," She moaned.

"No, it's not. I wanted to try it," I informed her, glumly.

"I'm not going to that house. I'll sleep here," I said.

Hawa talked me into going to the house.

"It's not that bad," she said. "...Cover the spot with the rest of your hair."

"No, I don't want to touch my hair it might fall out," I said, weeping.

She did it for me and we went to the house.

"Why.... Why did you undo the nice style Magainda did for you?" Ngor Yewa asked. "I...I had lice," I whispered.

She nodded.

"Have you been crying? I have the medicine somewhere, don't cry," she said.

Magainda was on the veranda talking with Guy.

"What, did the itchiness increase?" she asked.

I nodded, looking at her, nervously waiting for what her reaction would be. I walked slowly towards her.

"Come," She beckoned "Let me see if I can find any. We need to dry your hair first. My God," she screamed. "What have you done... did you try to shave your hair?" "No, I... tried to kill the lice with some native relaxer," I explained.

"What! Who told you that thing could kill lice? Now look what you've done," she scolded.

"I'm sorry. It was a mistake," I moaned.

"You should have told me before." She pulled me. "Let's go to Lansana's room.

Guy, call Ngor Yewa!" she ordered.

"Ah...ah what did you do?" Ngor Yewa screamed at me.

"Why did you do that stupid thing?" Samia asked.

"Sit down let's cut it. You will answer all the questions." Magainda informed me.

She cut it so low that I did not need to comb it. When Amara, Hawk and Laser saw me they screamed.

"What happened? Memuna, what did you do?" They asked.

The screaming went on and on.

"Lansana and Magic are coming today," Magainda said.

I looked at her and smiled.

"Don't be so scared Magainda, it will grow back," I said.

I took one of Ngor Yewa's scarves and covered my head.

"Why are you covering your hair? Are you okay?" Lansana asked, after they arrived back.

Magic asked the same question too. Guy jumped on his father as soon as he saw him.

"Memuna shaved her hair," he broke the news.

"What? Yewa what happened? Magainda?" Lansana asked in Mende.

"Memuna come here." We went to his room. "Are you crazy? Why did you cut your hair?" he asked.

"It was a mistake," I said.

Ngor Yewa told him what had happened.

"She could not wait and heal the lice? This is crazy, Everyday a new problem. I want to eat, Yewa, please give us some food," he said, not taking his eyes off me.

The look on Magic's face told me he was just as mad as Lansana was. I left the room and went to our room.

"Why are you crying? Why did you do that to your hair?" Magic asked as he walked in. There was silence as I looked at him.

"I did not intend to, it was a mistake," I said.

"Well you don't have to cry, I understand," he wiped my tears.

"It...it will soon grow. I'm crying because everyone is yelling at me," I said.

"I know," Magic said.

I took the scarf off and we went back to Lansana's room. We sat there and talked for hours then everyone else left.

"Memuna, I am sorry for yelling at you. You still look good with short hair, although I like the long hair better," Lansana said.

I did not say anything. Magainda and Samia came back to the room.

"Samia please call Yewa for me," Lansana said.

Samia returned with Ngor Yewa following.

"Yes, you called me?" Ngor Yewa walked into the room.

"Yes. I want to tell you something. We might be going on another mission soon. I want you to look after each other. Let Guy stay here until it gets calm; maybe next week," he explained.

That night they talked about their previous battles and victories.

"This one shouldn't be hard as long as we have enough weapons," Hawk said.

"It won't. It's my mission," Lansana assured him. "John and CO. Husain are coming. We are taking two missions with two weeks' interval between each mission."

Lansana was the frontline commander. Lt. Leigh was the company commander and Captain Speed was the battalion commander – Leigh and Lansana's boss. Kabbaty was the company base and Mattru Jung was the battalion base for Bo and Moyamba district (third battalion). There was a big hospital in Mattru Jung with about sixteen nurses and two doctors they had captured in Mattru Jung and Rutile. The hospital was just as it was when they took over the town; they did not spoil it as they knew they would need it. The wounded soldiers who got their legs amputated used the wheelchairs, some used crutches. Some of the rebels were so badly injured they stayed in the hospital so long they stank.

It was time for the mission in Sembehun Coco-Faylay, a little town near Bo Town. All the boys were in Lansana's room getting dressed. Lansana was up town at Lt. Leigh's with Lt. Titanium. Magainda, Samia, Ngor Yewa and I went to the room to keep them company. I did not want Magic to go.

"Memuna we are going to Sembehun Nes Tucker. You want to come?" Hawk said, trying to make mockery of me. They knew I did not want their brother to go.

"If you want to take me, take all of us. That includes Samia, Magainda, Komeh, Nyalay and our uncle," I replied smarting at the jibe.

Magic put his arms around me. "Don't mind them; we are going to Sembehun Coco-Faylay not Nes Tucker. I have to go, Memuna, I'm next to Eagle. I'll be fine. Look...." He reached into his pocket and took out a cassette. "This is for you, I recorded some songs I know you like. Listen to them when you think of me," he said and kissed me.

Dirty-boy was standing behind me. "I need a belt," he said. Hawk told him to look around. He saw me clutching the cassette.

"Hey give me that cassette, it's mine." He grabbed my hand. He had asked me out and got rejected so he went all out to do something to me. The room was noisy and smoky.

"It's not yours, it's mine. Magic recorded it for me," I protested, trying to pull my hand from him. He held my arm so tight, his fingernails pierced into my skin.

"Hey, hey. Dirty-boy man what's your problem?" Hawk yelled at him.

"Leave her alone Dirty-boy," Magic ordered.

"The cassette is mine," he demanded.

"You must be crazy. It's not yours. We brought that…" Magic said.

"It's my Bob Marley," Dirty-boy interrupted.

"Look, let her alone now!" Magic ordered.

When he saw the look on Magic's face he left my hand.

I cried when I saw my wrist bleeding. Magic held my hand.

"Look what you've done. What's your problem man?" he confronted Dirty-boy.

Everyone in the room was angry with Dirty-boy. He did not try to apologise.

"I'm going to tell Lansana about this," I said.

"Tell him. You can go tell your father if you want. Lansana won't do shit about it so go on tell him Hawa Queen. Who do you think you are?" Dirty-boy said.

"Don't talk to her like that," Magic yelled, rushing towards him.

His brothers told him it was not worth it.

"Don't talk about my father like that," I yelled at him. "Don't talk about him with your stinky mouth. Talk about your father because you know him and you know what he likes to be involved in. Maybe he will like to be a part of your bullshit," I screamed, running off to look for Lansana. Magic tried to stop me.

I found Lansana at Lt. Titanium's house.

"What's wrong? Why are you crying?" Lansana asked.

"Memuna, what's wrong?" Titanium asked.

I was weeping so hard I could not talk. I showed them my arm.

"Stop crying and tell me why you are bleeding," Lansana said. "It's…. It's Dirty-boy…he pinched me," I said.

"Titanium man, I'll be back. I need to deal with that bastard. Memuna let's go." Lansana stormed out of the house.

We passed by the cells and Lansana ordered two MPs to follow us. I told him every word Dirty-boy had said to me. The cells were about four houses away from where we occupied. It was someone's house which was built with a shop attached to it. That house was used as the MPs' office and the prison for Kabbaty rebel offenders. The cells for civilians were on the other side of town and were in the care of the Town's Commander.

"Dirty-boy, you son-of-a-bitch, come here," Lansana ordered. As soon as he came near, Lansana slapped him very hard across the face.

"I'm sorry Sir," Dirty-boy cried.

"You are not. From today you will respect women. I brought them here but have you ever seen me hit her?" He ordered, "Take him to the cell."

Lansana followed them to the cells. Lansana ordered Dirty-boy to stretch on the ground outside the cells. He gave Dirty-boy twenty-four lashes and ordered the MPs to lock him up until further notice.

Magic was upset with me, he accused me of "bypassing channels."

I should have let him handle it and he refused to talk to me. Two hours later Lansana told Soja to go to the cells and tell the MPs to let Dirty-boy out as it was time for them to go. They got in the pickup and Magic gave me a hard look and did not say a word to me, but he said bye to everyone else. Magainda was angry at Dirty-boy but she did not say anything to him.

"Don't mind that bastard. You did the right thing. Dirty-boy has no respect for women, that's why I don't speak to him," Magainda said.

"Ah….Ah, why did he pinch you? Lansana taught him a lesson," Ngor Yewa said.

"I hate him," Samia chimed in.

At-the-end stayed with us. "I'm sorry about what happened, Memuna," he said.

"Magic is siding with him; I will never talk to the two of them," I said.

I was upset with Magic and I missed him. Magainda and Ngor Yewa talked about the incident for a while. We talked until much later then went to bed.

Two days later on a hot sunny afternoon, I was in our room having a nap. I was woken by a lot of noise outside. I lay in bed staring thinking 'if I was home with my family this would not happen. Why is Magic upset with me? I miss him, but I need to be strong.'

Magainda came into the room red eyed.

"Have you been crying Magainda?" I asked.

She shook her head.

"Why are your eyes red? Are you missing home? We can ask At-the-end to sign our passes. Magainda you can tell me why you are crying," I said as I put my arms around her. I did not know why she was crying but she got me started. "Magainda your problem is mine, tell me," I said.

"It…it's Magic," she cried.

"What's wrong?" I demanded, suddenly very nervous as to why she was so upset.

"He is wounded; he is in the hospital in Mattru Jung. They say he lost his leg and he might die as he is in a bad condition. Lansana is badly wounded too. God, what are we going to do? Who is going to look after us if they all die?" she cried.

I felt like I had been punched in the stomach, so weak I started crying.

"Magainda, let's go to Mattru Jung, I want to see them. Let's walk," I said.

Magainda nodded.

At-the-end burst into the room. "Oh, you heard," he said seeing us both crying.

"What's going to happen now At-the-end?" Magainda cried.

"Please tell us the truth," I demanded anxiously.

"Bra just had a little wound in his leg. It's just a flesh wound and he is at the house in Mattru Jung. The RPG shrapnel wounded Magic. He just has something like scratches on his hands and some cuts in his head, but he is fine. He lost a lot of blood though. He is at home too. I swear I'm telling the truth, Memuna. He is fine he says he misses you," he explained, trying to console us. As we asked these questions, Samia just sat looking very worried but quiet.

"That's not what we heard. Someone told Ngor Yewa that Magic lost a leg and he might die and Lansana is badly wounded. So you better tell us the truth," Magainda cried at him.

"I heard the news this morning and I went to see for myself. I swear they are fine," he insisted. "Magic is my brother, I wouldn't be here if what you are saying was the case. I would have been by his side. I'd like to know the dog that gave you such miserable news so I can cut his tongue. That way he won't tell lies anymore," At-the-end said. "I knew the news would trouble you girls that's why I came as soon as I could. I've already made it clear to Ngor Yewa," adamantly he explained.

"They wanted to come back here," he continued, "but they need to rest. Old Ma'am Naffie said they should stay," At-the-end continued.

That night was a sleepless one. A few days later, late afternoon, Lansana, Magic and the other rebels arrived in Tricks's pickup. Seeing them, I stood in disbelief. Lansana wore shorts as his leg was bandaged just above his knee, but he could walk just fine. Magic had one of his hands bandaged and a bandage around his head and his head had been shaven. They looked tired. I greeted Lansana. "How are you feeling?" I asked.

"Alright and I can walk," he replied.

He took Guy and went to his room followed by his other bodyguards. Magic could not stop looking at me.

"How are you doing? You okay?" I asked.

He smiled and nodded. We all went to Lansana's room.

"Do you patients want to wash up?" Magainda asked.

"No, we did in Mattru Jung before coming. I just need some rest," Magic said.

"True," Lansana agreed.

We left Lansana alone and Magic went to our room for a nap. Five minutes later, "Memuna, Magic wants you," David said.

I looked at Magainda.

"Forgive him. Pretend nothing happened," she said.

I thought "that's not like me, to pretend nothing happened" but I nodded and went to him.

"I'm sorry," he said. "I missed you so much. I should have listened to you."

I told him it was okay. "Let's be grateful you all made it back," I said, caressing his hand. "Is it serious?"

He shook his head.

"I thought you wanted to rest," I asked, quietly teasing him.

"Yes, that's exactly what I'm doing," he said.

We lay in bed talking; he explained events leading to his injury until we fell asleep.

Magainda, Samia and the rest of the boys came to the room hours later and woke us. Magainda was extraordinarily nice to Magic; she liked him very much. We talked and the boys left, leaving the three of us with Magic.

"I like the boyish look. But our heads look the same,' Magic said, in reference to my new hair style.

We laughed.

"Should I be vexed?" I asked smiling.

"No, true, I like it although I liked the long hair better," he said.

"Are you saying it because you just have to accept it or you really mean it?" Magainda asked him.

"Well earlier when I first saw your head I thought I just have to accept it; but now I don't feel that way anymore. I like it," he said.

"Thanks," I said.

I was still sleepy so I snuggled next to where he was sitting in the bed and slept.

The next morning Magainda made Magic and Lansana some stew.

"Wow, you really are getting some pampering," I teased them.

"That's what my mother would have done if she were here. But I'm glad to have you and Magainda," Magic commented. We all used any opportunity we had to talk about our parents and families in the war. It gave us comfort.

I thought to myself, 'I'm glad to have you all including Magainda and especially you. I wish it were not this way though.' I looked at him and left the room.

Later that afternoon Magainda, Samia, Hawk, Magic, Laser and I sat in the hut. While Magic was recording some songs onto another cassette, suddenly the jet came. He stopped the music and left the recording on as we ran from the hut to the house. The jet went around and left.

Two days later Komeh, Sunshine, Storm - Bayo's girlfriend, Bayo and Nyalay came to visit.

"How is our man?" Komeh asked as we hugged.

I did not answer. I was too busy with Nyalay telling me what she's been doing.

"Huh? Memuna I'm asking you. How is Magic?" Komeh asked.

"Oh, he is doing fine. He is in there. He can tell you how he's feeling better," I said.

We went to Lansana's room talking and screaming. The room was too hot so we went out of the hut. Komeh and Sunshine greeted Lansana. Lansana had Nyalay on his uninjured knee.

"How are you doing Nyalay? Are you looking after Naffie?" Lansana asked.

We left Lansana and the kids in the hut and went to our room.

Komeh and Sunshine started mocking Magic.

"Please calm down when you go to the front," Komeh pleaded.

"True. Magic if it were not for Storm we wouldn't have you here today," Sunshine reminded him.

"The man was just doing what he was trained for. Hey Memuna I saved your man, you have to pay me. He ran towards the enemy shooting, they got angry and launched an RPG at my brother. Luckily it slammed into one of the houses behind him and the fragments went into his hands and his head. I ran and caught him," Storm told us.

Magic looked at me as if he was saying sorry. He did not say anything smiling wryly.

"Magic is your brother-in-law Storm, Bayo will pay you," Magainda said, making all of us laugh.

"Thanks Storm, my brother will pay you," Magic said.

"Komeh how is Max?" I asked, about Maximilian.

"Ah, he is there. He thinks I'm his mother. He won't stop moaning," she answered. The room was filled with laughter. "His mother is not here so you are in her shoes," Hawk said.

"No!" she said.

"I'll tell Max," Laser teased. Komeh told him to go ahead, that she did not care.

We had dinner, listened to music and went to bed. Some days we sat in Kabbaty and did nothing and days like those made me further miserable as I was used to being active. However, we were constantly afraid and anxiously ready to run for our lives at any time. The boys seemed to always be on their guard and ready to fight. In the morning, Lansana had to go to Africa's Ground to arrange the next mission - the one to Rutile. That is the one he is supposed to go on with Lt Husain, Lt. John and Lt. Strong. Magic was not going this time, as he still needed time to heal.

"I'm going to be like Captain Barrie now," Magic joked.

"That man is troublesome and he's become even worse since he got wounded," David said.

"What happened to him? I always see him with a bandage around his head," I asked.

"They got into an accident and he almost died, he burst his head," Hawk said. "So now he causes trouble and when Lion sends for him he ties his bandage around his head and says his head is still hurting and he can't travel. He'd tell the nurses to send a message and say the same thing backing up what he said."

"Yes, but the hole is still there though, I saw it," Laser said.

Kabbaty was packed with rebel reinforcements from Mattru Jung and Sumbuya. The following morning, the troops left for Rutile. Two hours later we could hear the bombing going on in Rutile from Kabbaty. We were all nervous.

"That sounds heavy," Magic said, looking anxious.

"Don't think about it," Magainda advised him.

"No, but Bra thought it was going to be easy," he said.

Two jets and a helicopter went to the front to help the Sierra Leone army.

"Shit, this is tough. These cowards have already called for their air force."

Kabbaty was now quiet as if there was a funeral. We all sat in the front of our houses. Magic was restless. Magainda told him to relax.

"I can't Magainda, my brothers are there and Lansana is out there too. I can say most of the people I grew up with are out there. I know they will make it though."

Sitting in the hut talking and listening to the shooting and bombing, the pickup pulled up with two wounded rebels. One had his testicle shot through and the other had a broken leg.

Panic ripped through all of us when we saw them. Magic went over and asked the men who brought the wounded how it was and they said it was a tough battle. They told him that they were not fighting the Sierra Leonean army, they were fighting the Guineans – from Guinea, Conakry. Magic came back to the hut.

"What did they say?" Magainda asked nervously.

Magic explained, "I knew it was not the Sierra Leonean army they were fighting, it's the Guineans. Those bastards know how to fight and they like using heavy artillery."

The pickup sped off, leaving dust clouds behind. The battle lasted all night and the following day. The rebels came back muddy and looking sad.

Lansana, Lt. John, Lt. Universe and the others were very sad. We greeted them but they only nodded. Usually Lansana would play loud reggae music and smoke with his bodyguards and friends after their battle, whether they won or not. If they lost they would celebrate and make new arrangements and go back if the area was still a threat. That day was different. Magainda, Komeh, Ngor Yewa, Sunshine and I wanted to ask what was going on, but we were afraid to.

"Sergeant, why is everyone so sad? What happened?" Magic asked.

"CO. Husain is missing, we looked but we could not find him," Hawk answered.

"Shit, those dogs," Magic groaned.

I could see the devastation in his eyes. The real RUF Rebels prefer getting killed to getting captured by their enemies. Sunshine felt so sad she cried. She had known CO. Husain for years.

"That battle was tough I almost ran away. You remember the time Laser cried and told Bra to take the gun from him?" Soja asked.

"Yes," Magic said, nodding slowly.

"Well, that's how tough this one was. I miss CO. Husain man. He was one of the good COs," At-the-end said.

He had mud and blood on his boots and so did Lansana but it was not theirs. That night the security was tight. They thought the ECOMOG force would follow them; we were all alert and ready to run. It was a sleepless night. Lansana, Lt. Universe, Lt. Strong, Lt. Sky and Lt. John were wondering how they were going to break the news to Ruby, Lt. Husain's girlfriend – he was a Lieutenant but they called him CO for Commanding Officer. Magic and the others were thinking the same. We all stuck together that night.

CHAPTER TWELVE

Missing Commanding Officer

The following day Lansana, Magic, Bayo, Storm, Soja, Hawk, Miles, At-the-end and Lt. John went to Mattru Jung with Guy, Komeh, Sunshine and Nyalay. Samia, Ngor Yewa, Magainda and I stuck together. Laser stayed but he was with his friends. He was sad too. He told us he would be with us should anything happen.

He returned in the evening and we talked a while and went to bed. I was scared and felt sorry for CO. Husain. I was trapped between my two inner voices. It was so sad to see them this way. They are all here but him; only God knows what has happened to him. But I also thought, 'They captured you too. In fact they captured you, your sisters and your uncle. Your family is still wondering what happened to you and whether you even had breakfast today let alone dinner.' The voices went on and on contradicting each other till eventually I fell asleep.

The following morning was similar to the previous one. Everyone was scared and sad. The jet came once in the morning and left. Lansana came, followed two days later by his bodyguards. They looked drained especially Magic who had gone with him this time.

"Are you feeling alright? You look exhausted," Magainda said.

"Who wouldn't be drained? After having an RPG launched at you and losing one of the nicest people you've ever known. I feel okay physically but not mentally," he said.

We knew we had to stay away and give the guys their space as much as we could but at the same time they needed someone to be there for them. At the end of the day we are all human. We did our best to help them through their difficult times and I tried not to ask too many questions. They had taken us from our homes but they were looking after us more than any of the other rebels looked after their captives. We all spent time with Lansana in his room and then went to our room. Magic sat in the bed caressing his wounded hand.

"Is it itchy?" I asked.

He nodded.

"It's healing," Magainda said.

"Do you want me to help you?" I asked.

He nodded

"Do you feel pain inside?" I asked.

"No. It's only a flesh wound," he said as we both tended to his wounds.

Two weeks later, they seemed to cheer up a little. In the evening Tricks came with Komeh and Sunshine in the pickup to visit, again looking all dusty.

"What's wrong with you? Have you been digging a grave or what?" I asked.

"We went to a farm. The old man and his wife were so nice. They were afraid of your sister Komeh. They thought she was a rebel. She had Lansana's pistol. I told them she was not a wyes (what female rebels are called), she was a civilian," Sunshine said.

"Komeh, what did you do to the people on that farm?" I asked

"Nothing, I was just excited. You know, these days being among old people makes me feel better," she said.

"You had a pistol," I said. "You are only a civilian. What is wrong with you? How did you get the gun anyway?"

"Lansana left it in Mattru Jung," she said.

I walked away from her. Nyalay was with Magic, she liked him and he and his brothers called her Small Soja.

The following day we did not have enough rice to cook for dinner. We had some rice that needed pounding. Lansana told Laser, David, Salifu and big Soja to pound the rice for us to cook.

"Memuna, all of you need to help," They said.

"I'll think about it," I told them.

"Hey old ma'am - you are going to help us. There is no thinking about it.' Laser replied, making everyone laugh.

"Who is Old ma'am?" I asked. I knew he meant me.

"You," he said.

"If you call me that again I will report you to Lansana. I'm younger than you are so don't call me old ma'am," I demanded.

Soja and Salifu also called me old ma'am even though I told them not to.

"We did not pound rice when we were with our family," I said "We had our rice sent over all ready to cook."

"Oh your father is one of those who are eating the country's money. I'll catch him," Laser said.

"You are crazy, Laser. You don't know what you are talking about," Komeh said.

"I think you had too much to eat this morning; your stomach is full so you don't know what to say. You will never see my father," I said.

143

Despite the back chat, we gave them a bit of hand. I spilt some rice on the ground while pounding.

"Stop wasting the rice or else we will take you on the next mission," Laser started up again.

"Why don't you just shut up? If you intend taking me on a mission let it be to where you took me from and I would like to go with my sisters and my uncle," I said angrily, wanting to be anywhere but here with them.

The following afternoon, Lt. Leigh came to visit Lansana. Spider and Julius had been watching Komeh each time they came, as the two were our neighbours. Spider had gone to Lt. Leigh's house to complain about Lansana. He claimed Lansana took his girlfriend he had captured and he wanted her back. If Lt. Leigh did not take any action he would do something. I was in the hut with Lansana and that afternoon Lansana had started his jealousy again. He made me wear one of his T-shirts and he kept me in custody in the hut with him. Leigh came with his girlfriend; she was very beautiful and quiet. She made compliments on my short hair.

"Memuna please call Komeh for me," Lansana said, managing a smile. He did not want Lt. Leigh to know what was going on between us.

I went to his room and found Komeh, Magainda and Sunshine were trying to sleep. I woke her up and took her to the backyard to give her a heads up. I could not let her go to the hut not knowing what was going on. I had to do anything to keep us together and besides, at Spider's house, they beat the women everyday be they pregnant or not.

"Komeh, this is it. Now you have to be brave and don't be afraid to talk. Spider and Julius want to take you away. They told Lt. Leigh that you are Spider's girlfriend. He said he captured you and Lansana took you away. So go there and say he did not. I don't know if they will let me talk, so good luck and don't be afraid," I said.

We went to the hut.

"Hello Komeh, you are growing up," Lt. Leigh said.

She grinned.

"Were you sleeping?" he asked.

She nodded. Lt. Leigh sent PJ to call Spider. PJ was one of Lt. Leigh's bodyguards who was on duty that day.

"Sir," PJ said and left.

Lansana's eyes were blazing at the sight of Spider. He was angry.

"Sir. Good afternoon Sirs." Spider saluted Lt. Leigh and Lansana.

They both nodded.

"Rest," Lt. Leigh ordered.

He was offered a seat in the hut. I stared at Lansana. He was furious and as I watched, I thought he is going to take all the anger, caused by jealousy, out on Spider. 'Spider you sure did pick the wrong time to step on Eagle,' I thought.

"Spider, what is your complaint?" Lt. Leigh asked.

"Sir. When we went to Sembehun Nes Tucker, I captured Komeh. But Bra Eagle and his boys took her away from me. When we got to Africa's Ground I tried to take her back but they took her again," he explained.

"Eagle, what do you say?" Lt. Leigh asked, forcing himself to question his friend.

Lansana was angry but he managed to stay calm; he kept batting his eyes though. "Well. When I first saw Komeh she was with Hawk crying. Then she stood, together with her sisters, clinging to each other and crying. Spider tried to take her when we got to Africa's Ground but I ordered my boys to bring her back," Lansana explained.

"I captured her ...not Hawk...I..." Julius interrupted.

Lansana had held on long enough. "If you talk while I talk I'll raid you out of here. Shut up, don't make me angry," Lansana threatened.

"Calm down, Eagle," Lt. Leigh said. "We will ask Komeh now. Komeh, please tell us who captured you?"

We all turned towards Komeh; I crossed my fingers while my heart raced. I knew Lt. Leigh and Lansana had been good friends for years so I knew he was not going to make Lansana give Komeh up. Still anger rose in me again - they were treating my cousin as some piece of possession and I did not like it one bit. Komeh was nervous but she managed to hide it. "Hawk took me to the shop where my sisters, my grandmother, my mother and Lansana with his bodyguards were. Spider tried to take me away from my sisters and Lansana twice - first in Kongo-Lorlu and then in Africa's Ground. He did not capture me," she said.

'Wow, thank you God. She is serious this time,' I thought. I could not help but smile as Lansana's face lightened. Spider's face went hard with anger.

"Well, that's it. Spider there is nothing I can do. You know in RUF we are ordered to take good care of our females, especially civilians. Komeh says it was Hawk who captured her, not you and she seems happy to be where she is, so I don't think I can spoil her heart. I'm sorry, dismissed," Lt. Leigh said.

"But Bra..." Spider tried to talk.

"Spider leave!" Lansana ordered.

"I will get her back. This is so unfair," he said and left.

"You will see who I am," Lansana said.

Spider blamed me for what had happened. Lt. Leigh left with his girlfriend and bodyguard. Komeh did not go back to sleep. She went to the room and woke Magainda and Sunshine and explained everything to them. Lansana looked at me for a while and I stared back at him. He could not stay upset with me; he smiled.

"What's wrong with you, why don't you want me?" he asked.

There was a moment of silence as if the jet was flying nearby. I can't give you what you want. I thought. "Nothing," I answered, thinking. 'You are very handsome, but you are 26 years old and you have a pregnant woman and a son.'

"I want to go to Komeh and the others. Can I go?" I asked, trying to be as polite as possible.

Lansana smiled and nodded. He kept his eyes on me till I was out of sight.

We sisters lay in bed and laughed at Julius and Spider.

"No-one is going to separate us until God says so," I said.

We played loud music and jumped around in the room. When Magic and the other bodyguards came, we told them about the incident. They too found it funny.

"Those two are ridiculous; Spider needs to have one of his legs broken," Laser said.

They roared with laughter.

Two days later Magainda, Samia and I went to Mattru Jung with Komeh, Nyalay and Sunshine. Hours later Lansana arrived with Magic, Hawk and Miles. We went to sympathise with CO. Husain's girlfriend -Ruby for her loss. Magainda and I spent the night with Ruby in her room. The following morning Komeh was a bit upset.

"Why are you upset? Are you hungry or what?" I asked.

"That boy Maximilian, he is not here, he slept out," she said.

I stood there wondering what to say to her to calm her down.

"I will find out what he's up to, I don't care how long it takes," she said, determinedly.

"Okay, maybe he will soon be back then you can ask him quietly. Maybe there's a good explanation. Don't let him get the best of you," I said.

"But he tried so hard to make me like him and now he is pulling hide and seek on me?" she said.

"Calm down Komeh. Take it easy," Magainda said. "You know we think we don't have dogs in this RUF territory but I tell you, we do. We just don't see them. All these men are dogs trapped in men's bodies. So just play low,"

Komeh nodded.

"Hey, we are leaving in the afternoon so cheer up and spend time with us," I said. Samia and Nyalay were with Naffie and Lansana in the room. Guy was with the boys. "Hey, Komeh, don't let his brothers know you are upset, or else they will find him and help him make up some story," Magainda pointed.

We went around Mattru Jung; we went to At-the-end's girlfriend's house. "Hey...wow. I've got visitors. Morning girls," she said.

It was my first time meeting her. Magainda had known her for years as they grew up together in Mattru Jung.

"Bateh, how is the morning? Where are your men? Oh and this is Memuna," Magainda said.

146

"Memuna, how is the morning? I knew who you were as soon as I saw you," she said. We both nodded and smiled. "Nice meeting you Bateh," I said.

"Those men were here ten minutes ago. They left and said they were going up town to the house. I'm glad they are gone; they are very noisy," Bateh said.

"Hey… tity (tity is Krio for girl) you look good oh…" Magainda teased. "So who is doing this good work?"

"Magainda you will never stop being silly. I have a man you know and he is always with you and I know you are taking care of him. I'm taking care of Twelve-round," Bateh said.

We all giggled. We talked for a while.

"Hey Komeh tity, why do you like Kabbaty so much nowadays? I asked for you when I went to see Ruby but they said you went to Kabbaty," it was Bateh's turn to tease.

"I just want a break from Mattru Jung," Komeh replied coyly.

"She is here now and I promise you we won't accept her in Kabbaty anymore," I teased. "So Bateh, when will you visit us in Kabbaty?"

"I'll think about it. But I will come," she assured me.

"Maybe you will make her come. I have been after her to come to Kabbaty for months. All she does is promise," Magainda said "I'll come. I'm just too busy. You know?"

We left and went further down town. We had two gross of cigarettes with us and we traded some for a big fish and some vegetables and Sunshine too had a box for her own smoking and to give away. We went to Lansana's girlfriend Josephine's mother's house. Sunshine introduced me; we spent a few minutes then we left.

Later that afternoon, we left for Kabbaty, leaving Nyalay, Sunshine, Komeh and Guy behind. As soon as we arrived in Kabbaty, Magic, Hawk, At-the-end and Miles pulled a disappearing act. They did not come back till after formation at 6:30pm. We were all very tired, we went to bed after dinner. Magic slept in our room again this night, he started caressing my arms and legs. This time it was more intense. I knew there was something different about this night. I could feel his body trembling. I felt scared, so I took his hands off me. Two minutes later he started again.

"Let's do it," he whispered.

I shook my head and took his hands off me. He looked at me for a while and went outside. After a while I followed him.

"I'm sorry but I'm not ready yet. I can sleep on the floor on the other mattress if you want," I said.

He shook his head. "No, you don't need to do that. I will have to deal with being with you and only kissing you. Maybe I should change rooms," he thought out loud.

There was a long silence. "The day will come. I just feel I'm still too young for it. We are still together so don't worry," I said, holding his hand.

He looked at me, smiled and nodded. I gestured him to the room. "Go, I'm coming. I want some air," he said.

"It's cold out here and you have no shirt on,"

"Please pass me one. I think it's going to rain tonight," he said.

I gave him his shirt and went back to the room, leaving him talking to Freedom, Bullet and Kekeh - the calibre guards. He came back to the room ten minutes later. By then the wind had gotten stronger and the calibre guards had run onto the veranda. He kissed me on my cheek and went to sleep.

In the morning I was a bit embarrassed. I lay in bed refusing to open my eyes. It was cold outside, but it was not raining. Magainda went out to the toilet.

"I know you are not sleeping. Nothing happened and you cannot look at me. What if we had done it? Open your eyes; I can close mine if you want," Magic teased me.

I smiled and opened my eyes. "Don't bother me," I said shyly covering my face with the blanket.

He laughed and tickled me. I hugged him as I giggled. "I will wait as long as you want," he said "I really love you. I want us to be together forever."

Magainda returned and interrupted our play, "What's happening here? You two look happy. Oh not forgetting you two are always smiling when you are together. Jesus, it's wet outside and a bit cold," she complained.

We snuggled under the cover and listened to music. "Those men will soon be here, formation is over now," Magic said, looking at his watch on the table.

"This room is going to be like the market," Magainda, once again, complained.

Soon, they came in.

"Oh, no," I groaned.

"Wake up, Magainda, what's for breakfast?" Hawk asked.

"NATCO biscuits and Peak milk. I'm tired and sleepy," she answered.

'What?' At-the-end was surprised. "Okay let's go to Laser's girl Yema. She will make us something better. Only Memuna can have NATCO and Peak milk for breakfast."

"Leave me alone," I snapped at them.

They laughed. "Where is she by the way? We can hear her voice but we can't see her," Hawk teased.

"That's because she eats NATCO and drinks Peak milk for breakfast, that's why she is that small," said At-the-end.

He pretended to look for me in the room making everyone laugh.

"Colonel, man I hope you are not telling her lies," Hawk said.

They all laughed including Magainda.

"What if he was? I think I should leave you all here and go out," I said as I took the cover off my head.

"Leave her alone. I like her size, she's like a baby - easy to carry," Magic argued.

"We are just bullshitting man, we all like her. Hey, Memuna you know we like you don't you?" Hawk asked.

I nodded.

They stopped talking about me and started smoking. "Hey, old ma'am Memuna, we are hungry. Magainda, are you still sleeping?" Laser walked into the room.

"Laser, I told you not to call me old ma'am. Hawk, Magic, At-the-end tell Laser to stop calling me old ma'am,' I demanded.

"Laser stop it," At-the-end warned.

"Hey, man," Hawk said, "we need your girl to make some breakfast for us. These two are on strike."

"I think they are all on strike including Ngor Yewa. She is in the kitchen making food for Bra," Laser said.

As they all left the room, Hawk said he would bring back Magic's share of the breakfast.

Magainda and I did not get out of bed for hours. Samia and Ngor Yewa had breakfast. She left some for Magainda and me. Ngor Yewa had prepared cassava and gravy. I was happy that Samia had enough breakfast; I really did not care much about myself. I knew I was ready for anything. I was worried about Samia as she was very sickly before we were captured and she and Nyalay are younger so I worried about them. But they were both doing well. Lansana left some of his food for me. He pointed at the plate when I walked into his room to talk to him.

"You seem to be in a good mood today," he said.

I smiled but did not say anything.

I went out and brushed my teeth, freshened up and came back to our room. "I'm hungry. Come let's eat," Magainda said.

"Did you freshen up or you want to eat first?" I asked.

"When you were in there talking to Lansana," she said.

We sat in the room talking with Lansana and eating. Samia and Ngor Yewa joined us. "So Bra what's going to happen, is Rutile cleared now?" Magainda asked.

We all listened carefully.

"Not yet. We will have to go there again. We need to keep attacking them till the place is cleared. We are planning another trip. Memuna please don't disappear again. Now is not a good time, those guys are strong. We don't know, but they might plan to attack us one day. We are just waiting for the advance team from Freetown Highway and Kenema Bypass, for our next attack on them," he explained.

I looked at him and nodded. We sat there for a while then left him alone.

After a while Soja came to call me. I went to the room. Lansana was there waiting for me. "I want us to read and write," he said as I walked into the room.

"What are we reading?" I asked.

He looked at me and smiled.

"'Chike and the River'. Then we will write whatever we want to write," he said.

We sat in the bed reading 'Chike and the River'.

"This is a nice book; I see why you like it," he said

"There is another one written by Chinua Achebe," I said.

"Things Fall Apart, you mean?" he interrupted.

I nodded and smiled slightly.

"I like it too. You know, I was in form three when I was captured," Lansana explained. He got my attention as soon as he started, as I wanted to know how they all ended up being what they were.

"The rebels who captured us were very mean. In fact they spoke French and a little English. They captured us on the border when they attacked Zimmi Makpele. My mother did not dare say a word in complaint to them, she had to hide to cry, so they wouldn't see her crying and then kill her. Those rebels were the ones who came from Liberia to Sierra Leone to help Foday Sankoh. They took us back to Liberia to train us. They'd kill you if you were unco-operative. Sometimes they would eat parts of the body and sometimes they'd throw it away. Every day one or two recruits must die. They'd tell us to stand in a single file and make sure the line was straight. They straightened the lines with their guns by then. They would lay the gun on the first person's shoulder and ask us if we were sure our line was straight. We had no second chance to straighten the lines. They would shoot on both sides of the line so whoever was out of line would die."

He stopped explaining. All I could think about was Karimu, Samba, Briama and the others – our brothers captured to be trained as rebels.

"Are they still doing that on the training bases?" I asked, I was afraid for Karimu and the other men.

"No. We've got laws now. no-one is allowed to beat girls or rape them within our territories. You just don't go around killing…you know those are some of our laws. You are scared I can see," he said.

I nodded trying not to cry.

There was a long silence.

"In those days they would send us to the front just after we came from the training base. They'd take us on a mission and put us in front. A lot of boys died but some of us, the lucky ones, are still alive. When they came to Sierra Leone and took over Pujehun – now our First Battalion, that's when we got stronger. Those Bay rebels still continued what they did in Liberia and they used to steal things from here and cross the border with them like they did in Liberia. When they trained a lot of us we turned against them. Some of them were lucky enough to go back to Liberia, some died. The nice ones and some of the ones we trained with are still here," he said.

I thought of what Magic had told me about his father and I thought 'although this was not the place I wanted to be, we were very lucky they captured us at the time they did'. I started crying, I imagined the rebels Lansana was telling me about and I remembered the ones I saw in Liberia.

"I saw them in Liberia, we left Monrovia in 1990. They really are scary," I cried.

Lansana held me close and told me he was sorry for everything. He had decreased the volume on the music during all this conversation.

When I came out of the room in what seemed two hours, the boys were in the hut.

"Hello old ma'am," Laser said, as I walked into the hut.

This time I was not in the mood. "I don't like it, I've told you. If you call me that again I will report you to Lansana." I snapped.

Leaving them in the hut I went to our room. Magic followed me later. "What was going on in that room?" he asked.

"Nothing," I answered.

"Did he do something to you?" he asked

"No, he will never do anything to me," I assured him.

He knew I did not want to talk about it so he stopped asking.

Laser did not stop calling me old ma'am. I grew fed up with him so I reported him to Lansana once more.

"Laser, grow up, I did not think you would be so stupid. Don't you understand stop? Go to the MPs and tell them to lock you up for two hours. If you let me do it you will regret it," Lansana said

"Permission Sir," said Laser asking for permission to explain himself.

"I don't want to hear it. Go!" Lansana ordered.

Laser left the room, he was angry with me. Later that evening Lansana had to go to Africa's Ground to arrange the new attack. He went with the other bodyguards and left Magic to look after us. Early the next morning, Magainda and I left our room and went to Magic in Lansana's room. Magainda sat in the bed playing loud music and I snuggled up under the cover next to Magic. A while later there was a knock on the door.

"Come in," Magainda said.

It was Mariatu, Two-Five's girlfriend and another girl.

"Hello?" the girls said. "Hello, how are you?" Magainda and I answered.

"Memuna you remember Mariatu," Magic said.

I nodded.

"The other girl is Fanta," he introduced.

I nodded and waved slightly at her.

"Magic, can I talk to you?" Fanta asked.

Magic nodded and jumped out of bed. They went outside to talk. When they came back into the room, Fanta was a bit upset.

"Mariatu let's go," Fanta ordered.

"Bye Magainda and Memuna, see you later," Mariatu said her hurried goodbyes.

They slammed the door behind them and I knew what was going on, but I did not say a word. I looked at Magainda and raised my left eyebrow.

Two days later Lansana came back. It was a sunny day. Samia was with Lansana. Magainda and I did not know the whereabouts of Magic, Laser and Dirty-boy. Later in the afternoon Magainda and I decided to take a walk around town. We went up to the clerk's office where we had our passes signed. Later, we went behind a little house as Magainda needed to use the rest room. There was one behind a house near the small house. "Let's go to that one," I said pointing at the thatch- built rest room.

As we passed behind the little house, we heard a voice, "Laser, I'm sorry I won't do it again."

The voice went louder and we could hear the person getting lashed at. "I'm sorry, I said I won't do it again. Stop for your mother's sake," the girl's voice came louder.

"Don't bring my mother into it," Laser's voice retorted.

We stood at the window trying to peer but we could not so we stood and listened.

"It's Laser, he is beating someone," I whispered.

"I'll go to the rest room and then we will go in there. This could be their secret house," Magainda also whispered. She ran to the rest room and came back.

The girl was still getting lashed at.

"Hey stop making noise," another voice ordered.

"That's Dirty-boy." The two of us said.

"Let's go stop Laser," Magainda said.

We pushed the door as hard as we could. The door was not even locked. Dirty-boy was in the little living room wrapping marijuana.

"What are you two doing here? Who showed you this place?" he asked, nervously.

The crying was still coming from the room. But Magainda was instantly annoyed about something else entirely. "Oh God! All our things you people stole are here. I will take them all back," Magainda exclaimed.

"We heard the girl crying," I said.

"Laser is torturing someone's daughter in that room and you are sitting here smoking?" Magainda said.

"I don't want to interfere in their enjoyment," Dirty-boy casually replied.

Magainda and I pushed hard at the door and it opened. "God, Laser. Are you crazy? Yema come out. Look at you. Why are you beating her?" Magainda asked.

Laser and Yema were both breathless. "Memuna........Memuna what are you doing here? You Magainda, what are you two doing here? He asked breathlessly.

We just looked at him disgust growing in our bellies. "Shame on you Laser. You are shameless," Magainda yelled.

Yema left. We looked around and saw all the missing things in the room.

"I'll come for these things one day," Magainda said as we walked out. "Laser, I'll tell Bra."

Amara came over that evening. We sat in the room that night as usual; the boys were talking about the reinforcement troop.

"Hey is anyone coming from Blama Highway?" Laser asked.

"I'm not sure. I only know about the ones coming from Freetown Highway and Kenema Bypass," Hawk said.

Magic was always close to me. When we sat in our room at night to talk before going to bed, he would sit behind me and cuddle, sit me on his lap or lie next to me if I was lying down. This night he sat behind me on the bed with his arms around me. Samia was with us most of the time. She did not like to be near the boys but I did not want us to be isolated and sad (even though we were sad) all the time. So when I dragged her along to sit with us, she would normally just sit there silently till I took her back to the other house or if she fell asleep she and myself would sleep together on the mattress on the floor.

"You two don't get a break off each other," Magainda said sarcastically.

"You're jealous. Tell Twelve-round to stay," Laser teased.

"Oh, listen, listen everyone. We finally know where your secret house...is" Magainda said.

"Don't go entering peoples' houses thinking it's ours, you will get into trouble," At-the-end said.

"It's true we found the house..." I said trying to describe the area.

"Don't. Let Laser tell them," Magainda interrupted.

Laser and Dirty-boy seemed guilty. They looked at each other.

"So? Laser, is it true?" Miles asked.

Laser nodded.

They tried to turn everything around on us.

"So now the two of you are going around spying on us? What else did you see?" Hawk asked.

"Yeah, so you two are spying on us now?" they all asked.

Magic turned my face towards his and gave me a questioning look. I turned from him to the others.

"Hey. We did not go out intentionally to spy on you,' I retorted defensively.

"Don't mind them they just want to turn it around for us to apologise. Tell them what we saw," Magainda said.

"We just went for a walk around town. We heard Yema crying, Laser was beating her and commanding her to shut up. Magic, your brother Dirty-boy was busy burning grass," I said.

They all turned to Laser. At-the-end could not help but slap Laser on the head. "You are stupid."

"Man, what's wrong with you? Yema is a nice girl and she is pretty. If you make her leave, you will never find anyone like her," Amara said.

"Look, let's establish a law. Laser, the next time you beat Yema we will beat you and jail you for days. You need to stop this. She is a woman," Hawk said.

"Memuna you and Magainda will pay for this!" Laser spat at us.

"Laser it's true, the girl likes you very much or else she wouldn't still be with you. I agree with what At-the-end said," Magic said as his grip got stronger on me.

"We need to tell Yema to let us know whenever he lays a finger on her again," At-the-end suggested.

They all left and Magainda and I went to bed.

Magic did not come that night. The following morning there was a vegetable and fresh fish trade on the other side of town. Money had no value within the RUF zone then. So it was barter - cigarettes or tobacco for a big fish or a bowl of vegetables. Almost all the women in the town were there.

"Let's go to the trade, Memuna. Where is Samia?" Magainda said.

It was a bright sunny and calm day. It was almost like a normal day to me. We left the boys and took two heads of tobacco and three boxes of cigarettes. En route to the trade we went to Marion and Mahawa so we could go together, but they had already left. Half way to where the trade was we met Captain Barrie. We greeted.

"Where are you women going?" he asked.

"Down there, to the trade," Magainda answered, pointing towards a group of women.

I stood next to Samia smiling and swaying the plastic bag in my hands behind me. He smiled at me and kept talking to Magainda while I turned my back to give them some privacy. Minutes later their conversation was over and we continued walking.

"He wants me to visit him some time. You know, he says he likes me," Magainda said, blushing.

I nodded. "What are you going to do?" I asked.

"I don't know, I'll think about it," She said.

"What about Amara? Magainda you have to be careful," I warned.

"I know. No-one else will know except us. Don't panic," she assured me.

The place was full; almost all the women in the town were there. Magainda and I pushed our way through the crowd. There were no fish left but we managed to get some garden eggs, eggplants and some pepper. We went back as now it was getting too hot to be outside.

On our way home Magainda was excited about her conversation with Captain Barrie. We took the vegetables to Ngor Yewa and went to the room. All the boys were in the room with Acid-Moe smoking. They did not seem very welcoming when we walked in; I saw the look on their faces and sensed something was wrong. So I turned to walk out.

"Where are you going Memuna?" Amara asked, coldly.

"Outside," I answered, calmly.

Magic was lying in the bed as all the others looked at me. Amara gave Magainda a hard look.

"Magainda, what were you talking to Captain Barrie about?" At-the-end asked.

"When?" Magainda asked, looking confused.

"Laser tell her what you told us," Amara ordered.

I felt my heart racing. I could not believe Laser would do such a thing. It was my first time seeing Amara so angry. I gave Lasera nasty look and turned away to the others.

"So, tell me. Are you cheating on me with him?" Amara asked.

Magainda shook her head. I stood shaking by Magainda, playing with the silver ring Sunshine had given me. All of a sudden At-the-end lashed at Magainda with the belt he had in his hand.

"We will find out. Go under the bed and stay there till we tell you to come out," At-the-end commanded.

Magainda and I started crying; both standing there with tears streaming down our cheeks. Magainda got on her knees to go underneath the bed.

"You too Memuna, go underneath the bed. You were involved in the conversation," At-the-end ordered.

We lay underneath the bed crying. I wiped Magainda's tears.

"Hey men, it's enough," Magic said, after a while.

"Yes, man. Maybe it was nothing," Acid-Moe added.

At-the-end told us to come out. We got out and went to the other house then went to the creek to freshen up. I was glad Samia was left out of the punishment, I didn't want anything to happen to my sister she had enough on her plate – just being taken away from home.

"Magainda, what's going to happen?" I whispered.

"Amara is a very jealous person; he's going to try to find out and I won't give up," she said.

"You have to be careful," I warned.

Left with me I would have told Lansana that they punished me but I could not do it for Magainda's sake.

She nodded.

The breeze was a bit cold, as it was late in the afternoon. Magainda, Samia and I always went to the creek together, apart from the times we went to Ndogbohun and left Samia behind, I would never go anywhere without her. Though most of the times she just went with us and said hardly nothing. If she had something to say she would whisper it to me. We cleaned up and got out of the water as fast as we could. That evening Amara was still angry. I slept with Hawa that night. I was still worried about Magainda but I did not say anything. The following morning Magainda told me he had picked on her all night. Two days later, one rainy night, they started arguing about nothing and, though I tried to stop them, no-one would listen.

"You don't have time for me anymore because you are fucking people in higher ranks now," Amara said.

"I'm not fucking any COs. and you can look for your own trousers," Magainda said.

I stepped out of the room to let them argue in private not expecting them to get physical. Suddenly, I heard Magainda screaming Amara was beating her. I went back into the room screaming and crying.

"Amara stop!" I cried.

I could see the bruises on Magainda's face in the candlelight. He did not listen to me and I could not dare go-between to stop them. I ran to the house and got Magic and Hawk. They finally got him to stop beating on her.

"Twelve-round, man what's the problem? Why are you so angry?" Magic said.

"She is very rude nowadays," Amara said. "In fact I'm going to fuck off from here tonight."

Amara searched for something to wear and leave.

"The rain is heavy man and you can't just go like that and leave her like this," Hawk said.

Magainda and I sat on the steps with our feet in the rain, crying. "I'm leaving him. I'm going to Ndogbohun and I might go back to Mattru Jung. From tonight Amara is out of my life, I swear to my mother's milk I sucked," she said.

"Magainda please! We can go to Mattru Jung together and when you feel better we will come back. You don't have to be with Amara but you can't leave me here. Please… Magainda, for God's sake, don't leave us here like this," I wept, clinging to her.

Magainda's swollen face was bleeding and the top she had on was torn. She held me close to her as we both sobbed. She got up and went to the room to pack an overnight bag so she could leave. I followed her crying and begging her to stay.

"What's happening here?" At-the-end walked in all wet, "What!" he exclaimed when he saw Magainda's face. He looked at Amara questioningly.

"What are you doing, Magainda?" Magic asked.

Magainda shook her head and took a deep breath. "I can't stay here anymore. It was good knowing you all but I cannot take it anymore," she cried and continued packing.

I kept on begging her.

"Magainda. Please forgive me. I'll never do it again. If I do it again then I'll be hitting my mother," Amara said, falling to his knees.

"Amara, don't touch me!" She snapped.

"I mean it Magainda. I swear to my life, by God I'll die on the front the next time I hit you. Please stay. I won't be happy without you," Amara begged.

We all kept quiet and looked at them. Magic held my hand tight. Magainda did not listen to Amara as she continued packing. Suddenly Lansana stormed into the room, the gossip must have travelled to his room. "What's happening here?" he demanded.

'It's Amara.' Magainda cried. She went into Lansana's arms.

"Amara, you lost your mind? You of all people know that this is not allowed. How can you beat a woman like this? What's wrong with you?" Lansana asked.

"I'm to myself Sir. I won't do it again Sir," Amara said, standing saluting.

Lansana looked at him in disgust, batting his eyes. "Why did you do it in the first place?" Lansana asked. "I'm taking her to the other house and you are going to apologise tomorrow."

We left Amara standing on the veranda wearing the shorts Magainda had torn into a skirt during the fight but without any shirt on. He watched as Lansana took us to the other house.

"That's what little boys do. They don't know what they have," Lansana said.

I knew that comment was meant for me. He sat Magainda on the bed while Ngor Yewa soothed her swollen face with a warm wet towel. I was so angry with Amara I wanted him to feel what he had done to Magainda.

The thing about RUF was that if a girl was captured from a town and the rebels make that town and the surrounding villages their territory and the girl had a good relationship with their captor like we had with ours then they have a choice to go home if they still had family in the area. This is what gave Magainda the option to say she was leaving Amara. Also with everything that was going on I guess he ended up loving her therefore he let her have options. My sisters and I however, did not have that, Sembehun was not RUF territory and we could have been taken by other rebels on the way, who could have treated us exactly the way rebels are known to treat their captives.

Magainda stayed away from Amara for a whole week. Samia and I begged her to stay and luckily she agreed. They solved their problem; Amara swore he would never lay a finger on her again and he went back to his assignment in Mattru Jung. Two days after Amara left for Mattru Jung, Magainda, the boys and I sat in our room late at night talking. I asked one of my questions.

"Can I ask you guys something?" I asked.

They all paid attention to me, but I looked at Hawk directing the question to him but not minding if anyone else would answer me.

"Yes, what's the question?" Hawk asked.

"Before you guys captured us, rumour had it that you guys had a pregnant woman leading you when you went out to fight. She was the voodoo and you also had a dead body in a hammock on your shoulders, he was also your voodoo. Also you had Foday Sankoh wounded. Is that true?" I asked.

They laughed. "Memuna, I think you can answer that yourself" Hawk said. "You know some people don't even get to see us. By the time they hear we are in town they run off and make up their own stories."

"But did you guys ever have Foday Sankoh wounded?" I asked.

"That man stopped fighting long ago; in fact I've never been on a mission with him. Besides you have to be an Oso (rebels who had been in the RUF for a long time and brave to face it all) to see him, he is far away," Magic said.

"Well I'm confused. I don't really know what this war is about, so why is this war?" I asked.

Hawk took a deep breath. "Well, Sierra Leone needs lots of changes. We want equal rights. We want everyone to be able to go to school, rich or poor. We want everyone to be able to afford medication. When you take a dying person to the hospital instead of the doctors seeing to the person first, they'd ask for money before they even attend to the person. A lot of people die because of that, so we want to stop all of that," Hawk said.

"Ok, don't you think there is a better way to do that instead of through war?" I asked.

"Well I don't think so. All those greedy leaders need to go; they all enter State House with something preconceived and it's not to benefit the whole country. When I say the whole country I mean everyone including the poor people. Don't get me wrong, I'm from a wealthy family but I feel for the poor," Hawk said.

"Equal rights and justice. No war!" Magic said.

"Ok, well so far everything you are saying makes sense. But what I don't understand is why do you capture people?" I asked.

"To liberate them," Laser said.

Everyone in the room laughed.

"No, tell me something, why?" I said.

"Laser just told you – liberation," Hawk said.

"Well, I've never needed liberation before but I need it now," I said. "I mean how can you go and take me from my family looking very clean and healthy and bring me all the way here saying I need liberation."

"Well, we did not liberate you from your family. We liberated you from the government," Laser said.

"This is crazy. I did not have anything that I knew of to do with the government and I did not ask to be liberated," I reminded them, suddenly feeling angry. "Ok, let's say you did liberate us. How can you liberate me and make me walk more than thirty miles in three days and it's not like I was having a ball while walking all those miles, my sisters and I were crying our eyes out while you rebels had the men tied up like animals? So now tell me, do you call that liberation?" I asked.

They were silent for a while.

"Well, is someone going to answer me?" I said.

"Hey, in order to succeed you have to suffer first," Hawk commented.

"Not necessarily," Magainda said.

"Tell him, Magainda," I said, looking to her now.

"What are you, some lawyer?" Laser asked me. "Your father is one of those government workers eating the poor people's money in this country, huh?"

"Just because a person knows what's right doesn't mean he or she is a lawyer or their father is a government worker," Magainda said.

"Just let Laser be," I said. "Hey I told you not to involve my father in your things."

"But is your father a government worker?" Laser asked.

"No and even if he was, he had never worked in Sierra Leone. My father left this country when he was very young so leave him alone with your Sierra Leone money problems," I said.

"The war will end before we enter Freetown," Magic said.

"How?" I asked.

"We are going to enter that city and take over Sierra Leone and change everything. This time the diamonds will be in good use for everyone. We are going to march into Freetown and not pull a trigger. That's the plan," Hawk said, asserting his rebel pride.

"Oh, okay. But I don't understand," I said.

"Well, we are going to fight and take over. Then it will be easy to walk into Freetown without pulling a trigger," he said.

I nodded raising my eyebrow.

"It's a good idea if we can get it to work, because Freetown is a one way town. So if we take over that road by force everyone is going to go into the sea and that's very nasty if you think about it," Magic said.

We talked on for what seemed hours and then went to bed. I still did not get a satisfactory answer as to why they had taken me, my sisters and uncle.

CHAPTER THIRTEEN

Lingering Threat

The situation in Rutile still had not changed. The jet visited us almost every day. One night, after dinner, Magainda, Samia and I went to visit Mahawa and Marion. Magainda just wanted a chance to see Captain Barrie. From there we went around town for a short stroll. Passing behind one of the houses we heard a voice.

"Magic, I've done all I could but you still don't understand," it was a girl's voice.

We heard Hawk and At-the-end talking with some other girls.

"What do you mean?" Magic's voice came, sounding upset. Magainda looked at me raising her eyebrows

"That could be his side kick," she whispered.

"Well good for them, let her give him what he wants," I answered.

"Are you alright?" she asked.

"Of course I am. It sounds funny to me anyway," I said.

"You're still a little girl. Let's go home," Magainda said.

We were silent for a while. "You sure you don't want to go there?" Magainda asked.

"Let's go and wait for them. If I'm going to react it will be between him and me not her and me, but I think it's funny. Let's tease them when they come back," I laughed.

The boys came home soon after we got there. Magainda looked at me; she thought I would be upset. I smiled slightly and shook my head to assure her that nothing was going to happen. Magic tried to hug me but I pulled away.

"Don't touch me!" I said.

"Why don't you want me to touch you? I just went out for a short while," he said.

I looked at Magainda. "Magic, I've done everything I could but you still don't understand," Magainda and I mimicking, together. They were surprised.

"Where is that coming from?" Magic asked.

No-one answered. They were all staring at us looking guilty.

"Yes. Where is that coming from you two?" Laser asked.

We ignored them totally. Kabbaty was a safe RUF base so Lansana did not always need his older bodyguards. Soja, Small Soja or Salifu would guide him at night while the others went around with their secret girlfriends.

"It's not what you think Memuna," Magic said, pleading and trying to explain.

"What do you think I'm thinking?" I asked.

He was silent

"It's true those girls are our friends," At-the-end said.

I was silent.

"Magainda, talk to her man," Hawk said.

They would say "man" to anyone as all of the RUF main men had Liberian accents. They would speak Krio but as most of them were captured on the Liberian/Sierra Leonean border, or had parents from both countries and often went to Liberia, or grew up there, whatever they said had that particular accent.

"Birds of the same feather," Magainda said.

"There is nothing to talk about, except if Magic wants to confess," I said, only looking at him.

There was silence.

"Those girls are our friends. There is no confession to make," Magic asserted. "I swear there is no-one else."

"Even if there is," I shrugged. "Why don't you introduce us to those girls?"

"Do you want me to tell you what she was talking about?" he asked.

"No," I shook my head.

"Okay, we'll introduce you both to them," Hawk said.

"I don't want to know them," Magainda said

"Neither do I," I added.

"Man. They are just our friends," Hawk said.

Magainda was tired of hearing them lie; she increased the volume on the radio. We did not talk about the girls anymore. Magainda and I went out onto the veranda to talk to the calibre guards.

"Freedom, how are you boys doing?" Magainda asked.

"Good." They all answered.

"How are you girls?"

"Good," we answered.

"Memuna is your hair growing?" Bullet teased.

"Leave me alone. You know I look better than you even with short hair," I said.

They all roared with laughter.

"You tell him, Memuna," Freedom said.

The boys came out onto the veranda. Hawk was smoking a cigarette, took it out of his mouth and held it between his fingers.

"Memuna, do you want to smoke with me?" he said, trying to cheer me up and making everyone around laugh.

"No Hawk I don't smoke," I said.

Magic hugged me from the back and kissed me on the cheek.

"Please leave me alone," I said, pushing his hands off me.

"Can we talk, please?" he said.

We went to the room; there was a long silence. He would not look at me.

"Um…look I'm sorry. Forgive me please," he said.

"Why do you need me to forgive you? What have you done wrong?" I asked.

"That girl that you heard talking was my girlfriend but we broke up long ago. We are just friends now," he explained.

"Since when did you break up, ten minutes ago or when? What would you be doing at her house at night if she were not your girlfriend? I don't care; it's your business," I really started to feel upset with him but I did not want it to show. It was confusing as some part of me did not want to care.

"Please forgive me. Her other friend wants Hawk, that's why we were there tonight," He said.

Just to close the topic, I said, "Okay, I forgive you. But please don't touch me, you've been touching her," I said

"No, I did not touch her," he said

"Okay, but I still don't want you to touch me," I said.

Hawk, Laser and At-the-end left us and went to bed.

The following morning Magic joined the others at formation, as this was an important one necessitating even Lansana to go.

Magainda, Samia, Ngor Yewa and I had breakfast in Lansana's room. An hour later they all came into the room. Lansana was in a hurry as usual.

"Lansana…Lansana are you going somewhere?" Ngor Yewa stammered.

"Yes. I have to go to Africa's Ground. I'll come back in the evening," he said.

"Is something wrong?" Magainda asked.

Before Lansana could answer, Laser interrupted. "It's not easy to trust some civilians."

"Which ones, what's wrong?" Magainda asked

Ngor Yewa, Samia and I listened carefully.

"Four civilian women confessed to being witches today, they came to us during formation. They said they've been tampering with the calibre at night in witch," he explained.

"What…. What?" Ngor Yewa stammered.

"We need to tie them up," Miles suggested.

"Bra, what's going to happen, I mean to them?" Magainda asked.

"I don't know," Lansana said thoughtfully.

"How exactly did they tamper with the calibre?" Magainda asked.

"They said they've been dancing naked in front of the calibre at night," Hawk said.

"How and no-one ever saw them?" I asked.

"That's because they were invisible," he said.

"What?" I asked, laughing "That sounds so mysterious and nasty."

"I swear it does," Magainda said "Are they old women?"

"Three old women, the town commander's mother is one of the old ones and one young one. The young one said she stooped naked in front of the calibre," Hawk said.

We could not help but laugh.

"Well, Freedom, Kekeh, Bullet and the others would have seen some backsides if they weren't invisible," I said, making everyone in the room laugh.

"And wrinkled ones too, while his girlfriend slept in their room," Magainda said.

"No, but this is really nasty. What's going to happen to them?" Ngor Yewa asked.

"We don't know yet. We sent a message to Zogoda. We are waiting for the reply," Lansana said.

"I'm scared," Samia whispered.

"They don't want you, they want the calibre," Magainda replied. "Don't be scared."

Lansana and his other bodyguards went, leaving Hawk to look after us.

Magainda, Sue, Mabinti, Hawa and I spent all day laughing about it. We sat in the hut playing Ludo talking about how horrible it must look. We teased the calibre boys about it.

"Memuna, leave my man alone," Sonia, Bullet's girlfriend joked.

"You are lucky he did not see their backsides," Magainda teased. "In fact, all of you in that kitchen, except Rita, are lucky."

Rita was Lt Universe's captive - girlfriend and all the calibre guards were Lt. Universe's bodyguards and all the girls in the kitchen were their girlfriends. She was very young; she seemed to be around nineteen or twenty years old. Their kitchen, unlike ours, was at the front of their house - it was a thatched hut. There were about seven women. All the men in the house except Kekeh had a girlfriend. We teased them about the witches all day. It was the talk of the town. No-one liked the town commander (the person in charge of the civilians that did not live with rebels) for what his mother had done. Some other young rebels caught him and beat him up as his mother was old. They accused him of knowing about what was going on but he denied it.

Lansana came back and left for Mattru Jung two hours later. That evening At-the-end came back drunk. He staggered into the room with a big packet of Maggi cubes in his pocket.

"I'm tired, I want to sleep. Magainda, please take the Maggi cubes out of my pocket. I brought it for you girls," he slurred.

"Do you have boxers on?" Magainda asked.

He nodded.

"Help me Memuna. Let's take off the jeans so he can sleep," Magainda asked.

We took off his pants and pushed him into bed. Magainda took the Maggi out of his pocket, hung the pants and put the Maggi cubes on the bedside table and we went to sleep. Hours later, early in the morning At-the-end woke up.

"Where is my Maggi? You stole my Maggi," he said, walking around the room looking for the Maggi. I want my pants, who told you to take off my pants?"

Magainda and I sat up in bed laughing at him.

"At-the-end, we have the Maggi. No-one stole it," Magainda answered him.

"I want my Maggi," he interrupted, "and I want my pants. I want to go to my house, I'm not coming here anymore and you people are thieves," he ranted.

He got out of hand so we gave him his pants and his Maggi cubes and he left vowing not to come back.

Trying to sleep again we heard people quarrelling; the girl was very angry and foul. It was Lt. Strong and his pregnant girlfriend. He had left her on Blama Highway as she was pregnant and he had come to Kabbaty to his assignment.

"Kadiatu, I can't believe you did this," Lt. Strong said incredulous.

"Why don't you? I'm a trained soja and just because I'm pregnant doesn't mean I'm sick," she yelled. She was speaking English with a Liberian accent.

"So his woman is a Liberian?" Magainda thought out loud.

I nodded, "And he is here with Ashleigh. I heard from Sunshine that those Oso wyeses can do anything for their men. They could kill if you try to take them away from them," I said.

"Where is the bitch," Kadiatu raged "I'll kill her. Strong, I can't believe this, we've been together for years and this is what I get?"

"Kadiatu calm down," Lt Universe's voice came.

"Universe, how can I calm down? I have been with this man for a long time and I have never done this to him. Instead of trying to bring me over, he takes another arsehole of a girl and forgets about his baby and me," she yelled.

"I've had enough of your foul language. Kadiatu I'll see you tomorrow and make sure your things are still packed because you will be leading your own convoy back tomorrow," Lt. Strong said.

"You must be crazy. You think I will spend five days walking to come here and let you chase me back? You and your bitch will die," she said. "She's lucky they disarmed me or else by now she is history."

They went on till daybreak as she followed them every step. Everyone in the neighbourhood woke up.

The next morning we were in the kitchen preparing breakfast when At-the-end showed up.

"Morning everyone," he said.

Magainda and I laughed as soon as we saw him.

"What's there to eat? I'm as hungry as if I'd never eaten all my life," he said.

"First of all, I thought you weren't coming here anymore?" Magainda said.

"Why wouldn't I come here? I live here," he said.

We all burst out laughing. He gave the packet Maggi cubes to Ngor Yewa.

"Magainda wanted to steal it last night," he said and went to Lansana's room.

Lansana came back the following day.

We saw Kadiatu. "Wow, I'm a woman but I don't mind saying how beautiful she is," Magainda confided.

"Magainda, she is Liberian, it's hard to see an ugly Liberian girl," I said. "Look at me, I have never been told I am ugly. Oh yes I have, by my one of my brothers and my father when they get upset with me."

"Give me a break about Liberia," Magainda said.

"No, she is beautiful and she looks good pregnant too."

"Poor Ashleigh," I said. "You have to be strong to take a Liberian girl's man away."

We went to the creek to freshen up. It was crowded. Everyone was talking about Kadiatu, Ashleigh and Lt. Strong. Some of those who had heard her talked about how foul-mouthed she was and could not wait to see her. Magainda and I just kept quiet, bathed and left, not wanting to be part of it.

When we got to our house we found Kadiatu, Lt Universe, Lt. Strong and Lansana in his room talking. They were trying to calm Kadiatu. They took her to Lansana because he is half Liberian so they treated each other like siblings.

"Eagle, I want you to know that Strong and I have come a long way under fire and all. I'm not going to share him. Not in my life time," she said.

We left them to it. They spent hours talking to her but she remained adamant. She gave Ashleigh time to clear her things out of the room.

The house we had a room in, which was owned by an old woman, needed maintenance. Our room's ceiling was leaking so we had to move three houses away to where Sabatu Sowah stayed. She was happy that we had moved in.

"Hey, at least we can have more time to talk and you can sleep with me if you want," she said.

"But you have Sabatu Sowah and Ashleigh here, don't you guys talk?" I asked.

"Well, I have Sabatu Freedom's company when Freedom is on guard. But I hardly have Ashleigh's," Sabatu said.

"Hey, name-sake I can hear you. I will tell Sabatu what you just said" Sabatu Freedom said.

We had too many people sharing the same name, especially if the name was African. These were mostly Mende women. Most of us girls still used our real names as opposed to the men who used nicknames. So because of the name sharing some had appendages or called themselves a completely different name. There were two Sabatu in our area - the one from Sembehun had lost the man who captured her (he died on a mission) so we called her by her real full name Sabatu Sowah and the other one was Freedom's girlfriend so we called her Sabatu Freedom. Magainda and I laughed and talked with them but went back to the main house as we still had things to do there.

The sun was burning hot. Kadiatu came to our hut to cool off. Lansana had told her about me and when she saw me she smiled. I could see she wanted to talk to me, so I walked up to her.

"Hey," I said.

"Hello, Eagle told me about you. I've wanted to talk to you but at the same time I'm trying to get back what's mine. So anyway how are you?" she said.

"I'm fine and you?" I said.

"Well I will be soon," she said. Kadiatu was fearless; she talked with a bit of an attitude.

"I'm Kadiatu," she said, giving me her hand to shake.

"I'm Memuna," I said.

"When did you leave Liberia?" she asked.

"Oh, long ago I left in 1990," I said.

"Okay, I'm Sierra Leonean but I was raised in Liberia," she said. "Girl, it was a nice country. I love that country."

I smiled but I did not want to talk about Liberia, the thought of my country was making me think about my mother which was bringing tears to my eyes.

"You are pretty," she said.

"Thanks. You are too," I said.

We both laughed. "I'm trying to cool off, the sun is too hot. I don't feel so pretty anymore. I'm a different Kadiatu from the one I knew years ago, but one thing's the same, I still don't take mess," she said.

I nodded, assuring her.

"I'm telling you my sister; I have been in this thing for years. If you decide to be too nice I see you far (an expression – which can mean it's your problem) because they will walk all over you. Stand up for yourself," she told me.

"True," I said, nodding.

"You see those country Mende girls in that kitchen; I'm ready for all of them. I know they hate me but I hate them just as much and I don't care, they will give me anything I ask for. If they don't, the real Kadiatu will come. I don't even want to eat their food. I know they won't put anything in the food because, if they do, the war will be between them and us the old wyeses," she said.

Kadiatu was Mende too from Kailahun, but she did not speak it very well.

"They won't do that," I said. "Relax, you are pregnant. Calm down, okay,"

She nodded.

"Okay, I'm going to the kitchen now," I said.

"We saw you talking to your Liberian sister," Magainda said, making everyone in the kitchen laugh.

"Magainda I'm stuck in the middle," I said.

"Of what?" Magainda asked.

"Well, Kadiatu is trying to get close to me and Ashleigh is my friend. What I'm I supposed to do?" I asked.

"Don't be friends with Kadiatu," Sue replied.

"Why? Is it because she is fighting for her man?" I asked. "All of you would do the same if it were you. Look, in this place you have to have a man behind you to even breathe properly, then not to mention you've been with a man everywhere…I mean through it all, under fire and all of a sudden he leaves you miles away pregnant and finds himself someone else. What would you do?"

They were silent for a while.

"I thought Ashleigh was your friend?" Magainda asked.

"She is, but I'm just being honest here. Anyway, Ashleigh did not know about Kadiatu," I reminded them.

"Well you see?" Magainda said. "Then she shouldn't come here and frustrate the girl."

"Don't blame her, blame the man," Ngor Yewa stammered. "And she is an Oso she can get her friends to do something."

"Hey, she is in the hut and she might come here at any time so let's change the topic," I suggested.

A week later Sunshine, Komeh, Guy and Nyalay arrived again in the morning for their routine visit again. That afternoon Lansana was on his way out to visit Lt. Leigh, so we sat in his room listening to music and chatting. Sunshine dragged on her cigarette and blew the smoke in Magic's face. He told her to stop, as he did not smoke cigarettes because he did not like the smell. She continued blowing the smoke in his face although he had told her to stop. So he got out of the bed and played the cassette he had recorded the sound of the jet on. There was Burning Spear's track "Lions in this Kingdom" on the tape before the jet's roaring sound. None of us knew what he was doing. Sunshine stopped blowing smoke in his face when she heard the song and she started dancing. I was rocking in my chair. Suddenly the loud roaring of the jet came on. Sunshine quickly stubbed out her cigarette and ran to the corner to duck for cover.

"I hope there is no smoke in the kitchen," she said nervously. Shaking in my chair, I could not move. Magic was calm as usual.

"Stay in the room, you can't go outside now," he said.

Magainda and Samia clung to him. Nyalay came to me and Komeh tried to go underneath the bed. The sound went on for ten minutes. It was terrifying.

"It is going around the town looking for something. Oh God please!" Sunshine whispered terrified.

Magic laughed and stopped the radio. He would not stop laughing

"Sorry everyone except Sunshine," he laughed.

"Magic, you dog. How can you do that to me? I'm a wounded soja. If you do that to me again I'll hurt you and get away with it. Give me the cursed cassette," she said snatching the tape from Magic.

It was funny and we all laughed. But Sunshine was afraid of the jet more than anyone I knew within the RUF, as she had been wounded by it. She had been close to a place the jet had bombed two years earlier. A big piece of fragment went into her leg under her abdomen and little pieces went into one of her thighs. The little pieces remained under her flesh when her wounds healed; she did not want the doctors to take them out. Like me, she did not trust their work to operate on her. Sometimes she would feel pain from the fragment under her skin and sometimes she let me feel them sitting under her skin. "Next time you won't blow your smoke in my face again," Magic said.

"What? It's you, Hindowa and the others who got me smoking. You used to blow your smoke in our faces on Blama Highway. So maybe I'll get *you* to smoke cigarettes," she said.

The following day, in the afternoon, I was in our room having a nap.

"Memuna, Memuna, wake up," came Sunshine's voice. I shook my head but she kept shaking me, "wake up. There is a man here from Sembehun. The MP has him, they are beating him!" she said.

I jumped and sat up. "Where is he?" I asked.

"Come."

She took me to the MPs. They had three young men tied up lying out in the sun.

"I know two of them," I whispered. "Where is Komeh?"

"I don't know. When I saw them I did not think of her, I thought of you," she said. "Talk to the MPs; they've been beating them. If you don't say something to the MPs and tell Lansana to stop them, they won't stop."

I stood for a while looking at them and they looked at me with familiar eyes but did not say a word. They looked so pitiful. Tears came to my eyes at the sight of them. The MPs were hard on Saidu.

Pleading but cautious I spoke to one

"MP…. I know him. He is not a bad person," I said.

"He ran away from the training base and went back, he almost got home but they caught him again," The MP told me as he gave Saidu another lash.

"It's not him," I spoke desperately, "the one on the training base is still there and this is his twin brother," I said.

"How do you know?" he asked.

"I know them. We've known each other for years," I said.

As I said this I thought of how rude the twins were. They would insult anyone who got in their way and if the person were not lucky, they would fight them. They had their group. The other boy, who was lying next to Saidu, was one of the group members - they were the troublesome boys in Sembehun though, at times the twins were nice to me.

"Are you sure this is not the one on the base?" Sunshine asked.

I nodded.

"Okay, I'll see what I can do," The MP said.

"Sunshine, please call Lansana," I asked. I did not want to leave just in case the MPs did something to them.

Sunshine ran to the house to call Lansana. Two minutes later she showed up with Lansana, Nyalay, Magainda, Samia and Komeh. He told the MPs to untie the men. I told him that we knew Saidu and the other boy though I never remembered his name.

"Memuna, are you sure this is his twin?" Lansana asked.

I nodded.

"Yes, this is his twin," Komeh agreed also.

"Okay. Give them something to eat, let them freshen up and make sure no-one touches them. I'll send a message to the base to ask for his twin," Lansana ordered.

The MPs took the men into their office and we left. Lansana held my hand as we walked to the house. He took a deep breath.

"They are lucky you are here and Sunshine saw them in time," he said. "I do not know what would have happened to them otherwise."

Later that evening we sat in our room talking as usual. "Maybe big At-the-end will come with the Freetown Highway reinforcement," Laser said.

"I don't think so. That man could be busy," At-the-end said.

"Who is big At-the-end?" I asked.

"At-the-end's older brother. He was Mabinti Sahr's boyfriend before she met Sahr," Magic said.

"Why did he not take her when he was going on Freetown Highway?" I was curious.

"He could not, because it was a tough mission and no civilians were allowed and Mabinti is still a civilian," he explained.

"Memuna, I heard you saved your boyfriends today!" Laser teased.

"Shut up. They are not my boyfriends. We all lived in Sembehun, although they were not nice to us," I replied.

"Don't mind Laser. He would give them up so the MPs would kill them if it were him. He is such a coward," Hawk said.

We all laughed.

"Yes. Man, I remember the day I captured Laser. He was so scared he did not know what to do. He would point at anyone and told us the person was in the army. He was like a crazy man and now my small soja (referring to Laser) is an Oso," Magic said.

We laughed at Laser.

"Hey old ma'am Sunshine, I hear CO. Speed is coming with the reinforcement. Did you see him before coming?" Laser said.

"Laser you stupid, I told you to stop," Sunshine replied. "I'm a wounded soja. You need to watch what you say to me and don't upset me."

"You got bombed years ago so don't try to use that as an excuse to harm me," Laser challenged her. Most wounded rebels would hurt others and claim they were traumatised and that is why they are short tempered and their judgement was clouded by that. That was how they got out of trouble when they were court marshaled.

I looked at her wondering who CO. Speed was. "CO. Speed? Why did he name himself Speed?" I asked.

They kept talking and no-one answered me as they continued teasing Sunshine,

"Why is he called CO. Speed?" I yelled to interrupt their talking.

"That is because he doesn't waste time on his missions. It goes as fast as okra and smooth," Hawk answered.

"Okay," I nodded.

Two days later our visitors went back to Mattru Jung leaving Guy with us. Lansana was very tired that night. He lay in his room with his son resting and listening to music after his friends had left. It seemed we were all tired. Small Soja, Salifu and Laser had spent hours smoking marijuana that evening. Magainda, Hawk and I were in our room. Samia had gone to bed, Magic and the others had gone to visit Rebel Daddy and the boys. Big Soja was guarding Lansana that night. Then, all of a sudden Small Soja stormed into the room. "Memuna, see I'm older than you," he said.

"Yes, you are older than me and shorter," I retorted.

170

Hawk and Magainda burst out laughing. "Where do you get off with your answers Memuna?" Hawk asked.

"I don't know. But isn't it true? He goes on about being older than me but I still see the centre of his head when we stand," I said, smiling at the boy soja.

We all laughed again. Small Soja stood there looking at us but he was more focused on Magainda.

"What are you laughing at Magainda?" he asked.

"At you," she giggled.

"If you don't stop laughing at me, I'll shoot your foot," Small Soja retorted.

"The condition you are in now I could take your own gun and shoot you," she said.

"He can't even carry the gun. He is so short that the length of the gun is his height," I had to join in. "And it seems too heavy for him."

"I will kill you and your sister if you don't stop Memuna," he said.

Hawk just went on laughing. As Small Soja raised his gun towards us, Magainda and I stormed out of the room. He ran after us cracking the gun but I hid in the kitchen at Lt. Universe's house while the calibre guards were laughing at us. Small Soja kept chasing Magainda and calling after her. I thought it was very funny but scary; the Small Soja we knew was not the same that night. Hawk, realising how serious the situation was, ran after Small Soja and caught him but by then, Magainda and I were in our room leaning against the back of the door.

"You are going to be disarmed for a week and if I catch you smoking you will be in trouble. So try not to upset me or anyone because if I tell Bra what you just did you know what he will do to you," Hawk said. "Now give me your gun and go to bed."

Small Soja handed his gun over and went to bed. "Warn them!" he said over his shoulder.

Magic and the others heard him on their way to our room.

"What is Small Soja talking about?" At-the-end asked.

"I think he's high. He almost killed Memuna and Magainda," Hawk told him.

"What?" Magic asked. He chuckled, then suddenly he got serious. "So what did you do about it?"

"I disarmed him and it's going to be that way for a while," Hawk replied.

"I told Small Soja not to put his foot in his bigger brothers' shoes," Laser said. 'So Small intended to burst your coconuts (meaning our heads)"

Everyone in the room started laughing. Small Soja's eyes were very red and sleepy looking, he had been smoking with the missing CO. Husain's Soja.

"Laser you need to go to bed too," At-the-end told him.

"I will. Soon," he said.

They sat with us for a while then went to their house.

Small Soja apologised in the morning, but he was still not allowed a gun. Magainda was a little grumpy that morning but it was quite unrelated to the situation with Soja and us as she was nice to him. She, Samia and Ngor Yewa were in the kitchen cooking while I was about my own business. Magainda bumped into me on purpose when she met me on the veranda. I saw the look on her face and ignored her. She went in the room and came back with something. This time I was on the rear veranda talking to Ngor Yewa.

"So you think you are a queen huh?" she said. "You sit on the veranda while we kill ourselves in this smoky kitchen."

I chuckled. "Magainda, I don't think I'm a queen, I'm not in the kitchen because I don't feel like being there," I said

"What do you mean you don't feel like being there?" she asked.

"You know…. I don't want to be there," I said.

"Don't you dare be cheeky with me," she said.

"There is nothing cheeky about that. It's simple, I don't want to be there," I replied.

She came and stood in front of me very angry looking and there I was very relaxed.

"There is nothing left for you to do so you will do the dishes or you won't eat any of the food," she demanded.

"No-one has ever told me to do a chore or I won't eat and besides, I hardly eat the food you people cook here so you can eat it because I don't want any of it and as from today, I don't want anything you cook and don't think I will let you treat me like a Cinderella," I said.

As I turned to walk away she slapped me across the face. I held my cheeks as I looked at her, telling myself to let this one go. I stood there for a while and walked away.

"Why didn't you do anything?" she yelled.

I could hear all the women in the kitchen telling her she was wrong.

"That's not nice Magainda," Salifu reprimanded her.

"It's not your business. So please try not to upset me," she said angrily.

Samia started crying as she followed me. Hawa and Sue also came to me.

"Why didn't you do something?" Sue asked.

"I'll let her get used to it but it won't be like this the next time," I said.

"Look at her hand print; it's on your cheek," Hawa said.

I nodded and went on crying. If I was home this would not happen, I thought. This made me cry even harder.

"Go and tell Lansana," Samia cried.

"No," I said, "I'll let this one go. I'm not going to tell even Magic," I said.

Magainda and I stayed away from each other all day. That afternoon, while I was having a nap in Lansana's room, Ngor Yewa came to console me.

"Sorry for what happened, you shouldn't have said anything you should have let her talk," she said

"Who is she to tell me to wash the dishes or I won't eat? My heart is very big and in our family no-one tells us to do our chores or we won't eat, they force us to eat," I said.

"Yes, but this is not home. When you are out in the world with other people things change. There is this saying: 'you drink dirty water and don't look under.'"

When she said that, I remembered my grandmothers saying that before.

"Yes my grandmothers used to tell us that," I said.

"So calm down and eat. Okay?" she said. "Are you going to tell Lansana?"

I shook my head. "I will leave it this time."

Later in the evening I snuck away from Samia and Hawa and went to the hut. Swinging in the hammock I was thinking about Sembehun wishing my sisters and I were home and wondering when we will get home.

"You shouldn't be alone," Magic's voice sounded behind me.

I forced a smile "I'm not lonely," I quietly replied.

He pulled a chair by the hammock, sat and held my hand.

"I heard about what happened today," he said.

"What happened?" I asked, pretending not to have a clue of what he was talking about.

"I'm sorry; I wish I was there to stop it," he said.

"It's ok I'm alive," I said. "I don't want anyone treating me like a Cinderella."

Magic was silent.

"She had the brave mind to slap me because I did not want to go to the kitchen," I said, holding back my tears.

"It's okay, we'll solve the problem," he said.

"How? Take the slap back?" I asked, sarcastically, as I knew that was impossible. "Because that's the only way the problem will be solved."

"Magainda will apologise," he said. "There is no reason for that," I said. He hugged me, knowing I was on the verge of breaking down.

Magainda apologised but I was still angry with her so I ignored her and stayed away from her for days.

A week after we had sorted out our differences, Magainda, Samia Magic, Guy and I were in our room when Rita – Lt. Universe's girlfriend - came in carrying a bowl.

"Who is that for?" Magainda asked.

"Is it for me?" I asked her.

She laughed and blushing, looked at Magic blushing. Magainda and I looked at each other and then at them both. She gave the bowl to Magic who lifted the lid and smiled.

"You are a CO's woman, don't put me in trouble," Magic said jocularly.

Rita smiled and turned to walk out.

"Thank you," he said.

She turned and smiled again.

"What's this?" I asked.

"Food, can't you see? I want to eat; it smells good," Magainda said.

"I don't mean what's in the bowl. I mean what's going on, am I dreaming?" I asked.

"Am thinking the same; I don't know what's happening," Magic said.

"I don't know. I think she wants you Magic. She is very daring coming here with food for you and knowing you are not single. Warn her, because we can eat the food she brings and beat her up," Magainda said.

We laughed. He got up, leaned over the window and called her to come for the food.

"No, Magic take it. I cooked it for you," Rita said.

"What, did you put something in it?' Magainda asked, pretending she was joking.

"No," Rita replied ignoring the implied insult.

Magainda and I stood by Magic at the window looking down at Rita. When she looked at me I bit the inside of my lower lip slightly and raised my eyebrow. The look on my face told her she was getting on my nerves.

"I don't think it's a good idea to take this. I don't want any bad name," Magic said.

Rita took her bowl and left.

Later that evening we were all in Lansana's room with Lansana while Magic was on the veranda with Hawk, Miles and At-the-end. Lt Universe came raging at Magic. We could hear his voice from the room.

"I hear you are after my woman. You better stop now if you know what I know," he said.

Magic did not say a word.

Lansana heard him, he smiled and lit a cigarette and I sensed then that he was getting upset.

"Bra, aren't you going out there?" Magainda asked.

Lansana shook his head, "I want to hear what he will say before I do."

"You young boys think you can just do anything but don't forget boy, I'm your superior," Lt. Universe roared at him.

"I'm not after your woman, I have a girlfriend. Your woman is after me; she just came out of nowhere and cooked for me," Magic defended himself.

"What do you mean she is after you? If you play around my woman I'll shoot you," Lt. Universe said.

174

"You don't know what you are talking about. In fact, I'm going to tell Eagle you just threatened my life and let me tell you, we will take it to the highest," Magic said.

"We will shoot you back," Hawk threatened Lt. Universe. "I swear you won't shoot my brother."

As Lansana heard Lt. Universe say he will shoot Magic he called out to Magic. Magic came to the room looking very angry and Lt. Universe followed.

"Eagle, warn your boy to leave my woman," Lt Universe said angrily.

"Hey, hey, man. Calm down and think. I heard you threaten my bodyguard and that's a big problem to threaten another Oso," Lansana said. "And why don't you ask your woman?"

"You are not enough for her that's why she's looking for someone else, man," Magic said, trying to make Universe even angrier.

"Look, be careful with what you say," Universe angrily shouted back.

"Look, we will talk about this tomorrow at Lt. Leigh's," Lansana said trying to get rid of Universe.

He stormed out of the room cursing. Moments later we heard Rita screaming for her life, which went on for hours. The following morning she had bruises everywhere and her face was swollen.

CHAPTER FOURTEEN

Rivalry

Three days later, early September 1995, we were still in Kabbaty when some of the reinforcement team arrived. It was still during the rainy season but the week had been a really good sunny one. Kabbaty was full and a lot of girls got beaten up for cheating with the new arrivals. Our house was full. Finally, I got to see the one and only Captain Speed. The Calibre guards saw him approaching the town surrounded by all six of his bodyguards. They were all very tall - about ten metres away from them – and they stood up and executed the courtesy.

"Good afternoon Sir," their voices sounded.

David stuck his neck out of the hut to see who they were saluting.

"Rest gentlemen, how are things?" he asked.

"It's CO. Speed Sir," David said.

"I can hear his voice," Lansana smiled.

I found it very fascinating the way the RUF were organised and the way the rebels respected and knew their entire force of superior officers. There were more than ten thousand RUF rebels in the country but they all knew where they belonged.

He met Lansana, Guy, Magainda, Samia, Ngor Yewa and me in the hut with David, Laser and little Soja. When they saw him, all of them including Lansana, stood up to give him courtesy. The boys made sure that Lansana led the courtesy. They were still on guard standing still but slightly behind Lansana and letting him greet CO. Speed.

"Good evening Sir," Lansana said.

"Rest," he ordered. "Lansana, how are you? Hey Guy soja how are you?"

"I'm fine Sir," his little voice came.

"Good afternoon Sir," the others said.

"Rest gentlemen," he ordered. They all went back standing at ease.

"I'm fine sir," Lansana answered.

He greeted Magainda as he had met her before. "Who are these beautiful girls?" he asked Lansana.

"That's Memuna and her sister Samia," Lansana replied, pointing at us.

CO Speed was a very energetic and charismatic man in his early forties. "I'm Captain Speed. Aa naamu yelleh," he said, with a lightning demonstration making us laugh. 'Aa naamu yelleh' is Mende for "it slips easily."

Lansana led Captain Speed to his room so they could talk in private and were followed by their bodyguards. Moments later, Lansana sent for me. He gestured me to sit by him. He only wanted to show me off.

"Lansana, where is my Sunshine?" Captain Speed asked.

"She was here days ago but she is in Mattru Jung now, Sir," Lansana replied.

"I saw Naffie two days ago. Her stomach is huge now," Captain Speed said. "And Guy, you have a small soja here. He is smart, he knows who I am."

Lansana smiled. "He is really troublesome now," Lansana commented.

The reinforcement team was in town for at least four days; they were still waiting for even more reinforcements. We were running out of food as we cooked as if we were running a restaurant. The boys were getting ready for a bigger mission so Magainda told me about a little town just a couple of miles away from Kabbaty.

"Let's tell the men and see what they will come up with," I suggested.

Suddenly Magic walked into the room. "What are you going to tell us?" he asked.

"You know we are running out of food and there is nothing else you people can do about it now. So I thought about this village, I think it's about two miles away from here. They have a lot of farmers there. Memuna and I can go there with Salifu and the two Sojas or whoever but we need people to help us bring the food. We will also need cigarette, tobacco and some Maggi cubes to trade for the food," Magainda explained.

Magic was thoughtful for a while then he took a deep breath. "I'll talk to Hawk and At-the-end about it. As for Bra I know he is too busy now to talk about food. This is why women are mothers. You people are very thoughtful," he said and went out to look for his brothers.

Ten minutes later they were all in the room discussing the matter. In another ten minutes we were on our way leaving Guy totally hysterical. We had tried to leave without him knowing but he would not let us. Samia followed us this time.

"Go, he won't cry blood. He will be fine," Ngor Yewa stammered as she tried to take him but her stomach was too big. So she held his hand. Salifu and I argued till we got to the town. I threw stones at him to stop calling me old ma'am.

The villagers knew exactly who we were. Nonetheless they were welcoming. An old lady let us sit on her veranda and she even offered us some water to drink.

"So, why are you here young women?" She asked.

"We want to buy some food. Rice, at least half a bag and some meat or fish," Magainda said.

I just sat there smiling at the old lady and the children who were passing by.

"I know some people who do trading. I ran out, the things I have left now are for me to eat and I want to save some for next year to plant," she explained.

Magainda gave her some Maggi cubes and some tobacco leaves for her to make her snuff. The colour of her teeth clearly indicated that she used snuff. Sierra Leonean elderly people held snuff in their mouths instead of sniffing. We sat on the veranda while she went around to her friends telling them about our visit. Minutes later we got what we needed and left. They told us we were welcome at any time for business.

When we got back to Kabbaty there was another cute little boy in our household.

"Whose son is this?" I asked.

"I'm thinking the same," Magainda replied.

I called Magic and asked him whose son the boy was.

"Yes, whose son is that handsome little boy?" Magainda added.

"Well, you left Guy crying as if you were going to die so the guys took him for a walk to a village. You know the one the jet bombed the last time? It is just a mile away from here; we have some men there. They took this boy from there," Magic explained.

"Wait…. Tell me something," I said my tone quickly changing from curiosity to challenge. "So you people capture people even within your territory, is that what you are telling us Magic?"

It was obvious Magainda wanted to ask the same question. We both stood in front of Magic with our hands akimbo waiting for our answer.

"His mother must be going crazy right now," Magainda said.

"No, it's not like that." He was quick to defend himself. "The boy's mother is At-the-end's friend's girlfriend. She will have her son back when he is ready to go back. He is only here to keep Guy company but it seems like Guy thinks the boy is a threat to him because he is not getting all the attention at the moment," Magic explained, smiling. "What's his name?" I asked.

"Isaiah, he is six years old. You women should make him feel at home."

Magainda, Samia and I went to Isaiah and talked to him.

"What's your name?" I asked, kneeling in front of him.

"My name is Isaiah," he shyly replied in Mende.

"Do you want to go home?" Magainda asked.

He shook his head and put his fore finger in his mouth.

178

"Do you like it here?" Samia asked.

He nodded.

Samia took him and Guy to the hut. This time Magainda was polite to me when she asked me to go and help in the kitchen. We sat in the kitchen preparing to cook. I offered to pound the chillies; she knew that it was an effort for me because I hated pounding. While doing that, Magainda emptied the steamed meat in a bowl by me.

"Ouch! You burnt me with the heat from the pot," I yelped at her, putting my hands on my ankle.

"Oh I'm sorry let me see. Don't rub it you will rub the skin off and it will turn into a big sore," Magainda said, pleadingly.

"Well, can I have a piece of meat?" I asked.

"Yes take one, let me see your ankle,"

I took the meat and ran off giggling, making everyone in the backyard laugh.

"I knew it was one of her crazy pranks. Magainda, you know your cousin is crazy," Ngor Yewa stammered as she giggled.

"Why are you so crazy?" Magainda asked.

"Well, it would have taken me a longer time to talk you into giving me a piece of meat, so I came up with that."

"Yeah, you like eating out of the pot when someone is cooking," Magainda said, shaking her head.

After cooking Ngor Yewa dished out the food. She dished some food out in a plate for Isaiah and in another plate for Guy. I offered to cool their food for them. I cooled the food and gave them benches to sit on and eat. Guy did not want to eat. Magainda told him if he did not eat that she was not his girlfriend anymore and threatened she would leave him for Isaiah.

"Okay Magainda I'll eat, don't leave me for him," he said, making everyone laugh. "I am going to marry Magainda when I grow up because I like her and she is nice to me."

After dinner we took them to the creek. Magainda bathed Isaiah before Guy and this upset him. "Why are you bathing him before me?" Guy asked. I was in the water with Magainda, Samia and Isaiah. The question made us laugh.

"Guy is jealous," Samia said.

"Guy is only showing us that he is truly Lansana's son," I said.

We all laughed.

"Guy don't be jealous," Magainda said, laughing.

When we got home from the creek, Isaiah and Guy kept up their little argument.

Captain Speed was at Lt. Leigh's house. We were in the room with Lansana and Magainda told him how jealous his son was. Lansana smiled guiltily when she told him. I looked at him and chuckled. Hours later we left him and went to bed. Guy and I slept on the double mattress while

Magainda and Isaiah slept on the bed. I suggested the idea but the jealousy continued.

"Magainda, I can see you don't like me anymore, that's why you chose to put me on the floor," Guy said.

"You are not lying on the floor Guy. You are lying on a mattress," I said.

"But it's on the floor," he said, sulking. "I will not wet the bed tonight but I know he will."

Laughing, we asked him, "Guy how do you know?" I asked.

"I know," he replied.

"I don't wet the bed," Isaiah snapped at him.

That was even funnier and Magainda and I laughed so hard. "We should let the two of them sleep on the bed Magainda," I said.

"No, I don't want to sleep with him," Guy cut in. "I'm a soja and he's not!"

We burst out laughing once again. "They will skin each other if we let them sleep together," Magainda said in Krio, as neither understood Krio.

We managed to get them to sleep. Late in the night Guy had a running stomach. He woke me to take him to the toilet. By the time I could take him out it was too late. I took him outside and put him on the chamber while Magainda cleaned the mattress.

"I hope he's not sick," Magainda whispered.

"Guy do you feel sick?" I asked.

He shook his head.

He was tired and sleepy and he almost fell off the chamber. I reached out and held him quick. I stood by him and let him lean his head on me. Magainda and I tried not to wake Isaiah but it was in vain as he woke up anyway.

"What's that smell?" he asked sleepily.

"Go back to sleep," I said.

"I can't sleep the room stinks," he moaned.

"Okay go and stand outside while I clean up, alright?" Magainda said.

Isaiah nodded and staggered out onto the veranda. There was a mat on the veranda. I told him to lie on the mat until the room is cleared.

"I did not wet the bed but Guy went to the toilet in bed," Isaiah said.

"It's not your business," Guy snapped.

"Okay. You two, you both are tired. Isaiah, go to sleep and Guy, toilet. Or are you finished?" I asked.

He nodded.

Fortunately the calibre boys had a bucket with them. I told Guy to sit on the chamber and don't fall asleep. Taking the bucket of drinking water we had in the room, I went back outside.

"Where are you taking the drinking bucket?" Magainda asked.

"I'm only going to use the water. I took another bucket from them," I said, glancing over to the calibre boys.

"Oh. I thought you were going to bathe Guy in it,"

"No," I said. "Did it go through the bed sheets?" I asked.

"Luckily, no," she answered. "We just need to wait for the smell to go out then we can come back to bed."

She opened the windows and changed our bed sheet. I poured the water into the bucket I took from the calibre boys and took the other one back to the room.

"Guy, you need to bathe, ok?" I spoke gently to the sleepy child.

He nodded "but I will be cold," he said

"The water is not really cold. It will make you feel freshened up and besides you really need to bath," I said, trying to talk him into bathing.

He finally agreed. Magainda took the chamber and the bed sheets to the back of the other house while I bathed Guy.

The following morning Guy refused to put on his trousers, so we gave him an oversized T-shirt to wear. He still had an upset stomach. He left us and went to the calibre guards and he was so pressed, he went to toilet by the pickup without telling anyone. When the guards noticed it he admitted he did it. Everyone started laughing at him. Magainda cleaned it up and grounded him for two hours. He and Isaiah still continued their fuss.

"You are such a baby. You pooped in bed last night," Isaiah said.

"It's not your business. I did not mean it," Guy said.

They went on and on. Lansana told Guy to stop it and be nice to Isaiah, as he was visiting with him and so he did. Three days later, Isaiah went back to his mother.

The reinforcement unit came from Freetown Highway making the town even more crowded. Early the next morning though they left for Rutile. The battle there went on for two days and three nights; they returned very early one morning. Once again they were very sad. They had lost some of their men and the heavy artillery they took from Kabbaty gave up on them (the one Universe's boys guarded). Luckily they had three more heavy weapons with them. They also returned with some wounded soldiers making them very angry. When day broke they blamed those witches who had confessed that witch craft had something to do with the artillery giving up.

About 11am that morning there was a group of roaring and screaming people on the front veranda of Lt Universe's house. Everyone in the neighbourhood ran to see what was going on so I went too. I stood on the veranda looking over the crowd. The rebels had the women who had confessed they were witches. They had shot one of them the day they confessed so she was in her house locked up, but now the boys were killing the other three. I saw David with a cutlass chopping off the young witch's rear end. She lay by a house with her hands tied behind her, fighting as she bled to death. David went on chopping at her as she twitched and turned, he chopped her at the back of her neck. Screaming at the sight, I ran into Ashleigh's room in our yard wanting to throw up. I sat in the bed shaking with the image going round and round in my head. I could still hear the roaring outside.

The other old woman was beaten to death. When I went back out on the veranda I saw Magic with a whip lashing the dead bodies. Everyone was laughing at him.

"They are dead Magic," some said.

I thought it was disgusting what he was doing. When I thought of David chopping that woman's rear end and neck I wondered how long it will be before I eat meat again. More upset, I went back to our house.

Hours later some rebels took the bodies of the three women and dumped them over the bridge. From that day I vowed not to ever go to that bridge to bathe again and I vowed that I would never look in the water. The MPs arrested everyone who was involved in the killing. Small Soja and Laser were involved but they hid themselves. Soja was only at the scene for a moment and he vanished but Laser was really involved. Rumour suggested he lashed the other old woman at least four times. The town commander's mother was killed at her house. Rumour had it she was hit just once, her arm broke, the bone stuck out and she died. Laser hid and went to Africa's Ground while Magic and David were imprisoned with the others who were involved.

Lansana was stressing out. He went to the jail trying to get them out but it was out of Lt. Leigh's hand. The news had gone all the way to Foday Sankoh and he had ordered their arrest. In the evening we took some food, a tooth brush each and tooth paste for David and Magic. We spent some time with them; MaHawa was there and we stayed with them till six in the evening. That night MaHawa had given her room to Magic as he did not want to sleep in the space they gave him in the jail. She slept with him sometimes under cover.

Magainda and Ngor Yewa made breakfast early the following morning so Magainda and I took the breakfast to them.

"David, where is Magic?" Magainda asked.

"He is somewhere around there," he said pointing at the back door.

We walked in the direction he pointed us. As we opened the back door we saw MaHawa and Magic standing. He was brushing his teeth with a towel around his neck.

"Morning, MaHawa," we said.

"Morning, you. How are you?" I asked, tapping Magic on the shoulder.

"I'm fine. I can't wait to get out of here. I did not kill anyone," he said

"I know," I said.

"So where did you sleep?" I asked.

He was quiet for a while. He swilled some water in his mouth and spat it out.

"I slept in MaHawa room," he said.

I looked at the two and nodded.

She smiled "I let him sleep in my room. I slept with Memuna," she said.

I nodded. 'Who asked you?' I thought.

She took us to the room while he went to bathe.

One of the MPs wanted MaHawa so Captain Barrie gave her to him. She did not, however, want him so she gave him hard times and cheated in his face. He would not do anything as she was RUF's one and only Lieutenant Colonel Mohamed's cousin. This man was second in command to Foday Sankoh.

"So MaHawa, you let Magic sleep in you and your boyfriend's room. What did your boyfriend think about that?" Magainda asked.

"Well, he knows that I don't want him; he did not say anything. But I can see that he is upset though," she replied without emotion.

I just sat there looking at her and Magainda and listening to their conversation. Magic came back to the room all dressed. We talked for a while and left him. He told us to tell Lansana he was sorry and he should try and get them out.

Two days, later they were out but Lansana's assignment was changed as was the other entire COs. The reinforcement went to Mattru Jung with the wounded leaving Kabbaty as if there was a funeral. They sent Lansana and Lt. Universe to a town called Mokabba about fifteen minutes' drive away from Kabbaty. We of course, had to go with him. It was a beautiful town and all the houses were new. The house Lansana chose to live in was big and brand new. It had three bedrooms, a furnished living room and two large verandas. The bathroom and toilet were outside. There was a big hammock on the front veranda and an even bigger one on the back veranda. When the rebels entered that town they did not damage a lot of the houses. The person who owned the houses we moved into was very lucky as both of his houses were left alone. We occupied both houses. The big one was for Lansana, Ngor Yewa, and the small soldiers (Salifu, Big Soja, and David.). Small Soja was Lt. John's bodyguard so he went back to Mattru Jung.

The little house across the road was for Samia, Magainda, the boys and me. It had four small rooms, a little living room and a small veranda in the front. The kitchen, the bathrooms and the toilet were in the backyard and there was a big hammock in the kitchen. This time there was no creek. We had a well in the backyard of the small house right in front of the kitchen. The landlord actually had three houses the other unfinished house was next to the one we occupied across the road from Lansana.

After moving everything, Lansana was called to report to Kabbaty immediately as all the COs from Africa's Ground and Sumbuya were ordered by Foday Sankoh to report to Zogoda immediately.

"I have to go, they say Lion is calling us," Lansana informed us that day. "Amara, Magic, all of you look after the women. I'll be back," Lansana said.

"When are you coming back?" I cried. Despite everything, he was the rebel whose protection we relied on. He forced a smiled and cupped my face in his hands. "I'll be back as soon as the meeting is over with Lion. I want you to be strong and stop crying," he said.

"Who is Lion?" I asked

"Foday Sankoh," he answered.

Lansana was deeply stressed. He chain-smoked. He started sweating and he took off his shirt and went to the veranda. Samia, Magainda and I followed him while Ngor Yewa packed his things for him. The commanding officers were ordered to take two bodyguards each. Lansana hugged me and we went to the room to the others.

"Look everyone, I don't want anyone crying. I'm going for a meeting and I will be back before you know it. I'm not going alone and we will all be back; we might get our assignments changed again though - this time far apart. Guys, take care of these women. Magic, I'm not here - you are in charge; anyone beats any of these girls send them to the ambush in Africa's Ground. That's an order."

Magainda, Samia, Ngor Yewa and I burst out crying when Tricks came for him. He kissed me on the cheek and got into the pickup with Laser, David and Salifu but he was stopping in Mattru Jung. It was going to be Laser's first time to see Foday Sankoh. At-the-end got in the pickup with them but he was only going to spend some time in Mattru Jung with his girlfriend and he wanted to see Lansana off too.

The rest of the boys laughed at us and begged us to stop crying. I went to Lansana's room, lay on the bed and cried until I fell asleep. Magainda woke me up when it was time to cook, as they wanted us to agree on what to prepare.

"Well, we have four cups of rice and a big pumpkin, though we have some cassava already cooked. So what should we do?" Ngor Yewa asked.

"I'm fine with anything," Samia said.

"So should we cook the pumpkin?" Ngor Yewa asked.

They all said yes.

"But Memuna doesn't like it," Samia said.

"Well, give her a cup of rice for her alone," Magic suggested.

"No, I will eat some cassava. The rice is not enough for seven of you," I said.

"Are you sure?" Ngor Yewa asked.

I only nodded, as I was about to cry but managed to hold it back. "Yes, I'm sure and I prefer the cassava to rice anyway," I assured her.

"Oh, Memuna don't cry. We all miss Lansana and he will come back; your eyes are swollen, you need to stop crying.' she said, trying to comfort me. I nodded and went to the room to listen to music.

Ngor Yewa, Samia and Magainda came to the room making noise. "So, aren't you people going to cook your rice?" I asked.

"We are waiting for those boys; they have gone around the town to trade some cigarettes for some fish or meat," Magainda said.

"God, please give them fish, there is no way I can eat meat now after looking at David cutting that woman up," I thought out loud.

Ten minutes later the boys came back with lots of fresh fish. They gave the fish to Magainda. Magic jumped on me on the bed trying to cheer me up.

"If you are worried about someone beating you, you don't need to worry because I won't lay a finger on you and no-one will. I meant what I told you that day in the hut," he said.

I looked at him and nodded.

"I want you to smile," he said, tickling me.

Laughing, I screamed making everyone run to the room.

"When you two are doing your thing you should keep it down," Magainda commented, making everyone laugh.

"We are not doing anything," I protested, seeing the shock in Samia's face.

"Hey Memuna, come out here and take the fish you want to eat with the cassava," Ngor Yewa stammered.

I took two fish and cleaned them. Magainda cleaned the rest and divided the quantity into two. She gave one part for the pumpkin to Ngor Yewa and fried the rest.

"Memuna don't you want to fry yours?" Magainda asked.

"No, I want to roast it and eat it with ground pepper," I said.

They all pulled a disgusting face. "It's better if you fry it," Samia said.

"You don't want to get sick again do you?" Hawk asked, reminding me of last time.

I fried the fish and it was so much better than I imagined it roasted. Magainda and Ngor Yewa cooked their rice and the pumpkin together in the same pot to make it plenty enough for all of them. They ate and made a lot of noise. When they started the war, their voodoo was against eating pumpkin, lime and palm kernel oil, menstruating woman and many other things. As they took over a lot of places and they started getting hungry, they ate pumpkin and palm kernel oil. Some of them caught malaria so they used lime in their native potions. While they ate, the boys made fun of their old rules.

"Oh, I just ruined my zaykay (zaykay is what they called the voodoo patches they gave them on strings to wear)," Magic said.

"Oh I just got shot," Miles yelled, holding onto his chest.

"Oh no, I'm dying! the bullet is going through my heart," Hawk said, play acting his pretend wound. "I wish I hadn't eaten that pumpkin."

Amara was busy making sounds of guns as if they were on the front.

We sat staring at them as they played around.

We used kerosene lamps in these houses. We made noise all night and went to bed early in the morning. The boys arranged to go to Africa's Ground for some rice for us. Around 7am, (after the 6am news not sure if it was BBC or VOA - Voice of America) Amara, Hawk and Miles went to Africa's Ground and came back two hours later with a bag and a half of rice. They divided it into three so the three of them could carry it. That morning we had cassava for breakfast. Ngor Yewa, Magainda, Samia and I went to the unfinished house to look around. While looking from room to room Samia and I played hide and seek. The landlord came, while we were there and we could tell that he was a bit nervous.

"Morning young girls," he said.

There was an unspoken pact between us that for the sake of our elderly relatives whom we were taken from, we would make sure we treat every elderly person with the respect we wanted ours to be treated with.

"Morning Pa," we said.

"I learnt you live in those two houses," he said, pointing at his two houses.

"Yes, anything wrong?" Ngor Yewa asked.

"Well, you seem like nice girls. I own these three houses and I just want to beg you girls to please take care of them as you would take care of your parents', please. I think I've lost everything I ever worked for. My family and I only have these houses left; we will rent them out after the war if they are in good condition," he said.

"Ok, we promise we will look after your houses as long as we occupy them," Magainda said.

"Is it only the four of you or you have men?" he asked, nervously.

"Yes we do, but the head of us is not here at the moment. I will show you to the others if you want to meet them," Magainda asked.

We took him in the backyard where all four of the boys were. Amara was lying in the hammock and the other three were sitting in chairs.

"Magic, this is the landlord," Ngor Yewa said.

Magic shook hands with him, introduced the others and told him there were more of them. He told them the same thing he told us about taking care of his houses.

"Don't worry old man, we will look after your houses, you can come in and check anytime you want," Amara said. "Feel free, we won't do anything to you, we have old family members too."

"God bless you young men," the old man said as he shook their hands one by one.

He took us into the unfinished house. "The people who lived here before were a bit careless, they burnt some of my furniture as fire wood and some of the plank in this place for the house. I was happy when they left," he said. "You people can use the little short planks for fire wood but not the long ones please."

"Ok, we won't," Ngor Yewa said.

We were all fond of the old man; he spent all morning packing the planks he thought were useful to him and then left promising to come the

186

following day. Later in the afternoon, it was cloudy and there was slight thundering. We cooked quickly, bathed and went inside before it rained.

Mokabba was a beautiful town; the area we lived in was not destroyed which at times made me forget I was in a war zone. The delusion, however, only lasted the longest at half an hour at a time. It went away any time I remembered I had a boyfriend and I had three sisters to look after and especially when I saw Samia's sad face. I sat every day, when I had the chance to be alone, thinking why there was a war and if what Hawk told me was the real reason for the war then why should so many people die for money. It made me very sad to know how cruel the world could be sometimes.

Samia and I had a room together in the small house. This time we did not share the same bed as the room had two beds in it. The room was once a shop during normal days; it had a door leading to Magainda and Amara's room. The other two rooms were between Magic, Hawk, Miles, At-the-end and Laser. Samia slept with Ngor Yewa most of the time when she was in a good mood. Some nights Magic would come to my room to spend the night. It was a bit scary for me because I knew very well that he was sexually active but I was not. So some of the time I would chase him out of my room and sometimes I would just get up and put on some shorts and not say anything to him, which did not make him leave though. He would sleep in the room with me and on the same bed. He would stay away and wait until daybreak before he would say something to me.

On our second day in Mokabba, after a heavy breakfast, we decided to walk around town so we could know our way around. We went into a deserted house down town. The whole yard was covered in grass and a fruit tree which caught our attention. We went into the house. It was dark but we could see a skeleton on the floor in the lounge area. When we saw that, we walked quickly out of the house. Most of the houses in that area were destroyed - some were burnt and some had bullet holes in them. The sight was very discouraging.

Later in the afternoon we all sat in the kitchen chatting while Magainda and I cooked. Magainda asked Ngor Yewa to take a break from the kitchen because her stomach had grown bigger and she had backaches sometimes. We had sugarcane in the yard; the boys littered the kitchen with the sugarcane.

"You boys are going to clean that place when you are finished," Magainda said, in her bossiest manner.

"Ok, we will," Hawk agreed.

That night at around midnight it rained. Samia slept with Ngor Yewa. I was in my room lying on the bed talking to Magainda as Amara was still with his brothers in the living room talking. "Do you like this place?" Magainda asked.

"Well…I liked Kabbaty better, but to be honest I don't like anywhere within this war zone," I said.

"No-one does, but what can we do?" Magainda said.

"I can't wait for this war to end," I said. "I hope by then I'm not all grown up with a child."

"By God's grace it won't last that long," Magainda said, sounding very hopeful.

"I really miss Lansana; I wonder when he will come back?" I asked.

"Well, maybe they are still walking to Zogoda. Let's ask those men," Magainda said.

"Oh… the rain sounds good on the roof," I said.

"Yeah, so you want me to call Magic for you?" Magainda teased.

"No… I don't want him to come here, call Amara for yourself," I said. "I hope Ngor Yewa and Samia are ok."

"Hawk is sleeping in Bra's room. They will be fine, he will keep an eye on them," Magainda said.

"That's a good idea for someone to sleep there with them," I said, feeling better knowing that Samia would be safe.

"It's cold, I'm cold," Magic said, as he walked in, "can I sleep here?"

Magainda laughed. "Amara try and come to bed," She called out to Amara in the living room.

"No, you are not sleeping in this room," I said

"Please, I just want to be with you," he said. He jumped on me on the bed laughing.

"I will close the door for you two," Magainda said, getting out of her bed to close the door between her room and mine.

We laughed.

"Goodnight," Hawk's voice came.

"Goodnight. See you tomorrow," we all said.

Hawk ran across the street in the rain to the other house. Miles and Amara were left behind.

"I'm sleepy now, so I'd better go to my room too. Goodnight everyone," Miles said.

"Goodnight, man," Magic and Amara said.

"Goodnight Miles," Magainda and I said.

Amara closed their room door leading to the living room and turned the lamp high to look for something.

"Oh, good thinking man. It's too cold to sleep alone," he teased, when Magic opened the door between our rooms to talk to his brother.

"I will send him to his room if you say that again Amara," I said

"True, Amara don't scare her," Magainda said, making them laugh. "What are you looking for by the way?"

"Something," Amara replied.

"Well, try and turn the lamp low I'm sleepy," she said. "Goodnight you two over there, Amara please close the centre door."

"Goodnight," Magic and I said together.

Amara turned the lamp low and closed the door between us whispering. "Magic, be good man. Memuna see you tomorrow," he said.

"Ok, goodnight," I replied.

Magic laughed.

The lamp in my room was already low, I closed my eyes and pulled the cover over my head and recited Psalm 23. "Goodnight Magic," I said

"Why, are you afraid of me?" he asked.

"I'm not afraid of you," I said.

"But you always try to kick me out when I try to spend the night with you," he said.

I yawned. "Magic you have your room,"

"You are my girlfriend," he said "would you prefer me sleeping with other girls?"

I was silent for a while. "It's up to you, if that's what you want to do then" I shrugged.

"That's not what I want to do; I want to be with you. I know you are afraid of having sex but I told you I was not going to push you. I'm ready when you are," he said.

"Ok," I replied

"I don't want you to get pregnant. I know you like children but this is not the right place or the right time. I know that's why you are scared of doing it," he said.

"Who told you I liked children?" I asked.

"You think I don't see you with Guy? You and your sisters like children, I know," he said.

I smiled.

"So is pregnancy what you are afraid of?" he asked.

I sighed. "Yes."

I was not thinking about pregnancy, it was a reason to stay away from sex but it was not the main reason why I did not want to do it. The reason I did not want to do it was because I did not feel like it and I was not ready for it at all. I just told him it was the reason why because I wanted to cut long matters short. We talked for a while, kissed and then fell asleep. Early in the morning, before formation, I was still asleep. Magic awakened me with a kiss, I turned and covered my head with the pillow.

"I was dreaming and now you have interrupted,"

"Ok, we are going to formation," he said.

Nodding, I waved at him.

Magainda was still asleep until Miles slammed the front door, "What's that?" she asked.

"They are going to formation," I said.

"Do they have to make so much noise?" she asked. "Is it seven o'clock already?"

"I know they did not listen to the six o'clock news this morning," I said.

I got out of my bed and went to Magainda's, "I'm still sleepy," I yawned.

"Me too," she added.

CHAPTER FIFTEEN

Registration

Unlike Kabbaty, the boys went to formation almost every morning and evening in Mokabba as they had eyes on them, though they did not know who exactly was keeping their eyes on them. That morning the place looked good to me.

"Magainda, it smells and looks good outside, come and see," I said, opening the window.

"Yes," Magainda said, stretching, "God is good. Let's go next door to those people."

I wore Magic's jeans and we went. "Look at you; you wear the jeans like Magic."

Magainda had to comment.

"No, it's dragging because it's big and too long for me but he drags his on purpose," I said.

"He says they restrict his legs when they are not dragging," Magainda said

"Ok," I said

We went to the house and knocked on the front door, Ngor Yewa was already up sitting in the living room.

"Morning Ngor Yewa," we said.

"Morning, how are you? Where are the boys?" she asked

"They are gone to formation," I said, keeping my eyes on her big belly.

"The rain was heavy last night, was it not?" she said.

"Yes, but it was good though," Magainda agreed

"Yes, it helped me sleep well," I said.

Samia came out to the living room rubbing her eyes and looking sleepy.

"Morning everyone," she said.

"Morning," we replied.

"Did you sleep well?" Magainda asked.

She nodded.

I turned back to look at Ngor Yewa's stomach, as I was fascinated at how big it had grown.

"Why are you looking at my stomach like that, Memuna?" she asked laughing.

"It's very big. Are you okay?" I asked.

She nodded as she rubbed her stomach. "Yes I'm...I'm fine. I felt it moving last night again," she stammered.

"Memuna, let's go and see what we have to eat this morning. We have a pregnant woman and four men to feed," Magainda said.

We went back to the other house. Samia was still sleepy and I was a bit energetic that morning so I volunteered to get water from the well. We had a drum outside which was half-full with rainwater but the drum needed cleaning.

"The drum is full of water but it's dirty," Ngor Yewa said.

"Yes, Ngor Yewa," Magainda agreed, "we forgot about the drum last night that's why we did not clean it, but it's September anyway so it will rain almost every day so we will clean it today before the next rain."

"I'll clean it," Samia volunteered.

"Okay that's good," Ngor Yewa said, encouraging her to be involved.

"So let the pregnant woman decide on what to eat this morning," Magainda said.

"Let's eat rice and fried fish gravy," Ngor Yewa suggested.

"Okay," Magainda agreed.

"Well I will be eating my cassava again this morning," I said.

"Eww...that cassava again!" Samia screwed up her face at me.

"Hey, I'm talking about the cassava we cooked yesterday," I said, "You think I'll eat some four day old cassava?"

Samia fixed her face, "Oh, ok," Samia said.

"I'm with you on the cassava Memuna," Magainda said. "I can't eat rice for breakfast and dinner. So we will cook the rice for the rice people."

The boys came back just after we finished cooking and eating our breakfast. They came talking and laughing. "Was formation that good?" Magainda asked them.

"Yeah, Magainda," Hawk said.

"Is there anything to eat? I'm famished," Amara said.

Samia told them, "Yes, rice and fried fish."

Magainda gave them their food, they ate and we all went to the veranda to talk. The sun was rising a bit by then. While sitting there talking, PJ and Ghost came to visit. The boys were happy to see their brothers.

"Hey, man how is this town?" Ghost asked.

"Ok, we are trying to get used to it," Hawk said.

They greeted us and came boisterously inside the house.

"Are you hungry man?" Magic asked.

"No, we ate before coming," PJ said.

They all went around town; they came back hours later with some girls and Fanta. When we saw them, Magainda smiled and looked at me. I shrugged. We did not say a word. When they came, the boys said hello but the girls did not want to say hello.

"We are fine. Hello girls, how are you?" Magainda asked, sarcastically, as if they had asked us how we were doing.

They laughed looking all embarrassed and answered back. In Sierra Leone, if you go to someone's house and pretend not to see him or her until they say hello to you it means they are just trying to let you know they think you are very rude. I looked at Magic and turned around, he was embarrassed but he knew he was not going to dare say a word to me at that time.

"Ngor Yewa, do you want to go for a walk?" Magainda asked her.

"That would be a good exercise for me," Ngor Yewa said thoughtfully.

"Memuna let's go. Samia you want to come don't you?" Magainda said.

"Yes, I'm coming," Samia answered.

I went inside to drink some water. Magic followed me to talk to me. When I saw him I used the back door and came back out to join Magainda, Ngor Yewa and my sister. We went to the other side of town where there was a dam. We wanted to sit by the water but the place was an open space and it was risky as the jet could come at any time. So we stood there for a while, walked around some more and then we went back to the house. On our way home we traded some tobacco for some greens. When we got to the house, the girls had left and Magainda and I totally ignored the boys. We sat in the kitchen for a while resting and then we started cooking.

PJ and Ghost knew what was going on; they knew we were upset about what had happened so they came to us in the kitchen to talk to us.

"Memuna what's happening?" PJ asked, cautiously.

"Nothing, I'm just tired," I said. I did not want to tell him how I was feeling, as he was nothing to me.

"Magainda, are you alright?" PJ asked.

"Of course," she answered.

There was a moment of silence.

"Man, we are sorry about what those girls did," Ghost said.

"Well, you boys need to teach them to greet people. They don't have to greet us in the street but when they come here they have to because we clean this place day and night," Magainda retaliated.

"Memuna, sorry," PJ said.

"Sorry about what! I don't care; there is nothing to be sorry about," I retorted.

"We brought those girls. Magic and Twelve-round have nothing to do with them," PJ assured us.

"Wow, be careful before you say the truth. I know that Fanta girl, so don't say Magic has nothing to do with it. Maybe if you say 'Amara' I will believe you. But hey, I really don't care," I said.

I just wanted them to leave me alone because if anyone owed me an apology it was only Magic, not PJ or Ghost. I stayed quiet; they talked for what seemed like twenty minutes and went to see their brothers on the veranda. Ngor Yewa however, had different ideas.

"Those boys are your guests, you shouldn't be angry with them so make them feel welcome," she corrected me.

"They are not my guests," I said.

"Not mine either," Magainda added.

"They are here to visit the boys and Amara and Magic are your boyfriends," Ngor Yewa said.

"Now I feel like a 1960's housewife. It's not easy to be a grown up, you have to put up with a lot of mess," was what I said.

The three of them laughed.

"That's not what I mean," Ngor Yewa said.

"She means you have to be patient," Samia added.

"I feel even older," I said.

Magainda just went on laughing. "Why are you so crazy?" She asked.

"No, honestly you people think what I'm saying is funny but I don't think so. Look at me I'm only still fourteen and I have a boyfriend. At the same time he cheats on me in my face forcing me to be jealous but notwithstanding, I have to do what my great grandma did – be patient," I said.

"True," Ngor Yewa agreed, "I understand what you are saying. But he is not cheating on you in your face."

"If I was home I will still be considered a child but here I'm not," I said, forcing my tears back.

I left them talking in the kitchen. I forced a smile, as I did not want Samia to know I was on my way to the unfinished house. I went and, sitting on the planks in one of the rooms and cried. I was not crying because of what Magic was doing, I was crying because of the thought of losing my childhood when I was still a baby. I cried and sat there till I was sure I could come out without anyone knowing I had been crying. Then I came out. Ngor Yewa, Magainda and Samia were eating guava in the kitchen while waiting for the food to cook.

"Can I have some guava?" I asked.

"It's so sour! There they are; take as many as you want you like sour fruits," Ngor Yewa replied.

I took the guava and washed it and sat on the bench by the hammock which Samia was lying in. Just as I was about to bite the fruit I saw Magic at the door looking at me. He beckoned me but I turned away pretending not to see him. "Memuna, I'm calling you," he said, sounding upset.

I looked at him as if he was someone I had not seen before. Everyone in the kitchen was silent; they looked from me to him.

"Go, Memuna," Ngor Yewa whispered.

I still did not move.

"Memuna, didn't you hear Ngor Yewa?" Samia asked, she sounded scared for me.

I nodded, took a deep breath and stood up to go to him, but at the same time he was walking towards me.

"Can I talk to you?" He asked.

I did not say a word while I stood there looking at him. He gestured me to lead him. "Let's go to the room," he said.

He sat on the bed and gestured me to sit by him, but I shook my head and sat on the chair in front of the bed.

"I know you are angry about seeing Fanta here and I'm sorry about that. I want you to know that there is nothing going on between us," he said.

"Look, I don't know what to believe, but tell Fanta to stay away from here or she should behave herself when she comes to this house. It's not my style to fight for a man and besides I never had a boyfriend before you, but if she wants me to start on her I will gladly do it. After all I might as well accept my new life," I said.

"That's not necessary, just look up to me. I can never cheat on you to your face, God will never forgive me for that and neither will I," he said.

I nodded and thought 'but you will cheat behind my back'. I looked at him and shook my head.

"But warn them to show some respect when they come here or they stay away," I said.

He nodded and watched me walk out.

That evening, after dinner, we talked for a while then everyone went to bed. The following morning it rained. We managed to cook dinner in the morning and spent the rest of the day indoors. Ngor Yewa and Samia came over to be with us at the other house. Ngor Yewa lay in my bed and Samia lay in her bed in our room. The boys were busy cleaning their guns and making noise in the living room while Magainda and I lay in her bed talking to Samia and Ngor Yewa. We talked till they fell asleep. Magainda and I went out to the living room to the boys as the rain had ceased for a while.

"I thought you two were sleeping," Amara said.

"How can we sleep when you people keep making so much noise?" Magainda asked.

I sat next to Magic to see what he was doing. "You want to learn?" he asked

"No. I don't like guns," I said. "I just want to sit by you."

"Oh. I better go and find someone to sit by me," Hawk teased, making everyone in the living room laugh.

He went out and tested his gun. I was frightened when I heard the firing.

"Don't be scared it's hawk, he's trying his gun," Magainda said.

"I need some more oil," Hawk said walking back in.

He poured some more engine oil into his gun and rushed out. "Well I'll be back soon. I'm going to find someone to sit by me," he said joking as he was going to visit his friends.

"Ok, man," his brothers said.

Miles left too just after cleaning his gun. PJ and Ghost sat around smoking and laughing. After cleaning their guns, Ghost and PJ went for a walk. Magic took me to his room to talk.

Two days later Ghost and PJ left after breakfast back to Kabbaty. Everyone was in the house eating boiled peanuts in the shell. I felt the urge to be alone so I snuck out and climbed the mango tree in front of the house. Once again they started looking for me. Magainda saw me in the tree but I told her to keep quiet. She told them that I was a big girl and they should not worry, I would be alright. Samia was getting a bit upset but Magainda took her in and talked to her. Magic was upset.

"She is going to be in trouble with me for pulling these disappearing acts," he said.

But I was in the tree looking at them on the veranda. He stood and put one of his feet on the banister with his hands in his pockets. Everyone else was eating peanuts but him he stopped because of me. I sat there for an hour then I climbed down the tree. They all laughed when they saw me climbing down. Magic could not help but laugh even though he was upset with me.

"I thought we talked about not climbing trees?" he said.

Smiling, I shrugged and said "I like doing it," I said, making everyone laugh.

"You are a boy, Memuna" Hawk said.

"Yes RUF need strong women," Amara added.

"Sorry I made you all look for me. Except Magainda, she knew I was in the tree," I said.

"You better stop climbing trees, the day you will climb a tree and meet a snake...then you will know," Ngor Yewa said.

I laughed and started eating peanuts.

Magic came to sleep in my room again. He would not let me sleep because he was not sleepy. He would open my eyes with his fingers when I closed them.

"If you don't leave my eye lids alone I'll bite you," I said.

"Look at your eyes they shine in the dark," he said.

"Magic please, I want to sleep. I'm tired," I said.

"You see, I told you not to climb a tree, that's why you are tired," he said

"No, that's not why; I've been climbing trees since I was ten so this won't make me tired. I'm just tired" I said.

"What did you do today?" he asked.

"Nothing but I'm human. So let's sleep now," I said.

"Ok. But," he said

"But nothing!" I interrupted.

"But can I have a kiss?" he asked.

I kissed him and turned to the wall so he would not start having ideas. I slept and did not wake up till I felt Magic's cold hand on my cheek. When I opened my eyes he was looking at me smiling.

"It's day break," he said.

I nodded. "It's raining. Why are your hands so cold?" I asked.

"I went outside. I don't think you girls will be able to use the kitchen today if the rain continues," he said.

"It's not a problem to me; I can spend the rest of the day in bed and eat gari (West African snack)."

I took my head off the pillow and rested it on his leg. "Are my eyes swollen?" I asked.

He looked into my face and shook his head.

The rain ceased later that afternoon and we all went to the kitchen and quickly cooked. We ate and went to bed early. The next morning was beautiful. The sun was calm and cool; Magainda suggested we cook dinner in the early afternoon as we could use the day for better things and so we did. Magainda and I ate and left while Samia and Ngor Yewa took a siesta. We went up town to Mariatu Two-Five's house, just to pick on those girls.

"Hello Memuna and Magainda, how have you girls been?" Mariatu asked.

"Fine, we were just passing by so we decided to come and see you since it's been too long," Magainda said.

The girls, they looked at us in disgust but made sure they were out of our way. "Mariatu how is Two-five?" I asked.

"I think he is fine; he is gone to Africa's Ground. Why, do you want to see him?" she said.

"No, I just want to know how he's doing."

"Well Mariatu, we will see you some other time," Magainda said.

We went the other side of town and saw Kekeh, Lt. Universe's bodyguard. We spoke to each other since he was very fond of me too. At times he called me little sister. "Memuna, can I talk to Magainda please?" he asked.

I nodded and excused them to talk for what seemed like half an hour and then we left. I wanted to know what was going on but I did not ask. "I know what you are thinking," Magainda spoke first.

"I'm not thinking," I replied.

"Liar! I was afraid to tell you but Kekeh and I started going out three days before we left Kabbaty," she said.

I was shocked; I did not know what to say. "What…wait did I hear you right? What did you say?" I asked.

"What? is it bad?" she asked.

"No, Kekeh is a nice guy. But aren't you scared?" I asked.

She shook her head. "It's RUF Memuna I don't care, maybe this war is going to last till I have my grandchildren," she said.

I laughed and walked four steps ahead and turned towards her. "You are a woman, Magainda," I said, "so tell me why you were afraid to tell me."

She shrugged. "I was not exactly afraid to tell you…I just did not know how to tell you," she said.

"Well I know now," I said.

"Kekeh is very fond of you, you know," she said.

"I know and I think he is a nice person," I told her.

We walked laughing, I didn't know why but I was happy for her. When we got home, the guys asked us why we were so happy.

"Although this is RUF, laughter is still contagious. We saw someone laughing so we got started," I said.

Magainda laughed even harder. We went to the room and fell on the bed laughing; the noise was so much in the house. Samia and Ngor Yewa came to ask what was going on.

"We went to those girls and we left them upset. We pretended as if they were invisible," Magainda said.

"You two shouldn't go around picking fuss," Ngor Yewa said.

"We did not pick any fuss Ngor Yewa; we went to Mariatu's house not Fanta's house as she has no house to talk for," I commented.

While in the room talking, "listen I can hear girls outside," Samia said "maybe they are here to fight you two."

We listened; they were laughing and screaming over their lungs. "I don't think so," I said.

"This won't suit them, over my dead body," Magainda said.

She grabbed me by the hand and we went to the veranda. The girls had brought two big calabashes full of shelled boiled peanuts. The boys had already started eating the peanuts.

"Girls, you are making noise in our house, would you keep it down?" Magainda said.

They looked at us reluctantly. Fanta said "sorry" with a bit of an attitude.

"So where are these peanuts from?" Magainda asked.

"We brought them," one of them said.

I did not wait for her to finish her sentence; I threw one of the calabashes out in the yard. Indignant one of them yelled at me, "What was that you just did," one of them asked.

"Ask my arse," I replied in Krio.

She rushed towards me. Magainda threw the other calabash in the yard and rushed to stand between the girl and myself.

"Pass through me," she challenged.

I ran and stood on the banister to confront the other girls.

"We do not ever want to see you girls here again. Fanta, if you have a problem with Magic not wanting you anymore be a woman and come to me alone. Leave your friends out of it. Don't bring your battalion here to turn this house into a whorehouse," I yelled at her.

"He wants me...he wants me," Fanta screamed.

"I can see that. You mean he is using you. That's what you mean Fanta because if he really wanted you then, by now, you are here in this house, living with us," I screamed back at her.

Magic pulled me into the house "I don't want to see you out there," he demanded.

"I don't need to go there - I've already done what I wanted to do," I screamed at him.

He looked at me and walked out slamming the door behind him. I smiled and shook my head.

'I don't blame you,' I said to myself, 'it is because I only talk and don't take action that's why. Now I've begun taking action, I'll carry on for as long as I'm here.'

Amara and Hawk told the girls to leave. Magainda, Samia and Ngor Yewa came to the room to me and we sat together laughing. That night, after eating dinner and before we all went to bed, the boys called us together to apologise.

"I'm sorry Magainda, Memuna, Ngor Yewa and Samia. I like one of the girls but I'm not serious with her yet that's why I haven't introduced her to you. I will, however, bring her one day soon," Hawk said.

We nodded and told him to bring her as soon as possible. Magic and Amara apologised that the situation came this far; they promised it wouldn't happen again.

The town was full of strange faces and some rebels were abandoning their assignment to roam around Mokabba. One morning the MPs summoned everyone to the town hall, stressing they will bulldoze anyone staying home without a good enough reason.

They started with the women and rangers. I was scared. I did not know what to say as I was not allowed to lie about being Lansana's sister because as far as they were concerned, I had no reason living with Lansana at that age. I was supposed to be with my man. So we talked about it before going to the town hall. Everyone, including Magic, wanted me to say I was his girlfriend but we were afraid Lansana would see the document Magic had signed to confirm my statement. Because of that we all concurred for me to say I was Lansana's girlfriend and considering Samia, she was not old enough to have a boyfriend. Ngor Yewa was the problem as no-one knew where the father of her baby was but we sorted it out. We had to. If we did not belong to someone they would have taken us away and given us out to other men.

When we got to the town hall it was full and noisy. Standing there all I thought of was the jet. When they called Magainda, Amara went with her and they wrote and made her sign. Then they called Samia and Hawk went with her. He told them she was only twelve and she was in our care as we are her sisters. So they wrote her name and Hawk signed for her. They called Ngor Yewa and all the boys went they spent half an hour talking. The MPs wanted to send her out of Mokabba not mindful of where she went just as long as she was out of Mokabba. So the boys told them that they wouldn't let her go like that. They insisted she should stay till Lansana came back, but the MPs gave her four days to leave town. She cried. We put our arms around her and told her she would be okay.

"You are supposed to go and have the baby in Mattru Jung anyway, so don't cry," Magainda said.

"But I did not want to leave like this," she cried.

We all cried for her. They finally called my name. When we went to the table they asked me what I was doing in Mokabba.

"I'm here because Eagle is here," I said.

"Who is Bra Eagle to you?" one of the MPs asked, sitting behind a table wearing an army jacket and an old red beret on his head and looking very serious.

I never thought I would hear myself say it but I did. "He is my man," I said, trying not to sound reluctant.

I signed and we left crying for Ngor Yewa. "Memuna, you see what I was telling you? You have to have a man in this nasty place," Magainda said.

When we got home Ngor Yewa wouldn't stop crying. "It's okay you are going to Naffie but we are still together," Magainda tried to comfort her.

"Old ma'am Naffie will be happy to have you. You two can do your pregnant women thing together," Amara said. Ngor Yewa smiled slightly.

"Why are they doing this? She is a pregnant woman, she has no assignment," I asked.

"I don't understand either; maybe the order came from Zogoda," Amara replied.

We made the most of the four days Ngor Yewa had with us. When it was time for her to leave, the news got to Mattru Jung and Naffie sent Salifu to come for Ngor Yewa. It was on a sunny afternoon when we took her to the junction where she was to board the pickup. We stood there till the pickup took off. From that night on Samia slept with me in our room.

The house was quiet as we all missed Ngor Yewa. Magainda was a bit changed she became quite distant. Four days later we ran out of food. Magainda and I were in the bed sleeping when Samia got up and went to the kitchen; she cooked coco yam leaves and cassava. She came to the room and woke us up to eat. She brought some for us to taste. We did and it was not really good but we thanked her for the initiative. Miles went to the kitchen to eat some of the food. When he tasted the food he spat it out.

"Fuck! You bastard! you just spoilt good food. The food tastes like medicine," he roared.

He reached out to slap Samia across the face but she was fast enough to dodge and ran off. He chased her, swearing at our mother.

"Miles! You don't swear at my mother and leave my sister alone, she is not your cook! She was just trying to make something for everyone to eat," I yelled.

Samia ran into Hawk's room screaming. I went to Magic and told him to tell Miles to leave my sister alone and he must also stop swearing at her. He looked at me. "What?" Magic asked.

"Miles is running after Samia and swearing at our mother," I said.

We went outside and met him and Hawk.

"Miles you don't respect women. If you dare lay a hand on Samia I'll send you to the ambush." Hawk reprimanded him, angry at Miles.

"The three of you are biased! just because I'm not Mende, you treat me like shit," Miles complained.

"Don't blame it on bias; you are a very rude guy," Amara said.

Hawk got even more angry and sent Miles to the ambush.

Two days later we still did not have food. The boys traded some tobacco for some wild yam but that was not enough. So Magainda sent Samia and me to Ndogbohun. I was upset. I did not want to go because I thought we were too young to go in the bush on our own. But there was nothing I could do. Samia and I walked the long distance about twelve miles, to Ndogbohun. At times we got lost because I did not know the way there from Mokabba. Samia and I would sit in the path and cry and start walking again. We finally found the way but later we went the wrong way again and got into a huge swamp. We were fortunate to find some men there who helped us out and told us how to get to Ndogbohun. By the time we got there anger boiled in me. The people in the town were happy to see us as usual. We got what we could carry and in the morning, took off back to Mokabba.

When we finally got to Mokabba we were both angry, I bathed and didn't bother to eat. Hawk had toothache. I went in his room to talk to him. I found him crying; I gave him a cup of salty hot water for him to hold in his mouth. He did that for close to an hour and he fell asleep. But I was still angry, I felt that my litter sister and I were taken advantage of being sent to look for food. I asked Samia if she was feeling ok and then I went to bed.

Samia and Magainda went for a walk and I lay in the kitchen hammock. "Where is everyone?" Hawk asked.

"Samia and Magainda have gone for a walk around town and I don't know where Amara and Magic are," I replied.

"Okay. Hey, Memuna can you please help me?" he said.

"With what?" I asked.

"With my medicine," he said.

I got out of the hammock and took the plastic bag from him.

"What's this?" I asked.

"This is the only medicine I can find to soothe the pain," Hawk said. "I got it from one old lady. She told me it was good for toothache."

"So which tree are these roots from?" I asked.

He shrugged.

"Okay, what am I supposed to do with them now?" I asked

"The old lady told me to scrape the roots, wash them and boil them and I will retain the brew in my mouth," he said.

He sat with me in the kitchen with his swollen jaw. "Are you feeling a bit better?" I asked.

He nodded, trying to force a smile. I smiled and emptied the roots in a big bowl. I scraped the roots. The last one was long so I tried to cut it in two halves suddenly the knife slipped into my left wrist leaving a deep long cut. Dropping the knife I squeezed my wrist, adding pressure to stop the bleeding.

"What's wrong," Hawk asked forgetting his tooth.

"I...I cut myself but don't worry it's not serious," I said.

"Let me see," he said "I'm very sorry."

I showed him my hand but did not let him touch it. "Leave it, I'll do the rest," he suggested.

"No. You are sick. It's all scraped, I just have to wash them and put them on the fire so don't worry I'll finish it," I said.

There was silence for a long time in the kitchen as I was in a lot of pain. I could feel my left arm getting weak but I did not say anything. Luckily I did not bleed as much as we both thought I would, but it was really painful – I felt the pain through my body but Hawk, Magic and Amara were good to us and they protected us and he was sorry that I was hurt and I did it because I was helping him.

"Samia, I can see you are sad, especially with Ngor Yewa gone. You've changed," Hawk said.

I did not say anything.

"Don't worry, things will be okay one day," Hawk said. "We get tired of the whole mess too but we just hope it will end soon."

I looked at him but did not say anything. I was deeply sad for all of us, including them. I washed the roots, put them in a pot and set the pot on the fire. Soon the others noisily joined us in the kitchen. Still in pain, I left them and went to the room. I was scared my wrist was changing colour but I did not tell anyone. Even now I don't understand why I did not want to tell anyone because usually I never hide my pains. I grew weaker as my wrist kept bleeding. Reaching underneath Magainda's bed for the little first aid box, I took out some bandages, I wrapped my wrist but it still went on bleeding. I was laying in Magainda's bed crying as I thought I was going to die, when Magainda walked into the room. "Why are you crying Memuna? Are you okay?"

Weakly, shaking my head I did not look at her but stared straight at the wall. She sat on the bed next to me.

"Did anyone do something wrong to you?"

I shook my head and showed her my wrist.

Shocked, her questions came tense and frightened, "What happened? Your wrist is swollen."

I cried, "I was trying to cut Hawk's medicine into half when I accidentally cut my wrist."

Magainda held my wrist and loosened the bandage.

"It's swollen and still bleeding. Let's see."

I nodded. "It's so painful."

"So you would have sat here and bled to death if I hadn't come into this room," Magainda said. "What's happening to you? You are changed nowadays."

"I don't know why I could not tell you."

"Okay. Have you had a bath?" Magainda asked.

"Why?"

"Because I want to dress your wound and I don't want you to wet it."

I quietly replied, "Yes I have,"

She cleaned the wound with disinfectant and bandaged it.

"The cut is not big it's just deep so you will be fine."

I nodded and thanked her. "I'm a bit sleepy and my arm is weak so I'll go to bed now."

"Okay," she said. "Tell me if it's still bleeding."

She went to the others in the kitchen. I could hear them laughing and talking. After a while Amara asked for me. Magainda told him what had happened.

"What?" Magic asked. "What is she doing in the room now?"

"She is tired so she is resting," Magainda answered.

Hawk felt guilty so he came to the room to me.

"Memuna, Memuna, I'm sorry for what happened."

"It's not your fault. Don't blame yourself."

"Can I have a look at your hand?" he asked.

I gave him my hand to look at saying, "I think your medicine is ready now. It's better you start using it before the pain starts again," I said.

"True," he said. "I'll go and get a cup of it."

He smiled and walked out of the room.

Samia and Magic came to me in the room.

"Are you feeling better now?" Samia asked, with tears in her eyes, she cried about everything since we left Liberia and didn't have our mother around and that was why I tried to hide things from her; we protected each other.

I nodded.

Magic sat on the bed quietly looking at me. Like Hawk, he looked guilty too. "I'm sorry."

I nodded.

"Sorry that happened," Samia said and she went out.

Magic sat on the bed giving me a questioning look. I looked at him and sat up.

"I'm fine," I said. "I'm just a bit tired."

"Okay. But in case something like this happens again, please tell someone."

Soon they were all in the room. I really wanted to sleep but I could not as the noise was too much.

"Memuna, I am sorry about your hand," Amara said.

I smiled slightly and nodded.

Magainda knew that I wanted to sleep so she took them outside. I fell asleep as soon as they left. Four hours of sleep and I woke in the late afternoon. We all sat on the veranda talking; Hawk, Magic and Amara were talking about their time in Burkina Faso. I had heard them talk about this so many times and really wanted to ask whether they were talking about Burkina Faso - the country.

"Magic, where is Burkina?"

He smiled and rubbed his head. "Burkina is Kailahun."

I was a bit confused. "But on the map Burkina Faso is a country of its own and Kailahun is one of the districts in the eastern province of Sierra Leone," I pointed to them.

Hawk laughed, as he could not talk because of his swollen jaw. He sat on the veranda with a cup of his potion for washing his mouth.

"Memuna, you still have more to learn about RUF. When the rebels came to this country they changed the names of some of the places so people won't know where our bases are. So Burkina is Kailahun district and Libya is Pujehun," Amara said.

I looked at him nodding thinking RUF really has a plan. I wanted to ask where Zogoda was but I did not want to push it.

We talked all evening. Hawk left us and went to sleep as he started feeling feverish. At-the-end came to Mokabba that night. We were all happy to see him.

"Memuna, what's wrong with your hand?" he asked.

"Just a little mistake I made with the kitchen knife," I answered.

The house was noisy they were so happy to see him.

"Man where is sergeant?" he asked.

"He is in the room sleeping, he's got toothache," Amara said.

Before Amara could finish his sentence Hawk was outside.

"It's for you Sir," At-the-end executed the courtesy.

Hawk smiled and hugged his brother.

"Where have you been man?" Hawk asked. "Is there any news from Zogoda?"

"There's rumour that all the officers who went to Zogoda are getting re-assigned. They say Lion is really angry about those civilians, man," At-the-end.

The boys were all happy about the change of assignments. "Yeah! Maybe we will be sent to Freetown Highway," Magic said.

"Yeah man. That will be really good," Amara added.

"If we get sent there we have to get ready for the fighter helicopters," At-the-end said. "I hear ECOMOG is not giving those guys a chance in that place and we all know that the helicopter is worse compared to the jet."

"True but we will be fine," Magic boldly assured the others, as he did not want anyone to ruin his day dream of having fun in RUF's Freetown Highway camp.

That camp was close to Freetown and being there for the rebels, meant they were one stage away from reaching their goal of taking over Freetown which meant that they would have taken charge of the country as well and the thought of this alone, for Magic and most other rebels was the best high.

"At-the-end how is Ngor Yewa and Naffie?" I asked.

"They are fine. Your sisters can't wait to come here."

"Let them stay there," I replied.

"Magainda, anything to eat?" At-the-end asked.

Magainda shook her head. "Sorry At-the-end, we can make something for you if you want."

"No don't worry I'll eat something when I go up town."

Amara, At-the-end and Magic left us with Hawk and went out that night. We knew precisely where they were going; they were going to those girls. I, for one did not care as long as they did not bring them to our house.

Within a few days my wrist was healing. Miles came back from his punishment a week later; he kept away when he came back. He tried his best to have less to do with the boys and us. One shining moonlight night they all went out and left the three of us alone in the house. Magainda had seen Kekeh in the afternoon.

"Memuna, can you please do me a favour?" she asked.

Looking at her I pulled a funny face. "It depends."

"Well, it's a big favour," she said.

"Then try me," I answered her.

"Well, I want you to please take a bucket of warm water to Kekeh for me," Magainda said. "He is not feeling well and he asked me to go to his house to warm some water for him but as you can see I can't. So will you please? Please?"

I took a deep breath. "Magainda you know if I get caught the three of us will be dead. Don't you?" I said.

She nodded.

Samia listened and laughed at us.

"Wow, Mama, wherever you are please be praying for me now," I said making the three of us laugh even harder.

"You are going to dress like someone else. We will cover you from head to toes," Magainda said.

"Do I have to walk like someone else too?" I teased.

"Yeah. That will help," Samia said.

"Hey, we need to do this quick before they come," I said.

Magainda went to the kitchen and brought the water. "Hey, Magainda pour it in a plastic bucket it's lighter. I can't tote that heavy metal bucket on my head up to Kekeh's house or else they will surely catch us," I said.

"Okay lazy Joe," Magainda said.

She poured the water in the plastic bucket and dressed me. She and Samia went with me to the neighbour's house then she set the bucket on my head and they both watched me walk in the street. I looked from one side of the street to another to see if there was anyone looking at me. I tried to change my walking. The street was absolutely empty. I walked faster and got to Kekeh's house. Everyone else was indoors but him, he was sitting on the veranda on the steps waiting for Magainda but I showed up instead. I felt embarrassed for the mischievous trick we played. I gave Kekeh his water and told him why Magainda could not come.

"I'm sorry you are sick. Are you feeling better now?" I asked.

He nodded. "But I still feel a slight headache."

"Magainda says she is sorry she could not make it but she promised to see you tomorrow," I said "I better leave now Kekeh. Sleep well."

I walked back to the house the same way I walked to go. When I got to the back door of our house I listened for the boys' voices but they were still out so I knocked on the door. Magainda opened the door and burst out laughing.

"Are you laughing at me?" I asked. "I swear I never thought I was capable of such mischief."

We both laughed. "Where is Samia?" I asked.

"She is on the veranda watching our backs," Magainda said. "How is he doing?"

"He was disappointed that I went instead of you, but I told him why and I told him you'll see him tomorrow."

"Oh good, thank you very much," she said.

"Yeah now, let's go and sit as if we've been telling each other stories all this time," I suggested.

Samia laughed when she saw me. The boys arrived in what seemed an hour later; Magic kissed me and sat on my lap. "Get off my lap you," I said.

He laughed, "Come let's go," he said.

He took me to his room; we fell on the bed and started kissing. "So why is this?" I asked

"Nothing," he answered. "Do I need a reason to kiss you?"

Before I could say another word he kissed me again. "Let's sleep here tonight," he said.

"I'll think about it,'" I said.

He chuckled. "Don't start playing games again," he said.

"I'm not," I said.

"Well I don't think there is anything to think about," he debated.

"Okay we will sleep here," I said.

The following morning Miles seemed to have gotten over his anger towards us all. We sat in the kitchen, ate and talked; afterwards Magainda, Samia and I had our morning bath.

CHAPTER SIXTEEN

Retreat

A few days later, late in the evening, Lansana and his bodyguards came back. He looked worn out but seemed happy to be back even though he did not bring the news the boys hoped for.

"Good evening Sir," they executed their courtesy.

"Rest gentlemen," he said.

They took his luggage into his room and Magainda offered him water to bathe.

"Memuna, we need to cook something for them to eat," Magainda said.

I nodded.

"I need to talk to you all," Lansana said.

"Now?" Magainda asked.

Lansana nodded. We went to the kitchen and sat outside while we cooked.

"Well guys, thank you very much for taking care of the women," Lansana started.

"They helped too Sir," Amara said.

Lansana smiled. "Well what I want to tell you is that….I've been demoted to sergeant and Lion sent me to Libya," he said.

"What?" Amara exclaimed.

"How can they do that?" Magic asked.

At-the-end was quiet.

"I should be going to Libya in a few days. So I want you all to feel free to choose whether you come with me or be on your own." Determinedly he quietly added, "I'm taking Memuna and her sisters though."

There was an awkward moment of silence and then I knew the boys were going to choose to be on their own. Everyone sat quiet for a while. Magainda and I went to the kitchen to talk while she poured some water into a big bucket for Lansana to bathe. We were both silent for the moment; I did not know where to start from. Magainda took a deep breath.

"So you, Nyalay, Komeh and Samia are going to Libya with Lansana, I will miss you very much."

I looked at her and looked at the sky trying to force my tears back. I took a deep breath and nodded.

"Oh, so you are staying," I said. "Magainda, please plead with Amara and the others to come with us."

This time I could not stop myself from crying.

"Don't cry," Magainda said. "Who knows, maybe things will change and besides Lansana doesn't need this right now! He is just as upset as anyone of us would be."

I wiped my face with the back of my hand and did not say anything. Lansana left us and went to bathe.

"Man, I don't think I want to go to Libya, I'm trying to advance not retreat," Magic commented.

I looked at him and then at Magainda and looked away from all of them.

"I'm very sorry for Bra man, I wish this hadn't happened," Laser said.

"So Laser man, what's your plan?" Amara asked.

"Well, I think I'm going with Bra," Laser replied.

'Well at least some one is loyal,' I thought. The rest of them said they were going to Freetown Highway; they did not want to retreat. I was very upset again that night I was going far away from the district I knew to another district I've only heard of and read about at school. To make things worse, we were going to walk to Pujehun District from Moyamba district about fifty miles away .

I thought, 'What if we fell into an ambush?' And the fact that Lansana was going back to where he had started just because his bodyguards got involved in a massacre. He was not only getting reassigned but also demoted; I thought he needed their support. He went to his room, got dressed and came outside to talk to us.

"Gentlemen, you can decide whatever you want, if you don't want to come with me, I'll understand. No hard feelings," he said.

"Yes sir," they said.

"Memuna, Samia are you ready to go to Mattru Jung tomorrow? Have you packed your things?" he asked.

I looked at him and did not say anything. He looked sad but he was trying to put on a brave face. He did not ask Magainda to pack her things because he knew that Magainda was not coming without Amara, but I could not stay with any man but him.

"Magainda can you please help me pack some clothes?" he asked. "I can't take all because I'm walking, so guys you can take the rest. But I need you to tell me what your decision is before tomorrow."

Magainda and I went to Lansana's room to pack his things. I was numb. I could not think beyond the fact that I was going further away from home, at least Mokabba is in Moyamba district same as Sembehun, so being here I was not far from home when we were in Mokabba or Kabbaty. Pujehun was further South of Sierra Leone and anything could happen. I kept consoling myself with the belief that God will protect my sisters and me because He knew what was going on and He was in control. I burst out crying at the thought; Magainda rushed to the other side of the bed and put her arms around me.

"Sshh, Memuna, everything will be okay, just leave it to God. Don't let Lansana see you like this," she said.

I nodded and wiped my face. Lansana walked into the room and peered intently into my face. He knew I had been crying but did not say anything. He turned to Magainda.

"Magainda I just want at least six pairs of jeans and twelve tops. As for my underwear I'm taking all of them," he said.

Once again he looked at me and walked out. Magic came to the room; he looked at me and smiled.

"We will talk later," he said.

After packing the things we went out to the veranda, Lansana got more support from Samia than he did from anyone. The two of them sat close together talking, she was glad he was back. He was telling her how the journey to Libya was going to be.

"So you mean I'm staying with old ma'am Naffie till the end of the raining season?" Samia asked.

"Yes. You, Nyalay and Komeh are staying with Naffie, Guy and the baby," Lansana replied.

Naffie had given birth to a baby girl two weeks earlier and she could not travel. Besides it was mid-September, rainy season in Sierra Leone. The rivers had swollen bigger than usual. Miserable, I walked away and went to the other house. Minutes later Magainda and the boys came.

"Memuna, can we talk?" Magic asked.

"Yes," was all I could say.

We went to his room. We sat on the bed facing each other. "I'm sorry I don't want to come to Libya. I can't take you away from Lansana so if you want to stay with me tell him you don't want to go," Magic said.

I looked at him for a while. "How can I say that to him?"

"What do you mean?" he asked.

"Well my sisters are going too," I said.

"Okay," he said.

"Why don't you want to come?" I asked.

"No RUF fighter wants to go to that place again. That place was first battalion – Phase 1. It is a dead end. If you run out of tooth paste that's it, you will have to use salt," he said.

"Please come, Magic. Maybe we won't be there for long, anyway," I said trying to change his mind.

"I'll think about it," he said.

"But Lansana wants an answer from you boys before he goes to bed," I had to remind him.

"I know but..." he leaned over and gave me a kiss that felt like good night and goodbye. The thought of it made me cry.

"Don't cry," he said. "It's not the end of our lives."

He wiped my tears and we went outside. He and his brothers discussed the news all night. Miles told Lansana that he could not come with us before everyone. Lansana seemed fine with it; they shook hands and wished each other good luck. Everyone was a bit upset but Samia, at least, seemed fine. She came saying, "Memuna, Bra is calling you. I'm going to bed. Goodnight everyone."

We told her goodnight. I looked at Magic and Magainda and crossed the street. In my thoughts I knew this was coming. I knocked at the door.

"Yes come in," he answered. The lantern was burning low and he was listening to Burning Spear.

"Yes. You sent Samia to call me?" I said.

"Yes," he smiled. "Why do you look so sad? How are you? Did anyone do anything to you while I was away?"

He asked one question after the other.

"I'm fine; no-one did anything to me," I answered.

Nodding he asked, "So did you do something I should know about?"

I looked at him; you are a nasty jealous man. I thought. "Something like what?"

"Anything, just anything," he said.

"No," I answered.

All this time I had been standing talking to him. "Can't you sit or something?" he asked.

"No, I don't want to sit." I shook my head.

"So are you going to stand all night?" He asked.

Then I knew I was going to sleep in his room again. I looked at him and did not say a word. He looked at me and turned to the wall.

"Why were you crying? I can't leave you here. Crying won't make me leave you here. So you better stop crying, because it's not going to help," he said.

I looked at him and thought 'God, why does this have to happen? Is tonight the night that I get pregnant?' I knew that anything could happen to me that night and this was not one of the nights that I took chances and pushed my luck. He was very upset tonight. He was upset with his bodyguards' betrayal and his demotion. As I stood there for a while without saying a word, Lansana seemed so sad and hurt yet in my eyes, he was the worse person I had ever seen. Something in me wanted to say comforting words to him but the thought of him taking us away from our family came to me again. Then I thought, 'why I should be kind to such a person. He took us away from our family and tomorrow he is taking us even further?' Then I frowned and clenched my teeth.

The room was quiet while my mind ran over time. He turned to me and stared at me but did not utter a word. He kept looking about every five minutes.

When he spoke his voice was quiet but cold "Why are you looking at me like that? I know you hate me now for not wanting to leave you here with your little boys but one day you will thank me."

I just looked at him as tears streamed down my cheeks. Shaking my head I kept thinking 'I hate you for better reasons. I hate you for taking my sisters and me from school. I hate you for thinking I'm old enough to have a man when I don't think so. I hate you!' Then I sobbed harder and squatting as I buried my face in my hands.

"What is wrong with you?" he was shaking as he held my arms for me to stand up. "Why are you crying as if I've done something to you? Stop. I can't think when you do that, I get confused. I'm sorry if I said something bad."

I looked at him pleadingly. "Please let us go back home. I need to go to school. I don't want anyone," I cried.

He looked at me and shook his head. "I'm sorry Memuna; it's too late for that now. I promise you, I will protect you and your sisters," he whispered.

Hearing him say those words I wished I was dead; they made me cry even harder. He released my arms slowly and sat on the bed while I stood there and cried.

It was time to start the journey. First we had to go to Mattru Jung to make final arrangements. It was obvious to everyone that I'd spent the night crying. Magic tried to stay away but he could not. Magainda cried each time she looked at me and she gave me a firm hug and told me that we will see each other again by the grace of God. She said she wished she could come with us but she could not because Amara did not want to retreat. That, at least, was what they, including Lansana, called it. The pickup came for us and we said our final goodbyes.

At Mattru Jung, Komeh and Nyalay seemed happy to see us, but all I did was cry. Komeh took me aside. "Why do you look like someone just bereaved?"

"I'm dead Komeh, I am the dead person," I cried. She hugged me tight.

"We've got to stay strong for our little sisters Memuna. The most important thing is we will still be together," she said.

That sounded better; we went inside. I tried to be part of the conversation but I was still screaming inside. Talking in Naffie's room that night, I noticed that she had not started packing yet. I wanted to ask but then I thought to myself, who cares? When it is time to go I'll just grab my sisters and our bags, whoever is ready or not will not be my problem. Then Lansana voice broke through my thoughts. "Memuna, only you and

Sunshine are coming with us. Your sisters are staying with Naffie until we get there and settle in and till rainy season ends. She will take care of them."

Screaming inside, louder than before, I looked at my sisters and cried thinking this could be the last time we see each other.

Suddenly, the room was filled with wailing from the Barnes girls. At that moment I wished I could find our uncle Karimu that very night, so he could follow me or keep an eye on Komeh, Samia and Nyalay. Hurting so much I could not breathe, my face felt hot and I ran out. Then my sisters followed me. We sat in the dark and cried for a while. Samia clung so tightly to me she just wouldn't let go. She and Nyalay were begging me not to go; I told them it was out of my control. When I looked at Samia I could see when we were younger in Liberia, two spoilt little girls who had everything their parents could give them and I shook my head. I put my arms around all three of them. "Nothing will happen to any of us. I will be careful and I want you three to do the same and look after yourselves."

I looked at the two little ones and then at Komeh. "Komeh, try and look for Karimu and tell him what has happened, okay? Promise me that," I said.

"I promise. I will look after them and I want you to know that God will not let us die. We will make it," she cried. When I looked at my little sister and thought of how spoiled she was, she seemed so vulnerable. So did Nyalay she was only nine years old.

We went to bed but did not sleep at all, we prayed and cried all night. In the morning I knew there was nothing I could do and I certainly could not cry forever.

"Komeh, Samia, Nyalay - God will protect us and we will all go home together. Let's stop crying and leave it to God," I tried to encourage them.

"Nyalay and Samia, I want you girls to listen to Komeh and don't give her a hard time; be good. When you see Karimu, don't forget to tell him. Komeh tell him to join Lansana's group or he can stay around until it's time for you to join us. Then you can all come to us," I said.

That afternoon Tiger joined Lansana's group. He made himself one of Lansana's bodyguards as his boss got demoted too. Tricks came with the pickup truck and took us to Sumbuya about twenty miles away, where we were meant to meet Captain Speed for some arrangement since we were all going together. He was very welcoming to me, as Lansana had told him I was his girlfriend, embarrassing me as he said it, CO. Speed had liked Sunshine for a long time so having her there made him happy as well. That did not, however, make me feel any better. Lansana was getting upset so he followed me to the room.

"Memuna, it's time you stop sulking and behaved yourself," he said.

I did not care anymore, for all I cared he could kill me if he wanted to. I looked at him.

"You should be used to this now, Bra. How many people have you snatched from their families?" I asked.

He looked at me, shook his head and went out slamming the door behind him as hard as he could.

The captain had five of his bodyguards in Sumbuya; Scholar, Ur-Pa, King, Kallon and Corporal Moses. Corporal Moses had a girlfriend called Salim and they had a little girl who was around twelve or thirteen years old, dark skinned and very tall and spoiled called Cecilia. Cecilia was captured by Corporal Moses. Salim was pretty and average weight, light skinned like Corporal Moses with pinkish lips and very short hair. But she was not a very friendly person, she was always by Corporal Moses's side. When he sat she sat very close to him and she dragged Cecilia along with her everywhere she went. She cared very much for that little girl never let her out of her sight and was very protective of her like I was of my sisters. Salim was at most 20 years old and Corporal Moses appeared to me in his mid-thirties. He was very mature in the way he spoke and carried himself. He mostly spent time mingling with Lansana and CO. Speed. Sunshine and I did not like Salim at first. Sunshine introduced me to them and she told me Kallon was her cousin.

Two hours later Kallon asked me out. I told him what I told Lansana, "I am not interested in any man, I am too young."

When he left, Scholar came to me and asked me out too and I told him the same thing. He was persistent; he would not take no for an answer. He sat close to me on the bench almost on my lap, so I moved away. We talked then I went and bathed from a bucket and went to the room they assigned to us. Sunshine joined me after she bathed. "Memuna, it's okay. Don't sit and cry every minute. I know you miss your sisters but leave it to God. Just think of the other girls who don't have any family member here and, at the same time, they get beaten by their men every day. I'm here, I will be here for you; we are sisters now. I'm not replacing the others but we are going to live together until God's decision. Maybe till the end of the war," she said.

I looked at her and nodded thinking 'she makes a lots of sense.'

Sumbuya was not the place I wanted to be but it was a beautiful town on the premise that one looked beyond the bombed houses and burnt vehicles. Half of the town was quiet and bushy because it was abandoned. We had been in town for four days. One sunny day Sunshine and I were tired of sitting in the house all day so we decided to go for a walk around town. I was a bit scared of going around because I did not want to get harassed. She told me not to be afraid because I was walking with her and she knew almost all the rebels. We went down a very quiet street with beautifully fenced houses. In West Africa the fences around the homes are higher than the houses. Some of the fences had been broken down. Looking at the houses I remembered something I overheard my aunties talk about.

"Hey, you know. I once heard my aunties saying my uncle's wife came from this town. Maybe one of these houses belonged to her family, I whispered to Sunshine as I was afraid there might be an ambush somewhere.

"Really?" she replied, "well let's look for her house," Sunshine said.

She looked at me smiling. I was usually a fearless person but next to her I felt like an amateur.

"I can see that you are scared," she said. "Why? In RUF only the fearless survive. If people see that you are always scared they pick on you. So even if you are scared don't let it be demonstrative, be like me. I only show my fear when Doodoo-bird comes," she said. When she said that, I thought of school.

"So how are we going to look for my Auntie's house?" I asked.

"Well, we will start by going into the houses and searching for pictures and letters," she instructed. "If we don't find anything and you still want to find the house, we will go around to see if we still have some of the people who used to live here in Sumbuya."

We looked into five deserted houses with expensive furniture that had been destroyed but we found nothing. It became fun reading other people's letters and diaries. The sixth house was huge with a nicely paved backyard with a little boys' quarters (a little apartment in the backyard which almost every West African house has for the older boys). It seemed everyone in the house was educated or at least getting an education. We went into the master bedroom, the bed had been taken away. Some of the paintings on the wall in the living room had been stolen. There were clothing and books (from primary school to high school) everywhere.

"It seems this family wished they could have put all their belongings in a safe place," Sunshine said, thoughtfully.

"Yes," I replied in the same tone thinking about my home and my books.

Sunshine found a huge photo album on the floor of the living room. She made herself comfortable on a little stool while I read letters. Some love letters, some invites, apology, obituary and some letters of appreciation but I never found anything that said my uncle's wife's name. So we went to the boys' quarters. It was typical boys' quarters with calendars of naked girls on the wall and a few pictures of two boys and their girlfriends. The poses on the pictures told us the relationship they had. There were jeans, t-shirts, shoes and underwear on the floor and the beds.

"I bet you, some of the young people of this family are with us in RUF. It seems they are some of the people who waited till the last minute to flee or at least tried to flee," Sunshine commented.

I was so lost in my thoughts that I could not say a word so I just nodded in reply. All I could see or think of was when we were attacked, how we tried to escape and got captured. I felt sorry for the family who owned that house.

We grew tired of searching in vain and the sun had begun to set. We decided to stop the search for the day and go back to our house. As we stepped out of the boys' quarters we saw a huge black snake wrapped up on the paved ground in the backyard. We ran and slammed the front door behind us and made no stop till we were at least five blocks away.

"Ok, that house is off the search list," Sunshine said panting. I nodded back, trying to catch my breath.

At night, after Lansana and the boys had talked about what route we were going to take to go to Libya, we told them about our day and they laughed at us when we got to the snake issue. Throughout the rest of the conversation I was there but my soul was not there, their voices were like noise in my ears. I sat with them looking straight ahead of me in the dark, thinking of my sisters, wondering over where they were taking me to and if we were ever going to see each other again.

I felt a hand on my shoulder tapping and shaking me slightly. It was Laser; he said Lansana wanted to see me. As if I was in a trance, I turned to him looking at him as if he was someone I had not seen before. 'Lansana, I'm not in the mood for his little conversation. They do me no good.' I thought to myself.

He was lying on the bed listening to Bob Marley. Laser closed the door behind me after I entered the room. "Yes, Laser said you wanted to see me?" I said, trying to fight back tears. He nodded and sat up in bed and looked at me for a moment.

"I just wanted to know how you are getting on," he said. "You don't look too good."

Looking at him I felt nothing but hatred. "Who would feel or look good in my situation?" I cried. "I want to see my sisters."

"I told you," he said, "they will come and meet us in Libya soon. It's just because of the rainy season and Naffie just had a baby and Samia and Nyalay are too young to survive the rivers."

"Well you should have thought of that before taking us from our family," I said firmly. I was not afraid of Lansana anymore.

I thought, since he thought I was old enough to be his girlfriend, there was no need for me to be afraid to speak my mind to him.

He got out of the bed and came to me standing by the chair in the corner. "Look, I'm very sorry about everything," he said. "Please stop crying, I get confused when you cry."

"I can only stop crying if you let us go back to our family," I said.

"Well that can't happen tonight," he said.

I was so angry; I knew that it would not happen even the next night. I looked at him in disgust.

"But can you bring them here so we can at least be together?" I asked. I was trying to be a bit calmer this time.

"I'll ask CO. Speed if that is possible. If it is not, then I will make sure they join us as soon as possible," he said. "Don't you want to sit down?"

I felt as if I was lost; we stared at each other as I slowly sat myself in the chair. There was only a short moment of silence in the room.

"Memuna, I'm very sorry about everything. no-one has made me feel so guilty as much as you have and I don't have any real answer to the questions you ask," he said, with his head down. "I'm very sorry."

I remained silent. I was wondering why he was so calm and I was so angry but then I answered my own question. He was the cause of my misery. Then I asked myself another question. Do the other girls have the same opportunity to get angry and say their feelings to the person who captured them and not get beaten up? As much as I hated to admit it, I, more than anyone else knew the answer that I was lucky that it was Lansana who captured me. I was so lost in my thoughts that I did not hear the rest of what he said.

"Memuna, please say something," he spoke holding and shaking my hand as I looked at him.

"You don't want me to say anything because all I have to say is that I want to go home and I want to go to school. What are my sisters and I doing here? We are of no help to this war. We are just here wasting time and who knows anything could happen to us."

He looked at me and wiped my tears with his hands. "I really like you Memuna," he said quietly. Almost shyly. "Don't," I interrupted, waving my hand. "Can I go now?" I did not want to hear any more of what he had to say.

"Ok," he said. I was surprised he let me go.

Four days before we were due to leave Sumbuya; there was an attack on two villages not far away from us. Some of us were ready to run for dear life and others were ready to fight. Some of the wounded fighters (rebels) from the villages were brought to Sumbuya for treatment. Two days after that Doodoo-bird came. RUF had attacked a town close to Bo. King, Scholar and Ur-Pa went on a mission in a very small group. The jet flew around Sumbuya three times and it flew very low. We were in the kitchen when it came. It was so low that we heard it before it got to our neighbourhood so myself, Sunshine and all the other women in the kitchen quickly put the fire out so that it won't see the smoke and bomb us. Together we ran into the house as the bush was too far off. The yard we lived in had about three more adjoined apartments in the backyard, we lived in the main house. The apartments in the backyard were occupied by other rebels and their girlfriends. We did not really mingle with them but Sunshine, Salim and myself shared the outdoor kitchen with them. All the girls in the house were crying. I was crying too but at the same time saying my last prayer. I knew the death was not going to be painful because the rocket was going to cut us into little pieces in a matter of seconds. Angry and scared Sunshine wished she could bury herself right there.

"I wish someone could just gun the nasty thing down with a missile," she whispered.

"Sunshine, if anyone is going to try they better not miss, because we will all become history and dust,' Salim said. While they talked, I was busy trying to remember the difference between The Lord's Prayer and Psalm 23. So confused and scared I tried to read Psalm 23 (as my last prayer) but I kept saying the Lord's Prayer instead.

Ten minutes later, when the whole ordeal was over we remained in the house for at least another fifteen minutes before coming out. The jet had the habit of hanging in the sky soundless, fooling the rebels to think it was gone. Then the fighters would come out and are bombed. This happened twice before and everyone remembered. We came out from our hiding place looking very shocked and worn out.

That night and the next day were filled with more frightening moments with the jet and helicopter making frequent trips over the town. The boys came back from their little mission with a boy about fourteen years old. He was so afraid of all of us that he prayed in Arabic almost every minute. His name was Lamine but we called him Kamor sometimes (kamor is Mende for teacher but it's mainly used to refer to Arabic teachers among Mende people). The boys teased him every day especially Salifu, who, at the same time tried to make Lamine feel comfortable; as did Sunshine and I. Lamine was particularly afraid of Lansana; I don't know why.

Two days later, at 4am, it was time to eat something and depart Sumbuya on foot. I told Lansana that it was too early for me to eat and that I did not want to go that far away from my sisters. He was not ready to put up with me that morning. He seemed too busy.

"Memuna, please don't make me angry with you this morning. I don't have time to go over this again just pack your things let's go," he demanded. "If you want to be stupid and say you won't eat, that would be your problem, because we will spend the whole day walking until we find a safe place to rest."

"You should be ready to talk to me whenever I want to talk because you brought me here," I snapped back at him.

Sunshine saw that the argument was getting heated so she left us in the room.

"We will talk about this when we get to Libya, so just pack your things. I don't want to get angry with you!"

He walked out of the room slamming the door so hard behind him that the clock on the wall shook. I started crying knowing I better not say anything more or I'll get hit.

I sat on the bed with my head in my hands and cried. The door opened, I looked up to see if it was Lansana but it was Sunshine .

"Memuna, don't cry. It's ok," she said. "Come out. Let's eat something before the others are ready."

I looked up at her feeling very sad and resentful with tears streaming down my cheeks. She kept telling me it was ok but nothing felt ok to me.

"What's there to eat? I don't like eating late at night and early in the morning," I said.

"Well in times like these you have to make lots of changes. We are in a war: you eat when you have the food and when you have the chance to eat."

I looked at her as if I had not seen her before. "So what's there to eat?" I asked.

"Rice," she answered.

"It is too early in the morning to eat rice! And am I supposed to get used to that?" I cried.

"Well, I'm sorry but you have to eat something now because we will be doing a lot of walking today. Libya is not around the corner it's all the way on the other side of the country - Pujehun district." This time she was firm instead of comforting.

"Ok, let's go," I said. I brushed my teeth half asleep. Lamine and Salifu had already dressed and were ready. The boys were laughing at me.

"Memuna let me eat your rice for you, I'll tote you when you feel tired and hungry," Salifu teased, making everyone laugh.

"Shut up Salifu. You can't even carry Guy, what makes you think you can carry me?" I retorted annoyed.

Everyone laughed at him even harder. Sunshine and I ate the rice as fast as we could and had a cold bath from two big buckets to wake us up.

It was a cold morning in September, getting to the end of the rainy season. We came out of the bathroom shivering. The boys were still in the backyard talking, some brushing their teeth; others combing their hair while some were tying their shoelaces.

"Hey drop those towels," yelled Tiger.

"Don't let Bra hear you say that to Memuna," Laser warned and they all laughed.

We both ignored them the best way we could, went into the room and got dressed in a hurry, as Salim and her Cecilia were ready and waiting for us. Sunshine, Salim and I said goodbye to our neighbours and set off.

We walked a day and a half non-stop. We only stopped when we arrived in a little deserted village with about twenty houses covered in tall elephant grass. The grass had grown over the village. It had been attacked a long time ago. Some of the boys in our convoy had been on that mission to attack the village because the villagers had soldiers living there to protect them. Even those boys could not recognise the village either.

"Where the fuck is this?" Scholar asked as we walked through the coffee and cacao farm.

"This place looks familiar," Kallon said.

We walked into an old camp on the edge of the river. Bullet shells were strewn on the ground. "Hey, remember this place, Ur-Pa?" King asked sounding excited.

"Yes," Ur-Pa answered, "it was a tough one."

"Oh…yes this is where we captured that pretty girl and we did not know she was a member of the Sierra Leonean Army until my man Alasan captured that little boy who told us who she was," Kallon said.

They kept on reminiscing till Lansana called them to make arrangements for us to cross the river. Being a branch of the Wa-a njai (Mende for bring water) River, it was full and strong. We had walked a quarter of the journey and we were somewhere between Bo and Pujehun district. The Wa-a njai River is the Pujehun river and being at one of its branches meant we were closer to Pujehun district more than we were to Bo district.

It was a little sunny but the sun was mild making me assume it was around 3pm. I wanted to ask Lansana a question but I thought the timing was not right. He was too busy ordering and helping to make two rafts for us to cross.

Salim, Cecilia, Sunshine and I sat on tree branches in the muddy camp watching the men make the rafts. I was not the least at ease as my legs were itchy from walking in the grass, I was afraid, tired and there were three skeletons lying about six feet away from where we sat.

Lansana and the boys were a bit nervous too. They did not want us to spend the night in the old camp, as there was a possibility we could get attacked as well as rain. The attack was the one thing that worried him most as we were by the river. We, the girls, were the cause of worry; if they were on their own they did not care.

They cut down a few trees and got some thick forest vines to tie the rafts. After hours of hard work they finally completed their work. By then I was famished because I did not eat so much of the rice that morning but I did not say a word of it to any one, not even Lansana.

Lansana sent the reinforcement team to cross the river on the rafts first taking up position as soon as they crossed. He was in the advance team too but he wanted us girls to be safe before he crossed. When it was our turn to cross on the raft I was so frightened it became hard for me to breathe.

"I can't do it," I said to him.

"Memuna please," Lansana said. "We need to get out of this place as soon as possible."

"Well, come with us," I said. Despite everything Lansana was our guardian.

He got on the raft with Sunshine, Laser and myself. I was still frightened but I felt a little better. He told me it would be fine and that nothing would happen so I clung to his hand. When we finally got to the other side I took a deep breath.

The village we arrived in on the riverbank was empty; we did not see even a chicken but it was clean and open. Walking further up town we saw footprints and suddenly the advance team took their positions. This time I too was ready for anything. No-one knew whom those prints belonged to and no-one knew which direction they were heading now. Nowhere in this town was safe for us. Everyone was tense. They sat us four girls somewhere and some of them followed the footprints. Lansana went with them and I discovered I was very frightened for him. 'God please don't let something happen to anyone especially Lansana. He is our parent here, my sisters and I. Otherwise the boys will have a big feast with us,' I thought.

"Keep your guard gentlemen, we don't know who we are facing," Lansana ordered the advance team.

Five minutes later we heard the loud sound of a single barrel gun followed by the sharp fire of the AK in response. People were calling out to each other in Mende "that the rebels are here, the rebels are here," as they ran off. The advance team came back telling us that it was only a few men who seemed to be looking for food. One of them got shot by Scholar but did not get killed.

We could not spend the night in this village so we ate some oranges and mangoes, had a bit of rest and set off in search for a safer place for a longer rest. This time my feet were painful and my legs were tired but I did not complain.

We walked another maybe ten miles and arrived in another village. We found women, old and young, children and some old men. The night was cool, calm and very dark. It was dinnertime. Oil lanterns and candles had been lit and some of the villagers sat in their huts to have dinner while others sat in the palaver hut (a gazebo) to eat enjoying the fresh air. When the villagers saw us they wanted to flee but it was too late. The advance team had already surrounded the little village. One of the village women came to the four of us girls as we stood in a palaver hut watching the drama around us. She came to us with her toddler clung to her chest pleading for their own lives as well as everyone in the village.

"Oh please don't kill us," she wailed. "This is our village and some of us could not flee sooner. Please think of my baby and besides I look after my parents, they are very old and my father is very sick."

When she said this I looked at Sunshine and forced a smiled. The lie about her parents was very common because everyone who thought they were going to get killed or captured used that line. We all knew the lie but even so it did not always convince the rebels from doing what they wanted to do. She carried on begging but we just stood there staring at her.

"Hey," Sunshine said laying a hand on the woman's shoulder, "Relax, we are not here to hurt anyone. We are going home and we won't hurt anyone as long as no-one shoots at us first, so stop crying and stop begging."

All this time Sunshine was talking to her all she did was nod frantically. She was so terrified her eyes wide open.

"Hey, Sis," Laser interrupted patting the woman on her shoulder giving her the fright of her life, "do you have some food in your house that we can eat? We are very hungry. If you give us some food, we will be out of your village before you know it."

"Yes, I have some food in the hut. Follow me," she said.

There was a tray of something that I had never seen before on a mat on the floor served with some stew on it. It was their dinner. "You can have that," she pointed to the food.

"Are you sure that food is not poisoned?" Salim asked.

"No, no it's not poisoned. It's the food we were going to eat tonight but it's fine you can eat it," she said nodding and shaking her head frantically.

I waited for Sunshine to put some in her mouth first then I did and I felt like spitting it out. The stew was tasteless and flavourless and above all I did not know what I had put in my mouth.

"What is this?" I asked with the thing still in my mouth I could not dare chew.

"It's yam," Sunshine said.

"But yam doesn't taste like this or look like this," I said.

"It's grated," Laser informed me.

So I swallowed what I had in my mouth and washed my hand.

"Memuna, eat something. We don't know when we will find some food next," Sunshine said.

I did not say anything I just stood and looked at them. By the time they got through eating Lansana and the advance team were arranging for us to continue the journey. The villagers could not get rid of us fast enough. As our convoy took off we could hear the villagers calling out to each other and asking if each other were alright.

It was so dark now some of us could not see.

"Lansana, I can't see," I said, closed to tears. Sunshine agreed with me.

"We have to find somewhere safe, so can you two be patient and try to stick to someone who can see," he said. We walked about five miles and arrived in another suspicious town. To my surprise they had kerosene lanterns and the moon was bright in this area. We saw a few men but luckily we saw them first. There were two at a checkpoint and others on the other side of town beyond the checkpoint. The area we arrived in was uninhabited; it was only a bit dark as the moonlight shone on this part of the town. Lansana told the four of us to sit somewhere in the dark with some of the boys while he went towards the check point with Ur-Pa, Kallon, King and Tiger. They were members of the advance team who wore army trousers or T-shirt; Lansana wore a pair of black jeans and an army T-shirt. The rebels were suspicious mainly because of the kerosene lanterns and the check points.

Because there were no markets around and in most of the war zones, money was of no value, so only rebels or their opponents would be able to have things that only money could buy and kerosene was one of those things. The rebels looted such things and the opponents got it as part of their support from the government. So the men we found in this town were either Kamajors (Mende for hunters) or the army, the rebels were sure they had no posting in this area.

Deceived by the rebel's attire, the guards at the checkpoint thought they were Sierra Leonean army; they saluted the rebels and talked to them. Lansana and the boys put the guards under gunpoint, telling them to put their single barrels down and run without saying a word or they would be killed. The two men did as they were told. By this time Corporal Moses, Scholar and the other rebels had managed to bring us close to the checkpoint. So when the guards ran off, Lansana and the others called out to us and they led the way to the stream in the village. The stream was big. Kallon had to carry me under his arm like a bag, Sunshine clung to Ur-Pa and we crossed quickly. Behind us we could hear the guards wasting their bullets and screaming swear words at us but they did not dare follow us.

Once we crossed the stream, we arrived on the top of a huge rock the size of a house. Beneath there was the heaviest waterfall I had ever seen and I knew to think of jumping down was suicidal. The forest behind us was thick and dark. All I could think of were snakes and wild animals. At this point even Lansana did not know what to do.

"I hope no-one is giving up. We will find our way out; we just have to try harder and I don't want you girls to be frightened. Stick together and stay with us," he said.

As we sat huddled together shivering on this huge rock, the advance team flashed around a very dim flashlight till they found a little footpath in what seemed like ten minutes later at the side of the huge rock. We were cold now as we had got wet crossing the stream. We walked in single file close to the trees so we would not fall in the waterfall. We arrived in an old farm there which seemed like the owners were re-cultivating it. We saw a boy at around ten or eleven years old in a pair of brown shorts sitting on something that farmers build using fresh strong tree branches and vines which resembled a four legged ladder to watch birds and chase them from eating their seeds in the farm. He was bird watching with a sling and a bag of stones to shoo the birds away. We had no idea where we were, so Kallon and the others decided to capture him for him to show us the way. As soon as he was about to scream he was put under gunpoint.

We continued walking through the forest with the boy leading us. He had to be honest and he was told that if he played any games his head would get cut off. So he led us to another town about two miles from where we found the guards at the check point. The boy was released as soon as we arrived in the town and he could not run fast enough away from us.

The village was lit; there were lanterns and candles. People were in the mosque praying, some were home praying and others were out and about. But once we arrived the whole town was in chaos; everyone started screaming and calling out to their families, some started shooting at us.

"The worst that could happen is to get killed by a civilian," Scholar said.

The rebels shot back at them and they all ran into the forest around their village. We four girls fell on the ground so we would not get shot. Before we knew it the whole village was on fire. There was an old man who tried to shoot us girls. King and Laser caught him just in time with his single barrel aimed at Sunshine, Salim, Cecilia and me. They threw him to the ground for us to keep him in custody and took his single barrel away.

"Why do you want to shoot us?" Salim asked him.

"I don't."

"Well you did, they just took your gun from you. Why?" I demanded. I was tired, angry and hungry. I could not be polite or kind, fear and anger ruled my words.

"Can you and your village people fight us?" Sunshine asked. He shook his head and pleaded for forgiveness.

"We will not leave you until we are ready to go," Salim said.

"Oh please don't hurt me I will never do what I did again," he begged.

"Of course you won't," Sunshine said.

With the village burning, the air was hot and the heat was so intense that our clothes got dried on us and warmed us up. The rebels had spread around the village and we could hear screams from every corner of the village. About an hour later, when at last it was time for us to carry on walking, we ordered the old man to get up and walk fast, as fast as possible, away from us and not to look back. Instead, he ran screaming, "Please don't shoot me," in Mende.

We continued our journey hoping we would find a place to rest as we had walked more than forty miles that day. We found another village on fire about a mile or more away from the one we left. The advance team had set the town alight when they arrived. Most of the villagers were fast enough and got out of their beds and houses and fled when they realised we were in their village. The advance team told us to walk on the sides of the road, that way it would be easier for us to hide in the bush if there was an attack.

We did as we were told. The rest of the villagers were trying to flee. We rushed through the other half of the town which was not on fire trying to see if we could stay for the rest of the morning as it was around 3am, but the village was too risky. We were in an enemy zone and the villagers could come back and attack us. We did find a father and daughter in a prison cell. When asked they said the villagers had locked them up and promised to take them to another village to the Kamajors as they were suspected to be on reconnaissance for the RUF.

"We live in this village too," the daughter told us. "but because they had not seen us for a while they think we came to spy on them for the rebels."

As for her father he just sat there in shock looking as if he was in another world. We took them out of the cell with their hands still tied behind them. It was a little cold that early morning. Sunshine and Salim could not take the girl's rings and bangles off her fast enough.

"What's your name?" I asked.

"My name is Ma Sallay," she said. She was tall, dark, slim and pretty. There was already one of the rebels called Koi, who wanted her. He came to us and asked us not to be wicked to her. The boys set two more houses on fire.

While talking to her, we heard a gunshot and a child scream. Sunshine and I ran towards the scream and found a boy about twelve years old.

"Hey are you hurt?" Sunshine asked.

"My mother, my mother..." he cried. "She is the only person I have in this world and my grandmother. You people have killed my mother so please kill me too."

I was so very sorry; I wished I could make it right and bring his mother back to life. I wished I had got there three minutes earlier so it would not have happened. Sunshine said the same agreeing with me. Tears streamed down my cheeks as, just then I thought of my mother. I put myself in that boy's shoes and I can't say that I knew how he felt but I felt his hurt.

"Please ma'am kill me, I want to go with my mother," he cried; this time he knelt down in front of me holding my feet begging me to end his life and making me wish I were dead. I became hysterical.

"Sunshine," I whispered. "who killed this boy's mother?"

"We have to go find out," she said. He ran to his mother's body as we walked over to Lansana.

"Why are you girls crying?" he asked concerned and sounding tired.

"Who killed that woman?" Sunshine demanded. "Her son is now begging us to kill him too and we know nothing about his mother's death."

"Standing here, I'm angry too as you can see" Lansana said, "it was Scholar who shot her. Apparently he found her in bed with her Kamajor husband and he fled so Scholar shot her. Where is the boy?"

"What are you going to tell him?" I asked.

He shrugged saying he did not know what to tell the boy. The boy was near Ma Sallay and now he was still begging Salim and Cecilia to kill him. They were as speechless as we were. He went to Ma Sallay wailing.

"Ma Sallay, they have killed Ngor Sue, my mother. How am I going to go to school, where can I find another mother who would feed me now?"

"Go to your grandmother when you can and be with her. I am very sorry," Ma Sallay told him.

He ran around town crying but he was not allowed to leave the village at this point, as we were afraid he would have brought back Kamajors to attack us, though I did not think we deserved any better.

Sunshine and I went to his house where his mother was killed. We saw her corpse lying in her blood at her door with her legs in the room and her upper body on the veranda still whole. She was shot in the neck.

We left the village soon after and we saw the boy running into the dark forest screaming his mother's name. I felt so horribly sorry for him watching him and I silently prayed for him to find peace and for my mother that no-one hurt her. I hated Scholar for killing the boy's mother and I did not want to talk to him anymore.

I was tired, sad, hungry and aching from my head to the sole of my feet but I did not say a word. In shock over what had happened, I could not stop thinking of that boy and his mother and the sight of her lying at her door. We continued walking till we got to the main road. Some of the rebels recognised the road; they said it was the Pujehun/ Koribondo Highway. There was not much vegetation and bushes alongside it so we assumed that it was still in use by vehicles plying the route. Lansana and the boys assumed the road was dangerous for us and so if we were crossing we needed to do it fast and we did.

We arrived in another village also covered in grass about half a mile away north from the road. It was burnt down with four houses and a mosque left standing. The tall grass surrounding the village was damp with morning dew and the air was cold. By this time it was around 5am so Lansana said the village was safe for a few hours. Salim, Cecilia, Sunshine and I went to the mosque with Lansana as well as his body guards and some of the other rebels to rest. "Memuna, we are almost there," he said. "I know you are tired now."

"Tired? My feet have blisters and my body hurts."

"Ok, we are almost there," he said, trying to encourage me to be strong.

"Bra, how far are we? Because I don't remember this place," Sunshine said.

"I think we will be there tomorrow," Lansana replied, sounding a little unsure.

I looked at him and did not say anymore.

Sunshine and I managed to get some sleep and woke up to Salim fussing about us resting while she cooked. I looked at her and said nothing because I was not in the mood for the little catty argument and neither was Sunshine. We just wanted to cook some rice to eat with some oil and set off for the rest of the journey but we did not have pots. Corporal Moses volunteered to go look in some houses for a pot or two and Sunshine and I went with him. I had blisters under my feet but I was trying so hard not to clash with Salim that I went with them. We searched three houses and we found a few little pots but we were looking for big pots. Fortunately we went to another house where, not only find a big pot but an old man as well.

"Pa, hello," Corporal Moses greeted.

"Morning son," the old man said.

"Are you here alone?" Sunshine asked. "I mean, are you in this town alone?"

The old man nodded. I sensed no sign of fear in him; he was old, a little shaky but strong.

"Yes, in the day and nights am alone but in the mornings my son and his friends come with some food for me," he said.

"What does your son do?" Sunshine asked.

"He is a Kamajor (Mende for hunter) and he brings his friends here every morning," he said.

A group of Mende men got together and decided they had had enough of the rebels tearing their districts apart, so they formed a force and fought against the rebels. They fought with single barrel hunting guns, machetes and spears, as most of them were farmers.

"Pa, do you know who we are?" Corporal Moses asked.

He nodded. "Yes, I know you are rebels. I saw you this morning when you arrived," he said.

"Pa, why did you not run when you saw us?" I asked. "My child I'm very old now," he said, "what would anyone gain out of killing me?"

I looked at him then at Sunshine and Corporal Moses. He was a nice and honest old man. He lent us two big pots and told us to hurry and leave the village as soon as possible. He said an hour was too long for us to stay, that his son would come soon and this meant an attack. I was very surprised and glad to know that there was someone who did not, for one reason or another, want us dead. We hurried to the others and told them the news. Lansana told Laser and King to go and tell the others to hurry and do whatever they had to do as we had to leave in less than an hour.

The rice was half cooked and it tasted horrible but we managed to stuff it down. We picked up our bags and set off. About three miles away from the village we ran into another convoy of rebels going on a mission from Libya. Lansana and the advance team told them what the old man had told us and warned them to be careful. We carried on.

"Sunshine, that old man is nice don't you think and he is very brave?" I whispered. She nodded.

We did not talk much while walking and if we did we only whispered because we had to listen in case of anything.

We walked in the forest for about four hours and finally arrived in what looked like an open land. I realised it was once a town when we arrived in the football field. It seemed the whole town had been set on fire though there was no-one in the town but us. We did not rest; in fact we walked faster than we had to, to get out of the town. The space was too big and open and anything could happen. Lansana was leading this convoy and he was trying as hard as possible to avoid any battle.

About midday we arrived in another ghost town; at this point almost everyone seemed to be in a better mood.

"Hey Memuna, we are almost there," Sunshine said. "You are going to see some of the people I have told you about."

"How close are we to Libya?" I asked.

"We are in Libya," she said. "We just haven't reached our precise destination yet."

She had a smile on her face and I believed her. After all, she was the only one I could trust next to Lansana because I had left my sisters behind. She was so happy it was clear to me that she was home. She was so excited; she knew where we were now and this was her home. Her brother and their family were Wanjama Mende and we were now in Pujehun district – Wanjai district. She held my hand, squeezing it slightly and letting out a quiet laugh. The boys urged us to walk faster so we could get to our destination and relax.

PART TWO

CHAPTER SEVENTEEN

Phase 1 - First Battalion

Except, Sumbuya the town was bigger than all the other towns we had come across throughout the journey. We walked in the grass and through a few skeletons here and there. Then we got to the police station and saw some human skeletons. I did not realise it was a police station until I saw a sign.

"These bones probably belong to some policemen," I commented.

"Maybe, maybe not," Sunshine replied.

"Only God knows now."

I agreed with her and we kept walking till we reached half way up town.

We headed for some orange trees we saw ahead. Lansana told me that this town is called Sahn Malen. Lansana and the boys reminisced about how hard they had fought to capture this town. Suddenly, we saw a couple of armed men running away from the advance team. The guys let them run away. I was shocked and frightened there was going to be a fight.

"Who were those men?" I asked Lansana.

"I think they were Sierra Leone soldiers from Pujehun. They must have been here in search of food," he replied, seemingly unworried about their presence in what was supposed to be an RUF town.

Fear written all over my face and he saw it.

"Don't be scared, I know they won't come back. We are very close to our base now.

In case of anything we can hide you girls somewhere and call for reinforcement," he tried to reassure me.

We stayed in the town for half an hour eating oranges as if they were running out of existence. We ate all the oranges off five trees then continued our journey.

Ma Sallay and her father were quiet. They did not say a word until they were asked a question and at times they hardly answered. For one part of the journey her father had pretended to be crazy and he made Laser, Kallon and Scholar upset.

"I don't blame him" Laser complained, "I blame Bra for being lenient on them and I blame our man there for liking his daughter," Laser whined, suddenly looking like a little boy.

We laughed at him.

"Laser, man you sure you don't have a bit of your heart on Sallay?" Lansana teased. Laser shook his head but he had a guilty smile on his face that sold him out.

We walked miles for hours before arriving in another village. At this time the weather was kind to us being sunny and cool, so we did not get too thirsty and irritated by the sun. But this new village was another broken village. We continued walking; we had crossed almost sixty miles in two days. Night fell and we were still walking. We were all very tired and no-one said a word as all we could hear was our own footsteps. At this point we could not even see ahead of us but Lansana was determined that we get to his base that night. After walking another four miles we heard the loud roar of waterfall.

"I think there is a river somewhere ahead of us," someone whispered.

We had to wait for the advance team to use their flashlight to lead us again. We continued walking on the road but suddenly the road disappeared and we were on a long steel bridge, the swift water underneath glowed and swirled beneath our feet.

The advance team found the path past the bridge and, staying close to each other, ten minutes later we arrived in a town covered in grass with lots of broken houses.

"Halt!" said a voice. "Identify yourself."

"Lt. Eagle's convoy," Lansana replied.

"Good evening Sir," was all I could hear.

At this moment it seemed they were expecting us or else they would have asked more questions. Some of the boys who knew people in Libya asked for them and those of us who did not even know the guards just sat and watched the reunion as best we could in the night darkness.

This town is called Bandajuma Sowah. The guards took us to the town hall; it was the cleanest building in the area. I was so tired I sat by the fire the soldiers had made in the hall and did not want to get up but I wanted to speak to Lansana. My very painful feet were covered again in sores but I got up and struggled over to him.

"Are we staying the night here?" I asked.

"No Memuna, we have to go," he replied quietly, but refusing to look at my tired face.

I looked at him and with tears streaming down my cheeks felt sorry I was alive.

"This place is safe. We are already in RUF territory why?" I cried. "Why do we have to keep on walking? I feel like I am walking on hot coal, the blisters under my feet have turned into sores and I can't walk anymore."

He looked at me, stood up and took me aside.

"Memuna I am sorry. Very sorry about your feet," he said, "but we have to go it's only a mile and a half left. I have to report tomorrow to CO. Speed in Senehun, so we have to go besides, when we get to Baoma you and Sunshine can rest all you want. We will take you girls to the hospital for your feet so please for God's sake just bear the rest of the journey and I promise I will make it up to you."

Looking at him I believed he would try to do something for me to forget about the pain in my feet but I didn't know if he knew that he could never make up to me for every other pain I felt.

He commanded the advance and leading the way, we followed.

"I could kill Lansana right now," Sunshine said, clinching her teeth and looking up to the sky.

I looked at her and shook my head thinking I could do the same. Well, the mile and a half was over in a flash but I was still in a lot of pain. Everyone was happy to see us, they gladly welcomed us. Sunshine, Lansana, Kallon, Salifu and King knew almost everyone in Baoma. As for Laser it was his first time in Libya so he only knew some rebels there. They showed us the house that we were supposed to live in and there was a very nice and welcoming lady called Ngor Mamie. Sunshine had known her for years and they were happy to see each other.

"Look at you, you are a woman now Hafsatu," Ngor Mamie said hugging her tight.

"Ngor Mamie this is Memuna, Lansana's girlfriend," Sunshine said. "Memuna, Ngor Mamie my auntie."

I said hello to this new lady and she hugged me. She told us she could help us with some water when we were ready to bathe.

Sunshine and I walked to our room and she had a sneaky smile on her face because she knew what she had done.

"I know you are going to kill me for introducing you as Lansana's girlfriend. I'm sorry," she said.

"But why would you?" I asked.

"Hey, come here," she said, pulling me to a corner. "Look, I'm only doing that to protect you from them; if they know you as Lansana's woman they would give you a break as for me I'm immune to their trouble I've been in this almost from the beginning and RUF started here. This is our first battalion base and you have to be strong here."

I understood exactly what she meant and I nodded.

"And let me tell you," she said pointing her finger at me like a big sister. "That is precisely how Lansana is going to be introducing you to people. Here he can't lie to anyone that you are our sister because this is our hometown. Pujehun district people know our family a lot. So try and get used to the wife thing."

She poked her tongue at me and we walked to Lansana's room. It was filled with welcomers. He introduced me to some of them (at least those who needed to know) as his girlfriend and Sunshine gave me that I-told-you-so look.

I did not care about any of this, I just wanted a bath and a good night's sleep. We had to wait for everyone to leave us before we could settle in and it was annoying. So I sat on the bed by Lansana and listened to them while Sunshine went out for what I don't know. She came back and told me that Ngor Mamie had offered us some water to bathe. So we took some clean clothes out of our backpacks and went to her room. She gave us two big buckets of cold stream water and we stood at the far end of the house in the moonlight naked and bathed, thanking Ngor Mamie. Then we went back to the room.

The welcomers had left and the convoy had split as the other people who were not Lansana or CO. Speed's bodyguards went their way. Corporal Moses was part of us as he was one of CO. Speed's bodyguards. He was given a room with Nyalay and Salim in a house opposite the house where Lansana and his team stayed – including Sunshine and myself. Tenneh and her father were left with the rebel who wanted her. Now they were property of RUF's so the old man was left with Lansana. Lansana arranged for a sergeant who was already in the town to look after the old man and make sure he ate something that night and in the morning something would be sorted for him. Laser came in and told Lansana that there was a bucket of water in the bathroom for him and he thanked Laser and went to bathe. By the time he came back there were about six bowls of food (rice and meat or fish stew) in the room for us.

Corporal Moses and his family joined us for the late dinner. Very hungry, but too tired to chew the food so I managed to eat a piece of fish and swallowed a few spoonfuls of rice. Everyone went to his or her room as soon as the food was finished. Lansana told the guys not to forget formation at 6am and he dismissed Laser and Salifu off guard duty. Sunshine and I thanked Salifu, Soja and Lamine for helping us with our bags throughout the journey and said goodnight to them and Laser. I can say Kamor and Salifu had enjoyed the journey more than anyone of us as they fooled around till we got to Baoma. Sunshine and I slept in Lansana's room with him. I slept between them.

"I think Lamine is not so afraid of us anymore," Lansana observed. "He seems to get along with Salifu very well."

"They are both stupid," Sunshine said.

I heard the screeching sound of the radio and opened one of my eyes.

"Can't the news pass you just this once?" I muttered.

"Morning, it's 5am I have to catch BBC news," Lansana said, "Sunshine is still asleep."

"Not really," she mumbled.

"Ok well, I'm going to Senehun today to report and I'll leave you girls with Salifu and Moana," he said. "You get enough rest and I will be back. I will arrange for someone to cook for the four of you till I return."

"So how long are you going for?" I interrupted, "I don't know anyone here."

All I had on earth in human form to care for me was Lansana and his going anywhere without me and my sisters made me very restless.

"Memuna I'm not leaving you alone, Sunshine and Salifu will be here. I could take you all with me but you need to rest and this is our home till my next assignment, so please understand I will be back as soon as I can."

All this while, his sister had been pinching my side slightly. She was indicating that I give him a hard time about going to Senehun without us.

"Ok if you promise to come back soon," I complied.

"As soon as I can," he said.

They called for formation and afterwards Lansana and the boys left for Senehun. They all said they could not wait to see us in Senehun. Salim, Nyalay, Corporal Moses and the rest of CO. Speed's bodyguards went along, leaving Salifu and Lamine with Sunshine and myself. They were all meant to go and stay in Senehun then Lansana and his bodyguards were to come back. Lansana left Sunshine, myself and the two boys with the sergeant in Baoma. We slept till midday and woke to lunch already prepared for us. The sergeant looked very mean but he tried to make us comfortable around him. It seemed to us his wife was afraid of him. She served him like he was some scary king or something and there was a little girl staying with them who was very much afraid of him. So we were a little scared of him too. His wife cooked for Lamine, Salifu, Sunshine and myself. We sat in their house, ate the meal, sat a little and left. We were glad to leave. We went to Lansana's room, talked with Salifu and Lamine and the two of us fell asleep. When we woke up we went for a walk in the swamp and at the creek, as we wanted to know the town.

"Did you see how she served him?" Sunshine asked.

"Yes, I think she is afraid of him," I said. "I feel sorry for her. Lansana better hurry up and come back soon I'm a little afraid of that man myself."

Sunshine agreed that she too was afraid of him a little.

The swamp was just at the back of the sergeant's house. So we could not walk past the house as if we did not know anyone there. After all, despite his male domineering behaviour towards his woman and the child who stayed with them, he was helping us a great deal and so was his woman. They cooked three meals for us every day till Lansana came back and we settled. Sometimes she even looked at the sores on the soles of our feet and told us how to care for them. There was only one doctor in town whose qualification I doubted - I didn't know whether he was academically qualified or only by RUF's standards. So we went and talked to her in the kitchen a little, as we did not have much to say to each other.

"You girls still look tired," she had said. "You got lots of time to know this town; it is a small town so don't worry about knowing it, just rest as much as you can."

We looked at her and nodded, she is so nice I thought.

"You know we are just tired of being indoors so we thought we could just walk a little," Sunshine said.

We told her we were just going to the swamp for a walk and that we would be back.

That afternoon although we still felt aches in our bodies and feet we tried to do some exercise and before I knew it, news had already gone through the town that I was Lansana's woman. It had only been two days since we had arrived in this small town. Everybody, including old women who could be my grandmother watched their words around me. They treated me with a great deal of respect, so much that I got upset and took it out on Sunshine sometimes.

On our way to the swamp, we saw the little girl who stayed with the sergeant and his woman. She was carrying a bowl of water and she smiled at us and said hello. We said hello to her and as she passed us we noticed that she had two fingers missing on her right hand. Although we wondered what had happen to her, we did not ask just then.

That afternoon there were some men germinating rice in the swamp while some women were planting vegetables. In the war the people of Sierra Leone who lived in towns and villages taken over by the rebels lived off the land – they grew their own food. We went as far as the edge of the swamp and climbed up a mango tree in the coffee and cacao farm close by and sat watching them.

"Hey we should ask that girl about her fingers," I said. Sunshine nodded but did not take her eyes off the people in the swamp.

"I wonder if those working over there would mind if we went there," she said, thoughtfully. We had lost our slippers on the way coming to Libya and all I had to wear on my feet now were the sneakers I had on when I was captured and it was starting to feel tight. So I wore Lansana's slippers or Sunshine's sandals, which were all too big for me, especially Lansana's. Unfortunately there was nowhere to get slippers from for me. This time I was wearing Lansana's slippers.

"I don't know if they would but I know I wouldn't," I said. "My sores are still not healed yet so if we go to that swamp and I slip off the path into the mud it's going to make my sore worse I think."

"What are you, some kind of doctor?" she asked sounding slightly annoyed.

"I'm not a doctor I just assumed that's what would happen and besides that's what my grandmother told us," I said. She looked straight ahead of us and kept quiet.

"If you want to go you are free to go," I said. "I'll sit here and watch so don't stay because I don't want to go."

We sat in short silence and Sunshine saw the sergeant's little girl coming towards us. "Hey Memuna, she is coming," Sunshine said.

Usually we would jump off the branches to sit on the ground but we managed to climb down slowly.

"Hey come here" I said in Mende.

The girl walked towards us slowly with her head down and the bowl hanging in her hand. She was going to fetch more water. Her hair was short and plaited all the way down her head. She had about six plaits. When she got close to us I started playing with her plaits she tried to hide one hand from us by wrapping it in the cloth that she was going to lay on her head to rest the bowl of water on it. "What's your name?" Sunshine asked.

"My name is Jeneba," she said, standing kicking stones.

"Jeneba, is the sergeant your father?" I asked. At this question Sunshine and I flicked each other a look. Jeneba shook her head; she told us that she was captured. "So what happened to your hand Jeneba?" Sunshine asked. "We saw it the other day."

Jeneba did not want to talk. She stood there for a moment and whispered, "I got burnt."

Looking at each other again, Sunshine seemed to know what was going on but I did not know.

"How did that happen?" I asked, kneeling down in front of her.

"Sergeant burnt me," she cried.

The shock hit me like a rock to my stomach. Looking at Sunshine I tried to fight back tears.

"Why would he do something so cruel?" I said, my imagination seeing the poor child screaming. "How did it happen?"

"I stole a piece of fish," she confided.

Sunshine held the burnt hand looked at it and shook her head. I could see sorrow in her eyes and Jeneba stood there with tears streaming down her cheeks. Mine almost came out so I looked up to the sky and rubbed my eyes. Poor Janeba had enough sorrow in her life she did not need me crying on her.

"So because of a piece of some fish he burnt the hand of someone else's child," Sunshine said, as if she was thinking out loud.

"That man is not human that's why everyone in his household is afraid of him," I exclaimed, bitterly fighting the urge to do the same to him. But there was nothing we could do for Jeneba. We told her how sorry we were and walked her down to the well. We both held the bowl of water till we got to the mango tree and then we set it on her head. She was just in their backyard now; all she had to do was take it to the kitchen and pour it in the container. We told her there was nothing we could do about the pain the sergeant had caused her. God in heaven could fight her battle for her so she should leave it up to God. She nodded and went with her bowl of water.

We still could not believe our eyes and ears. "Memuna, if you were staying with that sergeant you would have been dead by now," Sunshine said.

"Oh! The same goes for you too, he is too wicked. I'm not eating from his house today, I'll tell them I'm not feeling very well," I said.

We helped Jeneba with two more bowls of water and on our way to our house we could not escape without the sergeant's wife seeing us.

"Your food is ready girls. The two boys already had theirs," she said.

I nodded forcing a smile.

"Ok, we just want to get some more rest, we will come here to eat later," Sunshine said.

We went home, told the boys about the girl's hand and told them not to utter a word of it to anyone. They were both sorry for Jeneba and angry on her behalf. Lamine started saying something in Arabic but all I understood was "Allah!" Salifu being the fool he is never took anything seriously.

"So the girl is left with eight fingers?" he said, chuckling, "I'll catch some fish for her, today or tomorrow."

"Look, don't get her into more trouble, just act as if you don't know," I warned them. "God! Lansana better come back soon!"

"We don't want their food anymore," Sunshine said.

"So how are you two going to eat?" Salifu asked.

"God will provide," was her reply.

We talked about it for hours then went to Ngor Tenneh's room. She had a bowl of rice and stew for us.

"Girls I dished out some food for you."

We told her about Jeneba hand and our decision. It turned out everyone in the town knew about the child's hand but no-one talked about it. It seemed lots of the people were afraid of the sergeant. We did not bathe that night we went to bed as we were; I could not wait for Lansana to come back.

Salifu and Lamine slept on the mat at the foot of our bed. We talked till we almost fell asleep then we heard noise outside.

Some people were ma pathetic noises and we heard people saying "Thank God you are here."

We also heard moans, cries and grunting as if someone was in pain. Quickly we all ran round to the back of the house to where the crowd had gathered in the town hall, just between the mosque and our house. There were sojas from the convoy we'd seen earlier on the road going as we were coming to Baoma. Unfortunately, they had run into the old man's son and his friends in that village we had left and they fought. So the RUF sojas brought back the wounded rebels and the whole convoy had to retreat.

There were about seven wounded rebels and the doctor in Baoma could not accommodate them. He managed to treat them though before they were transferred to Senehun. Some had to be carried and others managed to walk. One of those who had to be carried was a boy called Nor-go-de. He'd been shot with a single barrel in one of his legs, arms and buttocks. He got temporary treatment and was taken to Senehun. I was so frightened I thought the Kamajors would follow the retreating rebels to Baoma. I could not sleep.

We became familiar with this new town. We found the creek that we could bathe in and made some friends who told us it was alright to pick vegetables from their gardens if we wanted. Sunshine knew the doctor's wife; they had been friends for years. Her younger sister was Sunshine's best friend, but she was no longer in Libya. We still got our meals cooked by the sergeant's woman and we also had food from Ngor Mamie. Lansana came back on the third day. He looked so worn out. He greeted us and hardly said much, which left us assuming the worst – were we going to be sent back to Rutile and had Lansana been demoted further? We asked Laser what was troubling Lansana. He said they had to go again and we might move to Senehun but he was not sure. He also said that they might have to go and attack that town to get rid of the old man, his son and his friends. When Lansana and the boys came back from Senehun they came with a flirty guy called Alasan. I had heard lots about him from Mattru Jung. He took every moment he had to eye me without getting caught by Lansana.

Lansana bathed, ate and had some rest and then he was ready to talk to us. He called Sunshine and me into his room and asked us how we were doing. I told him about Jeneba's hand and he was sorry for her.

"So apart from that, nothing went wrong with you girls," he asked.

"Nothing," Sunshine assured him, "except when Memuna decided to stay up all night when the convoy retreated. She was scared"

"Speaking about that," Lansana said, "we have to send a troop to that village, or else those people might attack us here."

As the reggae music played, I listened as the brother and sister talked.

"Memuna, Captain Speed says hello. He wants you girls to go visit him," Lansana told me.

Sunshine and I flicked each other a look as he said this.

We talked till dinnertime. Once again we had food from almost all the houses in the town. We ate and went to bed.

The house was cleared now of extra people and everything was getting settled. The older body guards (Alasan, Tiger, Laser and Soja) had the outside room on the veranda of the mud house opposite ours; that house seemed a little spooky to me. No-one ever went inside the main house. Sunshine and I had our room, it was a shop-room adjacent to Lansana's room with a door between the two rooms. As it was a shop prior to the war, our room was quite huge. There were two big beds so we let Lamine and

Salifu sleep in one of the beds until they found a room for them. They were not allowed in the room until bedtime. We started cooking our own meals using Ngor Tenneh's kitchen far behind the mud house.

Two days after that Lansana had to go to Senehun and this time he took us with him. This was to prevent the boys giving us a hard time just in case he was not coming back soon.

We woke up early in the morning for the trip to Senehun, ate something and set off. It was a cold morning and the moon was still out. All this time Sunshine and I did not know that Ma Sallay's father was still in Baoma. We took him with us that morning. It was a long journey, not quite what I expected. Baoma and Senehun were about ten or more miles apart. We had walked all morning and now, as it became afternoon, we arrived into an empty little village surrounded by a huge field of elephant grass. The boys asked us not to make too much noise, because apparently the men of Pujehun District refused to give up the fight. These men attacked the rebels anytime they felt like it. We saw some arrows on the ground and the boys told us about the bow and arrow attack by the civilians. Frightened out of my pants, I could feel my stomach turning. I just wished I could vanish from where I stood. The distance through the field of tall elephant grass was about two miles. Everywhere we went the boys had a story to tell - not very helpful ones but they felt they had to be told. All this walking worsened the sores on my soles. I started crying and so was Sunshine as the same thing had happened to her. But walking through a coffee and cacao farm leading into the town, Sallay's father decided to run off into the farm. The sojas had made him carry a bag of grenades and bullets. He threw them down on the side of the path and ran off into the coffee and cacao trees. This was so upsetting - he knew as well as we did that the safest place for him now was with us.

"What is wrong with him?" Sunshine said and grunted.

"He knows he would die if he returns to his town," I said, "so why is he doing this?"

Lansana just said "He can't even make his way back."

The old man seemed very frustrated and wanted to go home at all cost.

Upset and sore, all Sunshine and I wanted was some rest and some hot water to put our feet in but we had to wait while the guys chased after the old man to bring him back. When he was finally caught, the boys threatened to shoot him if he ran off again. For now though they tied his hands behind him. We continued the journey and finally arrived in Senehun at 5pm. At this point I was hungry and so thirsty there was hardly any saliva left in my mouth. We went straight to CO. Speed's house. Lansana, Sunshine and his bodyguards saluted him and Captain Speed's bodyguards and some other subordinates saluted Lansana. I must have looked so helpless, Captain Speed shook my hand and introduced me to his wife, as I was the only one amongst us she did not know and who did not know her.

"Janet, this is Memuna. Memuna this is Janet my wife," he said. She shook my hand while I looked at her and thought 'your husband is a cheat! Help me relax please, Janet'. She and Sunshine shook hands and they were very pleasant towards each other. We saw Salim and Cecilia. Salim was in the kitchen bossing some girls around as usual.

The boys called Janet "Mammy Jay". She took us into the house and asked us to see her after we bathed so she could treat our feet.

"What is she, Sunshine?" I asked.

"She is a nurse," she said, "I hear she was in medical school in Kailahun before she was captured."

"So does she know about you and her husband?" I asked.

"Well news goes around," she said, "I hear she confronted him about it. So I guess she knows."

"But she never asked you?"

"No" she said.

I looked at her and nodded not knowing what more to ask. We followed some girls down the creek, bathed and came back as fast as we could. We did as we were told. Mammy Jay treated our feet and we had dinner. Later we sat with CO. Speed, Lansana and Mammy Jay in the palaver hut then went to the other guys. Laser was on guard and Salifu was free to roam about town. Laser did not really like this - he stood on guard angry.

The town was lively, security was heavy and tight but a little friendly and it was safer than Baoma, because Baoma was not well secured. We only had two guards in the village ahead of us and it felt spooky to me. The moon was bright that night, the breeze was cool and there was reggae music flowing from every corner, with marijuana and cigarette smoke in the air. Kerosene and palm oil lanterns shone at every house in every veranda except the communication house. Those sojas used car batteries and solar powered system for electricity and while everyone else listened to reggae they listened to UB40. When I heard it I wished I knew someone there so I could go listen to the music because they were the only ones who had the tape and I was very tired of listening to reggae.

We went over to Kallon's house just opposite the captain's. They were all in the room smoking - Alasan, Tiger, King all of them except Laser and the two younger boys. The captain's other guards were guarding him, Yusufu, Corporal Moses and Scholar. Yusufu was new to me but after we were introduced we shook hands and he promised to catch up with me and especially Sunshine later. He was not allowed to engage us in a lengthy conversation with Lansana and the captain around. They all desired the same things - us.

There was a chubby girl sitting next to Kallon on the bed. When we walked into the boys' room she leapt to hug Sunshine. Sunshine introduced us.

"Memuna this is Amie, Kallon's girlfriend and my other sister-in-law. Amie this is Memuna, Lansana's girl."

She shook my hand and said "it's nice to finally meet you; I've heard so much about you these few days."

I looked at her, she was pretty and I wandered why Kallon could not be happy with just her. Smiling I told her it was nice to meet her too. I talked with them as much as I could till the conversation changed to some of their old stories. Then I listened till I fell asleep. When they were through Sunshine woke me and we went to our room. We slept with Lansana that night. He wanted to talk, but I was just too tired so I fell asleep while he talked.

My feet felt better in the morning. I could walk around without feeling too much pain. The house was so busy everyone had a chore to do especially the girls and the younger boys. They cleaned the yard, did the dishes, fetched water and some of them cleaned the house and the palaver hut. It was a little cold that morning. Sunshine the early bird had woken up and went to Amie before I woke up. So I was left in bed with Lansana, but I was not quite asleep. The noise of everyone busy woke me up but I did not open my eyes for an hour or so. I could feel that Lansana was looking at me. When I opened my eyes he was looking right into my face.

"Morning," I said looking at him too wondering why he was looking at me like that.

"Morning," he said, "I was just looking at you wondering why you ruined your hair."

I sighed, shook my head and said, "that was long ago and my hair is growing fast."

He rubbed my head. "Please don't cut it again."

I looked at him wondering why he was so worried about this hair issue . Then it occurred to me that maybe if my hair was this short on the day we were captured, maybe I'd be home by now. We sat in silence for a while.

"Where is Sunshine ?" I asked.

"She might be outside," he suggested.

I got up, wore his slippers and went out to look for her. I ran into Josephine and said hello. She looked at my feet, asked me how they felt and I told her they felt better. I kept walking around looking for Sunshine. I asked one of the girls and she told me to go to Amie's house.

The room was cloudy with marijuana smoke. She was talking to Yusufu, Amie and Kallon. The guys and I exchanged greetings and I sat a bit. Kallon was lying in bed smoking. Sunshine and Yusufu were too cosy with each other. Kallon grabbed me, "let's lie down," he said. "Amie, I want Memuna to be my second wife."

She smiled and nodded. I looked at the two of them and said, "You two must be crazy, you need to stop smoking. You know that, don't you?"

They all laughed. I was still a little sleepy but I did not want to sleep, so I asked Sunshine whether she had bathed already.

"No I was waiting for you," she said, "so I'm ready when you are."

"And what if I am ready now?" I asked.

"Ok," she said, freeing herself from Yusufu.

I was a little upset by this time. I did not know why Kallon did what he did and what was going on between Sunshine and Yusufu.

"So what's happening between you and Yusufu?" I asked once we were out of the room.

"What do you mean?" she said.

"Sorry I asked if you don't want to tell me that's fine," I said.

"I'll tell you when I can," she said, "don't worry."

I nodded and we dropped the topic and did not say anything for a while as if we were searching for something to say.

Suddenly she brought up Kallon. "Kallon likes you," she said, sounding as if she was teasing.

"Good for him," I said, sarcastically. "I'm glad everyone likes me. Thank God for that."

"Don't be like that," she said, "some people wish these guys liked them the way they like you."

"Well I think those people are mad," I replied, angry that I was even in this situation. None of this would have mattered if I had been at home where I was supposed to be.

We had reached the creek by now for bathing. She sat in the water looking at me and I knew she wanted to talk about me giving Kallon a chance, so I did not look in her direction.

"You know what?" I said, "I'm just so tired of guys wanting me, I'm only fourteen I'm still a child. I don't know how to have a boyfriend and I don't want to know. Well at least not just yet."

"But you will soon be fifteen" she said.

"I'm sorry for being honest to you, for telling you my real age," I said. "I should have told you I was thirteen."

"That won't stop them from liking you," she said,

"Sunshine don't push it," I said, this time looking at her. "I asked you about Yusufu, you said later and I respected that. So let's drop this topic and don't ever bring it up again."

"I'll try," she conceded, "but don't be upset with me."

"You are trying to bring it up again."

I was in no mood for her challenge.

We got out of the water, dried our skin and talked about my sisters in Mattru Jung. "I can't wait for Komeh to come," Sunshine said.

"Neither can I. I miss all of them very much and I'm worried about Samia a lot. She is always sick."

"They will be fine. Naffie is there with them."

She tried to comfort me.

"Oh my God they will feel the pain we felt from walking," I said thoughtfully.

"It won't be so bad on them if their convoy commander is not in so much hurry like ours was. That way they will have time to take breaks."

"But most of the villages and towns around Pujehun District are not safe to rest in," I quickly reminded her.

"They will find ways to do it if their commander is clever,"

"By God's grace they will have a clever one and they will come soon," was all I could say.

We went to the room, got dressed and went to Janet for our treatment and then we went to Amie for breakfast. I did not want to go to Kallon's house but Sunshine promised not to bring the topic up. As soon as we got there Kallon tried to hug me but I ran away from him. Suddenly the ridiculousness of it all seemed very funny. He and King chased me and caught me behind the kitchen. All the kitchens were outside and they both hugged me.

"Stop it you two," I said.

They did not stop till I pinched them. We went back to the room and Amie gave Sunshine and me some cassava and stew with fried fish in a bowl. I liked it; it was delicious and it smelt like it too. We ate and went for a walk around town with Amie.

We got to an orange plantation and, sitting in the grass eating oranges, everyone was relaxed and I was sure that the Kallon topic was left behind us in the room with him. I was very wrong as Amie brought it up. She seemed insane to me as she was begging me to help her boyfriend cheat on her or at least that's how I saw it.

"Memuna, you are pretty you know that?" she said.

Scathingly I replied, "No, but I hear it all the time and I'm losing my eardrum because of those words."

She laughed and Sunshine tried not to look at me, as she knew I was looking at her with dagger blazing eyes. She tried to pretend she did not know what was going on as if she was somewhere else.

"Sunshine did you hear that?" Amie asked.

Now we were both looking at her.

She nodded but still did not turn, in fact this time she looked up into the orange trees.

"Something will drop in your eyes," I said calmly. She flicked me a look and looked ahead of her.

"Sunshine, your cousin wants Memuna," Amie said. "He told me he was serious last night when we were alone."

"Well ask her," Sunshine replied, this time looking in our direction. "She is right here."

The look on Sunshine's face was weird. I think we were both wondering if Amie was mad.

"Amie you are good looking yourself," I said, "so why?"

"Nothing is wrong, this is what he wants," She said.

Sunshine said nothing she just sat looking at us.

"What about you?" I asked, "what do you want?"

She looked at me and said nothing. This was a relief for me as I thought she was lost of words so I caught a break. The oranges we picked from the trees had run out so we got about ten more and went back to the house. I did not want to go to Amie's house at that moment, so we said we would see her later in the evening.

"Think about it Memuna," she yelled out.

"Yes, you think of an answer to my question too," I yelled back. We waved and went our ways.

"See, I did not bring it up," Sunshine said.

Lansana was sitting in the hut, he flicked me a look that said lots but I knew what he was saying. He did not like me hanging around Kallon's house too much because of the guys but he did not know what Kallon was up to. I looked at him, gave him a teasing smile and walked away. I knew he would not do a thing about it at that point he was too busy with the captain.

Two days later, we left Senehun and went back to Baoma. Amie had already assumed I was her boyfriend's second girlfriend whether I liked it or not and she looked even crazier to me.

CHAPTER EIGHTEEN

Attack At Christmas

Baoma was the same spooky town to me and I got upset easily and often. We settled in as best we could and cooked our own food but the sergeant and his woman still helped us with vegetables. Sunshine and I did not like the kitchen. It was far away from the house and scary so we told Lansana how we felt and he ordered the boys to build us one near the house. The kitchen they built was built of zinc and we liked it. Two weeks later Ngor Mamie moved from Baoma and went far away to Sormu. There were more people and I heard life seemed normal there. She had her grandson to look after so she had to go. A Liberian man came into her old room with his pregnant girlfriend. His name was Fighter. He looked crazy: he yelled too much, ate too much and he always wanted to bother me. He said that after the war we were going to Liberia to get married. This annoyed me so much; it seemed no-one thought of anything but marriage. Soja did not like him because he sent him around every day on errands. On the other hand his girlfriend Rosa was so very quiet and pleasant.

We shared the kitchen with Rosa and sometimes she was entertaining as she told funny stories. She begged us to eat with her because she did not have appetite when she ate alone. So every day when we got through cooking we would eat our food and she would reserve something just in case she got hungry at night. Lansana and Fighter ate together too sometimes, when they felt hungry at the same time, which was not often. Everything was alright in Baoma. I was getting used to the spooky town and all the people in it. We played a lot; Rosa only sat and looked at us playing with the boys, as she was heavily pregnant.

This time, being in Baoma as the rainy season was nearing an end, we had more sunshine than rain and I began to accept the town.

Lansana had already sent out the first mission from Baoma and the vegetables in Ngor Mamie's garden were running out.

Amie came from Senehun to visit; it was good. As soon as she arrived I asked her not to discuss her boyfriend issue - well at least nothing about him and me. She slept with us for two days and later she and Tiger started going out. I was shocked but Sunshine was not. It seemed normal – girlfriends and boyfriends cheat vice versa.

It was livelier when sometimes the boys came to the kitchen to help us cook. Alasan let me get away with offending Salifu and Lamine like Lansana did. There were now four females with Amie around, we girls joked and laughed at each other a lot.

Sunshine and I had lots of tiny beads for our waists - which was a traditional adornment for young women. The beads were given to us by several people: some were given to us by the boys, I got some from when I visited Magainda's family in Matru Jung and we bartered tobacco and cigarettes for some. I loved waist beads. As a young girl living in Monrovia, before the Liberian civil war, waist beads were something I saw in pictures in books and now, here I was with thousands of these beads in my possession. But we needed to put them on threads before we put them around our waists.

We had some old ladies in Baoma who had thread they had spun themselves from pure cotton, some friends we had made in the small town led us to ask these old ladies for some thread and in an hour we had more than enough thread.

To thread so many beads we needed help so we asked Amie and in a day and a half we were through. We had a hundred strings in total; I got forty to add to the twenty I already had around my waist of what I got during my visits to Ndogbohun and before we got to Baoma. The amount of beads I now had on my waist was heavy but very pretty in variegated colours. So was Amie's and Sunshine's.

That evening, when we bathed at the creek, we had everyone looking at us. They admired our beads and some of the girls begged us to give them some strands of beads.

Back in our room, but having time away from the boys, we talked.

"Let me ask you both something," I said to Amie and Sunshine.

"What is it?" Amie asked, smiling. I liked her for that - she was very smiley and so was Sunshine.

"So do you girls say yes to every man that asks you out?" I asked.

They looked at each other and laughed. "Not really," Amie said coyly.

"Ok then," I said, "Sunshine, now tell me what is going on between you and Yusufu."

"What do you think is going on?" she asked, challenging me to answer my own question. Shaking my head I told her,

"No, no. I don't want to assume so why don't you tell me?"

Amie did not mind us. She was listening to Burning Spear's "Mek We Dweet" and dancing. She was still part of the conversation though. Sunshine and I were lying on the bed.

"Turn it down a little," I called out to Amie. She did not seem to hear me. Sunshine got up and started dancing with Amie, trying to get away from my question. A moment after her I got up and went to join them. After the track I asked her again and Amie asked her why she did not want to tell me.

"Because I know what she will say," Sunshine replied, calmly resisting the pressure, "and I can't lie about it now. Amie - you don't know Memuna. She already knows but she wants to hear it from my mouth."

"Stop accusing me of knowing," I challenged her again. "Why would I ask if I knew?"

Amie sat on the bed looking at us, this time the music was a little low.

"I know you," Sunshine said to me.

"Come on tell me," I said.

"Ok, ok. We are going out."

I looked at her in surprise though I already knew. I did not think I would be surprised when I heard it from her but I was. I looked at her as if I had not seen her before.

"You are going out with both him and his boss?" I said, "Bravo!"

"You see I told you," she said, turning to Amie. Pointing at me she said, "Now she will make me feel bad!"

"No, how do you girls do it?" I said laughing, in total disbelief of the scary world I now lived in.

"When it's time you will know how to do it without learning," Amie said with so much pride.

"And what do you think I'm doing now?' I challenged her, "I'm learning from you cheats, not so?"

I looked at the two of them, shook my head and we laughed. Our life in RUF was truly in God's hands and, in another way, it was in our own hands. It was up to us to know that we could not be immoral just because we could and would not be judged by any man on earth. Similarly it was also up to us to respect our bodies and know what was good for us and what was not. Thousands of the other girls in captivity were taken from their respective families by true animals and they were raped and beaten daily. Very few of us were blessed to not be in that situation. I was amazed at how grown I suddenly became when I was with RUF; I did very little things like a normal teenager.

Before I did anything, I always thought of my sisters first - especially Samia and Nyalay. I also always heard my own voice telling Komeh that the four of us were taken from our home and we should withstand the struggle and go back together. I realised I felt older than my age and I then understood what our grandmothers went through when they worried about us. I did not get worried about myself as much as for my sisters. For all the time we were apart I asked myself whether they had eaten something, was

Samia sick, or wondered if Nyalay's head was ok because she had the worst dandruff I had ever seen. After asking all these questions I'd then pray for God to guide and protect us through it all.

I looked at Sunshine and started teasing her. I sang a song for her about a woman who fell in love with her husband's driver and the driver could not say no to the woman because he did not want to lose his job. The song was titled: 'The Wife of My Boss'. I sang it for her because Yusufu was the Captain's bodyguard and she was with him too, though they hardly had much time together. Yusufu was good looking and friendly, tall, lean, nice smiles and fit. He became my friend the first time he saw me.

That night Lansana was very tired so he went to bed early. I think he was a little down too. Before he slept he called me to his room to talk. He looked worried. I asked him what was wrong but he did not tell me; he only said it would be alright. Once again he apologised for taking my sisters and me from our family and everything we knew. I listened to what he had to say although it was the now familiar story about how much he wanted me to give him a chance, to let him show me how much he liked me and how sorry he was for bringing us into RUF. Then I left.

He gave me something to think about and I thought all evening. While sitting with Amie and Sunshine we talked about what cheats they were and also talked to Amie about my sisters. Sunshine told Amie that Komeh was prettier than I was and we all laughed about it. Tiger came to us demanding a bucket of water for him to bathe.

"Go fetch your own water Mr. Man," I said.

"Wait, when did we start giving you water to bathe?" Sunshine asked, "Tiger, are you ok or what?"

"Look, I'm not joking," he said. "If you girls don't go to the creek and fetch me some water I will do something you don't want me to do."

"Well as long as it won't hurt us I'm fine with that," Sunshine replied nonchalantly.

Amie sat and let the moment pass her without saying a word for a while.

"I'm fine with it too," I chimed in.

He turned his back on us, stormed into their room and came back looking angry.

"Look, I don't want to get angry. I want some water to bathe!" he demanded again.

"No-one is responsible for that, but you," Sunshine swiftly reminded him.

He was getting to my nerves so I looked away, trying to get myself out of the conversation.

"Memuna, don't pretend as if you don't know what is happening," he growled at me.

"I can pretend if I want to as I'm free to do whatever I want," I snapped back. Still looking away, I had found something to look at - a big star in the sky. He came across to me and tried to get me to stand up. Holding tight onto my hand, he pulled me off my seat.

"Tiger, if you dare touch me again I will wake Lansana and you will tell him why!" I returned to my seat to look at the star. He looked at me for a long moment, then at the others and he walked away calling us bastards.

"Son of a bitch!" Amie yelled out.

"You are the bastard," I called out too.

"You got five fathers," Sunshine joined in.

Alasan came in from the other room and told us to stop what we were doing. We told him to advice Tiger that we were not his servants.

"Apart from Lansana, no-one forces me to do anything," I reminded him, "especially when it benefits only them."

"Ok, girls," Alasan said, "calm down. I will tell him to apologise."

"That's better," Amie said.

We swore at him all night and so did he at us till we went to bed. Soja, despite his being greedy, did not like being rude to girls. He was upset at Tiger for swearing at us.

He apologised in the morning and we were all good friends again. We had lunch and played Ludo. Lansana looked much better in the morning -he was the Lansana I knew, always smiling even when he knew what he was doing was in his own interest or wrong. We could hear cheers in the town hall. Lansana was sitting in a chair jotting some thoughts on a piece of paper; he got up when he heard the noise.

"I think the mission I sent out is back,' he said.

We ran to see what was going on. He walked behind us to the town hall that was in our backyard. We lived in the town chief's house.

They were back, looking dirty with mud on their faces but they seemed happy. There was a crowd in the town hall gathered around something and we wanted to see what it was. Everyone gave their opinion about what they were looking at but no-one said what it was. Women mostly had sad opinions while the guys had rude and funny opinions. So we pushed our way through to see what it really was. It was the head of a man, a penis and a hand of an army man. His eyes were still open. Screaming when I saw it, I quickly turned away and forced my way out of there. The body parts were the talk of the town for weeks. Some talked about how good the man must have been in bed, some wondered where he inherited such a thing from and I talked about how cruel and disgraceful I thought it was towards the man.

Amie went back to Senehun and promised to come back some time. We missed her very much. Sunshine and I were alone again with the boys. Salifu and Lamine had become thorns in our flesh. We had to beg them at times to fetch us firewood and help us fetch water to cook. We had to beg them for everything until we got tired and stopped giving them food; so they had to cook for themselves. Alasan solved the problem. Sitting out on the veranda eating oranges the guys talked about how scared I was to have a boyfriend and they wanted to know why.

"I just don't think I'm ready;" I said.

"Why not?" Alasan asked.

"She is lying," Tiger said, "she is still hanging on to Magic."

I looked at him thinking of something to say that will serve him right and that would offend him.

"Well, yes that's true but at the same time, before I go out with anyone, he needs to understand when I say no," I said. "Magic did. Before him I never had any boyfriend so I don't really know much about the whole boyfriend/girlfriend game."

A tall dark masculine sweaty man walked towards us smiling. It was a hot but beautiful day.

He shook hands with Alasan and Alasan introduced him to us. His name was Magic and he was originally from Sembehun. He was Mariama and Sue's family member and he was also captured in Rutile.

"How are you Memuna?" he said.

"I'm good," I said smiling. It was a pleasure to meet someone from Sembehun in Libya which I did not expect.

"Are you coping?" he asked.

I nodded and looked at him with a little smile. He nodded back and put his hands on my shoulders, by then Lansana was behind him but he did not know.

"I'm very happy to see you," he said. "I'm your brother. Whatever you need just let me know through Alasan. Even though I live all the way in Sormu and always busy, I'll always make time for you."

I was pleased and thankful to God that despite all the trouble I still had people offering to be there for my sisters and me. I looked at him and smiled and nodded. He turned around to take a seat then he saw Lansana. He gave Lansana courtesy and shook hands.

"Welcome Sir," he said.

"Thank you," Lansana replied. "You look good man. How is it treating you?"

"We are fighting the struggle sir, can't complain," he said.

"Came to see Memuna did you?" Lansana said.

"Yes sir," Siaka said, "I heard she was here from Zainab. So I thought I'd let her know I'm here too."

Lansana smiled and offered his hand for a handshake.

"Memuna, wow, I'm glad to meet you," he turned back to me. "There is this old lady who is like a mother to me. I know she would be glad to see you."

"Who is she?" I asked.

"Her name is Ma Marie. She is from Sembehun too."

"Oh well, o.k. I'd like to meet her so she can show me the way when I go crazy," I said and we laughed.

Siaka was a nice guy. He talked to me and asked me about his family and I told him about the ones I knew. He asked about people from my family and I told him they were fine. He kept asking about people from one family to another and it seemed he wished he were in Sembehun again living with those familiar faces. I told him what I knew about them: that some were dead, some going to school, some moved to the city to go to high school, college or to work in an office, some were out of the country like my auntie and some were married with children. He was excited and so was I. I was glad to have someone to talk to about the same things and we understood each other very well as if we had known each other all our lives. He and my aunties and uncles knew each other because they grew up together. I told him about how great Sembehun was before the disaster and how good everyone was doing in making something good for them.

As for me, I did nothing much apart from going to school, having a very good report at the end of the year and giving my grandmothers headaches. I was a tomboy who went every day to ride a bicycle and climb trees with the boys. When I came back home I often had bruises and my grandmother would feel sorry and worried for me. As for Grandma Memuna, she got tired of reminding me that I was not a boy. So she would pretend not to see me but from what I heard from her when it was time to discipline me, she was just like me at that age.

"So you are following in Gbondo's footsteps now," Siaka said, referring to one of my older sisters.

I nodded and smiled when he mentioned my sister's name.

"She is my sister," I said, trying not to cry because, despite our sibling rivalry, we loved each other but we never said it.

"Really?" he said, "I can see the resemblance. That girl is one strong headed woman."

We laughed. It felt so good. We talked for hours till he had to go. I asked him if he smoked, he said yes, so I gave him a gross of 555 cigarettes from Lansana's room. Hugging me, he told me not to hesitate to send for him if I needed anything and that I should let him know when Samia, Nyalay and Komeh came.

It is now a week since Siaka left. That night we were in the boys' lantern lit room listening to reggae music and having a chat as we always did.

Then Alasan, Sunshine and the other guys dared me to kiss Alasan. He had already told me how he felt about me weeks before. I said no, I did not want to kiss him and they started calling me a coward. This went on for an hour so I thought, 'what have I to lose?' All I needed to do was make sure Lansana did not see me. So I gave him just a peck. They all screamed after which I ran to our room.

A day after Siaka departure Ma Marie came. She walked about five miles, with a teenage boy, all the way from her village to come and see me.

She greeted Lansana and introduced herself to us all. She told Lansana she was there to welcome us, especially me and that she had a huge garden in the village which we were welcome to go and get vegetables from anytime.

"I heard you are from the Barnes family," she queried me.

I nodded.

"Pa Barnes was my Grandfather."

"Oh….Good God," she said, looking in the sky with tears in her eyes. "What a good family!"

She looked at me pitifully. I thought, 'Ma'am, I don't need that now!'

"Are you ok?" she whispered, drawing closer and holding my hands in hers.

I nodded.

"Your grandfather was a good man," she said, "but strict too. He was my father's friend."

"I heard he was strict."

She smiled, reminiscing.

"Child, my God will protect you and if you need a woman's advice or anything at any time come and see me; you are not alone." She changed tone saying, "I better go back now this boy has to go somewhere. So you look after yourself."

I asked her if she wanted some salt and sugar. She answered yes, so I gave her three packets of table salt and two boxes of sugar cubes. Then she left emphasising that I should look after myself.

Salifu and Laser teased me about my new grandmother for weeks. This was why I preferred Lt. John's Soja to Lansana's. He only joked with me when he wanted something like either food or smokes. He liked teasing but he did not want to be teased, as he looked choleric. One day, in the evening, a convoy arrived that I did not know about. Usually we are informed of the expected arrival of a convoy but not this time.

"Where is this convoy from?" I asked.

The boys wanted to lie to me but I saw people from Mattru Jung. I knew something was wrong.

"They are from Mattru Jung," Alasan admitted.

Sunshine looked at me bemused. Lansana had been called to Senehun early the day before and was due back that day. So I was waiting for him to come and tell me why he did not tell me about the convoy. At that stage something in me told me not to be hard on him as he had his children there too. I started crying and Alasan held me

"Alasan, where are my sisters and my uncle?" I cried.

"They will come," he said. "let's just keep looking."

"But why did not anyone tell me about this?" I asked. "Is there any bad news?

Sunshine shook her head, "At least not yet."

"Oh! God," I cried.

Lansana came, called me in the room and he hugged me when I walked in. He was frightened and angry I could feel him shaking.

"What's going to happen now?" I asked.

"I don't know yet," he said, "CO. Speed thinks we should go to Rutile and fight. But we are trying to get a response from Lion or CO. Mohammed."

"Did the army attack them?" I asked.

"Yes and the ECOMOG," he answered honestly. "We think they might need reinforcements."

I cried for my sisters and Lansana's family for two days. Someone came and told Lansana they saw Naffie and that she could not join the convoy because of my sisters especially Samia and Komeh.

"Why, Lansana?" I asked, "what's happened to them?"

"Nothing, Foday Sankoh is angry and he is taking it out on all the young civilians from twelve upwards.

"But why?"

"I'll find out."

"At least it's good to know they are alive," I said, as bravely as I could. Lansana nodded and told me to be strong.

About three days after the arrival of the convoy from Mattru Jung, Sunshine became sad and homesick; she wanted to go to Sormu to see her grandmother and other relatives. She asked Lansana and he said she could go so she went at the end of the week. I wanted to go with her but Lansana refused to let me go, so she went with Salifu. I stayed with Lansana and the other boys. Rosa gave birth to a baby boy late one night and her stupid husband made more noise than the baby did. He was a big baby and ate like his father; he would breast feed for hours. All the while Sunshine was away with Salifu and Soja, Lamine was good as he helped me in the kitchen and we were good friends. Sometimes I slept in Lansana's room just so I was not sleeping alone and scared.

Lansana sent messages to his friends in Rutile via the radio and told them to look after our family for him. They promised they would and they would keep in touch.

One morning I woke up in a bad mood - I was homesick. Lansana wanted to talk to me but I strained the conversation and he got upset. I gave him his food and went to my room. Another huge troop had gone out on a mission again and there were few men left to guard the town. Lansana came to my room and asked me if I was alright and if there was anything he could do. Looking at him tears came rolling down my cheeks. My hair was loosened and I needed to wash it. I felt numb where I sat, thinking of Naffie, the kids and my sisters.

"Memuna you need to go bathe and do something about your hair." Lansana said.

"I can't," I said.

"Why?" he asked

"I don't want to," I replied, words seeping through the numbness.

"Oh no, you do," he said.

"No I don't," I said, raising my voice. "Just leave me alone."

"The next time I see you I want you to be tidy," he demanded and walked out.

He looked like he meant it. So I went to the creek with a red plastic bucket to bring back some water. It would have been easier for me to wash my hair and bathe at the creek, but it was too quiet around there, so I came home with the bucket of water.

I carried the bucket of water to a ruined house we used as a kitchen because the rain had run through our little kitchen by the house. I put a big pot with some water in it on the fire. Sitting with my head bowed and my hands on my head, all I could think about was Naffie, the children and my sisters. Hearing footsteps I did not bother to look up thinking it was Lansana. It was Lamine.

"Memuna, are you feeling ok?" he enquired.

I nodded and still did not look up.

"Do you want to come watch me fish later?" he asked.

He was making a real effort to get me to talk so I looked up.

"Maybe, I'll tell you later if I can come," I said.

He nodded. "Have you eaten? I'm hungry."

I had some rice in the pot on the other fireplace warming up but I did not want to eat it. "There is some rice in that pot; you can have it," I said, weakly gesturing to the other fire.

While we talked about the rice, Jeneba came into the kitchen and she was hungry too.

"Hello Memuna," she said.

I nodded.

"What, are you sick?" she asked.

"No, I'm just tired. What are you doing here?"

"I just came to say hello," she said.

"Jeneba, do you want to eat?" Lamine asked.

She looked at him and me and then she nodded.

"Jeneba," I said, "it's ok you can eat."

They sat to eat the rice and Lamine started talking about Salifu.

"This kitchen is a good place to lay an ambush," he observed.

"What do you know about ambush?" I asked this young boy.

"I can't wait for Salifu to come back," Lamine said, "he teaches me things."

I looked at him and nodded. "The two of you are not very pleasant when you are together. You are very annoying."

"You know, you could just hide in that corner," he said, ignoring my comment and running towards a corner in the kitchen by the broken wall to demonstrate. Squatting in the corner, he pointed a piece of firewood out through the hole in the wall.

"Look," he said, "this is my RPG. You just sit here and wait till you see the enemies, then you launch."

Surprised I said,

"You, so you know all about this and you pretend to be so frightened of guns!"

We started laughing. Looking out through the hole I saw Lansana standing on the veranda talking to Fighter who was in his bedroom. Suddenly, a bomb exploded in the forest very close to the town and shooting rang out through the town. As everyone fled, Lansana ran through the house screaming my name and ran off towards the swamp with everyone else. Screaming at me to get up, Lamine and Jeneba fled the kitchen but I was numb - I could not move. I don't know why. I watched a group of strange looking men I had not seen before walk in the town with single barrel guns. Then I heard a voice calling me, so I got up and fled the kitchen through the garden. They quickly shot in our direction but I think the tall okra trees in the garden were covering my back. I was wearing only a T-shirt and a cloth tied around my waist. The cloth almost fell off so I bent, picked it up, wrapped it round my neck and ran up the hill behind the Sergeant's house.

Lansana was standing there crying for me and the others did not know what to do. Lamine was leaned against a tree with his head bowed.

"She is in the kitchen," he said. "She could not move."

Lansana, kicking at a tree, between gritted teeth he said, "Someone's daughter."

Then, looking up, he saw me out of breathe and panting. He ran and grabbed me, holding me so tight.

"Did you get shot, are you hurt?"

Shaking my head, I could not talk. I was trying desperately to catch my breath.

"Are you out of your mind? Why are you so stubborn?" he said, "why did you not get up and run?"

"I could not move Lansana, I'm sorry," I gasped.

"I was so scared. But now I'm worried about that mortar in the ground commander's house. I hope those fools won't take it with them."

Rosa was standing there with a small top on. She had nothing else on but her underwear and the top reaching at her waist. So I gave her my cloth because my T-shirt did not really cover me but it was better than what she was wearing.

The boys could not fight because the troop that went on the mission were well armed. Besides, RUF focused more on their other bases. Libya was old now so they had felt they had it for their own.

We found our way through the swamp and went to the other village where Ma Marie lived. Sunshine was due back in Baoma that day as was the mission troop. So we ran into her in the village - she was lucky. Ma Marie had stopped her. They were evacuating the town and going further towards the other villages far from Baoma. The RUF troop came and engaged the Kamajors in battle in Baoma. They chased the Kamajors but they could not get the mortar from them. They ran off with it taking their wounded men with them. The town was not safe for us to stay in anymore; they had looted our house and took everything.

"They came for Christmas shopping," Laser said.

"What's the date?" I asked.

"According to the radio it's the 23rd of December 1995."

"What?" I said, "I'm fifteen and I did not even realise." I broke down.

"Hey, hey, come here," Lansana said, "come and sit next to me."

Ma Marie had given me something to wear so I felt a little more decent. So I went and sat next to Lansana, he put his arm around me and said, "Happy birthday."

I nodded and Laser and Sunshine started singing happy birthday to me.

"You will have better ones to come. Sorry about this," he said.

We slept outside on mattresses that night. The following morning we proceeded to another village. But this time everything got tougher. The Kamajors decided to advance on us in a bid to kick us out of Libya and have their Pujehun back instead of RUF's Libya. The captain had been ordered to go to Kailahun District, which RUF named Burkina Faso. So he went with some of his bodyguards but Yusufu did not go. We went and stayed with Lansana's friend Owl and his wife. They had a very cute little son.

Weeks later Lansana was transferred to Blama Highway almost near Rutile. It was between Bo and Kenema. He stayed because he wanted us to settle before he left as Naffie and the kids were coming also. So we stayed with Lansana's friend Corporal Owl till they came. Corporal Owl always had a smirk on his face which when studied said a lot. I interpreted his smirk as: 'I can be very mean if I want to though I look like I am smiling every day.' We thought Samia and Komeh were coming too but Naffie only came with Nyalay, Guy and Lucia. They looked so very drained and tired especially Nyalay and Guy.

"Naffie, why did you not bring Samia and Komeh?" I asked

"They are there trying," she said, "they will be fine. They could not come because Lion said they should keep all the young civilians in custody. It's like he's blaming them for what happened to those civilians in Kabbaty. They are also training them while in custody."

I was so angry I took Nyalay for a walk by the swamp and there were still people coming from Mattru Jung and now even Libya was not safe anymore. They brought lots of wounded rebels. Lansana followed us to talk to me.

"Memuna, I'm sorry," he said.

I looked at him in his eyes, looked away and said nothing. All I could think of was how was I going to tell our family that Samia and Komeh were dead that is if Nyalay and I could go home one day. I turned to Lansana he was still looking at me.

"How am I supposed to explain this?" I cried, "I mean to anyone."

He held me and begged me to stop crying. He said that my sisters were not the only ones in that situation and that all the other rebels were asking Foday Sankoh to stop punishing their loved ones.

"In fact Magic, Hawk, Amara, Maximilian and At-the-end are there so they will look after them." He took us back home.

Sunshine and I cooked some food for everyone to eat and we later went for a walk. She and Naffie did not really get along.

"Now that Naffie is here you and Lansana won't have too much time together," she said.

"I'm not worried about that, I just want my sisters back," I said.

"Don't worry let's just pray for them, they will come," she said.

We walked around and went back to the house. We did not really want to be around Naffie too much, not because of Lansana but because I was not used to having her around. It was just Sunshine and myself with Lansana and the boys.

Sunshine, Nyalay and I went to her uncle's house, ate plenty of rice and meat and came back to the house. We found the boys in the kitchen cooking in a huge pot. "What are you boys doing?" I asked.

"Cooking," Laser said.

"Cooking what?" Sunshine said.

Alasan went to his girlfriend Zainab to take her to Sormu so she could be safe. He would come back and return to her every weekend.

"Do you want to taste what we are cooking?" Soja asked.

"If it won't kill us I'm sure we would like some," Sunshine said, "Isn't it Memuna?"

"Of course," I said.

"Ok," Soja said.

We sat with them and talked for a while then we went to the room. Lansana was lying on the bed looking a little drained. He was breathing fast and he was slightly sweaty. Sunshine and I looked at each other and I walked to him and asked him what was the matter.

"I feel sick," he said

"You are sweating," I said, taking the cover off him.

He held on to it as tight as he could and said "Memuna no, I'm cold."

"Lansana I think you've got malaria," Sunshine said.

He nodded and asked us to call Naffie. She came to the room and felt his forehead for temperature and she told us to get a bucket of cold water ready.

"It's just started so we can do something about it without the doctor; call Salifu for me please," she said.

She told Salifu to go to his uncle's house and get pawpaw leaves and some leaves which I had no clue about and some lemons. We washed the leaves, put them in a big pot and set it on the fire to boil and he had the cold bath first to bring his temperature down. Then his uncle brought some concoction in a bottle for him to drink. After boiling the leaves for about two hours we poured the extract into a big bucket and cooled it till it was lukewarm. We then took it to the bathroom for him to go and bathe again with some native soap his uncle brought. This was one of the native prescriptions for treating malaria. It is treated from both inside and outside. Naffie helped him bathe. He drank the concoction and threw up a lot and then we gave him some more and he fell asleep.

Sunshine and I went to the kitchen again for the meat the boys were cooking in the kitchen. It was dark and the weather was cold as it drizzled.

"Are you boys through with the cooking yet?" Sunshine asked.

"The stew in that bowl is for the two of you," Soja said.

"Thank you," I said, "but what exactly is this meat you boys cooked? It's a lot."

"Not anything that will kill you, old ma'am," Salifu said, making everyone in the kitchen laugh.

"Oh please don't start your foolishness again, Salifu," I said.

While I was busy investigating, Sunshine had already started eating. She asked no questions about the meat; as long as it is flesh she is ready to eat it.

"Anyway, thank you boys," she said, with her mouth full.

I looked at her as if what do you think you are doing. She came closer to me so we could eat the meat. I took a smaller piece and took a bite at it. It was delicious, but there was something unfamiliar with the taste but it was not bad. I just knew that I had not eaten that kind of meat before.

"This is delicious," I said, "what is this? Where did you boys get it from?"

"Tell us now; we are already eating the thing," Sunshine said. "I did not know you boys went out hunting today."

I shook my head in agreement. The food was very spicy but delicious.

"If you don't stop talking while you eat, the food will go up your heads," Laser said. "How is Bra? He shouldn't get sick we have to go soon. I'm tired of this dumpster. (Laser was Sierra Leonean but had picked up some Liberian words from Lansana and the other part Liberians around him) This place is a dead end I can't wait to go back to my comfort zone where I'll have familiar faces around."

They told me about Blama Highway while we ate the mysterious meat.

"Where is this Blama Highway?" I asked.

"Have you ever heard of a town called Blama or have you ever been there?" Sunshine said.

I shook my head.

"Well, it's somewhere between Bo and Kenema so our camp is only about a mile away from Blama in the forest. That camp is called Blama Highway because the camp is in the forest by the highway that runs through Meni-meihn, Sondu-meihn, Jui Koya, Bandawor and Waterworks and comes straight to Blama. We got all those towns and all the little villages close to them except Blama itself, but we are very close," Sunshine said.

"So, is there anyone living in Blama?" I asked.

"Yes, some very stubborn civilians," Salifu said.

"So how do they travel when RUF has the highway and all the little paths in their hands?" I asked.

"They got the other highway from Bo to Kenema," Sunshine said, "that one is more important than the one we have. They can still dare to travel to get food and other things they need."

I nodded.

We had finished eating the food.

"Now you can ask us to tell you what you just ate," Salifu said.

"I don't want to know anymore," I said.

"Yeah we don't care to know, it's already in our systems now," Sunshine said.

"Well if I said you just ate a very big black snake what would you do?" Salifu said.

Laser walked away from the kitchen when Salifu started talking. He did not want to be part of our trouble; they all knew what we were eating except Sunshine and I.

"Laser come back here," Sunshine called out to him.

I was busy forcing myself to vomit.

"I will hurt you boys when I'm through vomiting," I said.

"Well you haven't even started vomiting yet. So I guess we have more time to be prepared," Salifu said.

Soja and Lamine were too busy laughing their lungs out they could not talk.

Sunshine punched Salifu in his back twice and then she went to Lamine and Soja and landed both of her fists in their backs.

"All of you will pay for this," she said.

They brought the snake's skin out of hiding. They hid it from us so that we would eat the meat before we knew what we had eaten and they succeeded. It was a very long snake about eight feet long and black but they got rid of the head, they did not show us the head.

"So how did you boys get this snake?" I asked, shaking.

"We killed it when you two took Nyalay for walk," Lamine said.

"Weren't you frightened of it?" I asked, because I was frightened out of my pants of the empty skin.

"It was frightful but there were four of us. Laser was on guard a boy from down the other side of town helped us and he took his share," Soja said.

They said they were sorry for making us eat it without telling us what we were eating. They pleaded with us not to make a complaint to Lansana.

"Well I will accept your apology for now and give it two months to see if anything will happen to my skin. If anything happens I will tell him what you did, but if not then it's ok," I said.

Sunshine agreed with me and we went our ways.

Lansana woke up early the following morning feeling better but he still drank some more concoction and bathed with the native medicine. He told us to get ready as he was taking us to another village in Pujehun district called Sembehun. One of their uncles with his family stayed there and if we wanted to go stay with his grandmother and the others it was up to us. Naffie refused flatly as soon as he said that, she did not get on well with most of his family members especially his grandmother. I agreed with her because the further down we went the longer our journey would get when it was time to go to Blama Highway.

Sunshine and Yusufu got closer while we stayed in the village. Lansana and Laser had joined a convoy to go to Blama Highway. He promised he would look for Samia, Komeh and Magainda.

Naffie and I did not really get along too well; she tried to ban me from hanging out with Sunshine. She said we hung out too often and that I had other things to do, which I did not know of. Sometimes she would just get angry with the two of us. We thought she was jealous thinking Lansana would leave her for me. She tried to convince me to start going out with some guys but I rejected them and she got angry with me. She would not speak to me for days. We stayed away from her as much as we could and did our own thing most of the time. There were times we did things with her, but I still kept my eyes on Nyalay.

I missed Lansana so much I sometimes got close to screaming, because life got so tense when he was away.

Some days we ran out of food and Soja, Salifu and Lamine would go to the bush in search of wild yams or they would go to the other villages to Lansana's family for some rice and vegetables from the farm. I did not mind being hungry because most of the time I was so worried I had no appetite. I was mostly worried about the three children - Guy, Lucia and Nyalay - and I was also worried about my sisters on the other side.

Sometime in early February 1996, a message came that we should pack our things and go to Senehun. There will be a man waiting to lead us to Blama Highway.

We packed our things; Sunshine and I did not have much. We only had the things she had taken with her when she went to Sormu, which was a school bag full and about six pairs of underwear left between us. The same applied to Naffie and the children. Most of the times, Nyalay wore Naffie's tops as dresses. She was a big woman, not too big though. Guy was alright, he had some things to wear. We did not take Guy to Blama Highway; things were getting rough for RUF so Lansana told Naffie to leave Guy with his uncle, Kamor Ibrahim. He was an Alhaji (Muslim man who has completed one of the Five Pillars of Islam by going on the Hajj, or religious pilgrimage to Mecca) and a good man with a very young and beautiful wife who liked Guy very much. We took Guy to them and made sure he was settled before we left for Senehun as a prelude to our journey to Blama Highway.

Senehun did not look the same. There was no-one at the captain's house, the town looked like a ghost town - it was too quiet. There were very few people and the only household that was still lively was the radio house (the studio). They still played their loud UB40 and sometimes reggae music and GQ88 (a Liberian singer). We slept at the studio and early in the morning though it was very cold, we had to get up, bathe, eat something and start the journey. I was glad I was finally leaving the dead end and that I was going to see Samia, Komeh, Magainda as well as my uncle again and also Lansana.

Nyalay did not want to get up that morning crying when I woke her up. She begged me to leave her because she had a headache, but I told her that she had to wake up and get ready, eat something and take some Panadol.

Lucia cried when her mother tried to wipe her body with a warm towel. She fed her with some rice-porridge and changed her clothes. She did not have to stay awake as her mother was going to carry her on her back. On the previous night, I was told that the man who was leading us to Blama knew me only as Lansana's woman. So I should act like that till we got there or else I would have to stay in Pujehun District. They also told Nyalay to say that I was going out with Lansana just in case she was asked at any RUF checkpoint. This was all because I was still a civilian and in the age bracket of people that, according to Foday Sankoh (aka Lion), are to be punished. In order to consolidate the story it was presumed that Lansana and Naffie were not together anymore and that she was only following him because of the children- till Lucia became at least three then she would find her way.

The sad thing is that this lie almost gained credence and it was very disturbing to me. The reason why nothing happened between us was because I was afraid of being in a relationship I was still too young to sustain. He was ready to be with me anytime; he told me that the ball was in my court. 'Ready when you are' were his exact words.

The dew was still falling and it was very cold that morning when we started the journey. I made Nyalay rub enough Vaseline on her body, feet and lips and wore two tops to keep her warm and I did the same. The man came in a hurry wanting us to start early. That way we will get to Blama Highway within three or two days if we walked fast.

Everyone wished us well; they prayed that God would protect us on our way and even when we got to our destination. It was a little tearful. Some of them cried that they might never see us again - especially Nyalay and I as we were not from that part of the country. So there was no possibility of us going there again except if Lansana was transferred there. Such an occurrence was even remote as Lansana himself considered it a form of punishment, which he prayed should not happen again. I felt a little hurt and a little voice in my head told me to stop making friends because in parting we might not see each other again.

When we started walking I took my share of our clothes in a school bag – some of Nyalay's and some that belonged to Sunshine and I. The three boys had said they would help us. Sunshine helped Naffie with Lucia's porridge and clothes. Soja and Lamine helped her with their clothes. Salifu carried his, Lamine and Soja had the little or nothing they possessed in another school bag half full. We were all pretty relaxed; we did not have too much to carry. Nyalay asked Naffie to let her carry Lucia's two little bowls. As we started the journey I held Nyalay's hand while we walked and silently recited the Lord's Prayer. All of them, including Nyalay thought I was only holding my little cousin's hand because it was still a little dark.

It was harmattan weather in Sierra Leone. It is a cold and very dry season in the time of the year when people had the option to save their money or their skin. We had to use lots of moisturiser or our skin would crack, apply Vaseline to our lips whenever it felt dry or it would get so dried that it would crack and some people had bleeding sores on their lips and cracked heels. I could not wait to see my sisters and Lansana. I wanted so much to tell him how much I hated him for putting my sisters and me through this pointless and unwarranted pain. It was cold and we were all still sleepy so we did not talk until we really needed to; and to my greatest surprise, we absent-mindedly walked very fast. I concluded that the cold weather had a lot to do with this. The silence gave me lots of time to think and fantasise about going to Blama Highway and reuniting with Samia and Komeh and also going home very soon and telling my grandmothers the story. I also planned on what to tell Lansana when I saw him. I even thought of slapping him in the face, but I knew I was not going to do that.

The journey was not as tough on us like the one with Lansana, even though they were more or less equidistant. We had some blisters under our feet but not as bad. It took us three days to get to Meni-meihn, a town close to Blama Highway. It seemed this time we could take a little break as we were in RUF territory. There were not many people in the town, mostly guards, so we went to the bridge and got in the water to cool our feet.

Naffie put some water on Lucia's body to freshen her up. All of a sudden there was this loud noise and it was very loud. It was the jet spearheading an attack going on somewhere that we did not know about. We all ran into the bushes and hid under trees, it went on for twenty minutes then left. We got out of the bushes and walked as fast as we could to get to our destination before it came back. An hour later we were in Jui Koya. There were people there, we went to a house and they offered us some water to drink and we rested a bit while Naffie fed Lucia. Suddenly the jet came again, this time it was lower than before and the town was an open town with people everywhere. The whole town was in chaos. There were screams and people looking for their loved ones, some of us ran to the bushes for shelter. Nyalay sat clinging to Sunshine and me while Naffie sat under a tree with Lucia. As for the others, we did not know where they were. It went around the town for half an hour and flew off.

We got out of the forest and continued the journey in a convoy leaving those who were stopping at Jui Koya behind. I was so frightened and in so much shock that I forgot Lucia's baby food in the bushes. Naffie had made it from pan-toasted and pounded rice. I left it in the bushes where I was sitting when the jet came. We were about a mile and a half away before I realised that I had left the food.

"Sunshine, hey I think I left Lucia's food in the forest under that tree," I whispered.

She took a deep breath and said, "ah, don't worry we are already at our destination so she won't give you hard time about it. Lucia can eat something else."

Unfortunately, Sunshine was wrong about that. When Naffie found out that I did not have the food with me, she got upset and told me to go back to the bushes for the food or else I would be in trouble with her. I told her I was sorry and that I could not go back for it. Even though I was remorseful and polite, she was very furious, she made a scene and she started screaming out her lungs.

"I don't know what kind of carelessness is that," she said. "You are either useless or wicked."

"I am sorry. I was just so frightened when the jet came that I even forgot that I had anything in my hands," I said.

I was getting angry that I am someone else's daughter but she was comfortable calling me wicked and useless. I, however, managed to stay calm because we all knew that Naffie's anger was not all about the baby's food. Her anger was mostly because we were going to Lansana and she wouldn't be able to bully me anymore. So I guess she thought she'd better have a ball before we got there.

I kept quiet as tears streamed down my cheeks. I could not wait to see Lansana to take it all out on him. I blamed it all on him because he took us from our family and brought us into such mess. Otherwise Naffie would not have had the guts and opportunity to call me a useless and wicked person, more so when I was actually helping her in carrying the food for her. Besides I did not deliberately leave the food in the forest. She frowned so hard and kept grumbling. I walked past her because I did not want to argue with her, but Sunshine had had enough of her.

"Naffie, have you stopped to remember that Memuna is somebody's child too? She was trying to save her life and her little cousin's in that bush and she was very frightened. She has told you several times that she is sorry but knowing you Naffie, you only care about yourself. I guess you would rather she died saving your daughter's food," Sunshine said furiously and in a harsh tone.

"Sunshine, don't you talk to me like that," Naffie snarled. "And this is none of your business. It is between Memuna and me."

"It is my business, Lansana is my brother and he brought Memuna and her sisters into RUF. You are his woman but it seems you like bullying her, so I will stand for her while he is not here and I will tell you the truth; if you don't like it, tell Lansana and he will know the whole story and we will see how he feels about what you are doing," Sunshine said.

They went on and on. Sunshine refused to back off, as she was sick of Naffie and so was everyone. She picked on me because she thought that one day Lansana would leave her for me. It was true Lansana was ready for that. All he was waiting for was for me to say "yes I am ready to go out with you". Nyalay walked faster and came in front to walk with me. She had tears in her eyes and I told her not to dare cry that everything was going to be fine.

"I'm starting to hate her so much," Nyalay cried, "she is full of jealousy."

"Wipe your tears," I said forcing mine back.

Bandawoh was a little cold and dark; it was around 7pm. The guys at the guard-posts were very much alert. The breeze smelt of marijuana and cigarette. Some people were still in their kitchens cooking while some were sitting in their verandas talking. It seemed a little like a normal town that night without the guards. A young man I had heard Sunshine and Lansana bragging about so much came limping. His name was Drisa; he greeted us and took us to a huge house. Drisa was Sunshine's cousin, they were so happy to see each other. He told us how he had sat all day looking out for us. Naffie was sulking like a little girl, she only introduced Lucia and Sunshine introduced Nyalay and me.

Another very handsome young man walked into the room, he was an amputee and he used crutches.

"Hello Naffie. Sunshine, look how grown up you are now wow," he said, "and who are these pretty girls?" he offered a hand to me to shake.

"That's Memuna and the other is Nyalay her little sister," Sunshine said.

"My name is Den-Papa, nice meeting you," he said, "how was your journey?"

"It was ok?" I said.

They offered us all water to bathe and later we ate some rice. While eating Naffie brought up Lucia's food again this time no-one said anything. We just pretended as if she was not there and let her talk. This made her even more furious. After eating we went to bed.

CHAPTER NINETEEN

Phase Two

We went to Water Works the following morning as we were meant to live there. It was a mile and a half away from Bandawoh and it was a beautiful little town with identical houses surrounded by palm trees. It had a mill by the river. Now into 1996, January and New Year's Day had already passed with none of us realising it. The rainy season of 1995 had ended but it was still cold because it was harmattan. The sunny afternoon was still touched by a dry breeze. Nyalay and I liked the town the moment we arrived. I enjoyed seeing her smile.

"I hope Samia and Komeh will be here soon," I said.

She nodded. We were given a room in a big house, the first house as soon as one enters the town from Bandawoh. There was a forest on one side of it and we could hear the river in the backyard. It also had coffee and cacao trees in the backyard.

There was someone else living in the house - the alleged wife of Musa (aka Vayanga) who was also Sunshine's man. She was pregnant and she made such a big deal of it. She did not know me before but she could not wait to meet me because of what she heard of me from Lansana. She and Sunshine spoke but they did not really like each other. One could sense the strain in their conversation; it was obvious to everyone that they really tried hard to be civil toward each other. Naffie introduced us this time.

"Oh… Sia, how are you?" she said. "You look so good with that big belly. Look at you glowing!"

Sia giggled looking like a little girl. She was a small woman and pretty and so was Sunshine, but Sunshine was slim and tall and looks like an Arab. Her facial features looked very Arabian.

Sunshine and Lansana's family was a mixture of Mandingo, Fulani (a tribe of people spread throughout West Africa from Guinea Conakry, to Senegal, Nigeria, Sierra Leone, Liberia and Cameroon - most of them look

Arabian) and Mende. Lansana was very dark skinned like their father (I was told) but Sunshine, Lansana's twin Sao, and their other sister (both of whom I had not met) took their mother's complexion. But one look at Lansana and Sunshine one could tell they were related as they had resembling features.

"Thank you Naffie," Sia said, as she poked Lucia's nose, "So who are these pretty girls? Which one is Memuna?"

"I am," I replied, forcing a smile.

She came to me looking very cheesy when, all of a sudden, she was getting on my nerves.

"Oh, how are you? I have heard so much about you and I'm glad to finally meet you," she said, offering her right hand for a shake.

I took the hand, shook it and said, "Nice to meet you too."

I introduced Nyalay to her and she poked her nose too.

We went to the river, bathed in the water and came back to the house. Everyone in town could identify us by our names. They looked at us as if they had not seen people like us before. The town had about twenty houses and everyone knew each other. I did not have any footwear; those hunters that attacked us in Baoma had looted the last thing I had from my family: the pair of sneakers that I was captured in. I had also lost my slippers in the forest when the jet came so I used Sunshine's plastic sandals. Though they were oversized for me at least I had something on my feet.

Only problem was Salifu and Lamine teased me about them. Lamine stopped after I gave him an unexpected slap in the face. Lansana came to town from the camp that afternoon.

He seemed pleased with life. He gave Naffie a hug then Nyalay and then me. Sunshine walked into the room and accorded him military courtesies, after which they exchanged normal greetings. He asked us about the trip, how we were faring and whether we liked the town. I managed to get out of the room. I needed time to myself because I knew that he still did not have the girls with him. He followed me out to the porch ten minutes later. I was trying my best not to cry because I had a headache.

"I got a message that they are ok," Lansana said, "and I'm doing my very best to get you altogether again."

I turned around, looked at him and did not say a word. All I had were questions - questions now seemingly monotonous - so I said nothing. I just looked at him with tearful eyes.

He stayed with us for two days. The days were very hectic for me because I worried about my sisters and uncle, tried hard to stay away from Lansana, let Sunshine eat all the meat from our food to avoid an argument and I had to keep my eyes on Nyalay making sure she was not being sent around too much. I could not wait to be with Lansana and the boys again and, above all, I could not wait to see my sisters again. Samia especially was of grave concern as she was very sickly. I would have felt better knowing where she was, what she was doing and how she felt. When I was with Lansana, I didn't have to worry about him, I only had to worry about my sisters, uncle and trying not to make Naffie grow jealous so as to avoid friction with her.

I spent every night with Sia and she talked till she fell asleep. I liked her stories but I began feeling like I was in a tight corner. Musa had three women - Sunshine, Theresa and Sia - and they were all my friends. Theresa and Sunshine were friends which was a little hard for me to understand from the onset but later I knew what was happening. He was only really very close to Theresa and Sia. Sunshine, on the other hand, was always with her brother and she had other men, which was our little secret. I could relate to Sunshine and Theresa more and this, Sia was aware of so she did not gossip about them to me. She always told me stories about herself. But one night she thought we should talk about boys and me and why I did not want to get involved with anyone. She thought I had some problem with men. "You sure there is nothing going on in your head?" she asked.

I was beginning to get annoyed but I tried to stay calm and just said, "No, I'm just not ready. I can be good friends to guys but I don't think I am ready to be someone's girlfriend yet."

She lay in bed for a while as if thinking of something to say to me. Then she asked "What if this very good looking guy, with so much power comes up to you and asks you to be his girlfriend, what would you say?"

I knew just exactly what she was getting at because I had heard about this allegedly handsome and powerful Liberian boy Lieutenant called Lt Titan. Salifu, Laser, Sunshine and Soja had started teasing me about him the moment we heard that Lansana was transferring to Blama Highway.

"Oh, so you know about this Titan guy too?" I asked.

She laughed; Sia was so cute she always looked like a little girl. I liked it when she smiled and she made me feel so close to her; we talked as if we were the same age.

"He is a nice boy and he has never been so excited about any girl in this whole RUF. Girls ask him out and he turns them down and some of them beg to guard him," Sia said.

"Well, lucky him," I said, feeling worried.

"No Memuna, you are like a little sister to me now. You know what - there are so many people who want to see you," she said.

"Why do so many people want to see me? Is it because of what Lansana has told them?" I asked.

"Yes and it's all very true. He told Titan about you and the boy can't wait to see you. Lansana and Titan come a long way. We saw Sunshine and him grow up together. Suddenly he is now a Lieutenant commanding the whole Blama Highway. He is a descent boy," she proclaimed.

I looked at her going on and on.

"Why are you telling me all of this? What this boy has or doesn't have and what he is or not, has nothing to do with me."

"Oh yes it does. He is a good catch and you will be protected throughout this whole shit. Am warning you as a little sister, don't turn him down."

"Sia…." I sighed, "I don't. I don't even know this boy and I don't want anyone."

"You need to stop saying that because you will probably keep on saying it till you end up like me, not like I said that," she said.

"What, do you mean pregnant?" I asked.

"Yes!"

I laughed. "Goodnight, Sia."

She went on talking and I had to answer to everything she said. Eventually I fell asleep. The following morning I really liked Sia. Before he left, Lansana told Sunshine and me to get ready to go to the camp in two days. Theresa came that afternoon - she was a crazy one. We went down to the bridge with Arrow - one of Musa's bodyguards living in Water Works - to check his trap he had set in the river for fish. One had about three catfish in it and the other two a variety of different fish.

Naffie and her cousin (who came to visit her to make sure she was settled) had gone with Nyalay to visit a woman she'd befriended. The house was left to us, making Sunshine and me feel so free. Sia went to the camp as she could not stay in the same house with Theresa. We fried the fish, kept five pieces for Naffie to cook for dinner and took the rest to the room in a big bowl. Sitting on the bed, we ate while taking pictures with a camera we found in Lansana's luggage. No-one within RUF was allowed to take pictures as the enemy could find the pictures and look for the person to kill them. We did anyway and because there was no photo lab anywhere near, we were going to send the camera with someone we trusted. This could be someone in any convoy that was going to RUF's Kailahun base, so they could take it to Guinea Conakry for printing. RUF rebels from Kailahun (aka Burkina) went to Guinea once in a while to shop and came back without any trouble. Suddenly there was a knock at the door, as we made our plans about the pictures.

"Who is it?" Sunshine asked.

"Open the door and see," said the voice from the other side of the door. It was a young man's voice.

"Is it who I think it is?" Sunshine whispered.

"It's CO Titan," Theresa whispered.

Suddenly my stomach churned, I felt hot right away as well as sick but then an inner voice told me to stay calm, so I took a deep breath and continued eating the fried fish. I quickly slid the camera under Sia's bed as we were in her room. The girls looked at me as if they were asking whether I was ready to see who was behind the door. I looked at them and shrugged. We laughed and Sunshine told him to come in. He was just what Sia said about him. He was handsome and baby-faced with his head shaven, about six feet tall, brown skinned and smiling as he walked into the room. Two women were with him as bodyguards. They endeavoured to look bad forcing frowns. They wore baggy jeans; one of them had a T-shirt on and the other an army jacket. Sunshine and Theresa got up and gave him courtesy, they exchanged greetings and he hugged Sunshine. Sunshine, Theresa and the two guards already knew each other. They greeted and luckily enough no-one bothered to introduce me. He looked at me sitting in the bed and waved at me saying hello.

"Afternoon," I said, nodding at the same time.

"What, are you girls having a fish party or what?" he asked.

We laughed and Theresa asked if she could put some on a plate for him. He answered that he would have some.

"Hey, Sunshine, I just got an urgent call from Lion saying I should go, but when I come back we will pick up where we finished. Theresa can tell you all about what has been happening here," he said.

"I hear you all have been enjoying your life around here," Sunshine commented. "I hear you are now the company (from the Blama Highway camp to Water Works) commander."

They laughed. The two guards stood out in the porch while he talked with Sunshine and Theresa. I did not say much.

"Who is Memuna, I heard a lot about her. Is it you?" he asked, looking and smiling at me. He looked so sweet.

The girls looked at me and they knew that they had to leave that with me to deal with. "Oh, no," I said, "she is my sister, I am Nyalay. Memuna has gone for a walk, she likes walking about, looking for what, no-one knows."

To my own surprise I was so calm and every word came out as if I had planned it.

"Wow, is she as pretty as you are?" Titan asked.

"Well, that's for you to find out. But I think she is better looking," I replied, pretending not to care.

He looked at his watch and said,

"Well, Nyalay, nice meeting you, but I have to continue my journey now. Please tell your sister that I'd really like to see her the next time I come by and that's two days from now, maybe same time."

I nodded and kept looking at him; he was very handsome and I was not sure what to do. He said bye to the girls and he commanded his guards to follow him.

The girls could not believe their ears. I could not believe I did that either. Sunshine screamed as soon as Titan was out of sight.

"I can't believe you did that," she said. "What if he comes back and the real Nyalay is here?"

"Yeah, really tell us, you crazy girl," Theresa said.

"Then he will find out the truth; but if she is not here then I'm still Nyalay," I said, walking away from them.

"Oh my God, Memuna did you plan this?" Sunshine asked.

"No, I did not even know I was going to see him today. One thing I must say he is very, very good looking."

"So is it a yes?" Sunshine asked, peering at me intently. "Are you going to go out with him?"

"No! and knowing you Sunshine, I know you would want to talk about this all day. I don't want to talk about him anymore so let's drop the topic."

"I'm too hot, let's go to the bridge and lie in the water," Theresa suggested changing the subject.

The sun was setting and the harmattan wind started blowing. It seemed as though it was about to rain. So we dried our skin and walked up the hill home. Sunshine and Theresa still wanted to talk me into going out with Titan.

"I have not seen him with a girl before," Sunshine said through the wind.

I turned and looked at her; even I did not know whether to say yes or no. I liked him but I still had that voice telling me that I was not ready for a man yet.

"He still doesn't have a girlfriend. I was there when Lansana told him about you Memuna," Theresa said. "His face lit, he could not wait to see you and now you did this."

There was no-one outside except us three and two boys we did not know. Everyone was indoors because of the wind and it was a bit cold. I stopped and waited for them to come closer.

"Hey, Theresa, don't try to make me feel guiltier than I already feel. I'm confused enough as it is, so I need you two to help me out by giving up this topic till I ask to talk about it," I said.

We stood firmly on the ground trying to protect our eyes from the small particles blown in the wind. They finally agreed with me and we went home.

As we walked into the room Naffie flicked me a harsh look making me wonder again what I had done to her. Theresa, Sunshine and I looked at each other because we did not know what was going on. We did not expect her to know what had happened between Titan and I but, unfortunately, she knew he had been in town. She assumed that, knowing me, he had asked me out and I had already rejected him. The three of us did not say anything to her. Theresa went to the room she and Sia shared. Despite the proximity they did not touch each other's things. Sia had all of her belongings in the room, she lived in Water Works as she was a civilian and was pregnant. Theresa lived in the camp with Vayanga so all her things were in their shelter in the camp. Sunshine and I went to the room and got dressed. On our way out, Naffie came into the room.

"I heard CO. Titan was here today. So Memuna what do you think. Do you like him?"

"I don't know," I replied, trying to stay calm.

"What do you mean you don't know?" she said, the challenge loud and clear in her eyes.

"I mean I don't know if I like him."

"I don't blame you; you think you are just going to turn every man down. Lots of girls wish they had that opportunity. You think you are better than everyone," she said.

Sunshine said nothing but she listened angrily.

"I don't think I am better than anyone. I just don't want a man. Lansana brought me here and he will take care of me. If I were home I would not be forced to have a man; my family provided us with everything we wanted. At my age all I should be worried about is school, not men."

"All you think about school, school. Good for some. I will tell Lansana we need to give you to someone whether you like it or not," Naffie retorted.

"I don't think Lansana will agree with you on that," Sunshine stepped in.

"Stay out of this Sunshine; it is not your business. I'm doing my best to avoid you," Naffie snapped at her.

"We are going to the camp to be with Lansana and let me tell you something," my voice gained volume, "even if I decide to like someone I will still be with Lansana just like Sunshine. It is not my fault you don't understand what school is and those girls who want your so-called 'opportunity' can have it. Just so bad for them that no-one wants them," I screamed and stormed out of the room.

I had lost all respect for Naffie now. With her jealousy she wanted to get rid of me while all I wanted was to stay with my sisters and remain safe in a bad situation. I had talked to Lansana and he said I could stay with him even if I decided to go out with someone. Sunshine and I went to Theresa; she had heard me yelling at Naffie.

"What was that about?" she asked.

"Naffie can't wait to get rid of her rival," Sunshine stated.

"Hey, I'm not her rival," I butted in.

"Well that's how she sees you," Sunshine reminded me.

"I'll go out with someone when the time is right," I reminded her.

After that Sunshine and I tried to stay away from Naffie as much as we could. I kept my eyes on Nyalay always making sure she was alright. Titan did not come in the afternoon as we expected; he came in the evening and, unfortunately for me, everyone was home. Again I wished I could bury myself.

"Theresa I need you girls to help me. What can I do?" I said.

"Go to bed," Sunshine said.

"But he will see Nyalay and I know Naffie will be pleased to introduce the real Nyalay to him," Theresa said.

"Well, I think I will just have to face it. It is bound to happen sooner or later," I said.

He was in the house the moment the last word of my sentence was out of my mouth. Everyone greeted him but I walked away to the porch. It was a bit dark outside but I sat on the banister and stared into that darkness. I could hear him asking for me in the house. This time he was asking for Nyalay unaware that Nyalay and I were right there. Poor innocent Nyalay had no clue of what was happening.

"I'm here," she said.

"No I mean Memuna's sister - Nyalay," he told her. "The one I met the other day when I stopped here on my way to Zogoda."

Sunshine took him aside and told him what was going on and he said that he wanted to talk to me.

He touched me on my shoulders and said hello.

"Good evening," I said.

"I think we should start again," he said, offering me a hand to shake. "I'm Lieutenant Titan."

"Memuna," I said.

I wanted to tell him I was sorry for telling him I was Nyalay but I did not and he asked me if I was coming to the camp anytime soon.

"I thought civilians were not allowed," I asked, concerned at his reason for asking.

"But you are," he replied, though I was unsure what I could see in his eyes.

I nodded and turned away. He went back inside, said goodbye to the others then he left with his two guards.

Three days later, the day had come for us to go to the one and only Blama Highway I had heard so much about. I was excited to go there just because Lansana and his bodyguards were there. They were now like brothers to Sunshine and me despite the fact that each time I thought of Titan I felt nervous. We cooked a meal, ate and went down to the river and bathed.

Sunshine was so excited she could not wait to see all of her friends again. She could not stop giggling. Naffie was irritated when we got back to the house. She was upset that we stayed too long at the river. Since we did not care about her anymore; we ignored her as she moaned. She packed some clothes for Nyalay, Lucia and herself in a bag with some of Lucia's food and it was time for us to go. We had already done our packing the previous night indicating how much we could not wait to get away from Naffie.

The journey was about eight miles long and it was fun but a little spooky for me. Salifu helped Naffie with the bag and Sunshine reluctantly carried her niece Lucia, as she did not want anything to do with Naffie at the time. When we finally got to the camp I was both happy and nervous. I was always scared during our journeys, always thinking we would be attacked. The camp was in the forest on the highway linking Water Works and Blama.

Our shelter was really crowded with Lansana's four bodyguards, Lt. Cross's seven bodyguards Kasiloi (the senior bodyguard), Second-Phase, Mustapha, Ibrahim, Mbalu, Ganga and Hindowa. We had four shelters - each had either a double bed or a queen-sized bed with a doorway without a door. The four girls (Nyalay, Sunshine, Mbalu and I) shared the same shelter as Lt. Cross and Rain. It was a two-bedroom shelter with two double beds each. Naffie, Lansana and their baby shared the one next to ours while the boys had two left for them to share. This was convenient as all of them did not go to bed at the same time. At least four of them had to stay on guard all night and one of the two shelters – the one that was just a few meters away from the others - belonged to Hindowa. He built it himself.

Hindowa, like Magic, Hawk, Tiger, Second-Phase and their bosses was a pretty boy. He felt over the limit; there was a time when he just wanted a shelter of his own because he thought he was cleaner than the rest. He always kept his bed tidy and so did not like anyone going to his room. He eventually gave the room to us the girls and joined the rest of the guys. I was happy that there were so many of us together eliminating complete sadness or silence though we all had our personal hurt and inner pain. A day did not go by that I did not dream of Samia and Komeh, or did not pray for the four of us to be reunited. Also not a day went by that I did not give Nyalay a hug and ask her to stick around Sunshine, Lansana or me. Despite all this, I was still frightened out of my mind every day and I hardly slept at night.

This time I was scared of our situation, bombs and snakes. Those were the things I went to bed worrying about. Every morning we would all get up and clean the yard, shelters and kitchen. Salifu would help Nyalay do the dishes or, at times, we would take them to the wells in the garden and wash them, bringing them back hours later because Sunshine and Mbalu had their marijuana to smoke. We helped in the kitchen if we felt like it or we would dress up and walk around the camp all day annoying the "married" women. Sunshine, Mbalu, Theresa and I were the enemies of the camp to almost all of the married women except Sao (CO. Flomo's woman) and Edna (the ambush team's chef, Fambuleh's woman). These two were our friends and Sao was hated just as much as we were. They hated us because they said all of the men wanted us and were paying us too much attention. They did not know how much we, especially me, hated that attention. We pretended to like it because it drove them crazy.

It was a hot day but the camp was always cool as huge forest trees towered over it. After two days of sewing by hand I completed two white satin tops, one for Nyalay and the other for Lucia. These unisex tops were said to be talismanic for all RUF members. There were also two different types of necklaces which were also talismanic for RUF, one made of wild cat's tooth on a string of white tiny beads and the other was just two cowries tied together on black thread. I started on another top for Sunshine. She suggested we visit Titan and the other boys. Lansana was at Titan's shelter when we got there. We said hello and sat for a while. Titan was busy in the studio with Daniel and Robert while Lansana played chess with CO. Feel-good. The others sat under the trees and played checkers. Lansana did not want us to be there. He flashed us a look and I wanted to leave but I sensed that Sunshine was up to something though I did not know exactly what it was. She totally ignored her brother and focused her eyes on Titan in the studio. I kept sewing, looking up occasionally to keep up with the eye-game. It went on for ten minutes though by now Sunshine and Titan had started communicating through signs. Then I caught up with what was going on but was still unsure.

"Sunshine let's go," I said, "I don't want to be here any longer."

"Why?" she asked. "You let Lansana scare you away with those eyes of his?"

"I can't handle his arguments and he will blame everything on me even though I don't know what is really going on here," I said.

"Memuna please, listen to yourself. When did you ever let Lansana win your arguments?" she asked. "You better wake up."

I looked at her and shook my head.

"Maybe I'm not ready for one today, so I'm going," I said.

As I turned to leave she pulled my left arm and said "If you go now you owe me."

Then Titan called out to us from the studio asking us to wait, he wanted to talk to us. I flashed Sunshine a look and told her she was going to pay but she laughed.

Titan looked so good that day but I was not ready for a boyfriend. I imagined what he wanted from me so, though he is very handsome, that made me angry. I, however, kept my cool while my heart raced.

He walked up to us rubbing his head and he shook Sunshine's hand then mine. He asked what we were up to but I did not say anything. Sunshine told him that I was making a top for her and so she thought we should take a walk and get some fresh air. He asked me to hold up the top so he could see what I was doing and I did.

"Oh that's beautiful. If anyone told me you could do this I would have never believed it; you don't look like you do all these boring things. Can you make one for me? Please?" he said.

I looked at him and thought to myself should I feel insulted or flattered? So I said, "Well I'm a girl and, yes, if I still have some energy after I'm through with this I'll make yours."

He nodded and thanked me.

He said he wanted to talk to me so we went to a room in one of their shelters and sat on the bed. He was shy, he did not know where to start and he started shaking. I gained some strength from his nervousness. So I kept looking at him in his eyes, but he could not look at me. After a few minutes he mustered courage and then cleared his throat.

"Memuna, let me ask you something," he said.

I nodded and kept looking at him. By now we had our eyes on each other but he was still shaking.

"You know you are pretty, right?" he asked.

At first I did not know what to say; I thought 'even with my ugly boyish head?' but I said, "Well I've been told a lot of times."

"But what do you think?" he asked, "Look I've never felt this way about anyone before," he said. "I really like you, I think of you all the time since the day I heard about you and when I got to see you the feeling got intense. Please, would you be my girlfriend?"

Looking at him I did not know what to say. I could feel my pulse and my skin opening and sweat coming out, then I looked away from him. All this time Sunshine was at the studio with Daniel and Robert talking and really annoying Lansana.

"Look, I understand how you feel about this but this is not by force because I really want you and the fact that we are both Liberians has a huge role to play in this. So think about it but please don't take long."

I looked at him and nodded then we went outside. He asked me what I was going to do for the rest of the day.

"The usual, you know, annoy more people with my friends."

He looked at me and smiled, "Take care of yourself, while you're at it."

We walked up to the studio and Sunshine and I left.

"Now I know what you were up to you poppy!" I spoke to her through accusing eyes.

"I'm sorry and I promise I will help you get away from my jealous brother till he's calm," she replied, completely unrepentant.

"And just how is that possible? I asked.

She looked at me, let out a mischievous smile and said,

"Are you really interested?"

"In what?" I asked. "Your little trick you just pulled on me or what?"

"No, in getting away from the argument," she said.

"Oh yes, what are we going to do?" I asked.

"Let's look for Mbalu and Theresa," she suggested.

Around 3.30pm we went to our shelter and I told Nyalay I was going to be with Sunshine, Mbalu, Theresa and Vayanga's bodyguards (Turay and Amidu) at their shelter. This was only for her to know just in case she needed me but she was not supposed to tell anyone, especially Lansana. Unless there was an attack or anything she should stay with Naffie and tell Lansana where we are so he could go and get us.

We got to the boys' shelter and entered the cloudy room of marijuana and cigarette smoke. The reggae music was so loud that I could hardly concentrate. We asked for Mbalu and Turay told us to go to the main gate.

"What's she doing there?" I asked.

"She threatened to shoot Kasiloi if he did not stop teasing her about her spells," Turay said. "So Bra Cross armed her and put her on guard for a few hours; that's her punishment."

"Well we really need her," I said.

"We will have to go and talk to Kasiloi," Sunshine said. "Memuna if you talk to him he will do it."

Kasiloi, aka 'The wailer', was Lt. Cross's senior bodyguard. He was a very small guy who smoked marijuana a lot but was very sociable, especially with me. He and Second-Phase knew each other from childhood and they come from a small town between Kenema and Bo.

Sunshine and I went to look for Kasiloi and, luckily, we found him at Jackson and Franklin Morris' shelter. I pleaded with him to let Mbalu off guard duty because we needed her but I did not tell him why. We went to the guard-post and there she was sitting with her AK-47 leaning on her knee pointing to the ground. She was having a go at one of the guards at the guard-post. Sunshine told her that we talked to Kasiloi and he has released her to go home, but she needed to report with the arm back to the shelter.

Lt. Cross, Titan, Vayanga, CO. Flomo and Lansana were good friends so we were welcomed at any of their shelters at any time. We were always where the boys were which was either at our shelter or at Vayanga's. Everyone in the room was smoking and sucking on peppermint candy except me. I sat there sucking on peppermint candy and getting high on secondhand smoke. Initially, I thought no-one paid any attention to the fact that I was still not smoking after almost a year of living with RUF, but they were. There were about nine of us in the room and I was the only one who did not have a smoke.

"I think it's time you stop playing 'Holy Komeh' and started smoking, Memuna," Mbalu said.

Everyone agreed with her. Sunshine just looked at me and smiled.

"No I can't. I'm not a smoker I'll catch cough," I said, getting up to leave the room. "Ask Theresa, it's not that bad," Sunshine said.

I looked at Theresa and she nodded in agreement with Sunshine.

"Hey, this is a war zone - whatever we do God will forgive us and when we go back home - provided we live that long - our families will forgive us and accept their children again. Besides we are not killing anyone, we are just smoking grass," Mbalu said, trying her best.

"Shut up Mbalu, stop preaching," I said, making her and everyone in the room laugh. I was the youngest among my friends and they really cared for me, they looked out for me at all times but we all had to do foolish things.

"So what do you say, a roll for you?" Turay asked. Everyone in the room laughed, I just looked at him.

"No, she is just starting. So she will share with me," Sunshine said. "Besides she is my sister-in-law. We are taking this girl home to our family and Lansana will marry her!"

"I can see you really do need to get off marijuana, you are going crazy Sunshine," I said.

By now my eyes were really red and I was a bit high from the secondhand smoke. I took my first puff and expected to cough like the time I tried smoking cigarette in Kabbaty and the next day I had a horrible cold. Instead it was not like that, I did not cough at all.

"See, it's better than cigarettes. Although I smoke that too," Sunshine said.

I nodded and did not say anything. I was stunned. I could not believe I did it. Sunshine and Mbalu urged me to take some more puffs and I did.

An hour or so later Salifu came to call Sunshine and me as Lansana wanted to see us. I looked at Sunshine and giggled. By this time we had been in this room for more than four hours and everything seemed funny to us. We giggled about everything even the sight of Salifu was funny. We laughed at him and he was upset.

"Memuna, so you're part of it now, you wait till you go meet Eagle you will see," Salifu said.

"What? Is he going to sting me? I meet him every day so what's so different about today?" I said.

Sunshine laughed and sat on a tree root on our way to our shelter and then she gave Salifu a long hard look as if she had not seen him before and said,

"Salifu why are you so small? Look at me, you are older but I'm far taller and if you don't try to have lots more sleep and get off smoking, Lucia will soon be taller than you."

This made him really mad. He got a stick to hit us with but we ran off giggling.

Hindowa was busy trying to connect electricity from a car battery to all four shelters. He succeeded in doing it for the shelter he gave us, which is where all the electronic work was done. Though I was not sure of the wattage, it was glaringly bright. He was there with Tiger, Kasiloi and Ibrahim. Second-phase was on guard that night. We stopped at the shelter where they were and laughed at them a bit.

The batteries were used for flashlights and in the radios to play music outdoors and in the hut, while car batteries were used to power radios in the rooms. To ensure that the acid in the car batteries did not run weak, we used rain water to top them up. This we caught using a clean aluminium bowl set on a wooden high stool in an open space to retain its purity.

"Hindowa, have you ever lived in a house with electricity before?" I asked. "The brightness of this light tells us how excited you are to experience electricity." We laughed even harder.

"Sunshine, what's wrong with Memuna?" Kasiloi asked.

"Nothing is wrong with her! Look at her, do you see anything wrong?" she questioned.

"Well, if there is nothing wrong you better get out before I get off my seat," warned Hindowa.

We laughed at him some more. He was mad about me implying that he was a village boy who had not seen electricity before. This was only a joke, as we all knew that it was not true and that I was just messing with him. I knew he would not hit me but I ran to sit by Kasiloi because, like Lansana, he always defended me.

"I'm sorry, I was just asking?" I said.

"Shhhhh…. Hindowa is from Pendembu, he is not a village boy," Kasoloi said teasing him even more and making everyone laugh even more.

"These two have been burning goat caca with Mbalu and the others," Salifu said. (We called the marijuana stuck together like goat dropping 'goat caca' and it was said to be the best. I knew that it was strong).

"Good! Memuna tomorrow we are smoking together," Kasiloi said. "Where are you going?"

"Lansana wants to see us," Sunshine said.

"You are in deep shit, you got Memuna high and you two are going to see Lansana," Hindowa said chuckling.

"He won't know," I retorted, as I held Sunshine's hand and pulled her toward the door.

"And you are giggling as if someone is tickling you," Salifu said. "Let's go!"

As soon as we got into the room Lansana knew where we had been. He could smell it on us but he did not know that I'd done it this time. I tried not to laugh but when I saw him and Naffie sitting in bed I laughed. They asked me what I was laughing about but I did not tell them, I just shook my head.

"Memuna come here," Lansana beckoned me.

We heard the door open and Nyalay walked in asking where I had been that she had been looking for me.

He was smiling but his eyes were batting fast and I thought, 'oh, oh what now?' Lansana understood me very well; he knew all of my signals. Apart from my sisters only him, Magic and Titan knew when I was up to mischief. This is because sometimes I would give them signals that I was up to something but left them wondering what it was. I hesitated a bit but then I had a mint candy in my mouth so I went to him. We were both smiling at each other and Naffie started changing her facial expression while Sunshine, her naughty sister-in-law, stood by and watched.

When I got by his side of the bed I stood and kept my eyes on him. He beckoned me to come closer, so I took two steps further and stopped.

"Bring your mouth," he said.

"Why?" I asked. "I'm sucking a candy."

"Come on Memuna," he said.

He smelt my mouth. Our mouths were so close and when he looked at me this time the smile was gone.

"Have you been smoking?" he asked.

I looked at him for a second and shook my head. All this time he was holding my face in his hands.

"I don't believe you Memuna. Tell me the truth I know you did it this time," he said.

Sunshine burst out laughing and we all started laughing. I admitted I had just a few puffs and promised not to do it again. He nodded and held my face a while longer. He let go and told us to be careful and not get caught doing it. He asked us to sit by him and we did. Nyalay could not stop laughing and she gave me a hug. Lansana could not stop looking at me; his eyes were full of desire and tenderness. I saw that he was hurt and wanted more than just having me sit by him and smile. Unfortunately that's all I could offer him as it was all up to me to decide otherwise - that's what he told me but his desire was obvious to all of us in the room; no-one said a word about it.

"Lansana, have you heard anything on Samia and the others?" I asked, changing the subject. He shook his head.

"Titan and I are working on something, but I don't want you to worry just stay calm and pray," he said. He touched my hand and after a while Sunshine, Nyalay and I left them and went to bed.

"You see Lansana is dying for you inside. Why don't you want him?" Sunshine asked.

I looked in the dark for a while then at her.

"Sunshine, you still don't understand do you?" I replied. This is not about Lansana it's about the way I feel about having a boyfriend at my age. I'm just not ready."

"But you are not even trying and all the guys we come across want a piece of you. You try so hard to chase them away but it's not working."

"You think I don't know what's going on? I know that half of the men in this camp want us, but that doesn't change the way I feel. I know Lansana likes me very much - besides he reminds me anytime he gets the chance to." I tried to explain in a different way.

"But I don't feel good about ruining families. He has started a family with Naffie and she depends on him. Now if I get in the middle of that she and those children will never forgive me so I'm not going to help him leave her for me."

"Oh, I think Mustapha likes you too," Sunshine said.

"That's not possible, he is Magic's little brother," I said. "It's beyond nasty! Or maybe he's crazy?"

"You just watch and see," she said.

We talked till we fell asleep. Nyalay was not in a deep sleep by then so she listened to a little bit of our conversation while she sucked her tongue, clinging tight to me. I did not have to tell her to leave what she heard in the room because she knew that she was not supposed to talk about it.

CHAPTER TWENTY

Blama Highway Camp

The following day was cold, it had rained all night and the atmosphere around Naffie was tense. She was angry because of what happened the night before; she knew what Lansana was up to. Sunshine and I could not stand the tension so we took Nyalay to our shelter after breakfast and stayed till dinnertime. I did not even eat the food because I felt emotionally ill. So I ate some fruits for dinner and we hung out with the boys. I managed to stay away from Lansana. I did not want him to know what was going on in the house because he would get really upset if anyone made me uncomfortable.

The tension in the house went on for about two weeks which made the place very uncomfortable for Sunshine and me especially. Naffie had the habit of blaming Sunshine for anything bad that happened between her and Lansana because she was his sister. So she also blamed Sunshine for Lansana wanting me even though Sunshine was not with Lansana at 3pm on June 3rd 1995 when he saw me and decided to take me away from my family. She blamed Sunshine for him wanting to kiss me that night. Sunshine had been labelled the "bitchy" sister-in-law. It was also obvious to everyone that something bitter was going on between Naffie and me because Naffie scowled her face as hard as she could each time I was around.

As if the problem with Naffie were not enough, Titan wanted to know whether I liked him or not. This was all too much and I got very snappy. I had a headache and stiff neck from the tension and I tried not to direct my problems to Nyalay or Lucia. Lansana grounded me about five times and threatened to put me on guard (although I was still a civilian) if I did not stop snapping at people. Sunshine got snappy too and we were always together. Mbalu, for her part, did not care and she maintained the same composure – the annoying, cheeky person she was. We smoked anytime we had the chance to. It was dry season now and it got really hot in the camp. We would go down the highway where there was a little bridge with really cool and very clean water. One could see right through to the bottom. We would go there and spend hours smoking, eating and swimming. Although I was not a good swimmer I did more swimming and eating than smoking. As a neophyte I was afraid of getting too high.

I discussed the Titan issue with the girls and they told me to give him a chance. They assured me he was a good person, but all through this, I thought of Magic every day. I had really grown to like him and I was upset that he chose to stay in Kabbaty. On reflection I thought God made him choose to stay so he would look after my sisters; that was my personal consolation. I had sleepless nights and miserable days trying to decide whether to give Titan a chance or not.

As for Naffie I did not want her advice on the topic because I knew she just wanted me out of Lansana's life. I also knew that was the last thing he wanted. Though Naffie knew I did not want her to say anything to me about Titan that did not stop her for she went on anyway.

Anytime I thought about giving him a chance I would envision myself playing wife at his shelter. I'd freak at the thought and thinking about leaving Lansana and my sisters, left me gasping for breath. My thinking brought so much confusion to my mind it also made me bitter. I'd sit and imagine myself back with my family without the girls and I'd have to answer all the questions about their whereabouts, when last I saw them and what conditions they were in. I'd sit and burst into tears.

This went on till Theresa and some of the other girls we knew got sent to the actual Burkina Faso to complete a communication course. I was supposed to go with them too; it was only going to be for a few months. Titan and Lansana made all the arrangements but I pulled out because of my sisters. On a fine cool afternoon, after talking to Sunshine and Mbalu about Titan one last time, I decided he was going to be granted his wish, but with a few conditions. We had some smoke and the girls and I went around the camp looking for a pen and a sheet of paper or two so that I could write him a letter. I was too shy to say everything I wanted to say. Shyness was the last thing the girls expected of me, so they teased me about it. After two hours we finally got a pencil and two sheets of paper so I wrote him the letter. If I remember correctly it went like this:

Dear Titan,

How are you? Well I've been trying very hard to make up my mind and it's been a hard deal because I'm new to this boyfriend thing. I am sorry I behaved so badly towards you please forgive me; I think I like you too. But I would still like to stay with Lansana and we can spend some time together. We can take everything step by step till I'm old enough. So if that's ok with you then I'll be your girlfriend. Please reply as soon as you can when you get this letter.

Yours Memuna

I think I also told him that he was good looking.

We had dinner; I took Nyalay with us to the wells in the swamp and bathed. Then we sat a little while for me to tell the girls what I wrote because they could not read very well. They agreed that it was a good letter and Sunshine agreed to deliver it personally to make sure it gets to the right person. By now most of the guys had something against me because according to them, I was betraying Magic. They knew I was going to be with Titan - their reason was I like to be with the big boys (RUF officers) and Titan was also Liberian. Luckily I still had Kasiloi and Lansana on my side.

We got back to camp and we saw Titan's youngest bodyguard, Jonah. He was about eleven years old. We saw him walking past our shelter going up to theirs and, as it was around 8pm, it was getting dark. So Sunshine thought it would be less suspicious if we let him deliver the letter to his boss. I gave it to him and told him that it was for Titan only.

The camp was quite lively that night and after writing the letter I was in a better mood. Naffie seemed to lighten up a little and everyone sat outside the shelters on mats in the moonlight enjoying the cool breeze. I was waiting for his reply and it seemed so were the girls before we went for our usual late night walk.

Titan came to see me just after he read the letter. I was so confused I did not know what to say to him so I let him do all the talking.

"Memuna, can we take a walk?" he asked.

This left Naffie and Rain in shock eyeing each other but smiling. They were surprised that, all of a sudden, Titan and I were going for a walk in the moonlight because things had been pretty tense between us the past weeks. As for Naffie I knew it was her happiest moment since she gave birth to Lucia. I'm sure she thought that if I went out with Lansana's friend, things would change between him and I. Sunshine and Mbalu sneaked me a smile and I knew they had my back. Titan held my hand and we walked away but after a few steps I took my hand back. Standing by him I looked so small; he was a big man and quite tall.

"So did you write the letter?" he asked. "You sure about what you said?"

"Sure, I wrote the letter. I was already at the end of my first year in high school when I got captured. So I can write and read very well!"

There was a moment of silence as we walked on the path in the camp. He had Jonah and Jeff on guard that evening so they were with us but totally ignoring our conversation. He promised he would be there for me and he would do anything in his power to make sure I survived this war. All I had to do was to say the word. He kissed my hand and we came back to our shelter. Lansana and Lt. Cross were there so he sat with them and I went off with Mbalu and Sunshine leaving Nyalay with Naffie and Lucia. Naffie got upset with me whenever I kept Nyalay up late. She would say, "don't take my child (Naffie often referred to Nyalay and Samia as her children) with you when you are going on you secret trips around this camp."

The following evening the atmosphere was tense again. Naffie was angry with me and so was Lansana, but I did not know what for. In a conversation with Rain, Naffie referred to me as a green snake in green grass, but I pretended not to hear what she had said. It really bothered me that she'd said that about me. She meant that I was very sneaky; she did not say why she said that. So I told Sunshine what I overheard.

"Just leave them," she counselled me. "I told you to get on with your life and do whatever makes you happy. Life is short, especially here. You did nothing wrong to her – at least nothing that any one of us know about - so leave her. When it really bothers her, she will tell you what it is," Sunshine concluded and we went for a walk.

Lansana was due to go on his first big mission in a while and the boys were happy because they said he was a good boss and they were sure the mission would turn out a success. By then Sia had already given birth to a baby girl and named her Fatima. She looked so much like her father -she was a big baby girl. Sia moved to Water Works to take care of the baby. Naffie was also due to go to Water Works the following day so that she, Nyalay and Lucia could be a bit away from the danger zone.

Water Works is a small palm oil (that is what the mill they had there was used for) factory town, as I was told. It was in the middle of three little villages with a river running through it and near Bandawoh. There were men in all of those villages and a few grenade ambushes to protect the town while Bandawoh was the battalion base for the third battalion. So it was like the headquarters. Bandawoh was full of ammunition and I think there were about ten COs in that town. It was always lively; they did not sleep as they were always on their guard. One reason being because Zogoda - Foday Sankoh's camp (which some referred to as EMG meaning Executive Mansion Ground and some called it Lion's location), was only nine miles away. Zogoda was located in the thick forest of Jui Koya. Jui Koya was another big town and, as I was told, the battle to capture the third battalion was tougher in Jui Koya. I had been in that area once before on our way from Libya when I lost Lucia's food trying to hide from the jet-fighter. The town had very few houses left and bullet shells of different kinds still littered the ground. The guards looked very anxious as it was an open town (very few trees left) which made me imagine how beautiful it must have been during normal days. Now it was a ghost town because no-one wanted to be in the open.

We went to see Naffie and the children as often as we could. Sunshine and I were in Water Works every week because of the river and I wanted to check on Nyalay. The water was fresh and very clean, lying in it was very soothing. At times we would come and spend the whole day and then walk the two and half miles back to the camp in the evening.

Lansana made sure he was there at least twice a month. There was no need to worry as there was one of Vayanga's bodyguards, Arrow, who was a wounded soldier and could not fight anymore. Arrow was there to look after Sia, although they did not always get along. He would make sure Naffie and the girls were alright as well and they lived in the same house.

Women with children were safer in Water Works and Bandawoh. Arrow got wounded in one of his feet, which he almost lost. I was told that before he got wounded he was a strong fighter who operated only heavy weapons (like LMG - limited machine gun, RPG – rocket-propelled grenade, muter, etc). Sunshine told me that he got hurt on Blama Highway and at that same time Lansana, Titan, Drisa and many others got hurt. I wanted to ask him but he did not want to talk about it. Arrow's emotional hurt was more severe than his physical hurt. He spent his days fishing for Naffie and Sia. Sometimes he would go to the camp on Blama highway or Bandawoh. Arrow had a slight limp and he could not run as fast anymore but he once told us that if he were needed to fight he would go. In the eyes of RUF he was retired only without pension. Before Naffie moved to Water Works there was a day when Sunshin, Mbalu and I visited Sia after a swim at the bridge. We thought since with no other female in the house yet and she was a new mother she needed female company and no sooner had we returned to the camp when Naffie confronted me.

"I heard you wrote a letter asking CO. Titan out," she said.

"I don't know what you are talking about," I said.

"Naffie, but everyone knows that CO. Titan already asked Memuna out. So how is that possible?" Sunshine asked.

"Mind your business! You are another green snake in green grass. You girls think we don't know what you go around doing in this camp," Naffie snarled.

Mbalu just stood watching in disgust. The three of us looked at each other then at Naffie. We were surprised that she felt that way about all of us. It felt like it was not even safe in our own shelter, like we had no-one to trust.

"I wrote Titan a private letter but it had nothing to do with asking him out," I replied and turned to walk away.

"You did! I can't believe you are lying about it," Ganga exclaimed loudly. "I was standing behind him when he was reading it and I saw every word."

I looked at him, feeling so angry and violated new tears welled up in my eyes. I could not believe he poked his nose in my private business and, to add insult to injury, he ran his mouth.

"You are the worst man coming up. Men are not meant to gossip, it's a woman's thing," I yelled, "And on top of it you are so very stupid you can't read well. That's why you came to Naffie and told her rubbish. You are pathetic!"

I walked away crying. Lansana was not there either or else Naffie would not have dared to do what she did. Now I knew why Lansana was upset with me the days prior. He was jealous but I knew he would not talk to me about it in front of everyone.

Ganga and Soja liked listening to women's gossip and girls' talk in general. The difference between them was that you had to bribe Ganga with food or something to smoke so he wouldn't tell anyone. He just liked using his mouth to cause problems between people. As for Soja you only had to tell him that you did not want anyone to know and, at times, you did not even have to tell him. Sunshine defended me.

"You are a hopeless boy Ganga and I can assure you that you will pay for this, trust me," Sunshine warned him. She followed me into our shelter. I was hysterical.

Later that evening, Titan came around, saw, that I was not in a good mood so he asked what the problem was. I did not want to talk because I was only going to start crying again. When I thought of how Naffie and Ganga were conniving, I felt ganged up against and it made me sad. It was one more thing to remind me I was not at home and safe. Sunshine told Titan what had happened and he was furious. We told him that it was all under control, we had already told Kasiloi and all the boys were angry with Ganga. Tiger called Ganga a hopeless boy too for getting involved in women's business. Kasiloi just looked at him and promised to punish him when they came back from the mission. So we told Titan all this.

"Man Ganga all of us have seen our bosses do things but we don't talk about it, it's not our business," Tiger said.

Titan went home and we - Sunshine, Mbalu and I - talked to the boys till we fell asleep. Kasiloi, Tiger and Hindowa slept in our shelter on the bed with us that night.

The following morning we helped Naffie pack her things to go back to Water Works. Nyalay started crying because I was not going with them but I told her she would see me very often because Water Works was not far away from the camp. We walked with them up to the little village called Ngovokpahun on the main road between Water Works and the camp. Ngovokpahun was a very small village with a big RUF history. They were attacked by Guinean troops and Tommy Nyuma's troops in that little village and they lost two RUF lieutenants and some others but they killed lots more. I saw the skeletons of men in army uniforms in the bushes. Sunshine took me to see. There were also two burnt out army vehicles on the side of the road. On our way back to the camp Sunshine and Mbalu took me into the palm fruit farm where this heavy battle took place. They wanted me to see.

"When did this happen?" I asked because we could still smell the slight stench of dead bodies.

"On the other side of the road was the old Blama Highway camp. After this battle we moved to where we are now before Lansana was transferred to Mattru Jung," Sunshine explained.

"So, it was just almost two and a half years ago?" I asked.

"Yes," Mbalu said. "This was two weeks after Lansana, Drisa, Titan and Arrow got hurt."

Shocked and terrified, goose bumps rippled my skin thinking about what had happened here. I wanted to get away from there but I also wanted to hear and see more.

"So is this where they got hurt?" I asked.

"No, they got hurt on the Bo/Kenema Highway. By then we just arrived here to take over third battalion," Mbalu answered. "Lansana launched an RPG into the enemy's war tank and his own back blast burnt him. It was a tough one but Lansana's reputation got even better because of that war tank."

As she explained, I could sense the pride in her voice. They were excited and nervous to be there. Sunshine took over the story.

"Yes and for a while I looked after three patients: Lansana, Titan and Drisa and they ate like pigs!"

"Where was Naffie?" I asked.

"She was here, but she was busy with Guy and most of the time her friends while I looked after my brothers and Titan," Sunshine said. "But Magic, Hawk and the others were there to help me. That's why you see Titan and Lansana are tight and that's why Titan likes me like his own sister."

"How did Titan get hurt?" I asked.

"He was with Lansana, CO. Speed, Lt. Cross, Lt. Ninja, Musa, Drisa, Arrow and many other Lieutenants and Magic, Hawk, Amara and all of Vayanga's and Lt. Cross's bodyguards in the advance team. They went crazy because the enemy was strong, so strong that Lion had to send a reinforcement team," Sunshine kept going.

"Sunshine, remember how scared CO. Titan was of losing his leg?" Mbalu said laughing.

"Memuna that's a very scared man you have there," Sunshine said.

"After that battle he was promoted to Lieutenant and he vowed not to fight anymore," Sunshine said.

They took me to the other side of the road into the old camp and I saw some of the old shelters, but most were broken.

"So two weeks after RUF won the battle on the highway the enemies followed us here," Sunshine narrated. "We did not even expect them; they really manoeuvred very well to come right in front of our camp without us suspecting them."

"That's probably what they spent the two weeks doing," I said.

"That's the bravest the Sierra Leone army have been so far," Mbalu commented.

"Well, they had help from ECOMOG," Sunshine reminded us.

"Memuna, pray not to get caught in a battle between the Guineans and us. They will speak French or Susu and bomb till it's over; they don't have time to shoot."

This made me so nervous a sharp pain stabbed my stomach. I was afraid of bombs even though RUF was not the first time I had been in a war. It happened to me in Liberia only then I was not captured.

"Ok, can we go now?" I asked.

"Are you scared?" Mbalu asked.

I nodded. "Who knows they might just turn up again? See, they don't want to give Blama up,"

"And we are waiting for them," Mbalu said, with pride and confidence. "Now we know this area like the back of our hands and it is all guarded with grenades and ambushes!"

"Fine. Now I really want to be in the camp near Lansana just in case they turn up again, so let's go!"

They teased me all the way to the camp. I did not get upset because I had something to take my mind off what Ganga and Naffie had done. We were happy that Naffie was not in the camp anymore.

Titan and I tried to get used to each other but it was hard on my part because, at that time, I did not really like him the way he liked me.

Rain went to Kenema Bypass - an RUF camp in the mountains over Kenema. Sia and I were the only civilians over ten years old that I knew of allowed in the camp. This was mainly because we were connected with Commanding Officers. I stopped smoking for a few months.

When Lansana and the troops returned from their mission, Naffie and Rain came back to the camp. By then Sunshine, Mbalu and I had good times without anyone nagging us. I became good friends with Jackson Harden (aka Harder Than The Rock) and Franklin Morris. But even good times just meant making the most of this situation I had no choice over.

It was in late March 1996, over four months and we still hadn't heard from Samia and the others. Lansana and Titan did what they could to calm my nerves. Titan and I got closer. To my surprise I grew liking him and with him I always wanted things my way and that I got away with most of the time. We started playing games together like the Ludo game and at other times checkers. We also started going for long walks with both of us laughing; sometimes we took Sunshine with us. One sunny afternoon he went with Lansana to one of the places Lansana hadn't been to for a while. They also took me to the ambush; it was another small town between the camp and Blama itself. RUF ambush team took over the whole burnt out town, which had only about three houses left standing. We stood in the town and could see some part of Blama. While I stood there I gave credit to those people who bravely stayed in Blama.

"So there are still people living in that town up to this time?" I asked.

"They are very stubborn and troublesome. They come to the bridge at times and throw stones and insults at us," Lansana said.

Before he could finish his sentence we saw two women and some men on their side of the bridge and they started throwing insults at us, calling us bastards, as soon as they saw us. It was kind of fun to watch. At the time it reminded me of school, when girls got into fights in the corners.

We spent a few hours looking around. Titan and Lansana showed me where the land grenade was hidden and where the ambush was. It was frightening but adventurous. It was during the dry season so the sun was very hot; it was around 1pm and I was thirsty. Being hot and thirsty made me grumpy, so we got some oranges, lime and greens and then returned to the camp. I left Lansana and Titan and went to sit with the girls to get some rest. We still had not heard from my sisters. There were times I became very moody and resentful towards Lansana and I even questioned God.

Meanwhile Naffie still felt insecure because even though Titan and I were going out I still had Lansana's full attention all the same and always. Our group made the camp very lively as we always had something to laugh about with the guys. But each time I felt like I was having fun I felt guilty, got sad and sometimes burst into tears believing my sisters were dead.

Naffie moved to Water Works again, this time finally with Nyalay and Lucia. Lansana took another mission and Sunshine wanted to go so I begged to go too. But Laser had to speak his mind.

"Memuna, just because we are around your comfort zone you think you can trick us into taking you somewhere and you will end up running away."

"Why don't you think before you talk? Laser you are either just foolish or you like the sound of your own voice," I retorted. "You boys lost my sisters and you are afraid I will run off home leaving them, my uncle and Nyalay?"

Everyone looked at me with regret in his or her eyes and then at him.

"You sure you will come back?" Tiger asked.

"My sisters are here aren't they? I'm not that selfish."

"Memuna, cut it out!" Lansana demanded. "You and Sunshine are staying here and Titan will look after you girls, in fact Mbalu is here too."

Sunshine got upset.

"So after all that training I have to be a civilian now because of Memuna?"

Lansana just looked at her and she knew what it meant. I thought it was a bit harsh for her to say that, but she was upset and we were close so I did not want to make anything of it.

Rain was going to see her grandmother in the civilian camp called Target Q and she was going to stay for two weeks. We did not like Rain much because she was too loud and fussy though she was very pretty and friendly when she chose to be. So we were happy that, for a while till Lansana got back, we would be the captains of our ship. Titan did not really monitor us, so it was great. We did anything we wanted to do except having sex - that I was very terrified of. Although we were left alone it was still a little boring because the guys were away. So we went to Water Works for two days and came back.

The mission lasted four days. The boys arrived early one morning at about 4.a.m. and we were very happy to see them back, especially me. Although the only way we got most of the food we ate and other things (like toiletries and clothing) was because they went on missions, I was always very worried when Lansana went out on missions. He was my rock on earth in the war zone, so I did not have enough sleep till he came back in one piece.

They brought back a bale of new clothing and it was full of girls' clothing. They also brought some gold necklaces, food, medicine and smokes. Sunshine and I were like two year olds in a toy store only concerned with the clothes. We went into the other room and woke Mbalu up and then we started trying on miniskirts, shorts and T-shirts. We all had about twenty outfits each. I made sure we put some aside for Nyalay, Samia, Komeh and Magainda, still not losing hope that they would come to me anytime. There was no size for Lucia so Lansana took the rest to government property.

The following morning we could not wait to wear our outfits and annoy those women. I wore an aqua coloured flair mini skirt and a light blue little T-shirt that had the Pacific Ocean and the sunset painted on the front with the writing 'Pacific Ocean' that I liked. Sunshine wore a red T-shirt and a black mini skirt and it looked pretty on her long legs, Mbalu wore a blue T-shirt with one of her own skirts. We all always wore short things, which was why the other insecure women hated us so much. I looked good with a necklace but I was not really interested in them. All I wanted was some short things to wear.

A week later we went to Water Works to drop off the clothes for Nyalay, Samia and Komeh. We got there late in the afternoon and went to the bridge to swim. The current was a bit strong and the water had swollen a little as it had rained for three days earlier. I had on a white ripped denim mini skirt and it had black tights underneath it with a black T-shirt and a pair of aqua-coloured scholl mule on my feet – this time they were my size and mine, Lansana had brought them specifically for me. We stayed at the bridge till 5.30pm, which is not very good for women to do, especially young girls.

According to the old people in Sierra Leone, it is that time that evil spirits and lost souls go to bed or come out to play and if they saw a naked girl's body they liked they could possess it. That, they say, could lead to childlessness and miscarriages.

Mbalu was already under some sort of possession. Her's was by the spirit of the female secret society and she was not allowed to sing certain native songs anywhere between 4.30pm and 8pm. We were also not allowed to splash water on her. This possession comes with regular or sporadic fits. The one Mbalu had makes the possessed sing native society songs when under the spell. Sometimes they do not even remember those songs in normal circumstances. She will sing and even get very violent if anyone touched her without her request. Rumour had it she slapped Titan across the face and beat up another guy who later died in combat before I was captured.

That night we stayed at the bridge until Bypass and Turay came and got us. Naffie was furious, out of her mind, with us for being so daring because we knew what the consequences of our actions could be.

"Memuna, Sunshine, are you two crazy? Don't you have enough trouble in your lives with everything that's going on?" Naffie yelled. "And now you want to be possessed? You girls are too stubborn for your own good. You see what your friend Mbalu goes through, what more proof do you need?"

Naffie cared about us, it was just that she was afraid if she got too close to me she could lose Lansana but she did not know how to go about it. She thought that by making me miserable her relationship would be alright. She was angry with us; she kept walking back and forth in the house and to and from the room with Lucia on her back so she could put her to sleep. This time she was right to tell us off so we apologised and promised not to do it again. We also begged her not to tell Lansana because with him around we had our baths and swims at the appropriate time. He'd already told me off for bathing outside once in the early evening. One time in Kabbaty he took my bucket of water away from me and left me covered in soap foam because I was having a bath outside in the early evening. I ended up wiping my skin with a wet towel and went to bed. Naffie promised she would not tell Lansana this time but we should not do it again. I took myself away from the others for a time and just stood, staring into space, saying the 23rd Psalm to myself. I was terrified at the thought of being possessed.

The house was so noisy and there was smoke everywhere except in Naffie and Sia's rooms. Everyone seemed happy; apart from our little river drama everything was good. The children (Nyalay, Lucia and Fatima) were still awake because of our noise. It was not strange to see Nyalay awake at this time because she wanted to see everything that went on till the very last thing every night. Naffie would say, "Nyalay you better go to bed and stop trying to hear the last conversation.'" At first Nyalay felt shy when Naffie said it but she ended up getting used to it and she even used to Marion when Naffie said it to her but she made sure Naffie never saw her.

The house seemed like a bar only there was no alcohol. We had music and smokes; it suited us just right, except the little ones. We had dinner very late that night; we turned the music down after dinner and Sia tried to put Fatima to bed. Lucia, on the other hand, spent hours on her mother's back and absolutely refused to close her eyes let alone fall asleep. So Mbalu, Sunshine and I tried to make it up to Naffie by trying to get Lucia to sleep. Lucia did not want Sunshine or me to touch her and this frightened me, although she snubbed us at times for Nyalay. I was afraid she saw that I was possessed. People in West Africa believe that because of children's innocence God gave them visionary powers adults do not have. Sunshine and I left them in the room and went out closing the door behind us.

"Hey maybe we are possessed and Lucia can see it," I whispered.

"Don't even say that. Astafulai (Mende for God forbid)," she scolded me fast.

I whispered astafulai and did the sign of the cross and we went out to join the fun.

The boys were talking about when they were captured. During that time RUF was really horrible and it was especially easy for women to get killed because the rebels smoked marijuana, other drugs and gun powder freely and therefore were more reckless and were more tempted to kill anyone, anywhere, anytime.

"Nyalay go to the room and see if Lucia managed to put Mbalu to sleep," Naffie said making all of us laugh because we knew it was easy for Mbalu to fall asleep.

A minute later Nyalay came running and calling Naffie. Lucia was already asleep and Mbalu was lying next to her but a fit was starting. She was lying on the bed as stiff as a dead body with her eyes wide open, staring straight at the ceiling with clinched teeth and fists. Naffie took Lucia to Sia's room as fast as she could and we all tried to help Mbalu but no-one was allowed to touch her. So we took everything breakable out of her way so she would not get hurt.

With this entire event going on, Turay kept staring at me. Then he called Sunshine and told her he wanted to talk to me. So I went and stood by him.

"Let's go outside," he said.

I was afraid of going outside. I thought the evil spirit was outside waiting for me but he talked me into it and we went to the back veranda.

"Memuna I have something important to tell you but you've probably already noticed," he said.

"What is it? I haven't noticed anything," I said.

Some part of me knew what he was talking about but my other half did not want to believe it. So I urged him to tell me what he wanted to say.

"Memuna I like you, can you be my girlfriend? Please," he entreated.

I looked at him in the dark as I took backwards steps feeling confused and upset. "What?" I whispered.

"Honestly, I really want you," he said, walking towards me.

"Turay we are friends, very good friends and I'm with Titan," I wanted to remind him what everyone knew.

We went around the house with him walking toward me and me stepping backwards in the dark.

"Think about it please," he begged again.

Angry I told him there was nothing to think about. I just wanted us to be friends. I turned, ran into the house and to the room where everyone was with Mbalu. By now she was on the floor struggling and singing. Her voice was so beautiful I could not believe it was she. She repeated one line of the song in Mende and jumped to another song, which was not really clear. She called out to Sunshine and continued singing and crying.

"Sunshine, help me please. Bring a plate and set it on the floor by me," Mbalu said. "Pour some palm oil in it and bring a candle. Light the candle and stand it next to the plate. Hurry!"

She carried on singing and saying she was sorry. The next minute she was telling someone or something to leave her alone. As she was speaking she hit her head on the floor very hard and screamed for Sunshine.

I stood in the doorway, tears in my eyes, feeling sorry for her. I had not seen Mbalu this vulnerable. Sunshine rushed back into the room with a white plate and some palm oil with the candle.

"Mbalu the oil and the candle are here," she said.

Mbalu threw herself around the room a few more times and then she told Sunshine to take a slipper and hit her slightly on the head and feet three times (six times all together). Mbalu lay still and let Sunshine do what she had asked her to do. When she opened her eyes, they were red and she looked so worn out. She looked around as if everyone else in the room but Sunshine were invisible. She stood up, brushed her skirt off with her hands and calmly said, "They want the oil and candle."

She asked Sunshine to follow her with the candle and plate of oil. I was really scared as I watched them go to the bridge. No-one was allowed to follow them.

"Isn't it too late to go to the river?" I asked everyone there. "Someone should follow them."

Naffie agreed with me so Turay and Senesie followed them. They did not stay long but returned without the plate and the candle. Mbalu did not talk to anyone; she just went straight to bed.

"Sunshine where are the things you and Mbalu took to the bridge?" I asked my friend.

"Apparently the spirit wanted them so we left them there," she replied, unusually quiet.

I did not understand, but I just took it as she said. We did not spend more time outside because we had to wake up early to go back to the camp the next day.

In the morning, I let myself forget the truth of where I was and so the walk was fun. Sunshine, Mbalu and I jogged all the way to the little bridge by the camp. The morning was a little cold and the dew was falling but we were warm from jogging. As we got to the bridge we took off our clothes and jumped into the water.

"Oh God now I'm losing all my body heat," Mbalu immediately complained.

Sunshine stood in the water. She complained it was too cold to put her upper body in straight away, so she intended to do it slowly. She tried to sit in the water but we did not let her, we splashed water on her and she screamed. After skinny-dipping it was time to smoke. I did not want to smoke neither did Sunshine so Rain wrapped one roll for herself. I took a puff and left them to it. We sat by the bridge, smoked, then carried on our journey. We were only fifteen minutes away from the camp but we kept messing around and what seemed like almost half an hour.

Once there Rain wanted the full details on what we got up to in Water Works. We were not crazy to tell her the truth so we told her that it was boring. She did not believe us.

"You girls cannot be bored when you are together, you always have something to do or say," she said.

"Well Rain there is always a first time for everything," Mbalu said.

While we were on the topic, Titan arrived at our shelter. He looked at me and smiled and I stood there thinking does he sense my presence or what. He held my hand and asked me how I was doing; I told him I was alright. He spoke to the others as well. He took me to his shelter. On our way there he looked at me closely,

"You look tired,"

"I am. We did not get much sleep having to wake up early to come back to camp."

We spent the day together talking about my sisters and how much he liked me and I came back to our shelter in the evening.

Sunshine and Mbalu thought something had happened; they pulled me to our shelter to ask me what we did. When I told them that we just talked, they did not believe me.

"You know what, stop lying to us. There is no harm in having a little bit of sex," Mbalu said.

"I swear I did not do anything," I tried to convince them.

"Really? Why don't I believe you Memuna?" Sunshine asked.

"Well, that's a question that you can answer yourself. We tell each other everything so if something did happen I will tell you," I said. "But I won't make up a story for you, so I'm sorry but I'm still a virgin."

They still did not believe me.

"Well we are watching you; you know that thing is like honey. Once you taste it you won't stop so we will catch you and that day you are in trouble with us," Mbalu promised.

"Just leave me alone you two. I'm tired and take your minds out of the dirt."

It made them even more curious when I said I was tired. They said an ordinary conversation was not enough to make anyone so tired but I ignored them totally and fell asleep.

A month later, Lansana fell sick with malaria and this bout was more serious. We took him to Water Works and Mbalu stayed with him. There was a lady who knew efficacious native medicine for the sickness. We spent days and nights looking after him. I was worried he was going to die with the malaria making him very weak. He was in pain; he said his whole body hurt and he was too weak to walk. So I prayed for him every day and after a week of drinking the concoction from boiled roots and leaves, he got better. We had to stay a little longer for him to regain his strength.

Sunshine and I could not wait to go back to the camp because we hardly slept. There were too many mosquitoes and the place was too hot at night. In the camp even the snakes and monkeys knew they had to stay away and there were no mosquitoes.

One afternoon Naffie was busy with Lansana. They were in the hut on the other side by the house lying in the hammock to get some fresh air. So she asked Sunshine and I to cook dinner. I sat on the banister mindlessly looking straight ahead of me wondering what was going on with Samia and Komeh, especially Samia. I was cooking rice while Sunshine cooked the stew. She went inside to get something for the stew and asked me to keep an eye on the meat for her so that it would not get burnt. While sitting there a hand came from behind me and covered my eyes. Initially I did not want to say anything. I was not in a good mood that day so it was annoying me. The person kept holding on.

"When you are through with your childish game can I have my eyes back?" I said.

The person chuckled and asked, "is the diamond still mine?"

It was a whisper so I thought it was Laser.

"Go to hell Laser, I'm not your diamond. The person who used to call me that is not here," I said.

Magic used to call me his Black Diamond so I thought Laser was trying to mess around with me that afternoon.

"He is now," the person whispered.

Before I could say anything he took his hands off my face - it was Magic. We were so happy to see each other again we fell into each other's arms.

"Is the diamond still mine?" he said.

I nodded and asked him about the girls.

"They are fine. Your sisters are fine," he said. "You haven't even asked how I'm doing."

Smiling I asked, "How are you?"

"I'm alright. I missed you though."

Sunshine could not stop smiling. "So are you staying?" she asked him.

He nodded keeping his eyes on me and his arms around me and mine were around him too.

"I need to go talk to Bra in the hut so I'll talk to you later," he said. He kissed me on the cheek and turned to go to Lansana in the hut. As he turned I asked him if he was telling me the truth about my sisters and he nodded.

I could not believe it was happening. I was so happy I could not wait to sit and talk to him alone but mostly I could not wait to see my sisters. To me he looked even better, he knew he was coming to see me so he shaved his head just the way I liked it. The moment I saw him I had my hands on his head. I totally forgot about Sunshine I just kept smiling and she took the pleasure in looking at my every move. When I finally got hold of myself I gave her a big hug.

"What am I going to do now?" I asked.

"About what?"

"Him and Titan!" I whispered.

"Memuna, everyone in RUF who knows you very well knows that you like Magic more than Titan and Lansana more than all of them, so do what you want. Don't be scared we are here for you," Sunshine replied.

It was so true the way she said it but I did not know I was that transparent to her. "How do you know that I like Lansana more?" I asked.

"It's obvious! You think I don't see the way you two look at each other? And don't even deny it. The day you had your first smoke and he asked to smell your mouth you both wanted to kiss but you could not because we were there. I think even Lucia felt the connection between you two."

"Hey don't watch me like that!" I said.

It was true and I think Lansana himself knew and that was probably why he did not give up. I could not do it. He already had two children with Naffie and I was scared of going into a relationship with someone who was already in his mid-twenties while I was only fifteen years old. If he did not have Naffie and the children I would have been with him and no-one else. He was very handsome and he looked after me although that was the least he owed me and I was sure he understood my not wanting to have sex at that age.

We stopped talking about Lansana and me when we heard Naffie coming through the house dragging her slippers and praising God.

"My girls are in Koribondo Jungle and they are coping," she said.

"So how about the punishment that Foday Sankoh gave them?" I asked.

"Magic did not say anything about that, but I'm sure you will know everything," she said.

"So are they coming soon?" I asked.

"Well that is the next thing Lansana needs to put together," she replied.

I was very excited not only because Magic was in Water Works but also because I knew that my sisters were alive and would be joining us soon. I was so happy I was numb. I could not wait to ask Magic questions about Komeh and Magainda and particularly Samia as she was very sickly and to play with him the way we used to in Kabbaty. As climax to my happiness I went to the side of the house and cried, thanking God for keeping my sisters and also for Magic. I whispered to myself asking if this is what they call romantic love or that I just liked him so much. I wiped my tears quickly with my T-shirt and went back to cooking with Sunshine. After I saw Magic I was only in the kitchen in body, subconsciously aware of anything that went on around me. The only things I remember were the things I did with him that evening.

After dinner he managed to escape from Lansana and the boys so we could spend time alone. It was around 7.30pm and the moon was full and bright. We went for a walk we sat down in the gravel, by Captain Mon Fré's farm, on the road to Bandawoh, kissing and hugging each other so tight.

"I miss my Black Diamond so much," he said. "Are you ok?"

I nodded and told him that I missed him, my sisters and his brothers very much. I asked him if he was really staying.

"Well, yes but I have to go back to bring the girls,"

He stood up, helped me up and kissed me again as I stood up.

"I have to go to Bandawoh tonight and I will be back," he said, playing with my fingers. "Do you still bite your nails?"

"Stop teasing me about my nails! Why do you have to go to Bandawoh?"

In the moonlight he could see the tears in my eyes.

"Hey don't cry. I'm going to do something and I'm going with Mustapha and Laser. We are coming back tonight," he assured me.

As we walked back to the house I had on a ring that Naffie had given me. He felt the ring on my middle left finger and he put my finger in his mouth, sucked the ring off and placed it on his right pinkie. He knew that I was going to sit up till they came back from Bandawoh that night or very early the next morning, so he told me not to.

Sunshine and I were so excited that night we spent most of it talking. We fell asleep early the next morning in one of the rooms, which we had converted into a girls' room. We did this so that when we came to Bandawoh we would neither have to share the same room with Naffie and Lansana, nor sleep in the room the boys had slept in leaving it smelling sweaty. We had two mattresses on the floor - one double and the other single. The boys came back just after Sunshine and I had gone to bed and he came to wake me. I was too tired and told him that I would see him in the morning.

In the morning I had a very weird feeling that something was going to go wrong. Suddenly I was upset with Magic for making me miss him so much because if the other boys and him had agreed to stay with Lansana no matter what, Naffie and the girls would have followed us to Libya.

"What's wrong with you?" Sunshine asked. "One minute you are happy the next you are upset, what's wrong?"

I did not want to start crying again so I did not say anything. I just shook my head and looked away from Sunshine. She took me to the bridge so we could talk while we bathed in the river.

"Sunshine, I'm afraid he will not come back when he goes for the girls," I confided.

"He will Memuna; he is going to bring Magainda, Samia and Komeh, and the rest of the boys are coming too. I'm sure that's what Lansana is discussing with him, so don't get sad about that."

I nodded and went down into the water. When I brought my head out of the water Sunshine was standing in the water with her eyes fixed on me.

"What? Why are you looking at me like that?" I asked.

"You really like Magic, don't you Memuna?"

As much as I did not want to admit it I told her the truth.

"Yes. Don't get me wrong, Sunshine, you are my best friend but you are like a sister-best friend," I tried to explain. "But Magic, he is my first boyfriend and my best friend; we talk and cry together. He talks to me about his family and I let him cry if he needs to and he does the same for me. He is always happy, he knows when I'm sad, happy or upset and I know when he wants me to stop doing things I do that annoy him. We understand each other and I don't want to lose him."

Sunshine looked at me with understanding reflected in her eyes and nodded.

"You know every one of us knows that Magic is crazy about you and we all see how much you two understand each other," she said. "The painful thing is that we all have people we really want to have to ourselves in this place, but it's a war zone Memuna. We all know that we shouldn't be so attached but we can't help it."

"So who do you feel this way about?" I asked, knowing whom exactly she meant.

"Who else? You know it's Musa," she said. "But he is too busy with other women so I'm doing my own thing too."

I asked her why she could not tell Musa about her feelings and she told me that he was aware of her feelings for him but they just needed the right time to talk things over. Until then she would do whatever pleased her.

Magic stayed for another day then it was time for him to go back to the Koribondo Jungle. I was not worried or sad about him going this time because he told me he was going to get my sisters. I knew that this separation was going to last for at least two to three weeks before I could see him and my sisters again. The thought of being reunited with my sisters and having Magic back in a few weeks made me happy. I could see the glow on my face when I looked in the mirror and it was obvious to everyone. All the bodyguards teased me about it; they teased me more about wanting Magic back. Kasiloi got a little distant, which I think was because of how close he saw I was to Magic and though I could sense a bit of jealousy from him but I managed to keep our friendship going.

So Magic and I were the talk of the town. The few days we spent together became everyone's bedtime story and everyone had something to say. Titan did not say a word about Magic and I thought that even though he knew about us, he pretended to be in a different level as if he did not hear any of the gossip. He neither asked me any question nor made any comment on the matter. He did not even show any anger towards me or anyone else. I was scared of how calm he was and I thought he was being cold to make me feel bad; but again I thought it was because they knew each other since they were little and he did not want me to go between them. Titan would normally question my every move.

Lansana got better and regained his strength, though not fully and we went back to the camp. We were happy to go back to the camp because we could not stand the mosquitoes in Water Works anymore. There were about a thousand of us living in the camp including children. It was in the forest but I only heard about snakes twice.

Titan came to sit with Lansana and when he saw me, gave me a kiss and hugged me just as he always did. He told me how much he missed me but he did not really say much more to me.

Sunshine and I found Mbalu and asked for some food. She told us she was just getting ready to cook dinner so we went in the kitchen to help her cook quickly.

On his way home Titan came to the kitchen. Taking me aside he told me he was going to Zogoda as Foday Sankoh wanted to see him. He explained that he was going to Zogoda with some other commanding officers. They were going to organise a big mission and if Lansana felt well enough to make the journey he would go too. He promised he would be back in a few days.

"Anyway Lansana told me that the girls are alright and that they will be here soon," he said, encouragingly.

"Yes. Magic came and he said the same thing too and he has gone to get them," I said. There was a long silence. I was not sure why but I thought it was because I said Magic's name. I was not trying to hurt him; I just wanted him to know what exactly was going on.

"Has he gone back already?" he asked.

"He said they were leaving yesterday evening. I saw him yesterday afternoon, we arrived here this morning so he must be gone by now."

Later that evening news came to the camp that Magic's convoy had been delayed for four more days. His brothers were happy that they would get to spend some time with him and so was I.

I was, however, not too thrilled by the fact that, this time, he was coming to the camp. I was happy but worried that I was going to hurt Titan. In a way, I felt more of a girlfriend to Magic than I did to Titan. With Titan I felt like whatever it was between us was a duty to myself to keep protected and this hurt me a lot; because he really liked me while I tried to push him away. I did so sometimes by not speaking to him, ignoring him and doing a lot of hurtful things to him but none of that changed the way he treated me.

The following day Lansana, Lt. Cross, Titan, Sunshine and some of the bodyguards went to Bandawoh where they will convene at the meeting. Titan was going to Zogoda with the battalion commander - a Liberian called Captain Sniper. Snake, Titan, CO. Flomo and Lt. Feel-good were like brothers. Sunshine went just in case Lansana had a relapse and she could look after him. A few weeks earlier we heard on BBC news that the leader of the National Patriotic Revolutionary Council, Valentine E. M. Strasser had been overthrown by his own Brigadier General Julius Maada Bio and he was exiled from the country. RUF was really excited; they thought it was a sign they were winning the war and they made up a song swearing at his mother. The words of the song became familiar to even the youngest child who could talk.

I was left with Mbalu, Rain, Laser, Second-phase and the little bodyguards. It was a rainy day in the dry season and everyone - but our friends, the boys and us - seemed to be in a bad mood. We made a lot of noise and, as far as I was concerned, in a matter of weeks I was going to be reunited with my sisters. So I decided to stop worrying, start living, forget about tomorrow particularly as I had no guarantee that I was going to see the next hour.

We had so much to eat that I found it hard to breathe. Edna cooked and brought a big bowl of rice with lots of fish over for us to eat together and so did Sao. We deliberately started cooking at the same time just so we could finish together and eat together. Mbalu and I told Rain to relax and let us do the cooking. We smoked as we cooked. Titan and Lansana were not in the camp so I had nothing to worry about. Sao was in between our kitchen and hers for the smoke. She did not want her man to see her smoking; he was in their shelter.

"Sao where is CO. Flomo?" I asked

"He is in the room copying music for you and fixing other things," she said as she slowly blew out the marijuana smoke.

CO. Flomo liked me very much, he did his best to understand me and every day he visited me. There were times he would bring his food over for me to eat with him or he would come and get me and take me to his shelter to eat with him. He'd say, 'come here you Mende girl, you don't eat with your man but you will eat with your brother-in-law.' If I resisted he would take me anyway and make me sit watching while he ate which always made everyone laugh. Sao was always glad when he did that; she would have time to play around with the girls. He knew that I liked listening to Burning Spear and Lucky Dube and he wanted me to know all the words because Titan liked those artists as well. So he would sit and write the words for me and I liked that.

After dinner we continued to make noise with the boys and played games – Ludo and checkers. Jackson liked playing Ludo with me because he enjoyed it when I unsuccessfully cheated to win, as in the end I lost and he teased me about it. Early on that evening though the rain ceased, it was a little chilly and Mbalu and I were left with the guys. Edna and Sao were with their men. It was always like that: we would spend all day together but at night it was Sunshine, Mbalu and me left with the boys, which was alright for us.

Mbalu and I thought it was too muddy and disgusting to go to the garden in the swamp to bathe and it was too cold to walk all the way to the bridge to swim. So we had water in containers in the shelters so we could warm some water over the fire in the kitchen and bathe from the buckets. We both hated the bathroom, especially me. It was a little spot with zinc around it and lots of stones to keep the grass from growing but worms came out through the stones and that's what I hated. So, on good days, I preferred to bathe outside in my undies in the dark.

On this cold night, while sitting by the fire, I told Mbalu a lot about my sisters and how much she and Komeh had the same personality. Suddenly we heard the boys laughing loudly and heard them greeting someone. We knew it was not Lansana because the noise was too much. Then I heard Laser say, "'it's for you sir,'" (they said that when they saluted their superiors and sometimes they said Good evening or Good afternoon).

"Who is Laser giving courtesy to?" Mbalu asked.

"Go see if you really want to know but I'm not getting away from this fire until it's time for me to bathe," I replied.

Then we heard Magic's voice calling my name.

"Memuna, Memuna," he said.

Mbalu and I looked across the fire at each other in surprise.

"Is that who I think it is?" Mbalu asked.

Smiling we jumped to go and see him. I was shocked and confused, but I managed to stay calm. It was good that Titan was out of the camp so at least that issue was not too much of a problem. Mbalu and Magic met half way and gave each other a big hug and I stood there watching them.

"You are even finer and sexier Magic," Mbalu said.

He smiled but all this time his eyes were on me standing behind Mbalu. I knew that they knew each other and that they had not seen each other for a while so I was not bothered. He came to me, kissed me and hugged me.

"I thought you would have been in Koribondo Jungle by now," I said, through my smile.

"Yes... but we have to wait a little. Anyway I'm glad I get to spend some time with you my diamond," he said.

As the noise and the loud reggae music got louder, the cloud of cigarette and marijuana smoke got thicker in the boys' shelter and everyone got more excited. Magic asked me for a bucket of water for him to bathe. While he was bathing Mbalu and I had to cook another meal.

Later that night the two of us sat together in the new shelter. It was built in the form of a hut to sit in when people needed some fresh air and talk. It was mostly used by the men as we were not bored enough to sit in a hut for fresh air. Mbalu told me that when Magic comes back with my sisters, I should not let him go away from me again. She said she liked me more with him around because she thought he brought out a side of me she had not seen before.

"You know, he used to be my boyfriend but that was years ago," she confided.

"Oh, so why didn't you tell me this all this time?" I asked, feeling a little bit embarrassed.

"I did not think it mattered anymore because it was a long time ago when we just opened Blama Highway," she said. "Anyway he is much older now and he loves you so let's forget about it and you have nothing to worry about - we are like sisters."

She wanted to smoke again but I could not. The last thing I wanted was for Magic to get mad at me. So Mbalu went to Lansana's shelter where the boys were smoking as she was welcomed to smoke with them but I was not. So I went to tell Rain that I was going to be with Mbalu and the boys just in case she needed me for anything. Magic told us Lansana was in Water Works with Sunshine. He had gone into relapse but Sunshine was coming back to the camp in the morning leaving Lansana with Naffie. So I slept in Rain room with her and Strength till Sunshine was back. I did not want to sleep in our shelter alone as Mbalu was now going out with Laser and they slept together.

I went to join them in the cloudy room. Magic beckoned me to come to him when I walked into the room. Second-phase, Laser and Magic sat on the bed playing a game of cards. Mbalu had a big roll of marijuana in her hand; she winked at me and smiled slightly when I reached for Magic's hand. He kissed me on the cheek and mistakenly scorched me with his marijuana on the back of my hand. He apologised and indicated that I rest my head on his lap.

"Memuna is so spoilt with attention," Laser said.

"You always have something to say don't you?" I retorted.

"So you two are still the same?" Magic observed, smiling.

"Ask Laser, he is completely refusing to grow up and leave me alone."

"Laser is a big boy, he is grown up," Mbalu said jokingly.

"Really, or is it just wishful thinking?" I said.

Magic kissed me so I would not say anymore. He knew that when Laser and I started we went on for hours though we did not stay mad at each other. For most of the time he gave up because I'd threatened to tell Lansana who would scold him or put him on guard duty. In Kabbaty when Laser upset me, Lansana would jail him.

The game ended and Magic went outside. I thought he went out to use the rest room, but five minutes later Salifu came to get me.

"Memuna, Magic wants to see you, he is in the other shelter under the big tree," he said.

I was a little nervous but I calmed myself because we had spent nights together before and nothing happened.

"Magic, you can't ask me to sleep here with you tonight because when Lansana comes that will be the first thing that will come out of Rain mouth before hello," I said.

"Ok, so Rain is still talkative?" he asked.

"Well apparently they say the only two things that have changed about Rain is that she has a baby now and she doesn't go on missions anymore."

We talked about Samia, Komeh and Magainda for a short while and he asked me if I really wanted him to come back.

"Of course, why do you ask that?"

"I heard there is something going on between you and Titan and, honestly, seeing you two together will hurt me to death."

"You were not here and I did not think I would see you again although I hoped to. There is nothing much going on between Titan and me, nothing has happened," I tried to assure him.

"So you are saying that you are still a virgin?" he asked.

I nodded

"I don't believe you this time."

"Magic, I can tell you the sky is red when it's really blue and you would believe me without making any effort to verify it for yourself. But when it comes to my virginity you don't believe me," I said.

"Well make me believe you, after all we are going to be together again."

I lay down next to him staring at the ceiling thinking that I had to do something just for him to come back with the girls when he went back to Koribondo Jungle. He kissed me but I did not respond. The thought of losing my virginity that night at that age was not at all appealing. I was tense, still and afraid I could get pregnant.

"What's wrong Memuna? Don't you want me anymore?" he asked.

I looked at him for a short moment and looked away.

"No, it's not that, I'm just thinking," I replied.

"Please don't say no tonight," he said. "I will come back with the girls and we will be together so don't worry."

Then he kissed me again as he lifted my skirt up. There was still no response from me but I tried to give in because to me there was no way out this time. I had to do something to make him come back with the girls especially Samia because Komeh was with her boyfriend and so was Magainda. I was really worried about Samia though I missed all of them and I wanted us all to go home together. I kept telling myself that I had something to gain out of breaking my promise to myself – I had promised myself that I would wait till I was nineteen or twenty-one before I had sex. He tried, but it was too emotionally painful and scary as I felt him find his way along my inner thigh. I could not bear the situation for what seemed like two minutes or less and, crying for him to stop, he did and apologised.

I could see in his face that he was pleased to be the first man to touch that part of my body so he had no problem with getting off me. Just knowing that I was telling the truth about being a virgin was enough for him. I was angry with him though. So I got dressed, went to our shelter and got ready for bed. I did not tell anyone what had happened but he told Laser and asked him not to tell anyone. When I went outside to pee I saw the two of them talking in the hut and on my way back to Rain room to sleep he called me and I went to him. He sat me on his lap and told Laser to look after me. At this moment the sight of him was the last thing I wanted to see.

"Look I'm tired I need to go to bed. Laser can't even look after himself," I said.

I told them both goodnight and I went to bed vowing that sex was out of my vocabulary until I'm nineteen no matter what, I was sure that the shameful experience would make Magic bring the girls.

Early the following morning Magic was leaving. I woke up to wish him a safe journey kissing him on his cheek. Rain was leaving that morning as well to go to Naffie and then take off to see a friend of hers in another town where she was meant to spend two weeks. I was a little down and everyone knew that it was because Magic had left, but it was not entirely that. It was more because I felt guilty about how close I came to breaking my promise to myself, but I did not tell anyone.

Sunshine came back to the camp in the afternoon. It was sunny and dry so the three of us: Sunshine, Mbalu and myself, went to the garden in the swamp and smoked.

"So Memuna what happened?" Sunshine asked.

"What do you mean?" I asked.

"Well, did you and Magic do it?"

Shocked, I stopped smoking and held my smoke as I looked at her.

"When is this going to stop?" I asked, frustration and my earlier anger returning.

"Well we are friends and I'm just asking," she said.

Mbalu just sat there smoking; she did not say anything at first. I told Sunshine that we almost did but we did not do anything and the last thing I needed was for them to make me feel worse than I already did.

"Well that's not what I heard from that bitch with the big mouth," Sunshine replied. Mbalu chimed in,

"So, Rain took off from here early this morning to go talk about Memuna!"

I was so angry I was shaking and if Rain were in the camp that morning she would have seen a side of me she has not seen. I had lost all respect for her and I hated her. "Rain is lucky she is not here or else she would have me hot," I told them.

"Why is she like that?" Mbalu asked. "After all the beatings she's had for her mouth she will never change," Sunshine agreed.

"I was so angry when I heard her gossiping to Naffie I just wanted to tell her off. I mean even if you and Magic did something I wanted to hear it from you not by hearing her gossiping to Naffie," Sunshine said.

I kept rubbing my head so furious I just wanted to scream. All I wished was that Lansana never found out and I was glad that Magic and I did not go any further; and as far as I was concern I knew I was still a virgin.

"If Lansana asks me I will report Rain to her husband," I said. "You know she is the only grown woman I know in my whole life who doesn't shower twice a day and she won't tell the world how dirty she is, all she does is talk about others - people far younger than she is."

"Lucky she bathes in the evenings now-a-days because before she had her baby she had to be told when to clean her own body," Mbalu said.

It was disgusting and funny, but I was too angry to laugh. Sunshine and Mbalu laughed about it as I sat there staring into space while my smoke burnt away. Mbalu asked me whether I was ok.

"You know it's not only African men that get excited about virgins, the women do too and I just wished that everyone would leave me alone. I don't owe my virginity to anyone," I said tears rolling down my cheeks.

"Don't cry about this. Just let's set a trap for that foolish bitch and I know we will catch her poking her nose in our business," was Mbalu's idea.

Walking through the forest we smoked and got to the bridge to swim. When we got home Titan was in the camp. He sent his bodyguard to call me. Jonah came to our shelter as soon as I walked into our room to change my clothes, telling me that Titan wanted to see me and that he arrived an hour ago. I was nervous, but the girls told me that I should just calm down. So I got dressed and went over to his place. I was surprised at what I found.

His face lit up as soon as he saw me walking towards him in the studio. He got up and Daniel and Robert his house mates who were in charge of communication were smiling at me as well.

"Hello," I said to all of them.

Holding my hand Titan took me to his room.

"Why are you back so soon?" I couldn't help asking him.

"I didn't go to Zogoda. In the end I stayed at Bandawoh and talked to my brother about the mission. I missed you. Are you alright with Lansana and Sunshine away?" After this morning's trouble I felt he was so kind to ask.

"Everything is alright. Sunshine came back this afternoon just a few hours before you."

We both were on the bed talking as he said he just wanted my company.

"Your body feels warm, are you alright?" I had to interrupt our talking to find out.

"I feel a bit sickly but I just need to rest," he replied, still smiling at me.

I was not sleepy so we talked a little more and I left him to sleep.

CHAPTER TWENTY ONE

Unwell In a Rebel Camp

Our nights were always the same – Mbalu, Sunshine and me with Lansana and Lt. Cross's bodyguards listening to loud reggae music, smoking and laughing. This evening while we were at Lt. Vayanga's shelter Turay kept going to the toilet and the other guys, especially Laser, teased him about it.

"Man, Turay, by tomorrow your butt will be very sore from all the pooping and cleaning," Laser laughed.

It was funny the way he said it but Laser was really foolish. He was a very funny person who at times knew when to be serious. Turay went about six times within two hours. He was getting weak so we told him to go to the doctor. He, however, refused saying he would rather sleep on it because it could just be an overnight thing. With that we made him some (ORS) Oral Rehydration Solution and we let him go to bed.

It was a good night with just us - no bosses and no Naffie. No-one really cared about Rain but she was not there either. We had fun that night with the boys bringing up how happy they will be when Magic comes back with the other guys. They talked about how much they've missed their brothers. Tiger had come back from Water Works that evening sending Salifu and Soja to guard Lansana. He told us Lansana was getting better and that he would be in the camp before the end of the week.

It was a hot evening and we all had shorts on - the boys wore shorts and took off their T-shirts leaving their singlets on. It was Mbalu's first time seeing Tiger in a pair of shorts and she said she thought he was so sexy; she could not stop looking at his legs. Tiger was the most handsome of the bodyguard. When we were in Kabbaty it was not as obvious because there was Magic, Hawk, Amara and Maximilian, but here, his competition was elsewhere and we could all see how good he looked. Tiger was lying on one of the mats we had and he did not want anyone to even sit next to him.

"You are so selfish, don't bring that rich boy attitude here," Sunshine said. "You have been in RUF long enough to forget about your rich Kailahun life and start sharing."

"How long have you been here?" I asked him.

Being the usual snobbish Tiger, he looked from one person to another as we spoke and did not say anything to Sunshine or me; this made the other boys laugh at us. Anybody just had to spend an hour with Tiger to know that he was a spoilt rich boy before he was captured. His father, like Magic's, was said to be a diamond dealer in Kailahun and the fact that he knew that he was gorgeous was another factor in his behaviour.

"Try four to five years, Memuna," Sunshine answered for him.

I looked at him staring back at me from the mat and went to the room to get another one. The boys laughed at the way he and I were exchanging hostility with our eyes. "You are annoying," I said.

I was not really upset with him as Tiger was like Laser - a little boy who had days when he put up his occasional tantrums and tonight was one.

"I have been here longer than that," he said as if somehow that was in his defence.

Just to tease us Tiger left his mat, came to Sunshine and me and tried to force his way between us.

"Oh come on give me some space," he said.

I refused to acknowledge him even though he was annoying me. Sunshine too refused to say a word about what he was doing; she got up and went to his mat. I tried to do the same but as soon as I got up he held my foot.

"Come on Memuna, you're my little sister and I want you to do something for me," he said.

"Oh look, now he can open his mouth to talk to me and he even knows my name," I said, all of us laughing.

"What do you want?" I asked him

"It is a secret. I will whisper it to you."

I bent over for him to whisper but he asked me to sit down so I did.

"I want to give you a mission," he said.

"What is it?"

The music was loud so no-one could hear us.

"There is this girl, I don't know if you've seen her around. Anyway I like her," he confided.

I looked at him and laughed.

"Tiger if you want Memuna just say it," Mbalu said over top of the loud music.

We looked at her and laughed; the others thought the same. They thought he wanted me.

"This petite girl is my sister, man. I'm just asking her for something," he replied.

"Anyway who is she?" I asked.

"You just look around, you will see the new girl and if there are two of them then tell me and I will show you which one."

"You will get her," I said.

We continued talking about different things. At some point I just sat and listened because I did not know what the boys were talking about or I was not around when the event took place. Despite that they did not leave me out by making sure I understood everything. We sat there till early in the morning then we went to our rooms.

Laser woke up running to the toilet in the morning and he went every hour.

"I feel like using the toilet but when I go nothing comes, I just feel so much pain," he said.

He looked weak and lost his appetite so we told him to go to bed. He could not sleep so we called the doctor who diagnosed dysentery. He complained about the inadequacy of medication for it and identified some native medicine, which we could get from the forest. Laser could not keep his jeans on because he went as often as six times a day and he started passing blood. Mbalu took his pants off and wrapped a huge beach towel around him and she sat in bed by him all day. We were around just in case she needed us. I felt sorry for Laser. It turned out lots of people within RUF were infected by dysentery that month. We had no clue until it occurred to Turay and Laser, though Turay recovered quickly. Kasiloi went into the forest and got some leaves for Laser to chew and swallow the juice. We washed the leaves and took them to the room. I sat in a chair in the room watching Laser chew the leaves like a goat. Sunshine and I looked at each other trying not to laugh. Even Mbalu wanted to laugh at the sight of Laser chewing the leaves, but we decided to save it till he was out of bed and back to the normal Laser we all knew.

All these past few months, before the dysentery outbreak, there was rumour of a new presidential election in Sierra Leone and RUF was planning to attack every major town and every main highway. They already had bases in all the districts and on the highway of the capital Freetown itself. It was going to be huge. Laser wanted to be in the group that was going to attack Blama and the Bo/ Kenema Highway so he chewed an overdose of the leaves and within three days he was up again eating more food than usual. Lansana came back to the camp the same day Laser recovered. He came back with Naffie, Nyalay, Lucia, Rain and her baby, as did Sia and her baby.

It was just a nice day, the weather was nice and I felt good. Titan and I were growing apart and I was fine with it because I was pushing him away. The girls and I were confused about why Lansana came back with Naffie and the children. She said that she was tired of being in Water Works and was tired of the mosquitoes. I had run the scissors through my hair for the second time. Lansana did not notice but Naffie did. I thought Lansana heard about Magic and me so I was trying to distance myself from him a little but he called me aside to talk to me and he kept smiling at me. Everyone knew that whenever Lansana was away from me for more than a day he would call me aside to talk to me on his return. Even Naffie had to deal with that.

"How are you?" he asked.

"I'm doing well," I said. "How are you feeling now?" I asked.

"I'm o.k. I thought of you all the time I was in Water Works. Memuna, please don't do anything stupid. I need to trust you when I'm away because I won't always be around. I have to go on missions," he said.

I felt guilty and I could see that he really cared. The sincerity was clear in his eyes and tears welled upon mine.

"Nothing happened. I'm ok," I said.

I could not explain the whole thing to him because I knew how he would react; he would get so mad at me. Naffie would be the first person to say 'I told you' to him and I did not want that to happen. After all Magic and I only attempted, we did not really do it.

The following morning Lansana and his friends seemed happy and so did everyone else. Except for Rain - one of the women guarding Titan the first day I met him - hated me so much. From the day she heard that Titan wanted me, she stopped talking to me. On this day she decided to talk to me. She said hello to Sunshine and me saying our names when she saw us passing in front of her shelter. I said hello to her in return though I thought she was up to something.

"Sunshine, did you hear that or was I just hearing things," I asked.

"Don't start thinking everything is ok because she might just want to get close to us to know things about you and Titan," Sunshine warned me. "I know these women. See, I don't even trust my sister-in-law; they were all friends a long time ago.

"Oh well I don't even like her. I just said hello back for courtesy's sake," I said.

I had made three outfits for Sunshine and me by hand and one for Nyalay. That day I was embroidering a top for us and we both had on two of the skirts I'd sewed.

We went to the guard post and some boys and a corporal called Sin-child were there armed with knives in the huge orange garden eating oranges. The boys were excited to see us hanging out with them, even if it was only for an hour, because we did not go around with them. We only hung out with the commanding officers in the camp and their bodyguards and they all knew me as Titan's girlfriend. This way I shared in the respect shown him and Lansana. They peeled some oranges for Sunshine and me. She knew all the boys who had been with RUF for a long time and they all liked her because she was really easy going. With Sunshine around most of the time there was no problem with the guys. We sat with them for half an hour and packed our stomach full with oranges and even took some with us when we left them.

On our way back to the camp walking in the coffee farm, we kept burping like a couple of boys and giggling about it.

"There is something I haven't told you," Sunshine confided.

"What is it? That you are crazy and you are making me crazy?" I said, laughing.

"Look who is talking, that's the case of the ogirie calling the kainda stink," she said. "You are crazier than I am but that's not what I'm talking about."

"What then?" I asked.

"You see that guy Sin-child? Naffie cheated on Lansana with him," she said.

I was speechless and stood with my mouth agape.

"What! Sin-child is so ugly, why did she do it?"

"I don't know," Sunshine shrugged.

"So what did Lansana do or say?" I asked, still credulous.

"He was so angry he almost shot Sin-child. As for Naffie he almost left her but by then she had Guy," she said. "But he tied her up and beat her up and I think she is still paying for what she did."

"Oh…. my God," I said.

"The doctor had to visit her at home for days when he was through with her. He doesn't love her anymore," Sunshine stated, ignoring the seriousness of what she'd just confided. Shocked I did not know what to say; it was very shocking news.

We walked on to Musa's shelter. Mbalu and Laser were napping so we woke them.

"You two are having too much fun, wake up," Sunshine chided them.

"The two of you have your own men so go and have a nap with them also and leave us alone," Mbalu snapped back, covering her head with a pillow.

"Oh get up!" I said, throwing an orange at her.

She got up and got dressed. Laser was pretending to still be asleep so we lied that Lansana was looking for him.

"Ok when you and Memuna get out I will put on my clothes and go home," he said, his eyes still closed.

"Wow, you and Mbalu waste no time, do you?" I had to comment. "You do the deed any time you get."

We all laughed and Sunshine suggested to me we keep an eye on them and ruin their moments.

"Some of us are not getting any, why should you Mbalu?" Sunshine joked.

"You and Memuna can go to hell," Mbalu replied. "One of you is too busy being a virgin and the other is too big to tell her man that she has urges. So the next time I will have a stick for you two."

We carried on laughing about it as we walked down to the shelter. Mbalu confirmed the story about Sin-child and Naffie, but I was still in shock.

All the time I had known her Naffie acted as if Lansana was the only man she had ever been with. Naffie and Rain were laughing about something as soon as we got to the shelter.

"Memuna we were just talking about initiating you and your sister in the female secret society when they come here," Naffie said.

"It will be a ball," Rain insisted.

Even more shocked, I stood there with my eye brows lifted looking confused wondering what brought that up and what made them think they have the right to even think about it.

"Rain, are you going to be initiated too?" Sunshine asked, trying to shut Rain up.

It was a shame for a grown woman - especially one that did not live in the city - not to be initiated and still hanging out with women who were initiated. Sunshine knew that her question was insulting and shameful enough to shut Rain up. We looked at each other and I knew what she was doing.

"Oh, Rain so you are just like me. Well we can get initiated together," I said.

She looked at Mbalu, Sunshine and me and then went to her room.

"Naffie," I asked, "where is Lansana?"

I asked for Lansana because I was curious to know if he was in on the "society" arrangement. I was afraid of the whole ceremony. I liked the songs they sang and the beads they wore but the masquerade gave me nightmares. If I was going to be brave enough to do it, it was going to be with my family. Lansana, as it turned out, was with Titan at his shelter with Lt. Cross so I waited for him to come home so I could ask him. It seemed like Naffie did not wish to give me a break. Every day it seemed she randomly had something new to bother me with. We had lots of fabrics in the camp at our shelter and Naffie kept about ten yards for us to wear if the initiation took place. She was already making plans. Mbalu and Sunshine saw that it bothered me so they told me not to worry about it. I should wait, they said, till I speak to Lansana.

Having already had our second bath early that afternoon, we went to the shelter. Hindowa gave us smokes. Later that evening Lansana came home and he sent Salifu to call me into his room. He always had a sweet smile on his face when we were alone and not fighting. He smiled and asked me to take a seat; I sat next to him on the bed. Naffie was sitting outside with Rain on a mat with the little girls.

"Lansana what is this talk about female society?" I asked.

"What society" he asked, looking surprised.

"So you do not know about Naffie's plan to initiate my sisters and me," I asked. "She said she would take us to Target Q and have some old ladies and Rain grandmother initiate us."

Holding one of my hands in one of his hands and rubbing his head with the other, he then looked at his watch.

"I don't know what Naffie is talking about and, besides, it is women's talk," he said.

"But you brought my sisters and me here so you should know everything that goes on with us," I said.

"Memuna, I meant every word I said when I promised that I would do everything in my power to protect you and your sisters," he spoke calmly. "So if you don't want to be initiated all you have to do is tell me and no-one will touch you."

He looked at me for a long time and he said,

"You are so different and that's why I like you very much. Most girls would be happy about this but you are not."

"Well I don't think my parents would like it," I said. "Our grandmothers in Sembehun would have done it for us a long time ago but they said that my father did not want us to be initiated because our mother wouldn't like it. So I would like to keep it that way although I don't know what it's all about."

He said it was ok and that Naffie was just talking but it was not going to happen. We spent a few more hours together talking then Naffie walked in looking upset, so I left.

A week later Titan and I had an argument. He wanted me to visit him and spend the night which I did not want to do. So, that evening, he got upset despite his promise that he would not do anything. I still refused to go to his house. So he stayed away and I did not mind because it gave me some time alone. I did not have to think about him wanting anything from me and I was pleased, but Mbalu and Sunshine kept telling me that I should keep him interested. Sia was in the camp too, to take the baby away from the mosquitoes and for her to spend some time with her father. This made Sunshine really mad. Lieutenant Musa (nicknamed Vayanga) who was the same age as Lansana had formally asked for Sunshine's hand in marriage from Yea Zina (Sunshine and Lansana's grandmother) just after they were all captured by the Osos who started the RUF with Foday Sankoh. Vayanga was the father of Sia's baby and he and Sunshine never really spent time together and Sunshine now felt she was ready to be a woman to him. But there were two others. Sunshine and Vayanga had decided to wait for her to be old enough for them to have a proper relationship, although traditionally they were engaged.

Both her and Vayanga were angry at each other from what I gathered. He had two other women and she had several other guys including a top ranking officer – Captain Speed

The following day it rained a little but it was dry enough to go to the swamp. Naffie pretended as if she needed something from Sia. So she told Nyalay to tell Sunshine to give Lucia a bath when she got back and that she wanted to go with me to the other side of the camp across the swamp. Naffie and Rain took me to where Mbalu, Sunshine and I sat every day when we went to the swamp to smoke. It was the first day I ever saw Naffie smoke; Rain always smoked cigarettes but she was not allowed to smoke marijuana anymore. I thought they wanted to talk about the society so I told her,

"I've already spoken to Lansana and he said that I did not have to be initiated if I did not want to."

"I have already spoken to Lansana too," Naffie said. "He told me that you were not interested and the girls were not either."

"Then why am I here?" I asked not trusting her.

"I want you to do something for me and I want you to please forget about it the moment we are through," Naffie said.

She gave me two sheets of paper and a pencil and asked me to write a letter for her to Sin-child. I wrote the letter asking her not to ask me to deliver it for her because I did not want to do that to Lansana. I felt bad for him because he must have thought Naffie was through with Sin-child. He had a girlfriend and a child too. I looked at Naffie thinking Sunshine was not joking when she told me that story. Upset with Naffie I felt like I was betraying Lansana but I pretended it never happened and I did not tell a soul. All evening I remained confused and could not believe she got me involved in her affair.

While smoking, the guys told us about the attack on Election Day and I was worried about my family on the other side. I could not say anything though while we smoked and later went to bed.

Naffie tried to get too close to me, it was probably because she was worried I would expose her but that did not cross my mind. That same evening, during dinner, Sunshine did something very disgusting that upset me resulting in an argument between the two of us.

In the war zone we did not have the usual domestic meat to cook. We cooked fish or venison like wild pig or some other wild meat, most of which I had not heard of before the war. So that evening, Naffie cooked and we assisted. She dished rice for Sunshine, Mbalu and me in a medium-sized tray and put the stew separately in a bowl. This was because most of the time at least one of us – and it was me - would not be ready to eat. Today, however, it was Mbalu who was not hungry at the moment; so we dished her food out. I did not have much appetite but I wanted to eat because of the meat. Sunshine picked up the meat from the food and sucked each piece. It was not her first time doing this as she had done it to me about three times before.

"Why do you always do that nasty trick?" I challenged her.

"Don't say that word when we are eating," she said.

"What word," I asked. "Nasty?"

"If you don't stop I will leave this food for you to eat," she said.

"Too late, because I've left it for you already," I said. "You've spoiled the one reason why I wanted to eat. I was not afraid of telling you though I ignored you but it doesn't mean I am afraid to tell you. You are too greedy! Why do you always have to suck on the meat on our food?"

"What's the problem with you girls?" Naffie asked.

"Sunshine sucked on all the meat again!" I told her.

"I've been watching you both and yes, she has done it to you many times."

"I am not eating this food anymore." I got up and washed my hands.

"What about her? She doesn't know how to eat with her hands. The way she does it is disgusting. Who eats fufu with a spoon? It's just her I've seen do that," Sunshine yelled.

"I don't care," I yelled back. "You can eat all that rice in that tray and all the meat you've already put your spit on," I kept yelling, "and if you can't handle how I eat with my hand then bite me where there is no bone." I walked away.

We were really upset with each other. I was very upset at how inconsiderate she was and the fact that she refused to accept that she was wrong. She turned it around and said that Naffie and I were ganging up against her and that Naffie was sucking up to me. At that very moment I was glad I never told her about the letter. Lansana came home and heard us yelling at each other with Sunshine calling me a half woman - I was not a full woman because I was not a member of the female society. That was not her first time to say that to me. Lansana called us into the room and chastised her.

"Sunshine, you need to stop showing off with that society of yours because it is not going to take you anywhere. The only thing that can take anyone places is education and consideration," he said. "Don't attack Memuna about her eating again and I don't want to see you two girls sulking around here. Memuna – you need to let it go!"

Sunshine promptly went to Mbalu and explained her side to her but I did not bother. I just sat with Naffie and Nyalay not saying anything to them but took my book (Things Fall Apart) and read. Naffie said she was going to Vayanga to talk to Sia and Eliza so she took me along with Nyalay.

Eliza was the new girl Tiger wanted. She was as tall as he was and of the same skin complexion. She was a nice girl, very pretty and was fond of me. I was fond of her too, but she wanted Lansana not Tiger and Naffie did not know. I knew because I saw them flirting at the studio. She was staying at

Titan's shelter. I don't know whom she came to visit but rumour had it she was Robert's relative. We talked and they smoked but I did not. They talked about men and their babies and I was the last part of the conversation. I just wanted to dig a hole and bury myself.

"So Memuna my girl, it's been so long since you and I had our serious late night conversation hasn't it," Sia said, turning her face to me and bringing me out of my retreat. I nodded.

"Well we haven't had time together because you've been hanging around with a bunch of immature girls," she concluded.

Sia did not like Sunshine, not only because they both wanted the same man but also because Sia said that Sunshine was too primitive. Sia was at least in her late twenties and she liked talking to me. She treated me like her equal when she spoke to me and she hardly spoke Mende so most of the times she spoke Krio to me.

"Girl I hear you are playing games with my son Titan," she said. "Why Memuna? You are pretty and young and he is handsome. Honestly I can tell you that boy is really a nice boy. All this time I've known him he doesn't get in anyone's way and no-one has lodged any complaint against him."

"I don't know Sia," I said.

"Well you want to tell me that you don't like him, even a little?" she enquired. Naffie kept nodding in agreement with Sia.

"Memuna I don't know you that well but I can see you are a nice person. A little crazy from what I've heard, but nice and I think you two suit each other," Eliza freely commented.

She talked with her teeth clenched all the time. I realised that was how she spoke even when she was happy. I looked at the three of them and smiled thinking they set me up. Naffie did not bring me with her just so I wouldn't be alone.

"I can tell you, I'm not crazy I don't know what they are telling you," I replied.

"Believe me if you go over there to the studio all they talk about is you, so I know he really likes you," Eliza said.

"So this was all a plan," I said, nodding my head. "Did he send you people?"

They laughed.

"To be honest Titan asked me to talk to you he really wants you and I think, if these were normal days, he would be just as crazy about you. The feeling is from his heart and he really begged me to talk to you," Sia said.

Before I could say anything else Titan, Lansana and Vayanga were at the door. I was so embarrassed I just wished I could disappear out of there.

"Sia!" I said, making everyone in the room laugh. The men looked like they had been drinking. I could smell the alcohol but I was not sure because there was nowhere to get it from. Titan kept smiling at me and he touched my shoulder.

"I have been talking to her darling," Sia said, "and I think things will be ok."

I looked at Titan and deep down I knew I liked him but I was willing to fight it. I don't know why but I guess it was because he would take me away from Lansana and I would be separated from my younger sisters. We talked for a while longer and we left. As we walked out, Sia yelled out to me telling me to think about what we talked about.

The following morning I hung out with the boys and Kasiloi and I joked a lot. Tiger was a little upset with me because he did not succeed with Eliza and he was mad that Eliza wanted Lansana.

"Why does he always have to get all the pretty ones?" he sulked.

"Hey, man look at me and Memuna! I want this girl but she doesn't feel the same way and, because I like her so much, I will keep our friendship going," Kasiloi said.

"Hey you can always find another pretty girl," I said, trying to cheer him up.

Sunshine and Mbalu walked into the room and asked me if I wanted to come with them to the bridge. I looked at them for long time wondering what they were up to. They could easily gang up on me.

"Don't you want to come?" Sunshine asked.

I got up reluctantly and went with them, after all they have had my back for months.

"Hey I think you two should forget what happened yesterday," Mbalu said.

I looked at them and nodded.

"I'm sorry I won't do it again," Sunshine promised.

We said sorry to each other and got on as usual. I did not smoke that day, I just played in the water; we told stupid jokes and laughed. We talked about how great it would be when Magic, the girls and his brothers come. Sunshine told Mbalu about how horrible she and Komeh were and how she taught Komeh how to shoot a gun and load a magazine into a gun.

"She and my sister were so foolish they terrified civilians," I said.

"It's not true!" Sunshine objected. "The old people liked us."

"Mbalu believe what you want, the truth is a few weeks away," I said. "But I know she will tell you what ever Sunshine says."

We laughed about it, got dressed and went home.

On the day of the election 15th March 1996, I had been their captive for nine months. We listened to the radio all day. We listened to voters sending out prayers for their favourite party or their loved ones. There were thirteen parties: Sierra Leone People's Party (SLPP) Tejan Kabba's party, United National People's Party (UNPP) Dr. John Karefa-Smart's party, People's Democratic Party (PDP) Thaimu Bangura's party, National Unity Party (NUP) John Karimu's party, All People's Congress (APC) Edward Turay's party, Democratic Center Party (DCP) Amara Aiah Koroma's party,

People Progressive Party (PPP) Abass Hindowa's party, People's National Convention (PNC) Edward Kargbo's party, National Unity Movement (NUM) Desmond Luke's party, Social Democratic Party (SDP) Andrew Lungay's party, National People's Party (NPP) Andrew Turay's party and National Alliance Democratic Party (NADP) Mohamed Sillah's party. The first election had taken place February 22, 1996, which I was totally unaware of until this second round now being broadcasted on the radio. There was a run-off on this day because a party that didn't secure 50% could not rule.

Listening to them, I wished I was there on the other side of the country where there were no rebels. Although it was a little rough on the people living out of the war zone, they sounded happy on the radio and I wanted to be there. If I could not be there then at least I could be somewhere where I did not have to listen to that happiness. So I asked the girls if they wanted to go to the swamp to bathe because it was midday and we had not had our morning bath. It was necessary because we did not know what was going to happen once the attack Lansana and the boys had been planning, took place. So we went to the swamp that was inside the camp and closer to our shelter.

Naffie had done my hair the day before in rubber bands as she wanted me to stop cutting my hair and I looked pretty with it. The boys had gone to get ready to attack; they were ready in every part of Sierra Leone where the election was meant to take place. I told Lansana how scared we were and Nyalay went on to tease me.

"Nyalay, shut up before I pinch your ear!" I demanded.

"Not when I'm here," Lansana said, smiling and picking her up into his arms.

It seemed even little Lucia understood what was going on that day: she crawled from her mother and went to her father and held his foot.

"Lucia wants you to pick her up too," Nyalay said.

Lansana put Nyalay down, picked Lucia up and she hugged him. Lucia was a copy of Lansana; she looked so much like her father from head to toes. Unlike Guy she liked to cling to her mother.

Lansana and his team took off to Blama that morning and came back late evening.

"How did the attack go Lansana," Naffie asked, once the boys and him returned.

"It was good. no-one fought back and no-one died and we did what we went to do," he replied. "I think they will just count whatever vote they had before we attacked or I don't know what they are going to do."

"How are they going to count what they had before you attacked when you attacked them as soon as the voting began?" I asked, trying not to sound angry.

Lansana looked at me and did not say anything. He knew I was angry and that I was still struggling with the whole war episode and that I still did not support RUF. More here - the voting was supposed to free Sierra Leone to a new possibility but this war meant it was not possible to obtain peace without someone dying and I hated them. When they got back the boys gave us some of their marijuana. Naffie and Rain were in the kitchen with Nyalay but Mbalu, Sunshine and I were so caught up in the marijuana excitement. I got more than the others because Kasiloi gave me a lot. It was so much I felt sick just from looking at it. He offered to show me how to dry it.

"This is the real strong grass; you need to be careful and you need to handle it with care," he explained.

"How do you know that it is strong just from looking at it," I asked.

"Well considering how long I've played with this thing I should know. You see you can tell from the leaves; don't worry I will tell you later," he said.

While we stayed with the boys we also asked them what they saw in Blama. I had not witnessed an election so I asked Kasiloi and Tiger to tell me what it was like and they told me.

"What does Blama look like?" I asked.

"Just like any other town out of our zone," Laser said.

"What were they wearing?" I asked, wanting to know everything.

"Some people were dressed in normal everyday clothes - you know jeans, skirts, T-shirts, shirts. The old people and some young people were dressed in caftan and African suit," Kasiloi said.

"Why do you want to know all these things?" Laser asked.

"I just want to picture how things were, before you people entered their town and raided everything," I said.

The camp stunk of marijuana; the smell came from every corner. Everyone had some at their shelter. The camp was really noisy that day, they were happy that they had ruined the election in Blama. All they were waiting for were results from the other bases.

Naffie and Rain did not bother to call us in the kitchen. I guess they knew that nothing they did would have taken us away from the excitement. Besides Naffie was a good cook unlike Rain. The girls and I quickly put the attack on the election behind us and carried on with our usual foolish behaviour.

After dinner we sat with the boys plucking the marijuana leaves off the stems and spreading them on big pieces of cloth to get them sun-dried. It was a very hectic day full of anxiety and excitement and I was tired, so I retired to bed early that evening.

March is the start of the dry season in West Africa. It gets a little cold in the mornings in Sierra Leone and Liberia from December to late March.

We tried to dry the marijuana within two days as everyone else had run out or had less than a hand full left. But I still had a lot of mine left. I dried the leaves with Kasiloi's help, put it all in a plastic bag and hid it away. I was going to use it to make Soja, Salifu and whoever needed some smokes from me, to do things for me. I did it in a way that even the girls did not know that I still had some left.

Titan knew that I did not like going to his shelter anymore so he made it a point to visit Lansana everyday just to see me. Most of the times Naffie and Lansana would ask me to get him some water to drink if he was thirsty. Since Lansana, Titan, Lt. Cross, Daniel and Robert had dinner at each other's shelter Titan was welcomed at our shelter anytime whether it was dinner time or lunchtime. There was always food reserved for him. So if he got there just in time for dinner they would make me serve Lansana, Titan and Lt. Cross. That made me really upset but as I got used to it I stopped getting mad about it and complied with what I was told.

All this time we still had not heard from the girls, but at least we knew they were ok as Magic and others had brought news about them. All we were waiting for was Magic to come with them. Two weeks later Lansana was out of the camp. He went to Water Works with Naffie and the children. They had only come to the camp to be in a safe place while the attack on the election happened and he was due back in two days. Magic showed up the following day after Lansana had left the camp, but he came back alone. He wore a big T-shirt and a pair of black baggy jeans and a pair of white sneakers. Everyone was happy to see him but I had a sick feeling. I knew something was wrong yet I smiled at him and gave him a hug.

"Where are my sisters? Are they in Water Works?" I asked.

"No, I did not bring them, can we talk in private please," he said.

I went into the shelter underneath the big tree with him feeling very hurt and disappointed but I still wanted to hear his side of the story.

"I came back for you so we could go to Freetown Highway and be there together. Komeh, Magainda, Amara and Maximilian are going," he said. "And we can take Samia with us."

Speechless and shocked I could not believe it. I could not believe he was suggesting I just leave Nyalay and go play wife to him. I was so angry but I could not say anything simply because I could not think of where to start.

"What are you talking about?" I demanded.

"There is a convoy going in three days on a mission. They will stop midway but the Freetown Highway convoy will carry on. We will meet with another convoy from Kenema Bypass and join together as one convoy. We will carry on joining the ones from Koribondo Jungle," he said. "Then you and your sisters can be together again and we can all go to Freetown Highway."

I sat on the bed looking at him and feeling deeply disappointed.

"Did you forget that I have a little cousin Nyalay?" I asked, "And I can't leave her."

I looked at him thinking he knew this was important to me and he had disappointed me. How many more disappointments does he have up his sleeves? I had already made my decision that I was not going, but I wanted to cool down and tell him nicely that I did not want to go with him. So I thought of something to say to him.

"Thank you very much, but even if I wanted to go with you I just can't take off like that when Lansana isn't here," I said. I was standing in this room alone with Magic and I had to make him think I had agreed to go with him, because Lansana was not in the camp to protect me from Magic's rage if he got really angry and lost his temper, although I had never experienced that side of him.

He was so happy he gave me a hug but I did not hug him back and we went outside. He went on to tell all the guys that I was going with him. When I saw Laser I could tell he was upset with me but I did not know why. Sunshine and Mbalu asked me to go to the bridge with them and we left. All we talked about was me leaving with Magic. Sunshine was angry with me; she thought I was going to pack up my things and leave with Magic.

"Look, can I trust you two to shut up?" I asked.

"Yes," Mbalu said.

"What, you don't want us to tell Lansana?" Sunshine asked. "I wouldn't have to, Titan will find out and I'm sure he will walk to Water Works to tell Lansana since he is in the camp." She was really upset.

"Look, I'm not going with Magic," I told them.

"Then why did you promise him that you would and say that you are only waiting for Lansana? Memuna just tell us the truth," Sunshine asked.

"Let her talk," Mbalu said.

"Sunshine, I have not lied to you before so just listen and stop accusing me of lying," I said. "Look, I only said that because I was so angry but I did not want to say anything hurtful to him. I just wanted to leave him with his conscience."

"I think you should really give it to him," Sunshine said. "After he betrayed Lansana now he wants you to do the same thing."

"What he did was really wrong and it's strange to see you so calm. Normally your mouth will be going," Mbalu put her piece in.

"I'm still so angry and I can't believe he did what he did," I told them.

I tried not to cry and told myself not to ever depend on anyone but my parents and my family because they had not disappointed me in such a hurtful way - especially not my grandmothers and my mother. My father postponed promises at times but in the end I got what I asked for. We swam and returned to camp.

Later that evening I wanted to go up to Titan because I had not seen him all day. I guessed he heard that Magic was in the camp again and maybe he did not want to put me in a tight position so he had stayed at his shelter. He did not even attend formation that evening therefore I did not think seeing Titan was a good idea so the girls and I stayed in the shelter Hindowa gave us and talked about things. The boys thought we were spending time together because I was leaving in two days. I did not have much sleep that night as I lay in bed thinking how Magic could be so selfish.

The following morning the girls and I slept for a little while longer than usual, then we went to the swamp, bathed and fetched some water for us to use at the shelter. I wore my white denim skirt that Lansana brought and a T-shirt which had 'Pacific Ocean' written on it.

Magic was all over the camp. I could tell that he was over the moon as he was so happy. I looked at him and the girls and I walked around the camp all morning until Lansana arrived back. Magic could not even wait for Lansana to settle before he started urging me to tell Lansana about "our" plan. At first I told him to wait a little but he kept pushing and it made me uncomfortable so I had to tell him that I was not going with him.

"What?" he exclaimed. "Yesterday you wanted to go and now you are telling me something else?"

"You know what? I only told you that because I did not know what to say. I can't leave Nyalay and I can't do that to Lansana," I answered his anger with my own.

"Well we can take her," he said. "After all she is your blood and Lansana can't stop you from taking her. So tell him you want to take your cousin."

"I'm not leaving with you Magic! Lansana brought me into RUF and I will stay with him till my sisters, uncles and I go back home if God keeps us alive."

"So you don't want me?" he asked, his anger fading into something else.

"I want you, but if you really want me you will understand that I'm only fifteen and I can't look after two little girls on my own; and you can't look after us either," I said, "and you can stay here with me where everyone will be ok.'

"I don't want to stay here," he replied. "I want to advance, in fact we are all going to end up going to Freetown, that's RUF's mission,"

"Well if we are all going to end up there one day and maybe very soon, why the hurry?" I countered.

We kept on talking and asking each other questions but he would not give up.

"Do something before tomorrow morning because that's when we will be leaving," he said, his determination returning.

"I've already told you Magic, I want you but I can't go with you. I can't put Nyalay and Samia's lives at risk."

He was very disappointed and hurt, maybe even more than I was. I felt so sorry and drained of every strength I wished he would change his mind and stay. All we could have done was ask Lansana and Titan to tell his brothers in Koribondo to arrange a way to get Komeh and Samia to Blama Highway. But he would not budge. I talked to the guys to talk him out of going but they did not succeed either. Instead, he started telling them how much I shocked him and how I disappointed him and that he was not going to let go. So I gave up on begging him to stay and went back to our shelter leaving him at Vayanga's shelter with the guys. He cried when I turned to leave and the look in his eyes got to my heart. It hurt that we were parting so badly after all the times we spent together making each other laugh and crying on each other's shoulder. It hurt so bad that I burst out crying, but I could not do what he asked. I asked Laser to tell him I was sorry, that I wished him good luck and hoped to see him again.

I did not have a moment's sleep as I stayed up all night crying silently; I had been disappointed by my best friend in RUF and was losing him. It could be ages till I see Samia and Komeh again, I was so hurt I wished my mother was there.

Early in the morning Magic left and I did not see him. So I was left with the memory of both of us crying. It broke my heart any time I thought of him and that was almost every day.

Somehow Lansana found out what was going on. I did not know who told him but I had lost so much weight within only two days.

One afternoon in the camp Lansana saw me sitting and talking with the girls, "Memuna, is everything ok?" Lansana asked,

I nodded. He knew that I was not alright so he took me aside to talk.

"I heard Magic wanted to take you to Freetown Highway," Lansana said. "Is that why you are sad?"

I nodded.

"I wish he would stay," I replied, the sadness sweeping over me again.

"Well why don't you go?" Lansana asked.

I looked into his face when he said that but his eyes meant otherwise. I could tell that he was being sarcastic.

"I mean if you think he can look after you then go, but Nyalay is not going anywhere," he said. Crying I told him the truth,

"I don't want to live with anyone else so don't say that! You brought me here and you will take me back home."

I walked out of the room leaving him sitting there. I needed to be alone as this new pain was too great.

The next day, Lansana promised me that Samia would be in the camp as soon as possible.

"I can't promise you that Komeh will be here too because she is with Maximilian and where ever he wants them to go is where she would go but I will try."

I was a little relieved but the boys were upset with me, especially Mustapha. He had nothing kind to say to me.

"All this time you were with my brother and now because of someone with a higher position you are turning your back on him," he spat at me one day.

They twisted everything, blaming it on the fact that Titan liked me, saying that I liked Titan more than Magic because of his position. But they did not know what our arrangement was, what I did or almost gave up. I wanted my sisters with me now, more than ever.

It was early April 1996 and we had started running out of food. RUF – three battalions on Blama Highway - had discovered a new place with a few hidden villages in the Blama area and they all wanted to go there. So Lansana led a mission somewhere into that area and was due back in three days. Mbalu started talking about going to be closer to the man she really wanted to be with – Bob.

I was glad when they went on the mission. In fact, Sunshine, Rain and I went to Water Works and came back the same day. No-one was on my back. Titan in fact did not talk about the situation with Magic and I was sure he knew, I could bet my last penny on it. News went around easily in RUF, especially when it concerned a CO. Though this gossip did not concern Titan at all and only concerned Lansana a little, Magic's supporters made it all about Titan. When the boys came back they all had a message or two from Magic. They saw him in the town they went to attack as there were already some RUF men there from the Freetown Highway convoy.

"Memuna," Mustapha said, "my stupid brother, who can't leave you alone, said that he will come back for you."

I looked at him but did not say anything. Mustapha had also demanded his T-shirt back. He had brought me a new Tejan Kabba /SLPP T-shirt from Blama the day they raided the election and he wanted it back.

"Give me back that T-shirt," he said.

"Why? You gave it to me," I said.

"Why should I give you anything?" he said. "I'm sure Titan can do more than that if he stops being a coward and go to the front line again. You should be thankful to my brother because if it were not for him your prince here would be dead. Magic dragged him to safety the day he got shot in his leg and now what does he do but takes his woman."

Anger filled my veins again but I did not know what to say to hurt him as much as he was hurting me by his words. I went into our shelter, took the T-shirt and threw it at him.

"Here, sissy! Any man who reclaims things from a woman because he doesn't have his way is a woman," I said yelling at him. "You don't have a clue what your brother and I had and you will not understand. So why don't you get hold of yourself before you disgrace yourself? And if you think I'm going to explain myself to you, you better think again."

Completely speechless, he took the T-shirt and walked away leaving the rest of the boys looking from me to him as he turned his back. From that moment on I was ready for anyone who dared to interfere.

I went and sat down in a chair outside our shelter to calm myself. I went inside and took up my book "Things Fall Apart" and continued reading. After a few pages I was ok enough to have a conversation. Laser, who always looks for a chance to say or do something, came to me.

"Memuna, Magic said that when he comes back for you he will come with two squads of men to take you with him and he said he would be back in a few months," he said, looking at me to gauge my reaction. "He was so disappointed he had stomach ache from the shock."

"Well, I'm waiting for him and I did not mean to do anything bad to him," I replied quietly now.

But the disappointment and hurt continued. Every day after he left I dreamt of him crying, telling me that I had disappointed him and it made me sad.

Throughout this time I stayed away from Titan and it was upsetting him that I was pushing him away. He even once asked me to tell him if I did not want him instead of making him feel unwanted.

I still had my marijuana but it had been a while since I smoked and I did not want to smoke. Instead I used it to get Salifu to fetch water for the girls and me. We did not have to worry about firewood because they always made sure we had enough in the kitchen. The day for Mbalu's convoy to leave for Libya was getting closer and closer and we were starting to miss her already. Every day she and Sunshine assured me that I made the right choice about not following Magic; even though I was already sure I had done the right thing. I was only sad that a good relationship ended the way it did. I had no regrets.

The boys found their new target. They said there were pretty girls in the new towns they had discovered and the girls were not afraid of them. There was rumour in the camp that Rain was pregnant again and she took trips away from the camp to visit her grandmother in the civilian camp and to visit her friend. I think that was why people said that she was pregnant, but I did not see her stomach grow. Lt. Cross was always away as well. RUF was trying to make a new base in the two new towns so some of the rebels stayed and some, including Hindowa, went back after their mission. He went back mainly because of the girls.

"I'm glad we found some new girls, because I'm really tired of these three we have here," Hindowa said.

"Don't fool yourself Hindowa none of us want you," Sunshine said.

He got dressed in jeans, T-shirt and sneakers, loaded all three of his magazines and left. He went with some other rebels leaving us with the other guys.

We had the shelters all to ourselves. Lansana was with Naffie. It was nice to be our own bosses, but I was bored. All we did was join Edna and Sao in eating a lot and making lots of noise. CO. Flomo wrote the lyrics to lots of songs for me so at times I sat with him and we sang together. The ones I liked so much were: 'Crazy World' by Lucky Dube, 'Lions In This Kingdom', 'Mek We Dweet' by Burning Spears, and 'Stop the Cursing And Fighting' by Culture. I like "Lions In This Kingdom" and 'Mek We Dweet', but each time I listened to them I felt sad because those are the songs

Lansana and his boys were playing from the moment they captured us till they took us to Kabbaty.

"Why do you like 'Crazy World'?" CO. Flomo asked on one of these days. "Is it because my brother likes it?"

"No. I just like it; they're all very good lyrics."

We sang all afternoon in our kitchen making the girls sick of our voices.

"If I hear that song one more time I will never listen to the tape again," Sunshine complained, loudly.

A week later Rain came back to the camp with her baby, Strength and the child had mosquito bites on her cheeks and her legs.

"Oh…. Strength, darling how are you?" I cooed.

I took her from her mother's arms and hugged her. Strength was a beautiful baby, she looked like both her parents and she was very easy to deal with. She only cried when she was hungry, sick or needed a nappy change. Sunshine, Mbalu and myself played with her that afternoon.

"Rain, you need to stop taking Strength to Target Q. Look her cheeks are red from mosquito bites!" Mbalu told her off.

"Even on her legs," Sunshine pointed out.

"Yeah, we won't be going there in a while, I don't want Ranger to kill me if his daughter catches malaria," Rain replied.

CHAPTER TWENTY TWO

Unravelling

Two days later Mbalu, Sunshine and I went to Water Works. Hindowa was there but he had been shot in one of the towns they had discovered. He got shot in his leg and his butt by a rifle and he could not wear pants till the wounds were healed. He used a cane to help him walk. We saw him sitting in the hut with a towel around his waist.

"Hey Hindowa, what are you doing here? I thought you were enjoying with the new girls," Mbalu teased him mercilessly.

"Don't tell us you have dysentery," I said, chuckling.

"I don't have dysentery," he said, looking away frowning. Nyalay saw us and came running to the hut. She hugged the girls, then me and tried to get a piggyback from Mbalu. She went behind and kept jumping.

"Hindowa, what is wrong with you, why do you have a walking stick?" Sunshine asked.

"None of your business," he snapped.

"He," Nyalay tried to tell us what was wrong with him but he cut her off.

"Nyalay, go away. Just go back inside the house," he said. "I got shot."

We could not help ourselves laughing.

"Really? with what?" Mbalu asked.

"What do you mean with what? I said I got shot! It can only be with a gun or is there something else?" He asked.

"I know you got shot with a gun," she said. "What I meant was with what type?"

"A single barrel," he said.

We laughed even harder.

"So you went and got with a Mende hunter's young wife or daughter," I said.

"Shut up Memuna!" he said.

"But she is right," Mbalu agreed. "You are Mende and you of all people should know that it's not safe to play with a young Mende man's woman, let alone an old one."

"So he shot your arse and left you with all the okra seeds (the bullets the hunters use we called okra seeds because it looks like okra seeds)," Sunshine laughed.

We stopped laughing at him and sympathised with him. He said that he did get shot because of a girl and she was a hunter's daughter. They did not know that there were hunters in the town, but after Hindowa and some other rebels got shot, RUF planned to attack them and capture some of the men and train them. We left him in the hut and went to say hello to Lansana and Naffie in the house.

"What are you three doing here?" Lansana asked.

"Nothing, we just wanted to take a break from the camp and we are going back tomorrow," Sunshine informed her brother.

"Well we can go together. We are going with Hindowa," Lansana said, reminding her who was boss.

It had been a week and a half since Hindowa got shot. The doctor managed to take out the bullets and he could walk just right. He wanted to go to the camp because he was sick of the mosquitoes and scared of catching malaria. Later that evening a troop of rebels came from that area with about eighty or less men they had captured from those towns and with a lot of luggage.

When we got to the camp the guys laughed at him even more and they told us all the stories about how the girls sang, in Mende, for Hindowa.

"There are three girls in that town who are crazy about Hindowa and one of them made up a song in his name," Kasiloi said and he went on to sing the song. It went:

"Hindowa newa a.

A newa, Negy negy negy a, a negy."

It meant Hindowa is too sweet, too sweet, too sweet (newa is Mende for too sweet. Negy is Mende for how sweet). This made him so upset he went into the shelter he gave us. Within a few days he was well enough to wear his pants again. One afternoon Kasiloi suggested we go for a walk near Blama to the ambush town but Hindowa did not want to come and Sunshine and I started singing "Hindowa Newa". He got angry and threatened to shoot us. Kasiloi told him to settle and stop threatening to shoot people or else he would get punished.

Despite it was a really hot day but we went anyway and it was fun but dangerous. When we got back to the camp there was rumour that one of the men they captured from the new towns was on the loose. He was armed with what seemed to be a four-foot long iron rod and he had hit three rebels with it and ran away from the training base. He made his way into the forest and was now closer to the camp. He was making his way back home and that was not good for RUF because the training base was close to where

Foday Sankoh lived. The thought of him making his own way in the bush set our nerves screaming again. He would attack anyone. We stopped going to the bridge and Water Works late in the evenings and early in the morning.

Later that evening Lansana came to the shelter and told the guys that they were all needed to be at the formation that evening. They were going to arrange a way to catch that man before he beats someone else with the rod again. I was still a civilian so I did not go to the formation but Mbalu and Sunshine went. After the formation, security at the guard post and the ambush got tighter and everyone in the camp were on their toes. I was frightened at the thought of being caught in crossfire but I told myself to suck it up and just trust in God for anything. Within a week they got him. I don't know what happened to him but everyone had his or her own story to tell about the man. Some said that he got killed while others said that he got taken back to the training base. We believed that he was killed because it was not safe to take him back to the base.

We went back to our normal activities and one evening we dressed like the boys all in army uniforms. Sunshine and Mbalu were tall enough to fit in the guys' pants. I wore Kasiloi's army jacket and Salifu's jeans and I took Lansana's beret without him knowing and we went for a walk as far as the guard post. The moon was bright and we could see the stars. Sitting in the road we looked at the sky.

"That's my star," I said, pointing at the brightest star.

"That could be a satellite," said Sunshine.

"I don't think so," I said "it's too small to be one,"

We sat there for about an hour then went back to our shelter and went to bed.

In the morning we went to the bridge to do our laundry. I hated doing laundry because we had to hand wash the clothes and I was never good at that. The clothes I washed were never clean because it hurt my fingers. Before we went that morning, Titan came to our shelter, saw that we were going to do our laundry and so asked if we could do his. The question was directed to me but I just looked at him and tried to ignore him.

"Memuna, Titan is talking to you," Naffie said.

I nodded but I was annoyed with her and she knew it. They all knew I was not good at washing clothes using my hands. He went to his shelter to get his laundry.

"Memuna try to be nice to that boy," Naffie said. "He really wants you. Put the fact that he is a rebel out of your head and see him as a person."

"It's not that," I replied. "You know I don't know how to wash clothes."

"Well just do what you can, he will understand," Naffie said, as she left to get her clothes.

Nodding, I picked up an orange from the bowl in the kitchen. I did not know whose it was.

"Don't worry about the laundry you won't be alone," Mbalu said, encouraging me.

"Oh can I come?" Nyalay requested.

"No! I don't want to spend all afternoon telling you not to spend too much time in the water," I said.

She pleaded but I still said no and she insisted.

"Ok but if you give me a headache I will send you right back here, is that a deal?"

"Yes," she said.

"Well go and ask Naffie if it's ok for you to come with us to the bridge."

It was really sunny and hot. We took some biscuits, candy and smoke with us. Nyalay carried the food and we carried the clothes. Before we left the camp we had three big tubs full of dirty jeans and T-shirts. We were not going to do our laundry any more than Lansana's, Laser's, Tiger's, Kasiloi's, Second-phase's, Titan's, Ibrahim's and ours. When we got to the bridge Mbalu wanted to start smoking before starting the laundry but we did not let her or else we were going to do it alone. She and Sunshine washed the first dirt off the clothes and they passed them on to me for me to wash them for the second time and rinse them. I did and passed them to Nyalay because she was complaining that she was bored. So I showed her how she could spread them on the grass in the sun to dry. I let her into the water for a little while because she was hot. When we had done most of the clothes and had only a few T-shirts and our skirts left we sat in the gravel road and admired our work.

Wow they are really clean," Sunshine observed, full of self-satisfaction.

"Well I did not think I would ever be doing a boy's laundry at this age because I can't even do my own laundry," I said.

"Yes, I knew I wanted to ask you about that. Who did your laundry for you when you were with your family?" Mbalu asked.

"Why do you want to know?" I asked.

"Well, you really enjoy looking good in clean clothes but you don't want to see them when they're dirty," she said.

"It's not my fault I look good in them," I replied and we all laughed.

"You think you are the finest thing God ever created, don't you," Mbalu said.

"Well I'm just being grateful."

"She used to bribe our cousins to wash her clothes when we went to the bridge in Sembehun," Nyalay called out from the water.

"Nyalay - watch your mouth or you will find yourself sitting on this hot gravel like us!" I warned her.

Mbalu wanted to know more. She believed what Nyalay said but she wanted to hear it from me so she insisted. Sunshine started wrapping some marijuana and asked if I wanted some. I told her I did not want any because I just did not think the weather was good for me to smoke - it was too hot. She wrapped some for Mbalu and herself; Nyalay asked for some biscuits and we told her to help herself. The water at the upper far end, that we considered the head of the little stream, ran underneath the bridge and was cool and drinkable. There were little thatch trees growing among other trees on each side of the stream. So we drank the water in leaf funnels that we made ourselves.

"Hey, come on, tell me who did your laundry," Mbalu said.

"Mbalu you really serious about this?" Sunshine asked, her voice hazy with smoke.

She nodded.

"Ok. In Liberia we had a nanny and she and my mother did our laundry but my uniform went to the dry cleaners. Later there was my mother's sister, then here in Sierra Leone my sisters Gbondo and the others did it when they were with us in Sembehun for holiday. I did some because they wanted me to learn and if it was not clean enough I'd sneak and throw them behind our house," I confided the whole truth.

"Now you satisfied, Mbalu?" Sunshine asked.

"I can't believe it. If my daughter threw her clothes away I'd make her walk around naked for two weeks and then she'd learn her lesson," she said.

"Well I'm not your daughter," I said.

We left Baindu to smoke because she did more laundry than we did. Sunshine and I did the rest of the laundry and Nyalay spread the clothes in the sun. We asked her if she was hungry but she said the biscuits were enough and she could wait till we got back to the camp. We spread all the laundry in the sun then swam in the stream for hours. When we got out of the water and our skin got dried we started to flake and it was funny. All the time we were washing the clothes Mbalu was busy wrapping smoke after smoke and she needed to rest a little bit so we continued to play on the road.

Nyalay stood on the other side of the bridge where one could hardly see the water because of the grass. The bridge was only about five foot high over the water and the water was really shallow. She was saying that if we dared her she would jump into the grass. So I walked to where she was on the bridge and slightly pushed her, falling into the water,

"Oh....please get me out I'm scared," she cried.

"Ok, ok, wait I'm coming to get you. Don't cry," I said. I was sorry I did that. I thought she would not be scared because the water only came up to her chest. But her screaming was making me panic and it even woke Mbalu up. I called to the girls lying on the ground.

"Sunshine, pull Nyalay up for me! There is no path here to walk out like the other side."

I went in and, with Sunshine, we pulled her up. She was shaking which made me feel really guilty.

"Nyalay, sorry! I'm sorry, ok, don't be so scared - it's the same water you've been playing in," I said, desperately trying to comfort her. "This is just the lower end of the stream."

"But it's scary, all the grass," she cried.

I hugged her and rubbed her head for her to stop crying. Then I let her go to the other side to wash up and after that we went back to the camp with all the laundry dried. Nyalay did not tell Naffie what happened.

After a week we were left alone again. Lansana, Salifu, Soja and Tiger went with Naffie and the children to Water Works and Rain had gone to her grandmother again. The boys were due back in a couple of days. It was a few weeks more before Mbalu was to leave for Libya.

It was a cool afternoon and later, in the evening, it started to rain. After eating we went into Rain's shelter with Second-phase, Laser, Kasiloi and Ibrahim and smoked as if marijuana was becoming extinct. We smoked for hours; we were so caught up in the smoking we did not realise it was getting late. None of us remembered to get the oil lamp we used. None of us could remember where the plate we used as a lamp was, let alone the cloth. The cloth we used as wick for the lamp ran out so we needed to remember where the cloth was to tear a piece off to roll another wick. Unfortunately we were completely out of it. We had been smoking for hours and we were hungry but there was no cooked food so we needed to cook.

It was past midnight. Stumbling over each other Mbalu, Sunshine and I found our way to the kitchen. Luckily we found a pot of black-eyed peas we had boiled that morning so we could cook something nice for lunch the following afternoon. I was meant to cook the stew. I was not good at washing clothes but cooking was my field and we were all looking forward to the black-eyed peas stew - till we got really high. As soon as we saw the peas we forgot all about our plans for the next day. We sat on the kitchen floor by the fireplace and ate the peas, dripping with water, with our hands straight out of the three-legged pot. We ate as if we hadn't had food in weeks. I tried to talk with my mouth full and choked so I went to the room and drank some water. I felt my way out of the room so I wouldn't trip over something and fall. Luckily, I touched a box of matches. I took it out and struck one to light my way back into the room.

"Hey stop eating the peas like that, let's cook the rest," I said.

"I'm in no condition to be near the fire," replied Sunshine.

"Neither am I but we are hungry so let's do something, let's try and keep our eyes open and cook."

I had to take the pot from her and it was a struggle because I was tired.

We managed to cook something. We were lucky to have some steamed meat in the kitchen as well. If we had meat we used to steam it the day before because that was the only way to preserve it. But this was venison; they are pretty tough so we had boiled it. We managed to put something together; we cooked some rice as well and none of us cared what the food tasted like. All we wanted was something in our stomachs as we were very hungry and needed our energy back. After eating the guys thanked me for keeping the marijuana and they thanked us for the food. We went to the room and sat there listening to music. Before we knew it all seven of us were asleep on Rain bed and we slept through the morning routines. The boys woke up very early in the morning. They were used to getting very high and waking up early. They were still hungry so after formation, when they came home and found us still asleep, they decided to make a lot of noise so we would get up and cook for them. We woke up but none of us was in the mood.

"Memuna, go and cook - you like the kitchen," Mbalu stammered.

"I'm not smoking this crazy grass again! Last night was the last night," I said.

"We want you to cook for us," Mbalu said, our mumbled sentences crossing over each other.

"When I get up I'm going straight to Sao's kitchen before I go to the swamp to bathe," I said. "So whoever wants to eat better go and find themselves some food because I'm not going to hang myself over the smoke this morning."

The boys begged for us to cook for them and we told them to go to Lt. Vayanga's shelter to the other guys and eat whatever they had there, or they could go to Jackson and Franklin Morris' shelter. They thought it was a good idea and they pursued it.

We woke up a second time and went to Sao and Edna kitchens to eat. Sao had some food but she did not cook that much, she had only made something for CO. Flomo. So we went to Edna with Sao. Her husband, Fambuleh, had cooked for the ambush men. He cooked some wild yams and stew and he gave us some.

Fambuleh was an old Gissy man and we thought it was funny when he grumbled because it was like he was speaking some totally different language that none of us had ever heard. He grumbled that he did not understand girls of these days. They wake up in the morning and eat the food men cook when it should be the other way round and when we laughed at him even Edna laughed at him.

Edna and Sao asked us what was wrong. I told them I could not talk about it at that moment because I was still trying to put myself together, but Sunshine told them what we did the night before and they laughed at us but they wished they were there to get high too. I had such a hangover that I was not in the mood to wear any of our tight clothing. So I wore one of Lansana's huge T-shirts and we went to the swamp each with a bucket. Edna and Sao followed us; all we did was laugh. Then we got some very small eggplants, some greens and chilly from the garden. Having washed everything we brought them back to our shelters for us to cook.

"Why are these egg plants so tight?" Sunshine asked.

"It's because they are experiencing the war too," Rain said, making all of us laugh.

"Just like you and me," I said.

Titan came and saw how happy we were. He greeted everyone and called me aside. "How are you doing?" he asked. It seemed he wanted to touch me but was not sure I would be ok with it.

"I'm fine," I said.

"Well I can see that but I just want to know if everything is ok with you so if you need something just let me know,"

We went to the kitchen and he sat with us for a while. When Fambuleh and CO. Flomo saw him sitting with us they came to join him. CO. Flomo asked him if he had had breakfast, he said he hadn't, so they sent me to go and get the food from Sao's shelter. I came back with a bowl of boiled cassava with some palm oil and ground chilly in it. They ate and made noise. Fambuleh did not eat because he was already full. A while later Titan left as he had to go talk to someone on the radio. CO. Flomo sat with us till Sao came and got him.

"CO. Flomo! I'm alone over there, I need someone to talk to too so leave these girls and come talk to me too," Sao scolded. We laughed at him as he left.

"Hey Sao," I teased, "why are you taking my husband away from me?"

After cooking we all ate together as usual and sat at the back of the shelter and played games. The following morning Lansana returned to the camp and went straight up to Titan's shelter. Everyone in the camp seemed happy as if something was going on. The girls and I were desperate to know what it was. When Lansana came back to our shelter he came with Titan who had three little pocket-sized books in one hand.

"Is there anything to eat?" Lansana asked.

We did not have any cooked food ready so we went in the kitchen and made something. Titan came to the kitchen to talk to us. He had this broad smile on his face seemingly happy about something.

"CO. Titan, what is everyone so happy about?" Sunshine asked.

Since the day he asked me out I hadn't been able to look at him straight in the face. I was shy, so I was involved in the conversation but I did not look at him and he knew I was shy. Also when I spoke to him I made sure to find a way that he would know that it was him I was talking to because I did not want to say his name either.

"You remember the books we wanted to write about what RUF is about?" he asked. "Well it's done but just in a pocket size for now."

Sunshine and Rain jumped with joy as they did high fives and jumped around. "Now everyone will know what RUF is all about and they won't run when they see us anymore," Sunshine declared, as if prophetically.

I wanted to say that what they wrote and what they did were different but something told me not to push it so I just looked at them.

"Where are the books?" I asked.

There was a brief silence then he handed me one of the little black pocket-sized books. It had few other bright colours on it. It was called "Foot Path to Democracy".

I looked at it and read the title out loud. I was curious to read it; I wanted to know why they were putting us through all that hell - what was their sorry excuse. So I drew out a chair from the table in the backyard to sit and read. They all saw that the expression on my face had changed. I sat and read it; it only had in brief the details they thought were important. It had the date of the first day they attacked Sierra Leone and the first town (Zimmi). It had names of some of the commanding officers, (RUF's only Lieutenant Colonel Mohamed, Foday Sankoh the leader, etc.) I realised I had already met most of the people the book talked about. It also had RUF's anthem in it.

That day I learnt how to sing the whole thing again. I thought the fact that they wanted equal rights, free medication for the poor, free education, etc. was a good idea. But I also thought that the way they went about it was wrong because they were hurting the same people they claimed they wanted to help. Titan asked me what I thought.

"Are you sure you really want to know what I think?"

Both Lansana and Titan said they wanted to know what I thought so I told them and, as hard as it was for them to admit it, they agreed with me.

"But there is no other way, the government is too greedy," Lansana argued his case.

The girls joined in and we talked a little about what we thought of the then Sierra Leonean government. I became attached to the book and it was always with me because I found it fascinating.

Naffie and Rain came to the camp with the children three days later. We were getting a little annoyed that Naffie was almost always in the camp.

"Wait a minute! Was not Naffie meant to stay in Water Works?' Sunshine asked.

"Well, Memuna is here and so is Lansana so you think about it," Mbalu had to point out.

"Mbalu, somebody needs to sew your lips together," I said as we laughed.

That night Naffie, Lansana and Titan were in the room talking but we did not know what they were talking about. The moon was bright and it was beautiful in the camp. I wished I was just on a trip and that I could go home anytime I wanted. We could see the shadows of the trees on the ground in the camp and we could hear the birds chirping out in the night. Then Lansana left with Titan and Naffie called me into the room to talk to me. Naffie said that it was ok for Sunshine and Titan to be present in the room when she told me what she wanted to say. So we went and sat on the bed next to her. I was nervous as I thought Lansana was going to make me stay with Titan, so I started to shake. Seeing through the light of the palm oil lamp, Naffie could see that I was scared and she could see the fear in my eyes.

"Memuna I'm not going to eat you don't be so scared," she said.

"Well talk and tell me what is it? I said.

The girls agreed that the suspense was nerve-wracking.

"Ok, ok. Memuna, Lansana thinks it's time you go on the training base because we don't want what happened to Komeh and Samia to happen to you," Naffie announced. "If you are trained you can go anywhere any of us can go and the fact that you are with Lansana and going out with Titan you can even go to Zogoda. Normally newly trained people don't go to Zogoda so what do you think?"

It was not what I expected though but I preferred that to being a "wife" at my age but I was speechless. The girls thought it was a good thing.

"Memuna remember when we had to come here from Libya to join Lansana they almost did not let you come and we had to register you as Lansana's girlfriend," Sunshine said.

I knew then that I was ready to make sure the Libya drama was not going to be repeated, so eventually I agreed. I was a little scared though because, although Sunshine and Mbalu were not allowed to tell me what happened on the base, they had already told me a lot. So I knew what to expect and who was rude before I was even told that I was going for training. I even met one of the training officers CO. Michael Forest; he was a middle-aged man who found pleasure in talking about women's private parts. So I was kind of ready for what I was going to experience. The only thing that really worried me was the beating in the Halaka.

Lt. Cross arrived in the camp that night so our shelter was a full house just like the day we first arrived here. The guys greeted him and they all made noise. The noise got louder when we got out from talking with Naffie and told our news that I was going to the training base. They all had something to say.

"Good for you Memuna, now you can be my ranger," Kasiloi said.

"Man, I think we should take her on a mission when she comes back," Tiger said.

They all agreed with him.

"Good," Laser said. "Now we have one more bodyguard. When she comes back the three of them will start helping us to guard."

"Laser, just stop pretending as if I don't guard," Sunshine said, indignant. "I started going on missions and guarding Lansana before you were captured."

"Yes and now you are being a girl," Laser complained.

"Well I am a girl and I can do what I want! If you don't like it, you can give me your balls and make me a boy."

With us laughing at him, he got upset telling Sunshine not to be rude. She apologised and the conversation moved on.

"I don't think Memuna can make two days on the training base - she likes herself too much," Salifu challenged.

"Do you want to bet?" I answered, thinking he should have known better than make that comment. "Besides if I don't like myself whom should I like, you?"

"Memuna," Sunshine cut across my challenge, "I have one advice for you: the wyes commander Miatta Duke is nice and I'm sure she will like you but I should warn you don't show any weakness whatsoever. She can be a complete bitch if you act like a spoilt child. So be yourself and remember no brother in the army - not that you have any relative on the base."

"Don't be too friendly," Mbalu said. "Don't try to say hello to Martha every time you see her."

"And don't show your spoilt side," Laser said.

"Am I spoilt?" I asked, daring him to answer.

"Only when Lansana is around," Sunshine said.

I could not believe it; I looked at them with my mouth opened.

"Sorry but it's the truth," Mbalu said.

Our friendship was mainly based on honesty so I didn't mind. Laughing we carried on with our conversation. Salifu wanted to talk and I told him to shut up. The girls, Kasiloi, Tiger, Second-phase and Ibrahim told me not to worry; they assured me that it will happen so fast I would not even know it. None of us knew when I was going, but Lansana told me that I would be told two days before. I thought about the base every day since that night, but I did not get stressed about it. I told myself that I was human like Sunshine, Sao, Mbalu and the others and if they did it, I could do it too. That thinking kept me sane.

The RUF were having problems in those two new towns and the situation there got worse. The people in the villages turned against the rebels; they were ready to take back their villages. So RUF sent more men there as often as possible. Kasiloi was one of the guys who went on those trips. The day he decided to go on that mission was the day I found out I was to go to the training base. A week before that, Kasiloi brought up the topic of me being his girlfriend again and I told him that I did not think it was right for us to do that. So he asked me why.

"Is it because of Titan?" he asked.

"No," I said.

"Why then? Is it Magic?" he asked.

Barely nodding he could see tears welling up in my eyes. So we left it hanging for when he came back from the mission. He was the only one who knew how I felt about Magic and he kept it to himself. That afternoon we were standing and talking in front of the shelter that Medbongo gave us. Kasiloi did not look very happy; he had on a blue and red windbreaker and, taking it off, he put it on my shoulders.

"Take it with you to the training base, it will keep you warm," he said.

I thanked him, we hugged and then he left. Deep in my stomach I felt bad but he kept turning around and waving to me and when I waved back he finally smiled. Kasiloi was not a sentimental person, so it surprised me when he got that way with me and I did not know what to do.

The morning came for me to leave for the training base. Sunshine and Rain reminded me not to forget their advice, Naffie made some cassava for breakfast but I was too nervous to eat. I forced myself though because I had an eleven-mile (from Blama Highway camp to Target Q) journey ahead of me, then another nine miles from Target Q to the training base. Lansana told Soja to accompany me to the training base, but Soja was angry with me because a few days before we had an argument for my food. I was not ready to eat and he had eaten his food but he was still hungry and wanted mine. I called him a greedy-gut so he did not want to talk to me. That was not the first time he had tried to take my food, but this was the time I refused to give it to him.

Lansana, Naffie and Titan got me ready for the base. Titan gave me some tobacco leaves for me to trade for anything I needed on the training base; Naffie helped me pack some clothes, toothpaste and bathing soap and some biscuits and candies. She also talked to me like a mother.

"Stay away from group things don't go over there and try to be too friendly, be nice but not too friendly," she said. "And be careful don't let anyone touch you, some girls get raped on the base."

As if being friendly and touching was the reason for their rape.

Lansana got me to write a letter to a friend of both himself and Titan, a guy who lived on the training base. He was one of the trainers and his name was Lt. Viper.

"Memuna, I'm too tired to write. Come write this letter for me to Viper," he said,

It was sometime in May but we were not sure what the date was. Lansana told Viper to look after me and that I was his sister. Apparently Viper was very good to his woman so Lansana told him to treat me right like he did his woman, with respect.

"Titan said he would talk to him on the radio before you get there and even Sir Ace (one of the vanguards who helped Foday Sankoh start the war - he was like a brother to Titan, around Lansana's age but they all saw Titan as their younger brother and protected his interests accordingly) knows that you are coming so they will all look after you," Lansana said. "No-one will bother you so don't be afraid. Sir Ace is only a mile away from the training base. If there is any problem just let him know and we will know. That is if you don't want to tell Viper or the guys at the studio on the base to tell us."

Sir Ace was a Liberian young man and a known womaniser. The village he lived in was near the training base and the rebels name it Sir Miles Ground. Titan and Tiger walked Soja and me up to Ngovokpanhun. Titan told me he was going to be in touch with Viper every day and if I needed anything at all I was to let him know. We had our first proper kiss on the road and then Soja and I were left alone to continue the journey.

We walked through Water Works and did not go to the house; we only waved to the people who saw us. All this time we did not say anything to each other. He had his gun and I had my bag on my back. When we got to Bandawoh we went to see if Drisa was home. He was but we did not have much time so we spoke to him, drank some water and took off again. The journey between Bandawoh and Target Q was a long dry one.

"Are you still vexed with me?" I asked.

He stopped walking and nodded.

"I did not like what you said to me and anytime I think of it I get angry more and more," he said.

"Sorry, but you have to stop forcing people to give you their food," I said.

We sat in the hot quarry and talked for a while and he forgave me for calling him a greedy-gut. He helped me with my bag because the hill was a little steep and I was thirsty. When we finally got to Target Q it was around 6pm, it was my first time in the civilian camp and it was beautiful. They made it look like a little village by building mud huts with thatched roofs, verandas and kitchens. They even had windows and doors and they had farms and gardens around them. There was a stream running through the camp and the farms. Some of them cooked in a big space they made under a few huge trees.

We stayed at Rain's grandmother's hut; she cooked black-eyed peas with palm oil and some new rice from the farm. It was delicious it reminded me of when I was in Sembehun and the other people who had farms would give my grandmothers new rice during harvest season. We did not have a farm, but our relatives in the villages did and they brought us produce from their farms in the harvest season that was when I realised it was harvest time. Our food was sent over from Freetown with money for other things at least twice a year and we always had more than we wanted. My grandmothers shared some of the things with people in Sembehun sometimes.

There was a very scary old lady in the civilian camp. I was afraid of her eyes - they just seem evil and looking at her gave me chills. She came to Rain's grandmother's hut to greet the guests (Soja and I) and I managed to look at her that once. We got some water in the bucket from the stream to bathe. Soja waited for me to bathe and he went and got his. That night we went and joined the other young people under the trees by the fire. I listened to them tell stories, some of which I already knew. I was very absent-minded I was worried about the rest of the journey and how it was going to be on the base. Rain's grandmother gave us a room in another hut next to hers; it had two straw beds with thin sheets on them. We took one each. There was an oil lamp in the room and two linens for us to cover with. The room was cold and there were lots of mosquitoes. We could not sleep so we talked and tried to kill the mosquitoes all night. As soon as we heard the cockcrow in the morning and the Imam calling for prayers, we got up, went to the stream and got some water to freshen up.

"I'm not bathing this morning it's too cold I'll just freshen up," I said.

We brushed our teeth and changed our clothes. The old lady offered us something to eat, but it was too early for me so I only drank the coffee. The coffee was fresh and natural; they had coffee trees everywhere so they were able to process their own coffee. The only problem was that she used her sugar with great care because she only had some when Rain visited and that was if we had sugar from the loot the boys brought back from their missions, so the coffee I drank did not have enough sugar in it. Soja and I thanked the old lady for her hospitality and we left. We walked for a few more hours and Soja told me not to worry that the three weeks was going to run fast and before I knew it I would be back in the camp. He told me that his training lasted for a month and a half and it was tough but it went fast.

"Sunshine told me that she and Mbalu's training lasted three months," I said.

"Yes, I think she was in the third group of wyese to go for training in RUF and they did the real guerrilla training," he said. "And it's the same thing you are going to do but the only change is I don't think you will be eating leaves or drinking dirty water as part of your training but everything else you are going to do."

"Well, thank God I won't be coming back to the camp with a huge stomach full of dirty water and leaves," I said.

"And besides, you have all the COs catering to you. We had no-one to call when things turned to shit at our training bases," he said.

We kept walking and finally we were in a forest but it seemed closer to a town. In Sierra Leone in the Mende regions it was always obvious when a village or a small town was nearby, because there was always a coffee farm with some cola nut and cacao trees in between the coffee trees at the entrance and exit of every village and small town. So a few metres out of the forest we arrived in Sir Ace's Ground. It was a little busy village and Sir Ace was sitting in his mud house porch on a chair. He was wearing a white singlet, a pair of black jeans and sneakers, listening to reggae music and smoking a cigarette.

He knew who I was as soon as he saw me. I'm not sure why but I think it was because he already knew Soja and he knew that Soja was accompanying me. He was exactly everything I had heard about him; the only thing I heard about him that I did not get to see was his bedroom manners. He was a small masculine but energetic man who enjoyed talking loud and he laughed a lot, very flirty too. He was very dark - as dark as Lansana - and good looking.

"Wow you are exactly what I was told," he said. "My little brother is finally getting it right."

Meaning Titan was finally getting his taste in women right.

Soja gave him courtesy. "Good afternoon Sir," he said.

"Rest, soja," Sir Ace said.

He shook my hand smiling. "How are you my sweetheart?"

"Good thank you," I said.

He took me to the veranda and Soja walked behind us. He called out for someone to bring us some water to drink. A very pretty round faced girl with short Afro came out with two cups of water in a tray. I took mine and thanked her and then Soja did the same. Sir Ace was a very sociable man like his friends, Lansana, Lt. Cross, Titan and CO. Flomo. His bodyguards did not follow him around town. They were on their own business but some of them were around just in case he needed them. As for CO. Flomo he had only one bodyguard and he was an eight-year-old boy called Lamine, whom we bothered a lot.

Sir Ace left us for a minute as he was going to arrange something at the back of the house.

"Where are his bodyguards?" I asked.

"He is like his friends, they are really laid back," Soja said. "Some of those guys over there are his bodyguards."

He pointed at some guys sitting under a mango tree playing checkers games on three boards. Sir Ace returned and asked if we could stay a little but we could not. I was meant to start training and Titan and Lansana were meant to call that evening to see if I was there and everything was ok.

"No Sir, Memuna should start training early tomorrow morning," Ranger said.

"Ok, well Soja you can come back and spend the night here then," he replied. Sir Ace shook my hand. As we turned he said he was going to call Viper and tell him that I was untouchable and that he should look after me.

"Memuna when you come back I will steal you from my brother and you will be my personal bodyguard," he said confidently. Smiling I waved at him.

"Sir Ace is exactly what I was told," I said to Soja.

"Yes and he is a good man as well; he always smiles about everything," Soja said. "Like Bra and CO. Titan but when he gets angry it's not a good sight. He is also a damn good fighter that's why he, Bra, CO. Titan, CO. Viper, Bra Cross, CO. Ninja and even CO. Speed are friends. Even Lion likes him."

I confided, "It's hard not to like someone who makes you feel comfortable the first time he sees you."

Soja told me stories about the little he knew about Lansana and his friends and it was a good story to hear.

The next day I was on my way to the training base, Foday Sankoh was getting into a helicopter and flying to Ivory Coast. He was advising all the commanding officers of RUF that his sorcerer had told him that there was a force coming to attack RUF and this time, if they survived it, then RUF would have Sierra Leone; otherwise they shouldn't fight it. Who is able to run should run and save their lives and those who could not run should surrender because this force was going to enter places no other enemy had been able to come close to. Soja told me Lion was in tears when he told his army these words and he got on the helicopter and left.

The training base was in the Jui Koya hills, a mile and a half away from Zogoda. A helicopter was just outside Zogoda in a field. Guards patrolled the area from the helicopter to the base and from Zogoda to the base. When we got closer to the training base it was a little frightening as security was tight and they were really serious. I knew there was trouble and I was grateful I made no fuss about training because this was no time to play around. There was serious war ahead of them and I had to be part of it to stay alive, get my sisters and get home. Everything we had been through was just a preamble. The real thing was imminent. RUF was expecting some new guns so we were all going to carry our own guns.

Soja knew all of his superiors and his subordinates. He greeted all of them in the appropriate manner and it was fascinating as I watched him do it. I thought to myself, 'This is what I'm going to have to do all the time'. The worst thing is that you have to give courtesy even if you did not like the person. He took me to Lt. Viper shelter. The training base was a camp like ours so they had zinc shelters like we did on Blama Highway. Viper was a tall big man, well built, masculine and with a broad chest. He came up to me and shook my hand which he was not supposed to do because they should not shake hands with the recruits. He shook my hand and showed me my room. I was not even going to sleep with the rest of the recruits. He gave me his bodyguards' room - it was well tidied up. He introduced me to all the guys at his shelter but his wife was absent as she was in Zogoda. In effect, I was the only girl among ten men; I was scared and so I asked Soja to stay the night. One of the men at Viper's shelter was a nice man - he was a Temne, called Ali, who said he liked my name.

"Memuna, where did you get that name? Are you Muslim?" he asked.

"No, I was named after my grandmother and she is Temne like you," I replied.

He laughed and said, "I can see the Temne in you; you are a strong woman coming up."

He told Soja not to worry about me, that as long as he was there he would look after me.

"Ali, she is my sister so please look after her," Soja requested, but we knew there was also a challenge in his voice.

"Sure, who knows? Maybe her grandmother is my relative; so I will look after her and one day she will remember," Ali said.

Weeks before I was sent to the training base, RUF had sent Captain Mon Fré out of Sierra Leone with a five gallon drum of diamonds. He went away and did not come back. He was the topic on every RUF base, including this training base, for a long time.

Here I had no time to sit because they had to show me around and introduce me to the necessary people. The wyese commander was beautiful. She was a small woman with lots of hair and you could tell from looking at her that she took no mess from no-one. I liked that about her.

"Memuna, I know you've already heard about me as I have about you but, anyway, I'm Miatta Duke," she said. "Come to me with any problem."

She was feeding her baby porridge from a feeding bottle. I smiled at the little boy and Soja and I moved on.

We went to Michael Forest's house; he was playing a game of checkers with another man. They were both dressed up in a casual but nice way. They both had Seiko watches like Lansana, Titan and Lt. Cross. Michael Forest had on a polo shirt and a pair of khaki shorts with a pair of brown shoes. The other had on a plain white T-shirt and with a pair of long blue jeans and a pair of black leather slippers. He was handsome - he looked a little bit like Tiger. I was introduced to them both. I already knew Michael Forest. The young handsome man was introduced to me as Sergeant Duke (Miatta's boyfriend, the one she had her son by) and we could not stop looking at each other. He shook my hand and smiled in a pleasant manner. I took my hand away from him because I wanted no trouble with the wyes commander or else I would stay longer than planned.

"Memuna you look familiar," Duke said.

It was true, I thought he was familiar too.

"Yes, have we met before?" I said.

"Duke, you like pussy, leave this girl. In fact she is your CO's woman – Titan," Michael Forest said.

"You know Tiger don't you?" he said.

I answered "Yes."

"Weren't you in Kabbaty the time the huge group of reinforcement went to help the guys there fight the Guinean troops in Rutile when the calibre gave up?" He asked, still looking at me intently.

I looked at him and I remembered. He was with Tiger and he was one of the guys who tried to look scary by frowning. I looked at him again and smiled and he knew what I was smiling about so he smiled too.

"Nice to see you again," he said. "I'm around if you need me."

"She will not need you man; there is a wyese commander you remember her," Michael Forest said to Duke, over his shoulder. He was standing under an orange tree catching some fresh air.

Soon I was introduced to everyone I needed to know and then went to the shelter.

That evening Ali brought me a delicious meal he said was from Miatta. Everyone wanted to do their share in making sure I was ok on the base because of Titan and Lansana.

"Child you are a lucky girl, you are blessed," Ali said.

Soja asked Ali to eat with us but he said he was full. He had a huge tray of rice with his friends and I did not need to worry about him, so we ate.

I saw some girls going to the creek and I followed them so I could bathe. It was a little dirty around the water. There were dried leaves everywhere and it was creeping me out so I bathed in a hurry and went back up to the shelter. After Soja had his bath and got tired talking with the guys, he came to the shelter to sleep. He was going to spread some clothes on the floor to sleep but I did not think it was right because, as it was early rainy season and late dry season; it was cold. I told him to share the bed with me, he was like a brother to me and it was a strange environment, there was no way I was going to fall asleep. We talked a little more. He told me not to worry; that I should get some sleep because I was getting up at 5am to start my training and he was leaving at 6am.

The first session of the training was two and a half hours of jogging. I was really thin but I was not fit at all. I ran out of breath but I did not dare stop. We jogged and then we learned the parade (left turn, right turn, about turn, attention, at ease). We did some more jogging. I recognised some of the men on the base. They were the men who were captured from the two new towns. There was a boy who could not stop slapping his own face - he slapped his face and cried to go home.

"I'm not a war fighter, I'm a farmer and I want to go home to my family on our farm," he cried.

Sometimes he would sit on the ground and ignore all instructions and carry on slapping his face. I felt sorry for him I wished they would just let him go because his face had gone red from him slapping himself.

While jogging I saw two more women I knew – Mariama I knew from Libya at CO. Speed's house. She was now dating one of RUF's captains who was in Ivory Coast. She told me he called every day to see if she was ok and if she needed anything. The next person was Ngor Nyahanga ; a lady who we met when Sunshine and I went to visit Sandy, Magic's brother; she was Sand's friend's woman. She was happy to see me and she said that we should stick together. She was pregnant and I was wondering what she was doing on the base. I guess everyone wanted to get ready and, besides, Sia had just left the training base three weeks before I went there. She was pregnant with her second baby. She was getting on everyone's nerves talking about the hard training she did. Meanwhile she did not get trained like everyone else because she was pregnant; she was treated differently.

Most of the recruits, including Mariama, on the base thought I was there for advance training even though we all carried sticks on slings as our guns. They thought I was just there to advance my skills because they all knew that I was from Blama Highway camp and no civilian above twelve years of age was allowed in the camps. Most of the Commanding Officers knew me, so the recruits on the training base gave me courtesy and I did not tell them to stop. I wanted to but I was embarrassed so I told Ali.

"I told you that you are blessed so don't fight it, just go with the flow," he said.

Later that afternoon everything was set in the kitchen for me to cook I don't know how but Ali just came to me and took me to the kitchen.

"We heard you like cooking so here," he said. "You are God sent. While training you will help us with some things please,"

"Ok. Wow you brought fresh greens and all. Who told you I liked cooking?" I asked. "Soja told me some things about you – like things that you don't like and things that you like and he said that you are a little complicated," Ali said.

"Well, men always think women are complicated but I think I'm just like any other girl," I assured him.

Ali went inside and brought some steamed meat, palm oil, seasoning and some onions and chillies. He told me, "if you need help with anything all you need to do is call any one of the guys if I'm not around."

I cut the greens asking the guys to help me make the fire because I was hopeless at setting fires. Sitting outside to avoid the smoke while I cooked, Mariama came by and I asked her to stay and keep my company which she did so. When I got through cooking we ate quickly because we were due for training in twenty minutes. We ate as fast as we could with our hands and cleaned up. I dished out food for the younger boy, Ali, the other man and then for Viper. I called Ali, told him which bowl was for whom and Mariama and I ran off to the training ground. I was so full I almost threw up and the fact that I ate so fast made my stomach ache.

We were told to go in the forest and fetch firewood for our night session. We needed the wood to keep up the warmth and for us to see by. Ngor Nyahanga, Mariama and I formed a group with another girl Ngor Maria had become friends with on the base. It was disgusting being in that damp forest. There were faeces almost everywhere and it was smelly. We kept screaming 'ewe, ewe.' Quickly we got our wood and ran back to the base. No sooner had we delivered the wood than we ran to the creek to bathe. The thought of seeing all that faeces made my skin crawl and I began scratching and bruising my skin.

I had nothing to do at the shelter. Our next training session was five hours away, so we spent a lot of time cleaning up. I still felt sick after the long bath in the creek. When I got to the shelter Lt. Viper told me that Lansana and Titan called on the radio to check if I was alright.

"I hear you are very sickly and they are really worried about you," Viper said, "so please, if you feel sick or any pain just let me know or you can tell Miatta ."

"I get fever sometimes but it doesn't last long and so far I'm alright," I could only reply politely to his concern.

He smiled and I went to the room to rest a little, but I had barely touched the bed when I heard the whistle blow for training. It was annoying but I had to go or else I'd stay longer on the training base. Everywhere we went we had to carry those stick- guns. Even when we went for fire wood and when we went to the creek. If we forgot them anywhere we would either get beaten or punished in some way - either bring more wood or fetch water for the kitchen where they cooked for the recruits.

In training the commanders taught us how to sing the RUF anthem, how to give courtesy and we did some more jogging. They'd whip us if we did not lift up our feet high enough when we jogged. I thought it was stupid and an unnecessary punishment. I was afraid of being whipped so I did what I was told even though my legs and calves were aching. I forgot myself sometimes though and I got whipped for that. Then we were taught how to use our guns. The trainer had a real A.K while we had our sticks on slings hanging on our shoulders. After the session my skin felt sticky so I took a bucket of water from the shelter and freshened up but tied and aching I showered and went to bed. I managed to sleep for a few hours and then just after midnight the whistle went off again. Getting up I wore the jacket Kasiloi gave me and went outside.

"What are we going to do tonight Ali?" I asked

"It's ideology time," he said.

In my head I thought, 'What ideology do they think they know? I mean how can you go out, kill people, loot their homes and businesses and then you wake me up to teach me ideology?'

"Ideology!" I exclaimed and Ali nodded.

So I waved and went to the training ground. There were about three places of huge fire and the other recruits were around them. I walked towards the group of people searching for my friends but Ngor Nyahanga saw me and called out to me. She had saved seats for Mariama and me on her mat. Some people did not have mats and some did not have clothes to spread and sit on so they sat in the sand.

There were recruits coming from every corner of the base, some did not have anything to keep them warm - they were shivering so they ran to the fires. I managed to stay awake for at least half an hour but I fell asleep behind Mariama. I asked her to hide me. The three of us thought that it was hypocritical of them to try and teach us how to treat civilians when we go on missions and when we capture them. We thought that it was foolish of us to listen. But we had to be there so we sat and fell asleep when we could not help it. It turned out the ideology lecture went on for three hours and at the end of it, it was already 3.30 am. The girls woke me up. I went to bed and they went to their shelters too. Ngor Nyahanga was in the female recruit shelter; Mariama was staying with someone on the other end of the base around where the radio house was. Viper came to my room to check if I was there and saw me lying in bed with my eyes opened. It was my time for meditation.

"I just came to see if you are alright," he said. "Is it warm in here?"

"Yes the blanket is warm," I said.

We said our goodnights and he left closing the door behind him. All of his shelters had doors.

Early the following morning we went jogging and they told us to get prepared for the following day because it was going to be a tough one. We went over the same things we did on the first day of training and they divided most of the recruits into groups. Some went to clean the creek, some cleaned around the training ground and others were sent to work in the garden. I was not asked to do anything; neither were Ngor Nyahanga or Mariama. I asked Ngor Nyahanga if she ate the recruits' food because it was not food for anyone especially not a pregnant woman. She said that she brought her own food and sometimes she gave some things to the Weise commander or some other woman she knew on the base to add to theirs and they dished some out for her. She also told me not to worry about her, that she was ok. I asked if she was sure, she assured me she was and so did Mariama. So we went our separate ways and promised to meet later. Mariama was only going to clean herself up and come over to me.

When I got to the shelter the kitchen was ready for me like the first day and Ali was sitting on the bench in front of the kitchen. We looked at each other and smiled. I took a bucket of water and went to the bathroom to bathe. The water was cold but it was refreshing and good for the pain I felt in my legs. Moaning throughout because of the cold, I then went to my room and rubbed my legs with Chinese tiger balm and Vaseline. Then I went to the kitchen to cook because I was starving too. Ali sat with me for a while then left to go run some errands Viper had assigned to him. A girl walked by with her thumb in her mouth. She was very thin and tall, she was malnourished and she looked weak. She stopped when she got past the kitchen a little, turning to look at me. I looked at her and smiled so she would come to me and she came over.

"Can I get you a bucket of water from the creek so you can give me some food? Please" she requested.

I thought it was too sad and it brought tears to my eyes. Looking up at her I shook my head.

"No they are cleaning the creek and you don't have to work for food," I told her. "Just take that other bench, sit with me and let's cook ok."

Nodding she thanked me and she told me how the person who captured her just took her to the base and abandoned her there. She was not fast enough to eat with the other recruits.

"They eat everything before I get there and sometimes I get there on time but before I put my hand into the tray they fight and clear everything," she said.

My eyes were full of tears mostly because I was grateful to God for not making me go through that. Though we were in the same war zone my situation was far better. In my heart I asked God why, why was life so

347

unfair? So I managed to force a smile and talk to her. I asked her name and she said that her name was Wuatta.

"Wuatta, you're now my new friend, so you have to come help me cook every day as long as you are here, is that ok?" I said.

She consented and we talked about different things. She talked about how hard it was for her to keep up with the training when she was hungry. Ali came and saw us. Wuatta started to run when she saw him

"Wuatta, it's ok, you don't have to run," I said. "Ali, is it ok that I help her out while she is here?"

"Of course Memuna, do whatever if that is what you want."

So Wuatta was happy. Mariama came but she did not stay long and after cooking I was not hungry so I dished out some food in a bowl for Wuatta. She ate and left some but I told her to take it and keep it somewhere just in case she felt hungry again. She helped me with the cleaning, thanked me then she went off.

I went over to Ali and his friends at the other shelter behind Viper's. They were smoking, listening to music and talking. The music was not loud because no-one was allowed to play loud music on the base as it was not that far from the enemy zone. On the other side of the creek, there were Kamajors (hunters) in the villages near Kenema. I was told they also had a strong ambush set up there to protect the base. Ali asked me if I wanted to smoke but I said no. So I just sat there and talked with them. We laughed about how people gave me courtesy while I was just a recruit like them. Then Wuatta came around. She had been looking around for me and when she saw me sitting on a table in the shelter she came running. She looked happier but she was still sucking her thumb. Wuatta was a pretty girl and tall; she had short hair but it looked good. All she needed was some food for her to get her energy and someone to talk to. She was shy when she saw all the guys I was sitting with but she started to smile.

"Wuatta, come here don't be shy," I said.

She took her time to walk to the shelter. One of Ali's friends teased her saying that he wanted her so she bowed her head, refusing to look up again. We all teased her about being so shy and she laughed. I got her to lift up her head eventually.

"Memuna I can't believe that all this time you don't remember me," Ali said.

"What do you mean?" I asked.

"Well we met before in Kabbaty," he said.

I looked at him shaking my head smiling because I don't easily forget people I've seen let alone people I've met before. So I could not believe what Ali was saying.

"No Ali this is my first time meeting you, I did not see you in Kabbaty. Did you live there?" I asked.

"No but I went there," he said. "Remember the day the reinforcement went to Kabbaty and CO. Speed was there too?"

I nodded and looked at him with suspicions.

"Were you there?" I asked.

"Yes I was and I saw you and all your sisters; you are all pretty girls. So," he said, "did Captain Speed get what he wanted?'

"What did he want?" I asked

"You, the day he saw you in those pants," he said.

"What! He wants Sunshine!" I said stunned. I did not like this news.

"Well we all knew that the captain had his eyes on you too," Ali said enjoying my surprise.

"Well I'm glad I was kept in the dark because that is really scary," I said.

We laughed about it and Ali went on to tell the guys about how men wanted Komeh, Magainda and me.

"That Magainda one is the one who has the butter-like skin isn't she?" he asked.

I laughed and asked him what he meant about butter-like skin. He said he was referring to her complexion. I laughed even harder wishing Magainda and Komeh were here to hear him.

"And that Komeh one too she got the same skin but Magainda's is lighter," he said. "Komeh now is feisty and her eyes are pretty and that is what most men I knew liked about her."

"But you and Magainda have the same skin colour so you think you look like butter?" I asked, laughing at him.

"You look like chocolate and you are feisty and fearless that's what they liked about you and your hair too," he told me.

"Hey were you watching us or what?"

"I saw you only twice but I saw your sisters a lot and I saw Magainda before you girls were captured," he said.

He told me that he only saw me twice but he heard a lot about me, Magainda and Komeh. We told the other guys about Mattru Jong and Kabbaty. All Ali could talk about was Mende girls and I laughed at him for that.

Later that night we went for some more ideology and I did not pay attention at all because what the trainer was saying was not what they did. Besides, I already knew what they were teaching because Magic and his brothers used to give me training either in the room or in the backyard when we moved to Mokabba. Most of the rebels were really brutal towards civilians. My sisters and I fell into good hands though we did not need it.

A week and a half went by and it was time for the manoeuvre lessons. I was so nervous; they woke us early in the morning and made us jog for hours. We later went to the obstacles. There was a huge log with some mud on it to make it slippery because we had to run across it. Then there were the drums cut on each end - about four - that we had to crawl through as fast as possible or else we would get whipped. The monkey bridge was one long stick on two other sticks across a pile of sand. We had to jump and hang on and manoeuvre across the sand. Then there was a rectangular hole and a well that we had to jump over without thinking. Then we had to crawl in the mud under barbed wires two feet or less above us. The wires were razor-sharp and some people got cut. I managed to squeeze my tiny body underneath.

All this time we were yelled at and there were trainers, including Miatta, standing to see who would stop so they could give them some lashes. We went through all these obstacles three times and then we went to the Hakka. This is a huge pile of sand surrounded with cement bricks. It is meant to represent a beach, a desert or any sandy area. We had to run in the sand in circles for about twenty rounds with the trainers behind us shouting "halaka" repeatedly and whipping whoever they wanted to whip. I got whipped about four times by some stupid boy I had rejected. Pain ripped through my back and I almost cried. So I slowed down and told him that if he laid another lash on me I was going to punch him in the face and tell Viper. He apologised and Miatta saw us talking so she asked him to get out of the halaka.

Almost everyone was crying. There were lots of us and so some had to watch us go through it while they waited for their turns. The sight of us made them cry too. I was whipped by someone else but I don't know who it was and the day didn't stop there.

After all this we went to the forest to manoeuvre on our stomachs on the forest ground between the trees. When we did the forest manoeuvre we were shot at with pistols but no-one got hurt. They threatened to shoot us if we did not do it faster. We did when we heard the gunshots. I cried and some people actually crawled in faeces. We did the forest manoeuvre twice that day. We undertook all this training with our stick-guns hanging on us.

At the end of the session my skin was tingling and aching because the day before we did a hundred push-ups and a hundred sit-ups each. My stomach and arm muscles were sore. I felt pain everywhere. We ran to the creek but we did not stay long as there were so many of us the water got muddy. I could feel the burning sensation when I sat in the water. I had bruises on my elbows and knees from crawling in the mud, the drums and the forest.

I went back to the shelter feeling like a totally different person and angry. Viper told me that Titan called to check if I needed anything and if I was ok, but when he called I was in training. I managed to cook and Wuatta came over but I was not much company and she understood. I told her that my whole body was aching and that I was really tired. We cooked and she left with her bowl and I went to get some sleep. Mariama did not come to eat because she was tired too. She went to sleep then get prepared for the evening training.

We were assembled late that night for some more ideology and arms cleaning lessons. But not all of us could see what the instructor was showing us. I knew most of it because Lansana and the boys taught me how to clean an A.K and how to clean and load a magazine. They taught me how to get the advance shot from the magazine and into the A.K and also how to get it out before you hurt someone. I already knew how to dismantle a pistol. Sunshine taught me using Lansana's pistol. That was exactly what they taught us that night. I could not see the instructor but I listened to him for as long as I could. The fire was warm and nice and it put me to sleep before I knew it.

That night during formation the boy who slapped his own face managed to flee the base. He only had one more RUF checkpoint to escape for him to find his way to Kenema when he got caught. At the checkpoint they almost killed him but when he told those rebels that he had run away from the training base they brought him back the following morning screaming and slapping his face. They beat him a lot before bringing him. He was all bruised and was bleeding from his head. The sight of him was really sad and I cried when I saw him.

The trainers asked us recruits to beat him up after training session that morning. I watched some of them pounce on him but I walked away crying for him. They beat him, branded "RUF" on his forehead with a blade and locked him up. When it was all calm, I went to his cell to talk to him. He stood there crying for his parents in Mende. I told him not to worry, that he should just do what he was told and one day God will help him and everything will be ok. I asked him his name, he said his name was Hindolo. There were a few of us talking to him and Mariama was there too.

"God will punish them for what they are doing to us. They will not go free," he cried.

We told him not to say it aloud before he gets tortured some more. He was there all day. The cook brought his food to his cell for him and later that night he was brought out for "ideology".

We had one more week left for training and later that night after the ideology session I went to the shelter to sleep. Hours after I went to sleep and I heard the squeaky sound of the door opening. I opened my eyes slightly and I saw Viper. He asked me if I was warm enough.

"I am warm enough, yes," I said. "I have a pair of socks on, I took two pairs of Lansana's socks with me." I used one pair for training and one to sleep in.

"Do you want me to spend the night here with you?" He asked me.

"No," I said.

He stood by the bed for a few more minutes and then he walked out.

In the morning I did not really see him but he left a message for me that he spoke to Titan and he wanted to know when I was going back and if I was alright. I had felt sick as I thought of him begging me to spend the night together. Ali gave me the message and the message made me feel better.

We did one more manoeuvres session and sit-ups and push-ups. We had one more to do and it would be graduation time. I could not wait.

From the night Viper asked to sleep with me I stayed awake all night when I was at the shelter. As a consequence I slept through the ideology lecture. I was grateful though that he did it later than at the start of my training because I could handle him until it was time for me to go home.

It rained the next day and the shelter leaked on the bed. I could not sleep there, as the bed got wet. So Viper asked the guys to clear their things out of the shelter next to his so I could use it till it was time for me to go home because I only had about five more days to go. I was a little afraid sleeping in the shelter next to his, but I liked it because it was warmer. There were more blankets on the bed.

After another session of firearm lesson I went to the shelter to sleep. When he heard me open the door he called out to me and asked me to go to his room; he wanted to have a word, so I did. He was sitting there with one of his friends who I thought was really sleazy, they were smoking.

"Good evening," I said, paying them courtesy. They greeted me back and I stood there waiting for him to talk. I was very tired and I yawned. He asked me to sit but I told him that I was tired and I had an early training.

"I just wanted to ask you how your training was going," Viper said.

I told him it was good and everything was going well. All this time he could not stop smiling at me.

"Your boyfriend called again this evening, he calls twice a day and sometimes three times to see how you are doing. I think he is missing you," Viper said.

I let out a slight smile and I said goodnight. He said goodnight to me too and I went to the room. The bed was so warm I struggled to stay awake. I had lost so much weight from the hard training and the lack of sleep. Also I wanted to go back to the camp as I could not stand being away. All I thought of was "what ifs" and it worried me. I managed to sleep a little but as soon as I heard Viper and his friend saying their goodnights I woke up.

He went to his room for a few minutes. The whole base was quiet we could only hear the birds singing in the trees in the dark. There were guards on guard. I was lying in the bed with my eyes closed but I was not asleep when Viper came into the room. I opened my eyes when I heard his footsteps. Shocked I saw him naked down to his briefs and he had an erection. I could not believe it. I was only fifteen and very tiny and here was this huge masculine man, probably in his late thirties, doing whatever he could and making a fool of himself in the process, to sleep with me. I was terrified, I sat up in the bed as fast as I could.

"What's happening?" I demanded, my voice shaking in the cold night.

"Nothing, I just like you. Can you come and sleep with me in my room?" he said.

I was so scared I did not want to say another word because I knew I was going to scream. I shook my head frantically but he kept asking me to go to his room and I panicked more and more.

"No I don't want to, I'm happy with this bed and Lansana and Titan wouldn't be happy about this," I said.

"How would they know?" he asked, as if they didn't matter.

"Titan is my boyfriend and we talk about everything and I tell Lansana everything. They both have a way of making me talk. They both know that I'm a virgin so please stop," I begged. "Just leave me alone."

Looking at me, he called me "La Petite Virgin" in French accent and walked out. He stopped, looked at me again when he got to the door, then left. I waited for a few more minutes then ran in the dark to the female recruits' shelter to Ngor Nyahanga.

"What's the matter?" she asked. She could see I was shaking and scared.

"Someone almost raped me just now."

"Who was it?" she asked.

I did not want the news to go around so I told her that I did not see his face. She made some space for me on her mat and I slept next to her by the fire.

Early in the morning we went for training and I came back to the shelter to cook with Wuatta. I did not sleep at the female recruits' shelter with Ngor Nyahanga that night I slept in that same shelter but I did not have a second of sleep. I had only three days left so I could cope with three more sleepless nights. Viper was angry with me but it seemed like he was more embarrassed than angry. He did not come to the room again.

The following day we did our last session of manoeuvre and we did the parade. That night we attended another session of ideology. Later they put some people into groups to clean up the training base for the next group of recruits that was coming. As for us we were officially RUF rebels. I was so excited to get out of there and so were Mariama and Ngor Nyahanga. Mariama's boyfriend was already making plans for someone to come and get her. That afternoon someone from the studio came looking for me.

"Who is Memuna? Lieutenant Titan's girlfriend," asked the man.

Before I could say anything Ali pointed me out.

"I have a message from Lt. Titan ma'am, he wants to know if you need someone to come and get you? CO. Eagle asked the same question too," he said.

"Tell them I'll be fine, that I'll be coming home with my friend when I'm allowed to leave," I said.

"But you don't know when you'll be leaving yet?" he asked.

"No, I have three days left to go for my training, thank you though," I replied politely. He talked to Ali and went back. He did not come back with any message from Titan or Lansana. I was so excited I did not sleep that night. I could not wait for the last day. The following morning we had some more beatings ahead of us. They made up a song saying that we promise not to tell anyone what we did on the training base, not even our parent or grandparents. The song went like this:

Po… po, po, your Ma po…

Your Pa po…

When you go home your Ma ask, your Pa asks you say, "I don't know."

Bu Ye ke…. Bu Ye ke.

We repeated this song over and over and again and they had their whips lashing us on our feet as we sang. I was really annoyed but I was glad it was all over.

That night we had our last ideology lecture and it did not take long. I went back to the shelter and to the room. I could not stop smiling. I had two more days. We did not do much the next morning as they only called us out to do the parade again.

"This is when some people stay and end up repeating their training so you all better do it well," Miata warned us.

We did the whole parade, sang the anthem, did some jogging and that was it. All we had to do was have some papers signed for us and we were on our way. Everyone returned to where they came from. As for those men who got captured from the two new towns, they were going to be assigned to different areas. I was worried about Hindolo, the boy who kept trying to run away and kept wondering whose bodyguard he was going to be. I asked God to look after him.

CHAPTER TWENTY THREE

Trained At Camp Lion

The following morning there were very few of us left as some people went home just after our last parade. We went to formation with the very same people who trained us and it was fun. To my surprise I could not stop smiling. After the formation Miata and I talked a little.

"It was nice knowing you. I hope we keep in touch," she said. "Oh and you were really strong for that little body of yours, you did great - no -one has to worry about you."

"Thank you Miata," I said.

When I went to the shelter everything was ready for me to cook but it was too early. "Why do you want me to cook so early?" I asked.

"Viper is in a meeting with some commanding officers right now and, when he is through with the meeting, he is going to Zogoda for a few days. So I thought it would be good if he ate before he left," Ali said.

Wuatta came over; she was back to normal as she only needed some food. She was smiling because she was waiting for her boyfriend to come and get her. She said he was already on his way from Jui Koya. She helped me cook very fast. I let her cook the rice and I cooked the stew; and we were through in an hour. We dished out everything and I was too happy to eat. Wuatta gave me a tearful hug; "I wish you good luck Wuatta," I said. "May God bless you and may he keep us alive to meet again."

We prayed for each other and hoped to meet again in good times. "May God bless you Memuna, if you were not as kind as you are to allow me to eat your food I might have died," Wuatta said with tears streaming down her cheeks.

"We need to look after each other in this place," I said. "You gave me someone to talk to when you came around."

"I pray we live to see the end of this war and may your kindness follow you," Wuatta said.

We were both in tears at the end of it all, but we managed to smile. Ali came to me and wiped my tears.

"You are a nice girl Memuna," he said and he gave me a hug.

I sat with him and the other bodyguards while they ate. Feeling hungry when I saw them eating, I took my bowl and sat next to them as we ate, talking together. While I was eating Ngor Nyahanga came to me and asked if I was ready to go or if I was waiting for someone to come pick me up. I told her that no-one was coming for me.

"Then do you want to walk with me?" she asked.

"When?" I asked eagerly.

"Now, all you have to do is ask someone to sign your paper," she said.

"Please give me a few minutes," I said.

For the first time in my life I already had my things packed so I ran to Miata and told her that I wanted to go home, that I had found someone to walk with. She told me to go to CO. Michael Forest for some paper that was supposed to say that I was a graduate and allowed to leave the training base. Running like the wind to find him, he gave it to me but I needed to take it to Viper for him to sign. He was the head on the training base and he was my guardian. I wanted to wait but something told me not to wait, that he won't refuse to sign it in front of all those people. I ran to him in the meeting, there were a few familiar faces but we were all too busy to say anything to each other.

"Good morning sirs," I said. "Sorry sirs, Lt. Viper can you please sign my pass, I need to go home?"

"Do Titan and Eagle know that you are coming home now?" he asked.

"Yes," I said. It was a lie but I did not care. I needed to go. If I had told him the truth it wouldn't have saved me. He took the pass from me reluctantly, signed it and gave it to me. I saluted him, thanked him and ran back to the shelter. I gave Ali a big hug and he said that he would really miss me.

"Well you know Blama Highway and you are always welcome Ali," I said running off to Ngor Nyahanga .

We met half way as she was already on her way to meet me at the shelter with her things. Ali hugged me again and told me to be careful and look after myself.

Ngor Nyahanga and I walked as fast as we could. We only stopped to drink some water and by 5pm we were in Bandawoh. Drisa made me stop in Bandawoh for half an hour. Ngor Nyahanga stayed for the night with a woman she referred to as her sister. She needed a break because we had walked nine miles that day and she was tired. The guys at the radio house in Bandawoh were all happy to see me.

"Our woman is a trained soja now," one of them said. They were all Titan's friends.

I drank a cup of water and asked them if they had seen Titan since I was on the training base. They said he was in Bandawoh the day before but he left and went back to the camp. I told Drisa that I wanted to go to Water Works before I got lazy, so he took me.

The two of us had been talking the whole time. Half way to Water Works, Drisa laughed at me about how thin I was.

"I never thought you could get any thinner," he said, looking me up and down, pulling faces like I was almost invisible. "Leave me alone Drisa, I will gain all that weight back," I said.

He was carrying my bag and his gun.

"What weight are you talking about?" he teased.

"Well, the little I had that I left on that training base,"

"Oh, Memuna did you see CO. Titan?" Drisa asked.

"The last time I saw Titan was when he walked me to Ngovukpanhun and I hope I'll see him tomorrow."

"But you know he has chicken pox?" Drisa said.

"What are you talking about?" I asked surprised. "Titan has been in touch with me all this time and he did not tell me anything about any chicken pox! Are you joking Drisa?"

"Well maybe her did not want to worry you he was sick," he said. "But now he is ok. All that's left is a few scars and they will disappear soon."

I kept quiet wondering why he did not let me know he had chicken pox and why he did not tell me he was in Bandawoh.

"Maybe he is in the camp now," I said. "He'll probably come to see me tomorrow morning or tonight when he finds out I'm in Water Works. I'm sure he knows by now - if he calls the training base they will tell him I was on my way. Maybe those guys at the studio in Bandawoh already told him."

When we arrived at the house Naffie had just finished cooking dinner. I spoke to her like I always did.

"What, you are not a civilian anymore, you are a soja and I'm your superior so give me the courtesy I deserve," she said, teasing me.

She knew I was tired, I gave her courtesy and she hugged me.

"Oh my sister, you look so small and tired. How was it?" she asked.

"Every bit of me is aching," I confessed.

Even Lucia was happy to see me; Nyalay and her were all over me. I hugged Nyalay but Lucia demanded I take her so I held her and she was smiling. I was about to ask Naffie about Titan but she asked me first if I saw him in Bandawoh.

"Are you sure he is still there?" I asked.

"Yes, I saw him yesterday evening. He said that he missed you," Naffie replied looking at me knowingly.

"But why did he not tell me he was in Bandawoh?" I asked, confused. "Even Drisa asked me if I saw him. Is the chicken pox bad?"

I thought he was ashamed of me seeing him with the chicken pox. It did not matter to me; I just wanted to see him.

"No he is fine. He just needed to recover from a few more spots," Naffie assured me.

No matter what Naffie said though, I was getting upset with Titan because I really wanted to see him and now he was playing games. I sensed something was wrong, but I did not say anything. Nyalay volunteered to fetch me a bucket of water for me to bathe. After bathing I had some food and thanked Drisa for bringing me to Water Works then I went to bed. I was fast asleep as soon as my head hit the bed. A few hours later I heard Naffie and Daniel talking.

"Daniel, come to the room I've got something for you," she said in Krio. Titan only learned Krio when he was captured and brought to Sierra Leone. He managed to learn how to at least speak Krio unlike CO. Feelgood. Daniel was Mende but he spoke Krio more than Mende.

"What do you have for me Naffie? Make my day, that son-in-law of yours is the reason why I'm travelling tonight," Daniel said.

Daniel was really noisy; he got that way when he was excited. He spoke so loudly it woke me but I covered my head with the blanket. Naffie brought Daniel to the room but he did not see anything.

"What is it Naffie?" he asked.

"Lift up the cover," Naffie said impatiently.

He lifted the cover and saw me pretending to be asleep.

"Get it up soja and talk to me!" Daniel almost shouted, grinning. "You don't need to salute me just give me a hug. We missed you, you crazy girl."

I smiled,

"Ooh I'm tired Daniel," I moaned.

Pulling the cover off me I got up and gave him a hug while he said what he had to say about my weight.

"Have you seen your man?" he asked.

"No!" I said.

"Well how can that happen when you came through Bandawoh?" Daniel asked.

"Well the guys at the studio saw me and they told me that he left and was in the camp," I explained.

"What? I'm going to bring him. Just give me and hour and a half and we will be back here. Don't sleep!" Daniel said and left to find Titan.

I was sure something was going on but I still did not say anything. Lucia and Nyalay were very energetic that night and happily kept me awake. I changed my clothes and wore a T-shirt and a pair of shorts. I spread a sheet on the floor in the room to sleep because it was a very hot night. Before I knew it Daniel and Titan were in Water Works. I looked at him and saw a few spots on his face and his hand but he was fine; he hadn't lost that much weight. He looked very guilty. I asked him,

"Why did you keep in touch with the people on the training base and made sure they looked after me but told the guys in Bandawoh to tell me you weren't there?"

He did not know what to say and we just sat there looking at each other. I just felt more and more disappointed by him and I went back to lie on the floor.

"Memuna I'm sorry," he said.

I did not say anything and he came and sat on the floor next to me. He kept rubbing my head trying to talk to me. I asked him to tell me why those boys lied to me. But he could not find the words to say and he could not even say he was not involved. I guess he knew I'd see right through his lies. So I told him to take his hand off my head. He got angry and walked out.

"Goodnight, I'll see you later or when you are ready to see me," he said.

"Goodnight, come back when you are ready to talk," I said back.

Naffie came into the room as Titan left.

"You are not going to do that Memuna. You are going to talk to that boy - he's been so worried about you so follow him now," she demanded.

I felt a little guilty and so ran after him. He stood and waited for me when he saw me following him.

"Are you cheating?" I asked.

He looked at me and did not say anything and then I knew he was. So I turned to leave.

"I will do something to you that will make you bite your finger and don't feel the pain," he called out after me.

I spun to face him.

"What would you do that for? You are the one doing the wrong so do what you want. Maybe your own actions will make you bite your finger and don't feel the pain," I calmly said, almost on a cold tone and we both went our ways.

Daniel was upset with him while Naffie was upset with me.

"Memuna I like you very much and I won't hide the truth from you," Naffie said. "All these men who are behind you like flies behind poo feel nothing compared to what that boy feels for you. I think you have to start being nice to him or else you will lose a lot."

I looked at her and smiled.

"He has someone else. That's why he told his friends to tell me that he was not in Bandawoh and he is threatening to hurt my feelings so bad that I will bite my finger and don't feel the pain."

Naffie looked at me and could not understand how I thought Titan was cheating.

"Memuna, that boy is very good looking and commands a lot of power and women ask him out all the time and yet, all this time, you are the only one he's asked out and I don't think anyone can beat that. You are the first person he's asked out in his life," Naffie informed me with no less of a telling off.

"I know that and I'm feeling different about him but I'll wait and see what is it that he will do to hurt me so bad," I replied.

Naffie went on and on at me and I left her to talk while I slept.

The next morning Lansana, Soja and Sunshine arrived in Water Works. There was no-one else but them - all the other bodyguards were in the camp. I gave them courtesy and it was weird to all of us. Sunshine was happy that now she could try to bully me, because I was not a civilian anymore. She had the right to demand courtesy from me. We joked about it and she told me that Mbalu had left for Libya and Kasiloi had made two trips to those two new villages. He said he wanted me to go and spend some time with him there when I got back from training.

"So how am I supposed get there?" I asked.

"Well he said he could come for you or you could go with Second-phase and the others when they are going," Sunshine said.

"I think it's a good idea we will go together. Finally I don't have to stay home because of you. We can go with the guys on missions."

"That is if they will let me, anyway I don't want to go on any mission," I said.

Soja was happy to see me. We hugged each other after I saluted them. I told him that I had some marijuana for him but he had to wait till I went back to the camp. He and Lansana left us and went to Bandawoh. Lansana informed us he was going to meet Titan; that they had something to do and they left in a hurry. They did not come back that night, but Naffie knew that Lansana and Soja were staying the night in Bandawoh with Titan and Daniel was still there.

Sunshine asked me so many questions about my training; she wanted to know if Jui Koya training Titan was still giving the very good training they were well known for within RUF and among some of their enemies. I told her everything we did and she was pleased that the only thing she did that I did not do was that I did not eat weird leaves or drink dirty water and I only spent three weeks.

"But Memuna you were already a rebel before you went to the base. You knew how to do everything. All you need is to stop being too nice but you are brave," Sunshine said.

"Well I went and got beaten and learned some new things which I'm not ready to talk about now," I said.

We moved on to talk about something else. Naffie had told Sunshine about what happened between Titan and me so Sunshine too got mad at me. I told her that I thought he was cheating but like Naffie, she did not believe me.

Later that afternoon, Naffie asked us to cook but we did not have enough firewood. So I decided to go into the coffee farm just a few meters away from the house and fetch some wood while Sunshine decided to cut the potato greens. Nyalay and I went; I was afraid because it was only around 1pm, the sun was hot and that's when snakes come out. I was afraid but then I wanted to do it. We fetched the wood and came back to the house. When I arrived Lansana had come back from Bandawoh with Soja,

Daniel, Titan, Jeff (Titan's bodyguard) and two girls – one pregnant. The pregnant one could not get off Daniel even though it was obvious he wanted his space and the other one was all over Titan. I was a bit upset but I was not surprised because I knew it all along. I just needed to see.

"Oh my God how did you know?" Sunshine wondered.

"Well just instinct," I said. "It was weird how his friends in Bandawoh acted so then and there I knew something clandestine was going on."

Naffie came to the kitchen. "Oh Memuna you've got nothing to worry about it's obvious he is only doing it to hurt you, he doesn't like her," she said.

"Well he's going to regret this and I think he looked stupid. Besides I'm not hurt so if that's what he meant by me biting my finger and not feeling anything then he needs a new plan."

I was surprised that he could be so foolish and deep down I knew that maybe he might tell her what he told me. However I knew he meant it when he said it to me more than he did when he said it to her. So honestly I did not care, as long as he was there when I needed him. She could give him sex I did not care.

We used the veranda of the house we lived in as a kitchen because the kitchen got flooded in the rainy season and it was close to the toilet. The house was a brick house like all West African houses in major towns. It had two verandas one in the front and one at the back; we used the front one to cook. Sunshine decided to let me cook the greens because she was not really good at cooking at the time and she did not really care. She cooked the rice and I did the stew. I was quiet for almost an hour and she felt bad for me.

"Memuna what are you going to do?" she said. "Because knowing you I know you are not just going to take this."

I looked at her and laughed. "I'm not going to do anything," I said.

She said she did not believe me.

It was really hot in Water Works that afternoon and the swamp at the side of the house had dried up. While Sunshine and I were on the veranda talking and cooking, Titan, Lansana and Daniel decided to give their guests a tour of the house and the swamp. They came through the house to the veranda then Titan stopped to make some small talk.

"What are you girls cooking?" he asked.

Sunshine was angry with him she did not want to talk to him. "We are cooking some potato greens and rice for you and your guests," I said.

He looked at me for a moment and did not know what to say. He was shocked that I was not blowing the roof off but I was better than that. I smiled at him and I asked him if he was having fun. He looked at me and walked away saying that he would come back to talk to me.

"Who cares?" I said.

"Memuna you are so cold about this it's scaring me," Sunshine said. "I never thought you would react like this to this kind of thing."

"Sunshine, for God's sake what do you think Titan and that whore would enjoy most?" I said.

"You are right if you start talking now you will make their day," she said.

"Here you go," I said.

We cooked and served them. Sunshine and I just dished out the food and Naffie did the serving.

"I better serve them before you girls pour hot food on someone here," Naffie said.

It was funny thinking about what Naffie said so we laughed and Titan came and saw us laughing.

"CO. Titan I've known you for a long time but I think you will really regret this," Sunshine said.

"What?" he said. "I'm not doing anything. I'm not with any of those girls."

"Well she can't seem to keep her hands off you," I said.

"I don't know why," he said.

"Why don't you ask her and she'll tell you or do you want me to?" I said.

He looked at me and told me not to but I should ask Lansana. I told him that I had no time for that and I could do better with my time. They finished eating before us, I decided to eat in the pot that I cooked the stew in and I ate with my hand sitting on the floor on the veranda. Titan came and saw me sitting on the floor eating from the smoke-black pot. He stood there looking at me.

"I have not seen you eat like this before," he said.

"Appetite and besides there's a lot you haven't seen me do," I said.

"Normally you are shy when I'm around, what's happening today?" he asked.

"I'm grown," I said.

He smiled and stood a while longer I told him to go and not to leave his guest waiting while he watched me eat. He was embarrassed and he could not turn to leave but eventually he had to because she came yelling his name through the house. Sunshine and I looked at him and laughed. Lansana, Daniel and the pregnant girl came along and they went to the swamp. There were some orange trees around there so they went to pick some oranges.

"Memuna you are a strong woman with self-respect," Soja said.

I smiled and he joined me to eat from the pot; he still hadn't had enough.

They brought a bucket full of oranges and took it to the rear veranda. Nyalay and Naffie were with them while Sunshine and I cleaned the kitchen and the dishes. After that we went to the rear veranda just to watch the drama. When I got there she was lying on Titan's lap while Nyalay peeled oranges for her to suck. Just to be sure I stood to see where the one she was peeling was going. I was disgusted when I saw Nyalay give it to Titan's guest, Tity.

"Nyalay I hope that's the last orange you are peeling and I hope it's yours," I said, when I saw her pick up another one.

Naffie took me to the room to talk to me.

"Memuna I really like the way you've been handling this whole show so let's just keep it that way," she said.

"I don't mind him doing whatever he wants with her whenever or wherever but I can't watch Nyalay working for her. What is wrong with her hands?" I said. "I don't know if he fed her the food I cooked but my little sister won't peel oranges for her to suck."

We went back outside, I saw Nyalay reading a story for them and she seemed to enjoy it more.

"I read that story when I was a little girl," she said.

She was lying on his lap with her hands under his T-shirt rubbing his body. The book was a little paperback with several stories in it – Cinderella, Snow White and a few African stories put together in the book.

"Nyalay I think you've read enough if you still want to read out loud you can go to the room but no more reading," I said.

Everyone looked at me but I looked straight at Lansana because he was the only one who mattered. He saw that I did not like what was going on so he let out a slight smile indicating that he understood. I smiled back, took an orange from the bucket and threw one to Sunshine.

"Oh I'm sorry my name is Tity and this is my cousin Marion," she said, introducing herself and the pregnant girl.

I looked at her and nodded. "Good to meet you," I said.

I could not be bothered telling her my name.

She was forcing to have his attention and when she spoke she had to hold up her hands wiggling her fingers and playing with the big Seiko watch she had on. She twisted her body when she walked. I could not be bothered with her; I knew she had nothing on me because I believe in being myself - take it or leave it. We left them playing and watching their own show. Sunshine and I took Nyalay to the bridge to bathe. We spent hours there and they left. We were in the water and heard Lansana calling out to us. He said they were going back to the camp and he hoped to see us soon. Titan waved but no-one waved back. His new woman waved and said it was nice to meet us and she hoped to see us again, but no-one answered her. When we got back Naffie tried to talk to me so that I won't worry about it. She did not know where to start but talked to me anyway.

"Memuna you are a very pretty girl and needless to say so many people want you so I don't want you to dwell on what Titan is doing because you are better than that," she said. "So talk about it, yell if you want but don't hold it in. All of us have enough on our minds."

"I won't lie, I'm a little upset because I feel disrespected but if that's what he wants then I'm really fine with it. Besides I don't want a man anyway and I don't like him that much."

Naffie, Sunshine and Nyalay spent all evening trying to talk to me even though I told them that I did not mind. I did not worry about what Titan did and for three days I did not say a word about him, as there was nothing to say. I just missed Magic and my sisters.

On the fourth day in the afternoon we went to the bridge again and Tity came. This time she was going back to Bandawoh alone without her pregnant cousin, she was with Jeff. They called out to us and waved. Now I knew that she knew she was with my boyfriend – again instinct.

"What is Jeff doing with her?" Sunshine inquired. "Oh I'm forgetting that he's a suck-up who likes gossiping."

"Maybe he's her new bodyguard. I know that by now he already told her about Titan and me" I said.

"So, he is yours," Sunshine said.

"She can have him I really don't care besides I can't give him what he wants," I said. "But I'm through with that arse licking dog Jeff."

We dried our skin and went to the house and Naffie asked us if we saw Jeff and his Madame. We told her that Tity made it a point to wave to us.

Captain Mon Fré and Captain Barrie lived in the biggest yard in Water Works. They had their families there with them. MaHawa who used to go out with Magic was in Koribondo jungle with some guy they tried to force her to go out with but she was finding her way to come to Water Works. Her cousin Halima, her younger sister Yayea and their mother were in Water Works with Captain Barrie.

That afternoon Halima met us at the bridge and she asked Sunshine and me to visit her. So we did after we changed our clothes. We told Naffie that we wouldn't be long and she said it was ok for us to go. Halima told me that Tity was coming and that she would be in Bandawoh in two weeks. I was happy to hear that. She asked me how Titan and I were doing and I told her that everything was ok. She was busy with her father and her boyfriend and Yayeaa was sick too so we left her and went home.

Captain Barrie had a hole in his head, which had been there for more than a year and he used it to get away with the mayhem he got up to. He, some other commanding officers and their bodyguards were involved in a car accident. They were in a jeep speeding and he got hurt in the head. So when he caused trouble and Foday Sanko asked him to go to Zogoda, he would start going for treatment all over again and say that he still had sores in his head. But sometimes he did have headaches from the injury and that day was one of them.

Two days later on a calm dull day after eating a pot of hot spicy stew with fish, Sunshine and I were on the veranda reminiscing about Mattru Jong and talking about how we could not wait to see Samia and Komeh again. We did not expect Magainda because she was with Amara and she went with him wherever he wanted to go. Although Magic had told me that Komeh was going to Freetown Highway I did not believe it. Then we saw one of Titan's bodyguards the tallest one called Pasineh (who I sometimes called 'Cabinet' when I was mad at Titan and he kept delivering messages to me from Titan). He was very tall - over six feet tall - lean and very dark. He was a nice guy but a little shy when he first meets someone. He hardly talked to me even when I talked to him. He would give one-word answers and look away. Sunshine told me that it was because I was dating his boss he did not want to get too comfortable. We laughed about it but stopped when he approached the veranda so that he won't think we were laughing at him and feel uncomfortable. He greeted us and asked for Naffie. We told him that Naffie was in the house and he went inside and greeted her. Naffie liked Pasineh. She said he was very respectful and that he was from a good home. She offered him some food and he told her that he came with a letter from Lansana demanding that he wanted Sunshine and myself in the camp that very night.

Naffie told him to give me the letter, when I read the letter, it was addressed to me alone and not Sunshine. I thought there was something fishy about that letter but since Pasineh said Lansana wanted the two of us in the camp I told Sunshine that he wanted the two of us to go. I did not want to go because Titan was the last person I wanted to see at that point. Going to the camp meant that I was going to have to serve him food when he came to our shelter and talk to him by force and he could demand I guard him for however long he wanted. Now I was forced to talk to Titan or any other Commanding Officer because I was no longer a civilian. "Naffie I'm not going," I said.

"Memuna I don't want to deal with that boy's drama, you know how Lansana can get," she said. "So please you two pack your things and go. You can even come back tomorrow. But let him have his way today."

"Pasineh, please do me a favour, can you go back to the camp without us and tell him that I'm not feeling very well?" I said.

He looked at me wanting to say something but he could not get it out while I stood there looking at him.

"Memuna let's not put Pasineh in trouble let's go," Sunshine said.

I agreed with her reluctantly and changed the clothes I wore and we took off without a bag because we had some clothes in the camp too.

"I just want to scream," I said.

"You don't have to talk to him when we get there," Sunshine said. "When you see him you give him courtesy and that's it. Keep it like superior and subordinate if you want."

I agreed with her, she and I talked and talked but Pasine did not say a word. So we asked him if he could not talk and he said he did not know what we were talking about and therefore he did not want to interfere. So we stopped talking about how much I disliked Titan and asked Pasineh to tell us what was going on in the camp.

He told us there was a mission but the boys were due back the next day. We thought maybe that's why Lansana demanded we got back, as we could help Rain so she won't be alone. Then we started talking about how lazy Rain was. Soon we were in the camp. It was a little sunny in the camp and it seemed a little lively. I was glad to be back there and things seemed a little strange. I guessed it was because I had spent a month away and there was no Mbalu. Sunshine and I saluted Rain when I saw her and she smiled.

"It's so strange to see you giving courtesy Memuna, you lost so much weight," she said.

I asked her about Struggle and she said she was with her father and Lansana at Titan's shelter. Pasineh left us and went to his house. Rain smiled.

"Speaking about Titan," she said. "He was the one who begged Eagle to write that letter. He said he missed you and he wanted to see you. All of his friends told him off, none of them like the girl."

"Well they are going to have to deal with her," I said. "See if I knew I would have just stayed in Water Works."

"Memuna you are not a civilian anymore you can't just do what you please anymore," Sunshine said. "Just in case you forgot the words Pasineh used, he said that Lansana ordered him to take that letter to us and that means the letter was an order to sojas"

I looked at her and Rain and shook my head and before I could sit Rain told us Lansana said the moment we arrived he wanted us to go and meet him at the studio.

"Oh Rain it is so obvious that it's Titan who wants me to go to the studio not Lansana," I said.

"Hey I'm just a messenger," Rain said.

I asked Sunshine to go with me to the studio. As soon as the guys saw us walking up the hill they started smiling at us. We stopped at CO. Feel-good's shelter and greeted his wife Amirah. She was pregnant and wanted a quiet afternoon alone so she had chased him away and he went to the studio to his brother. Amirah was a very tall, beautiful and feisty Temne woman and she was very fond of my what-you-see –what-you-get attitude because she was just the same. We left her and went up to the studio. As we approached them we could see them through the coffee trees laughing.

"Good afternoon Sirs," we said as we got to the studio. The worst part was that I had to stand in front and say those words "Good afternoon Sirs" because I was shorter. Titan was in the studio talking on the radio to someone. He smiled and winked his eye when he saw me. But I gave him a hard look and turned away from him. Robert was happy to see me. He rushed the person he was talking to off the radio and came out of the studio to hug me.

"Obviously that was not important," I said.

He shook his head and smiled. "Look at you, you look prettier by the day, don't be angry ok that thing was just a game" he said. "How was it soja?"

I smiled and told him that it was great. Lansana and Daniel could not stop smiling at me. Sunshine went into the studio to tell Titan off. Soon he was off the Radio. "Pasineh you are a good soja!" he said.

"Hello Memuna did you not see me?"

"No, where are you? I can only hear you," I said.

Everyone laughed. "This girl and Amirah should be friends, they are the same," CO. Feel-good said.

I told him she could hear him and he covered his mouth with his hand. Titan took me aside to talk to me. I did not want to talk to him but then I did not want to make a scene in front of his friends so I went with him to his room.

"Look, I don't know why I'm in here with you but you are the last person I want to see now let alone talk to," I said.

"I'm sorry," he said. "Please let me explain."

"What, what do you have to explain?" I said. "You wanted to do it, that's why you told your friends to lie to me about you being in Bandawoh and you threatened you were going to hurt me so bad that I would bite my fingers and don't feel it. Well I'm hurt but I'm more disappointed in you. I thought you could do better and I thought you had taste."

I turned to walk out of the room and he pulled me back. "Look I'm sorry I'll try to end it," he said.

"So there is something going on, I thought she was with Daniel and now you're promising to end it?" I retorted. "You know what, just leave me alone. In fact who is she and where is she from?"

He did not want to talk. "I'm waiting, I asked you," I said. "There is nothing to hide now because in front of me she had her hands under your shirt."

"She is CO. Mohammed's cousin and she works at the studio in Zogoda. She just came from Freetown Highway a week after you went to the base," he said.

"You know what I don't want to hear any more, keep her and enjoy yourself and stay away from me," I said and I walked out forcing a smile.

I waved at everyone and I continued walking home. Sunshine followed me she knew I was angry. When we got home I told her what happened in the room. She and Rain asked me not to worry because everyone thinks that Tity was just one of those girls you have temporary fun with. I told them that I was not looking for a husband but I had just started liking him and he did that so I wanted nothing more to do with him. I also begged Rain not to ask me to serve food again if Titan was around at our shelter because I did not even want to give him a cup of water to drink.

"Memuna don't worry I won't put you through that," she said.

Titan came to our shelter a few minutes later to apologise further but I completely ignored him. He wanted to use his position as a commanding officer to get me to give him some time to talk to me. I asked him if that's how it was going to be between us (if he was going to use his power to force a relationship between us). This made him feel guilty and he went home.

Later that evening we went to formation and I think because he knew that I was going to be there he sent CO. Flomo to close the formation saying that he was sick. I was now trained and that was my first formation outside the training base. I had to attend every formation twice a day and if I did not I had to provide an explanation to the wyes commander Satu Rocket who hated me so much because she wanted Titan. She was called Satu Rocket because Sergeant Rocket was her man's name and there were lots of other Satu as well. Mende names are really popular.

That evening after formation Titan came to our shelter again just to see me but he pretended as if he was there to see his friends. It was obvious to everyone that he was there because he wanted to apologise. He could not stop looking at me and he was not paying attention to their conversation. He asked if he could talk to me in private and because Lansana was there and I felt sorry for him I agreed. He asked if we could go to his shelter and I asked Lansana who said I could so I went. He held my hand and I so badly wanted to pull my hand away from his because I was getting really angry with him, but then he was begging too hard and looking too sad. Everyone was begging for him and I don't like people begging too much so I let him hold my hand. As we got up to his room he wanted to kiss me but I rejected him. We sat on the bed side by side and he held my hand.

"Memuna I'm very sorry please let's put this aside," he said.

But I could not forgive him and I was tired of talking about it. So I told him I did not want to talk about it anymore and that we should wait and see what happens the next few days. I said this because Tity had told us that she was coming back in two weeks. I told him I wanted to go home and he asked me to please think of letting the whole Tity thing go.

The boys arrived in the afternoon of the following day and we were so happy to see them. They were all so excited about the fact that I was trained now. Kasiloi said he wanted to know everything that happened to me on the base. Sunshine and I cooked and ate a lot and talked all night with them. Jackson could not take his eyes off me. I asked him if he enjoyed the mission, he said that it was fun and that he wished Sunshine and I were there. Rain went to sleep and left us talking with the boys. The following morning Sao seemed very excited when she saw me. She said, "I have a very juicy message for you and I'm sure you will like it."

"What is it?" I asked, curious.

"Ah no, this is private," she said. So I went to her shelter when CO. Flomo was at Titan's with the other men.

"Hey I know someone who likes you." She was gleaming with her good news.

"I know who that person is too," I said.

"Really?" she asked, now she was surprised.

"Yes," I said. "It's you, Sunshine, Mbalu, my sisters, the guys and the two women at my shelter."

Laughing, she pointed her finger to my forehead and poked me with it.

"You are a very cheeky girl," she said. "Everyone knows we like each other very much, but that's not what I meant."

"What did you mean then?" I asked.

"My cousin likes you," she replied matter of factly.

"Who is this?" I asked.

"He is your good friend," she said.

"Well I see why, you can't be friends with someone if you don't like them."

"He wants to go out with you." She looked at me hoping that this would happen.

"Well who is this?" I asked.

"It's Jackson," she stated.

I held my breath; I could not believe this was happening. I mean he was a good-looking guy, very nice and friendly but why? Can't they all just be friends with me? I looked at her and ran out. She chased me demanding an answer. I told her that I was going to think about it. Jackson was my friend but he also had a pregnant girlfriend who was very fond of me. Her name was Matilda. I started feeling uneasy around him from that day on. I managed, however, to make myself comfortable because we had the same friends and we had to hang out together. Besides I did not want anyone to be suspicious. Jackson and I hung out with the others as usual but I tried not to look him in his face for as long as I could until the news about him wanting me became stale. Then I felt more at ease around him. Sao eventually stopped bothering me about going out with her cousin.

A week after I got back to the camp, Sunshine and I went to our usual spot in the swamp. We sat in the grass talking about how much we missed Mbalu and from nowhere she asked me if I was confident enough to shoot.

"What's that question all about?"

"I just want to know if you are brave enough to protect yourself."

"I'm sure I could shoot if I need to. Besides I had been taught even before I went to the training base." I spoke more confidently than I truly felt.

"Ok, well take that AK and shoot," she said.

"What? Why?" I asked still surprise by her train of thinking.

"You are a soja now and you can't tell me that you don't know how to shoot," she replied stubbornly.

I could not believe it, but she was smiling and smoking her cigarette.

"I don't want to," I said.

"If you don't shoot I will tell Lansana and you will go back for two more weeks of training," she quickly threatened.

So I took the gun and shot twice. It was heavy for me and the force of it shook right through me, but I thought it was fun to shoot as long as I was not shooting at a person.

Once I got back from the training base Naffie, Sunshine, Rain, Laser, and Soja were always threatening to send me back for advance training because I was very defiant. Threatening me was the only way they could get me to do things. Titan did it too when I refused to give him courtesy. He said that if I was really trained I would respect my superiors and I told him that he was not my boss, he was my boyfriend.

It was July but it did not rain as much as it should have. Still the water beneath the little bridge swelled and it was good to bathe in but as it was rainy season I did not like going to the bridge anymore. I did not want to see anything nasty, so we spent less time than usual at the bridge in the camp.

The two weeks came and it was time for Tity to come. Everyone in the camp thought she was not coming while I got myself prepared for anything. I was hoping she wouldn't come because Titan had promised to put an end to whatever it was that was between the two of them. I told Sunshine that it was two weeks and she knew what I was talking about. We sat out on the veranda of our shelter waiting to see Tity and her new bodyguard Jeff arrive but they did not come. Titan made himself really scarce that day so that was a sign that he hadn't kept his promise to me but I did not say anything about it. That evening we could not attend formation because it was raining, we were tired of waiting for Tity and it was late so we went to bed.

After formation the following day Titan hurried home and that's when Rain told us that Tity had arrived very late that night. She heard it from one of the girls at the studio who did not like Tity. I was upset, not because she was there with him but because he did not keep his promise to me. I stopped trusting him. I tried to make the best of my day and the guys were all in the camp. We had fun doing our usual things but I did not smoke. CO. Flomo called me over to talk to me.

"Memuna, I'm so sorry, I mean I'm really embarrassed," he said.

"Why are you embarrassed?" I asked. "You did not do anything, you only helped him talk to me when he wanted me and now he doesn't anymore. There is no harm in that; you can't force someone to like another person."

"I swear Memuna, that boy doesn't like you he loves you but I don't know what this is all about. Don't worry it will be over soon," he said. "Please don't let it worry you."

I nodded and smiled and I told him that it was not worrying me, then I went back to try and get into a game we had been playing. When I got back it was too late so I had to wait for the next round.

That day I could not be in a good mood because of the drama that was going on between Titan and me, because I was worried about my sisters and I was home sick. Still we played two more games of chess and went to formation. Neither Titan nor his woman was there. CO. Flomo covered for him. We came back from formation laughing about something the boys had said.

"Hey Franklin, we still want to play. Can you boys come over after dinner or when you can?" Sunshine said, as Franklin and Jackson walked into their shelter. Matilda was on her veranda rubbing her belly and staring in space. When she saw us she snapped out of her thought and spoke to us.

"I need some chillies and I've been standing here waiting for you girls to come so I could ask you for some," she said to us.

Jackson wanted to stop and talk to her but when we started talking about pregnancy and chillies he just went inside.

"But Rain is there why did you not ask her?" Sunshine said.

"Did you even go to the shelter?" I asked.

"Yes, but I was shy to ask her," Matilda said.

We asked her to follow us to our shelter and we could give her the chilly. Tity was at our shelter with Lansana, Titan, Daniel, Lt. Cross and Robert. They were talking and laughing and we arrived talking about why pregnant women like eating lots of chillies.

It was a little awkward when we arrived. There was a short moment of silence and I looked away after saluting them quickly going to the kitchen to give Matilda Jackson the chilly. I was really upset but Sunshine was more upset than I was. She wanted us to leave the shelter and go to Musa's shelter to be with the boys but I told her that we did not have to leave our shelter because of Titan and his woman.

So we went to our room and we soon had something cheerful to talk about. We talked about the last time I smoked, the night we got so high that we had to crawl to the kitchen and eat boiled beans with water dripping down our elbows and we laughed.

"Will you smoke again, Memuna," Sunshine asked.

"I don't think so. I don't intend smoking again," I laughed.

Luckily we spoke in Mende because Titan walked into the room without knocking as soon as I finished my sentence.

"Hello," he said.

Sunshine looked at him as if she would tear him apart then walked out of the room.

"I'm going to get Strength so we can help Rain," she said.

I told her to come back soon because he was not staying long.

"Memuna please let me talk to you," he begged.

I looked at him thinking of what to say to him because, to be honest, he would not want to hear what I had to say to him.

"How was formation?" he asked, trying to make small talk. He sat next to me on the bed.

"Well CO. Flomo took your place at the formation, I'm sure he would tell you everything about it," I answered. "And you have nothing to talk to me about until you are through with that girl so just get out."

He looked at me and tried to touch my hand but I did not let him and he went outside.

Sunshine walked into the room with Strength as soon as he got out. We played with the baby and soon Titan, his friends and his woman were gone. Tity stayed in the camp for three days then went back to Zogoda. Sao, Edna, Rain, Naffie and Sunshine were regretting that I did not go for the communication training. They thought the fact that Tity worked at the studio in Zogoda meant she had something I did not have. I told them that just because Tity was working with the communication group did not make her more important and, besides, I could do it too but I refused. She was not getting paid anyway and she did not have any responsibilities. Her mother was there with her going everywhere she was sent. Most people in the camp did not like her because she tried too hard to make people like her and to be recognised. At some point I felt sorry for her. I decided to get on with my life and not let this whole business of Titan and Tity worry me. I just let it go because I got what I wanted and so did he – he wanted to be with two women (one with whom he could be intimate) and I had him whenever I wanted him whether just to talk or to help me out with anything, I needed his power to protect me. Although I had started to like him, I became so casual about the whole situation and decided not to make a fuss about it.

Several weeks later Titan, Lansana and some of the boys went on a mission. Sunshine went to visit her old time friend Maya in Bandawoh and I was left with Rain, the baby and some of the boys. But one night before he went Titan was at his house and he came over to check on us. Tity was due to visit in two more days. I had heard it from CO. Flomo, because he was annoyed that his brother wouldn't put an end to his and Tity relationship. I was in bed, feeling very sleepy and trying to read my book from the palm oil lamp which was too dim and started giving me a headache. Rain was getting Strength ready for bed. She was putting her nappy on her when Titan, Daniel and Robert walked into the room. I covered my head when I heard their voices. He greeted Rain and asked for me. He could not tell someone else was in the bed because I was so small and I covered my head.

"What do you care, CO. Titan?" Rain said.

"What do you mean, Rain?" Robert asked. "You know this man belongs to Memuna."

I could not bear hearing that he belonged to me anymore, not from him or anyone else. So I got the cover off my head and snapped at him.

"What are you, a paramount chief or what?" I yelled. "What do you want with two women?"

As I said this I tried to get out of the room leaving everyone laughing at him. When I got to the door it was too dark and scary outside and he held onto me begging me not to walk out on him. So, breaking free of him, I got back into bed again throwing the covers over my head. He wanted to talk but, because of the others, he asked if he could talk to me in the morning. In reply I told him I would give him the time if I had it.

"How would I know that you've got time to talk?" he asked.

"I'll let you know," I said, with no intention of bothering myself to talk about that girl.

That morning I did not attend formation; the guys went and gave some kind of excuse for my absence because the wyese commander was getting angry. She said that I thought I was better than all the other women who wake up early in the morning to go to formation and participate in other RUF activities. The "activities" included fetching greens and carrying them on their heads to Zogoda, helping to fetch water for Fambuleh to cook for the ambush men and even carrying their food. I did not think I was better than anyone and she knew it. She only said that because I had that one man she wanted more than anything. Besides Titan, Lansana, Musa, Lt. Cross and CO. Flomo did not let us do any of those things. Even one time Lansana said that, since all of the women at our shelters were known to be dating a commanding officer, asking us to do things like that meant you were asking the commanding officers to do it. But Satu did not care she wanted to get back at me.

The Kamajors and some other civilians started threatening the RUF camp again. Four more civilians escaped from the training base. Three of them got caught at the guard post right in front of the camp. The other got caught in the ambush town that was his last obstacle otherwise he would have been in Blama. The boys brought him to the camp and handed him over to the guards at the guard post without letting him into the camp. Someone came into the camp to let Titan know that there was something going on at the guard post but, before he knew, Rain and I took the baby and went to the guard post just to nose around. The two older men claimed they were Kamajors and before Titan could say anything, the boys started beating them. In a short moment their faces were covered in blood but he asked the rebels to stop beating and ask some questions. The men wouldn't answer important questions; all they said was they wanted to go home and that they were proud Mende Kamajors. Rain asked them what they knew about RUF.

"We know that you people have diseases, you don't bathe, you eat people and you eat dogs and you drink blood," one of them said.

I was speechless; the sight and smell of blood made me feel sick but I was also sorry for them – they were old men somewhere in their late fifties. Rain held Strength in front of him.

"Look at my baby; do I look like someone who has a young child? Do I stink, do I look sick to you," she asked, challenging his age and his stupidity.

The man looked at us and turned his face away. Giving me the baby, Rain stood up on the banister in front of the men. She stepped on the chest of one of them, lifting his chin to look at her when she spoke to them.

"Look at me! We don't eat people, we bathe two or more times a day and it's entirely our choice like you people on the other side of the country and we don't eat dogs, plus we don't have them. We move around a lot so we don't want to punish them. So if you live to go home tell all your friends that Foday Sankoh is not sick and everything they know about us is a big fat lie."

She got down from the man's chest and we left them with Sin-child and the other boys.

We went to have a look at what was going on with the other boy. He was tied lying next to the man the boys had brought from the ambush. He looked like he was in his late teens; all the rangers in the camp including Jonah (Titan's little body guard) surrounded him. He was talking too much and Titan was really interested in what he had to say.

"What is going on with him and why are you so interested in him?" I whispered.

"He is a soja, he is with the Sierra Leone army," Titan said. "You just listen to him you will know the rest."

Rain and I pushed through the rangers and stood right next to him. I looked at him lying on the hot ground in the sun outside the little booth the guards had at the guard post. The other man refused to say much. All he said was that he had a family to go home to and that was what he wanted to do. As for the boy he claimed that he was the one who shot Titan in the leg - the wound that made him stop fighting. He did not know it was Titan who was sitting on the stool next to him; all he knew was that he shot a rebel in the leg and he got away. He described the fight and we all knew that it was Titan he was talking about.

"I have fought a lot for my country," he cried.

"Really! Where and how?" Titan asked.

"I'm a small soja in the Sierra Leone army and I've been to the front," the boy said.

"Really, I thought RUF was the only one who had young sojas – or child soldiers as they put it," Titan said, sarcastically.

"But we don't have eight-year olds or ten-year olds in the army," the boy answered.

"What's your name?" Daniel asked.

"Edward," he said.

"Well Edward these eight and ten-year olds can do more than you have done," Rain said.

I was scared. I stood next to Titan as close as possible. Titan asked the boy to tell him how many battles he's been to and where the battles took place.

"Well the one I can't forget was the one where I shot that bastard in the leg," he said. "It was on the Bo/Kenema highway and it was really tense. At first I regretted going but when I shot him I was happy; I felt useful. The rebels you people sent were strong; they damaged our war tank."

"So what did this bastard look like?" Titan asked.

Daniel looked at Rain and me and smiled. At this time Titan could not stop rubbing his head. His ears were red I knew his face was too but I could not see his face because he was staring straight at the boy. Titan rubbed his head when he was angry or confused about something and sometimes he bowed his head when he rubbed it.

"Oh he was really light skinned and tall and he looked very young. I was in the bush so I did not get to really look at him but I think if I see him I'll recognise him," Edward said.

All this while, I did not believe this boy. At most, I think his father must have been the one who fought that battle and went home with the story and the boy must have listened in on his father's conversation.

"You sure?" Daniel asked.

The boy nodded and started looking frantically from one person to the other. Titan was really angry. He lifted his head and looked at me then took a deep breath and handed the boy over to Sin-child asking that the rangers take care of the boy and make sure he was taken back to the training base under high security.

"Oh and Edward, I was that bastard whom you shot. My name is Lieutenant Titan and I'm Liberian," Titan said. "Take care."

The boy screamed apologies while Titan and Daniel walked away into the field on their way to the school building. Within five minutes Edward's face was unrecognisable. The rangers beat him up with anything they could lay their hands on. It got too bloody for Strength and me and we turned to leave. Rain was afraid the baby would have nightmares so we decided to go back into the camp.

No sooner had we turned to leave than Titan called out to me. I did not want to go but I felt sorry for him and thought he needed someone to talk to after his little chat with Edward. So I went to him in the school building. He had blocked out everything that was going on in the field with those civilians; all he wanted to talk about was him and me. He begged me to stop pushing him away,

"Please Memuna, just open up a little more to me. That's all I want," he explained. "It's the only reason I got involved with Tity in the first place."

I felt bad that I was ruining my own relationship. Yet I was not ready for one although I needed one because of the situation. I told him,

"I'm sorry for pushing you away but you should be patient with me instead of going off with someone else." I had to tell him everything. "I know you like all the other people I'm close to in RUF. But they know I'm new to this relationship thing. I am still learning to treat a boy like one should treat a boyfriend. I am only fifteen years old."

"I'm sorry. I really am, Memuna."

This time I saw sincerity in his eyes more than all the other times. I was ready to forgive him deep down and let him carry on having whatever it is that she gives him. We sat there for a while not saying anything but staring at each other.

We walked slowly back to the field where the others still gathered.

"Memuna, Titan loves you, we've all known this guy for a long time and it's like we have grown side by side of each other. We all know that you are the first girl he ever asked out," Daniel said, "and it takes a lot for the Titan I know to do that. Normally women ask him out. So don't let these things with that girl take all of that away."

I looked at him and did not say anything for a moment.

"I have to go now," I said.

As I walked in the field hearing the screams of those men being tortured, Titan yelled out to me saying that he was coming to the shelter later. I nodded and continued walking without looking at the men getting beaten or at Titan and Daniel.

No sooner I was at our shelter than I told Rain that Titan was still begging. She told me,

"The best thing for you to do is let Titan do what he's doing but you shouldn't let it to pass the sex that is between him and Tity. It should just be that and nothing more since you are not ready for that kind of intimacy at the moment."

Later that evening Sunshine came back to the camp and we told her how our day was. She wished she were there to see the boy who made her play nurse and mother to Titan. Later, when, we were alone I told her about my conversation with Titan and she thought that what I had decided and Rain advice was the best thing to do. In fact they were all doing almost the same thing, just that in their cases their men did not do it because they wanted sex but because they were just unfaithful.

"At least he runs to you when you need him but when did you last see me and Musa talking," Sunshine moaned. "All he does is make babies with Sia; they are having a second one. Whoever your family voodoo man is, he is very good at his work."

"Not a voodoo man, it is God's grace. I have never seen my family (both sides) do voodoo. I have an aunt who is married to a man who owns churches, my father is an elder at his church and my mum prays a lot. I guess they are praying. Things will get better with you and Musa." I tried to assure her.

She asked me how.

"I do not know how things are going to change for the better but with faith everything will work out."

She agreed.

The mission crew got back in two days and this time they brought back lots of money, food, cigarettes and medication. It was my first time seeing sugar in ten or more months. When I had a cup of coffee at Rain's grandmother's hut at Target Q, I did not even see the sugar she put in the coffee for me but I could smell it and taste the little amount she was able to put in the coffee. I opened the box of sugar and took five cubes to suck on. I hadn't seen money since I left Mokabba, which was almost a year ago. The guys gave me lots of money - a few American dollars and the rest were in Leones (Sierra Leone currency). Kasiloi said he did not know how to count money and he had no use for it.

"Why did you bring it here then?" I asked. "The people on that side could use it."

"I don't know. I just wanted to take it," he said, laughing.

We had no use for money. Everything we used was looted apart from the meat, oil, vegetables and wild yams. As far as I am concerned even those things were looted as well because RUF had chased away the people who originally lived in all of their territory. So, in my opinion, if we stole their homes and forests then everything that came out of that soil was stolen.

The following day in the afternoon Tity arrived in the camp. She came with Jeff and they were both in the same T-shirts (two red large T- shirts). Everyone laughed at what a suck-up he was. This time I did not care; I think I was getting used to it and I ignored it totally. Titan did not bring her along to our shelter this time; he came alone and talked to everyone. I did not want to talk to him so I stayed away. Tity, she spent two days on this visit. The night she left, he came to spend some time with me but I told him to go home. I did not want to push him away but I could not pretend as though nothing was going on. To my surprise I had really started liking him and it was upsetting me. Sao brought up the topic in the evening about Jackson liking me again.

"Memuna, why are you doing this to yourself? He is cheating so what is stopping you?" She asked.

"Sao, as much as I hate to admit this I think I really like Titan and I don't want anyone else. I don't know how to keep two boyfriends at a time especially when Jackson lives right next door to me and Titan is always here."

She looked at me for a moment and shook her head.

"Look, I used to be very innocent like you," she said. "But the only difference is that you are only innocent when it comes to relationships with men."

We laughed about it and I told her to just give me some time to see if I can do the two boyfriends at a time thing and she consented.

A week later Sunshine, Lansana and Titan took a two day trip to Water Works and they refused to let me go with them. I was upset but more surprised. It was not like Lansana to leave me alone without Sunshine or someone he thought could keep an eye on me. But I was not alone; I was with Rain but I kept wondering what was going on. I was sure that Samia and Komeh had come to Blama Highway and they wanted to bring them to the camp as a surprise for me. They returned two days later and I waited for them to tell me but they did not. My sisters were still not anywhere close to Water Works.

"Why did you people leave me? Why did you not want me to come with you?" I demanded.

"Nothing, no reason. Lansana just thought leaving Rain here alone to deal with the boys was a little too much, that's all," Sunshine said.

Titan and Lansana were in the room laughing and listening to loud reggae music. Titan came out with Strength. She was all giggly, it was my first time seeing him with a baby and it was a good sight.

"CO. Titan," Rain said, "you look good with the baby. You should try and get one," While he, Rain and Sunshine laughed I just looked at them. He turned and looked at me when Rain said that. But shaking my head, I walked to the room and came back. "No Rain, I think I will play with Strength and Lucia for now and wait for some more years. I still have time," he said.

"What? Isn't Memuna ready yet?" Rain asked.

Rain was notorious for stirring things up. She knew the answer to her own question. But she would do anything for some drama.

"What? Am I the only one?" I interrupted. "Oh and the answer to that is 'no!'"

We laughed about it but Titan said "I don't think I'm ready."

As I waited for my sisters the camp was still boring, our daily routine was just the same and Titan and I kept having occasional fights about Tity. Naffie did not come to the camp much while Rain was a little more stable living in the camp and it turned out the pregnancy rumour was just that.

Several weeks later Titan and Lansana took me to Water Works leaving Sunshine alone. This time Rain was with her grandmother in the civilian camp, Target Q. She cried when Lansana insisted on making her stay though we pleaded with him to let her come with us. I asked them why they did that.

"It was her turn to stay in the camp while you spend some time with us. Besides," Lansana said, "you and Sunshine are not twins."

It was a sunny day in the raining season and it was good. We set off around eleven in the morning and an hour and a half later we were in Water Works. Walking with the two of them was too much for me; they walked so fast I had to ask them to slow down. At one point I called out to Lansana and he held my hand as it was annoying him that I was not walking fast enough. I pulled my hand away. When we arrived I saw someone in Naffie and Sia's garden at the front of the house and I could not believe it.

"Is that who I think it is?" I asked him.

"Who do you think it is?" Lansana asked, looking suspicious with his usual sneaky smile. Before I could say another word Magainda looked up and saw us. She came running down to us and immediately jumped into Lansana's arms while Titan and I just stood there looking at them. I could not wait to go to the house to see Komeh and Samia. When she was through hugging Lansana, the two of us, screaming, hugged each other. Surprised, Titan just stood with a smile on his face while Lansana told him about Magainda although he'd already heard about her.

"Wow, what a family to be in huh?" he said.

Looking at him I smiled. Lansana introduced Titan to Magainda before I could and I was fine with it.

Magainda and I, holding hands, ran to the house. I asked for Komeh and Samia but she said they were still in Koribondo Jungle. Though deeply disappointed she told me not to worry, that she was sure we would all be together very soon. I believed her because she was already there with me and I was sure the others would join us.

Naffie and the children were not home. Magainda said Naffie took them to visit her cousin in Jui Koya and she was spending the week there. Lansana had lots of questions to ask Magainda and they were all the same questions I had to ask. I let him ask while I listened, helped with the cooking and kept Titan's company at the same time. Titan was listening to what Magainda and Lansana were saying as well so it was not that hard.

"So Magainda, how come you are here and where are Komeh and Samia?" Lansana asked.

"They will be here soon. I managed to come here because I told the commanders in Korribondo camp that I wanted to come and train as a nurse aid," she said. "Because I'm Samia's guardian they will let her come soon. I think Komeh is also trying to do the same nursing thing so she can come too,"

I wanted to ask Magainda about their journey to Freetown Highway, if it was not going to happen anymore, but the timing was not good.

"So how long is this nursing course supposed to go on for?" Lansana again asked my question.

"Two to three months to learn the basics," Magainda replied. "After that they will send me back so can you please help me with that? Don't let them send me back."

Lansana turned and looked at Titan - he was in charge of Blama Highway and his brothers were in charge of Bandawoh, Jui Koya and Sir Miles Ground - almost the entire RUF second battalion was in the hands of him, his brothers and friends. Titan nodded back and told Magainda not to worry; everything was going to be ok. She did not have to go back or do the course if she did not want to.

We could not wait for the girls to come.

"I wonder how Samia is?" Lansana said. "Magainda has she been sickly?"

"Yes but she is trying to cope. She was not very well when I left," Magainda said.

After we ate we sat in the hut with Lansana and Titan to talk some more about Samia and Komeh and how we have all been. Titan loved asking questions; he was just naturally curious wanting to know everything. After a few hours we left them and went for a walk. I took Magainda to the oil mill. I knew some people who lived in the few rooms around the machine. Magainda requested that we sit in the grass outside the mill and talk a little.

"So, that's the new guy," she said. "What a jump, from a private to a lieutenant what did they put in your bath water at birth that makes you so lucky?"

We laughed and I told her that I did not see it as luck. 'You know if it were up to me no-one would be attracted to me in this place," I said.

"Well they find you attractive and it's not up to you. God did that job a long time ago, he made you a pretty girl," Magainda said.

"I've just started liking him and I think he is nice he is easy to deal with," I said.

"I heard about you and him," she said.

I did not want to talk about Magic and I knew he was the one who went and told Magainda something else rather than the truth.

"If you did not hear it from Naffie then just wait and see for yourself," I said.

I could tell that Magainda did not like Titan and I knew that she was jealous on behalf of Magic but I did not say anything about it. I only told her to relax and get to know Titan. We went to the mill and I introduced her to my friends but she had already met them as Naffie did the introduction for me. We did not stay too long as it was getting late and we needed to bathe.

We went back to the house, went to the stream behind the house, bathed quickly and came back to the house with some water.

In the rainy season the river swells up so much that the swamp behind the house got covered with water. The stream came as close as four meters to the house. Late that night Lansana and Titan used the water we brought to bathe. Titan insisted I stood by him and talk to him while he bathed, at first I thought it was strange because he had not done that before. I had not seen him naked before. I asked him if he did not need his privacy and he said he did not need it from me.

"Well I want you to have your privacy," I said. I was shy at the thought of me seeing him naked, I did not want to do it.

"Well if you don't stand and talk to me I won't bathe tonight," he said.

We went on and on about it and I agreed to stand by him. It was too dark for him to go to the bathroom so he stood at the side of the house. Magainda and Lansana were inside talking. I stood on the bricks on the side of the house holding the towel for him while we talked in the dark. I was glad it was too dark for me to see anything. We gave up the bed to Lansana. Titan and I slept on the mattress on the floor in front of the bed. It was our mattress from the other room that Sunshine took to Naffie's room because Arrow had started using that room. There were more mosquitoes in the room than there was outside and it was really hot. I covered myself from head to toes just so I won't get mosquito bites but I could not breathe because it was too hot. I struggled till 4am. Titan woke up to listen to the news; he got out of bed looking for a bed sheet so he could wrap it around himself and I heard him searching.

"What's the matter?" I whispered.

"It's 4am and I want to go outside to listen to the news," he said. "But I need a sheet to snuggle in I think it's cold outside. Will you come and sit with me?"

"I'd be glad to," I said. "The heat in here is killing me."

I got up and found us a sheet and we went outside to the front veranda. He sat on a small bench, leaned on the wall, I sat between his legs and we wrapped the sheet around us. We listened to some music, then news from VOA and BBC, but I fell asleep on him. After the news he woke me up so we could talk. He apologised about Tity and said that he cared more about me and he promised to always be there and again he promised to put an end to it. I did not say anything I just listened to what he had to say and besides I thought we were having a great time together – too good for argument - I really liked him. He was very affectionate and polite; he did everything with care. Titan was like me very hungry for education, he had his own teacher in the camp. The old man was a qualified teacher who got captured too. Titan used to make sure that he and his partner always had food and anything else he could help with. He really looked after the old man and he liked him and called him Teacher.

We sat on the veranda in the shadows of the moonlight and listened to the river as we talked.

"I'll do everything I can do to make your little sister and your cousin Komeh come here too. I've not seen you so happy before and I can't believe I'm sitting here with my arms around you early this morning," he said. "I really appreciate this moment."

"I'm not always cranky and difficult you know," I said. "I'm just finding it so hard to accept being here and everything else,"

"I know, the same thing happened to all of us but now I've accepted it all. I'm glad I was promoted because it gave me the chance to choose not to fight anymore," he said. "And I pray every day that my family will be ok."

I did not for once hear him talk about his mother and I did not want to start the topic because I thought maybe something was wrong. We sat there until 7am when Lansana woke up. Magainda asked if they wanted to bathe before going back to the camp but they could not wait to go back. They would just brush their teeth and start walking.

"Can I stay a bit longer?" I asked.

"How long?" Lansana asked.

I told him that I wanted to wait till Naffie came back and he said that it was ok.

"Make sure you come back to the camp when she arrives," Titan said.

It was still dark and a little cold, we walked with them to the bridge and then we went back to the house to sleep.

CHAPTER TWENTY FOUR

Territorial

Magainda kept talking about Titan in a bitter tone but she could not stop saying how handsome he was. I kept telling her to calm down and get to know him, because of this I did not tell her about Tity. A few days later Naffie came back; she seemed relaxed and so did Nyalay, Lucia was just her normal self – quiet and calm. She was a good and easy going baby and she grew fast looking just like her father and as tall as he was. I took Lucia to play with her and she started giggling. I love babies but I only played with Lucia, Strength and Fatima, because their parents were always near so that in case of anything I could just hand them back their children and run for dear life.

The last thing I wanted was to watch a baby die. We told Naffie that Lansana and Titan were in town with us and that I came with them. She asked me if things were getting better between Titan and I and I told her that they were. I told her what I had decided.

The next day, Magainda and I took off to go to the camp in the evening. I did not go to Water Works with a bag and I did not have one to bring back with me. Arrow gave Magainda some catfish that we could not wait to cook when we go to the camp.

We got some cassava leaves and chillies that Naffie brought back from her cousin's. On our way to the camp Magainda was frightened. She thought that the road was too quiet and spooky and she felt worse when I told her the story about the old camp and the man with the steel rod.

"What if there are more of them in the forest?" she asked, sounding so terrified.

"Well we look like any other innocent girl so we could just start crying and tell them that we were captured a short while ago and if they have to take us home they will," I said. "I mean that's better than getting killed isn't it?"

"Oh stop making me scared," she said.

"I'm surprised to see you so scared Magainda," I said. "Relax."

It was still early in the evening but because of the rainy season it got dark early and as soon as we arrived in the camp it started to rain. Sunshine screamed when she saw Magainda; she hugged her and did not want to let go.

"Lansana tells me that Komeh and Samia will come soon," Sunshine said. "How was your journey? This is the wonderful Blama Highway you've heard of for so long."

I asked Sunshine if there was anything to eat, she replied that she did not cook. "So how are Lansana and the boys going to eat?" I asked.

"They are not here, last night I was so scared sleeping here all by myself," she said. "They have gone on a mission. Lansana took the mission and they all said they wanted to go and Rain is going to be away till maybe the end of the rainy season."

"So have you had anything to eat?" I asked.

"Of course, your men CO. Flomo and CO. Titan came for me to eat with them and Sao and Edna took good care of me," Sunshine said.

"So Sunshine , you are still afraid of the kitchen," Magainda asked smiling.

"What can I do? I don't know how to cook and I don't give a damn," she said. "But I will protect you new sojas when there is an attack. I swear on my zakay."

Magainda put down her bag and we went to the kitchen to cook but it was too wet even the fire place. Sao heard us laughing and talking, Sunshine and I were calling out to Edna and her baby - we called the baby little Fambuleh and she ran over.

"You, I missed you," she said, slightly slapping the back of my head. Then she turned and saw Magainda. "Who is she?" she whispered.

I told her Magainda was my cousin and I introduced them. "Hey CO. Flomo is in the room with his brother let's go," Sao said.

"Who, CO. Feel-good?" I asked.

"No CO. Titan," Sunshine said. "I was there with them for dinner."

They told me that Titan missed me and we went to Fambuleh and Edna so I could introduce Magainda to them, then we went to Sao's shelter. Sunshine introduced Magainda to CO. Flomo while Titan interrogated me about why it took me so long to come back to the camp. I told him that he and Lansana said that it was ok for me to wait for Naffie to come and that's what I did.

We went to the kitchen to cook but Magainda changed what she and I had planned to cook and she and Sunshine decided to cook something else and I got angry and told them that I was not going to eat the food and I turned to leave and go back to our dark and scary shelter but Titan stopped me. He took me to CO. Flomo and Sao's room and begged me not to put up any tantrums about the cooking that I should just manage whatever they cooked because it was late.

"But Magainda knows that I hate cassava leaves and the only way I'll enjoy it is with palm kernel oil and that was our arrangement. Now she and Sunshine want to cook palm oil I don't want any of it," I said.

"Well let them cook it and you can eat something else but don't be upset about it just let it go," he said.

I was upset because we did not get cassava leaves that easily and although I did not like it, I appreciated it once in a while and we only took enough for one day to the camp so it was really upsetting me.

"But why can't they make the sacrifice for me," I queried. "Because it doesn't matter to them how we cook it, they will eat it and enjoy it but I can only enjoy it with palm kernel oil or burnt palm oil."

He told me that Magainda was my guest and that I should just let it go this once so eventually I agreed but I was still upset. I sat in the room eating the food Sao cooked and he went out to tell them that I was fine and they could cook it their way. Sao came in to bother me.

"You foolish girl you are so damn picky," she said.

"Just leave me alone and go join those two," I said, "In fact the food you cooked tastes really bad."

She smacked me on the head and ran out, "I'll come in there and take the bowl from you," she said.

"I got up, stood at the door and told her that CO. Flomo wouldn't let her. She said that I was missing some screws in my head. Titan did not know I was standing at the door and he nodded at what Sao said. I told him that I saw him and I went to our shelter. It was too dark and I could not stop looking at the big tree so I went to Edna. Titan came looking for me and took me home. He lit the oil lamp and we went to Rain room, which was now Lansana's room.

"I'm sorry I did not mean you are crazy you just get a little difficult sometimes and I want you to leave that cassava leaf thing for me ok," he said.

I nodded and we snuggled up in bed. The girls came to bother us and they took us back to the kitchen.

After cooking and cleaning Sao's kitchen we came back to our shelter and left Sao and her man alone. Titan was with us and his body guard Jeff was guarding him that night so he was with us too. Titan was trying to get close to Magainda because he knew she was not happy and she was my family. The camp was really dark that night and windy. We wanted to sit outside but it was too windy for the lamp and it did not have a shade it was just a piece of rolled cloth in a plate of oil. So we went into the room and sat on the bed to talk while Jeff sat on a chair at the door but inside the room with the door ajar.

To my surprise Magainda got really close to Titan initially making me wonder what was going on. Sunshine thought that Magainda wanted Titan, she could not stop pinching me and I knew she wanted to say something so I asked her to walk with me outside so I could pee.

"Why don't you ask CO. Titan?" she said.

"No I want you," I said. "Let's leave him and Magainda to talk."

We went outside. "I think it's time you got closer to your man," she said. "The in-law chumminess is too much for me now and you are so naive."

I just smiled and thought it was a very silly and somewhat disgusting thought.

We went back and I sat between Magainda and Titan, I lied down on his lap but deep down I kept telling myself that Magainda wouldn't do that but Sunshine was right, they were getting too close.

A few minutes later Magainda started acting like she was having a seizure. Titan was scared and was really afraid of Mbalu too. During his injury Mbalu had one of her attacks, got violent with him and slapped him. So when he saw Magainda doing that he got up and went to the door. But Sunshine and I thought she was joking because she had not had any of those attacks before. We pinched her but when we saw tears running down the corners of her eyes and heard her humming similar songs to those Mbalu sang, we knew it was real and we were surprised. Titan intended to run but I asked him if he was going to leave us to deal with it on our own. Instead he asked Jeff to help him and Sunshine hold Magainda down while I ran to ask for help.

I ran to Edna and Fambuleh, he asked for Magainda to be taken to his shelter. I ran back to the room and found her a little calm but still stiff and refusing to open her eyes. She also had her teeth and fist clenched. We managed to take her out of the bed and when we got outside she said that there was a tall man with long hair standing underneath the big tree and he was calling her. He wanted her so she started to fight. I was very scared so I closed my eyes. I did not want to see whatever it was that she was seeing.

"No, no leave me alone I have a man I don't want to go with you," she cried.

Fambuleh was an old strong masculine man. He came out and helped us take her to his shelter. We told Edna that we regretted the trouble and she said it was ok.

"That's what friends do and we are friends, we should help each other," Edna said.

She asked if Magainda had experienced that before. Sunshine and I told her that that was the first time we'd seen her do that. Fambuleh got out a huge native blanket and cut a piece of it. He lit the piece on fire and passed it in front of Magainda's nose; he asserted that the smoke would drive the evil spirit away. I was frightened. Ten minutes later Magainda was ok. She was bruised on her knees a little and she was crying.

"Magainda when did this start?" I asked.

"This is the first time," she said thoughtfully.

"Fine girl, have you been bathing outside or at the river in the early evenings?" Fambuleh asked.

Fambuleh was a Gissy (his tribe) man from Liberia and whenever he forgets a girl's name he would call her "fine girl" like most Liberians do. He called me "fine girl" many times and one day I told him that the next time he forgot my name and called me fine girl again I would give him a hard time. So whenever he forgot he would ask Edna because I was a very stubborn teenager and Fambuleh did not want me to start bothering him. Magainda said that she went to the bridge once around 5.30pm and she found a shining silver ring but she did not bathe.

"So what did you do with the ring?" I asked.

"I played with it a little, tried it on and I dropped it there. I went there early the next morning but did not find it there and since then I always have nightmares about the river," she said.

The side of the river on which Magainda found the ring was behind the mill and people hardly used that side. It was quiet and scary and I did not understand why she was there alone.

"Magainda why did you touch that ring; you are a Mende girl and we all know that when you go to the river and find jewellery you don't touch it just ignore it," Sunshine said.

"So are you telling me that this stupid spirit goes all the way to Water Works from underneath that tree to cause trouble?" I asked.

"It's the same river and he can go to any branch; that's why you girls should be careful," Fambuleh said.

We stayed for an hour at Edna and Fambuleh shelter and when we were sure that Magainda was alright we went to our shelter. I asked Titan to spend the night with us, so he took his gun from his bodyguard and sent him home. The bed was huge so I wanted us all to sleep in the room but Sunshine and Magainda opted to give us privacy. So they slept in our room and they assured me that if anything was wrong they would know besides they were just next door. That was the first night Titan and I spent alone together. I had said the words - asking him to spend the night before I could think of how he could interpret it. I was nervous but he knew that I did not want to have sex so we kissed all night and cuddled, fully dressed. I still had all fifty strands of beads around my waist and when he felt it he sat in bed and caressed them on my waist.

"How many are there," he asked.

"Fifty," I said.

"Isn't that too much?" he said. "Aren't they heavy?"

"No, I like them," I said.

He did not say more about the beads, but he just kept caressing them.

None of us went to formation the following morning we slept in. Unfortunately Magainda and Sunshine woke up before us and got Sao to come and wait for me when I woke up. Titan got up had a bath and went home; he said that he had some things to take care of. When I got up Edna was waiting for me to get out too.

"How was the first time, my newly deflowered friend?" Sao asked.

"Sao run back to your shelter before I jump on you," I threatened.

I told them that we did not do anything but they did not believe me.

"Tity is finally out of his life," Sao said.

"If that's what he has her for then I'm sure we will be seeing more of her because we did not do it," I said.

We went on and on about it, they did not believe me so I ended up giving up and letting them assume whatever they wanted.

Magainda spent three days in the camp and she cried throughout the three days, because she could not believe it was happening to her. On the third day she needed to go back to talk to the head nurse in Bandawoh so I went with her. It was my first time visiting the hospital in Bandawoh; it was awful – children crying from every corner, sick people, wounded soldiers and women in labour screaming their lungs out. I could not wait to get out of there; it was heart-rending. Luckily I saw MaHawa from Kabbaty, she was so happy to see me. I did not recognise her at first as she had lost so much weight. She did not look as pretty but she was alright. We hugged each other and went away from the hospital.

"So what are you doing here?" she asked.

"At the hospital or in Bandawoh," I asked.

"At the hospital, I know you people were transferred here," she said. "So how have you been?"

I told her that I was doing just fine.

"Well girl I haven't seen you in a while but I've heard a lot about you," she said.

"What exactly? I hope it's all good," I said.

"Well I heard about your new man and I've seen him," she said. "He is edible."

"Hey Mahawa, I'm right here," I said, smiling.

It was true Titan was really handsome he had a baby's face and he looked way younger than his 19 years.

"Hey I heard there is a little problem though," she said.

I knew she was talking about Tity and I did not want to discuss my private business with everyone. So I tried to avoid it by asking her how things were in Koribondo jungle. But she still wanted to talk about whatever problem it was that she had heard about.

"Hey I know that he is playing around with Tity," she said.

I nodded and asked her how she knew this.

"Well she is my cousin but not my favourite one," she said.

I got up to walk back to the hospital to see if Magainda was ready for us to go and Mahawa followed me. I pondered over the thought of two cousins having just messed with me, though I messed with the Mahawa. I could not wait to tell Sunshine that the two were related.

"So how are you two related?" I asked.

"We are cousins; CO. Mohamed (Second in command to Foday Sankoh) is my cousin too. He left me with Captain Barrie when he was going to open Freetown Highway camp because I was still a civilian then. As it was a tough battle he left me, Tity, her mother, and her little brother who was captured in his absence," she said.

"She and I did not get along, she always acts as if she is better than everyone else."

It was true what she said about her cousin's behaviour but I did not know what to say so I just kept quiet. She kept talking and telling me how annoying and desperate her cousin was and how she was always on the radio trying to get Titan to visit her or agree for her to visit him in the camp. She also told me that Tity's mother is trying hard for Tity and Titan to end up getting married if they both survive the war or maybe they could do it as soon as possible.

"Well good for them I think Titan would be very happy," I said.

We got to the hospital right in time. Magainda came out with a piece of paper but she did not seem happy. At this point nothing but a guarantee that the spirit was gone away from her could make her happy. She tried to be polite to Mahawa; we said goodbye to Mahawa and left. She promised to visit us when she came to Water Works.

Magainda and I walked to Water Works without talking much. I spent most of the trip recounting in my head how drastically my life had changed. Like a tornado with me standing in the middle. From the last day I saw my mother (on her way to Lofa while I and my sister were on our way to school), to giving my paternal grandmothers a headache to now living in the middle of a war zone where I was having to talk about how I could sustain a romantic relationship. Something I was raised knowing that a child my age should not be concerned with.

I needed to stay alive; why did I need to fight to stay alive? That was not my job. I was a child and keeping me alive was the concern of my parents and family, not mine. This was the chaos that went through my head as we walked back to Water works.

Magainda broke the silence, she told me she was sure that Titan and Lansana were talking to the people so that they won't send her back. That was one of the many things I liked about Titan, he kept his promise to make me comfortable although I wanted more. He treated everyone who meant something to me with respect and care and he got the same in return. When we got home Naffie was not there - Arrow told us she was on her friends' farm. This is the lady living with her husband in the rear room of the house. She and Naffie came from the same town and they knew each other very well so they passed for sisters. Arrow told us where the farm was and we went there. When we got there the man had just come back from checking on his traps and he brought game caught in one of the traps which I could not take my eyes off. We ate some boiled cassava with palm oil and chillies. I wanted to go back to the camp but Magainda did not want to go so Naffie asked us to spend the night.

The next morning after we had something to eat, Magainda packed a few things and we took off for the camp. She was more relaxed and we laughed and talked on our way back. When we arrived in the camp everyone was happy; it was lively as it hadn't rained for three days. Our shelter was busy, all the boys were home, Lansana was there, Rain came back and she and Sunshine were in the kitchen cooking. I introduced Magainda to Rain and I don't know why I just could not wait to see Titan. So I went straight to his shelter and Magainda came along with me. She said she wanted to thank him for talking to the people at the hospital who ran the course. Lansana was in the room with Lt. Cross smoking, I told him where I was going and he was ok with it. I went to the kitchen and told them that I was going to see Titan. Titan's shelter was busy as well when we got there, but he was not in the studio. I asked the guys for his whereabouts and they said he was in the room searching for his promotion document. They all really seemed happy. Robert asked Magainda to sit and talk with him in the studio.

"Robert leave my sister alone," I protested.

"Just because I was late to get you doesn't mean I cannot get anyone else in the family," he said.

We laughed about it and I went to Titan's room looking for him, but he was not there so I went to the kitchen to ask if they saw him.

"He is behind there with Jonah," Eliza said.

I went behind the bodyguards' shelter and Titan was there standing with his A.K pointed at Jonah' head.

"What are you doing," I asked running to them.

"He lost my paper, my freedom," Titan cried.

His eyes were red it was obvious that he had been crying long before I got there and Jonah was in tears too begging for his life.

"Without that paper I could get demoted and that means I would have to fight to get promoted again," he said.

"Please Titan listen to me," I said. "You know when you search desperately for something you sometimes don't find it; but when you are calm and search for it again you will realise that you did not really lose it? Well don't make a stupid mistake just give Jonah a chance to look for it because if you shoot now you will end up doing what you are so afraid of doing."

I started crying too because it was too much for me – looking at him with the gun on the boy and the two of them crying basically for their lives. Titan did not want to fight anymore because he did not want to shoot anyone anymore or get killed on the front. Jonah was begging for his life at the moment, so I walked to Titan and asked him to look at me and try to take the gun off Jonah. He looked at me but he did not move his hands, so I walked to him and slowly laid one of my hands on his slowly pushing the gun away while my other hand was pushing the boy in the other direction. When the gun was finally off Jonah he fell on the ground begging Titan for a chance to look for his papers and also for forgiveness. I got him to lay the gun on the ground and when he did he hugged me tightly and broke down harder and we were all in tears. He asked me to forgive him. Then he asked God to forgive him for even thinking of doing that to Jonah.

"Go Jonah, pull yourself together and look for the papers," he ordered.

"Thank you sir," Jonah said. He stood at ease and thanked me then he wiped his tears and ran off. Magainda came and when she found us crying she asked what the problem was. I told her Titan was just about to do something he would regret for the rest of his life.

"Magainda your sister just saved me from killing a boy," he said.

I wiped his tears and we went to his room. Jonah was there still crying searching frantically, I held his hand and told him to stop crying and take a break. Magainda told him to sit next to her on the bed. Titan could not look at Jonah he had his head bowed down when he spoke to the boy.

"Jonah, leave it take a break and when we are both relaxed we will look for it together," Titan said. "Jonah I'm very sorry for doing that to you but next time stay away from that bag, leave it with the big boys ok?"

Jonah said he was sorry too and dried his tears and went outside still looking terrified. We sat for a while and I later took Titan to our shelter. He seemed really shocked and was really regretting the fact that he pointed a gun at Jonah. Lansana asked him what the problem was but they went to the room to talk and I told Sunshine what had happened. Titan slept with us at our shelter but in Lansana's room with him.

Early the following morning we went to formation. Rain was due to go to her grandmother again. I did not spend too much time with the girls or my friends; I saw that Titan needed me so I went up to his shelter with him. He thanked me a lot for saving him from hurting the boy; he had his hand on my hip and when he felt the beads he asked me to take some off that he did not like it that way.

"I think it's too much," he said.

I told him that I liked them that way but I agreed to take twenty off just for his sake and he agreed reluctantly that thirty was ok. I left him and went to our shelter. When it was lunch time at his shelter, I was invited but I thanked them and left. I did not want to eat there I was shy. There were more people coming to the camp every day. None of these were civilians they were all old RUF members. I found Corporal Maseray Robert and Corporal Zainab Alasan when I got to our shelter from seeing Titan. I knew the two - Zainab Alasan from Libya was happy to see me.

"Hey big woman you all grown up look at you," she said. "I hear you are Mrs. Titan now."

I smiled and gave them courtesy. Maseray Robert was one of the women who lost their boyfriends in the old camp when the soldiers engaged the rebels; his name was Lt. Robert . I talked with the two women and they told me that everyone in RUF knows about Titan and me; that they heard about it in Kenema Bypass. I was surprised at how they would hear about me all the way over there when I had not been there and I knew no-one there. I smiled about it and I turned to go to the room for some food.

"Memuna you and Titan really suit each other," Zainab said.

I ate my food and Sunshine and I took off to our hiding place in the swamp. We talked about what happened between Titan and Jonah.

"He was lucky you got there in time," Sunshine said.

"I don't know why he would do that, I think God wanted me to stop him because suddenly I could not wait to come back here and see him," I said, "but I'm glad I came."

We bathed and went back to the shelter, got dressed and went up to Vayanga's shelter. The moon was bright and we were very energetic. The guys were not there they were at Franklin Morris and Jackson's so we went back to our shelter.

Early the following morning Rain went back to her grandmother and Maseray and Zainab returned to Bandawoh.

Titan came over that night and he was with us in our room. The boys were getting upset with me because of Titan; they were still dwelling on Magic's problem and me while I was trying to get over it. They said I was acting as if I was better than they were since I did not want to go out with them. It turned out Second-phase wanted me too. Kasiloi was not upset with me he was just the same as usual and I was glad that he was not on my back. They tried to stay away from us only because Titan came to visit me and they went to the shelter Fambuleh gave us. Lansana was with the other men up at the studio. We sat in bed and talked till we felt sleepy and I asked Titan to go home that we needed to sleep.

"No I want to spend the night with you, "he said.

"How?" I asked. "There are four of us in this room," I said.

"If he wants to stay let him stay the bed is big enough," Sunshine said.

"But no adult acts," Magainda said.

Titan slept in front and Sunshine and I slept in the middle of him and Magainda – I was next to him. That night he complained about my beads and he said that he only wanted me to get rid of everything and keep only one. I told him there was no way I was going to do that and it was late for us to talk about that, so we forgot about it for that night.

I was still awake with my eyes closed when Lansana came home. He knew that Titan was in our room and he opened the curtain to spy. I opened my eyes slightly to peep back at him. He stood there looking at only Titan and me for about five minutes and he went to his room looking sad. The next morning Titan woke up to go to formation, he woke Lansana up and they went together. We stayed and I was dreading looking Lansana in the face when he got home. I lay in bed staring at our room's ceiling and Sunshine noticed that something was bothering me.

"Don't worry Memuna, stop being sad," she said. "Magainda is here the others will come soon."

"It's not that," I said.

"What is it then?" she asked.

"Lansana was standing out there looking at Titan and me last night," I said.

She told me not to worry.

"I know he will be jealous but he should know that the day would come," she said. "I mean he knows that Titan is your boyfriend and besides he helped Titan get you so he should try and control his feelings."

I still felt bad that he saw us. "But I wish he hadn't seen us like that," I said.

"He shouldn't have looked," she said.

I agreed and got out of bed. As soon as I stepped out Lansana and Titan came back from formation and the feeling came back to me but I had to deal with it. Titan went home to bathe and Lansana told us he was going on another mission in two days. He acted as if nothing had happened; I hate it when people act like that but that day it suited me so I was fine with it. That night Magainda, Sunshine and I were in our room talking about boys and sex. When it came to sex I did not say much I only had questions to ask but I had a lot to say about boys. I was really sleepy though but the conversation was really interesting. The night was windy and the rain was threatening, the camp was dark so we did not sit on the veranda, Lansana was at Titan's. While talking someone came knocking on the table out on the veranda.

"Knock, knock Memuna," she said.

We had a fright when we heard the voice

"Who is that?" Magainda asked.

I said I did not know because the voice was not clear due to the wind. "Well ask who it is," Magainda said.

"No I prefer to listen," I whispered.

Sunshine was already finding a place to hide in the room; we thought it was a spirit calling my name. But the voice got closer and it was Paegie, Franklin Morris' girlfriend.

"What is it Paegie?" I asked.

"I need to talk to you," she said.

It was cold outside and I did not want to get out of bed; besides I could not think of anything she would want to talk to me about. I thought she wanted something but she was shy to ask in front of Magainda.

"Come in and tell me Paegie don't mind these two," I said.

"No please come out it's not going to take long," she said, popping her head into the room.

I managed to get out of bed complaining and I went outside.

"Memuna, Jackson sent me to tell you that he likes you," she said.

I looked at her feeling really upset, not with her but with Jackson. I could not think of a reason why he would send his girlfriend's friend to tell me that he likes me. "Paegie I have someone, so please thank Jackson for me," I said.

She tried to say some more but I cut her off and told her goodnight and I walked into the room.

"I can't believe it," I said.

The girls asked me what it was that she wanted to tell me and I told them how upset I was and they agreed with me.

"What, isn't he man enough to ask you out?" Sunshine said.

"I think he lost one of his balls along with his mind if he could send his girlfriend's friend to ask me out, in fact if he can ask anyone to ask me out for him."

We talked about it and I told them that I was not going to talk to him anymore.

That morning after formation, the guys had to stay because they had to make plans for the mission; we came home to prepare breakfast. We cooked some wild yam to eat with palm oil. I liked wild yam, it was one of those I wouldn't have known a thing about if I was not captured and there was something unexplained about it that made me like it. Maybe it was because I had to eat it or maybe because it was strange to me, which would be a weird reason because I never liked eating things I'm unfamiliar with.

Jackson came to our shelter after he'd had his breakfast to talk to the boys. Everyone talked to him but I acted as if he was not there although he tried to talk to me. In the afternoon, he came again and suggested we play a game of Ludo. I told him that I was cooking and he insisted.

"I have played with you so many times while you were cooking so what's different about today?" he said.

"I don't know, I just don't want to play," I said.

He insisted so I played. "What is the problem?" he whispered in Krio.

"There's no problem," I whispered.

"But why are you avoiding me?" he asked.

"I'm not," I said.

"Yes you are, it is obvious to everyone," he said.

I told him he was imagining it and he told me to stop being a child and tell him what was wrong. "We are all adults," he said.

As I was about to tell him that I was not an adult he told me that I was and I shouldn't deny it.

"Look I don't want to talk about it now before I say something I don't want to say to you," I said and left the game.

He looked confused, he looked at me and he went to the guys. Later Sao came and asked me what was going on. I told her and she did not believe it saying Paegie was lying.

"She must have been sent by her friend Matilda," Sao said.

394

Jackson came to our shelter and asked Magainda what was wrong and she told him. He denied sending Paegie, saying Matilda had been on his back insulting him and his mother at the shelter because she thought he was cheating on her. He said she thought it was me he was cheating with, so she must have been the one who sent Paegie just to be sure. Magainda was so upset when she told me the whole story.

"I see why she's been keeping her distance these few days," I said.

"I thought it was just the pregnancy getting to her," Sunshine said.

"What, was she close to you girls?" Magainda asked.

"Well not too close but we were nice to each other," I said.

"Poor boy what role did his mother play in this," Sunshine said.

I told Jackson to advise Paegie to stay away from me, I did not mind speaking to her but I did not want to play any foolish childish games with her. Jackson told Franklin Morris what Paegie had done and he dealt with her.

Titan and I spent some time together that afternoon and he went home. Jackson was at our shelter while Titan was there. We all sat and talked about funny things and at some point I sat and listened to their stories - some funny and some sad yet they managed to laugh about them.

Jackson was in his twenties but I was sure that Lansana was older than him and Titan was younger. He was a tall dark lean masculine guy and very likeable.

As soon as Jackson went home Matilda started screaming insults at him and she even insulted his mother saying some very dirty words. He tried to get her to go into their room to talk but she wanted to say those words for everyone including me to hear. She stood on the hill by their shelter looking towards our shelter and screamed filthy dirty insults.

"Jackson you bastard, your mother gave birth to you in the gutter," she said.

He felt so embarrassed he left their shelter with a cigarette and came to our shelter. The boys were sitting outside with us listening to her in disbelief.

"Jackson man, what is going on," Kasiloi asked.

"She thinks I'm cheating," he said, "and I'm not, I tried to talk to her and this is what came out of my effort."

"So what has your mother got to do with it?" Tiger asked.

Jackson let out a deep breath and shook his head. "I don't know but I'll let her get away with it today. When she's calm I'll advise her not to ever involve my mother in her bullshit," he said.

I felt sorry for him and I could not believe all of that was happening because of me. I wanted to talk to him but I did not know what to say to him so I told him not to worry and not to get angry and do something he would regret. Soon Franklin Morris came to join us looking very upset with a smoke as well. He stammered and it was easy to upset him though he was a nice person.

"I don't know why she's being so rude," Franklin said, "and that Paegie wants to start her own but she knows me, I don't have time for shit."

The boys asked him what was it that Paegie wanted to do.

"She asked me if I was cheating too," he said. "I told her not to ever ask me that question."

Jackson ignored Matilda's carrying on and she carried on for hours while we played games with the boys at our shelter listening to her and the music.

"I will tell her boyfriend and when he kills you I will find another man and maybe he will look after me and your child you son of a bitch," Matilda said.

That made the boys laugh. "Good luck Matilda," Jackson said.

That afternoon while we sat there, Jonah came running to our shelter and when Matilda saw him she stopped because she thought that Titan was coming.

"Memuna I found it," Jonah said.

He ran and hugged me thanking me while I was still on the bench playing Ludo.

"Where did you find it?" I asked.

"In CO. Titan's room underneath the bed," he said.

"God bless your arse," Sunshine said.

"Good," I said. "Give it to him and don't you ever touch that bag again,"

He told me that he already did that and that he was not going to touch the waist bag again and that it was in Pasineh's care. The boys asked what it was that we were talking about; I told them that it was nothing. But they did not believe me they insisted so I told them to wait that I was going to tell them later.

"Memuna, CO. Titan wants to see you," Jonah said.

I told him to go and tell Titan that I'd be there as soon as possible. Jackson flashed me a look when I said that, but I ignored him. Jonah ran back home.

"So tell us what it is," Laser said.

"As for Laser he can never let go," Sunshine said.

"It was only Titan's promotion papers that he thought were missing and concluded it was Jonah' fault," I said.

"Laser, now you will have a good night's sleep," Sunshine said.

"So how did he react?" Tiger said. "A man can kill for that paper."

As soon as he said that the girls and I looked at each other and realised that we had nothing more to say. After so many games Jackson and Franklin went home, the boys went to Vayanga's shelter, they told us that they did not want us there they wanted to have a "boys only" time and I left Magainda and Sunshine playing a game of Ludo and I went to Titan.

"Are you alright?" I asked.

He said that he was alright but he just wanted to see me.

"We found the waist bag," he said, holding my hand for me to join him in bed. I sat and he put his arm around my neck asking me to lie down and I did.

"Where did you find the bag?" I asked.

"Underneath this bed," he said.

I looked at him for a moment. "So if I hadn't arrived in time you would have just killed that boy or hurt him and then after you found the bag what exactly would you have done?" I said.

"I'm sorry, I swear to my mother whom I haven't seen in years, I will never do that again I'm sorry," he said. He had tears in his eyes; I leaned on him and told him to stop crying.

"I'm so very glad and lucky to have you, please forgive me," he said.

I told him that it was ok but seeing him like that made me scared and I told him that he should keep his promise and never do it again. He agreed and we stopped talking about him and Jonah's little drama. We talked a little more and I told him that I was hungry and I wanted to go home. Every time Titan was around me he had an erection and it scared me away, it was the same with Magic.

We did not go to formation the following morning; we had to cook some food for Lansana and the boys to eat before they went on the mission. They ate and we wished them good luck advising them to let go if they could not do it because we needed all of them. When they left we were sad for a short while; I went into Lansana's room to pray for his return. I did that anytime he went on missions and Magainda and Sunshine knew it so they just left me alone when they saw me like that. The mission was meant to last five days. They were going to a town near Kenema. Soja had his relatives living in that town so he did not really feel good going to attack the town but he had to. So he went but he was praying hard that they wouldn't see him. Titan checked in on us as usual when Lansana was away, but the day after Lansana went on the mission Titan came with Jeff to our shelter early in the afternoon he ordered me to guard him. I told him that I did not want to guard him.

"It's an order soja, I'm not asking I'm telling," he said.

"I see why you were so anxious to get me to train," I said.

"Sorry this is not the reason but it comes in handy," he said.

I told him that I was not going to guard him but he threatened to punish me if I refused his orders. I started to cry but he wouldn't budge and Magainda and Sunshine started laughing at me. They told me to do it and they were happy that he was forcing me to spend time with him but I was not. That afternoon Sao was with us she laughed at me. He had two of his AKs and he gave me one while Jeff had the other.

"We are going for a walk to Tobanda, so get dressed if you want to change your clothes," he said.

I was so upset but there was nothing I could do, I had on a T-shirt and a pair of shorts so I went into the room and wore one of the skirts I had sewn for Sunshine and myself. It was a hot day so I wore a unisex singlet – a red one. He smiled when I got out on the veranda; I took the AK from him and we took off. I said I wanted to walk behind him but he insisted that I walked by his side. As soon as we passed the guard post and walked all the way to the bridge toward Ngovokpahun he took the gun from me and tried to hold my hand but I pulled away, Jeff was ahead of us.

Titan spoke to the men on guard when we got to Ngovokpahun and asked them how things were and if they had enough food. They said that everything was fine but they were running out of food, he promised to solve the problem and we carried on walking. When we got to the palm nut farm across the road from the old camp he told Jeff that he wanted me to take a break although I did not say anything of the sort. We sat on some leaves on the ground by the path in the farm, with Jeff a few feet away down the path from us; it was the short cut to Tobanda.

"Memuna, don't get vexed with me I only forced you because I wanted us to spend some time together," he said.

"But you don't need to force me," I said.

"But all these days you haven't said a word to me and it really hurts and I knew that you were going to turn me down today that's why I decided to order you," he said.

"Well I hope you are satisfied now," I said.

"I want you to have a good time I don't want you to be upset," he said.

"Oh yes, I forgot it's all about what you want," I said.

He said that he was sorry and begged me to smile, when I did not he tickled me. We got up and continued walking to Tobanda.

The ground commander in Tobanda was a young man in his mid to late twenties and he was very friendly. We spent the day at his house in his bedroom after we went around the town for a reason I did not know. Tobanda was a small village surrounded by palm trees, cacao, coffee and orange trees with about thirty houses. It was very sunny and hot, Titan and I went to the room while Jeff and the ground commander stayed on the veranda and played checkers

We talked about us and I was worried he was going to start complaining about my beads again but he did not. We talked about different things and then he fell asleep. There were a few books on the table in the room so I went to the veranda and asked the ground commander if I could read one of his books and he said that it was absolutely fine. I fell asleep reading a book that did not have a cover. I did not sleep long, when I woke up Titan was covered in little sweat bobbles. I reached into his pocket, took out his handkerchief and wiped his back and he woke up.

"You are sweating," I said.

"Thank you," he said. He closed his eyes and asked me if I was ready to go back to the camp. I said I was as the sun was calmer then and I was a little cold.

"I'm cold - I hope I'm not getting sick," I said.

"Why, is something hurting on you?" he asked.

"No I'm just cold," I said.

He suggested we swap our tops and I agreed. He gave me his T-shirt, which went almost down reaching my knees and luckily the singlet I had on was big enough to fit him and it was unisex. On our way back I was well behaved and it was good.

When we arrived into the camp the girls were having dinner with Sao and Edna and as soon as they saw me with Titan's T-shirt on and mine on him they started teasing me for crying when he asked me to go with him. He left me and went to his shelter. "I was cold that's why we swapped," I said.

But it did not matter to them. "I think you two should stop playing around and just be together," Edna said. "I mean it's obvious that you like each other."

"They are not playing around," Sunshine said. "Memuna is playing around and CO. Titan would like nothing more than for them to be like this."

"Wow it's nice watching all of you talk about what I should like," I said. "Where is my food?"

As I sat down eating they kept talking about how great Titan and I looked together. "Look to be honest I like him but I don't know how to do this whole boyfriend thing," I said.

We talked for a while and Magainda, Sunshine and I went to the swamp to bathe. Titan spent some time with me that night and he went home to sleep. The following morning Magainda was temperamental and was snappy towards everyone especially me. I neither knew why nor did I know how to ask her; I was finding a way to ask her.

We did not have clean rice at the shelter, the rice we had needed to be pounded before cooking, as it still had husk on it. The mission Lansana led was because we were running out of food. The ambush men had no rice and they were complaining about eating wild yams. Salifu did not go on the mission; he was meant to stay and watch over us at all times.

We needed to pound some rice; enough to last us at least till Lansana and the boys came back. Left with Sunshine and I we would have just put the rice in the mutter and pounded it to get what we needed. Magainda, on the contrary, suggested we steamed and pan toasted the rice before we pounded it. It was a nice way to process rice because it smelt good, but I hated the whole idea of pounding rice. Anyway we agreed with her, the two of us were really hungry as if we hadn't had dinner the night before. Edna brought over some yams and palm oil for us. We sat around the fire watching the rice steam when she came. Magainda refused to eat the yams so Sunshine and I ate it and went back to sit by the fire.

"I think I'll call Jonah to help us with this pounding," I said.

"What about Pasineh?" Sunshine asked. "I'm sure he will help us if we asked."

"Yeah he would if he isn't on guard," I said.

Sunshine and I had shorts on with T-shirts ready for the hard work. I dreaded it; I was worried about my hands because anytime I pounded something for long I got blisters in my palms. Magainda looked at me for a while and she asked me why I broke up with Magic. I could not handle talking about what happened between Magic and me anymore. I felt upset when she asked me but I did not want to fight about it so I tried to calm myself down.

"I don't know what Magic told you but I did not break up with him," I said.

"You betrayed him," she said.

"Magainda you have no right to talk to me like that," I said. "Magic made a promise to me that he did not keep and then he came here trying to take me to Freetown Highway."

"So because you found someone with a higher position you turned him down," she said.

Sunshine looked surprised she just sat there looking from one person to another. I could tell that she wanted to say something but she did not want to get involved. Magainda would have definitely thought we were ganging up on her, because Sunshine knew the truth whereas Magainda did not care to know.

"Look Magainda, you have a man don't you," I retorted.

"Yes, one that I'm very loyal to," she said. But before she could complete her sentence I cut her off.

"Well good for you; the day you get pregnant for him let's pray you have a boy," I said. "And you can name the child Magic after his uncle but leave me alone. I own myself and only I decide who to let into my life not you or anyone; and besides stop trying to play mother because you are not my mother."

By now Edna heard us arguing but she did not come to the kitchen because Fambuleh stopped her doing so. He said as long as we were only fighting verbally and not using rude words it was ok to let us carry on and maybe we needed to talk about it. As I got up to leave the kitchen, Magainda took a piece of wood from the fire place with fire on it and threw it at me. Luckily the wood missed me but the hot coal that broke off it did not. I took the Same wood and threw it right at her and it hit her foot.

"Magainda, remember I warned you in Kabbaty the time you slapped me," I said. "I warned you not to do it again because you won't get away with it."

I went to the room, she followed me insulting me and I insulted her right back we said filthy things to each other.

"Magainda, stop saying those words you are older," Sunshine said.

But Magainda snapped at her, "Fuck off!"

Sunshine did not say anymore to Magainda, she talked to me. She told me to just leave it.

"Memuna stop, go to the studio and sit there" she advised.

"No Sunshine, Magainda thinks I'll let her run my life. She doesn't care about me she only cares about Magic. I don't know why she won't sleep with him instead," I said. "You all know how disappointed I was when he lied to me but to mother Magainda here, I still should have taken off with him, and besides I can't go to the studio because I don't want to bother Titan with this."

Magainda came to the room and slapped me across my face and I slapped right back. She tried to tear my T-shirt but it was too strong for her to tear. So we kept slapping each other till we got out of the room and went out in front the big devil tree. We stood there slapping and swearing at each other until someone got CO. Flomo and Sin-child.

Magainda liked swearing at people's mothers so I swore right back at her mother. CO. Flomo and Sin-child were just in time to hear her swear at my mother and called me a fucking dog. They parted us and punished us to fetch water for Fambuleh's kitchen, for him to cook food for the ambush men. They told me that for the fact that I did not think of Titan and just cool myself down I had to fetch twelve buckets of water and because Magainda was older and she was caught saying all those nasty words she had to fetch eighteen buckets of water.

"She said those words back to me," Magainda yelled.

"Look lady you don't know how things are here on Blama Highway," Sin–child said. "That's why only sojas live here so if you want to violate your orders you must be a civilian and that means you shouldn't be here."

Magainda was so angry she was ready to take on anyone and she thought that everyone was sucking up to me because of Titan but they were not. She was making everyone upset with her. She started crying and she wouldn't stop swearing at me. On our way to the wells in the swamp she pushed me and everyone saw her do it; I almost fell. CO. Flomo nodded to me indicating that I let go. After we both brought five buckets, she was still crying and throwing little insults at me. Honestly I did not want us to fight and she was older than me but I was angry. CO. Flomo saw what she did so he suggested I wait for her to come out of the bush with the water before I go. This way I would be going while she would be coming.

"I don't want to punish anyone further, so do it that way or else I will whip someone," CO. Flomo said.

She did hers as fast as she could just so we would meet on the way and when she finally succeeded she bumped into me as hard as she could throwing my bucket off my head and called me a bastard child. I managed to call her a bastard without anyone hearing me but her. She was the given six lashes and was ordered to continue fetching her water while I was ordered to stop. At this point I was really mad at her; I could not believe she would take Magic over me and worse of all to make us fight. I started crying because I was angry.

"Memuna, calm down, let's just leave the rice," Sunshine said.

Edna and Sao came to help her calm me down. "What am I going to tell Titan when he hears about this?" I asked.

But before I could finish the sentence Sao told me while he was on his way to visit me he saw us fighting so he went back when he saw his brother and Sin–child handling it. I could not believe my ears; it made me angrier with Magainda. I vowed I was not going to have anything to do with her anymore. They took me to Sao's shelter and CO. Flomo told Magainda to stop after she had fetched twelve buckets but she refused, she carried on.

"Memuna, you should never do this again you need to set an example after all you are our commander's woman," Sin–child said.

"And I'm also human," I said.

He looked at me and he left. I was only worried about how I was even going to begin explaining to Titan what had occurred. Sunshine and I had lunch at Sao's and she took some to our shelter for Magainda.

"I took the food for her and found her still crying. I think she is sorry it turned out like this," Sao said.

"That's her business," I said. "She will cry and when she feels really hungry she will eat."

Sunshine left me and went to calm Magainda. She returned after a few hours and said Magainda said she was sorry and wanted us to talk about it and forget about it.

"I don't think she is sorry or else she wouldn't have been on my back about Magic," I said. "I don't know why she could not ask me rather than venting her anger towards me; she trusts him more than she trusts me. She doesn't even like Titan and he is so nice to her."

Jonah came to call me saying Titan wanted to see me at that very moment. I felt like I was at home again and that I had done something for which my father was calling me. I tried to think of what to tell him but I decided to just tell him what exactly happened and why. He was in his room waiting for me when I got to the studio. I knocked on the door and he told me to come in.

"Hello," I said.

He looked at me and I answered, "I don't like it when you look at me like that," I said, "I think you should at least give me the chance to tell you what happened and I also need your support."

"You have my support and I'm ready to listen to you," he said. "But what's upsetting me is the fact that you fought outside."

I did not know what to say so I told him I was sorry.

"She started it," I said.

I told him what it was about and he told me that he knew Magainda did not like him or at least she did not like me and him being together.

"Don't worry about it," I said. "It's not up to her and I don't want this to change anything between you and her please."

He agreed that he wouldn't get involved and I promised that I would try to walk away if it ever happened again. It was not as hard as I thought and I was glad; we spent the rest of the day together and I went back to our shelter.

Magainda started crying as soon as she saw me but I was too angry with her to forgive her because she swore at my mother. So I walked passed her and went to Lansana's room and laid on the bed. Sunshine came to talk to me.

"Memuna, I know that you are really upset but Magainda won't stop crying until you speak to her," Sunshine said.

"Well I think her eye balls will fall out but I have no intention to," I said. "I can't believe she would open her mouth to swear at my mother when she knows how frustrated I am about finding my mother. I'm sure that even Magic - with whom I have the problem - would not swear at me."

Sunshine tried to talk to me so that I could forget it.

"Until she apologises for swearing at my mother I don't want anything to do with her," I said.

"But she is here in the camp because of you," Sunshine said.

"No, she only came here to see if what Magic told her was true and now she's got what she came for so she can do whatever she wants," I said.

Sunshine felt very sorry for Magainda I did too but I was still angry with her, so I stayed away from her. That night she and Sunshine slept in our room and I slept in Lansana's room. I was scared out of my mind so I did not have much sleep; I spent the night reciting Psalm 23. I got some sleep but each time I heard the slightest noise I would wake up and recite the Psalm again.

I did not go to formation the next morning so when they got back Sunshine called me to go out so we could pan toast and pound the rice. Luckily Jonah came by and I asked him if he was on guard. Since he told me he was not I asked him to help us do the rice. He said he would so I advised him to go back to their shelter and inform Titan where he would be. We did it faster than I thought because Salifu helped and Sao helped a little.

We cooked, but I was not hungry at the moment so they dished out my food. Titan did not come to our shelter that day but I went up to see him. I knew he was upset and wanted to give Magainda her space because she did not like him and had that brought about the fight. I went to his house to talk to him.

"I thought you promised it was not going to change anything?" I asked.

"Well it's hard because she fought you because of me so I don't know if I'm ready to be around her now; maybe later," he said.

When I got home Magainda and Sunshine were playing Ludo do and Sunshine asked me to play with them but I refused. I went to the room to get my food and Magainda followed me.

"Look I'm sorry, I should have asked you in a better manner," she said.

"It's not your business in the first place since you don't care about me. You should have just kept what Magic told you to yourself and not to bother me with it."

"I know that I was wrong and that's why I'm telling you that I'm sorry," she said, "and I don't care more about Magic."

"Magainda honestly I don't care whether you care about Magic or not and believe it or not I don't want to talk about it at all," I said.

I tried to walk past her so I could go and sit on the veranda to eat and she followed me.

"I'm sorry please let's put this behind us," she said.

"Yes, it's behind me already so let's just forget it," I said.

"I know you don't mean it, please for God's sake let it go," she said.

I looked at her for a moment and she looked like mess. She looked sad and it almost brought tears to my eyes. I did not need someone drumming Magic's name in my head. He claimed to have loved me but in his actions, he basically wanted my virginity in return for him helping me bring my sister and cousin to where I was. Love does not go like that and her siding with him was like a stab to my heart.

"I will forget about it but please just leave what happened between Magic and me to us and he and I can deal with it," I said. "Only God, he and I know the truth."

As I said these words I thought of how hurt I was when he came back without my sisters and he asked me to go with him. I almost cried I started choking on my words. I could not believe she would do this to me because we had been through a lot in the short while we were together and I liked her so much. So I forced a smile and I went back into the room to leave the food, I lost my appetite.

"Memuna, are you sure this is over?' Sunshine called out to me.

"Yes I'm fine I'm just putting this food away I don't feel hungry anymore," I said. I walked out trying not to look at them and I went to Sao and cried.

Magainda apologised to Titan, for everything and we tried to go back to normal.

CHAPTER TWENTY FIVE

Not Getting Along

Magainda had another attack by the devil on the morning that the mission was due to come back to the camp. This time she was standing on the veranda as we had just got back from the swamp. It was serious and this time we were able to identify which one was after her. She had the same problem as Mbalu - the female society's one. She sang and rolled from the veranda to the tree and she was lying there hitting her head on the tree and the ground in frenzy. I felt really sorry.

We intended holding her but she did not call on anyone for help. There was an old man living with Franklin Morris and Jackson close to where Titan's teacher lived called Karmor - he was a Muslim man. He came and suggested we needed to help her because it hadn't been long so she did not know who to ask yet. Sunshine took a broom with which she hit Magainda slightly on the head and then on her feet. She calmed enough for us to carry her inside the room. She continued to fight for a short while and later regained her composure.

She felt so embarrassed by her condition she wouldn't stop crying. We convinced her it was not her fault and that she could not help it. She sat on the veranda and cried for a few more hours.

The old man came to us and offered to write some prayers in Arabic and wrapped it in a piece of leather for Magainda to wear on her head. This he said would help drive the devil away. The thing is called a lasimoi in Mende. He said he did it for Mbalu and that's what helped her a little but when she lost her lasimoi and refused to take another the attack came back. Magainda did not want to do it initially, she said she would think about it and then she would get back to the old man. He went back to the shelter.

"I think I will take it because having fits in a war zone is something no-one wants," Magainda said.

She went to the old man and told him; I was afraid of him so I did not accompany her. When she came back she said the old man told her I was in great danger and I needed protection.

"Of course I'm in great danger as he also is," I said, "we could be attacked at any time; as for protection I don't believe that anything can kill me if God is not ready for me so I already have protection."

I did not want to hear of it I was afraid his work may be voodoo, I did not like it. Magainda tried to talk me into it but I told her that I did not want anything to do with voodoo that God can protect me more than anyone or anything else.

"He said that the danger was from insiders," Magainda said. "Other women some of whom want to kill you."

"I know that a lot of women hate me in this place but I'm not the only one who is experiencing this hate and I did nothing to them," I said. "These are more reasons for God to protect me. They all hate me because of men and they add by the day. Now Matilda and Paegie are two of them so I can't be bothered."

Sunshine laughed at Magainda and told her that we are the most hated women on Blama Highway and that nothing could happen to us.

"You know the reason why they hate us is that we are blessed with something they will not have. See Sao, Memuna, Mbalu, our other friend Theresa, Daniel's sister and me," Sunshine said emphasising, "we are the most hated women only because the men that mean something in this place only care about us and soon you will be one of us."

We talked about how hated we were till the boys arrived. I gave Lansana a big hug when I saw him, they were dusty but they looked pleased. They brought food, money, jewellery, and lots of other things including a few loaves of bread. Morris and Jackson dropped their bags at their shelters and came back to ours. At the time we already had pots on so we could cook something for them to eat. I was more attracted to the bread; it had been almost a year and a half since I had eaten some bread.

"Enjoy yourself with that bread Memuna no-one knows when we will get some more," Franklin said.

"Thanks Franklin," I said.

He smiled; he liked it when I called him Morris. He came and sat next to me and he had army suit on, which looked good on him.

"You look like an albino, with the dust on you," I said. "It's only obvious on your hair, eye brows and lashes that you have dust on you but your skin and the dust are almost identical in colour. He laughed and rubbed my head; he was accustomed to me teasing him about his skin. Sunshine and I did the same to Titan, Tiger and CO. Flomo - they were all light skinned.

"We were on Bo Highway where we fought one of the toughest battles. This time though we had women offering us jewellery and money so we would stop; they gave us food and all. Most of the passengers that went past in long distance vehicles were business women," he said.

He opened his jacket for me to see the gold chains he had on, he had four necklaces - all real and expensive gold.

"So you better enjoy that bread because who knows maybe the soldiers followed us again this time," he said.

"Damn all the business people were women; I think women have more guts than men on that side. They risk their lives and cross our line to go to the other side just to do business."

"You know why the women are braver?" I said. "Because RUF is more likely to kill the men so the women are doing the business instead."

Lansana was the first to bathe and as soon as he got dressed he went up to Titan to report and to arrange the government property. He promised us he would be back and he hoped that by then the food would be ready.

Jackson interrupted Franklin Morris and my conversation. He came and put a very pretty gold necklace on my neck. It had two pendants – a cross and a heart.

"How are you doing?" he asked.

"I'm fine and you?" I said. "Why are you doing this?"

"What have I done?" he asked.

"This," I said, feeling the necklace on my neck.

"Because it looks prettier on you," he said, "and I won't take no for an answer."

I smiled and thanked him; he said he wanted to see me with it always. I promised I wouldn't take it off. He went back to the boys to talk and I went to the kitchen.

"Hey Memuna I will need to talk to you later," Franklin said.

I nodded and started talking to Sunshine. Kasiloi came outside with a lot of money in his hands and just put it all on my lap.

"How are you my favourite girl?" he asked. "Have you been looking after yourself?"

I told him I was doing fine and I got up and gave him a hug.

"What am I going to do with all that money?" I asked. "We have no use for money here."

"You can keep it so that when we take over the country, which we are sure will be soon then you can use it," he said.

"Damn' the women on the other side are pretty too," he said. "Why are African women so beautiful?"

"Ask Hindowa he should know, he got shot in the butt for a Mende girl," Sunshine said when she saw Hindowa coming to the kitchen and we all laughed about it. They all had money and they gave us all of it. By then I had two grocery shopping bags full of money.

It was a busy day in the camp and it was noisy especially at our shelter. Ranger was tired but he was happy to be home. Laser was the usual energetic person he was. He came to the kitchen, gave us money, slapped the back of my head and ran off. I told him there was no food for him because of that. The excitement lasted two days and I really liked the necklace.

Lansana and Titan spent time together as usual, somehow Lansana found out about Magainda and I. He told me that someone else told him and he asked Titan if it was true and Titan told him that it was but everything was ok. He called me into his room and asked me why Magainda and I fought and I told him. He was mad at me for letting it go that far and he told me not to let that happen again. I told him I was sorry and that was it.

Franklin Morris got to talk to me saying he liked Magainda and he wanted me to help him tell her. I told him I did not think it was a good idea for me to tell her but if he wanted me to put in some good words I could. I told him to ask her out for himself and he agreed with me. Then he went on to tell me that his friend liked me.

"Jackson really likes you Memuna, think about it and do something," he said.

I nodded and we went our separate ways. That day I told Sunshine that Jackson liked me. Knowing her she was really care-free, she did not like to worry about anything for too long.

"So what are you going to do?" she said.

"What do you mean?" I asked.

"Well you know the man and you are being wrongly accused already so why not make them right if you like him," she said.

"We are all good friends and I'm sure we understand each other."

I told her that I was going to leave it for a while and she agreed.

That night Titan came over, he said that he was lonely and that he wanted to spend the night with me. So we were in bed talking with the girls and kissing and he felt the necklace on my neck. He asked me who gave it to me; all I could say was that it was a gift. So he took it off my neck and wore it on his, I did not say anything because I knew I was going to take it off him in the morning. While lying there and talking Jonah came to call him. Daniel had sent him for an important call for him on the radio so he kissed me and took off. He came back a few minutes later all dressed in dark colours with Pasineh and Jeff. He said he was going to Zogoda as there was something he needed to go and help take care of. So I wished him good luck and told him to travel safely. In the morning on my way to formation I wore something that did not show much of my neck. I tried to hide my neck from Jackson all day but he finally caught me and he knew who had it. I told him that I was sorry and that I would have it back as soon as Titan got back.

Two days later Titan came back to the camp, but before he got back Corporal Maseray was already in the camp and she told me where he was. He was in Bandawoh with Tity she had miscarried. The night he got back I was standing on the veranda in the big T-shirt I slept in, it stopped at my knees so I had no shorts under. It was dark and by mistake we blew our lamp off so I went out to light it using the lamp on the veranda.

"I don't think that is you standing out there almost naked at this time," he said.

It gave me a fright I was not expecting him.

"Oh yes it's me," I said and I went inside.

He came to the room and spoke to the girls and me. Lansana was at the studio with Daniel and Robert. He tried to tell me off but I told him not to try it because I knew why he ran out on me and told lies saying that he was going to handle something important. He looked tired but he was trying to hide it. I told him to go home and we would talk in the morning.

I went to his house after breakfast because he sent Jonah to call me. I did not want to go but I went anyway. He was in the studio when I got there and we went to his room.

"Why are you upset with me?" he asked.

"I can't believe you will sit here with straight a face and ask me that," I said. "I know that you ran out on me to go and be with Tity."

"I don't know where you got that from but it's not true," he said.

"Don't lie," I said. "I know she had a miscarriage. What was it a boy, Titan Jr?"

I turned to leave and he held my hand. "Please just listen," he said.

"I'm tired of listening, just let me go," I said. "The two of you almost shared a child and you look really hurt that it did not happen."

"It's not that," he said. "I just felt sorry that she had to go through that pain like I would if it were anyone I knew. You know how I feel about having a baby in this place. I told her I did not want it but she refused to take an abortion. I want you Memuna."

"Well you shouldn't have gotten someone else pregnant then," I said and I walked out.

He followed me begging me, I told him that I could not handle it and I asked him what would have happened if the pregnancy had survived. He said it was not going to change things, Tity was still going to be where she was and he went on to say that he was still trying to end it between them. So I told him he was not trying hard enough. I looked at his neck and the chain was not there.

"Where is my chain?" I asked,

As soon as he tried to say something I cut him off at this time I was really upset.

"Don't answer that because I know the answer and I really don't want to hear it from you," I said. "I want to see my necklace on my neck before tonight."

"It's not what you think," he said.

I turned around and looked at him.

"I took the necklace off my neck this morning when I was going to bathe and I forgot it," he said. "I swear I did not give it to her."

"Well you better send someone to go and get it now," I said. "I don't care if she is in Zogoda or Bandawoh I want it back today."

He told me that he was sending someone to go and get it but he needed me to calm down, I left him standing there and went home.

Magainda knew he was coming over for breakfast so she dished some food out for him. When I got home I called Soja and I ate Titan's food with him.

"Why are you doing that?" Magainda asked.

"He will not have any food in this house anymore," I said. "In fact I will tell him not to come here anymore but I know that is impossible."

When he came to the house Magainda told him that I ate his food. He said he was fine with it, that he already had breakfast at his shelter. He took me by the hand and took me to the room to talk to me.

"Memuna, I'm very sorry I did not mean to do this to you," he said.

"Well it's not like you could not put a stop to it and don't even stand here and tell me that you did not mean it," I said. "You promised you were going to hurt me so bad that I would bite my finger and don't feel it. Well I am hurt but I see no reason why I should bite my finger because I know that I would feel it. Also you know that in the process of hurting me you were going to hurt a baby by bringing it into this world at this time."

I was getting tearful but I held back and did not let my tears drop. I told him that I did not want to talk about it so he should just let it go.

Corporal Maseray went back to Bandawoh.

Later that evening Titan came to me with the necklace and tried to wear it on my neck but I did not let him. I took it from him and asked Sunshine to do it. Mustapha was happy that I was having problems with Titan. I was angry with him for days, I avoided him and I gave his food away every day except when he was eating with Lansana. If, however, Lansana ate before him or after him because he was busy or just not hungry there was no food for him as I gave it away.

Corporal Maseray and Zainab came back to the camp two days later, they arrived at night. Sunshine and I took off and went to Vayanga's shelter. Magainda was with Lansana and his questions. He was not in a good mood and everything was getting to him. The moon was a bit bright, on our way to meet the boys at Vayanga's shelter and we ran into Corporal Maseray and Zainab.

"Memuna, I have a message for you," Corporal Maseray said. "Young lady you have to try and get rid of that Tity girl."

"What did she say?" I asked.

"Well she knows that you know that she lost CO. Titan's baby," Corporal Maseray said and before she could finish her sentence Zainab cut her off.

"Who doesn't" Maseray said.

"She tells anyone who would listen. Memuna keep your man because I think he wants you. He is just with her for whatever reason, men cheat but don't leave him."

I nodded and laughed at the fact that Tity was telling everyone that she had miscarried.

"So why is she trying so hard?" Sunshine said.

"Well to get attention," Maseray said.

"So what's the message?" I asked.

"She said that the next time she comes here she will bring something for your pretty little face," Corporal said. "She said that I should tell you that it's not hard for her to get something to harm you because she works at the studio."

I laughed and shook my head but the women told me that even if I did not think she could do it, it was better for me to let Titan know. Zainab and Maseray said they wouldn't deny that they brought the message if I told Titan and he wanted to ask them.

Sunshine and I went straight to his shelter that night. He was in bed reading a book. I asked to talk to him. Sunshine greeted him and she went out to talk to Daniel. "What is the matter?" he asked.

"I'm getting threatening messages from your woman saying that the next time she comes here she would bring something for my face," I said.

He got out of bed and stood up to give me a hug. He told me that he was sorry and that he was going to deal with her. Titan cared too much about me, so much that he needed to ask no-one anything when I told him something, he always believed me and I did not lie to him. He told me how sorry he was when Sunshine came in. I asked him why he let the whole thing go so far. But all he could say was that he was trying to end it and I just needed to be a little patient. Sunshine told him that she was with me when I got the message and he told her that he believed me. We left him to sleep and we went home.

A few days later I was at Vayanga's shelter, I went there to look for Sunshine but we missed each other as she went home using the other way while I passed through Jackson and Franklin Morris' backyard to go to Vayanga. Zainab and Corporal Maseray were in one of the shelters in Vayanga's yard, I went in there to ask if Sunshine was there when I heard them laughing and they asked me to stay.

"So, Memuna I hear you are now playing with the older boys," Corporal Maseray said.

I did not know what she was talking about and I told her just that.

"Don't lie to us," Zainab said. "I know how much the men in this camp want you and your friends and we know that CO. Titan is not the only man you have."

I looked at her and wondered what they were up to.

"I don't know who you two think I'm going out with," I said.

I turned to leave, and went back to our shelter and told Sunshine and Magainda. I was a little upset about the gossip but I soon got over it.

"Corporal looked a little upset when she asked me that question," I said.

"Well she tried to get something out of me too when I was there and I told her that I did not know what she was talking about," Sunshine said.

We talked about it for a while.

"I wonder who is spreading this news," I said, "and what is it to them, why do they want to know?"

Sunshine said she did not know why Corporal Maseray was so upset about it, but she suspected Hanna to be the one who was spreading the news. By now Magainda knew that Titan was cheating on me and that I bothered him to leave Tity. After our fight she got close to Titan.

The two left the camp a week later and returned to Bandawoh. Sunshine and I left Magainda with Ibrahim, Tiger, Second-phase and Laser and we went for a walk to the guard post. Jackson was at the guard post with Kasiloi and Morris. They had buckets of oranges in front of them and they were making pigs of themselves with the guards at the guard post. When they saw us they asked us to join them, sucking some oranges.

"Where are you two going anyway?" Kasiloi asked.

"We just came here for a walk," Sunshine said.

I was making another top for myself that afternoon; I had the top in my hand while we strolled around.

"Are these oranges sweet?" Sunshine asked.

Jackson told her to try one and Sin-child told her that they were really sweet. I spoke to them but I did not look away from my sewing.

"Can I have one," I asked.

Jackson handed me one and it was really sweet. I folded the top I was sewing and paid attention to the oranges. After a while Jeff came to call me saying Titan wanted to see me. I told him to go back and tell Titan that I would be with him as soon as I could. He went back and did not come back. A few hours later we had enough oranges and enough of the boys teasing about how Titan's bodyguards followed me everywhere. Jackson did not think it was funny he just looked at me and turned away, but I could not be bothered and I just carried on sucking oranges till I'd had enough. Sunshine and I took off and went back into the camp leaving the boys at the guard post. She was tired so she went to bed to take a nap as the sun was hot.

I went into the room to put my sewing away and I went to see what Titan wanted to see me about. He was in his room having a nap when I got there.

"Why are you in bed at this time?" I asked.

"I was on the radio late last night," he said.

I did not want to ask whom he was talking to because I already knew. That day I was wearing an aqua flair mini skirt with my favourite T-shirt. He asked me to have a nap with him. I was not sure what was happening to him because he only did that when he was not feeling well. So I asked him if he was sure nothing was wrong with him.

"No I just want us to sleep, the sun is too hot and I want your company," he said.

I believed him and I lied on the bed next to him, but something was weird he wouldn't look at me. I lied on my stomach and turned my face to the wall wondering what was going on. To my surprise I felt sleepy so I closed my eyes and tried to sleep, then I felt him moving in the bed though I did not turn to look. I thought he was going out to use the toilet or something. But then I felt him lying on my back.

"Are you sure you are alright?" I asked.

He nodded and did not say anything. Then he sat on my legs with his legs on each sides of me. I did not mind I kept my eyes closed and I liked the weight on my legs. He caressed my legs gently and a few minutes later I felt little sharp pinches, I thought it was an ant biting me so I told him to get the ant off me. He told me that there were no ants on my legs but then the pinches went on for about three more times so I asked him to get up so we could check the bed.

"This room is clean I just got my sheet changed today," he said.

He got off me and I rubbed my hand at the back of my thighs because I could still feel the spots burning, I could feel bumpy bits but there was nothing else. It was not strange to me because my skin did that at times, so I lay on the bed again this time on my back. He sat on my legs again and I felt the pinch on my upper thigh again but this time it hurt more.

"What are you doing to me?" I asked. "Why are you pinching me?"

I was getting annoyed with him because I was already dealing with the burning sensation at the back of my thighs and he was doing it again. He looked at me and said nothing. The pinch on my upper left thigh was bleeding; it was a very tiny cut but it hurt and I was angry that he was physically hurting me.

"What are you using to cut me?" I asked.

"What is going on between you and Jackson?" He asked.

"What?" I said. "Is this why you are cutting me? Did I do anything when I saw you with Tity? There is nothing more than friendship going on between Jackson and myself."

I turned to leave and he pulled me back by my arm.

"What, are you going crazy?" I said. "I need to get out of here before you cut me into pieces and I don't want you at my shelter."

"You are cheating on me with Jackson," he said. "Every day you have a mini skirt on or something attractive and men have their eyes on you all the time and finally you are going with Jackson."

"The clothes are all I have," I said. "What do you what me to wear, your jeans that will cover me from head to toes? Look all you had to do was ask me instead of cutting me."

He tried to say some more but I cut him off by telling him to remember not to come to our shelter and leave me alone, then I stormed out of the room.

I got home looking very angry, luckily Lansana was not there. He was in Water Works and he was due back in the evening. Magainda and Sunshine asked me what was wrong and I told them what Titan had done to me. They could not believe he would be so jealous and stupid. I went to the room, took three band-aids and covered the cuts.

Before I knew it he was standing in front of our shelter requesting he wanted to talk to me. An apology was the last thing I needed after he deliberately hurt me. I told him to get out of my face that he was the last thing I wanted to see. I was so upset I could have slapped him across his face but I just looked at him and walked away from him. He stood for a short while and went back to his house.

A week later Tity came to visit Titan again, I did not say or do anything because I had told him to stay away from me and I hadn't let him talk to me since the day he cut me.

The morning after Tity arrived, Magainda, Sunshine and I decided to go to the bridge to do our laundry. As usual the boys gave us their clothes to wash as well and as I went passed Jackson's shelter on my way to Vayanga's shelter to borrow a huge plastic tub.

Jackson called out to me. He was in his room lying on the bed with his door opened. He was wearing a pair of shorts and a singlet. He asked me where I was going. In reply I told him I was going to borrow a tub so the girls and I could go and do our laundry. He asked me if I could do a pair of shorts for him too, I said I could and he gave me a pair of shorts.

"Is it ok if I come keep you company at the bridge?" he asked.

"Well it's a public place," I said, smiling.

I told the girls about Jackson's shorts and they had no problem with that; but teased me about Matilda, Jackson and Titan finding out. A few minutes later Jackson arrived at the bridge.

"Hey Jackson, have you two thought of what will happen if Titan and Matilda found out about you giving Memuna your laundry to do?" Sunshine asked.

He said he did not care; he sat with us till we were half way through the laundering.

When we took a break to have some food he took the time to talk to me about our situation. He asked if we could walk toward Tobanda and I walked with him a few feet away from Sunshine and Magainda and we sat on the gravel.

"Memuna I hear you are having trouble with the Lieutenant too just like I am having problems with Matilda because of something we haven't done," he said.

I nodded and did not say anything.

"I want you Memuna and you haven't said no all this time; so I need you to tell me what you think," he said. "Tell me now please because you've had enough time to think about it. So tell me no matter what the answer is, just tell me what it is because the suspense is killing me."

I looked at him and pondered about it a little. I could not think of anything else to say but yes; and besides Titan was cheating on me. Jackson could not believe it when I told him that I would give it a try.

"Are you sure?" he asked. 'I don't want you to say yes because we are alone here."

"No I'm not sure," I said.

"And we have been wrongfully accused for a long time," he said. "So are you sure?"

He was so excited he stood up and raised his hands to the skies while I sat and watched him asking myself if I could do it as I wanted to do it. He sat down by me again and kissed my cheek.

On our way back to join the girls I told him that Titan was my boyfriend and we did not have to demonstrate our relationship in his face and he agreed to be discreet.

"And please no jealousy because Tita and I might do things in your face," I said, hoping all the terms would repel him.

"Oh I have borne it for months and I think I can handle some more as long as we can find time for each other through all of that," he said.

I agreed. Both of us were smiling when we got to the bridge.

The girls knew me well enough to know that something went on because I had that shy look on my face. I did not want to look at Jackson in the face anymore. He took his shorts and left us at the bridge, they had already been washed. When I got home I was a little thrilled.

I did not know why Titan came over again to apologise and I told him to leave me alone. I was too upset with him to just forgive him like that because what he did to me was really scary. This time he refused to leave and he sat on the veranda and talked to Magainda and Sunshine - they were pleading for him too.

"Are you not going to entertain your guest?" I asked.

He looked at me and told me that what he was doing was more important and he asked if we could go to the room and talk. I felt sorry for him and he knew that when I said no I meant it. I went to the room with him; he got on his knees to plead with me.

"Memuna I'm really sorry please find it in your heart to forgive me for God's sake," he said.

"Well it's easy to do wrong isn't it when you can use the name of God to get away with it," I said.

"No, no Memuna it's not like that I don't know what made me act so stupid. Since that day you got so angry at me and walked out I haven't been able to sleep. I feel bad about myself and I'm really sorry," he said.

"You feel bad? You should feel sick," I said. "Cut me and you are feeling bad. What is wrong with you?"

I saw the sincerity in his face and I forgave him. He promised that it would not happen again and he promised not to hurt me in any way again. He asked me if I told Lansana and I told him I did not. He was very grateful that I did not because it wouldn't have been good for him. He thanked me and spent more time with us and returned to his shelter a few hours later. Tity spent two days and went back to Bandawoh. Titan tried for us to get as close as we were before but I had to take my time and he kept apologising for what he'd done to me. On the other hand Jackson and I took every opportunity we had to spend time together. I wanted to change my mind initially as I saw no point in being that close with him while I was still with Titan. I stayed away from him for a few days to think about it then I decided to have him.

Matilda Jackson stopped talking to me for a while but we did not argue and I still liked her. I stayed away from her too and she did not stop swearing at Jackson and his mother.

"I wish her man will find out about you and her. He will then send you to the ambush to be killed there; then I can find another man to look after me and my child," Matilda would always say.

Jackson got angry she said that and he beat her that day. A few hours later he came over to our shelter and he wanted to talk to me.

"Jackson, why did you beat her?" I asked.

"Did you not hear what she said? Also I told her to stop swearing at my mother?" he said. "So maybe this will teach her to deal with me and leave my mother out of it."

"But she is pregnant, if you are going to beat her again I'll just put an end to this," I said.

He promised not to beat Matilda again no matter what she said or did, he would just walk away. After talking for a while I told him to go home and talk to his pregnant girlfriend, he looked at me and told me that I was something different and he left.

That afternoon Titan asked me to go and see him at his shelter. I wondered what it was that he was going to do again, but went anyway.

"What have I done again?" I said. "We better talk about it because if you do something out of hands again I swear to my mother this time I will tell Lansana and this will be it for us."

He knew that when I swore on my mother I meant what I said.

"No Memuna, I told you I would never do that to you again and God in heaven knows that I won't," he said. "I just want to spend time with you I miss you. All the time you were angry with me our time was wasted and I want to make up for that."

I believed him and laid on the bed next to him on my back, but I was waiting to see if he was going to break his promise. He saw that I was not comfortable; he put his arm around me.

"Believe me Memuna," he said. "We have never lied to each other, I will not break that promise I just want you so relax."

He rolled over me, kissed me and whispered an apology while he told me to please relax and I did. We kissed and talked about our families on the other side and about things that were happening in the camp.

"Memuna," he said, looking at me underneath him with his hand in my short hair.

"Yes," I said.

"Will you marry me after the war if we are still alive?" he asked.

I was shocked and a little frightened. I did not know what to say but I wanted to say something so I just looked back at him with my mouth open.

"I know you would want to go back to school and get an education," he said, "and so would I. Being together will not stop us from doing that because we both want to be educated so much."

"But what about my family?" I asked.

"We can be with them maybe in the same neighbourhood," he said.

"Well that is something to think about," I said. "You do remember my age right?"

We started talking about something else, but I was still thinking about the proposal. Magic had said that same thing to me but his was more casual and I could handle it but Titan's seemed serious. He knew that it worried me so he told me not to think about it too much and that we had all the time in the world. We ended up beating each other with the pillows and I went home laughing.

I told the girls about the proposal and they thought it was sweet.

"Wow I have a permanent brother-in-law now," Magainda said. "He has to come and pay the dowry to me first before we go home to the family."

"Oh I think he has a lot of dowries to pay for this one woman because he has to pay to me and Lansana as well," Sunshine said.

"Ok you people are scaring me," I said.

"I don't understand why you are so afraid of men," Magainda said.

"Well maybe it's because I spent too much time playing with them from childhood till now," I said. "It is not that I am scared of men, it is just that I am way too young to be thinking of them or having them in my life in that respect at the moment."

Titan came to the house that evening and Sunshine and Magainda bothered him about the proposal.

"Yes, I will marry her and then I continue with the rest of the female cousins and sisters," he said. "From what I have seen your family is full of beautiful women."

"I can tell you," Magainda said. "I don't think you can handle two women from our family."

417

"I know because I'm still trying to catch up with this one," he said, pointing at me. "She is my natural star, always shining."

I thought it was so sweet for him to say that and I smiled. We talked more about it and CO. Flomo and Sao joined us - they all bothered me more about it. CO. Flomo and everyone started calling me natural star and I told them not to call me that. Weeks passed but Tity did not come to the camp and I did not ask why. CO. Flomo used to set traps to catch wild animals for food and he used to go slightly out of the camp. I got a share each time he caught something, but he only caught the smaller animals - things like squirrels and other little animals like that. I had my own special meat almost every day and I shared it with Magainda and Sunshine. They, however, still complained that I got special treatment.

"She is my sister-in-law and I have to pamper her," he said.

We were still being threatened by the Kamajors from the other side. Some of the escaped civilian men the RUF had captured showed them the way to come to our zone. One day when CO. Flomo went to check his traps he bumped into one of the Kamajors who gave him a message to deliver. He came back that morning looking shocked. Titan was at our shelter with Lansana; he came to our shelter and delivered the message.

"I bumped into a man who claimed he was a Kamajor," he said. "He told me that they were planning to attack us any time soon and the only reason he spared my life is because he wanted me to deliver the message. I did not even bother to check my traps anymore."

We all started panicking, it was unbelievable that the man managed to get pass the ambush and the grenade ambush and he got that far. CO. Flomo said that the man told him that there were three of them sent out on the reconnaissance work.

"I can't believe they are in our territory," I said.

"This place was theirs before we came along; chased some of them away and captured some," Sunshine said. "So they know the forest more than we do."

We concurred with her. While standing on the veranda listening to what Lansana, Titan and CO. Flomo were saying and making our own plans, Lansana called out to us. "Look, you girls need to stop using that short cut," he said, "especially you Sunshine and Memuna."

"We are going to tell everyone in formation this evening that now the law about shortcuts is serious," Titan said.

"So I hope this time you two will take it seriously," Titan said. "You know it's because we know how stubborn the two of you are that's why we haven't planted a grenade there yet but we might have to, so please stay away."

The shortcut we were warned about was a little path that Sunshine, Mbalu and their other friends had made from the main road to the camp through the swamp. It is very close to the upper part of the water which ran under the bridge where we did our laundry. When I came Mbalu and

Sunshine showed me the place and that's where we passed to hide and go to Water Works each time they refused to sign our passes. This shortcut was far from the guard post and we did not have to show anyone any passes. When Mbalu left we did not show the place to Magainda.

The rain got heavier and the water in the wells in the swamp got muddy because the rain washed dirt and everything into the wells. During this time we only used that water to water the vegetables in the garden. We had to walk barefooted through the forest to the deeper ends of the swamp to fetch clean water to cook and drink. I hated going to that place because it required walking barefooted in the mud not knowing what I was stepping on. We had to stand in the water to dip the clean bit. I was afraid of leeches even though Sunshine reassured me over and over again that there were no leeches in the water.

The first time we went there Magainda saw our secret shortcut and asked where the road was leading. We told her that it was an old entrance to the camp, but the day CO. Flomo bumped into the Kamajor we told her that it was our short cut and only very few people knew about it. We also told her that we were not ready to tell her that was why we lied when she asked and she understood, because she started to feel left out.

The boys suggested that they launched an attack first, but Lansana and Titan declined on the grounds that they would need an arrangement that should involve Lt. Cross because he was Titan's assistant. He was away and he left Lansana to handle his job for him. Lansana was glad because he wanted his position back.

Two weeks later they had already set some more grenade ambushes and assigned some more men to the ambush team. While the arrangement was still going on Lansana, Lt. Cross and the boys went on a mission to find a way around this problem and our food situation. Titan was left to take care of us again. At this point Naffie and Rain were told not to come to the camp because it was not safe for the children and we still hadn't heard from Samia and Komeh.

Two days after Lansana and Lt. Cross left for the mission, Magainda, Sunshine and I wanted to go and see Naffie and the children. We asked Titan to let us go but he refused. I spent hours pleading with him but he stood on his words. I got CO. Flomo to persuade him, he tried but he ended up agreeing with his cousin. Titan did not want me to go because he heard that a boy called Cut-neck was in Water Works. Cut-neck was one of Foday Sankoh's bodyguards and Naffie had tried to get me go out with him before I agreed to go out with Titan. Cut-neck on the other hand wouldn't give up on me even though he knew that I did not like him. He was slightly good looking and rough looking as well and he was very temperamental. He liked slitting people's throats when they went out to fight, that's why he was called Cut-neck.

Though I told Titan several times that he had nothing to worry about as far as Cut-neck and I was concerned he did not believe me. I got tired of persuading him to let us go; I even told him that we were not going to spend the night. We were only going for a few hours and we would be back 6pm but he wouldn't budge. So Magainda, Sunshine and I made an arrangement - one of us had to stay and because they knew that it was hard for me to lie to him we decided that Sunshine should stay and Magainda and I would pretend as if we were going to the bridge to do our laundry while Sunshine stayed and cooked dinner. We packed some clothes that we were tired of wearing to take to Water Works and bring some more back in a plastic tub as if we were going to do our laundry. That way no-one would ask us for a pass since we were only going to the bridge down the road. When we arrived at the guard post the guys asked us why we always had laundry to do. In replying we told them that most of the clothes we washed were for Lansana and the boys and we carried on our journey. The guards in Tobanda asked us for our passes but I told them that it was an emergency and since Titan was in a meeting and he could not sign a pass for us. They believed me and they let us go. Magainda and I laughed when we got past them. Naffie had cooked a big pot of some sort of wild meat stew when we arrived in Water Works. I did not bother to ask what kind of meat it was. It was delicious and very spicy. Even little Lucia liked it.

"You two are lucky," Naffie said. "You arrived right on time, or else you would have just smelt the stew and not eaten any."

She asked why we were in Water Works and where was Sunshine. We told her that we missed her and that Titan wouldn't let us come because of me and that he was still jealous of Cut-neck.

"Well if he goes to the shelter and asks for you two and you are not there he would send someone after you," Naffie said.

"We told Sunshine to tell him that we were at the bridge doing our laundry," I said.

"He will send someone to check," Naffie said. "That boy is too jealous."

I told her that I did not care and that it was unfair of him to bother me about other men when he was openly cheating.

"Memuna you are very stubborn and that's good in a way but I think you should be careful," Naffie said. "In fact Cut-neck was only in this town for a few hours and he has gone back, he left almost an hour ago."

"Titan can do what he wants but I know he won't do anything that will lead me to leaving him," I said. He's tried it before and I warned him so he is on probation."

Naffie and her friend laughed and said we needed more stubborn women. Naffie did not want us to go back that evening she wanted us to stay the night. We had to go or else Sunshine would be in big trouble.

So we took off and when we got to the bridge I suggested we use our shortcut so we wouldn't have to bump into Titan on his way to formation.

The shortcut led to the swamp garden and the garden was right behind our shelter. It was already 6.30pm and formation was in progress, so I thought Titan would be there. When we got the to the bushes between the garden and our shelter in front of Edna's kitchen, Magainda decided that I stay and hide among the trees while she went home to check if Sunshine was alone. As soon as she got out of the bushes she saw Titan and CO. Flomo sitting on the chairs at the table in our backyard. They were bombarding Sunshine with questions and she was trying hard to answer their questions about our whereabouts.

Magainda was too slow because they saw her too with the plastic tub of clothes we had exchanged from Water Works on her head shamming tiredness.

"Just one of the women I've been waiting for," Titan said. "Where is your stubborn sister?"

"Ah… ah, she is washing her feet in the garden she stepped on something," Magainda said.

I was standing behind a cacao tree listening to every word they said.

"Where have you two been?" Titan asked.

He questioned Magainda as she walked towards the shelter. Edna and Sao were in Edna's kitchen watching and laughing.

"We were at the bridge washing our clothes," Magainda said. "We told Sunshine."

"Yes I told him," Sunshine interrupted, sounding nervous.

"Try again Magainda, because I sent someone to check on you two at the bridge," Titan said. "CO. Flomo is my witness, ask him."

I was in the bushes laughing at how nervous Magainda and Sunshine were, but then I felt guilty because they were in trouble because of me. It was me who he did not want going to Water Works because I wanted to go more than anyone as I wanted to see Nyalay, after so long. So I decided to come out.

"So what did Memuna step on that she's taking so long to wash off?" Titan asked.

"Here am I," I said.

I was trying hard to wipe the smile off my face but when I saw him I smiled. He smiled back as I walked towards them.

"So you defied me," he said.

"I did not, we were at the bridge," I said.

"Don't say that or you will make me even more upset," he said. "Don't start that now, because I know you were not there."

I turned and looked at Sunshine and Magainda. "Ok, the truth is we went to Water Works," Magainda said.

"Yes I was desperate to see Nyalay and Lucia," I said. "I'm sorry I lied to you and I'm sorry I went."

"Memuna apart from the fact that we are together, you are a soja and if you defy me I have to punish you," he said.

"But this is personal," I said.

"Not entirely because we told you not to use that shortcut again and you did it anyway," Titan said.

"Luckily we did not plant a grenade there," CO. Flomo said.

"I know Memuna and Sunshine too well and I knew they just stood there and heard us that day. They were not even listening when we told them to close that short-cut because they were not going to close it."

We pleaded with him to please let us go this last time but he refused. Instead he and CO. Flomo punished the three of us - Sunshine for lying and Magainda and I for defying him. They made us jog, we did pushups and Magainda and I were made to squat while we held rocks. Because Sunshine did not defy him that punishment was for the two of us. We went on our knees four times from where we stood to the veranda. Then he made us do animal impressions – I would bark like a dog, then Magainda would meow like a cat and Sunshine would say that she wouldn't lie again. It went like this:

Roof....mew....I won't lie again.

We did it five times and I was very angry at Titan. While I did what I was told I thought of a way to make him pay for that. After we did that, he made us jog again, then he told us to stop.

"Now the next time this happens again the punishment will be real and severe," he said. "You will be punished like sojas."

I looked at him as if I was going to throw up on him and I went to the kitchen and got some water to bathe because I was sweating. He knew that I did not want to see him but he stuck around to justify his actions. He told me that he was sorry but he had to do it because I needed to know that he was my superior and if he told me not to go anywhere I should listen to him.

"Besides the camp is not so safe anymore you can't go running around as you like," he said.

"Anyone else can go running around and you wouldn't care so don't give me that," I said.

"Well I care about you and what you do because you are my girlfriend," he said.

"Really, am I your girlfriend," I said. "For the whole of today I've felt more like your child." I was furious and I raised my voice at him.

"I did not mean to make you feel like a child," he said.

"Well you did and I don't think I'm in the mood to have any adult conversation with you now. You want me to be an adult when it suits you just leave me alone."

"I'm sorry about that," he said.

"You know what just stop talking because I don't want to hear anything you have to say for yourself now," I said. "So go to your house and in a year from now when I feel like an adult I will come over to talk about it."

He looked at me for a moment and then at the girls, they had already forgiven him. But I could not because I felt humiliated, I was his girlfriend and he punished me like a child instead of leaving it for us to handle it like adults, so I was really mad at him.

"Look if you need me in anyway please try and contact me," he said. "For example if you feel sick or if you need food or anything please let me know. If you don't want to talk to me just write me a letter but I'm sorry."

I watched him leave and some part of me wanted him to stay but I could not ask him because he made me feel low so I let him go. I knew he would be back the same day so I did not worry about it.

"Wow Memuna you really are blessed," Magainda said. "Because I can't call that luck it's a blessing."

"What are you talking about?" I asked.

"You have a man who loves you so much that he begs you to let him take care of you," she said. "In this place of all places, that is every woman's dream within RUF."

I looked at her thinking, I know and this is what you did not know and you wanted me to leave him and my sisters to follow Magic. I smiled.

I knew that Titan's feelings for me were very strong but he did not always know how to deal with me and that was why I forgave him so often.

It was a slightly windy cool night and the camp was really dark as usual, Lansana and the boys were due back in two days. Magainda, Sunshine and I were sitting on our bed talking. They told me to let the punishment go and forgive Titan. I told them how humiliated I was but they thought it was funny and they made me laugh about it.

Jackson came over that night to spend some time with me but I did not really want him around that night because I was upset with Titan and I wanted to be with the girls and try to forgive him for what he did and having Jackson around was only going to make me more upset with Titan. So I tried to find a way to get rid of him without hurting his feelings.

"What are you doing here this late," I asked.

"I want to see my sweetheart," he said.

"Shouldn't you be by Matilda?" I said. "She might come here looking for you."

"She won't," he said, sounding very sure.

He asked me how I was and I told him that I was not feeling well and that I had a headache. I started faking my yawning, laid on the bed, closed my eyes and told them to talk and I would listen. Jackson felt my forehead and it felt a little warm and he believed me. I did not want him at my shelter, Titan could come over at any time and most of all Matilda Jackson deserved him to be home especially when it was such a dark night.

"Ok I better go to bed then," he said. "You two please look after her, Memuna you get enough sleep and I will see you tomorrow."

All my friends knew how much I hated taking tablets and that's why Jackson did not say anything about medicine that night. He just wished for me to have enough sleep. He tried to give me a goodnight kiss on the lips but I turned and gave him my cheek. I got up and walked out to the veranda with him and as soon as he disappeared into the dark Jonah showed up.

"Where are you going Jonah at this time of the night," I asked.

"I'm coming to you," he said.

"Why, what happened?" I asked.

I thought he was in trouble again. "CO. Titan sent me to give you this," he said, handing me a letter. Titan was still apologising. Jonah tried to run back home as soon as he handed the letter to me but I stopped him. I wanted him to wait until I was through reading the note.

"Jonah you can go now and please tell him not to worry that it is alright," I said.

"What is?" Jonah asked.

"Just say that to him," I said.

"I hope he will understand because I don't want to come back here," Jonah said.

I told him that Titan would understand and he ran off.

Two days later Lansana and the boys got back and that afternoon Titan decided to dress in a school uniform ready to go to school - brown shorts and a blue short-sleeved shirt with a pocket on the left side of the chest and a pair of black school shoes with white socks. He came over to our shelter, making his friends and the boys laugh.

We were in the kitchen at the time but when we heard them laughing we went to the room that used to be Lansana's room. Lansana, Lt. Cross and the boys were there smoking and Titan was there too showing them his uniform. It was really funny he looked like a little boy. I called him outside and asked him if he had been smoking.

'Have you seen me smoke?" he said. "I just think it's fun."

"Well I think you need to go home and get back to normal," I said.

He went home and changed and then came back but we still thought it was funny. Mustapha tried to use that to annoy me; he came to the kitchen and made some remarks. "Memuna, why is your man finding it hard to grow up?" he asked. "That is something my brother would never do."

I ignored him because I would have uttered something against Magic and to be honest with myself I still liked Magic - he had also been my friend. Mustapha did not know our original situation before Magic did what he did to me and I was not going to explain myself to him or any of them. Sunshine told him off for me and he went away laughing.

Tity came a couple of days later and Titan tried to explain to me that he did not invite her. I told him there was no point because it was just not going to end. The next day it rained all morning and we could not go to formation. When it ceased around 5pm in the evening we went to formation.

Titan sent a message saying he was really busy and could not make it to formation so CO. Flomo took his place. Sunshine and I arrived late to formation and we squatted because we were tired of standing. We immediately stood up when we saw Titan coming. CO. Flomo was not pleased that we could not stand to give him courtesy but we stood up when we saw Titan. As a consequence he punished us by making us go back to where Titan was when we saw him and crawl in the mud back to join the formation. Titan saw us being punished but he did not say anything. I thought that was very professional of him and I did not mind it. Sunshine and I were mad at CO. Flomo because we were wearing very nice T-shirts. Magainda and Sao laughed at us from where they stood.

After formation CO. Flomo was upset with us and he ignored us, so we went home cleaned up and went to his shelter to apologise.

"I don't want you girls to ever do that to me again, I like you two girls too much and I don't want to be mad at you," he said.

"We are sorry we won't do it again," Sunshine said and I nodded. I did not know what to do because he had not been mad at me before. I regretted doing that to him and he pardoned us. Titan came to our shelter to ask why we were punished and we told him.

"You girls shouldn't do that," he said. "Sunshine you should know better."

We told him that we were sorry and he stayed to spend some time with his friends and us; after a while they all went to his shelter.

Tity spent two days and went back. Titan, Lansana and Lt. Cross ordered some of the rebels in the camp a week later to build a long building to be used as a school. They considered it really seriously as they brought some new sheets of zinc over to the camp and it was built in two days. It was situated right on the intersection from Jackson's and Franklin's shelter to Vayanga's shelter and right opposite Satu Rocket shelter. It was the brightest and biggest building on the camp. Trees were cut down to use as benches and some people brought their own benches when they had classes.

Magainda came up with some extensions she used to braid my hair and it was my first time to have my hair braided with extensions and I liked it. When I was home, my aunties and grandmothers did not let us use extensions because they said it was too adult and also because it was not allowed at school.

The day after the school building was completed, we went to formation in the morning. On our way back to the shelter Satu Rocket asked me to stay because she had an assignment for me. I was confused I did not know what to say. Lansana did not go to formation that morning and Titan just went, did what he had to do and went back to the shelter as usual. Sunshine saw that I wanted to say something as I was getting upset; so she decided to interfere.

"Satu why do you want Memuna to stay?" Sunshine asked. "What assignment do you have for her?"

"It's not your business," Satu said.

"Oh I think it is because she is my family," Sunshine said.

"Don't argue with me soja," Satu said.

"Yes Sir," Sunshine said. "But permission Sir."

According to RUF there was no female in the army so every commanding officer was referred to as Sir.

"Yes what do you want to say now," Satu said.

It was obvious that she hated me and she was only looking for a way to hurt me because I had something she wanted - Titan did not want her, she was too old for him. She told Sunshine that I was just in the camp and not participating in any activity and Sunshine told her that I was.

"She is the company commander's woman and she looks after him and that's more than you do as a wyes commander," Sunshine said.

She threatened to punish Sunshine. Sunshine asked her to point out a hundred wyeses living in the camp for years who hadn't done anything.

She told me to go and join the group of girls she had gathered. They were going to the ambush town to fetch some greens meant for the wounded soldiers in Zogoda. I did not move a muscle and the sooner she said that than Magainda ran home to call Lansana and Titan. Kasiloi came and got me out of there.

"Satu you are crossing the line," he said. "All the people these girls are involved with are all lieutenants and Memuna is the one of them who is with the company commander and you ask her to go fetch greens. Don't ever do that."

"But the other girls are doing it," Satu said.

"Well these three women are nothing like those other girls," Kasiloi said, "and what I have told you is just from me. CO. Titan and Eagle said that I should tell you not to ever think of doing that again."

Magainda held my hand and we walked away. When we got back to the shelter Titan and Lansana appointed me as one of the teachers to help the children with spellings. I told them that I did not want to.

"Memuna please share what you know with others who need it," Titan said.

"I don't have the patience to teach anyone," I said.

"But you love children," Lansana interrupted. "So please help us, I will help too and Teacher will be the head of the school."

I asked them if they were going to pay the old man and they told me that they were arranging benefits for him. The girls thought it was funny and they teased me about it.

"I will be in your class Memuna." They both teased.

426

The boy smoking with Lansana and Tiger said he was going to be in my class too. "Memuna don't mind that ugly wyes commander," Tiger said. "I think she is just jealous of how pretty you girls are. Bra I think we need a new wyes commander."

We all laughed when he said that.

"I think she will listen to what I just told her," Kasiloi said.

They all looked so high and happy. Titan looked especially happy and I suspected he had been smoking, but it did not show. I decided not to bother him about it because I smoked too and he has not for once caught me or asked me, so I thought it was only fair.

It was cloudy all day but it did not rain. Everyone at our shelter seemed excited. I was excited about my new hairdo although I only had about twenty-five single braids. The boys smoked with Lansana and Lt. Cross in the room and Titan was with them. I was sure he was smoking too. Daniel came for a short while and Robert came soon after he left. He spent some time, ate and went back to the studio because it was a busy day for them. Magainda, Sunshine and I sensed there was something going on but we did not ask.

Titan went home that night and early in the morning, while we were on our way to formation leaving Lt. Cross and Lansana behind, he came to our shelter en route to formation .

After formation we went to open the school and it was the first day of teaching. We had two classes and I was meant to have only children in my class but Salifu, Sunshine, and some other grown-ups with the children were there. It was hard for me to keep a straight face because each time I looked into my friend's faces I laughed. Kasiloi was guarding Lt. Cross and Laser was guarding Lansana that day. They both said but for the fact they were guarding they would have been in my class.

I managed an hour of teaching basic spelling and Teacher took over. I was one of his students. I was wearing a dress that day, the first time in a while. It was one of Magainda's dresses that I used to wear in Kabbaty. I looked pretty and I was complimented by everyone at my shelter and all my friends. Even some of the people from the other side of the camp who knew me, including Titan and Jackson, could not take their eyes off me.

While we were in class a helicopter flew very low over the camp and we saw it. This time there was something weird about how the commanding officers, the boys and the other men in the camp reacted. Normally we would be very nervous and rush to find a hiding place but that day while Sunshine, Magainda, some other women, children and I were struggling to hide for our lives the men were shaking hands and roaring with laughter. We were threatened more by the war helicopter than by the jet, because the helicopter could raid every corner. It came very low but the jet was too large to fit into some places. Any time the helicopter attacked any RUF base it did not go away without killing or hurting someone.

"What is going on now," I asked. "Is the war over?"

They seemed so happy to see the helicopter, no-one tried to shoot it down. I saw it fly fast and that was very unusual.

"I don't know," Sunshine said.

Magainda could not say anything. We stood there looking lost until the excitement wore down. The class had dispersed by then. We asked Lansana why they were excited about seeing the helicopter.

"It just brought the ammunition and medication we have been waiting for," he said.

"Yeah and now all of you are going to have your own guns," Titan said.

"Memuna would like an Israeli AK," Laser said, "because it's not heavy."

I looked at him and rolled my eyes at him.

"I will let this go," I muttered.

"I will like a sister Beretta," Sunshine said. "A brand new one."

"Well everything in that helicopter is new," Titan said.

A sister Beretta is a gun called Beretta and it is very dangerous; not as small as a pistol but not as big as an AK, it is medium-sized. I liked it I think because of the name and it was Sunshine's favourite gun.

Everyone in the camp was excited and I got excited too but I did not know if it was because they were excited or whether it was because of the delivery but I knew that it was hard for anyone to stay serious among so many excited people.

That day our shelter was smoky, it stank of marijuana and we had to cook a lot of food; so did the women at the studio. I tried to get Magainda and Morris to start going out; that was the mission he had for me - he wanted me to tell Magainda that he wanted to go out with her and he would take it from there. All he wanted me to do was to initiate the move. But she was playing hard to get though she liked him too, so Sunshine and I were trying to talk to her.

The following day Tity came to visit Titan in the camp and in the morning someone came with a message that Samia had arrived in Water Works! Sunshine and I hastily packed our bags and went to Water Works leaving Magainda to take care of the men.

Samia was not feeling well and she had lost a lot of weight. When she saw me, she just smiled and she did not look at me. She managed to hug me, she was shy. She had sores on her head, Naffie had already started treating it and she had a rash on her skin. She isolated herself from us that evening but we got her to sit with us anyway. I asked her about Komeh and she told me that Komeh was with Maximilian and that they were going to Freetown Highway.

"So who did you come with?" I asked.

"I hid and joined the convoy that was coming here and no-one gave me anything to eat but I found some food," she said.

It was too sad for me so I tried to change the topic.

"Well you are here now and don't worry all those sores will heal soon and you will get back to your normal weight," I said. "I'm very glad that you were brave enough to join that convoy."

"I missed you and Nyalay so much," she said.

This time it was too much on my heart I was hurting inside seeing her like that and I was grateful that God gave her the brave mind to hide and join those people to come to us.

Tears streamed down our faces as we looked at her.

"Hey, you two need to stop crying, Samia will be ok soon," Naffie said. "We did some native medicine for her to bathe with and some for her to drink. As for her head the sores are drying up now. It was worse when she arrived two days ago."

I thanked Naffie and Sunshine. Nyalay and I tried to cheer Samia up. Lansana was due to come and see her in three days and when we told her that she was glad.

"Samia, I want you to know we did not forget about you," Sunshine said, "Lansana and CO. Titan have been trying to get you here. Oh and by the way CO. Titan is our new brother-in-law, Memuna's husband."

"Shut up you," I said, smiling.

"Really Memuna," Samia said. "Is he a CO?"

I nodded. "He is a lieutenant and he is Lansana's friend."

"Good because Magic did not really care about me," she said.

Again it hurt me that even at this point he was still disappointing me. I had lost trust in him and most men by then so I believed her when she said that.

"Well don't worry now. You are here and you are trained so we won't be separated again," I said, trying to put another smile on her face. "I'm sure Komeh will be fine, she will miss us very much but she will be fine."

As I said those words tears came from my eyes because Komeh was not only my cousin, she was also my best friend. The two of us used to do naughty things together in Sembehun and I loved her very much. My heart ached when I thought of her. I was very happy to see Samia but at the same time it hurt so much thinking about Komeh alone with those boys. I just wished I could fly to go and get her. I cried every day.

Samia told me that they did not really train them; it was more like a punishment. She told me about how she used to go and work for one of the RUF's captains called CO. Ramona who was a Liberian. CO. Ramona was not nice and she mistreated them. I told her to just try and forget about all the bad things that happened to them in Koribondo Jungle where they had been held. Instead she should focus on getting better and then, when she was back to normal, we could talk about it. I was hurt in my heart when I matched the picture of what she was telling me to the way she looked. Naffie was really good though and she took care of Samia as if she were her own.

429

"You girls have seen Samia. Now try and go back to your camp you are crowding up my house," she said. "I have three daughters now to look after."

The herbs they concocted for Samia to drink really gave her appetite and so she was gaining weight fast. Naffie gave her lots of food to eat and her sores were healing fast. I was really grateful to Naffie. I thanked her and we left two days later. Sania wanted to follow me. She cried when I told her I was going back to the camp. As I stood outside Naffie's house ready to leave I could not bear Samia's tears, we were separating again.

"Don't cry Nyalay is here," I pleaded with her as my heart hurt so much. "Samia, you are a soja and you can come to the camp any time you want; all you have to do is ask Naffie," Sunshine told her.

"But try and get well first and gain some strength," I said.

Nyalay held her hand and they went back to the house.

"Lansana is coming to see you," I said as I waved goodbye.

When Sunshine and I arrived at the camp, there were a few new faces in the camp but also one old friend. On our way home we bumped into Ma Tenneh - the old lady I met in Libya who knew my grandfather. She was living in the house of the commanding officer called Vamboi. They lived close to the entrance of the camp and we always had to walk through their yard to go to our shelter if we did not use our shortcut. She was sitting in the kitchen with Vamboi's young girlfriend. I was so excited to see her and when she saw Sunshine and me she was very excited and gave us each a big hug. The whole time I spoke to Ma Tenneh, I spoke in Mende.

"When did you get here my child?" she asked.

"We've been here six months since the beginning of this year," I said. "I could not say goodbye to you when we were leaving Libya because we were in different villages."

"So how are you, Ma Tenneh?" Sunshine enquired.

"Thank God I'm here now my child but I'm a bit sore in my body from the long walk from Libya," she said.

Vamboi's girlfriend was a young girl but she was not friendly and she liked to frown. All the while we were there talking to Ma Tenneh she did not say a word to us and we did not bother to say anything more than "hello" to her. She was not like us, how we talked and joked with each other. I was glad that Ma Tenneh was now in the camp. She kept a close watch on me just to make sure I was taking good care of myself and that I was treating myself with respect. She wanted to go with us to our shelter but because she was helping the girl in the kitchen and we had just arrived, she asked us to take her later.

We told Magainda about Samia and what she told us, but I did not bring out the bit about Magic not taking care of Samia because it was unnecessary. I did not want us arguing about Magic again and I still hurt anytime I heard his name. Magainda could not wait to see Samia but she was too scared to walk alone to Water Works. We told her Samia would come and visit us in the camp when she felt better. Lansana was getting ready to go to Water Works but he was a bit cranky because he was hungry.

"He's been giving me a hard time all morning," Magainda said. "He thinks that I have just been playing around the yard."

She had been busy trying to make something for Lansana to eat before he left and she was already done. We found her dishing out the food when we arrived.

"Memuna are you feeling better now?" Lansana asked, when he came for his food.

"Yeah, but I'm worried about Komeh and I miss her so much it hurts," I said.

"Well, who knows, we might see her again soon," he said. "So how is Samia? I hear she is sick."

"Yes. She has sores on her head and rashes on her skin, but Naffie is doing well with her," I informed him, without my usual scorn.

"I'm going to see her," Lansana said. "I hope she won't be mad at me."

"I told her that we did not forget about her," Sunshine said, over her shoulder, she was trying to cook.

Lansana thanked her. Lansana and I were really close and I understood why Naffie was so insecure because Lansana was always ok when I was around him. When we arrived that afternoon he was like a little boy, giving Magainda trouble because he was hungry but when he saw me he was calmer. He ate and warned me to look after myself; his tone was very strong but sweet. We all knew what he meant when he said that and he said it every time he went away. He was warning me not to have sex.

"My brother wants you to keep your virginity for him," Sunshine would tease me. We all knew that Lansana never gave up on his feelings for me.

Titan slept at our shelter that night and he got really serious about me reducing the beads on my waist but I refused.

"Why do you want so much?" he said.

"Because I like them and this is my first time having them so I want to keep them all," I said.

"Well I don't like them," he said.

"You don't have to," I said. "Just pretend as if they are not there." Getting upset he told me that I only needed one strand but I did not mind him. I let him sulk till he fell asleep. My beads were so many that one could see the thick line around my waist when I wore something tight and very often a few strands would pop out of my skirt or pants. The first few nights when I had just got them it was a bit hard for me to sleep with them. I used to jokingly call them 'my heavy anchor chain' but I soon got used to having them on.

Just in time for us to go to formation Ma Tenneh arrived at our shelter. She was always well dressed and she always wore her head-tie matching the clothes she wore. I was glad I bumped into her as soon as she was entering the veranda.

"Morning girls," she said.

"Morning Ma Tenneh," we said.

Magainda did not know her but greeted her anyway. I introduced Ma Tenneh to Magainda and I told her we were going to formation. She asked for Lansana and we told her he was in Water Works. She walked with us on our way to formation as the formation ground was just next to her shelter. I was glad that she did not see Titan because I did not know how to introduce them. I did not want to give her a shock, as she did not know I had a boyfriend. So we left Titan in bed; he did not want to go to formation that morning.

When we got home he was still in bed. I sat on the bed next to him and rubbed my nose on his. As he did not utter a sound, I tickled him and he smiled.

"Are you still sulking about my beads?" I asked.

"I really don't like that many of them," he said.

"Well we need to reach a compromise," I suggested. "I always liked these things when I was in Liberia. I used to see them on those girls who did the tribal dancing on TV in Sembehun - I wished I'd had some. Then I got a lot when we went to Libya and now you are telling me to get rid of them."

"Not all," he said.

"You are telling me to get rid of forty nine strands, why?" I said. "If I'm going to do it, it will take time."

He agreed, got up and went home to bathe and change his clothes.

"I will see you soon," he said.

It was a rainy day and I thought about whether I was prepared to lose my beads because he did not like them. I sat in the kitchen with Sunshine and Magainda as they cooked and that thought ran through my mind all evening. So I decided to smoke but the girls told me to wait till the evening.

Later that evening Titan insisted I lose forty-nine strands of beads and I told him that I had tried but I could not. He got upset with me and told me that Tity only had one strand.

"Oh, so you want to compare me with Tity now," I said.

"No," he said. "But I'm sure that if this was her she would listen to me."

"Well she has no mind of her own that's why," I quickly retorted, "if you want Tity with her one strand of beads then have her because I'm really tired."

I stormed out of our room wanting to compare him with Magic in his face but I could not bring myself to say Magic's name because just thinking of him brought tears to my eyes. I sat in a chair with the girls but on the dark side of the veranda, where the lamp could not show my face. I missed Magic so much I was in tears. At that moment I wished he were here. I

432

stared into the darkness as the cold wind blew my face and calmed my heart. When I was strong enough to talk, I told Magainda that I was sleeping in Lansana's room alone. We had a smoke and I went to bed. Titan did not stay the night.

CHAPTER TWENTY SIX

Unexpected Feeling

The following morning after formation Titan came to our shelter for us to talk but as I did not even want to look at him I told him to leave me alone. I could not believe he would do something so rude and stupid by comparing me with that girl. I refused to have anything to do with him for almost two weeks. He got his brother to ask him to please forgive him.

Lansana and the boys were back so I got too busy to bother myself thinking about what Titan had said to me. I missed Magic very much but I kept it all to myself because I did not think Magainda was willing to listen to me. In my heart I wished I was home then all I would have to worry about was waking up in the morning to go to school.

"Please forgive my brother," CO. Flomo said.

I looked at him and smiled because I did not know what to say. The first thing that came to my mind to say to CO. Flomo was that Magic would have never said what Titan had said to me. I was sure of it, but at this point I did not want to talk to anyone about Magic.

"Please Memuna, say something," CO. Flomo said. But I didn't.

A few days after Lansana came back to the camp from Water Works, Naffie came with Samia, Nyalay and Lucia. We were so excited we were jumping and screaming around. Titan was visiting Lansana that morning after formation. Titan liked Samia. He greeted her politely and they talked. But I was still mad at him. He took Samia up to his shelter and when she came back she was really fond of him and I was pleased. The camp was getting dangerous so Naffie and the girls only spent a night and went back. Three days after they left, Lansana was sent away again, so we were left with Titan in charge again.

In the morning as I woke up I was feeling so home sick, I did not want to get out of bed. It was a cloudy day and I was in a very complicated mood. I had this huge feeling of want. I knew that I wanted my mother but deep down it was more than that, but I did not know what. I did not want to talk to anyone in the camp except Magainda and Sunshine. I finally got out of bed and, walking to the backyard, asked them if they wanted to go to the bridge for a swim.

"It's a bit chilly, I don't think I want to swim," Sunshine said. "Why don't you and Magainda go while I will cook today?"

Magainda and I went to the bridge and stayed there till 5pm. She could see the pain in my eyes and we talked a little about what I was going through that day. I soon changed the topic to boy-talk; because I was close to telling her that I missed the way I had fun with Magic. We talked about Franklin Morris and her and my two men and me - Jackson and Titan - and we laughed about it. When we finally got home I felt so physically bad that my jaws could not open for me to talk. I was very weak. Sunshine was dishing out the food and asked if Magainda and I were ready to eat so we could eat together in the big tray as usual but looking at the food and inhaling the smell I just felt sicker.

"Sunshine, can you dish mine aside please and I will eat later," I asked

"You look tired Memuna, are you pregnant?" Edna teased from her kitchen.

I looked at her, smiled and shook my head. Titan could not stop looking at me. I left them and went to bed. A few minutes later I was really sick, I was feverish but my temperature was not that high and I was cold. I could not let out a word. I was too weak so I stayed lying down hoping that someone would come and talk to me or just keep an eye on me.

Titan came to talk to me but I couldn't say anything. So he climbed into bed and lay next to me but in snuggling up to me he was shocked at how hot my body felt.

"Memuna, what is the matter?" he asked.

They had finished eating already and were just chatting. I could hardly keep my eyes open; deeply frightened I was screaming inside. I did not know what was happening to me. I had tears streaming down my eyes and I could hear everything said to me but it was like I was paralysed. We all thought I was possessed but I could not see things or hear anything strange.

"Memuna talk to me," Magainda cried. "You know, I'm Magainda and you can talk to me."

I wanted to tell her that I wanted to talk but I could not talk. All I did was look at her as tears kept spilling down. She cried too and even Titan had tears in his eyes. He thought I was angry because of what he said to me so he asked Magainda to please excuse us.

"Memuna, I swear to God and my life I really regret saying what I said,' he said. 'I did not mean it. Please talk to me and forgive me."

I wanted to tell him so much that something else was happening to me, but I could not. Getting hysterical I managed to move my hand to touch my forehead.

"Do you have a headache?" he asked.

A slight headache had started so I batted my eyes. He called out to Magainda again and asked her to go and call the doctor. As Magainda ran off to Vayanga's yard Sunshine and Titan tried to get me to keep my eyes open and try to talk. Titan kissed my face and massaged my jaw so I could say something. All this time he was shaking.

"Memuna please think about Nyalay, Samia and Komeh and us," Sunshine said, now also crying "And try to get better."

Titan thought the doctor was taking too long so he told Sunshine to keep on talking to me as he ran off to get them. A minute later I was able to let out some words.

Struggling I said, "I'm so… weak Sunshine."

"Oh, oh talk to me," she said. "Take your time."

Titan and Magainda came running into the room with the doctor. He checked me and gave me some pills and a few Panadol tablets.

"Keep her cool, keep an eye on her and let her sleep," he told them.

According to him I was going through a lot of stress and had a fever as well. Titan did not leave my side that night. I spent the night with him in Lansana's room and I had a sound sleep. I woke up very early in the morning. Titan was fast asleep so I just lay in bed thanking God for giving me a second chance.

At the crack of dawn Magainda knocked at our door to see if I was better, and when she heard my voice she was very happy. She greeted Titan and told us she was going to formation with Sunshine.

"Memuna are you better now my sister?" Sunshine asked.

"Yes I feel a little tired but I'm fine," I said. "I know what it feels like when people lose their speech, though."

"Well thank God you are alright now," Magainda answered, relief in her voice.

"Magainda let's go before we run late," Sunshine said.

As they walked out I looked at Titan. "You really shook me yesterday you know," he said.

"I don't know why I could not talk," I said. "I was really scared."

"Please try not to be so stressed," Titan said.

"The only way that could happen is for my sisters, uncle and me to be taken back home," I replied.

Titan promised I would go home one day and that I just needed to keep my faith and be strong. He was a very affectionate person and he gave me a lot of attention and affection.

Two weeks later Titan went to Zogoda again. He said he was going for a meeting with Lion. When he told me, I just nodded and wished him a safe trip because I knew he was lying to me. He came back a few days later, late in the night, with a little boy around eleven years of age. He passed by our shelter to say hello to me and see if I was doing ok, and then he went home. The following morning he came to our shelter after formation with the boy and introduced me as his girlfriend to the little boy.

"Memuna this is Jeremiah," Titan said, introducing the boy to me.

He held my hand and took me aside to talk to me about where he got Jeremiah.

"I want to tell you something," Tity said.

"Yes," I said.

"But please don't get upset," Tity said.

I promised him I wouldn't get upset.

"Well Jeremiah is Tity little brother and he threw a tantrum to come with me," Titan said.

Disbelievingly I just looked at him, completely lost for words.

"You are vexed," Titan said.

"Oh, no I'm not," I said. "You have your own shelter you can keep him there."

"I am really sorry," Titan said. "I'm not doing anything to annoy you; I promise you will like the boy, Jeremiah is very interesting. Just give him a chance."

I did not have anything against Jeremiah it's just that I did not want to hear Titan say the word 'Tity'. Jeremiah seemed to be an interesting little boy. That evening he stayed with Magainda, Sunshine and me for dinner and we enjoyed his company. Jeremiah talked about his life before with his mother and Tity. He was captured with his other sister and he told me some names of his friends.

The evening after formation, Titan wanted to take Jeremiah home to their shelter to sleep but he refused.

"No, can I please stay with Memuna," Jeremiah requested. "I like her CO Titan,"

Shocked, but in a good way, I told Titan it was ok for him to stay.

"Memuna is that lucky with children, they like her and she is good with them," Magainda said.

Jeremiah was too spoilt but was a funny little boy. He told the girls and me stories all night until I had to tell him to stop talking and close his eyes as it was time to sleep. He snuggled up to me and fell asleep. In the morning I sent Jeremiah to Titan's shelter to brush his teeth, bathe and change his clothes. He went but before I knew it Jeremiah was back at my shelter. Magainda, Sunshine, Sao and Edna teased me about my new son, especially when Sao and Edna found out that he was Tity's brother. They teased me, but they liked Jeremiah too. That afternoon Jeremiah told me a lot about his sister and Titan.

"My mother is trying to get CO. Titan to marry Tity," Jeremiah said.

"How do you know about this?" I asked.

Magainda and Sunshine pinched me because they knew I was going to tell Jeremiah that I did not want to hear anything about his sister. I ignored them and listened.

"I hear them talking," Jeremiah said. "I think CO. Titan really likes you Memuna, more than my sister. I overheard him and Tity quarrelling one day because he called my sister 'Memuna' by mistake."

I laughed. This was the best news since Tity decided to interfere in my life. Magainda and Sunshine were also happy to hear that Titan had called Tity 'Memuna'. It was then I knew that Magainda had finally accepted that Titan and I liked each other.

"So Jeremiah what did Tity do?" Magainda asked.

"She was really angry and when CO. Titan came back here to the camp she told our mother and she was in tears," replied Jeremiah, unaware of the importance of this information he so freely gave to us.

Jeremiah told me about how Tity thought she was possessed and that she saw 'things'. She thought she saw evil things like what happened to Magainda and Mbalu. He also told me that Titan went to the civilian camp and got a white cock and a silver ring which they took to Zogoda and performed a sacrificial rite to get rid of the evil spirit. Since the ceremony Tity had had no more attacks from the evil spirits.

When I heard this I was really disappointed and angry because all this time Titan had been entreating that I do not bathe at night for fear that I would get possessed too.

That night I confronted Titan about everything Jeremiah told me. He said he was just an observer. He told me that he did not have anything to do with the events that took place. Of course I did not believe him. He was having an affair with Tity so why would I believe him. He swore that he did not have anything to do with the ceremony and I gave him the benefit of the doubt.

"Fine but leave me to bathe whenever I want! You can't protect me and then be involved with something that will hurt me when you are not here, including your lies!" I screamed at him.

"But I love you or else I wouldn't bother," he argued back.

"Do you really know what you feel? Because I think you are confused," I snapped, not caring about his stupid love.

"Well you don't know what's going on in my head. Just believe that I had nothing to do with it," he argued.

He stormed off in a huff. He promised to come back to spend the night, which he did and we continued our conversation about the sacrifice. Before he returned there was another conversation I had to have.

"Memuna, why do you argue with Titan all the time? It's your fault that he's cheating! You are not ready for sex and the man needs sex, so you should let him get it from somewhere else!" Magainda had no qualms saying what she wanted to say. Sunshine agreed with her.

"He knew I was not ready for sex when he asked me out!" Was all my argument with them was going to be.

Jeremiah went back to Zogoda after a week. Two weeks later Tity came to visit. It had rained that day and the camp was empty because it was becoming too dangerous. Some Kamajors had tried to attack the camp a few times but we but stayed on. Lansana and Titan were planning to move a few of his bodyguards and us to Tobanda.

Tity left the morning after she had arrived and I asked Titan why she left so suddenly considering she had travelled eighteen miles on foot just to see him. He told me that he did not want her to be there. I hadn't seen Titan for hours since I was at his hour that morning so I decided to go and visit him so we could spend some time together. When I got there he was nowhere to be seen and no-one could tell me his whereabouts. The moon was full that night so the girls and I decided to go to the other side of the camp. I went to Sao's house first and that's where I saw Titan talking to CO. Flomo. I heard a strange woman's voice in the background and CO. Flomo telling Titan to get rid of her because I was in the house. They left together but I went outside just in time to see them disappear into the bushes heading to the other side of the camp. Sunshine and I followed but they ran off but I could see him heading towards his shelter so I followed him. He told his bodyguards not to let me through. But I told them not to touch me as he would not like them touching me, so I got past them and all they could do was repeat to me what he had said that - that I was not allowed through. He told me that nothing was going on between them and he was just talking to her.

"Why did you run from me if nothing was going on?" I asked.

He repeated himself over and over again but I was so angry I went to the studio to talk to Daniel and Robert. On my way back to my shelter I got the chance to confront CO. Flomo.

"Why did you tell Titan and the girl to run away from me?"

"That girl's ex-boyfriend was Titan and Lansana's friend," he said. "This is not about you."

"Well running off just made them look guilty," I said, trying not to get angry with him.

To my knowledge he did not see her again. Titan and I argued about it but a few days later I dropped it because I ended up believing his story.

The guys went on missions less often and we started running out of food. We had to make do with the food from the forest. A few weeks later they moved Magainda, Sunshine and me to Tobanda with Soja and Salifu to guard us. We moved into an unfinished house which was not painted and the living room windows, and front and back doors, needed to be installed. The doors and windows in the other rooms were already installed. There were three rooms in the house: one for Lansana whenever he came over to check on us, one for the boys, and one for us girls. We were excited to be in the town as it was as close to normalcy as we could get. Ma Tenneh had moved to the town a week before we did. There were a few old ladies, poultry and goats. I was happy to be in a proper house although it was unfinished. We made brick bed bases and put our mattresses on them.

There were two in our room; one in Lansana's room and Salifu and Soja had theirs in their room.

Two days later, Fina and CO Feel-good moved into the house next to us. We were not pleased, as he checked on our every move and then told on us. Even the boys were upset he was in Tobanda but we still managed to have fun and have guests over. Jackson came over to visit us and he spent the night.

One morning Sunshine and I went for a walk around town while Magainda was home with Franklin.

We went to a house at the other end of town. It was a little isolated with lots of orange trees and grass around it. It seemed a little scary but the orange trees were too much of an attraction. As we walked closer to the house it seemed more and more as though there was no-one living there. We got to the house and called out in Mende.

"Hello... is anyone here?"

After a few calls, we heard an answer in Mende. The person sounded like an old lady. "I'm here," she said. "Who is it?"

"Just some visitors," Sunshine replied.

We gently opened the squeaky door and went into the first room. The door was ajar and we could see the old lady's legs. She was sitting on her bed staring straight through the window. We walked towards her slowly as she was shaking in fear.

"How are you Mama?" Sunshine said.

"Am alive, thanks be to God," she replied gently.

The house was clean though it smelt weird. The old lady's room was bright with her window open the morning sunlight shining right through. We told her we were drawn to the house because of the orange trees.

"Why, did you just see those trees after all this time?" she asked.

"We just moved here from the camp," Sunshine said.

We did not tell her we were rebels as we did not think she could handle it. She started relaxing as we spoke to her. Sunshine and I sat by her on the bed - one person on either side. Sunshine held her hand but because I was still scared of strange old ladies I sat there trying to build up the courage to hold her hand. But then she reached for mine. She told us she was blind and that was why she did not know that we were strangers in Tobanda.

"You young girls sound like two well brought up Mende girls. God bless you," she said.

We told her our names and she told us her name but we called her Mama as she was an old lady.

"I live here with my brothers," she said.

"Oh really, where are they?" I asked.

"They said they were going to check the nets they set last night for some fish or they might try to do some fishing at the stream in the forest near the village," she said.

"How long have you been here?" Sunshine asked.

"This is my village," she said. "My children and some of my other family members ran to Blama when we were first attacked by the rebels. I think my children are now in Bo."

"But you stayed?" I asked.

"Well I'm old, I can't run, so I told them to go and leave me," she explained. She could still see on the day of the attack and she told us how she witnessed the rebels killing many people she had known.

"After I saw all of that I ran to my room and did not go out. For months I stayed in the dark. I would have been dead a long time ago. My brothers ran in the forest trying to go to Blama but they were not successful so they came back after a few weeks of living in the cold forest."

I was so sad and ashamed that I was now one of the rebels. Sunshine and I could not help our tears streaming down our faces.

"My brothers have been looking after me since then and I still don't like to go outside," she said. "They take me out to use the rest room and they do everything else."

"How do you and your brothers get food?" Sunshine asked her.

"I don't know because I can't see anymore and I don't ask many questions," she said. "Food was not really a problem for my brothers and I but sometimes they'll cook without salt because we do not have any."

"Well as long as we are here you will not run out of salt anymore," I promised.

"Yes Mama, and please tell us whenever you need something and we will do our best to help," Sunshine added kindly.

Her brothers arrived back calling out to her from the backyard.

"I've got two young visitors, come and see them," she answered.

When they saw us they looked frightened although we were just two teenage girls. I think they knew we were rebels. Sunshine and I greeted them as we would greet our elders in normal situations. The old men introduced themselves to us.

"We just moved here from the camp on Blama Highway," Sunshine said, "and we were just walking around town and saw your oranges."

"Oh do you want to pick some?" one of the old men said.

"Please can we have some?" Sunshine asked.

"I think they are good children although I can't see them," the old lady said.

Her brothers agreed with her and volunteered to pick us some oranges. We left the old lady to rest and went to the backyard. As one of them picked the oranges with a stick he told us the same story his sister had told us but with a little difference.

"My sister's skin was not that light but because of the terrible things she saw on the day of the attack on us she only comes out to bathe or use the lavatory," the old man said, "and now she is blind and pale."

441

Chasing the oranges that rolled into the bushes, I whispered to Sunshine, "What are we going to say now?"

"Pa, do you smoke?" Sunshine asked.

"Yes," he said, "when I have it. I tried to grow some tobacco but it did not work out."

"Well we will bring you some salt and tobacco in the evening," I promised him.

"Do you have some salt to cook with?" Sunshine asked.

He said that they did not have salt so we took the basket of oranges and went home. As soon as we got home I ran back to their house with a cup of salt.

"We will bring the tobacco as soon as we can but for now here is some salt," I said.

They were really grateful and they all started praying for us but I had to run back to the house as we had some guests over.

"Amen, God will answer," I said over my shoulder as I ran off

Kasiloi and the other boys had come over from the camp and I did not want to miss the excitement.

We visited the old people every day and we always gave them tobacco and salt.

A few weeks after we moved into the house I was not well. Magainda was cooking but I knew I could not eat so I asked her to leave me out when she dished out the food. I was becoming unwell again because a few days earlier I had accidentally kicked a sheet of zinc and I now had a huge cut on the back of my foot. I had lost a lot of blood. Refusing to go to the hospital because it was in the camp and far away, the following morning when I woke up, my ankle was swollen and I could not walk.

"Magainda," I begged my sister "run to the camp for some medicine for me please."

Magainda went to the camp and a few hours later she returned wearing only her half-slip and brassiere she had on when she left.

"Where are your clothes?" I asked.

"Paegie attacked me; she had a razor blade, Magainda explained, still shaking, "she laid an ambush for me near the bridge telling me to choose between my skin and clothes so I just stood there. She tore up my skirt and top with the blade."

Magainda was lucky that one of the ambush guards found them there and took them both back to the camp.

"Paegie was punished and made to go on guard for two weeks."

Two days later I was able to walk so I went to the camp for my treatment. I was given a shot for tetanus and some antibiotics for the swelling.

Kasiloi and his brothers were not at the camp. They had gone to the newly found town. We went to visit Naffie and there we found out that someone we knew had died but we did not know who it was.

We returned to Tobanda and the boys came to see us in tears. They told us it was Kasiloi. He suffered a gunshot wound to the head and though he lived through the night, he died the next afternoon. Devastated, I could not stop crying. I could not eat for two weeks. I could not believe I had lost another person. After that Magainda and I went back to Tobanda.

A month later we had to move from Tobanda to Water Works because the camp kept being attacked. Everyone left to find a new camp, town or village where they knew someone to stay with. We went to the new camp and everything was different. This camp was between Ngovokpanhun and Water Works about a mile and a half away from the old camp.

One sunny afternoon I went to the camp with Lansana and I was meant to stay for a few weeks. That night I had a dream that the Kamajors attacked us. The following morning, while we were in the kitchen eating wild yams, I told Rain and the boys about my dream. Scoffing, they laughed at me telling me that I had too much to eat the night before.

Minutes later we heard gunshots. We thought the shots were from one of Lieutenant Colonel Mohammed's bodyguards on their way back to Zogoda. Again we heard gunfire but this time it did not sound like it was fired from an AK. It sounded like a single barrel hunter's gun. Panicking I rushed to the room to pack some things preparing to run. Fortunately Magainda had just arrived from Water Works in time to leave with us. But before I could say anything to her I saw Lt. Cross running towards our shelter screaming for his daughter Strength. He screamed for Rain to take her, take her and run because the hunters were coming. Everybody came running out of the shelters screaming and crying. Magainda grabbed one bag, I grabbed another and we ran to the other side of the forest, bypassing Ngovokphun, trying to reach the motorway towards Water Works. As we ran I lost both my slippers and stepped into someone's faeces. Still running I was trying to clean my feet. They were getting sore too from running barefooted in the bush. Magainda kept urging me to run faster,

"Faster Memuna faster."

Lansana was in the advance team with the other men but we were stuck in the bush trying to make our way through with Second-phase and CO. Flomo. Quickly Fambuleh swung his machete cutting down trees and bushes to clear the way for us. Babies and adults cried in the chaos. My body was aching everywhere, while the grass cut my legs through the skirt I was wearing, but more importantly I was scared.

Hours later, exhausted, bruised and still running, we found ourselves in a huge swamp near Ngovokphun used by RUF to germinate rice. The swamp was deep with mud that came up to my waste. Crossing it we trampled the rice and it all sunk to the bottom. We formed a single file and tried to get out of the swamp quietly without the Kamajors hearing us. CO. Flomo, Sao, Magainda, Rain and the baby, and I followed Second-phase, behind the advance team with the other group of strong fighters - Lansana had asked Second-phase to stay behind for us. I chose to stand in third position because we were all depending on the two in front. If anything happened to them I would die fast and painless too. As we emerged from the swamp we heard a voice in the darkness asking us to identify ourselves.

"Shhh," Second-phase said to the rest of us.

"Let's answer. They could be looking for us," I said.

"How do you know they are not Kamajors using our password?" he demanded.

I remained silent. We spent the night at the shallow end of the swamp. Though it was very cold there were lots of mosquitoes. Angry, at Lansana for bringing us into the war and at Foday Sankoh for starting the war, I wept all night. Early the next morning we carefully continued on our way to Water Works.

For hours we roamed in the forest searching for a way out and wound up in a cacao farm. Despite having got out safely we bumped into a group of rebels who almost shot us thinking we were the Kamajors.

"We have been in ambush all night searching for you lot," the sojas complained at us. "We heard voices in the swamp, but no-one identified themselves."

"We stayed in the cold all night," complained one.

I looked at Second-phase, "You see, I told you."

"When this is all over we will make you a lieutenant," he replied sarcastically.

"All I want is to go home to my family," I reminded him.

We arrived in Water Works to find the whole town in chaos with everybody screaming, packing and crying. The men were really serious and ready to shoot. There was no refuge here so we continued walking to Bandawoh, four miles away. Drisa and some of Lansana's friends had arranged some rooms for us in Bandawoh. We stayed there for a few weeks but then returned to Water Works thinking it was safe. We were attacked again just a few weeks later. This time the attack happened between Bandawoh and Water Works in a place called Kpetema. The Kamajors had made their way from the camp through the forest to Kpetema using the back forest route. Two grenade ambushes and a man ambush guarded the town but the Kamajors were unaware of this. They triggered one of the grenade ambushes setting off one of the bombs. Frantically we ran to the entrance of Kpetema on the highway between Bandawoh and Water Works. This way we escaped to Bandawoh before they attacked from the other direction. Gunfire rang out through the whole of Water Works and everything and everyone was in chaos. RUF reinforcements came from Bandawoh to help the men in Water Works attack the Kamajors in Kpetema before they reached the highway to Bandawoh. They had to protect Bandawoh as it was RUF's third battalion base.

My feet were sore and cut up underneath from all the running and my legs were quivering. Samia made sure she was close to Nyalay and I kept a close watch on them urging them on as we ran. Bandawoh was about a mile and a half away so we got there in an hour.

We sat for a while, huddled together in Bandawoh to rest as the shooting in Ngovokphun went on for hours. The rebels there retreated to Bandawoh with a few of them wounded. They said the Kamajors had retreated as well but we still had to be ready for anything. Sick and weak I was really tired from all the running. We ate dinner and Naffie sent the younger children to get some sleep while we sat in readiness.

There was now a new person in our group called Salamata. She and her sister had come from Senegal to visit their grandmother in Sierra Leone when they got captured. Her boyfriend(captor) was Lieutenant Colonel Mohammed's (RUF second in command) senior bodyguard called Cyclone but she had run away from their group because she had a miscarriage and needed time to think. She decided to stay with us for as long as she wanted.

Nothing more happened that night and it stayed quiet for a whole month. I was relieved but still anxious and scared because I knew that anything could happen at any time. Food was really hard to come by in Bandawoh.

One afternoon I walked to another part of town to visit a friend of mine called Edith. She was not in the house but a girl called Manja spoke to me. She asked for my name and said she wanted us to be friends and I agreed. We would often meet together and talk as if we were not in the middle of a war zone. It helped us forget and grab some semblance of normality even though fear still ruled our lives. Any time we got together Manja, Salamata and I made it obvious we were against everything RUF stood for. This way we had something meaningful to talk about.

Cyclone made another attempt at begging Salamata to go back to him and she agreed but she stayed with us and only visited him when she felt like it. He understood that she needed to take her time to go back to him.

A month later the Kamajors attacked us again. This attack was the most intense yet. Cyclone came running to us and scooped up Salamata.

"Please let me help. I can't leave you like this," he pleaded.

Salamata and I were sick on that day; she suffered from sickle cells and I had a terrible headache. She let him help and so, in tears, we all quickly said our goodbyes and wished to see each other again.

We ran. We ran faster as the gunfire increased and got closer. Suddenly I could not feel my headache any longer. All I felt was anger and the urge to pick up an AK and put into action what I was taught during training. As I ran in tears I was more and more convinced that's what I should do. Before that day I believed that any troop that fought against the RUF was right - that they fought for their country and the innocent people of the country; people like my grandmothers and others who could not stand for themselves. But on that day I just wanted to kill every Kamajor seeing them as my real enemy. I believed I was a real trained rebel and I had to be loyal to myself. Later, when I heard the Kamajors singing that they were happy they had chased us out of our battalion base, I was filled with hatred for the Kamajors. In the September rain I had never felt so much like a rebel before, or after, that day.

The rebels could not shoot at the Kamajors because they had used some kind of voodoo preventing the rebels from using their weapons. Running as fast as we could before I knew it we were in Target Q about twelve miles away from Bandawoh. Total chaos was here as well but a few RUF commanding officers told the people of Target Q they had nothing to worry about. The rebels asked them to tell the Kamajors that they were all civilians and the Kamajors would not harm them.

Out of breath, angry and frightened it was really hard for me to breathe. Nyalay, Samia, Naffie, Magainda, Lucia, Rain and I made sure we were always together, running and hiding. We could still hear the blasts from the bombs and sharp screech through the air of the shooting coming from Bandawoh and around Target Q civilian camp. The Kamajors did not use bombs at that time; it was the rebels who were bombing. This gave me some courage that we were going to get some breaks from running in the September rain. As soon as I could breathe properly, some rebels came running and yelling loudly, terror filling their voices.

"Run…run! They are coming! We can't stop them!"

Tears streaming down my face, I frantically searched through the running crowds of men for Lansana. We could not afford to lose him.

Another rebel came screaming past me, "They caught Captain Sir Ace and CO. Bai Bureh and beheaded them!"

Sadness filled me and my mind quickly flashed back to the day I first met Sir Ace and deeper tears rolled down my cheeks. Frozen on the spot Naffie pushed me to get me running, yelling at me,

"Run Memuna, do you want to die you stupid girl?"

Naffie ran with Lucia tied to her back. She was a good baby and, even with fear and confusion in her eyes, she stayed calm but clung closely to her mother's warmth.

Chaos and fear broke everyone. Running through the forest and coffee farms a woman screamed at her rebel boyfriend to help her carry their young daughter, threatening to leave her on the side of the path. He tried to ignore her but she soon took the baby off her back and placed her on the side of the path, quickly turning to run. Panicked he took up the baby running after the mother screaming, "We can do this together."

Soon we were in Sir Ace's ground thirteen miles away. We did not spend an hour because it was time to keep running further away from the attacking Kamajors.

While we rested we were told the Kamajors had captured two RUF members in Bandawoh - a trained wyes and a five-year old boy. I knew the little boy's father, his name was Kamanda. Kamanda and Sin-child lived in the same yard on the Blama Highway camp and they were friends. That little boy knew all the camps in that area including Zogoda. He also knew all the commanding officers and their partners, most by name and some he could match the face with the name.

The Kamajors captured the wyes with her baby. She had the cowries around her neck so they knew exactly who she was when they captured her. We knew the Kamajors would use them to find and attack every RUF base in the third battalion including Zogoda.

I knew from their words that though RUF was going to fight, this was the end as no enemy troop has ever entered Bandawoh before. These were tiny in comparison but a powerful group of Mende hunters and had managed to reach this far and they were heading for Zogoda. I realised then the Kamajors were the new force that Foday Sankoh spoke of, warning his rebels there was a force stronger than them and they did not have to fight. He had also told them it was alright to surrender because this new force was going to do things no other force had ever achieved against them.

Running and running and running. We ran for miles and miles finally arriving in Sondumei, another small town in the Bo/Kenema district over twenty miles away from Bandawoh. I had more cuts underneath my feet and I was tingly and aching from head to toe. The little village was already occupied with wounded RUF rebels, some having lost a limb in previous battles. There were not many of them and they had been brought to the village before we were attacked in Bandawoh so that they could be ahead and safe.

We were given two rooms in two houses in the village. Salamata was with us again as Cyclone was ordered to join the advance team. Lansana was on the front with some of his bodyguards while Salifu and Soja stayed with us. The two boys took one house and all eight of us females took the other. The nights were sleepless for us older ones but Samia, Nyalay and Lucia slept with Naffie reassuring them it was alright to sleep.

A week and a half later we had cooked some rice and eaten heaps but I had developed mild diarrhoea. Magainda, Sunshine, Salamata and I sat outside in the hut to braid each other's hair. Samia and Nyalay had their hair cut and Naffie'd had her's braided the day before by Magainda. No sooner we were finished than a girl came running struggling to breathe. She ran to us in the hut collapsing on the floor.

"They, they are coming," she cried, pointing in the direction she came from. Naffie told Nyalay to go get the girl some water to drink while the whole village broke into chaos. Our things were already packed so we just grabbed our little bags and ran to the other side of the village, through the village stream, toward Zogoda. Running through the water I slipped and fell very hard on a rock.

"No! Memuna get up and run. Are you ok," Samia cried.

Nyalay tried to stop when she saw Samia trying to help me up.

"Run! Nyalay step over there not here, we are coming," I cried as I tried to prevent her from slipping too. I thought one of my legs was broken. I could not feel my legs as I ran with blood pumping out of my knees.

It was drizzling and we ran in the rain. We ran for miles making it safely to Jui Koya

When we arrived in Jui Koya we could still hear the battle going on in Sir Miles's ground and Sondumei. It was really heavy as there was nonstop shooting and bombing. I was so scared I could not stop crying and I was in so much pain. At first I thought the stomach ache was hunger but I was not hungry as we had eaten just before the attack. But as soon as we arrived in Jui Koya, my case of diarrhoea progressed into very violent dysentery.

The town was used by the ambush team that guarded it before we were attacked, even though there were only two houses left standing. Zogoda - Foday Sankoh's camp - and the training base were both in the town's forest. The guards were too many for the buildings and, because they hardly stayed in town, they built shelters in the forest. We had to be careful making our way through the town, as there were grenade ambushes around most of the forest As soon as the men were sure that we were all in Jui Koya they laid two ambushes at the junctions of Sondumei and Camp Lion - the training base. This left us only one way to run: towards Kenema.

Naffie decided that we had better cook and eat something before the next attack. It was clear to all of us the enemy was not going to retreat until there were no more RUF or none of them left. We knew that it was surrender, run or die. As they had attacked us so fast, and hurt and killed so many of RUF's strongest within the third battalion, we knew we had no option but to run. Broken-hearted, my knees hurt and I had dysentery. I had lost so much weight my small body was like a walking skeleton with just some skin on.

Food was not a problem during the Sierra Leone war. There was no shortage of rice, potatoes, cassava, banana and wild yams. Basically we had no shortage of any kind of food that can grow on the soil of Sierra Leone. But sometimes we needed time for the food to grow and time to cook. So we settled in one of the buildings which I was sure was a school hall.

I felt like using the toilet so I quietly got up and went outside to look for a toilet. Though I was in pain I took it step by step. Walking through the coffee trees in the rain I saw faeces everywhere. I managed to increase my pace and went into the camp in the forest to use the toilet. I asked a woman (who thought she recognised me as Titan's partner) and as she saw that I really needed to go, quickly pointed out a little cubicle to me. I told her I had dysentery and she understood.

Some people were dying of it and I was worried as I had been ill for too long now and I hardly knew what was going on around me. It was cold in the toilet and I was in a lot of pain as I passed blood. After cleaning up with some leaves I walked out in tears and feeling nasty. I just kept telling myself that I needed to bathe.

As I walked past the woman who had helped me I felt my stomach ripping apart but I waved and nodded thanks to her. I tried to find my way back to town and I felt really tired, so I sat down on a rock by the road. I looked at my badly scraped knees as I cried in pain and thought I was going to have an infection and lose my knees. Standing up I continued walking again. I could see the town a few yards away and heard the people talking but it was too far for me because I had no energy. Malnourished, I blacked out and fell down in pain. I felt myself digging my fingers into the ground because of the pain ripping through my stomach. I urged myself to scream for help but I could not. For a moment my eyes were open but I saw nothing. When I finally got my sight back, Sunshine was standing over me.

"We have been looking for you," she said, barely holding back her own tears. "You just got up and left without telling anyone and you are sick. What if something had happened?"

I cried, "I passed a lot of blood and I'm so tired I think I'm going to die. Please look after my little sisters, Sunshine."

I told her that although my eyes were opened I did not see her when she walked towards me or anything around me. I was sick, still grieving over the loss of my friend Kasiloi who cared for me so much, but though my knees were swollen I could still walk. I was in so much sadness I felt I was the only sad person in the world. All I did was cry every minute.

"You remember the leaf that Kasiloi gave Laser and Magainda to chew when they had dysentery, don't you?" Sunshine asked.

I nodded. "But I don't recognise any of these leaves right now," I said, looking around. "I don't know the difference between coffee leaves and any other leaf."

"Well I'm here so you sit here and let me look around," Sunshine said.

I sat on a tree root as she walked among the trees; a minute later I leaned on the tree and fell asleep.

Waking me up, Sunshine said, "I got the leaf Thank God. Let's go!"

I was covered in mud from the fall when I collapsed so she suggested we go to the river to clean up.

"We will wash the leaves too and you can start chewing them on our way back to the building," she said.

"Are you sure you got the right ones, before I chew some kind of poison," I asked. Having survived so much already, I was not prepared to die by eating the wrong leaves.

"I'm sure. I will chew some to prevent me from getting dysentery too," she said.

We chewed the leaves as we bathed in the water. The river was not very clean as it had rained a whole week but it was not very dirty either. We cleaned up as fast as possible and headed back to join the others. The leaves worked fast and relief came quickly. I felt hungry and felt myself gaining strength as I chewed them. Magainda was on her way to look for us as no-one knew where we were so they were worrying about us.

"I've been waiting for the two of you to come so we can eat and CO. Titan and Lansana are here but they have to go back soon," Magainda said, concerned but as bossy as always.

I had not seen Titan since the attack on us in Bandawoh. He was the head of the Blama Highway Camp so I understood that he was busy. We hardly saw Lansana as well as all the strong fighters, the commanding officers and their bodyguards who were not wounded, were very busy on the battlefield which was now Bandawoh. I did not want Titan to see me in the condition I was in but I had no choice, as it could have been the last time we would ever see each other.

"But you know that I went out to look for Memuna," Sunshine objected to Magainda's attitude. "Lucky I did too, as she had collapsed and I found her on the ground in the coffee farm."

"But I feel better now, Sunshine got me the leaf," I said.

I did not want to say 'the leaf that Kasiloi got you' because I did not want to say his name as it only made me sadder. He had been like a brother to me although he wanted more. But Magainda knew what leaf I was talking about. I told her what happened when I went to use the toilet and she was really sad and thankful that Sunshine went looking for me.

Titan and Lansana were shocked when they saw me. Lansana asked what was wrong with me and I told him.

There was no privacy in the building so I took a clean top and a pair of shorts out of our bag and I went behind the building to change. I spread the wet skirt and the top out on the grass to dry.

I wanted to take that outfit home as a remembrance of my agonising days with the RUF because I sewed it with my bear hands. I only had a few colours of thread and some needles and I had a pair of dual scissors. There were times I used the kitchen knife to cut the style in the camp before we got attacked. That outfit was the last of my handiwork that I had left with me, the rest were in Bandawoh and the camp.

After eating I felt better. I chewed the leaf for hours and the next morning the pain was gone. I was able to break wind which meant I was rid of the dysentery but I continued chewing the leaves. I was still a little weak as I needed nutrition but I was ready for the journey that morning. We had to leave the town and head forward North. We walked for miles till we came to a new RUF camp in the hills. I did not really know what was going on around me, but I saw Titan and Tity having an argument. He had broken up with her a few weeks before the hunters attacked us in the camp because, I was told, she was cheating with one of his best friends. Lansana and Titan found us a shelter in the new camp; it was raining so we made a fire under cover and sat around it to dry ourselves out. A few hours after the officers' meeting, Titan called me aside to talk to me. He had his AK and three loaded magazines attached to it.

"Memuna, I'm sorry that you are sick and there is nothing I can do about it but I hope you get better. I know that you have your family to go back to," he said, with tears in his eyes. "We have made an arrangement to split us all into two groups. Some of us are going through Kailahun and the other group is going through Pujehun but we are all going to meet in Liberia."

Looking at him I said nothing but cried. I had so much to say but did not know where to start.

"I'm in the Kailahun team, because it is faster and I don't have anyone to worry about, just myself," he said. "But because of you and the others Lansana has to be in the Pujehun team to keep you girls and his child safe. I assure you that I will be fine and so will you and we will see each other again. I love you very much and the times we spent together in the camp are very precious. I will never forget. Take care of yourself."

My heart broke as I looked at him. I could only nod as tears streamed down my face and he tapped me on my shoulder. He forced a smile and told me to go and sit by the fire and warm up. As I turned away from him I buried my face in my hands.

I saw Titan two more times but we had to flee that camp too because the Kamajors were advancing toward us. They had taken over Zogoda and were happy that they were in Foday Sankoh's camp where no enemy had ever been. Magainda also decided she was not coming with us that she was joining Ghost and some other rebels to go with the Kailahun group and branch off to Freetown Highway so she could be with Amara. I was in tears as I pleaded with her but she gave me a hug and walked away. This was the last time I saw Titan, Magainda and their group as they went their own way and this added to my sadness.

Despite my grief I had gained some energy so I was able to run. As we ran, it rained on us and the sun dried us. I almost lost the new pair of slippers I was given again so I took them off my feet and held them as I ran. Making sure Nyalay and Samia were in front of me, we ran in the bushes and in water, as it was the rainy season. The rivers had spread onto the paths and almost every RUF path was in the forest. Finally two and a half days later, we arrived in Kenema Bypass, another RUF camp in the hills of Kenema. When we got there we found the people of Kenema Bypass under attack as well and preparing to run.

We were all very hungry, especially the children Samia, Nyalay and Lucia. We had some rice, salt and oil and borrowed someone's kitchen to quickly cook what we had.

The shooting stopped for a little while and we thought we could spend the night and rest. A few hours later bombs exploded into our sleep and again we ran into the forest. As we ran a little boy fell hard on the rocks hitting his head. I knew his mother and when I saw her standing over her son, screaming his name with his blood on the rock, I stopped. His mother and I watched as he had a seizure and died. I knew I could not leave her standing there but I did not know what to say to her – we just watched in horror and cried. Someone came and pushed us to run. Still crying she was screaming his name as she ran carrying her younger baby boy in her arms.

My sisters had already gone ahead with Naffie. I ran fast and caught up with them. Sunshine and Samia hid under a tree to shelter themselves from the missiles. Nyalay, Salamata, Naffie, Lucia and I were underneath another huge tree. I had a very bad feeling and urge to leave the place we were hiding.

"Naffie let's go and sit somewhere else," I cried.

There were missiles flying everywhere and because it was still in the day we could not see them. We could only hear their violent whistling as they flew around us. She did not argue; she just looked at me and agreed. The moment we ran down the hill a missile fell on our spot. Watching the blast I was in tears and grateful to God. The burnt gaping hole that remained looked as if there had never been a large tree on that spot.

"Memuna, Sunshine take the girls let's go!" Naffie yelled.

"Run! Let's run!" I cried.

Terrified we ran further down the hill. The September rain was intermittent but still we got wet and the ground was slippery. A few hours later the bombing stopped and we had no option but to go back up to Kenema Bypass camp deep in the forest in the rocky mountain.

Naffie always made sure we had something in our stomachs. As soon as we got to the camp we made a fire to cook some more rice but we had to eat the hot food fast. We tried to freshen up but now more missiles were flying at us.

These were so close the gunpowder went straight up my nose and I coughed as I ran. The missiles were coming from Kenema so we were told by the men to run in the direction they were coming from. A lot of rebels, women and children were killed and hurt. Some children were trampled over and killed; the fragments from the missiles killed the adults.

So frightened I cried until I had no more tears left. I did not know what to do. I could not feel anything because of the severe stress and fright. I could smell nothing but the gunpowder from the missiles. I kept yelling for my sisters and Naffie, crying their names into the fiery night. As soon as Salamata heard the first missile, she ran to Cyclone. The only good thing about that night was that in the darkness we could see the missiles so we managed to evacuate the camp. Lansana always told us to run but he also said we needed to pay attention, be fast but that we did not need to rush. I guess that's why none of us got shot or wounded by any weapon.

As we walked in the hills and forest it rained and then stopped. Our group needed to find a place to rest as we had some more wounded people among us. The doctors did not have enough medication because they did not manage to clear out ammunition and medicine for us before the Kamajors took over Zogoda.

We arrived on the Kenema Highway about five miles away from the camp. That highway was still used by the army and some business people living on the normal side of Sierra Leone. The army escorted travellers at night. We had to be careful as the men were sure that we could run into an ambush. As I heard those words, my mouth went completely dry.

It was a cold night but the rain had stopped. Luckily for us the moon was shining but at some times we had to hold onto each other to walk as it was very dark in some places. We finally crossed the highway in single file and fast. Going back into the mountain forest we could hear vehicles in Kenema town below us so we stayed on the mountain that night.

We all formed our little family groups the way we were in our camps. Lansana came to check on us but he was always in the advance team so he was very busy. Fragments had seriously hurt one captain who was Titan and Lansana's friend. He left Salifu and Soja with us and he was with Laser. Lansana and Tiger had had a fight in the camp over Magainda just before Kasiloi died and Tiger stopped guarding Lansana so he was gone with the Kailahun team. We watched the missiles fly from Kenema into Kenema Bypass as we sat, all night on the mountain.

It was an open space, the bush was a few metres away from the mountain and there was some at the foot of the mountain. We watched the stars and the missiles like fire rockets as we sat by the fire. The sight of the violence that was being inflicted on us hurt my heart so badly and when I thought of that little boy, tears ran down my face.

"We are human beings," I whispered to myself.

I was sad and very angry but I knew that it was the beginning of the end of RUF. I thought about Magainda, if she was alright. It is strange to think that one will be alright in a situation like that, but being alive with a few scratches meant you were alright. We spent the night in the mountain. I was very scared to close my eyes and sleep so I tried to stay awake but it did not work I fell asleep.

We had to leave the mountain very early in the morning; it was too close to the highway. We went further into the forest and the men had ambushed everywhere. They formed a camp for us in the forest and the doctors attended to the wounded all morning and all night. Some died and some were in difficult conditions begging to die. There was a girl about Magainda's age, complexion, height and weight. She looked so much like Magainda but they did not look alike in the face. I met her long before the attack on Blama highway. She lived in Kenema Bypass. She lost her face and her eyes that night when we got bombed in Kenema Bypass. She was lying on a mat on the ground in the forest. From her voice I could tell that she was crying. The fragments from the missile had burst her eyes and she had several cuts on her face. The sun had risen but she did not know. I went around and spoke to her in the shelter they made around her.

By this time some of the people who were wounded in the Bandawoh attack had started to smell. The place stank of blood and infected sores.

"I just want to die" she said, in Mende.

Sunshine knew her better than I did so we sat by her and talked to her. There was nothing the doctors could do about her eyes they were gone. I could not keep my eyes on her. I was so sad on her behalf as all she wanted was to die.

We had to leave our new camp that night and I do not know what became of that girl. Rumour went around that she did not live through the afternoon.

As we walked in the forest near Kenema I wanted to flee and go to Kenema so that I could go home to my Auntie and my grandmother in Bo. I could grab Nyalay and Samia and we could hide somewhere and wait for the Kamajors to capture us and take us home to our family but it sounded suicidal, knowing the Kamajors had Tamu's son. I could tell anyone that I was a Barnes and that my grandfather was J.C. Barnes and that my father went to Bo school. I could go on about my family but as long as I did not have any proof and Tamu's son knew me as Lt. Eagle's sister and CO. Titan's woman I could not pull it off. The Kamajors would have killed me if they had caught me at that moment. So I urged my sisters to run.

CHAPTER TWENTY SEVEN

Day Of Reckoning

We were heading for Libya. We had not been in that forest before the attack so we had no paths there which meant we had to make a new one. We were ordered to keep together and we ran in one group. It was rough; I got more cuts on my legs by the grass and more sores under my feet. My feet had blisters and cuts but they were numbed. They only hurt when I took a break and it was time to start walking again. I had little stones in some of the sores under my feet but I ran anyway to save my life.

I kept telling myself that I needed to go home to my family, I needed to see my parents and grandmothers again, I needed to go to school and be an educated grown woman and I needed to get married and have children. All of this gave me the courage to forget my physical pain and run. Samia was very helpful; she did not give me much trouble. When we got attacked in the camp and we fled to Bandawoh I told Nyalay and her they should run as fast as they could and follow the group whether they saw me or not as Lansana was in the advance team. I told them that the advance team kept the rest of us safe so it was alright for them to run ahead.

"But when you run far, you stand and take a break while you wait and look for me, Naffie or Sunshine. Ok," I said.

They did exactly that. Nyalay was little and frightened so she sometimes lagged behind waiting for me. I had to keep yelling their names and urging them to run telling them I was behind them and that I could see them.

All the rivers had expanded because of the rain. We ran into a very deep tributary and luckily for some of us a tree had fallen over it. The tributary was about ten yards wide and it ran through the forest. We had some people whose villages were near that town and that was their river so they knew about it. They told us that it was just a branch and that it happened every raining season and disappeared in the dry season.

Samia was fast enough to be among the first group of people to walk on the tree, which bridged the river branch and she was standing on the hill screaming out Nyalay's name and mine. She got insulted, punched and slapped when she stood in front of some people to ask if they saw us. I saw a woman hit my sister and she was crying my name. I was so angry and I called out to her in tears.

"Samia stop asking them we are here, we will be in the next group of people to cross and Naffie and Lucia are crossing now," I said.

I was so angry I shook in anger. I told her to get out of the way and stand somewhere while she waited for us. She ran to Naffie as soon as she crossed. Nyalay and I were not so lucky. I had a school bag on my back with clothes in it and I held Nyalay's hand as she stood in front of me on the tree. As soon as we got in the middle the tree broke and we went into the water and surfaced and then back down. All this time my arms were wrapped tightly around Nyalay and each time we surfaced I could hear Samia screaming my name. The wave was rough and the water was carrying some people. Nyalay also had her arms around me so I managed to take the bag off my back. The third time we surfaced, someone lifted us up. Sunshine was with Samia and Naffie, they pulled us as those strong arms - which I refer to today as the arms of my guardian angel - pushed us up.

I did not let go off Nyalay until I saw Samia reaching for her and I told her to catch Samia's hands. I was pulled up by Sunshine and as soon as I got on the hill I asked Sunshine if she saw the person who lifted us from the water. She said she only saw the strong arms.

"I think it was a man," she said.

"I think so too, his grip on me was very strong," I said. "God bless him to live and tell this story."

It was terrible when we fell into the water. People were pushing others down so they could climb on them to surface.

We were told by the advance team to wait at that spot so we had some time to rest. Nyalay was trembling and so was I because it was really cold. We took a change of clothes from the bag Sunshine had on her back and changed. I was wearing my outfit I made when I fell in the water. So I wrung it and put it in the bag pocket. Sunshine was angry that I lost the bag in the water and we had an argument about it.

"I'm sorry about the bag but Nyalay's life is more important than a few pieces of clothes," I said.

"How would you feel if I lost your last prized possession?" she said.

"You were hurt that you did not have your beads on your waist when we got attacked in Bandawoh and now all you have that is really important to you is your outfit, how would you feel if I lost that."

"Sunshine if you do that I will tell Lansana that you did it on purpose and you know what will happen," Naffie said. "And the clothes you are complaining about belonged to both of you so what is your problem. Leave Memuna alone she is not well."

I saw the woman who hit Samia and I went up to her and told her that if I saw her anywhere near my sister again let alone watch her hit her again I would shoot her. I meant it. I insulted her and walked away. She knew who I was so she said nothing.

Sunshine did not say any more. I told her that as soon as we could sit somewhere I would dry my outfit and let her have the clothes I wore so that I would be left with only my outfit. My sisters and I were sad at Sunshine's reaction. Samia told me to be patient and forget Sunshine. I was really sick and I was the only one who looked like a living skeleton. I was thankful that Samia and Nyalay were alright. They had lost some weight but they were not as sick and thin like I was.

There were faeces everywhere in the forest as we walked and some people died on the way mostly children. We went further away from the river and settled for a few hours and then we had to flee again. The Kamajors were coming. We arrived at a creek as we walked down the hill from the forest. The water was clean so Sunshine and I drank some. I could not stay long standing in the water even though I wanted to, because it was stinging the sores I had under my feet and on my legs. As I walked out of the water there was the body of a dead man. The rest of his body was bloated and his head was covered in maggots. I first saw the head; it was white because of all the maggots. The body was almost in the water I wanted to throw up when I saw it.

"We just drank that water," Sunshine said.

"I don't even want to think about it," I said." I think he got shot in his head because the flies must have gone into the wound in his head and deposited eggs to make maggots."

We talked about how disgusting it was to see a decomposed body lying by the water we drank.

We ran for hours and settled near a little village that night. We could hear the Kamajors singing in the village. They were celebrating their victory over the guerrillas (rebels). Matilda, Jackson's girlfriend, had just given birth to a baby girl a few days before we got attacked in Bandawoh and she was in much pain through the entire ordeal. She was among the group following the wounded soldiers because Jackson was in the advance team too.

We made fire in the woods and sat in the rain by the fire; we managed to cook some rice and we left early in the morning.

The missiles were still flying. We went to another forest and there was a path that led to a village. The water in the bamboo bush in the forest was clean and cool and there was a field with orange and grapefruit trees and a couple of mango trees. We could not just go to the trees, as it was a little suspicious the way the field was. Lansana and the other men were convinced that someone had been there before us. We sat for a few minutes and the bombing ceased. So we decided to go to the field and climb the trees.

There was a plane far away in the sky but we could still hear it and see it. It was like an ordinary transport plane. It went around us three times and then we got suspicious. The plane was a spy plane. The enemy had stopped using their war jet and the helicopter. This time they were sending a spy plane to spy on us and phone them telling them our location so that they could throw missiles at us. Before I knew it two missiles flew at us. The plane got faster as it went round and round. I looked up at it as I screamed for Samia to climb down the orange tree.

"Samia run, let's go," Sunshine yelled.

We left Lansana in the forest with Laser, Naffie, Lucia and Nyalay. The rest of us were in the field.

"I'm waiting for Samia," I answered.

Samia climbed to a lower branch and she jumped down. I grabbed her hand and we ran to the forest. They were still bombing us. They ceased fire when there was no-one left in the field. Lansana was angry with me way before we left Tobanda. CO. Feel-good had told him that we had men come over to the house in Tobanda. Lansana got angry when I lost my appetite because he thought I was pregnant. I stopped eating three weeks before we moved from Tobanda. I did not know what was wrong with me but I threw up any time I had a proper meal so I lived on cacao and oranges, basically anything sour. I used to go and sit in the cacao tree and pick ripe ones to suck on, cacao fruit is sweet and sour.

I had all the symptoms of a pregnant woman but I was not pregnant; as I did not once have sex with Jackson even though we spent some time together. Titan and I did not have sex either, but only Magainda and Sunshine believed that I was not pregnant.

Lansana looked out for me during this entire ordeal but he was really angry with me and he gave me no chance to explain. He was angry when we ran back from the field, and he blamed me for it.

"You are a greedy pregnant woman," he said. "And you have gone all out looking for something sour to eat and you almost got killed."

I did not say anything I was angry with him for saying that to me and I was also shocked. I watched him as he talked. We all sat in the forest close to the path.

"Why did you decide to come with me and not the father of your child?" he asked.

I was tired of telling Lansana that I was not pregnant, because anytime I told him I was not pregnant he got very angry and yelled at me and called me a liar. Naffie believed that I was pregnant because it had been several months after my first ever period in Water Works and I did not have another for months. I told her about my first period because I did not know what to do and she was the mother for all of us even though she sometimes saw me as her rival. When I first had my period I told Magainda and she advised that I let Naffie know, as she was our mother figure.

"I chose to follow you and not Titan because you brought me into this war not him," I answered Lansana, sounding very angry.

I looked at him in his eyes as I said these words to him. He could sense that I was sick of him. Naffie just watched us both from one person to another.

A minute later a missile flew through the forest, about two yards away from where we sat and about two yards off the ground. I saw it. Samia was sitting next to Lansana and I was opposite him with Nyalay and Naffie next to me. As soon as Lansana saw the missile he grabbed Samia's hand and scooped Nyalay and myself and ran with us across the path to the other side of the forest yelling to the others to stay down and follow us. We all fell underneath a huge tree. The missile flew some yards away and exploded. Everyone ran to the other side.

It was time again for us to leave that place and continue our journey. They continued bombing that forest as we left and an hour later, they stopped. By now the pressure was decreasing as we were getting into RUF zone again. We were close to Pujehun district and we were in one of the villages where RUF had men in an ambush. There was another huge river that we had to cross. First we sat by the river and ate some fruits and coconuts while they transferred the wounded in canoes to a small village across. Samba was there with Briama and some other men. I was so glad to see them; it was a long time since I last saw them. They peeled us some coconut and brought them to where we were sitting and Lansana thanked them.

I went to the corner where Samba and Briama were sitting and we talked. They asked me why I was so thin and I told them that I was sick. I asked Samba and Briama about Karimu and they told me that they had not seen him in a while but the last time they saw him he was alright. It was getting dark and almost everyone had crossed the river to the other village which was now RUF territory. I do not know how Naffie, Lansana and everyone crossed without me, but while I was talking with Samba and Briama I was left on the other side of the river.

It was really dark before I noticed that I was left alone on the other side of the river after I started calling out for my sisters and Naffie and no-one answered. I was glad that my sisters had crossed, I started to feel really sick and dizzy again and my jaws were stiff; it took me a while to say anything and everyone was now rushing to cross and the Kamajors were getting closer.

It was dark on our side, we were not allowed to have light on our side because the Kamajors were getting closer to us they were following our tracks. The RUF commanding officers had told the rebels we met on guard in the town to join our team and leave the town. As we ran, we ran along with all the rebels on our side of the country.

I was left behind on the other side of the river with about twenty men. I was so cold and weak. Luckily for me Jackson came back in a canoe with a flashlight; he was one of those put in charge of making sure every woman, child and wounded crossed the river to the other side and make sure there were no canoes left behind, so the Kamajors would not use them to reach us.

I saw Jackson and he waved his flashlight in my face as he waved his flashlight around asking if there was a female left behind. It was all too fast and he did not see me. So he put some men in the canoe and all this time I was fighting hard to unlock my jaws and call out to him. In time I did.

"Jackson I'm here," I said, sounding very helpless as I pushed my way through.

"Where are you Memuna?" he asked. "What are you still doing behind here?"

"I don't know how I got left behind, I'm very sick and weak," I said.

He told me to search for his hand in the dark as the battery was dying in the flashlight. He shook the flashlight as he reached out for me. Luckily there was a flick of light and he reached for me with both hands. He lifted me and put me in the canoe and urged the man to row faster as they needed to come back for the others. Some people could not wait for the canoe so they swam as we crossed.

Everyone on the other side was warming up by fires. When we crossed, I was very cold and too tired to walk up the hill to join the others. Jackson saw that I was tired, so he told me to lean on a tree while he got some leaves. I did not know what he was doing; I just saw him piling leaves on the wet ground. When he was through he took off his jacket and lay down on the leaves.

"Memuna, come and lie down on me," he said. "You need some heat and you are tired. We are safe on this side so we can spend a few minutes."

I was surprised that he would do that for me but I was also grateful, the minute I laid my body on his I fell asleep.

We walked three days non-stop in the rain and sun after we crossed the river. I had blisters between my legs on my undies line, from walking in the same pair of undies for three long days. They were cutting into my skin. As we carried on the journey a boy about the age of twelve who looked as thin as I did, lay on the side of the path and died peacefully. It was very sad as he took his last breath. Naffie, Nyalay, Samia, Sunshine and I saw it while we were waiting for a go ahead to continue walking. I felt really sad for him as I thought it could be any of us, especially me. I turned to Nyalay and Samia.

"You see what just happened? Please don't think about food just drink clean water and when there is food we will eat."

They nodded and Nyalay said that she was not thinking of food. Samia said she was thinking of going home.

On the fourth night we arrived in an abandoned village in the evening. We could not stay there because no-one was familiar with the village and the men did not think it was safe. We were all very hungry and tired but we could not stop running, we carried on walking as fast as we could. After a few minutes of walking in the forest we arrived on a farm and there was a boy about ten years old with his parents. They ran off as soon as they saw us and left him. He was sitting on a high stool they had built on the farm driving away the birds from eating their rice. Since we were not familiar with the area the men decided to capture him. He cried for his parents and they told him that if he wanted to see his parents again he had to show us the way. He walked with us through the forest and a couple of hours later we arrived at another very dangerous river.

The river was calm when we got there that evening and some people crossed. They walked in the water but before we could, it got really rough and it swelled so we had to spend the night on the other side while the others had to wait for us. There were glow worms on the ground and they stung us as we walked in the forest. We had no choice as the ground was covered in glow worms. I had lost my slippers again in one of the rivers; they had fallen in the water and went away in the current. I stood on the glow worms with my bear feet and made sure they did not climb up my thighs. It was still raining. Lansana had a lighter, so we gathered some wood and made a fire and so did everyone else. It was drizzling but the forest was thick enough to cover the fires from the rain. The glow worms disappeared when we made fires. I leaned on a tree and fell asleep as we sat by the fires. Naffie gave Samia and Nyalay a lappa (wrap around the waist cloth) to sleep on by the fire while Lucia slept in her arms.

We set off early in the morning. There were a few rebels among us who recognised the river. They said that the spirit of that river was very proud and that what happened to us that night always happened to strangers. They said that it was wrong when the first group that crossed talked about how shallow the water was.

"When that happens it swells because the spirit gets angry," one of them said.

I was frightened by all of the superstition and at the same time angry that the country has all these spirits but they allowed the war to happen. I just wanted to get out of there. As we waited for the men to make crossing arrangements we went down to the river and freshened up. I took off those undies and washed them and put them away. A few hours later, the water was calmer and the men bridged two logs across the water and we crossed.

We were still being chased but there was no more bombing, because they did not know our precise location. There was not much pressure on us to walk faster like before and the rain had ceased but we were hungry -it had been four days without food. We drank water I guess that was what kept us going. Strength, Fatima and Lucia did not cry. They were very quiet maybe because they knew what was going on and they were terrified too. Other babies were crying through it all and some of the rebels were telling the mothers to shove something into the children's mouths or they would do something to the children. As we got closer to Libya, we took a break in a thick forest with the advance team.

Sia's other baby began to cry; she said that the baby was cold. One of the rebels yelled from the back.

"Put the father's thing in its mouth or lose it. We are tired of these foolish children."

Vayanga and Lansana got angry and they went to the back to him and threatened to kill him. They also told him to apologise to Sia, Vayanga and the baby. He was so terrified he said he did not know it was a C.O's woman he was talking to.

"Well you should not even talk to anyone like that," Lansana said. "That is how babies communicate, they can't talk to us."

The rebel got a few slaps in his face. It was time for us to continue walking again. We were all excited when we were told we would have to walk another day and a half to get to safety. I mustered courage to hold on.

As we arrived in Libya, people left the group and went home to their family members; wounded soldiers went home to their families. It was like a group of children coming home from school, but there was too much emotion.

I felt lost, as no-one knew Samia, Nyalay and me in that part of Sierra Leone. We are from Moyamba and Bo districts and this was Pujehun district. There were tears and laughter and people were happy to be home. I was happy to be somewhere safe but all I really wanted was to be with my family again. I wished I were home.

There were more and more people leaving the group as we arrived in every town. We finally arrive in a village and Mbalu was there. She was very welcoming as usual, but when she saw me she knew it was me but she could not believe her eyes. Neither did Bob, Kallon, Yusufu or the other guys. I told them that I was sick. Sunshine told Mbalu that I was thin because I was under a lot of trauma. She told her about Kasiloi and everything.

"Oh Memuna I'm really sorry," Mbalu cried. "Sunshine and I basically grew up in RUF with those guys but in the short time you knew Kasiloi you two got closer than all of us. You really liked each other."

I started crying for him again. I wished he had survived to tell the story. Kasiloi was a very sociable person it was hard not to like him.

Mbalu being the person she was – did not take anything seriously - started teasing me as soon as we stopped crying.

"My sister was not all that fat and now look," she said.

I laughed. " Mbalu shut up you are never serious."

We laughed and I introduced her to Samia, she already knew Nyalay. Mbalu asked Bob to help her to cater to us. She told him to get us some water to freshen up while she cooked us some food. Mbalu was a giving person, she never held onto anything while someone else was in need, except when it came to her smokes. She gave us so much food. She gave Sunshine, Samia, Nyalay and myself some clean clothes to change into after we cleaned up. Lansana was left with Bob and the other boys when it came

462

to that. The house was noisy as they were very happy to see each other and we were all tired and sick but alive. It was good.

"Memuna survived the toughest battle RUF has fought in years," Bob teased.

"She was trained in camp Lion, what else would you expect?" Mbalu stressed.

I did not have the energy to talk too much, so I listened to them and smiled. It had been a month or more since we were attacked in Sondumei and that was how long it had been since I'd had a proper meal. A meal with some meat in it, a meal to fill me up not only to give me strength, also it had been that long since I drank some clean water. I was happy that we saw Mbalu, but we were not spending the night. We had to carry on to Sembehun in Pujehun where Lansana's family lived as he was going to be assigned again. I was angry and amazed that after all the torture RUF was still not ready to surrender, I thought it was pointless.

We did not get to Sembehun that night; Lansana's plans changed when we arrived in the village next to Sembehun. So we spent the night. That night I soaked my feet in a bucket of warm water and took out all the stones from my sores, there were up to sixteen tiny stones. I kept my feet in the water for a few minutes, dried them and put some oil on them. Two days later my feet were better, as I did the same thing every night.

A week later we went to another town to live with Lansana's granduncle Kamor Ibrahim and his wife whom Guy lived with. Naffie was glad to see her son again; she hugged him and did not want to let go. Guy had a lot to tell his mother, he told her how well his great granduncle and his wife had looked after him. Naffie thanked them and it was easy for us to settle in. It was hard for me because I was still traumatised.

The following morning I saw Jackson standing in a veranda two houses away from Kamor Ibrahim's house. I looked harder to make sure my eyes were not deceiving me, but he saw me and walked towards me.

"When did you get here?" he asked.

"It is you," I said. "Last night."

I asked him about Matilda and the baby and he said that they were still asleep and that she had been taking some native treatment and the pain was gone. I was happy for her, Matilda and I had started to become friends again in Bandawoh before she gave birth. I told Jackson that I would go over to see Matilda when she was awake so he should let me know.

Lansana was not in town and Kamor Ibrahim and his wife had gone to their farm that morning. They left us in town to rest.

Jackson suggested that we go for a walk, so I told Naffie that I was going for a walk around town. We went to the cola nut and coffee farm on the main road. We had a talk and Jackson teased me about my weight.

"Are you really pregnant?" he asked.

"I am not pregnant, I have only had my period once in my life but that doesn't mean I'm pregnant," I said.

"But that is the news around," he said.

"Well, Jackson do you believe the news?" I asked. "You and I have not gone beyond kissing. Titan thinks I'm carrying your child because he and I did not go beyond kissing either. Everyone else thinks I am carrying his child."

"Really? You two did not do it?" Jason asked.

"Unlike you Jackson, I told him I was not ready and he was willing to wait but I had to pay a price, Yoyo was the price," I said.

He laughed. "So you are not pregnant?" he asked.

"Except God is making me the next Holy Mother, I'm not," I said.

A few minutes after teasing me he leaned over to kiss me.

"Why do you want to kiss me when I look like this?" I asked.

"Well I know who you are and I have kissed you before, so what is a little weight loss?" he said.

I was pleased that he was not superficial. I kissed him and he continued teasing me as we walked back. I visited and played with the baby in the evening. Jackson always made sure he had some private moments with me but I was getting tired of it all.

Sunshine changed, she and I argued lots more and Naffie told her to stop. Samia, Nyalay and I became closer to Naffie. I missed Magainda so much and each time I thought of her which was quite often, I prayed for her.

I felt like the weight of the whole world was on me and I felt like God was punishing me for something I had done. I lost friends, my best male friend had died a brutal death, all the people I knew were vanishing from my life. First it was my friends from Liberia my childhood friends, then the ones from Freetown and Bo then it was Sembehun and then Kabbaty, then my uncle Karimu, then my cousin Komeh, Magic and then Kasiloi, Magainda, Ma Tenneh, Titan and everyone else I was close to on Blama Highway, I was crushed.

I started to gain weight. Naffie still thought I was pregnant, I did not know what was going on in her and Lansana's head because my belly was not growing. She used to force me to eat, so that the "baby" would grow.

"Memuna you are going to have a beautiful baby," she said. "You are pretty and Titan is good looking so look after yourself."

I looked at her in anger and tried not to talk because I would only be wasting my breath.

A week later we moved to a town near Sormu. We were more relaxed in that town and I had put on a little weight.

I had one more problem to deal with. I had lice I did not know how I got them but I did. They made sores on my scalp; I thought they played a part in my weight loss.

The relationship between Sunshine and me improved, because she needed me to cover for her when she was with Yusufu. I asked Sunshine to cut my hair a little shorter. Naffie was awesome with the children so it gave me time to take care of myself. I had lots of sleepless night and nightmares. We started to run out of food and we needed to be closer to the Liberian border while RUF was still trying to convince the people on the other side to let us into Liberia. So we had to move to a tiny village deep in the forest behind Sormu where Lansana's grandmother Yea Zina and her other brother, Ngor Bundu and his wife and children lived. It was a tiny village in the forest with about six houses.

I used to think that wild animals would attack us. It was funny considering we lived in the camp on Blama Highway and I was not scared at all. I talked to Sunshine about it and she told me that she felt the Same and that she could not wait for us to get out of there.

"The camp was far, far bigger than this place and at least we knew when it was sunny," she said.

The forest was so thick around the village that it covered the village from the sun. It was always cool and calm in the village but very cold at night. We had to move from the village as the Kamajors were already in Libya and they were advancing. So we moved to Ngor Bundu's farm and lived in the thatched hut on his farm with his family. The men slept on the ground outside around a fire and the women slept in the hut by another fire. The other villagers went into the forest around the farm and built shelters. We had a shelter in the forest as well but I did not go there. There was a stream between the village and the farm. We went to the stream to bathe, we fetched our drinking and cooking water from the head of the stream.

One day Salifu and Soja caught some fish from the other end of the stream and Naffie wanted to cook it.

Sunshine was told to put Lucia to sleep so she could have her afternoon nap. I was told to go to the stream to fetch some water to cook.

"I'll come with you Memuna," Sunshine said.

It was a sunny day and I was feeling a little nauseous, I sat on the side of the path and threw up on our way to the stream.

"Good thing you did not vomit at the hut," Sunshine said, "Naffie would have said you were having morning sickness."

"It's her business, since she thinks she knows all," I said.

As I tried to dip the water I felt something crawling up on one of my legs. I thought it was just a fly, so I shook my leg and carried on dipping and then I felt a sting. Just in time Sunshine and I saw that it was a huge leech. I screamed and ran off the log and up the hill.

"Sunshine help me," I screamed.

She put Lucia down and grabbed a piece of sharp splinter to help me scrap it off. It was making its way into my skin, as we tried to scrape it off.

"Help me scrape it off," Sunshine said.

I was terrified, this had not happened to me before, I had only heard about it. When we got it off there was a bit of blood on my calf from the scraping and from the tiny whole the leech made in my skin. I vowed not to step into that water again till I had to. I took Lucia; Sunshine went to fetch the water after we crushed the leech.

I used to sit up by the fire and stare in the moonlight on the farm every night while everyone slept. While I did that I meditated on my life and I asked God if I was going to make it through the war and why won't he just kill me, why was he letting me go through this.

We had to leave the farm a week later, we had to leave the forest and carry on to the border. The deal had been made; it was time for some people to cross over to Liberia. I had malaria by then and I could not walk fast, so Lansana decided to leave me with his granduncle Ngor Bundu. Lansana paid him US$200 to take care of me and abort my "baby".

"Memuna, I will come back for you no matter what but for now I need to take your sisters to safety. We are going to Liberia," Lansana said. "I will come back for you. Ngor Bundu is going to look after you and by the time I come back you will be healthy again."

We were standing in another village and I saw Sia, Rain and the others who I had not seen since we arrived in Libya. I nodded and turned to talk to Nyalay and Samia. They did not want to go without me, they were crying.

"I want you two to stop crying, because I can't look after you two. It is better for you to go with them and I will see you soon," I cried, "Samia, they are taking you two to Liberia. Look after yourself and Nyalay and try not to be too shy and trust some people. Ask for Mama and try to find her so she can look after the two of you until I get there. I'm sure she is still alive."

Now I was trying to convince myself that I was going to see my little sister and my cousin again but one side of me thought that I was fooling myself. I could not breathe I was losing the two most important people in my life at the time. I collapsed on the gravel road and wailed and so did they. I gave them a hug and told them that only God knew why we were experiencing that entire trauma. I told them that we had to believe that we would see each other again.

"Remember Samia, when you get to Liberia you only have each other until you find our mother so look after Nyalay and always stay together, share whatever you have and God bless you," I cried.

They both gave me a long hard look.

"Are you pregnant Memuna?" Samia asked.

I shook my head as I cried. "No I'm not," I cried. "I'm just sick."

She nodded and turned to leave. "We don't want to go," they cried.

"But you have to. So we can survive," I said.

It was time to go now and everyone was in a hurry. I had to watch my sister and my cousin leave and that was the most painful experience of my life. I gave up on life as they disappeared into the forest. I felt alone and crushed. I was left with strangers that I had only known for a few weeks.

We went into the forest and they built shelters in the forest by a farm. I did not know whose farm it was and I did not care, it was the least of my worries.

I felt like a zombie, I had lost so much for no reason whatsoever. I had so many questions and there was no-one to answer them so I refused to talk. I was always alone; sometimes I played with Ngor Bundu's baby. His wife was a good woman, she never pretended to know what I was going through but she never kept me out of her sight. Even though I hardly said more than two words to her she always talked to me. She told me that I was going to see my sisters again; all I had to do was keep the faith and pray. In my head I thought 'I have done nothing more than that lately and things just get worse'.

Ngor Bundu fed me a bowl of some sort of nasty native medicine every day hoping that it would get rid of my "pregnancy" and I would have my period again but it did nothing, it just made me sick and I threw up a lot. One time he took me for a walk in the forest so we could talk.

"Memuna did you have sex?" he asked, "with Lansana or anyone else?"

I looked at him and I did not want to talk. He told me that I had to talk to him because the medicine he was giving me was not doing anything but making me sick. I told him that I knew that I was not pregnant and that I was just sick.

"Well I think you are telling me the truth, so I will make you some native medicine for malaria," he said, "so you can regain your energy and when Lansana comes back for you at least he will see that I did something."

I was so traumatised that I was unaware of most of the things that went on around me. I made a friend but I did not remember her name; she was a nice girl. I did not say much to her but she always had something to tell me.

Several days later the Kamajors attacked us on the farm. I was on the farm with Ngor Bundu's wife helping her spread out the laundry she had done. They surrounded us and there was no way out. Two other teenagers and I were the only trained rebels among all the civilians in the forest. When I saw these men with their strange voodoo and their single barrel guns walking down the hill towards us I was terrified. I knew who they were although it was my first time to really look at a Kamajor. I was shaking like a leaf and all I felt for them was hate instead of being thankful.

"They are here, they are coming and they look so nasty," I cried. "I don't want the enemy to touch me."

"Shhh, they won't know what you are just try to calm down," Ngor Bundu's wife said, without taking her eyes of what she was doing. She was frightened too but she had nothing to be afraid for she was just a civilian.

We stood there as they approached us and they yelled at us to go into the forest to the shelter. I was close to telling them that I did not take orders from a group of men with crazy voodoo hanging all on them, but something in me told me that it was suicide. I wanted to see my family again, so I kept quiet. I found them very rude, I guess it was because I saw them as the real enemy. I hated the voodoo and the intimidation. They ordered us to pack whatever belongings we had so they could take us to one of the villages that they had made their base. They were all Mende men. None of them said a word to me for a while, an old man noticed how hysterical I was so he came to me and told me to stop crying that the war was over. I looked at him and thought, it would be over when I have my uncle, my cousins and my sister back and when we were all home with our family again. I wiped my tears but they kept flowing.

We arrived in a town miles away from the forest. There was Mende music from every corner.

"God! From living with reggae music for almost two years of my life now it's Mende music," I whispered to myself.

They kept us in the sun a few hours while they made arrangements. Minutes later a strong old man about sixty or more years old came to talk to us. He was the leader of that group. He was a good looking and pleasant old man like Kamor Ibrahim. He talked to us and told us that all the Kamajors were Mende men, our own brothers and fathers. He encouraged us to feel free to talk to him about anything.

"This war has been tough on our country but mostly on Mende people and that is why we formed the Kamajor organisation to free our people and then the country and we need you people to help us any way you can," The old man said. "You can all call me Kamor."

Kamor is Mende for teacher or medicine man but it was mostly used to refer to Arabic teachers and other elderly Muslim Mende men. I liked Kamor the moment I saw him. I felt like he was a family man and easy to approach. But somehow I was scared of him; I guess it was because he was a Kamajor. We sat in the sun for a while and we were all allocated to houses.

I washed my hair everyday with hot water to get rid of the lice but it did not work. Whenever I was alone I took a scissors and ran it through my hair. I thought that keeping the hair short would make it easier for me to get rid of the lice.

There was one young Kamajor around his early thirties by the name of Alusine who was very strict on me. He told me that he knew who I was and that he sensed it the moment he saw me. He threatened to kill me if I tried anything. I hated him, but he tried to confuse me. Sometimes he would go to our house to have a conversation with me and other times he would threaten me. One time I confronted him and told him to leave me alone when he tried to find out if the family I was living with was my real family.

"I have proof that you are a Camp Lion trainee and that you are a truly trained rebel so don't get smart with me," he said, "I know that you see us all as your enemies and I am ready for you. Just stay there I will bring the proof."

I was so scared but I tried to hide it. He went away and a few minutes later he came back with Jonah, Titan little bodyguard. Jonah had told Alusine and some other Kamajors a lot about all the people he knew in the camp. He told them about Lansana and Titan's status and all of us, he told them about my relationship with Titan.

"You see this boy, you two know each other," Alusine said. "He told us everything and you are lucky you never hurt anyone otherwise you would have been in a lot of trouble."

I looked at him as tears streamed down my face. He told Jonah to leave us alone when he saw me crying.

"Memuna I'm sorry," said Jonah.

I nodded.

"What do you want from me Alusine?" I cried.

"Nothing, I just want you to know that I know who you are," he said.

"Well I did not make myself the person you think I am," I said, "I was someone else before I became this person you think I am now. So why don't you try and see that person and let me breathe."

He apologised and we became friends. I went to see Jonah later. He was living with a young Kamajor who promised to help him look for his family. I asked Jonah to tell me why he had talked so much. He apologised and told me that he was asked to talk when they caught him. I believed him because Jonah was a clever boy. I saw Jonah every day and sometimes he told me about how much he missed Base. I did not talk about my feelings to Jonah, he was a child and I did not want to burden him. I always shared my food with him.

Alusine and I talked every day and sometimes he got me to tell him about my sisters and my pain. He assured me that everything would be fine. I also became friends with another Kamajor he was an old man called Kamor Hindowa Massaqueh, who was just fond of me. I guess he saw that I was going through a lot of trauma. He used to come over to the house to talk to me.

One day I was walking around town just to be alone and think and I passed in front of Kamor's house down town. He was on the veranda and when he saw me he called me over.

"Hello young girl, come," he said, in Mende.

I was a little scared but I went over to him. I greeted him and he asked if he could offer me some tea.

"No, thank you Kamor," I said.

"Ok I have been watching you and I really want to talk to you. You look really sad," he said. "Are those people your real family?"

I was shocked, some part of me wanted to tell the truth but the other side wanted to lie so I lied.

"Yes," I said.

Kamor knew that I was lying but being as wise as he was he did not say more. He just let me go.

"Memuna don't be afraid to talk to me and it's ok to come and say hello anytime you want," he said, "I better pray now."

He was going to take his ablution and say the last prayer for the day.

I went back to the house wondering what was going on.

A few days later Kamor Hindowa came to me.

"Memuna, you told me that you have your grandmother in Bo and I'm going to Bo in two days to take some children home to their families. Do you want to come?" he asked.

"Yes I do but I will have to ask Ngor Bundu first," I said.

Kamor Hindowa agreed and he told me that he was waiting to hear from me the next day. Before I could open my mouth Ngor Bundu told me not to think about it. He had been eavesdropping on my conversation with Kamor Hindowa . I cried and his wife begged him to let me go to my family.

"No," he snapped. "you are a woman, stay out of this. I promised Lansana that I would look after her until he comes back for her and I will do just that. I don't want to hear it anymore."

Just like that, I was dismissed.

At first I was shattered I thought it was all over for me. When Kamor Hindowa came to see me the following evening he was not allowed by Ngor Bundu and he was furious. I saw him on the day of the travel and we had a moment together. He promised me that I definitely had a space in the next group of children he would take to Bo and he asked me to describe my grandmother again.

"Her name is Mama Adama Barnes and she is light skinned and very small. She is short like me," I said as tears rolled, "She lives a few minutes away from Gbongo market and everyone in the market knows her, she is always very dressy."

"Ok Memuna don't worry, I will look for her if I don't see her I will ask around for her. I promise," he said.

"We have a big yard in Bo as well but I don't know the address and my Auntie Sewa lives there," I said. "Oh God I wish I knew."

We said our goodbyes and I turned to leave as he left. Alusine kept my company even though Ngor Bundu banned me from talking to Kamajors. Ngor Bundu had started hating me. At one point he called me an ungrateful child.

"Well what would you say if you were the one who looked after me from when I was a child, when I was in nappies?" I asked. "I was taken away from my family, from a good life and environment by your grandson. I never asked to be here. I have only been in your care a few weeks and besides you got paid to look after me."

I was shocked at myself that I talked back to the almighty Ngor Bundu and there was nothing he could do about it. Everything I said was the truth and he did not like it a bit. I did not care, all I wanted was some peace if there was any. I was already going through a lot.

Alusine knew what was going on, as he was very observant, but it did not stop him from talking to me. He would go to the house and put up a demanding attitude when he asked for me. No-one questioned him they just let me go and sit somewhere with him. Alusine and Kamor Hindowa were the only two people I talked to about my family, Nyalay and Samia.

I could not sleep, I was so anxious waiting for Kamor Hindowa to return and as I imagined myself among my family again. It made me happy and worried at the same time. I was so anxious I could not wait. The two weeks seemed like a decade. He finally came back one night and I was so happy. We were sitting on the veranda when he arrived and he came straight to me.

"Memuna how are?" he asked.

"I'm good and you?" I said.

"I'm very tired but I have good news for you," he said.

I saw him the following afternoon and he told me that he saw someone who knew my grandmother and he was told that she knew lots of Kamajors and that she was always crying for her granddaughters that had been captured by the rebels.

"I think your grandmother knows Kamor Lahai," he said. Kamor Lahai was like the leader of the Kamajors. They sang his name in their songs and they had lots of respect for him.

"I am leaving here again for Bo in two days so get ready," he told.

I was so excited I thought I was dreaming. This was not how I imagined my reunion with my family. I imagined I would go home when RUF took over Sierra Leone. Komeh, Samia, Nyalay and myself with our Uncle Karimu would just go home and introduce our friends to our family.

I was happy but nervous about how I was going to answer the questions about Samia, Nyalay and Komeh's whereabouts and the questions about Karimu. I gave it a long hard thought and I decided I was going to just tell them exactly what happened.

Ngor Bundu was not very pleased and he was ready to put his feet down when I told him that Kamor Hindowa had found out about my grandmother and that he was going to take me home. Ngor Bundu still wanted to keep me for Lansana even though I had a family that missed me very much. I was worried that I was not going to be allowed to go home again this time. I was excited but then not sure if it was only a dream or reality.

CHAPTER TWENTY EIGHT

Home Coming

The day came for my return home. Although I was not sure that I would be allowed to go home I got myself ready anyway. I went to the creek early that morning, bathed in the cold water and washed my hair.

I said my goodbyes to the town and to my life with RUF as I bathed. I fetched my last bucket of water for Ngor Bundu's wife and I went back to the house. I got dressed in the outfit I had made. I was proud of myself that I was at least able to save it and now I was taking it home. I sat down anxiously waiting for Kamor Hindowa. He came to the house and asked if I was ready. I told him I was but Ngor Bundu forbade me. As I spoke to Kamor Hindowa , Ngor Bundu came out to the veranda.

"This girl is not going anywhere," he interrupted.

I could not believe him I thought he was being very wicked to my family and me because I needed my family and they needed me.

"Why do you want to keep someone else's child here?" Kamor Hindowa asked.

He could not answer the question because that would mean he was admitting that he was related to a rebel.

"Memuna take your bag and let's go," Kamor Hindowa said.

I did not have many belongings then; I only had about two outfits that I really wanted to keep out of the four I was left with. I had already packed them in a plastic bag. I could not believe that was all I had in my life. Before I was captured I used to throw my clothes away when they were too dirty so I would not be made to wash them and I had lots and lots of clothes. The night before I was supposed to leave I packed my clothes and burst into tears when I saw my things in a plastic bag. I knew that I only had them till I got back home I knew that everything was going to change for the better.

As I tried to leave the veranda, Ngor Bundu stood in front of me to stop me from going. This made Kamor Hindowa very annoyed, he warned Ngor Bundu. Ngor Bundu would not listen, he proceeded to yell at me, calling me an ungrateful girl and he said that God would punish me for being ungrateful. Kamor Hindowa got angry and went off towards the other side of town. There was a group of people waiting for him and they had a smile on their face. A few minutes later Kamor Hindowa turned up in front of the house with Kamor. By then I was in tears, I was hysterical I thought that I was never going home to my family again. Kamor was angry when he saw me crying. He called Ngor Bundu and warned him.

"Bundu, I know that this child is not a part of your family," he said. "First of all I realised that a few days ago and I made sure of it when I spoke to her. The way she speaks Mende is too different from the way you or anyone from Pujehun would speak Mende. I know that her kind of Mende is from Moyamba or Bo. She is not ungrateful because I asked her and she never denied your family."

Ngor Bundu was speechless, he was shocked and he just stood there.

"How would you feel if someone took your child away just because they could and never let them go?" Kamor asked. "This girl's grandmother is crying for her everyday so if you know what I know you would let her go if you don't want to get in trouble. I know your grandson was a rebel."

Ngor Bundu let me go. He nodded at me reluctantly and made a gesture like he was shooing me away. He did not want to look at me. I thanked his wife and I joined the group.

I was so happy I could not stop crying but they were tears of joy. I thanked Kamor in tears and he smiled at me.

"God bless you my child, go home and get back into society," he said.

I was so happy. At that moment Kamor and Kamor Hindowa became my heroes. Alusine was so happy for me.

"So who am I going to be insulted by now since you are going?" He asked. "Did you leave someone to do your cheeky things?"

"I did not use to insult you?" I said.

"But you are cheeky and sarcastic and I will miss you," he said.

"I will miss you too," I said.

Ngor Bundu was very angry with me; he gave me the nastiest look anyone had ever given me. I felt bad that it had to end that way but I needed to go home.

We walked for hours over about thirty miles or less. We arrived in a town that was filled with Kamajors and Kamor Hindowa suggested we spent the night. We ate and we spent the night. I did not sleep that night.

There was another lady who Kamor Hindowa was taking home as well, she was quite fond of me so we spent all night talking and I think she was as excited as I was.

Early the following morning we had to start walking again. I was tired but I did not care I just wanted to go home. I still had lice and I was still a bit weak and I still needed to gain weight but I was much better.

After several miles we arrived in Zimmi Makpele, a town in Sierra Leone close to the Liberian border. I was lost for the first half an hour. It had been a long, long time since I saw functional vehicles, a market, well-dressed people with different hairstyles and no guns. I was happy to see real buildings and power poles.

Yet I knew that I had to work at fitting in, emotionally and physically. I did not like the thought of having to work to fit in. I did not make any effort to fit in before and yet I had lots of friends. I decided I was not going to try hard to fit in with anybody because I had my family.

Things had changed so much in the year and half I had been away, fashion and music. It was really busy as usual, as it was 22nd of December 1996. Everything in the market was on sale and there was so much noise.

We were tired, Kamor Hindowa took some of the people to their families and he took some to another house to stay until he was ready for us to go. He took the lady and me to his house in Zimmi, because he had space there for us. Kamor Hindowa really looked after me he kept his eyes on me and he reassured me about four times a day that he was going to take me home. That day he left the lady and me in the house cleaning up and he went to the market.

There was a very nice lady in the house who he introduced to us as his sister. She gave us water to bathe while she cooked us a meal. As soon as I ate I fell asleep. I was soon awakened by a nightmare. From that day on I started having nightmares of what happened during my last days in RUF. Kamor Hindowa came back from the market with some clothes for us. I was really grateful and he also brought me a pair of plastic slippers.

"I'm sure you need some private women things," he said. "I will give you some money in the morning. Are you sure you can be on your own in the market?"

"I will try," I said. "Thank you very much Kamor Hindowa ."

"I will go with her," offered the lady.

I thanked her as well. I was really happy about the clothes. He had bought me two tops, two lappa - everything was new to me again. I found it strange to switch the light on. Every time I did something I had not done since I was captured I believed I was really in the normal world. In the morning Kamor Hindowa was very busy he had a duty call. He gave me some money and hurried out.

"I will be back Memuna, soon," he said. "Relax and I promise I will take you home before Christmas."

I was escorted to the market, I bought five undies and I wanted to buy a bra or two but I was embarrassed. As we walked around window-shopping, I was nervous but the lady I was with tried to calm me down; she blended into the normal world well. I could not, because I had pretended that I was always in the normal side of the country while I was with the RUF. Besides I did not look like I had so I refused to try. That evening Kamor Hindowa came home, he apologised to me and said that he could not take me home before Christmas but he would try to take me home before New Year's

Day. I was a little disappointed but I accepted it. He was very good to me so the least I could do was acknowledge it.

I went to the market about twice every day to stop myself from falling asleep as I was running away from the nightmares. On the afternoon of the 24th December 1996 while I was in the market with the lady I saw Sunshine. At first I did not believe my eyes, but she yelled my name and we ran into each other's arms. The first thing I asked her about was Nyalay and Samia.

"They are fine they are doing well. I just got here yesterday from Liberia to pick up some things from my brother's shop and I will go back this evening," Sunshine said.

I was in tears, I just wished I could go with her and get Samia and Nyalay but it was the wrong idea. She asked me if I had anything to send to them or if I wanted to go with her.

"Lansana would be happy to see you," she said.

"No, I just got here a couple of days ago and I will be going home soon. I don't have anything to send for them but please tell them that I miss them so much and that I'm still alive," I said. "Tell them that I will make sure they get home soon."

Sunshine asked me how I was going to make sure my sister and my cousin get home but I told her that I did not know but I was going to try. We spent some time together and she told me that no-one in Zimmi but her family knew that she was a rebel. Like the lady that I was with whom Kamor Hindowa was taking home, Sunshine did not look any different from the people of Zimmi. Her family was known in the town, as it was her hometown. She did not look sick and thin like I did. The people in Zimmi were still angry with RUF; they beat them and jailed some of them who survived the beating when they caught them. We went around town and we saw them beating a man who they thought was a rebel but we did not know him. We could not risk him seeing us because there was no guarantee he did not know us. Lots of rebels knew us we did not know.

I spent all night thinking about Nyalay and Samia and I prayed hard for God to bring them home. On the 26th December I saw Sunshine again. She was getting ready to go back, she just wanted to buy some things from Zimmi.

"Laser, Salifu and everyone miss you," she said.

"I miss you all too but I have to go home," I said.

I came back to the house and cried, Kamor Hindowa saw me crying.

"Why are you crying?" he asked. "I know that you want to go home but please give me some time, ok."

"It's not that," I said. "I just saw someone who knows that my sisters are in Liberia and that they are doing well but they are still with the rebel who captured us."

"Ok, first I will take you home and then I will go and get your sisters," he said.

I believed him, as he was really kind and honest to me. I could not stop thinking about them and wishing they were there with me.

On the 27th December in the evening, he told the lady and me to get ready as the following day was the day of our journey home. I was so excited; time could not go fast enough. Early in the morning he had another duty call. He came back and said that he could not be in the same vehicle with me, as he had to do some things their boss wanted them to do.

"I will be on a motor bike but I have arranged a seat for you on a truck," he said. "The driver is my friend he will make sure you are safe. I will meet you in the car park in Kenema so just wait there for me. We will get another vehicle to Bo together."

He brought with him a whole black deer he bought from the market.

"Here, take it home with you this is your celebration meat. You and your family should cook it and eat when you get home," he said.

He took me on the bike with the black deer in a sack and my clothes in his bag. There was a pocket on the bag that he warned me not to open under any circumstance. He said that he had something in it.

The lady who was meant to go with me had changed her plans so she was staying in Zimmi a little longer.

I was scared in the truck but the driver told me that there was nothing to worry about. Kamor Hindowa was running out of time so he had to run, he got on the bike and sped off.

The road was bad but a few hours later we were in Kenema. I was confused, it was really noisy and busy and I wanted to get off in the first car park but I was not sure which one so I asked the driver. He told me that the other park was better so I got off in the other park. The truck driver allocated me to a spot.

"Sit here he will see you as soon as he gets here," the driver said.

I sat in the park all day until all the vehicles left and all the business people left but luckily Kamor Hindowa had given me some money to buy some drink in case I was thirsty. I was scared when I did not see him. There was a man who lived very close to the market, who apparently had been watching me all day. At 6pm when he saw that I was still sitting there looking lost and frightened, he came up to me and asked if I was alright. I told him that I was waiting for my uncle and that I was meant to wait for him in that park so that he could take me to Bo.

"Do you want to come to my house and spend some time with my wife until maybe he will come for you tonight?" he asked. "I will be here till late at night so if he comes I will see him. My name is Abdulraman."

I told him my name and he took the sack with the black deer in it, as it was the heaviest. He led me to his wife. She was a young girl in her early to mid-twenties and she was welcoming, she introduced herself to me.

"My name is Rama," she said. I told her my name. The black deer had started to rot so she suggested we cut it up.

"You know, just in case your uncle doesn't come you can sell the meat and use the money to pay your way home to your grandmother in Bo," she said.

We cut up the black deer that night and Rama's husband took the pieces around his area and sold it for me. I was so amazed at how nice they were. I told them that I needed to keep a piece of the animal for myself and they kept a huge piece for them and some for me.

They had a single bedroom shack by the market. I slept on a mattress in the room in front of their bed. I did not sleep, I was worried about Kamor Hindowa and I thought that something had happened to him. I closed my eyes but I did not sleep. A few hours through the night I felt someone touching me in the dark. I was scared and I opened my eyes. It was Rama's husband; he was standing over me naked with a huge erection. I almost screamed.

"What are you doing?" I asked as I sat up.

"Shhh, please," he said as he continued to feel my shoulders.

I was shaking and I told him to leave me alone or I will scream for Rama to hear. She was sound asleep while her man was trying to rape me. He left me and went back to bed. I sat up through the rest of the night.

As soon as I heard the first cockcrow I was ready to get going. Ramatu woke up and gave me a bucket of water to bathe. She cooked me some food, as I got dressed. She did not have a bowl to put the food in for me so I used my own money and bought a lunch bowl and a drink bottle. Her husband was a friend of another truck driver who was taking passengers to Bo that morning. He negotiated price with his friend for me. I thanked them both and got on the truck.

I was so anxious. We finally arrived in Bo at the junction of Gbongo Market. I asked someone to please show me the way to the market. The last time I was there I was eleven years old and I did not really remember the road. The person I asked told me to cross the street and walk straight ahead. I was lost and afraid as I walked down the street. I was intimidated but I tried to hide it. Soon I was in the market.

I wanted to ask someone about my grandmother but they were all too busy bargaining. So I closed my eyes and tried to remember the last time I was there with my grandmother Mama Adama. I did and I did exactly what I saw when I closed my eyes. I recognised the house as soon as I stood in front of it. I went into the veranda slowly and looked around to see if someone was watching me. I looked very different from everyone so I thought they were all watching me. There was no-one watching and there was no-one on the veranda so I pushed the front door to the house and got in. I remembered that my grandmother's room was the first room on the right from the front door. I arrived home on the 28th December 1996 in the afternoon.

Everyone was in the backyard and I thought she must be there too or in the market because she was a morning person. So I decided that I would go to her room whether she was there or not. I was just going to sit down until she came back. She was in the room with her back turned to the door. She was wiping the table.

"Mama, hello," I said.

She nodded and said that she was not in the mood that she missed her grandchildren and that she hoped God would bring them back from the war.

"I'm back Mama," I said.

"From where and who are you?" she asked without turning to look at me.

"Mama it's me Memuna, I'm back from the rebels," I said.

Before I knew it she already had her hands on me checking to make sure it was me. I looked different and she was very old so she had to be sure.

"Oh God thank you. My child is this really you J.C. Barnes' granddaughter?" she cried, "Is this really you, where are your sisters?"

In Sierra Leone we treat our cousins like our siblings, this was why my cousins Nyalay and Komeh were always referred to as my sisters added to my sister Samia. Mama Adama held me by my wrist and took me to the backyard. She was so excited she could hardly breathe.

"The child is back!" she said, "One of Sam's daughters is back from the war people."

Everyone in the yard turned to look at me but before they could say anything she had already pulled me back to the lounge. We were on our way to our other house where Aunties Sewa was. On our way to the house, through the market Mama Adama screamed all the way.

"Thank you God, the child is back," she cried.

She took me to her niece's house and yelled the same thing and we almost got run over as we crossed Prince William's Street. Soon we were at the house.

There was chaos in our yard, my Aunties were rushing to go to the radio station to announce my name as a missing person on the radio. My Auntie Mamie worked at the radio station in Bo - and she was going to get on the radio and announce that I had got lost on my way to Bo. Kamor Hindowa had arrived in Bo before me and he had found my Auntie Sewa from what I told him and he told them everything about how we had lost each other.

"Where were you, Memuna? I looked all around for you?" he asked.

"I was in the second park your friend the truck driver told me to wait there," I said.

"Well you are home now that is good," he said.

They were so happy when they saw me, all of my cousins who knew me came and hugged and so did Auntie Mamie and Auntie Sewa. Grandma

Ngaya was shocked she did not have a word to say other than 'God thank you.' She just sat in her chair and stared at me. I greeted her and she asked me about Samia, Nyalay and Komeh. They all did. I told them that they were in Liberia and I explained to them briefly what had happened, as I was very tired.

Kamor Hindowa told them to let me rest and they did for a while. I thanked him a lot and so did Mamas Adama and Ngaya and everyone. Auntie Sewa took the meat and my bag from me and arranged for me to bathe. Auntie Sewa's husband tried to pay Kamor Hindowa but he refused the money. I was in the house listening.

"I do this for God to pay me and to bring happiness to families. Just look after that child and don't ask her too many questions just leave her she will talk when she is ready because she is very angry right now," he said. "She is a trained rebel and I'm sure she did the real training at Camp Lion so she is very angry."

I listened as he warned them and I was surprised as how right he was. He called out so he could say his goodbyes. I emptied his bag and gave it back to him.

"You did not put your hand in that pocket did you?" he asked. I shook my head as everyone watched.

"You are a good child. Calm down and get back into society ok. God bless you I will see you anytime I come to Bo. I have to go now as I have to take some more children to their families."

I cried as he left and he reminded my family not to forget his warning.

I was now left with a group of curious and excited people. Everyone in the neighbourhood knew that I was back and I knew none of them. Auntie Sewa asked me if I was telling the truth about Samia and Nyalay's whereabouts. After a while Ngaya decided it was time for her to talk.

"Where is the baby?" she asked.

I thought she was asking someone else, so I did not say anything.

"Memuna, where is the baby?" she said.

"What baby?" I asked.

My own family was staring at me like I was a stranger. I guess they were shocked too.

"Someone told me that they saw you and you were pregnant and you had a gun on the war front," Grandma Ngaya said.

"I don't have a baby and I have never been pregnant whoever told you that Ngaya, made it up," I said, to my grandmother. "They never even saw a rebel."

My family did not really listen to Kamor Hindowa's advice because they kept asking me questions and I just sat there not answering any. Finally they got tired and I went to the bathroom and cleaned up. I was too tired to eat dinner. So I went to sleep. I slept in Ngaya's room with her. I talked to her about some of the things that happened to us and reasons I did not go to Liberia with Samia and Nyalay.

"So you were very sick were you?" she asked. "I see why you look so sick. But don't worry you will soon go back to normal. I know your grandfather is happy in heaven right now. God bless that Kamajor."

She told me how sad they all were when the rebels took us away and how hard it was for them to tell our father that Samia and myself were taken by rebels and how hard it was for them to tell Auntie Sewa that Nyalay had been abducted.

Grandma Memuna was not in Bo she was still in Sembehun so I did not see her. My father was in Freetown; Auntie Sewa told me that she would send a message to him as soon as possible.

As soon as I closed my eyes to sleep the nightmare started again. I was running in the forest and getting bombed just like it happened to us.

"Memuna, wake up you are having a nightmare," Grandma Ngaya said. "You were crying in your sleep kicking. What was happening?"

I told her that I was dreaming of what happened to us. I did not want to bother my grandmother so I decided to sleep on some blankets on the floor. There were other rooms in the house but I wanted to sleep with her because she was the only one listening to what Kamor Hindowa had told them. She asked questions but she took her time and chose her words carefully.

"Memuna I want you to tell me the truth," she said. "If you did have a child you would tell me wouldn't you? You know that we would accept the child don't you?"

"I know but I swear to you and God I did not have a child, I wish I knew who told you such lies," I said. "Don't worry Samia and Nyalay will come home as soon as something is arranged and they will tell you. But believe me I did not have a baby."

"Ok don't worry let's sleep," she said.

She did not sleep as my nightmares continued.

Early in the morning I woke up to guests after guests. Most were Auntie Sewa's friends and members of our family. They all brought something and they all wanted to play a role in getting me back into society. Some brought copybooks; one of Auntie Sewa's friends was a nurse she volunteered to give me some medical treatment. That day she brought me some vitamins. Another lady brought me some clothes. One of the ladies offered to take me shopping. I looked at Auntie Sewa for approval and she nodded her approval.

I liked it that they all cared so much but I just wanted some space. The pastor and his wife came over with some groceries. Auntie Sewa took me with her everywhere she went. We had to go around thanking everyone and although I looked so thin she still wanted to show me off. She killed the lice in my hair and treated the sores I had on my scalp. We went to the market and she bought me some shoes. We were happy that all those people had come to help put me back on track because she and my father had to put some money together so that I could go with them and a Kamajor or two to Liberia so that we could bring Samia and Nyalay back.

I threw up every day, Auntie Sewa said that it was because I was getting back into the food I was used to before we were captured. The first time I drank some milk after months of running in the forest I threw up. So Auntie Sewa decided to give me some laxative.

New Year's Day was awesome but I was a little sad I wished Samia and Nyalay where there.

Grandma Memuna could not come to Bo because the rebels had held up the main road. There were still some of the rebels left in some parts of the country. There were still some on Freetown Highway and still some in the Moyamba district, which was why my grandmother could not come. They were also still in the Temne districts.

I was happy to be home and it was really emotional. Sometimes I got really anti-social and I got angry and I could not pay attention to one thing for more than ten minutes. Each time I thought of what we went through I'd burst into tears and get very angry and refuse to speak. I was angry at how unfair life was.

I made a few friends and I soon got very close to one. Her mother and Auntie Sewa were good friends.

Soon I was back in secondary school only I was almost three years behind. I was crushed at the thought. When I went to class I realised that I was not the only one who was years behind. I met my friend Batu from my school in Kongoma, who was meant to be in form three but had been delayed by the same number of years as I was. She had not been captured but it was still due to the war that she was delayed.

I was happy I had friends at school, at church and at home; normal friends. I tried to be normal but deep down I knew that I was not going to be as normal as they were. A lot of my innocence had been taken away; I knew too much for a child my age. It brought me tears sometimes, but I still wiped my tears and got right back up, I had my family to back me up. I laughed and smiled and soon I was my normal weight but I was still going through a lot, I was living in my own private world of sorrow.

Life was not easy; there were some people who thought that I was dangerous and that they were better than I was. They used to whisper gossips when I walked by. I did my best to ignore them. I did not bother myself to talk to people I did not know. Sometimes they would initiate a conversation and I would walk away. I knew that talking to most of them would have been a waste of my time. Some just wanted to know what happened in the war and whether I got raped or whether I killed anyone. I was not about to convince any stranger, as it would make no difference. They would have thought that I was lying anyway. Some labelled me a snob.

A few weeks after I arrived in Bo I went to visit my friend one day and I bumped into Kumba and Manja. To my surprise Kumba was nice to me. In

RUF she saw me as a rival because she liked Lansana. We talked about our RUF boyfriends and then about how we were struggling with normal life. Manja did not go home she followed us for a walk and on my way home Kumba walked with us, she said that she was going to her family home. As we passed the market, she branched and went to our relatives' home, which was my grandmother - Mama Adama's - niece's home. I told her that the old man was related to my grandmother.

"That means we are related then," she said.

I nodded and looked at her. She knew why I looked at her the way I did. She gave me a hug and apologised.

"Sir Corporal Kumba," I joked. She was an RUF Corporal.

"That was in another life, let's just forget about all we did to each other," Manja said.

I nodded and we went our ways. The next time I saw Kumba she introduced me to her mother.

I got to know Theresa, Vayanga's girlfriend's brother and cousin at the school. That afternoon her brother missed her and he was crying for her and his cousin went to console him. There was a ring of students around them watching. I went there too. After they were all gone and there was only Batu, the boy, Theresa's cousin and myself left. I asked him to tell me her name and he told me her first and last name.

"Well all you have to do is pray that Theresa finds her way from Ivory Coast to here but she is alive," I said. "She's been out of Sierra Leone since the beginning of 1996."

They did not believe me and I called out Theresa middle name. I told them what she was like and I took off my shoes and socks and showed them the scares under my feet and I lifted my uniform dress up to my knee and showed them my scars. They believed me. I told them why Foday Sankoh sent her out of Sierra Leone. He stopped crying and the two of them thanked me and they went home to tell their parents.

A few weeks later my father came to Bo from Freetown and I was so happy to see him, he was well dressed and he smelt good. He and his sister arranged to go and get Nyalay and Samia and they needed me to go with them. He was meant to go back to Freetown and come back with the money.

I was getting myself emotionally ready because I was not at all ready to face Lansana again, but I had to do it for my sister and cousin. My nightmares continued, so Auntie Sewa gave me a room in one of the apartments. There were five apartments in the yard, another building and a kitchen with a wild berry tree and water well. I still slept with my grandmother most of the times as I could not sleep alone, I was afraid. A few weeks later one afternoon, on our way back from school my friend asked if I could go with her to the market. She wanted to get a top or two.

"I just want to get some more casual tops to wear in the house," she said.

"Ola the sun is hot," I said, "and I am hungry I want to go home."

"But it is on our way home please," she said.

I had a few Leones so I bought a pack of cookies as we walked through the market looking for her tops. We stood in front of a shop and she asked my opinion about a top. As soon as I said it was nice, a voice came from behind me begging me for some cookies.

"Can I have some?"

It was Samia when I turned around. I was so happy I thought I was dreaming at first. I shoved the whole pack in Samia's hand and I gave her a big hug.

"Let's go home, let's go home," I said. Where is Nyalay? How did you get here?"

"A Kamajor brought us, he said that Grandma Memuna sent him," Samia said. "We have been here in Bo a few days now and I'm here in the market with his wife. Nyalay is at their house."

Samia pointed me to the lady. She was standing at a table buying vegetables in the market.

"Ola this is my little sister," I yelled in Krio.

"This is Samia. She is here."

Ola left the top and ran toward me as I ran to the lady. I spoke to her and she told me that the girls were with her and her husband. She gave me their address and Ola wrote it.

"Samia we are coming there for you and Nyalay, today ok?" I said.

I did not want to leave her but the lady said that she would not let Samia go with me until there was proof even though she could see the resemblance. I was upset but I was happy she gave me the address. I ran home singing, "Joy Overflows my Heart". I was thanking God. I got to the house before Ola, I was breathless and I sat on the steps on the veranda.

"What is the matter?" Auntie Sewa asked.

"Samia and Nyalay are here in Bo Town. I saw Samia in the market," I said.

My auntie did not believe me.

"Why don't you believe me? I have not lied to you before," I said.

Grandma Ngaya asked me if I was telling the truth if it was not Samia's look alike I saw.

"No I swear it was her I talked to her and the person they are staying with gave me her address," I said.

Ola came and gave Auntie Sewa the address. We took off our uniforms and we went to look for the house and Ola came with us. It was a hot day and we went round and round.

While going around looking for the street we went to a popular boutique in Bo. The old man who owned the boutique was very happy he was jumping around praising God with a letter in his hand. He gave us a minute to ask him for directions. Auntie Sewa told him what we were looking for and he showed us the letter and the picture of his daughter. I knew her too, we were not best of friends but we always gave each other a minute or two to say hello and talk a little before she was sent away along with Theresa to learn the communication course. The moment I saw the picture I said her name.

"She is in Ivory Cost learning how to use the radio," I said.

That made her father really happy, because he was sure.

"Oh… God thank you," he said. "Now I really believe that this letter came from my child. I have confirmation."

He thanked and blessed me. He prayed that we would find the street we were looking for. It was a dramatic evening and a good one. A few hours later we found the house.

It turned out the lady and Auntie Sewa knew each other from way back. She said she did not know we were related to Samia and Nyalay because our grandmother in Sembehun had pleaded with her husband to go and get them for her. She said that if she knew Auntie Sewa's address she would have brought them home. Her husband was there and I guess Samia and Nyalay had told him about me.

The two girls did not look as bad as I did when I got home. In fact, they looked way better than I did and I did not mind. They came home with us and so did the Kamajor and his wife - they came to see our other grandmothers. Someone was sent to call Mama Ola from the other house and everyone thanked the Kamajor for bringing them home. Samia and Nyalay had their Kamajor and mine was Kamor Hindowa. I missed him and every day I wished to see him. I could not thank him enough, he was a Godsend.

When I came back from the war zone, Grandma Ngaya told me that Uncle John joined the Kamajors along with one of our teachers, Mr. Solomon and Dembie a man who lived in Sembehun. They joined mainly because of what happened to us. I ran into one of my friends from SLC School in Kongoma, James and he told me two of our teachers - Mr. Tucker and Mr. Sowah - joined the Kamajors when they heard about my abduction. I was surprised to know that so many people cared about me and it touched my heart. He told me he would ask his father for help so he could get news of my return across to Mr. Sowah and Mr. Tucker. They both came to our house in Bo to see me when they heard the news. It was a few weeks after I returned home and I was not much company, especially when it came to talking about RUF. They came on different days and we talked about the old days at school and they left promising to visit anytime they were in Bo Town. They, most importantly vowed to end the war.

A few months after I started school, I had to stop attending school because RUF was in Bo Town. They had associated with Johnny Paul Koroma to overthrow the government. I knew a lot of them so I had to hide at home so they would not capture me again. They could have used military force saying I was a trained rebel meant to be on duty and would have taken me to the barracks.

Samia and I left Bo Town about a month after the Kamajors and the RUF clashed in Bo Town for the first time. During this battle, while the shooting was going on and three jets flying over the town we were in our house.

That was the last thing I wanted, but I was more worried about Grandma Adama and Grandma Ngaya's hearts. Everyone in the house asked me to suggest to them on what to do. I told them to stay down in the house and pray. I slept with my Grandma Ngaya some nights and she would talk to me all night; she would tell me that it would be alright.

They ceased firing but it was still the same; people were scared and I stayed home until I left for Freetown. It was the same there too, I saw a lot of them in the city so I hated going out. I went to church and came back home.

A couple of weeks after I arrived at Bo Town to Auntie Sewa from the RUF, Auntie Sewa told me that my father and his partner had applied to the United Nations for resettlement. They had sent applications through the United Nations to the United States, England, Australia and New Zealand (who had newly opened its doors to Liberian refugees following in Australia's footsteps) and New Zealand was the first to answer that our applications were accepted by New Zealand in 1996 but at the time we were still in captivity so they temporarily closed our files. My father and his partner were trying to get the New Zealand government to reopen the files now we had returned home.

We travelled to Guinea Conakry Republic in November on our way to Banjul - The Gambia - in 1998, so we could wait for completion of our documents to get to New Zealand. The paperwork for our visas took two years from the time we got to The Gambia. I do not know why it took so long for them to grant our visas, all I know is that we went for a lot of medical checks including blood tests, injections, x-rays and more poking and prodding - we were told this was all to ensure we did not had HIV or tuberculosis, and that we'd had our malaria vaccine, etc. Samia and I were given a lot of documents to sign but we were not given any reason for signing the documents and we did not ask.

I loved it in The Gambia, it was awesomely lively and the people were very kind. I did not know about New Zealand until I was told that I was travelling to New Zealand. I knew about Australia though. I asked my father about New Zealand and he told me the little he knew about the Maori people and he was sure that I would speak the language when I got to New Zealand because I was fast with languages.

I did not intend to leave Africa because the further I went from Liberia, the further I felt I was away from my mother. Some part of me wished I would not be granted my visa for New Zealand.

Two years later our passports arrived in the mail with the visas stamped in them. I had a mixture of feelings; I was grateful, shocked and disappointed. Though I never told anyone how I felt. The night before we departed Banjul, I did not want the night to end. My friends and family and I cried and hugged each other before we left for the airport and when we got there, it was the same.

Our journey to New Zealand lasted four days, we changed planes five times. As we flew from Banjul my heart broke because of all the people I was leaving behind and also for my mother. We flew over Liberia and I could see the houses and trees. This was so hurtful; I thought to myself my mother could be in one of those houses down there provided she is still alive.

I could not believe it when we arrived at Wellington airport; tears began to stream down my cheeks. I had at no time in my life felt removed so far away from my mother but no-one knew why I was crying.

The first few months after we arrived in New Zealand, all I thought of was how long it would take me before I went back to Africa. I also contemplated on how I was going to find my mother. I went on the Internet and typed her name and sometimes, I would read Liberian news on the Internet hoping to find something.

Early 2001 I found a soccer magazine among a pile of old magazines in the house. I looked and I remembered that my mother's brother used to play soccer before the war in Liberia and he knew lots of the main players.

Every time I tried to let go of my mother and get on with my life and accept that she was dead, I would dream of her reaching for me and asking me to take her hand. That started two years after the last time – on 28th March, 1990 - I saw her in Liberia and it happened about three times while I was with the RUF and several times, before I was captured. Each time I had this dream, I woke up in the morning with so much faith, strength and will. That was the dream I had two days before I found the soccer magazine. This time I told myself to be ready for anything I was about to dig up. Maybe my mother was dead, someone could pretend to be her because I was in New Zealand and these are all the things that went through my mind every night.

I was hoping to find Mr. Gregory's office telephone number in it or anyone who knew my uncle or could help me. I did not find Mr. Gregory's number but I found the telephone number to the Liberian Football Association (L.F.A) in Monrovia. I wrote the number on a piece of paper. I sat on the floor and looked at the number for about five minutes, slowly took a deep breath and went in our room planning on what to say when I dialled the number. I prayed with an open heart that God would end my years of crying for my mother with good news. I told Samia about the number and she said by God's grace some good result will come out of it.

I bought a NZ$20 telephone card in the morning and I could not wait for night to fall to make the call. After three unsuccessful tries at calling the number I got through the fourth time. A man answered the telephone and there was a lot of noise in the background. I asked who he was and he said his name but I forgot it. I asked if he was the boss and he said he was not, so I asked him to please put me through to the boss. He did but the secretary answered. She was nice on the telephone, he was not in his office but she told me to call back in half an hour. I thanked her and asked her to please tell him to wait for my call, that my call was very, very important.

I was sleepy at this point but I tried to stay awake. Exactly half an hour later I called again and the secretary answered again. When she heard my voice, she put me through to her boss. I greeted him and introduced myself; I also told him that I really needed his help.

"What can I help you with, young lady," he asked.

"I am trying to find my mother, I have not seen her for over ten years and it really hurts. I just want my peace of mind. It would be good to at least know if she was buried somewhere," I said.

I told him my uncle's name and asked if he knew him. He was familiar with the name but he only knew my uncle's father not him.

"But I promise you I will do all I can to help you. Keep in touch. My name is Mr. Musa Yankuba call me any time," he said.

"Thank you very much Mr. Yankuba, thank you very much," I said.

I gave him my mobile phone number.

While Mr. Yankuba did his search for my mother in Liberia, I got on the Internet and got the telephone number for the Liberian embassy in America. I asked for the ambassador but I think they put me through to the assistant. They told me that the ambassador was out of his office. I asked the person I spoke to if he heard about my mother or her brother, if they were in America. He knew a man by the same name as my uncle and his sister lost her children too. He gave me this man's number. I thanked him and called the man but there was no-one home. A few hours later I called again and he answered. I explained my problem to him, he sympathised with me and he told me he was not the James I was looking for. He told me his sister's name was Viviane not Cynthia and she found her children. He prayed that I would find my mother and we said our goodbyes.

Since the first day I spoke to Mr. Yankuba, I always had about NZ$30 to NZ$40 worth of telephone cards with me. I called him once or twice a week, so he would not feel pressured. Every day I prayed that we would find an answer - a good one. For the first three months, he asked people who came to his office if they knew my mother, but he found nothing. So I called him and suggested that we put an article in the newspaper in Monrovia. He said that he was thinking the same thing. I offered to send US$100 via Western Union for him to pay for the article but he told me not to bother. I insisted but he refused, I could not believe how this stranger was so willing to help me. I was already very grateful to him.

Almost three weeks after he put the article in the paper in May 2001 a woman called our house in the morning. By then, there was no-one home; we had all gone out on our various activities.

When I got home at about 4pm, our father's partner was sitting on the steps at the front door. When I got home, I was feeling sad. After I greeted her, she told me that there was a message on the telephone for me from a Liberian and the person said that she was my mother. She asked if I wanted to listen to the message. I did not know what to say for a moment. I was shocked and I could feel myself shaking. I wanted to hear the message but some part of me felt unready for it all. I nodded and we went to one of the rooms and she dialled the number and the pin for me to listen to the message. I did not know the pin to the answering machine.

As I listened to the message, I struggled desperately to recognise the voice that I heard. I tried remembering my mother talking to me but I still could not recognise the voice. I got frustrated and scared and I hung up.

"When Samia comes we will listen to the message together," I said and went to our room to change my clothes.

My mind was really busy as a lot of thoughts ran through. I thought what if she was not my mother and she was only calling because she thought there would be some money in it for her. Then I thought, but God I do not have any money!

Then I thought well Mr. Yankuba must have been sure this woman was genuine before he gave her my home number. Before he put the article in the paper, we agreed that he would not put my sister's, mine or our father's full name and our telephone number in the newspaper. That he would use our names to test the person who reacted to the article before he gave them the number provided they pass.

As I thought about all these things I knelt down and thanked God, choking on my tears while I was at it. I thanked God for the answer although I did not recognise the voice.

I was anxious, happy, scared and nervous. Half an hour later Samia came home and I told her. I was suddenly so excited I could not talk fast enough; as I talked I pointed frantically at the telephone.

"Oh God. Really?" she asked.

I nodded and we asked for the pin to be dialled again so we could listen to the message again. Samia could not recognise the voice either, but she listened to the whole message.

"I hope this person is Mama," she said.

"I'm praying the same too," I said.

We both agreed that we would wait for our father to come home so he could help us with the voice. The time was not fast enough; he got home about four hours later at almost 9.30pm. As soon as we heard him walk through the front door, we stood at the top of the stairs and waited for him to come up. We greeted and asked him to listen to the message for us. We could not explain fast enough. He smiled.

"Oh…you sure?" he said.

We nodded and stood by him holding each other's hands, squeezing tight, hoping that the answer would be what we had wished and prayed for over the years. Finally, he smiled and said "yes, it is her. Oh…Cynthia."

He looked at us jumping hugging each other and we went to our room. I suggested we waited until 10pm local time before we dialled the number she left.

The message went: "Hello, hello Memuna and Samia, how are you doing? This is me, your mother Cynthia; call me on this number as soon as you get this message. I will call back, God bless you."

She left her telephone number. I was so happy and scared at the same time, I could not believe how easy it was. I was thankful to God and Mr. Yankuba. Ten minutes later the telephone rang and I answered, it was her again.

"Hello Memuna is that you or your sister?" she asked.

For a second I did not know what to say and then I told her it was me. "Are you really my mother?" I asked.

She said she was and before I asked another question she asked for Auntie Stina by name and she asked for my father. She asked to speak to Samia and we were all in tears. I asked if she was alright and why she did not look for us. She said that it took her a while before she was able to get to Monrovia city from Lofa. She told me that a lot of people told her that they saw our father killed - that he was beheaded. Some said that we got killed together. She said that a year or so before she saw the article in the paper, someone told her that we were in Canada. When we finally got to hear our mother's voice, my life felt complete.

I still do not know how I felt on that first day – 31st May 2001 - when I spoke to my mother after so many years. I know that fear was one of the mixture of feelings I had. I know that I felt wonderful, I felt lighter, which I think was caused by all the excitement and anxiety.

I called Mr. Yankuba on the phone to thank him for everything. I told him no matter what I did I could not thank him enough. I told him that he was very important to me and I hoped that God gave him whatever good he wanted. I could not stop thanking him. I promised to keep in touch with him and we hung up. I told my mother to please keep in touch with him when I was on the telephone with her.

I was so happy; I wanted the world to know. That night I prayed for others who were searching for something or someone and then I went to bed. Samia and I talked about how happy we were until we fell asleep. I have been in touch with my mother since then and I have made several attempts to go and see her.

We wanted more than anything to go to Liberia to see our mother and the rest of our family that very night, but we had a lot more to sort out. By then we were not yet eligible for citizenship though we were residents, which means we would have needed to pay for our return visa back into New Zealand. We needed money for flight tickets and pocket money for when we were away. We had only arrived almost a year in New Zealand and our father had just started working. Samia and I did not have jobs and our student allowance was just enough for our weekly expenses so our father said we should wait until we found a job then save for our tickets to go. With all this, we settled with being happy that at least our mother was still alive and we could talk to her on the phone.

When we arrived at Wellington from The Gambia, our father suggested I should go to high school with Samia to get an idea of the education system in New Zealand, especially because I had only really done a total of one year of high school before we left West Africa, as I was interrupted several times by the war. I did not like this high school experience, it was a very rough environment where teachers seemed to be afraid of the pupils and the pupils had not an ounce of respect for their teachers.

The first time I heard a student use the F-word in a conversation with one of the teachers was a very confusing day for me. I found this was very strange and disgusting especially when the pupil in question was a boy and he was talking to a lady teacher.

Another reason for my reaction was that where I came from our teachers were our parents while we were at school. Meaning, you speak to them as you would your parents, because they were allowed to discipline us for disrespect and other misconduct. A student who was disrespectful enough to verbally abuse a teacher would be lashed with a whip on their bottom and suspended for a few weeks or in some situations expelled. Also students in Sierra Leone or Liberia are very scared of their parents being called to their school because they had done something wrong because then the parents would be the ones doing the whipping.

Samia was doing very well at school. She was involved in hockey and basketball. She had made friends at school and seemed to be getting on very well.

I, on the other hand was still having the most confusing time of my life. I tried to appreciate my new home, New Zealand. However, we arrived to this strange country in autumn and I had never in my life experienced such cold. I learned the use of a hot water bottle, drank a lot of hot beverages and wore a lot of clothes (which I hated). I would wear three layers of tops and a jacket to school, a pair of stockings or knee high socks under my trousers and I was still very cold from the tip of my toes to my waist. I hated every moment of this. I found it strange that senior students did not wear a uniform to this school, though I liked that part because then I could wear whatever - I was admitted to the sixth form. I hated school, I did nothing while I was there. I did not pay attention at all. Sometimes I would do my assignment. Most of the time I had no idea what was happening around me and I did not care. I hungered for education and I really wanted to go to school but not the way I was and not in that environment. I could not tell anyone about it, no-one asked me how school was going, so I just went with the flow till the two semesters I was made to do there was over. I just wanted to be home watching television, eating, sleeping, keeping warm and talking on the phone.

At night I would not sleep especially if I had watched something on television involving shootings or if I heard a car tire backfire or a very loud noise while I was out that day - this sometimes meant two or three nights of me reliving the last battle I experienced with the RUF or the day I was captured or me searching for my sisters in the forest in the middle of a battle. I spent most nights walking around the house looking for chores to do at night when everyone was asleep.

In 2002 I moved out with my sister Samia, then a friend of mine joined us. Then I enrolled at Victoria University of Wellington to study Information Systems as I had grown an interest in computers. I liked my new life however I did not understand why we needed to attend tutorials and it was mandatory. I, however, would endeavour to attend one tutorial out of twelve, I wanted to exist and be useful but I hated life, everything was confusing, too much information for me to gather in this new life of mine. I felt like I was watching my life being lived by a stranger and it was all too fast.

Two things that I liked was that the government encourage local students to study by supporting them financially through student loans and allowances. Also this is the first country I had lived in where young people were encouraged to go out and work while studying. I did not understand the concept of part time work as I had not heard the words before. All I knew was that adults in Sierra Leone and Liberia went to work early in the morning and came home at night. Young people who I knew of who worked were those who helped their parents who owned small businesses. They would go and work in the shop after school which means they did not get paid. Then there were other poor children who would be taken from villages by a relative to do house chores and/or sell for the people who brought them from the village - these children did not get the luxury of going to school, they carried trays of fruit or confectionery and cigarettes all day in the blazing African sun and went home to a tiny plate of food and that was their life until they were old enough to stand on their own.

I on the other hand, only had to go to school and help with chores around our home. I sometimes hid in the ceiling from dish washing and pounding cassava leaves. I would offer to peel onions and pound peppers for Grandma Memuna when she prepared our dinner but I always ran and climbed the ladder up the ceiling through the access cupboard we had in the dining room at the family house in Sembehun Nes Tucker when I saw her coming from the market with a basket hanging on her arms with cassava leaves.

I had never work for pay in my life and now I was expected to write up a curriculum vitae and apply for jobs. I liked the thought of making my own money but I was called to only three job interview appointments in Wellington and they kept asking for experience. I told them I had never worked in my life but was a fast learner - that did not get me the opportunity I wished for and I became increasingly angry that no-one asked me whether I wanted to come to New Zealand before dragging me along.

Eventually, I was introduced to a lady who owned a salon in Wellington City that I could braid hair very well and this one day called me for a trial. That was the first day I enjoyed in New Zealand outside of our home. She was very nice and she took me home after work.

I then went to the clubs with my friend for the first time. I did not have to ask my father to let me go out as I had done all my teenage life. It was 2002 and I was twenty-one years old and flatting. It was an amazing experience going to a club for the first time in my life. I tried cocktails and discovered I love tequila, margarita, mojitos and vodka. It was amazing. On my first night out Samia, my friend and I went home at 5am. My friend and I were very drunk and Samia was sober as she did not drink. I had a shower while very drunk and went to my bed. I woke up in the morning feeling as if I had been in a boxing match but I loved it. I then discovered I was hung-over for the first time. To me, it was worth it. Nothing made me smile as much as I did when I was in the clubs dancing and drinking all night. I was never allowed to go clubbing before we came to New Zealand but every now and then my father and his brother Uncle Henry (when we were in Liberia) would give me a few sips of their beer so I knew what beer tasted like.

For the first three years I changed my degree twice and did not attend tutorials and most of my lectures. I could not sleep at night my mind was busy struggling to find an answer as to why I was created, why did I have to go through what I had gone through. This went on for years and I never used the sleepless nights to study so I failed. Eventually, I dropped out of university and by then I had gained experience in working with the New Zealand public where jobs were concerned so I still helped out at the salon. I had attained employment elsewhere and was slowly merging into life in New Zealand but I got annoyed every time anyone showed what I thought was too much interest in me. I did not like my reaction because this was a new country and I needed to make friends but at the Same time I did not want anyone knowing about me at all and I thought it was fair enough that no-one gave me the chance to know them either. I had my sister and one friend and that was enough.

I did not tell my mother about my sleepless nights because I did not want her to worry. I told Auntie Yenie and she suggested I write my thoughts in a diary; that way I could clear my mind to an extent. I thought it was a good idea and two days later I told my eldest brother Sam , about Auntie Yenie's suggestion and he agreed with her.

"Actually, how would you feel about making that diary into a book and publishing it," he said. "I don't think there is any other book like it."

Sam 's suggestion frightened me but he did not give up. Two other times I spoke to him on the phone he asked me whether I had given his idea any further thought and eventually I agreed. As I wrote, I became less anxious but I still could not sleep. Those sleepless nights started giving me constant migraines and my doctor asked whether I was sleeping well and I told her I couldn't. She asked whether I wanted sleeping pills prescribed for me but I refused them and told her I would try and stay in bed when I woke up at 3am, maybe I could fall back asleep. Then she suggested counselling and she saw I was going to turn her suggestion down so she booked an appointment for me. I smiled and thanked her but I did not attend the session.

About a few months later I called and booked a counselling session. I simply did it because my doctor and a friend kept suggesting it but I had no faith in it, because what can a counselor know about what I was struggling with - this was my thought. But I was tired of being in pain, not sleeping, not liking people and just having my life itself feel like one long agony and I was willing to try and make a change.

There was a day when I got really angry with myself and started talking to myself. I decided to count my blessings and appreciate the fact that God, the United Nations and the government of New Zealand had chosen to give me a second chance of life and I had no right misbehaving the way I was that I had a lot to be thankful for.

How many girls were taken by the RUF rebels and had a say in keeping her virginity (only about 5% of us female captives had this opportunity, because our captors felt something for us)? How many were not beaten every day? How many got the opportunity to travel to a western country with a pre-approved resident permit after coming home from captivity? What makes me think I am so special that I was behaving the way I was? These were the questions I asked myself, I got on my knees, prayed for God's forgiveness and asked for his help in giving me the grace to see his favour upon my life and appreciate his blessings on my head. I promised to try my best and live the life God has planned for me and stop trying to have back what I had before the war. After all I now had my mother, my search was over.

After I decided to change my behaviour toward my new life, I still enjoyed going out for a few drinks and a dance. However, I slowly started losing interest in dancing all night and only wanted a drink and a nice spot in the club where I could sit and people-watch.

So I went for counselling and my doctor admitted she had no idea about what I endured during my time as a captive but she would do her best to help me adjust to my new life. She suggested other techniques such as chamomile tea with a mug of warm milk and honey and milo to help me sleep. Today, my sleeping pattern is much better I can sleep up to five hours a night without waking up to look for chores. The nightmares are at a minimum and life is getting better. I am fully adjusted to my new life and I see New Zealand as my fourth home now. I went back to university; it was still a struggle but much better as I adhered to the mandatory requirements and completed a Bachelor of Commerce and Administration majoring in Commercial Law and International Business at Victoria University of Wellington, and graduated in 2012.

In 2009 I made it to Sierra Leone and Liberia to spend time with my family.

Made in the USA
Middletown, DE
24 October 2020